WRITING AFRICAN AMERICAN WOMEN

WRITING AFRICAN AMERICAN WOMEN

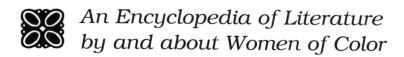

*An Encyclopedia of Literature
by and about Women of Color*

Volume 1: A–J

**Edited by
Elizabeth Ann Beaulieu**

GREENWOOD PRESS
Westport, Connecticut • London

Library of Congress Cataloging-in-Publication Data

Writing African American women : an encyclopedia of literature by and about
women of color / edited by Elizabeth Ann Beaulieu.
    p. cm.
   Includes bibliographical references and index.
   ISBN 0–313–33196–0 (set : alk. paper)—ISBN 0–313–33197–9 (v. 1 : alk. paper)—
ISBN 0–313–33198–7 (v. 2 : alk. paper) 1. American literature—African American
authors—Encyclopedias. 2. Authors, American—20th century—Biography—
Encyclopedias. 3. African American women in literature—Encyclopedias. 4. Women
and literature—United States—Encyclopedias. I. Beaulieu, Elizabeth Ann.
   PS153.N5W756 2006
   810.9'928796073—dc22   2005031487

British Library Cataloguing in Publication Data is available.

This book is included in the *African American
Experience* database from Greenwood Electronic Media.
For more information, visit www.africanamericanexperience.com.

Library of Congress Catalog Card Number: 2005031487
ISBN 0–313–33196–0 (set)
    0–313–33197–9 (vol. 1)
    0–313–33198–7 (vol. 2)

First published in 2006

Greenwood Press, 88 Post Road West, Westport, CT 06881
An imprint of Greenwood Publishing Group, Inc.
www.greenwood.com

Printed in the United States of America

The paper used in this book complies with the
Permanent Paper Standard issued by the National
Information Standards Organization (Z39.48–1984).

10 9 8 7 6 5 4 3 2 1

This work is for Lee Burdette Williams—friend of the second half, sister of my heart's heart, my poem.

❖ Contents

Preface

My introduction to African American literature came when, as a high school student, I was assigned Frederick Douglass's 1845 *Narrative of the Life of Frederick Douglass, an American Slave.* Knowing little about slavery other than what conventional history texts presented, I looked forward to reading the firsthand account of a famous American, intuiting even then the importance of personal stories in supplementing the historical record. At the time, I did not know the word *patriarchy*, but I was astute enough to recognize the truth in the cliché that history has always been written by the winners, and the winners were almost always white, male, and educated.

What I remember most about reading Douglass's *Narrative* is being captivated not so much by his story as by the anecdote of Aunt Hester with which he concludes his first chapter. Douglass identifies the beating of his aunt as crucial in his awareness of his own position as a slave, calling the episode "the blood-stained gate, the entrance to the hell of slavery" through which he is reluctantly and violently ushered.

Douglass never mentions Aunt Hester again, and I finished reading the text wondering about her fate and the fate of countless other enslaved black women like her. Who told their stories? How were their stories different? How incomplete would our understanding of American history remain if we were not afforded the opportunity to place their lives and their stories side by side with Douglass's *Narrative* and other tales of heroic American masculinity?

My questions remained unanswered until I read Harriet Jacobs's *Incidents in the Life of a Slave Girl*, which was published in 1861 but not widely available to twentieth-century readers until the mid-1980s. Jacobs offered me the companion piece to Douglass's example of physical bravery, heroic struggle, and escape; her work (now routinely read alongside Douglass's *Narrative*) provides a woman's perspective on slavery, suffering, connectedness, and motherhood and is straightforward in outlining the multiple sites of oppression faced by black women. Her voice, long absent from the historical record, was finally available.

This encyclopedia, then, echoes and amplifies Jacobs's voice, attempting to provide, for the first time, a reference work that focuses specifically on feminist and womanist approaches to African American literature. Not all of the writers included can easily be labeled feminist; increasingly, that definition is difficult to pin down, especially when applied to women writers of color. The term *womanist*, introduced by Alice Walker in her 1984 book *In Search of Our Mothers' Gardens*, is useful as an alternative to describe an emphasis on survival, wholeness, and inclusivity that conventionally held definitions of *feminist* sometimes preclude. What these writers of fiction, nonfiction, drama, and poetry have in common is their insistence that the lives of black women are worthy of examination.

From Lucy Terry, who wrote the first known work of literature by an African American (the poem "Bar's Flight," composed in 1746 but not published until 1855), to popular contemporary novelists Bebe Moore Campbell and Terry McMillan, black women have been telling their stories for centuries. Only recently, however, has African American literature become widely taught in American high schools, colleges, and universities. With the rise of black studies programs in the 1980s, African American literature finally entered the academy; around the same time, black women novelists began producing works that captured the attention of popular reading audiences as well.

Barbara Christian, in her seminal essay "But What Do We Think We're Doing Anyway: The State of Black Feminist Criticism(s) or My Version of a Little Bit of History" (1989), identifies Mary Helen Washington's 1974 *Black World* cover story "Black Women Image Makers" as a defining moment in the growing visibility of black women writers. In that essay, Washington issues a challenge to her readers, stating, "We should be about the business of reading, absorbing, and giving critical attention to those writers whose understanding of the black woman can take us further." For Washington, those writers were not only contemporary black women; she alludes as well to literary foremothers whose works could offer valuable insight into the image-making, life-transforming intersections of black women's lives and creativity. (It is interesting to note that the cover photograph that accompanied Washington's *Black World* story was of Zora Neale Hurston, who was still virtually unknown at that time.) Christian also points to Barbara Smith as initiating, through her 1977 essay "Toward a Black Feminist Criticism," a conscious insistence that black women's writing be analyzed and interpreted through the lens of feminist theory, in order to explicate more forcefully the triple oppression of race, class, and gender to which black women have always been subjected and about which they have always written.

Washington's and Smith's essays are only two examples from what has become a substantial body of feminist/womanist criticism; it is not my intention here to provide an overview of the scholarship, as there are several entries in this encyclopedia that do precisely that. However, it is important to note that at the same time women such as Toni Morrison and Alice Walker were establishing their writing careers, paving the way for what some consider a new black renaissance in the 1980s, scholars had already begun the important project both of reclaiming the black woman's past through their literary production and heralding a new generation of writers and critics who would, it turns out, reshape the American literary canon. It is my intention that this reference work will recognize and contribute to that reshaping.

In nearly 400 alphabetically arranged entries that are appropriate for scholars as well as for advanced high school students, college-level students, and general readers, *Writing African American Women* profiles writers as diverse as the eighteenth-century poet Phillis Wheatley, Harlem Renaissance folklorist-author Zora Neale Hurston, and contemporary playwright/novelist Suzan-Lori Parks. The encyclopedia features early slave narrators and spiritualists, numerous children's authors, political pamphleteers, and journalists, poets, and dramatists; the most well known contemporary black women novelists—Toni Morrison, Alice Walker, and Gloria Naylor, among them—receive significant attention, as do their contemporaries, including Toni Cade Bambara, Gayl Jones, Paule Marshall, and Rita Dove. Separate entries analyze their major works. Shorter entries present lesser-known writers such as Kate Drumgoold, Becky Birtha, Mae Cowdery, and Carolivia Herron. A number of black male writers who deal with themes from feminist or womanist perspectives are included as well.

In addition to biographical entries and feminist/womanist analyses of specific works of literature, the encyclopedia includes dozens of thematic entries with special relevance to African American literature. Lengthy pieces on topics such as race, stereotypes, motherhood, sexuality, memory, literacy, Christianity, slavery, violence, and the South provide context for the study of both African American literature and African American lives from a women's studies perspective. Movements and periods receive treatment as well, and a 6,000-word section titled "Literature" provides a chronological overview of major African American contributions to the broader field of American literature. Entries on black feminism, womanism, black feminist criticism, historical fiction, and masculinity offer a theoretical framework for understanding this subgenre of American literature that has rapidly established footing both in the academy and among lay readers worldwide.

Entries are arranged alphabetically, and cross-referencing of all the encyclopedia's entries is provided. A boldfaced name or term indicates that it is the subject of a separate entry in this reference work. Where possible, authors' birth and death dates are provided, although in the case of early African American writers this information often remains only speculative or approximate. Entries on each author conclude with a selective list of his or her works, and most entries provide a short bibliography of books and/or articles that readers may wish to consult for further reference. In both cases, the lists are not exhaustive; individual contributors have selected which works by writers to highlight and which resources to include at the end of their entries. This supplementary material is meant to provide a starting point for readers who desire more information than a reference work such as this can offer. Additionally, most entries are followed by a "See also" list that points readers to other relevant entries in the encyclopedia.

Writing African American Women concludes with two important apparati: a timeline of women's significant contributions to and achievements in the field of African American literature and a selected bibliography of book-length studies of African American literature from a women's studies perspective. These are necessarily subjective and incomplete; I am limited in my own awareness of what is out there, and the field continues to grow as it gains status in the academy and amasses an increasingly loyal following of lay readers. Nevertheless, it is my hope that these features provide some measure of the powerful force black women writers represent in literary production.

A word about contributors: A work like this would not be possible without the combined talents and effort of many scholars. When I distributed the initial call for contributors, I received hundreds of inquiries and offers of assistance. While I had already devised a working table of contents, many contributors suggested additional authors, themes, and works to include. Several offered to write their entries right away so that their pieces could be edited and distributed as models. Others, after completing their own assignments, took on additional entries when contributors already under contract could not complete work to which they had committed. Several patiently revised, and all offered a steady stream of encouragement and support for the project; when I felt overwhelmed, there was always someone there to remind me of the value of a reference work like this one.

When Sojourner Truth cried out in 1851, "Ar'n't I a woman?" she voiced a question that Douglass's Aunt Hester surely must have asked; it is one that generations of African American women have sought to understand, and it has become a primary impetus in shaping black literature and literary criticism. The contributors to this encyclopedia have attempted to demonstrate that while responses to Truth's question have many iterations, the resounding answer to her provocative cry is yes.

Works Cited

Christian, Barbara. "But What Do We Think We're Doing Anyway: The State of Black Feminist Criticism(s) or My Version of a Little Bit of History." *Changing Our Own Words*. Ed. Cheryl Wall. New Brunswick, NJ: Rutgers University Press, 1989. 58–74.

Smith, Barbara. "Toward a Black Feminist Criticism." *All the Women Are White, All the Blacks Are Men, But Some of Us Are Brave: Black Women's Studies*. Ed. Gloria T. Hull, Patricia Bell Scott, and Barbara Smith. Old Westbury, NY: Feminist Press, 1982. 157–175.

Washington, Mary Helen. "Black Women Image Makers." *Black World* 23.10 (August 1974): 10–18.

❀ Acknowledgments

I wish to thank the following programs and individuals for making this work possible:

The Cratis D. Williams Graduate School, the College of Arts and Sciences, and the Department of Interdisciplinary Studies at Appalachian State University for research time and technical support to prepare this manuscript.

Colleagues, contributors, and friends who provided suggestions, advice, encouragement, much to read, great conversation, and the occasional headache, all of which shaped this reference work in ways I initially could not have imagined.

And finally, James and Sebastian, who understood the importance of this project and were, as always, generous in their support and love.

✖ List of Entries

Thematic List of Entries

Dramatists

Bonner, Marita
Bush-Banks, Olivia Ward
Childress, Alice
Dunbar-Nelson, Alice Moore
Franklin, J. E.
Gibson, Patricia Joann
Grimké, Angelina Weld
Hansberry, Lorraine
Jones-Meadows, Karen
Kennedy, Adrienne
Miller, May
Parks, Suzan-Lori
Rahman, Aishah
Shange, Ntozake
Smith, Anna Deavere

Genres

Autobiography
Black Feminist Criticism
Children's and Young Adult
    Literature
Detective Fiction
Drama
Epistolary Novel
Fiction
Film
Historical Fiction
Neo-Slave Narrative
Poetry
Slave Narrative

Male Writers

Baldwin, James
Baraka, Amiri
Bradley, David
Brown, William Wells
Chesnutt, Charles Waddell
Cullen, Countee
Dickey, Eric Jerome
Douglass, Frederick
Dunbar, Paul Laurence

Ellison, Ralph
Gaines, Ernest
Haley, Alex
Harris, E. Lynn
Hughes, Langston
Johnson, Charles
Johnson, James Weldon
Kenan, Randall
Komunyakaa, Yusef
Major, Clarence
Malcolm X
McKay, Claude
Reed, Ishmael
Toomer, Jean
Wideman, John Edgar
Wilson, August
Wright, Richard

Novelists

Allen, Clarissa Minnie
    Thompson
Angelou, Maya
Ansa, Tina McElroy
Austin, Doris Jean
Bambara, Toni Cade
Brown, Linda Beatrice
Butler, Octavia
Campbell, Bebe Moore
Cartier, Xam Wilson
Chase-Riboud, Barbara
Clair, Maxine
Cleage, Pearl
Cliff, Michelle
Collins, Julia C.
Cooper, J. California
Crafts, Hannah
Danticat, Edwidge
Fauset, Jessie Redmon
Golden, Marita
Harper, Frances E. W.
Herron, Carolivia
Hopkins, Pauline
Hurston, Zora Neale

A

ADULTHOOD RITES. See Xenogenesis Trilogy

AI (1947–)

The poet Ai was born Florence Anthony in Albany, Texas, in 1947. She spent the first seven years of her life in Tucson, Arizona, but it was when her **family** moved to Las Vegas and then to San Francisco that she was first introduced to the complexities of racial **identity**. While her family included Native American and African American ancestors, she realized that she looked like none of them. As a child, she experienced racism for looking "different," and these experiences helped her uncover the reason when, at the age of twenty-six, she confirmed that her biological father was Japanese. She would eventually adopt the Japanese word for **love**, "Ai," as her name. In a sense, the process of renaming herself was also a way of remaking herself. She could break free from the past and create a new palette on which to paint her word portraits, the first-person narrative poems that she would develop as her personal style.

The process of breaking free from the past began when she majored in oriental studies at the University of Arizona, graduating in 1969. And though she had started writing **poetry** in her teens, she formalized her training by earning an M.F.A. in creative writing from the University of California, Irvine, in 1971. After sending her poems to poet Galway Kinnell, she published her first book of poetry, *Cruelty*, in 1973. *Cruelty* was highly successful, and soon after its publication, she was awarded a Bunting Fellowship (1975–1976) at

Radcliffe. The collection of poems that followed, *Killing Floor*, published in 1979, helped to secure Ai's critical reputation. It won the 1978 Lamont Poetry Award from the Academy of American Poets.

Her success has only grown from there. Published in 1986, her third book, titled *Sin*, won the American Book Award from the Before Columbus Foundation. From there followed *Fate: New Poems* in 1991 and *Greed* in 1993. Ai was awarded the National Book Award for Poetry in 1999 with her collection *Vice*. Additionally she has received awards from the Guggenheim Foundation and the National Endowment for the Arts. Her latest book is *Dread*, published in 2003.

Ai's poems have found such success for a number of reasons; among them is how accessible the voices of her narratives are to readers. She updates Robert Browning's form, the dramatic monologue, by giving voice to the sinners and saints that populated twentieth-century American life. From the Atlanta mass murderer to J. Edgar Hoover to rioters in L.A., her personae reveal the beautiful ugliness that can exist in American culture. Shifting from one voice to another, Ai inhabits the voices of others, inhabiting their identity, allowing us to hear from them—though always through her. The overall effect of these collected voices creates an edgy, sometimes sensationalized panorama of American existence where **race**, gender, **violence**, and politics all roil together to create the very individuals for which she speaks.

Works By

Cruelty. Boston: Houghton Mifflin, 1973.
Dread. New York: Norton, 2003.
Fate: New Poems. Boston: Houghton Mifflin, 1991.
Greed. New York: Norton, 1993.
Killing Floor. Boston: Houghton Mifflin, 1979.
"On Being ½ Japanese, ⅛ Choctaw, ¼ Black, and 1/16 Irish." *Ms.* 6.11 (May 1978): 58.
Sin. Boston: Houghton Mifflin, 1986.
Vice: New and Selected Poems. New York: Norton, 1999.

Works About

Becker, Robin. "The Personal Is Political Is Postmodern." *American Poetry Review* 23.6 (1994): 23–26.
Hueving, Jeanne. "Divesting Social Registers: Ai's Sensational Portraiture of the Renowned and the Infamous." *Critical Survey* 9.2 (1997): 108–120.
Ingram, Claudia. "Writing the Crises: The Deployment of Abjection in Ai's Dramatic Monologues." *LIT: Literature Interpretation Theory* 8.2 (1997): 173–191.
Leavitt, Michele. "Ai's Go." *The Explicator* 54.2 (1996): 126–127.
Mintz, Susannah B. "A 'Descent toward the Unknown' in the Poetry of Ai." *SAGE: A Scholarly Journal on Black Women* 9.2 (1995): 36–46.

Moore, Lenard D. "Poetry Reviews." *Black Issues Book Review* (March/April 2000): 44–45.

Ostriker, Alicia. Review of *Sin. Poetry* (January 1987): 231–237.

Seaman, Donna. "Poetic Fire and Ice." *Booklist* 95 (1999): 1028.

Seshadri, Vijay. "When Bad Things Happen to Everyone." Review of *Dread*. *New York Times Book Review*, May 4, 2003, 7.

Amy Sparks Kolker

ALBERT, OCTAVIA V. ROGERS (1853–1889)

Octavia Victoria Rogers was born a slave in Oglethorpe, Georgia, in 1853. Little is known about her childhood except that she remained in her hometown until after the Civil War when she attended Atlanta University and studied to become a schoolteacher. She was a member of the African Methodist Episcopal Church and, in 1874, married a fellow teacher and a Methodist minister, A.E.P. Albert. The couple soon after moved to Louisiana, where Octavia Albert embarked on a thirteen-year project of interviewing many of the local formerly enslaved men and women in an effort to remember the **history** of American **slavery**. Her interviews were collected as *The House of Bondage; or, Charlotte Brooks and Other Slaves*, a work first serialized between January and December 1890 in the *South-western Christian Advocate*, the paper for the New Orleans Methodist Episcopal Church. Octavia Albert died sometime around the time her work was first published, although the circumstances and exact date of her **death** are not known. After her death, Albert's husband and their only child, Laura T. F. Albert, published *The House of Bondage* in book form.

The House of Bondage relates the stories of seven different individuals interviewed by Octavia Albert, although the longest section deals with the life of the woman featured in the title, a slave named Charlotte Brooks, or "Aunt Charlotte." In keeping with Albert's goal of remembering the history of slavery, the stories emphasize the brutalities endured by a courageous people, the hard physical labor, the separation of families, and the various acts of resistance. Taken together, the stories display the importance of **community**, of a people with a shared history. In this sense, Albert's approach to combining multiple interviews into a collective narrative is different from the pre–Civil War **slave narratives** that focused on the experience of one individual. The theme of community, as well as the triumph over slavery, fits within Albert's post–Civil War purpose of recognizing the achievements of the **race** as a whole and the ability of a people, not just of individuals, to not only survive but succeed in a white supremacist **South** still intent on keeping them down.

Although she chose to write history rather than **fiction** or **poetry**, Octavia Albert's work is part of the same tradition of increased literary production by African American women during this period as part of the reform project of "racial uplift." As a university-educated former slave, an author, and the wife of a minister, Octavia Albert herself was evidence of an alternative and positive ending to the story of slavery. Even as an educated member of the black middle class, Albert's status and authority to produce this text were not assured, however. As a black woman and a married woman, Albert stepped out of the boundaries of proper womanhood in writing and publishing a historical text, especially one challenging white narratives about slavery and racism. Albert negotiated this situation and deflected attention away from her own role as author by presenting a collection of tales told by other people, her role being only that of interviewer and master storyteller. Albert's primary work was, however, ultimately a political act of recovery and a challenge to the dominant white narratives of southern history.

Work By

The House of Bondage; or, Charlotte Brooks and Other Slaves. New York: Hunt and Eaton; Cincinnati, OH: Cranston and Stowe, 1890.

Works About

Foster, Francis Smith. Introduction to *The House of Bondage.* New York: Oxford University Press, 1988.
———. *Written by Herself: Literary Production by African American Women, 1746–1892.* Bloomington: Indiana University Press, 1993.

Tiffany K. Wayne

ALEXANDER, ELIZABETH (1962–)

One of the most accomplished African American women poets born after 1960, Elizabeth Alexander is the author of three **poetry** collections, a book of essays, and a play, *Diva Studies*, which premiered at the Yale School of Drama in 1996. Her debut poetry collection, *The Venus Hottentot* (1990), was favorably reviewed in the *New York Times Book Review*, and the title poem has been widely anthologized since. Her two subsequent collections of poetry, *The Body of Life* (1996) and *Antebellum Dream Book* (2001), explore **history** and African American culture through the intersection of interior consciousness and historical moment in both lyric poems and those written in the voices of historical personas. The lyric themes of her early work include **sexuality**, travel, **identity**, and self-discovery; the later work mines the physical and psychological realms of **motherhood** and the **body**, invoking such woman-mother-artist figures as Sylvia Plath, Betty Shabazz, and **Toni Morrison**. Alexander's persona poems invent voices for characters ranging from the Hottentot Venus to Mohammed Ali. Her poems have appeared in over twenty anthologies to date. A reading of her poetry is available on the video recording *Furious Flower: Conversations with African American Poets* (1998).

   Alexander's poetry and criticism are both informed by an intense appreciation for visual art. She pays homage to the masters of African American modernism—Romaire Bearden, **Gwendolyn Brooks**, and Robert Hayden—in *The Black Interior* (2004), her collection of essays, as well as present-day artists such as Denzel Washington. Alexander's approach to criticism is exemplified in the title essay, where she explores representations of the living room by both verbal and visual artists in order to examine the overlap between public and private selves in this "presentation space." Her essays, as well as a number of short stories, have appeared in numerous periodicals and journals ranging from the *Village Voice* to the *Kenyon Review*, from the *Women's Review of Books* to *Callaloo*.

   Born in Harlem, New York, Alexander grew up in Washington, D.C., in a distinguished **family** where education and achievement were important values. Her father, Clifford Leopold Alexander, Jr., who served as secretary of the army under President Jimmy Carter, has had a distinguished career as a lawyer, business consultant, and diplomat. Her mother, Adele (Logan) Alexander, is a historian and writer whose work has been nominated for the Pulitzer Prize. Alexander received a B.A. from Yale University, an M.A. from Boston University (where she studied poetry writing with Derek Walcott), and a Ph.D. from the University of Pennsylvania. She has received grants from the National Endowment for the Arts and the Guggenheim Foundation, as well as two Pushcart Prizes. She has lectured abroad and taught at Haverford College, Smith College, and the University of Chicago, where she was awarded the Quantrell Award for Excellence in Undergraduate Teaching. She is currently on the faculty at Yale University. During the summers, she teaches at Cave Canem, a retreat for African American writers, of which she is a founding member. Recently she was elected to the board of the Poetry Society of America.

Works By

Antebellum Dream Book. Saint Paul, MN: Graywolf Press, 2001.
The Black Interior. Saint Paul, MN: Graywolf Press, 2004.
The Body of Life. Chicago: Tia Chucha Press, 1996.
The Venus Hottentot. Charlottesville: University of Virginia Press, 1990. Reprint, Saint Paul, MN: Graywolf Press, 2004.

Works About

"Elizabeth Alexander." The Academy of American Poets. March 30, 2004. www.poets.org/poets/poets.cfm?45442B7-C000C046100.
Furious Flower: Conversations with African American Poets. San Francisco: California Newsreel, 1998. Video recording.
Phillip, Christine. "An Interview with Elizabeth Alexander." *Callaloo* 19.2 (Spring 1996): 493–507.

                                                              Ann Hostetler

ALEXANDER, MARGARET ABIGAIL WALKER. See Walker, Margaret

ALLEN, CLARISSA MINNIE THOMPSON (?–?)

If Clarissa Minnie Thompson Allen's *Treading the Winepress; or, A Mountain of Misfortune* had been published as a single volume, she would have been the second African American woman to publish a novel. Instead, *Treading the Winepress* was serialized in the *Boston Advocate*, on the front page of forty-one issues between 1885 and 1886. In *Treading the Winepress*, Allen offers a noteworthy critique of specific social concerns within the African American **community**, including African American elitism and racial loyalty. Though the plot of *Treading the Winepress* is frequently melodramatic, full of unrequited **love**, madness, and murder, Allen's tale advocates morality, the virtues of womanhood, and respect for all people regardless of color or gender. To date, Allen's *Treading the Winepress* has still not been published as a single volume.

Allen was born in Columbia, South Carolina, to a prosperous middle-class **family**. Her mother, Eliza Henrietta Montgomery, bore nine children, of which Clarissa was the oldest. Her father, Samuel Benjamin Thompson, was a justice of the peace and state legislator. Allen was educated at the Howard School, then attended the South Carolina State Normal School, part of South Carolina University. After she completed her education, she accepted a teaching position at the Howard School and later went on to serve as principal of the Poplar Grove School in Abbeville, South Carolina. She then took a position at Allen University, where she taught Latin, physical geography, algebra, and ancient and modern **history**. Allen left South Carolina in 1886 to teach at a public school in Jefferson, Texas. After three years, Allen took a position as the first assistant in the Fort Worth City School System.

Allen began writing at an early age and published essays in the *Christian Recorder*. The first three chapters of *Treading the Winepress* were also published in the *Christian Recorder*, but the paper felt the novel's plot unsuited for its ecclesiastic audience and withdrew further publication. She also published **poetry** and letters for a variety of black newspapers, sometimes under the name Minnie Myrtle. Allen was also an essayist, and her "Humane Education" was presented at a teachers' convention in Ft. Worth, Texas, in 1892. Parts of the essay also appeared in the *Afro-American Encyclopedia*. One notable poem, titled "A Glass of Wine," demonstrates her intolerance for alcohol and was printed in the Texas *Blade* in 1886. She also published a novella titled *Only a Flirtation* in the *Dallas Enterprise*.

Allen was first and foremost an educator. She placed particular importance on the education of the African American community, especially women, whom she felt were regularly deprived of the opportunities to raise themselves. Allen used her literary skill to celebrate her high ideal of womanhood, which is reflected in her **poetry** and the characters in her novel. Above all,

Allen advocated knowledge as paramount to the elevation of the African American community, and she dedicated her life to that end.

Works By

"A Glass of Wine." *Blade*, 1886.

"Humane Education." *Afro-American Encyclopedia, or the Thoughts, Doings, and Sayings of the Race*. Comp. James T. Haley and Booker T. Washington. Nashville, TN: Haley and Florida, 1895. 267–270.

"In Memoriam—the Grand Old Man." *Afro-American Encyclopedia, or the Thoughts, Doings, and Sayings of the Race*. Comp. James T. Haley and Booker T. Washington. Nashville, TN: Haley and Florida, 1895. 549.

Only a Flirtation. Dallas Enterprise, n.d.

"A Simple Tale of Simple Trust." *Christian Review*, October 8, 1885.

Treading the Winepress; or, A Mountain of Misfortune. Boston Advocate 1–2 (1885–1886). Serialized.

Works About

Monroe, Majors. *Noted Negro Women, Their Triumphs and Activities*. Chicago: Donahue and Hennberry, 1893.

Shockley, Ann Allen. *Afro-American Women Writers, 1746–1933*. Boston: G. K. Hall, 1988.

Debbie Clare Olson

AMINI, JOHARI (1935–   )

Johari Amini (Jewel C. Latimore) is a poet, writer, teacher, and chiropractor. As a poet, she seeks to celebrate her black heritage and to reject the racism that was so prevalent in American society during the 1960s. She and other poets protested the unequal treatment of blacks by turning away from traditional approaches in American **poetry**. They rejected formal English grammar, experimented with free verse that avoided the use of traditional metrical patterns, and implemented elements found in the everyday speech of many African Americans. Some features of the vernacular included shortened word endings, multiple negations, slang, the unvaried use of "be," and a lack of possessives. In Amini's poetry, one finds little punctuation, unconventional capitalization, the use of equal signs, the ampersand, ellipses, words separated with large spaces or no spaces, and abbreviated words. Although Amini's poetry did not conform to traditional standards, as a teacher she encouraged her students to master orthodox English so they would have the proper background to excel in society.

Amini was born in 1935 in Philadelphia, Pennsylvania, where she was the oldest of six children. Her father was a clergyman and her mother, Alma

Bazel McLawler, was a songwriter who specialized in gospel music. As a young girl, Amini was considered by some to be a child prodigy and was encouraged to write by the adults in her life. She met Haki R. Madhubuti (born Don L. Lee) at Wilson Junior College, which marked the beginning of a significant literary and political alliance. Amini, Madhubuti, and **Carolyn Rodgers** cofounded the Third World Press in Madhubuti's apartment in Chicago with only $400. The Third World Press has become one of the oldest and most prestigious publishers in the nation that has promoted progressive black thought, critique, and **literature**. After meeting Madhubuti, Amini changed her name from Jewel Christine McLawler to Johari Amini. In Swahili, *Johari* means "jewel," and *Amini* stands for "honesty and trustworthiness." This name was thoughtfully chosen because Amini believes that a name is connected to a person's character and personality, and it was her hope that this name would be a reflection of her personal behavior. Among her accomplishments, she holds an A.A. from Chicago City College (1968), a B.A. from Chicago State College (1970), and an M.A. from the University of Chicago (1972).

Amini used the name Jewel C. Latimore when she first started her writing career. Her poetry can be found in such works as *Images in Black* (1967), *A Folk Fable* (1969), *Let's Go Some Where* (1970), and *A Hip Tale in the Death Style* (1972). Her essays are in *An African Frame of Reference* (1972), and she also wrote *A Commonsense Approach to Eating* (1975). Her background in psychology and training as a chiropractor provide her with the knowledge to address the whole person in her writing. She is particularly concerned with the survival of African Americans and believes that survival is most likely when people understand their **identity**.

See also Black Arts Movement; Black Nationalism; Race

Works By

An African Frame of Reference. Chicago: Institute of Positive Education, 1972.
Black Essence. Chicago: Third World Press, 1968.
A Commonsense Approach to Eating. Chicago: Institute of Positive Education, 1975.
A Folk Fable (For My People). Chicago: Third World Press, 1969.
A Hip Tale in the Death Style. Detroit: Broadside, 1972.
Images in Black. Chicago: Third World Press, 1967.
Let's Go Some Where. Chicago: Third World Press, 1970.

Work About

Reid, Margaret Ann. *Black Protest Poetry: Polemics from the Harlem Renaissance and the Sixties.* Studies in African and African-American Culture 8. New York: Lang, 2001.

Deborah Weagel

ANCESTOR, USE OF

The concept of the ancestor is important in the study of African American **literature**. Explanations of the ancestor can be attributed to **Toni Morrison**. In her essay "City Limits, Village Values: Concepts of the Neighborhood in Black Fiction," Morrison defines the ancestor and places the ancestor in relationship to the roles of the city and the country in African American literature. Morrison believes that because black men and women have not contributed to the growth of the American city, they are outsiders in that city. On the other hand, it is the village, the neighborhood within the city, that often empowers the African American, and this idea is illustrated by many African American writers. As well, Morrison points out that while the ancestor is often absent in literature that places itself within the city, the ancestor can often be found in the village within the city.

However, regardless of the setting of a work, the ancestor is frequently a key element. In her essay "Rootedness: The Ancestor as Foundation," Morrison explains that ancestors are not necessarily parents; they are grandmothers, grandfathers, and healers, among others. Morrison defines the ancestor as "benevolent, instructive, and protective." She explains that when the ancestor figure is absent, the characters often fail to succeed; when the ancestor is present, however, the characters are more likely to survive, succeed, and find happiness.

There are a number of works in African American literature in which the existence, or absence, of an ancestor figure has significance. For example, Mama in **Lorraine Hansberry**'s *A Raisin in the Sun* is perhaps the best example of the ancestor figure. Many attribute the strength of the Younger **family** to Mama, and it is as a result of Mama's wisdom that her son Walter acknowledges his black roots and experiences growth. Similarly, Janie in **Zora Neale Hurston**'s *Their Eyes Were Watching God* is another character who benefits from the wisdom of the ancestor in the form of her grandmother. As well, Mattie Michael in **Gloria Naylor**'s *The Women of Brewster Place* is the sustaining element for the **community** of oppressed women in this urban environment. On the other hand, Lutie in **Ann Petry**'s *The Street* is a character who fails to succeed because she has no ancestor figure to empower her; in fact, the solitary Lutie longs for the wisdom of her deceased grandmother as she tries to make the right choices. Without the ancestor, her life follows a tragic path. The use of the ancestor can also be seen in the work of **Toni Cade Bambara** and **Ralph Ellison**, among others.

Works About

Morrison, Toni. "City Limits, Village Values: Concepts of the Neighborhood in Black Fiction." *Literature and the Urban Experience: Essays on the City and Literature.* Ed. Michael C. Jaye and Ann Chalmers Watts. New Brunswick, NJ: Rutgers University Press, 1981. 35–43.

——. "Rootedness: The Ancestor as Foundation." *Black Women Writers (1950–1980)*. Ed. Mari Evans. Garden City, NY: Anchor Press, 1984. 339–345.

Diane Todd Bucci

ANDERSON, MIGNON HOLLAND (1945–   )

Mignon Holland Anderson was born and raised in Northampton County, Cheriton, Virginia, to Frank and Ruby Holland, who owned and operated a successful funeral home in the area. Exposure to the intimacies of **death** heightened Anderson's understanding and compassion for the debilitating affects of racism and economic poverty on African Americans. These experiences infused Anderson with a desire, exhibited in her writing, to represent the truth of African American heritage and experience and the strength developed and displayed in the struggle to withstand the onslaughts of segregation, which inevitably lead to feelings of helplessness, inadequacy, and vulnerability.

Anderson depicts the impact of potentially crushing outside forces upon the African American man and the significant role of the African American woman in that equation. She not only celebrates the power of African American womanhood but also what that strength brings to the African American male and **family**. In a 1968 short story, "In the Face of Fire, I Will Not Turn Back," Anderson honors the strength of the African American woman through a depiction that chronicles her fortitude through captivity, **slavery**, her husband's despair of his situation, and the need to hire herself out in order to support her family. Throughout Anderson's writings, the African American woman serves as the foundation for the man as she gives support in his struggle against the world. She likewise acts as a freeing and **healing** force for the African American man and a mainstay for the children.

Anderson's first book, a collection of short stories titled *Mostly Womenfolk and a Man or Two* (1976), contains stories that bring to life the intricate role of the female African American within the family. As the stories move from various accounts of birth, childhood, struggle, and death, Anderson weaves these representative roles of woman throughout the book, ultimately ending with a female child physically supporting an elderly man during a funeral. Anderson's second book, a novel titled *The End of Dying* (2001), continues, in part, this exploration of the significance of the African American woman in her family as it follows the impact of overt racism leveled upon one child, Carrie Allen, and the people she loves.

Anderson continues to write and publish and has dedicated herself to enriching the learning experience of students, especially college freshmen at the University of Maryland Eastern Shore (UMES), a historically black land grant university, where she resides as the only instructor of freshman English honors courses. She earned a Master of Fine Arts degree from Columbia University and has served as the associate editor and editor of the *Maryland*

Review, UMES' literary journal. Anderson has won several teaching awards, among them UMES President's Teacher of the Year and the President's Top Ten Teachers of the Year, and has appeared several times in Who's Who Among America's Teachers. Anderson is currently working on her third book, *The Summer Calling*.

Works By

The End of Dying. Baltimore: AmErica House, 2001.
"Gone After Jake." *Carry Me Back: An Anthology of Virginia Fiction*. Ed. Mary MacArthur. Arlington, VA: Gallimaufry Press, 1978.
"In the Face of Fire, I Will Not Turn Back." *Negro Digest* 17 (1968): 20–23.
Mostly Womenfolk and a Man or Two: A Collection. Chicago: Third World Press, 1976.

Wanda G. Addison

ANGELOU, MAYA (1928–   )

Born in St. Louis, Missouri, the multitalented and prolific Marguerite ("Maya") Johnson spent the majority of her childhood in Stamps, Arkansas. While living with her brother Bailey, her physically handicapped uncle, and her entrepreneur grandmother, Angelou was quickly immersed in the matrix of fear, surveillance, and racially centered **violence** that defined black life in the segregated **South**. The early divorce of her parents made for a rather unstable relationship with both, although her mother, Vivian Baxter, eventually emerged as the more influential parent. *I Know Why the Caged Bird Sings* (1970), the author's first published work, was the recipient of widespread critical and public acclaim. It generated five subsequent volumes of the same genre: *Gather Together in My Name* (1974), *Singin' and Swingin' and Gettin' Merry Like Christmas* (1976), *The Heart of a Woman* (1981), *All God's Children Need Traveling Shoes* (1986), and *A Song Flung Up to Heaven* (2002). A consistent theme is the struggle to maintain a healthy sense of individuality amid the unrelenting social terrors faced by black Americans from within a national machinery of racial and sexual oppression. Angelou's victimization is held in equipoise with her heroic drive for self-actualization and her desire to succeed. Of key importance is the belief that through intelligence, perseverance, and acquired skills, the fulfillment of seemingly impossible goals is possible and, indeed, imperative for survival and ultimate growth.

As a public figure, Angelou has been extremely aware of her office as a positive and enduring role model for women, especially women of color. By participating in worldwide speaking tours, educational projects, corporate ventures for companies like Hallmark, and various artistic and social endeavors, Angelou has morphed into a kind of American institution. Like the Horatio Alger books she explored as a child, hers is a narrative of uplift and (feminist) transcendence beyond the poverty and circumscription of early life. Even when faced with indignities (racism, abusive relationships, job stress, depression, intense personal loss), her actions have exemplified how inner resources, no matter how atrophied or abused, can be revivified through a mixture of initiative, creative thinking, and common sense. This mutable spirit suggests a very American kind of optimism. Angelou, in turn, is an emblematic figure, especially in what may be called the "self-made, self-help" tradition of American literary heroism. Her symbolic currency as a strong black woman has been duly suggested by her role in the **film** *How to Make an American Quilt* (1995). The **quilting** ritual serves as an occasion for her character, one voice emanating from a circle of female peers, to speak about ancestral wisdom, the dignity of folk tradition, and the nurturing, matrifocal bonds that can exist between women of different generations, backgrounds, and **races**. Art remains the nucleus of this creative and interpersonal exchange.

In an ongoing repudiation of the narrow roles that black women of her generation were expected to fulfill, Angelou's career stands as a veritable patchwork of life encounters. They have been in artistic performance (singer, dancer, actor, composer, film director), creative and critical writing (essayist, poet, journalist, playwright, editor, screen and teleplay writer), social welfare advocacy (northern coordinator for Martin Luther King's Southern Christian Leadership Conference), education (endowed professor, university writer-in-residence, motivational speaker), transportation (streetcar conductress, chauffeur), food service (cook, waitress, **domestic**), and miscellaneous employment (unpaid laborer in the **family** store, whorehouse madam, prostitute). As *Gather Together in My Name* attests, **motherhood** has remained an undeniably central aspect of her life, although as an urban woman seeking the twin goals of self-sufficiency and financial stability, the management of her son's life has been difficult. She dedicated *I Know Why the Caged Bird Sings* to her son Guy, whose birth in San Francisco occurred shortly after her graduation from high school at sixteen.

Both movement and emotional flux characterize Angelou's autobiographical journey. Especially during her teen years in California, she finds switching jobs and traveling routine occurrences. Her career would lead her to Canada, Europe, and Africa, among others, primarily by dint of the *Porgy and Bess* production (1954–1955) that she details in *Singin' and Swingin' and Gettin' Merry Like Christmas*. At times, she encounters resistance from others based on her refusal to muffle her assertive personality in conformity with her perceived station (that is, a young, black, unwed mother). Another reason for her early unsettledness lies in her failed romantic relationships. An intriguing section of *Gather Together in My Name* deals with the disparity between fantasy and reality in amatory relationships. Her human environment is littered with troubled males: drug users, pimps, pushers, gamblers, and the despondent, the latter category being one that includes her brother. While she acknowledges the dehumanizing pressures on many of these men, she finds her relative naiveté, loyalty, and straightforwardness abused by those who profess to care for her. Her **body** becomes a tool for the furthering of their personal and professional goals, an often sexist breach of trust that requires **healing** and much positive support from her mother as well as a cluster of female friends.

Her marriage to a Greek American (that is, a white man) would substantially affect her perceptions, especially with regard to interracial relationships and the disparity between good intentions, bad outcomes, and what might aptly be called "the mourning after." Whether it is the elaborately spun 1950s dream of a nuclear family that paired a working father and homemaker mother with a happy, well-adjusted child, or the more fundamental desire for respect and reciprocity in **love**, Angelou's hopes for sustained and salutary interaction with men falter due to their inability to commit wholly, monogamously, and with a necessary level of compromise. In the case of her first husband, the point of contention is religious belief, something the staunch atheist Tosh forbids. For feminist readers, the semiotic field of religious devotion is most closely aligned with the sanctity and security of her grandmother, Momma Henderson. Tosh's patriarchal intolerance for Angelou's right to worship gestures to greater curtailments of her personal freedom over the rapidly dwindling course of their partnership.

Conversely, in the case of the two lesbians for whom she briefly serves as brothel madam, the relationship appears at least mutually satisfying. Between employer and employees, however, the rapport is less about sisterly cooperation and female empowerment than material gain, competitiveness, and eventually, shared disdain. The lesbian characters Johnnie Mae and Beatrice are eccentric and bawdy, and Angelou's hardly tight-lipped ambivalence about their frank **sexuality** is reminiscent of **Ann Petry**'s portrayal of the queer landlady in *The Street* (1946). This episode, however, does provide a decidedly heterosexual (and arguably, heterosexist) coda to the agonizing qualms about **lesbianism** that the writer faces at the end of the first autobiographical installment. In *The Heart of a Woman*, lesbianism resurfaces briefly with reference to **Billie Holiday**, showing that homosexuality was a pervasive aspect of many prominent black artists' lives. In the third text especially, a widening of Angelou's social network makes more room for a spectrum of individuals; many are gay, and yet most of them are talented and memorable enough to be immortalized in her work. Such continuity functions in a more expansive, metacritical sense as well. At the end of *A Song Flung Up to Heaven*, the reader is taken to the point in Angelou's life when she decides to begin writing her first **autobiography**. Coming full circle, the textual act mimics the recursive nature of the writer's **memory** and the desire to reconstitute the past through a life-giving, life-affirming document of personal ascent.

From her early training in drama at the California Labor School, Angelou has danced, sung, and written herself into being as a consummate performer. During her artistic coming of age, she undergoes a name change (the adopted marital surname "Angelos" becomes "Angelou"), a profound metaphor for the refashioning of the female self. It is not through marriage but through the alembic of multiple formative experiences that this occurs. If the name stands as a sign of assertive individuality, the newly formed "Angelou" consolidates the importance of the writer's quest for an **identity** apart from the coercive influence of her husband or her prescribed role as wife. "Maya" also becomes her name proper, a tribute to the continuing love she has for her absent brother who originally used "maya" in lieu of "my" to signify an affectionate claim on her as sibling and charge. Her son also changed his name, an indirect testament to the influence of a strong female and mother on a growing son and a hearkening back to the importance of naming in African American **history** and **literature** as a means by which power relations have been imposed, subverted, or affirmed. The significance of naming initially emerges in the first volume when Maya refuses to accept a new, supposedly more convenient name from her employer as an adequate substitute for her own.

For readers, this textual resonance between mother and son reiterates the importance of Angelou's commitment to her child and the possible unconscious effects that absences—temporary or prolonged—have on the psyche of loved ones. During her theatrical tour of Europe, the writer rarely fails to remind the audience of her devotion to her son and the attendant guilt of leaving him with her mother in California. This scenario proves to be a repetition of her own situation as a child, handed over to her grandmother while her parents pursued their own goals from a distant shore. While Angelou comes to a clearer understanding of her mother's motivations and her probable emotional turmoil, she struggles with the double imperative of furthering her own inchoate career and attending to her only child. Privileging the latter need facilitates the recovery of Guy's psychosomatic skin condition but prompts Maya's descent into neurasthenic illness. In the end, however, she realizes with gratitude the extent of her life's path thus far, her blessings by the grace of God, and the joy that awaits both in the continued pursuit of her ambitions. In some ways, her fight to guide her son as a single mother shares many qualities with Gloria Matthews's struggle in **Terry McMillan**'s phenomenally popular novel *Waiting to Exhale* (1992).

These volumes stand as vital historiographical documents for their ability to bring together in continuous narrative form some of the most pivotal incidents and figures in African American history. Much has been said about the assistance **Langston Hughes**'s chapters on Harlem life in *The Big Sea* (1940) provided for literary historians. Angelou's contribution is hardly different, except that she strives to move beyond the scope of the merely literary, and her personal anecdotes tend to flesh out the characters and events more vividly because of the serial nature of her project. Her earlier texts contextualize, among others, the importance of Joe Louis, Charlie Parker, **James Weldon Johnson**, Paul Robeson, **Paul Laurence Dunbar**, and Jesse Owens in the readerly imagination. They also emphasize the influence of black music and social struggle on West Coast life, stressing how a culture beyond Harlem and other urban centers of the North did indeed exist. The later texts go on to mention southern lynch law, bus boycotts, Emmett Till, **Malcolm X**, Elijah Muhammad, the lure of the Pan-Africanist movement, the Du Boises in Ghana (where Angelou ventures in *All God's Children Need*

Traveling Shoes), Kwame Nkrumah, and a host of other crucial avatars of revolutionary social change. What sets her rendition apart from those of her male precedents is the way in which her story showcases her own investment in, and involvement with, these movements, leaders, and ideas. In other words, she is not simply the passive female observer, the assistant, or the secretary. Her gendered presence is crucial. While the **Harlem Renaissance** poet **Countee Cullen** wrote wonderingly about his alienation from the African continent in a poem like "Heritage" (1925), Angelou goes to Africa and directly interrogates the lost centuries, doing so in the context of her *female*, as well as her male, ancestors. Like many autobiographers, her mode is certainly confessional, but her tone shuns sentimentalism, remaining shrewd, measured, and at times, tersely philosophical.

In the fourth volume, building on a theme of arrival and leave taking, Angelou relocates to New York with her son. She joins the Harlem Writers Guild, a stellar opportunity for her to renew her interest in literature and forge more profound ties with writers like **Paule Marshall** and **James Baldwin**. This would be a precursor to her move to Africa, appearances in Jean Genet's *The Blacks* (1960), editorial work for the *Arab Observer* (1961–1962), print journalism for the *Times* of Ghana and the Ghanaian Broadcasting Corporation, and a climactic decision to return to America in order to continue her civil rights activism. *A Song Flung Up to Heaven* reveals how her work straddled two continents, interrogating the meaning of bicultural identification (African and American) at such an incendiary time as the 1960s. From a feminist vantage point, she takes up and reconfigures the work of similarly cosmopolitan individuals like Olaudah Equiano, one of the early writers of the transatlantic **slave narratives**. His travels during the European Enlightenment indexed what was to many the paradoxical status of being African and yet highly literate, intelligent, and indeed, a *human* citizen of the world.

Although the full impact of her **poetry** has been somewhat overshadowed by the popularity of her memoirs, this important aspect of Angelou's repertoire was underscored by the honor of being the first female and first African American to read at a presidential inauguration. "On the Pulse of Morning" ushered in the Clinton era in January 1993. Her collections include the Pulitzer Prize–nominated *Just Give Me a Cool Drink of Water 'fore I Diiie* (1971), *Oh Pray My Wings Are Gonna Fit Me Well* (1975), *And Still I Rise* (1978), *Shaker, Why Don't You Sing?* (1983), *Now Sheba Sings the Song* (1987), *I Shall Not Be Moved* (1990), and *Phenomenal Woman* (1994). The lyricism of her verse and the incisive commentary of her memoirs have been consolidated and transmitted into essay form, yielding *Wouldn't Take Nothing for My Journey Now* (1993) and *Even the Stars Look Lonesome* (1997). Many of her poems are succinct meditations on female strength, the refusal to submit gently to grief or failure, and the inimitable bonds that exist between family, friends, and lifelong acquaintances.

Angelou's artistic territory has extended to plays (*And Still I Rise* [1978]), television acting (**Alex Haley**'s *Roots* [1977]), spoken-word recordings (*Been Found* [1996]), children's books (*Kofi and His Magic* [1996]), a PBS series (*Black, Blues, Black* [1968]), screenplays (*Georgia, Georgia* [1971]), film direction (*Down* *in the Delta* [1998]), and manifold other efforts on the national and international scenes. She has become a cultural icon, receiving a lifelong appointment as Reynolds Professor of American Studies at Wake Forest University. Apart from prizes and honorary degrees, she was awarded a lifetime membership to the National Women's Hall of Fame in 2002. Her career has exemplified a drive for honesty, self-validation, and visibility both as a female and as an African American artist and public intellectual.

See also Civil Rights Movement; Work

Works By

All God's Children Need Traveling Shoes. New York: Random House, 1986.
And Still I Rise. New York: Random House, 1978.
The Complete Collected Poems of Maya Angelou. New York: Random House, 1994.
Even the Stars Look Lonesome. New York: Random House, 1997.
Gather Together in My Name. New York: Random House, 1974.
The Heart of a Woman. New York: Random House, 1981.
I Know Why the Caged Bird Sings. New York: Random House, 1970.
Just Give Me a Drink of Water 'fore I Diiie. New York: Random House, 1971.
Shaker, Why Don't You Sing? New York: Random House, 1983.
Singin' and Swingin' and Gettin' Merry Like Christmas. New York: Random House, 1976.
A Song Flung Up to Heaven. New York: Random House, 2002.
Wouldn't Take Nothing for My Journey Now. New York: Random House, 1993.

Works About

Burr, Zofia. *Of Women, Poetry, and Power: Strategies of Address in Dickinson, Miles, Brooks, Lorde, and Angelou.* Urbana: University of Illinois Press, 2002.
Cudjoe, Selwyn. "Maya Angelou and the Autobiographical Statement." *Black Women Writers (1950–1980)—A Critical Evaluation.* Ed. Mari Evans. Garden City, NY: Anchor-Doubleday, 1984.
Elliot, Jeffrey M., ed. *Conversations with Maya Angelou.* Jackson: University Press of Mississippi, 1989.
Hager, Lyman B. *Heart of a Woman, Mind of a Writer, and Soul of a Poet: A Critical Analysis of the Writings of Maya Angelou.* Lanham, MD: University Press of America, 1997.
Lupton, Mary Jane. *Maya Angelou: A Critical Companion.* Westport, CT: Greenwood Press, 1998.
McPherson, Dolly A. *Order Out of Chaos: The Autobiographical Works of Maya Angelou.* New York: P. Lang, 1990.
Williams, Mary E., ed. *Readings on Maya Angelou.* San Diego, CA: Greenhaven Press, 1997.

Nancy Kang

ANNIE ALLEN

Gwendolyn Brooks's second collection of **poetry**, published in 1949, tells the story of the early life of the title character, a girl who comes of age during the 1940s. This focus on a single character represented a significant shift from the emphasis on setting in her first book, *A Street in Bronzeville* (1945), which realistically portrayed a broad cross section of black people on Chicago's South Side through carefully selected details. By contrast, Brooks depicted Annie Allen's environment through symbols that suggest how Annie's perceptions are colored by romance and fairy tales. The second book also represented a stylistic departure for Brooks; her already careful language and attentiveness to form were dazzlingly heightened, earning both praise and criticism from the literary establishment. The collection won the Pulitzer Prize in Poetry in 1950, making Brooks the first African American—female or male—to be accorded this honor.

After opening with a poetic memorial for Brooks's friend who was killed serving in World War II, the collection is divided into three sections corresponding to the phases of Annie's maturation. The first, "Notes from the Childhood and the Girlhood," includes ballads and other short poems describing her earliest years, in which she absorbs the romantic ideals that teach girls to aspire to **love** in lieu of active, self-determined lives. Annie clings to these illusions, despite the evidence her parents' marriage gives her about the realities of domesticity. The young Annie learns to suppress her feelings to gain her mother's approval and dreams passively of escape into a fairy-tale marriage.

The title of the second section, "The Anniad," purposefully recalls Greek epics like *The Iliad*. Written in exquisitely crafted variations of the rhyme royal stanza, the single long poem composing this section depicts Annie's troubled marriage, implicitly comparing her struggles to the heroics of great warriors. Annie's battlefield is the gloomy little apartment where she fights to save her marriage, challenged by poverty, the draft, infidelity, and finally, the illness that leads to her husband's **death**. Critics disagree about whether this poem is a mock-epic, suggesting that Annie's battle is trivial compared to traditional, masculine epic subjects, or a feminist revision of the genre, employing its conventions to recast her as heroic.

"The Womanhood," the third section, portrays Annie as a mature mother, devoted to providing for her children. Through her trials she has gained a sense of self, independent of illusions of rescue by a Prince Charming. Having learned that poor, dark-skinned black girls are not the intended heroines of fairy tales, she teaches her children, in a series of poignant sonnets, to approach life's pleasures and pains directly and pragmatically. The remaining poems illustrate scenes in which she and they face loss, racism, colorism, and economic oppression—and survive. Brooks revisits many of this book's themes in her novel ***Maud Martha*** (1953). Though she later dismissed her achievement as overly interested in technique at the expense of content, *Annie*

Allen remains an aesthetically and historically important representation of societal issues confronting African American women.

See also Beauty; Motherhood

Works About

Jimoh, A. Yemisi. "Double Consciousness, Modernism, and Womanist Themes in Gwendolyn Brooks's 'The Anniad.' " *MELUS* 23 (1998): 167–186.

Melhem, D. H. *Gwendolyn Brooks: Poetry & the Heroic Voice.* Lexington: University Press of Kentucky, 1987.

Stanford, Ann Folwell. "An Epic with a Difference: Sexual Politics in Gwendolyn Brooks's 'The Anniad.' " *American Literature* 67.2 (June 1995): 283–301.

Tate, Claudia. "Anger So Flat: Gwendolyn Brooks's *Annie Allen.*" *A Life Distilled: Gwendolyn Brooks, Her Poetry and Fiction.* Ed. Maria K. Mootry and Gary Smith. Urbana: University of Illinois Press, 1987. 140–152.

Walters, Tracey L. "Gwendolyn Brooks' 'The Anniad' and the Indeterminacy of Genre." *College Language Association Journal* 44 (2001): 350–366.

Evie Shockley

ANNIE JOHN

"I always say it's completely autobiographical, including the punctuation," **Jamaica Kincaid** has remarked of her 1985 coming-of-age novel *Annie John* (Muirhead 45). "The point wasn't the truth and yet the point was the truth," she insists, describing *Annie John* as, at once, a fictional work and as autobiographical (Perry 494). First published as a series of stories in the *New Yorker*, *Annie John* is a fictionalized account of Kincaid's life as she grew up in Antigua in the 1950s through the mid-1960s. Haunted by memories of her mother-tormented past, Kincaid was moved to write because of the "immediate oppression" of the mother-daughter relation. "I wanted to free myself of that," she states (Bonetti 32). Writing gave Kincaid a way to talk back to her internalized mother and also a way to take control of her obsessive ruminations over the past.

Presented as a series of vignettes, *Annie John* chronicles the early life of Kincaid's daughter-character, Annie John, from ages ten to seventeen. Although *Annie John* may seem, at first glance, a simple narrative in its linear but episodic account of the childhood and coming of age of Annie John, many readers find an emotional puzzle at the heart of the work as Kincaid describes Annie's intense **love**-hate relationship with her all-powerful mother. If Annie as a girl feels physically and psychically close to her mother and secure in her mother's presence, she also is extremely sensitive to maternal rejection and slights. Just as Annie comes to divide her mother into the idealized good mother and the angry and rejecting bad mother, so she divides herself—and her girlfriends—into good and bad identities, seeing Gwen as an embodiment of her idealized good self and the Red Girl as her unlovable and defiant bad self. While Annie excels in her studies in school, she also defies her teachers as she actively resists not only her English colonial education but also her mother's efforts to make her behave in a socially acceptable feminine way. But behind Annie's defiance lie deep-rooted feelings of shame and despair.

Living in the shadow of her contemptuous mother during her troubled adolescence, Annie comes to identify her bad and rejected self with Lucifer. Accused by her mother of behaving like a slut, Annie becomes not only angry but also depressed. Retreating into herself, she collapses into a prolonged depressive illness and is ultimately cured by her maternal grandmother, Ma Chess, a practitioner of obeah, who restores Annie to health by comforting and mothering her. In the novel's closing scenes as Annie prepares to leave Antigua to go to England, where she will train to become a nurse, she is almost overwhelmed by a flood of contradictory feelings as she recognizes the finality of her leave-taking from Antigua—and from her mother.

"Clearly, the way I became a writer was that my mother wrote my life for me and told it to me," Kincaid has remarked of her writing (O'Connor 6). A mother-obsessed and female-focused novel, *Annie John*'s coming-of-age story sets the stage for Kincaid's continuing exploration of her mother-dominated Antiguan past in novels such as **Lucy** and **The Autobiography of My Mother**, and it also marks the emergence of Kincaid's distinctive voice as she talks back to the contemptuous mother who wrote her life. If Kincaid was profoundly injured by her mother, she also traces the roots of her writing to her mother's storytelling, and Kincaid's characteristic angry and defiant voice also finds its roots in her mother's contemptuous voice. It is this voice that Kincaid uses to great effect in her next novel *Lucy* as she, in describing her experiences after leaving Antigua and coming to the United States to work as an au pair, continues to tell the story of her early life lived in the shadow of her powerful mother, Annie Drew.

Works About

Bonetti, Kay. "Jamaica Kincaid." *Conversations with American Novelists: The Best Interviews from "The Missouri Review" and the American Audio Prose Library.* Ed. Kay Bonetti et al. Columbia: University of Missouri Press, 1997. 26–38.

Bouson, J. Brooks. *Jamaica Kincaid: Writing Memory, Writing Back to the Mother.* Albany: SUNY Press, 2004.

Caton, Louis. "Romantic Struggles: The Bildungsroman and Mother-Daughter Bonding in Jamaica Kincaid's *Annie John.*" *MELUS* 21.3 (Fall 1996): 125–142.

Ferguson, Moira. *Jamaica Kincaid: Where the Land Meets the Body.* Charlottesville: University Press of Virginia, 1994.

Mistron, Deborah. *Understanding Jamaica Kincaid's Annie John: A Student Casebook to Issues, Sources, and Historical Documents.* Westport, CT: Greenwood Press, 1999.

Muirhead, Pamela. "An Interview with Jamaica Kincaid." *Clockwatch Review* 9 (1994–1995): 39–48.

O'Conner, Patricia. "My Mother Wrote My Life." *New York Times Book Review* April 7, 1985, 6.

Paravisini-Gebert, Lizabeth. *Jamaica Kincaid: A Critical Companion.* Westport, CT: Greenwood Press, 1999.

Perry, Donna. "An Interview with Jamaica Kincaid." *Reading Black, Reading Feminist: A Critical Anthology.* Ed. Henry Louis Gates. New York: Meridian-Penguin, 1990. 492–509.

Simmons, Diane. *Jamaica Kincaid.* New York: Twayne-Macmillan, 1994.

J. Brooks Bouson

ANSA, TINA McELROY (1949–   )

Tina McElroy Ansa has carved a niche for herself among the current generation of African American novelists. She has created the fictional **community** of Mulberry, Georgia, and populated it with an interesting array of strong African American women who struggle to come to terms with themselves and with their places in their community. Ansa's women work against common **stereotypes** of African American women, especially the stereotype of the downtrodden but morally superior superwoman, and the **myth** of the black matriarch as the head of the **family**. She also works to refute the image of loving, giving black **motherhood** with some of the mothers she creates who, far from being eternal nurturers, at midlife turn inward, seeking personal expression and connection with nature and with the nature gods that form their heritage. Ansa is also interested in material culture as an expression of personality and historical tradition and in folk traditions that reinforce connections between people, especially women, and nature.

Ansa was born in Macon, Georgia, and grew up in the predominantly black Pleasant Hill section of that city. The youngest of five children, her family's middle-class background is reflected by the fictional McPherson family that is prominent in her first and third novels, **Baby of the Family** (1989) and **The Hand I Fan With** (1996), as well as by the Lovejoy family of **Ugly Ways** (1993) and the Pines women in **You Know Better** (2002). Her parents were Walter J. McElroy, a businessman, and Nellie Lee McElroy, a teacher's assistant. Her grandfather ran a juke joint in which she heard many of the stories that find their way into her fictions, especially those featuring the fictional McPherson family's bar and grill called "The Place." Ansa always wanted to be a writer, and following her graduation from Atlanta's Spelman College in 1971, she began a career in journalism, first at the *Atlanta Constitution*, where she was the first black woman to work at a daily morning paper, then in North Carolina at the *Charlotte Observer*. In 1978 she married filmmaker Jonee Ansa, and in 1982 she retired from newspaper work to become a freelance writer, commentator, and promoter of literary and artistic efforts by other young African Americans. Tina McElroy Ansa and her husband make their home on St. Simons Island, Georgia, where they are a vital part of the area's artistic community. Her novels are all dedicated to her husband, "whose love sustains me," and her acknowledgments, in addition to recognizing Ansa's debts to family, friends, and editors, always include thanks to St. Simons Island for its "beauty, peace, and acceptance of home."

Ansa's growing reputation rests on her four novels that offer vivid female characters struggling to come to terms with who they are as individuals and as parts of their families and communities. This struggle is personal and emotional for the most part, reflecting characters that have advanced up Abraham Maslow's widely known hierarchy of personal needs beyond physiological and safety levels to deal with their needs for **love**, esteem, and self-actualization. The needs for economic security and shelter are not central issues, even though they may form part of the background of her characters' lives. In *Baby of the Family*, young Lena McPherson is the central character whose life is traced from birth to adolescence. In this coming-of-age story, Lena struggles with the "gifts" that being born with a caul over her face have brought her while she also observes and hears much of the life of members of the African American community of Mulberry, thus telling us the stories of their lives. The other novels deal more with adult women in various stages of self-discovery; in addition, the connections among the stories are obliquely referenced from tale to tale. *Ugly Ways* focuses on the Lovejoy women, the recently deceased mother Esther and her daughters Betty, Emily, and Annie Ruth, all seeking independence and struggling with the problems created by decisions the others make. References to the McPherson business, The Place, tie this novel to *Baby of the Family*. In *The Hand I Fan With* we revisit Lena McPherson as an adult facing her own midlife crises and coming to terms with her personal emotional needs. Lena, remembering her parents' funeral, offers the mortician, Mr. Parkinson, the opportunity to contrast the dignity of the McPherson funeral with his embarrassment about the debacle of Esther Lovejoy's funeral, tying this story to *Ugly Ways*. Finally, in *You Know Better* we meet three generations of Pines women, each of whom, in an oblique reference to Charles Dickens, requires guidance from the spirit world to see her life for what it is and to begin positive change. Nurse Bloom, important in *Baby of the Family* and mentioned in *The Hand I Fan With*, is one of the spirit guides in this story. The spirit world is an integral part of all four of these novels, with Lena haunted and helped by ghosts, with the deceased Esther having her own voice, and with the Pines women each being visited by a spirit who serves as guide and mentor. Ansa helps us to believe that this spirit world is a resource available to us if we open ourselves to its powers. She also celebrates the female connection to the natural world by the gardens and landscapes to which certain of her characters are intimately connected.

Ansa's style, in addition to celebrating black expression and black vernacular language, is characterized by her attention to the specific details that characterize her people. Food abounds in all of the stories, especially the soul food that sustains her characters when they need the comfort of particular flavors and textures on the tongue or when they celebrate family occasions with traditional foods whose recipes have come down through generations. Clothes characterize her people from the fashionable designer clothes that Nellie and Lena McPherson wear to the gauzy pastels that Grandmama McPherson and Esther Lovejoy favor. The interior design of the homes in which the McPherson, the Lovejoy, and the Pines women live also tells us a lot about the women who surround themselves not only with specific pieces of furniture but also with particular rooms and color schemes that allow them to express their individuality.

Ansa's work has won many awards. *Baby of the Family* and *The Hand I Fan With* have both won the Georgia Authors Series Award; Ansa is the only author to have received this award twice. In addition, *Baby of the Family* was named a Notable Book of the Year by the *New York Times* in 1989, and after its paperback publication, it made the African American Best Sellers List for Paperback Fiction as well as being named a Best Book for Young Adults by the American Library Association. The African American Blackboard List named *Ugly Ways* Best Fiction in 1994. In addition, she is gradually becoming more well known as critics and scholars include her in bio-bibliographical sourcebooks and write scholarly articles that include her work, specifically those that compare her with writers such as **Zora Neale Hurston** and **Alice Walker**. Ansa herself has said that Hurston was a model for her. When she read Hurston as a student at Spelman, she realized that **literature** could be written in black vernacular, a language that Ansa explores and celebrates in her novels.

In addition to her four novels, Ansa has written various essays and short stories and has coauthored with her husband the screenplay for the **film** version of *Baby of the Family*. The film, directed by Jonee Ansa, came out in 2002. Ansa also conducts writing workshops and actively mentors other writers and artists. The cover art for Ansa's novels is by African American artist Varnette P. Honeywood, whose work is also admired by Lena in *The Hand I Fan With*, representing yet another way in which Ansa connects to the world of African American artists.

Influenced by models such as Zora Neale Hurston, **Toni Morrison**, and Alice Walker, Ansa writes stories about real women, who happen to be African American, struggling to make sense of their lives in a small city in southern Georgia. She paints vivid pictures of the settings and details that define the characters' lives and depicts their situations with humor and love. Over her four novels, Ansa has gone more and more deeply into the spiritual and emotional needs that women face and has especially tried to open herself to the issues that younger women face in the twenty-first century.

See also Sexuality; Spirituality

Works By

Baby of the Family. 1989. San Diego: Harvest, 1991.

Baby of the Family. Screenplay by Tina McElroy Ansa and Jonee Ansa. Dir. Jonee Ansa. Perf. Cylk Cozart, Salli Richardson, C.C.H. Pounder. DownSouth Filmworks, 2002.

The Hand I Fan With. 1996. New York: Anchor, 1998.

Ugly Ways. 1993. San Diego: Harvest, 1995.

"Women in the Movement." *The Prevailing South: Life & Politics in a Changing Culture*. Ed. Dudley Clendinen. Atlanta, GA: Longstreet Press, 1988. 184–193.

You Know Better. New York: William Morrow, 2002.

Works About

Bennett, Barbara. "Making Peace with the (M)other." *The World Is Our Culture: Society and Culture in Contemporary Southern Writing*. Ed. Jeffrey J. Folks and Nancy Summers Folks. Lexington: University Press of Kentucky, 2000. 186–200.

Cherry, Joyce L. "Tina McElroy Ansa." *Contemporary African American Novelists: A Bio-Bibliographical Critical Sourcebook*. Ed. Emmanuel S. Nelson. Westport, CT: Greenwood Press, 1999. 1–5.

Green Tara T. "Mother Dear: The Motivations of Tina Ansa's Mudear." *Griot: Official Journal of the Southern Conference on Afro-American Studies* 21.1 (Spring 2002): 46–52.

Mosby, Charmaine Allmon. "Tina McElroy Ansa." *Contemporary Southern Writers*. Ed. Roger Matuz. Detroit, MI: St. James Press, 1999. 12–14.

Town, Caren J. " 'A Whole World of Possibilities Spinning around Her': Female Adolescence in the Contemporary Southern Fiction of Josephine Humphreys, Jill McCorkle, and Tina Ansa." *Southern Quarterly* 42.2 (Winter 2004): 89–109.

Warren, Nagueyalti. "Echoing Zora: Ansa's Other Hand in *The Hand I Fan With*." *CLA Journal* 46.3 (2003): 362–382.

——. "Resistant Mothers in Alice Walker's *Meridian* and Tina McElroy Ansa's *Ugly Ways*." *Southern Mothers: Fact and Fictions in Southern Women's Writing*. Ed. Nagueyalti Warren and Sally Wolff. Baton Rouge: Louisiana State University Press, 1999. 182–203.

Harriette C. Buchanan

AUNT JEMIMA

The events that sparked the creation and rise of this icon, the twentieth century's most recognizable image of black womanhood, began in 1875 when an African American musician named Billy Kersand composed the song "Old Aunt Jemima." Its colorful portrayal of a stereotypical **Mammy** figure helped to make "Old Aunt Jemima" one of the most popular songs of its time, especially on the minstrel stage, where white male performers in blackface and drag brought the title figure to life. The image of the lively Aunt Jemima caught the attention of Chris Rutt, a former journalist. The year was 1889, and Rutt and his business partner, Charles Underwood, had recently acquired a bankrupt flour mill that they intended to use for producing their latest creation, a self-rising pancake flour. Rutt, who first saw the Aunt Jemima performed at a minstrel show, realized that her lively wit and comforting image would make the perfect trademark for his new product.

Rutt and Underwood were unable to develop their flour business into a successful enterprise, and the company was eventually taken over by the R. T. Davis Milling Company. Davis's generous financing and marketing expertise breathed life into the Aunt Jemima product line. He hired Nancy Green, a former slave, to play the role of Aunt Jemima at public appearances. At trade shows and promotional events, Green served pancakes and told animated stories of life on the old plantation. Green's international debut was at the Columbian Exposition in Chicago where she performed in a barrel-shaped kiosk, serving pancakes and telling stories of the "good old days" in the antebellum South. Aunt Jemima was a hit. Her popularity spawned a spate of imitators who used only slightly modified images of the jolly and corpulent Mammy to sell everything from produce to cleaning products. Meanwhile, seizing on the obvious appeal of their living trademark, the Davis company created a family of spin-off characters—Uncle Mose, her husband, and her "pickanninies," Diana and Wade—to increase the marketing options for their most widely recognized icon.

In 1925 the Quaker Oats Company bought R. T. Davis Milling and expanded its promotion of the Aunt Jemima pancake line even further. After Nancy Green's tragic death in a car accident in 1923, six other women would play the role, interpreting the character Green made famous at trade shows and fairs and even at elite venues like the Waldorf Astoria. As popular as the real-life Aunt Jemimas were, though, the true heart and soul of Quaker Oats marketing strategy was the printed image of that figure, the smiling, middle-aged woman in her bright red kerchief, gazing out from the front of the package.

As awareness of stereotyping increased during the middle decades of the twentieth century, the dozens of corporations who used images of African Americans in the marketing of their products responded, most by removing images not only of Mammies but of black butlers, "pickanninies," and grizzled Uncle Toms from their packaging and advertising campaigns. By the end of the 1960s most such figures had disappeared, but Aunt Jemima remained. In response to decreasing tolerance for the Mammy, however, her appearance has gradually transformed. In 1968 Quaker Oats unveiled a thinner, younger-looking Mammy, with a few locks of straightened hairs poking out from beneath her trademark head wrap. The year 1989, however, marked the most dramatic transformation in the icon's physical appearance. Over the course of her century-long marketing presence, Aunt Jemima had largely remained static, but Americans' perceptions of **slavery** had changed. When she first emerged, the United States was experiencing a wave of nostalgia for the perceived innocence of the plantation era, but in the century between Aunt Jemima's inception and her 1989 makeover, the Jim Crow era exposed the notion of the benevolent South as an illusion; the **civil rights movement** called attention to black Americans' dissatisfaction with the very same subordination that Aunt Jemima and other figures of plantation **myth** seemed to embrace; and the success of **Alex Haley**'s *Roots*, first as a novel, then as a widely viewed television event, offered a vision both of slavery's cruelty and of black slaves' rage and dissatisfaction that contradicted the humble contentment that Aunt Jemima and other mammies symbolized.

The modifications that produced the current incarnation of Aunt Jemima were made in the 100th year of her existence. She retains none of the plantation iconography of the original figure. He brightly colored scarf has disappeared to reveal a stylishly curled hairstyle. Her overall appearance has been feminized, her tasteful makeup and neatly trimmed eyebrows now accented with pearl earrings. Once a grinning Mammy with laughing eyes, today's Aunt Jemima would seem more comfortable in a boardroom than behind an ironing board. Even as her image transforms to reflect the beliefs and sensitivities of a new generation, however, nostalgia for the Aunt Jemima of the past has reached unprecedented levels. Original Aunt Jemima memorabilia and other reproductions of her image are increasing in popularity and value. Collectors of all ethnicities seek and find affirmation of either the racism of the past or the simplicity of times gone by in the comforting absolution and approval of her gaze, the suggestion in her smile and in the glint of her eye that between white people and black, between the enslaved and the free, between the servants and their masters, all is well, and if ever there were transgressions, ill will, or abuses of power, all is forgiven.

See also Plantation Tradition; Stereotypes

Works About

Buster, Larry Vincent. *The Art and History of Black Memorabilia.* New York: Clarkson Potter, 2000.

Kern Foxworth, Marilyn. *Aunt Jemima, Uncle Ben, and Rastus: Blacks in Advertising, Yesterday, Today, and Tomorrow.* Westport, CT: Greenwood Press, 1994.

Manning, M. M. *Slave in a Box: The Strange Career of Aunt Jemima.* Charlottesville: University of Virginia Press, 1998.

Ajuan Maria Mance

AUSTIN, DORIS JEAN (1949–1994)

Doris Jean Austin was an essayist, critic, and novelist. Central issues explored in her writing included the nature of kinship, relationships, recovery, **healing**, and wholeness. Austin published one novel, *After the Garden*, and short stories. She also wrote articles for *Essence* magazine, *Amsterdam News*, and the *New York Times Book Review*.

Austin was born in Mobile, Alabama, in 1949 and at the age of six moved to Jersey City, New Jersey. She grew up in a loving, supportive extended **family**.

Austin began writing in her teens and continued to write throughout her life. She was a member of Harlem Writers Guild, a MacDowell Colony fellow, and received the DeWitt Wallace Reader's Digest Award for Literary Excellence for her novel. Women figure prominently in her writing whether her subject was fictional or she was writing about herself. Austin's writing frequently addressed the psychological states of women and how these states impacted their **identity** and sense of well-being.

After the Garden was Austin's first and only published novel. **Motherhood** and surrogacy are central themes in this novel as well as **class** and **religion**. *After the Garden* is a coming-of-age story set between the 1940s and 1960s in New Jersey. The text revolves around Elzina, who has been orphaned and was raised by a surrogate, her bourgeois, domineering, religious, strict grandmother Rosalie. Rosalie dreams of Elzina being able to attend Tuskeegee Institute and is upset when Jesse, a popular classmate from a working-class background, impregnates Elzina. To Rosalie's dismay, Elzina and Jesse marry and move into her **home**. The marriage is troubled as Elzina and Jesse fail to reconcile their differences in expectation and worldview resulting from differences in class and religious orthodoxy. Rosalie's overt disapproval of Elzina's choice of a mate compounds the tension between Elzina and Jesse.

Jesse is convicted of armed robbery and goes to jail, Rosalie dies, and Elzina suffers from poor health. Elzina eventually goes to live with Jesse's mother, Truselle, who serves as a second surrogate mother to Elzina. Truselle's world is more socially liberal, open, and spontaneous than was Rosalie's. Elzina heals while living with Truselle and continues to develop her sense of self. The narrative comes full circle when Elzina becomes a surrogate mother for an orphaned girl whom Jesse had fathered with another woman.

Aside from the novel, Austin served as an editor and contributor to *Streetlights*, a collection of fifty short stories about the urban experience. Many of the magazine articles that she wrote were drawn from her own experiences and focused on recovery from traumas such as **rape**, divorce, and alcoholism. Austin died in 1994.

Works By

"The Act behind the Word." *Wild Women Don't Wear No Blues.* Ed. Marita Golden. New York: Doubleday, 1993.
After the Garden: A Novel. New York: New American Library, 1987.
Streetlights. Ed. Doris Jean Austin and Martin Simmons. New York: Penguin Books, 1996.

Work About

O'Meally, Robert G. "Naughty Kearney Avenue." *New York Times Book Review*, August 16, 1987, 20.

Kimberly Black-Parker

AUTOBIOGRAPHY

Autobiography as a genre has held a contentious space in literary theory almost since its inception and particularly since women have joined the fray of memoirists. The purpose of an autobiography used to conform to a fairly simple formula: White men would write the story of their own lives, showing their success stories and the "universality" of their human experience. These were public documents with little room for the ordinary or the daily, but they were full of the man's interactions within the public sphere and his shaping of that sphere. Ever since voices other than that of the white male have turned to autobiography, a theoretical and critical battle over what constitutes a "true" or "good" autobiography has been fought. The critical establishment has long argued that autobiography, when it takes turns toward the private (as it does in many works by nonwhite men), is an inferior literary form.

It seems that no matter the criteria, women, and African American women in particular, are always writing just outside of the "appropriate" boundaries. Premodernist conceptions of "good" writing held that unity of plot, character, and theme were requirements. Later, the privileging of fragmentation and alienation during the modernist and postmodernist period has carried over into the assumption that abstract and depersonalized writing is the superior model. But it is Western, white men who claim the **death** of the author, not marginalized voices that have not yet been given authority (Fox-Genovese 162–163). Clearly, the same rules should not apply to women and minorities who have only relatively recently been given the space for their voices to be heard. Because social and historical conditions play a part in women's and minorities' lives, they must necessarily also play a part in autobiography. In other words, the context and voice change the type of autobiography, and the same criteria cannot apply to all forms.

African American women have had to struggle with dual models in the creation of their own literary selves through autobiography: the public male **slave narrative** that details an individual's victory over struggle, and the private white female confessional of daily life. In the nineteenth century, in particular, women like **Harriet E. Wilson** and **Harriet Jacobs** had to find ways to discuss the double oppression of being black and a woman, and they did this through borrowing from both the male (slave narrative) and female (sentimental) traditions, creating interesting new generic hybrids that best fit their own voices and positions in society. Jacobs's ***Incidents in the Life of a Slave Girl***, for instance, has been called public confession, spiritual autobiography, seduction novel, narrative of captivity, and a text following the traditions of both abolitionist rhetoric and sentimental fiction.

In addition to the already hybrid form that is a product of following the male slave narrative and the female sentimental novel, there are two major strains in African American women's autobiography: secular and spiritual (Andrews 34), though these strains are often combined as well. Whether slave narrative, travel writing, or cultural criticism, it is clear that the lines between secularism and **spirituality** often blend in these texts, particularly in earlier works. Another duality found in this genre is the mediation between "I" and "we," between the personal and the political. **Black feminism**'s basic tenets of survival through **community** networking and adaptation are regular features in African American women's autobiography. The genre is adapted to fit the varying and various conditions of the woman's life, and the woman is never a lone individual striking out on her own; she is a self only in relation to others (Sorisio 6). In the most successful autobiographies, both the unique and collective selves are given voice (Goldman xxvii).

A few distinct time periods emerge in relation to African American women's autobiography: the slave narrative period, the ex-slave narrative period, the **Harlem Renaissance**, **Black Arts Movement** revolutionaries, and the personal autobiographies of the late twentieth century (Andrews 36–37; Bassard 38–39). Each period can be defined in some ways by the historical and cultural context of its authors. In relation to today's writing, many female slave narratives feel conservative due to their insistence on following the tenets of true womanhood: piety, purity, **domesticity**, and submission. Underlying the surface-level conservativism, however, lie some of the most radical authors, for their task was to convince a primarily white audience of their selfhood. In the slave narratives of Elizabeth, Harriet Jacobs, and **Sojourner Truth**, a strong commitment to religious faith and **freedom** for themselves and their families underscores their writings. This religious faith, though, is one that has remained strong through challenging the dictates of contemporary religious practice against their own beliefs about justice and God. In the same pre–Civil War time period, free (and thus more privileged) women like Mrs. Nancy Prince and **Charlotte Forten Grimké** write of their travels.

The ex-slave narrative was popular after the Civil War and into the 1930s. The Works Progress Administration (WPA) project of transcribing ex-slaves' stories helped make this genre even more prolific and accessible. Women's memoirs of slave life were often written through amanuenses, as in the cases of Bethany Veney and **Mattie Jackson**. But other women in this time period were writing autobiographical work that overlapped with cultural criticism and memoirs of personal scholarly activity (like **Anna Julia Cooper**) and activism (**Ida B. Wells-Barnett**). The Harlem Renaissance brought forth a new forum for and interest in African American writing, and gave birth to works like **Zora Neale Hurston**'s autobiography ***Dust Tracks on a Road***. Coinciding with the 1955 Montgomery bus boycott and official beginning of the **civil rights movement**, **Pauli Murray**, a civil rights activist, wrote *Proud Shoes*, her family's **history** and a personal memoir.

Still more innovations to African American women's autobiography came about with the Black Arts Movement. Revolutionary work and cultural commentary rooted in personal experience by writers like **Angela Davis**, and statements on life and **poetry** from writers like **Nikki Giovanni**, led the genre into different and new hybrids. Always maintaining an interest in both the political and the personal, but becoming more intimate, are autobiographies from **Maya Angelou** and **Audre Lorde**. Also typical of later autobiography is the hybridization started by Lorde's "biomythography."

Women like Michele Wallace, a literary critic, today combine autobiography and cultural criticism in moves that are starting to be recognized as "autotheory." Also prominent are **family** histories by writers like **Lucille Clifton**. Furthermore, the fictionalization of family and personal stories is quite common. **Jamaica Kincaid**, for instance, in the novels *Annie John* and *Lucy* writes of her own childhood but, with the freedom of **fiction** is able to move exactly where she wants to. In her later books, like *My Brother*, Kincaid deals directly with the family she indirectly struggled with in her earlier novels.

Despite the inherently personal connection between an author, her life, and her writing, there has never been an easy connection between reality and autobiography. All authors see their own life's story through lenses of distance, self-**love**, and authorial purpose. Many have relied upon conventions of changing names, omissions, and creation in order to have textual unity and personal sanctity. Harriet E. Wilson's pseudo–slave narrative *Our Nig* tells her own story, but through the character of Frado; the horrific Haywards become the Bellmonts, and she manipulates their story by omitting their abolitionist ties, by combining characters, and many think, by omitting her own sexual abuse. In the same way, Kincaid tells the story of Annie, a young girl forever distanced from her mother after the birth of a younger brother. Annie goes to England, while Kincaid goes to America. Later, Annie transforms into Lucy, an au pair like Kincaid, but Lucy is able to do and say things (regarding her **sexuality** and family relationships) that Kincaid might be uncomfortable making public. The novel packs a metaphorical punch that a "true" recollection would not be able to maintain.

Lorene Cary's *Black Ice* (1991) is a straightforward autobiography, unlike **Marita Golden**'s work or Kincaid's early novels. This text is an appropriate place to end this discussion, since it dramatizes, in a contemporary sense, the dualities and dichotomies of being a black woman writer struggling to write her self into American history. *Black Ice* exemplifies the struggle between the two traditions of women's and African American's autobiography. Cary is at once working within a tradition of women autobiographers, who write their painful and private experiences for the common good of women, and the African American autobiographer who writes out of a collective battle for racial equality, making politics of **race** more important than those of sex. The places where readers feel unsatisfied with Cary's withdrawal, such as when she only goes so far in discussing her parents' marriage, are precisely the places where the gaps in her two traditions show. *Black Ice* is critiqued for this split in purpose, but this same split demonstrates the tensions in her text based on her subject position as both woman and African American. The confusion in purpose between the two traditions, which can be felt as confusion or slippages in the text, are in the details she chooses to tell and withhold about her life. She is a complex person with a multiplicity of pressures and prejudices working against her, and because of this, she almost never fits neatly into other people's categories describing her work. In the end, she is writing her own story, a story that will be added to the stories of her people, her family, her community as an African American. Cary may not hit this balance consistently, and at times we as readers may be frustrated with the tensions in the text. But the tensions are her tensions, her struggles between the private and the public, between her fight against sexism and racism.

Multifaceted, hybridized, transforming, and personal, African American women's autobiography is a genre to be reckoned with; these personal voices form one of the bedrocks of the African American literary tradition, yesterday and today.

See also Religion

Works About

Andrews, William L. "Secular Autobiography." *The Oxford Companion to African American Literature*. Ed. William L. Andrews, Frances Smith Foster, and Trudier Harris. New York: Oxford University Press, 1997. 34–37.

Bassard, Katherine Clay. "Spiritual Autobiography." *The Oxford Companion to African American Literature*. Ed. William L. Andrews, Frances Smith Foster, and Trudier Harris. New York: Oxford University Press, 1997. 37–39.

Fox-Genovese, Elizabeth. "The Autobiographies of Afro-American Women." *Feminist Issues in Literary Scholarship*. Ed. Shari Benstock. Bloomington: Indiana University Press, 1987. 161–180.

Goldman, Anne E. *Take My Word: Autobiographical Innovations of Ethnic American Working Women*. Berkeley: University of California Press, 1996.

McCaskill, Barbara. " 'To Labor . . . and Fight on the Side of God': Spirit, Class, and Nineteenth-Century African American Women's Literature." *Nineteenth-Century American Women Writers: A Critical Reader*. Ed. Karen L. Kilcup. Malden, MA: Blackwell, 1998. 164–183.

Rodriguez, Barbara. *Autobiographical Inscriptions: Form, Personhood, and the American Woman Writer of Color*. New York: Oxford University Press, 1999.

Sorisio, Carolyn. " 'There Is Might in Each': Conceptions of Self in Harriet Jacobs's *Incidents in the Life of a Slave Girl, Written by Herself*." *Legacy* 13.1 (1996): 1–18.

Nicole Lynne Willey

AUTOBIOGRAPHY OF MY MOTHER, THE

An unremittingly bleak and bitter novel permeated with feelings of despair, contempt, and rage, **Jamaica Kincaid**'s 1996 novel *The Autobiography of My Mother* is at once a continuation of and a departure from her autobiographical-fictional project, her attempt in *Annie John* and *Lucy* to use **fiction** to write herself a life and make sense of her troubled relationship with her mother. In part, Kincaid had a conscious political agenda in telling the story of her seventy-year-old narrator, Xuela Claudette Richardson, whose mother died the moment she was born. Explaining that Xuela's life can be read as a metaphor for the African diaspora, Kincaid remarks, "At the moment African people came into this world, Africa died for them. . . . The birth of one is the death of the other" (Lee D3). But there is also something highly personal about this novel, which can be read at least in part as Kincaid's written vendetta against her "bad" mother, Annie Drew, and indeed Kincaid said that after writing the novel, she felt that she had made sense of her own childhood.

Continuing to investigate the formative influence of her childhood relationship with her powerful and destructive mother begun in *Annie John* and *Lucy* in *The Autobiography of My Mother*, Kincaid incorporates **family** stories into her narrative. Like Kincaid's mother, Annie Richardson Drew, Kincaid's narrator, Xuela Claudette Richardson, is from Dominica and is part Carib Indian, African and Scots, and she bears Kincaid's mother's family name, Richardson. Kincaid also incorporates into the life of her character obeah stories told to her by her mother. If Kincaid is intent on examining her matrilineal roots as she includes family stories and looks back to her mother's Carib Indian roots in *The Autobiography of My Mother*, she also is driven by the daughterly imperative to assert herself and assume power by talking back—or, more accurately, writing back—to her powerful and powerfully destructive mother.

In *The Autobiography of My Mother*, the loss of the idealized, good, and protective mother is experienced as a crippling, festering wound that never can be healed, and this loss puts the child at the mercy of a series of persecutory bad mother figures, who not only fail to nurture or confirm but also seek to dominate the child. Like *Annie John* and *Lucy*, *The Autobiography of My Mother* splits the mother into good/bad figures. Growing out of Kincaid's troubled relationship with her mother, *The Autobiography of My Mother* also deals, in a more self-conscious and extended way than her earlier novels, with the damaging impact of cultural forces and internalized colonialism on her character's developing personality. For as she describes Xuela's obsession with her idealized but dead mother and her abuse at the hands of a series of bad mother-substitute figures, Kincaid makes a conscious connection between her fierce hatred of maternal domination and her colonial upbringing, seeing the relationship between the powerful mother and powerless daughter as a prototype for the relationship between the colonizer and colonized.

Existing in a maternal—and colonial—world of dominator and dominated, Xuela determines to survive as best she can: by becoming one of the dominators, seeking empowerment through her **sexuality**, including her sexual power over the white English man whom she eventually marries and dominates as she plays out in her marriage, just as she does in all her significant relationships, a victor/vanquished power script. A motherless child and a woman who refuses to bear or mother any children of her own, Xuela remains self-possessed and defiant to the end, standing in the text as both an individual and also a representative voice as she breaks the long silence imposed on vanquished peoples.

See also Healing

Works About

Anatol, Giselle. "Speaking in (M)other Tongues: The Role of Language in Jamaica Kincaid's *The Autobiography of My Mother*." *Callaloo* 25.3 (2002): 938–953.

Bouson, J. Brooks. *Jamaica Kincaid: Writing Memory, Writing Back to the Mother*. Albany: SUNY Press, 2004.

Donnell, Alison. "When Writing the Other Is Being True to the Self: Jamaica Kincaid's *The Autobiography of My Mother*." *Women's Lives into Print: The Theory, Practice and Writing of Feminist Auto/Biography*. Ed. Pauline Polkey. New York: St. Martin's–Macmillan, 1999. 123–136.

Lee, Felicia. "It's a Time of Change for Ex–*New Yorker* Writer Kincaid." *Atlanta Journal and Constitution*, February 20, 1996, D3.

Paravisini-Gebert, Lizabeth. *Jamaica Kincaid: A Critical Companion*. Westport, CT.: Greenwood Press, 1999.

Simmons, Diane. "Coming-of-Age in the Snare of History: Jamaica Kincaid's *The Autobiography of My Mother*." *The Girl: Constructions of the Girl in Contemporary Fiction by Women*. Ed. Ruth O. Saxton. New York: St. Martin's Press, 1998. 107–118.

J. Brooks Bouson

 **B**

BABY OF THE FAMILY

Baby of the Family is **Tina McElroy Ansa**'s first novel, published in 1989. The story of the McPherson **family**, the baby Lena especially, *Baby of the Family* deals with African American **community** life during the 1950s. The main settings are the McPherson family **home**, a middle-class two-story house on a large lot, the **beauty** parlor Lena visits on a weekly basis, the McPherson family business, "The Place," and the church school Lena attends. All of these settings play their parts as Lena struggles to overcome the curse of being born with a caul and to live a normal life.

The McPherson family is definitely part of the middle **class**. As part of this class awareness we see the conflict between a spiritualist tradition and middle-class education. Lena is born with a caul across her face. Although Nurse Bloom and her grandmother understand what this means and honor the rituals that must be followed to avoid having the spirit world affect the baby in a negative way, Lena's mother Nellie regards their precautions as super-stition and, asserting that she is a modern woman, destroys the carefully preserved caul and the caul tea that Nurse Bloom has prepared for the baby to drink. Without the protection of the caul tea, Lena is subject to haunting by the ghosts of dead **ancestors** who frighten her.

Lena is indeed the baby of the family, being the youngest child and the only daughter. Her two older brothers are allowed adventure and **freedom** denied to Lena, who must be protected, both because she is a girl and because her thick hair reacts badly when it gets wet outdoors. Wrapped in the cocoon of her family's **love**, Lena's main conflicts come from the loneliness she experiences outside of her family's domain.

Lena's best childhood memories beyond the family circle center on the beauty parlor, where she meets people who encourage her curiosity and where she hears about women in the community, and on the family business, The Place, where she overhears other stories about the life of Mulberry. On one trip to the beach, Lena wanders away from her family and meets Rachel, the ghost of a slave who had drowned herself rather than submit to enslavement. This ghost, Lena's first experience with a positive spirit, comforts her and becomes a permanent part of her life. Only after the **death** of her beloved grandmother does Lena begin to accept, as her grandmother's ghost promises, that the spirit world can be a positive force in her life.

Ansa's first novel introduces us to her fictional community, Mulberry, Georgia, and to the McPherson family, particularly its baby, Lena. The descriptions of people and place vividly connect us to the tangible reality of the characters' lives and make us believe not only in them but in the spiritual forces that are part of their lives. Ansa's love for these people infects us, and we feel a similar affection for her people and places.

See also The Hand I Fan With; Spirituality

Works About

Irven, Krystal K. Review of *Baby of the Family*. *School Library Journal* 36.6 (June 1990): 144–145.

Jordan, Shirley M. Review of *Baby of the Family*. *American Visions* 5.5 (October 1990): 38–39.

Sayers, Valerie. Review of *Baby of the Family*. *New York Times Book Review* 94 (November 26, 1989): 6.

Steinberg, Sybil. Review of *Baby of the Family*. *Publishers Weekly* 236.10 (September 8, 1989): 56.

Harriette C. Buchanan

BAILEY'S CAFÉ

In her fourth novel, *Bailey's Café* (1992), **Gloria Naylor** castigates the long-venerated Judeo-Christian tradition, boldly revising scripture that has historically pinioned women to the limited roles of their biblical cohorts. In this veritable Gospel According to Gloria Naylor, the author keeps a record quite different from the original Bible. Instead of the diametric and stringent gender positions depicted in scripture, gender roles in Bailey's Café form a symmetry even to the point of androgyny. As Naylor presents her tale, humanity is a balance of genders.

In this work are characters named for Old Testament women such as Eve, Esther, and **Jezebel**. The New Testament Madonna is even implicated in Mariam, and Mary reminds the reader of Mary Magdalene, also of New Testament **memory**. Naylor's *Bailey's Cafe* is laden with key names and allusions to the patriarchal system induced and/or supported by the Judeo-Christian tradition. However, in this novel Naylor also indicts a repressive matriarchy in which communities of women are complicit in other women's oppression.

As *Bailey's Cafe* unfolds, the narrative makes its way across a world of women's stories, stories surviving in a penumbral collective that includes Bailey's Café, Gabe's Pawn Shop, and Eve's bordello/boardinghouse. The plot of *Bailey's Cafe* is guided by the proprietor of Bailey's Café who buys the place after his return from World War II. The café serves as the axis of the novel's events where people facing the consequences of reaching life's nadir either step into the void in the back of the café, committing suicide, or become whole before daring to face the world again.

A cast of interesting characters streams through Bailey's Café. The first customer is Eve, who arrives at the café after being evicted from her **home** in Pilottown by her guardian, Godfather. Located down the block from Bailey's Café, Eve's brownstone is a refuge for single women with the exception of "Miss Maple," a man who loosens the boundaries of gender, for he is as comfortable in a dress as he is in his manhood. Entering Bailey's Café on her way to Eve's is Esther, who comes to Eve's after twelve years of sexual and emotional torture. Jesse Bell arrives at the brownstone with a heroin addiction and the embarrassment of a failed marriage and a much-publicized **lesbian** relationship. Mary is the ultimate conundrum in the novel. In protest to the name expectations that she is unable to meet, she chooses self-mutilation. Mary is expected to be the biblical virgin but is more akin to the assumed prostitute, Mary Magdalene. Although Eve's place is full of aberrant personalities, Mariam can be categorized as phenomenal; she is a fourteen-year-old mentally challenged Falasha Jew who arrives at Eve's a pregnant virgin.

The imperfection of both patriarchy and matriarchy accounts for Naylor's move toward androgyny especially in Miss Maple, who is the last major character to tell his story. Furthermore, the Christ child that is born at the end of the novel offers hope that the next millennium will embrace liberation through **sexuality** that does not insist upon confining gender roles. As the characters who frequent Bailey's Café realize their sexual selves, they are positioned in a strangely liberating limbo. Only in another world can a cross-gender arrangement be made that accepts the sexuality of everyone.

Works About

Brown, Amy Benson. "Writing Home: The Bible and Gloria Naylor's *Bailey's Cafe.*" *Homemaking: Women Writers and the Politics and Poetics of Home.* Ed. Catherine Wiley and Fiona Barnes. New York: Garland, 1996. 23–42.

Chavanelle, Sylvie. "Gloria Naylor's *Bailey's Cafe*: The Blues and Beyond." *American Studies International* 36.2 (1998): 58–73.

Rummell, Kathryn. "From Stanley to Miss Maple: A Definition of Manhood in Gloria Naylor's *Bailey's Cafe*." *Diversity: A Journal of Multicultural Issues* 2 (1994): 90–96.

Sharese Terrell Willis

BAKER, JOSEPHINE (1906–1975)

Josephine Baker was born Josephine Freda MacDonald to Carrie MacDonald and Eddie Carson in Saint Louis, Missouri. They met at a theater performing as "natives" in a production called *A Trip to Africa*. But Carson did not stick around long, and Josephine, the oldest of four children, was at work earning money for the **family** by age thirteen; she would later recall herself as "the big man of the family." The East Saint Louis **race** riot of 1917, the worst in American **history** at the time, deeply affected her. Her refusal to tolerate **violence** of any kind after that perhaps prompted her to end her first marriage to Willie Wells (whom she wedded in 1919), a man known for his violent outbursts. Once again set on establishing her independence, Baker began getting engagements with touring groups of black performers. In 1921, having traveled to Philadelphia with the Jones Family Band, she met Willie Baker, who at twenty-five was ten years her senior. They married in Camden, New Jersey, and from this point forward, she was known as Josephine Baker. She learned about a black musical called *Shuffle Along* playing in Philadelphia, and when the show moved to New York, Josephine left her second husband to follow it. By 1925, she was performing with the Broadway production *Chocolate Dandies*. As the end girl of the chorus line, Josephine clowned up the role so much that audience members could not help but notice her, and they liked what they saw. Prone to improvisation often to the distress of directors and producers, Baker was nevertheless wildly applauded by audiences.

"Discovered" in New York by Carolyn Dudley, Baker traveled to Paris in 1925 to join Dudley's *La Revue Negre*. To sweeten the deal, Dudley offered Baker a weekly salary of $250, a huge sum at that time. But Dudley, a wealthy socialite and lover of French culture, felt secure in her investment, knowing that all things African were a big attraction in France and that Baker was sure to be a hit. For Baker, conversely, France's "negromania" was not a reason to expatriate. Rather, the promise of a country that was supposedly blind to race attracted her, and she was often told that in France "people would think she was white." Here begins what brings both criticism and praise to Josephine Baker for the rest of her life, and which continues today—her ambiguous position with regard to race. Did Baker's expressed desire to transcend race, **class**, and for that matter, sex mean that she was a traitor to her race, her class, and her sex? Or was she, as others have opined, one of history's greatest champions of human rights? On one hand, there are many examples of Baker's apparent deference toward **whiteness**. Often considered too dark for success on stage, Baker took to covering her face with white powder to audition—a scene played out in Baker's first successful French **film**, *Zouzou* (1934). One of her famous songs is titled "I'd Like to Be White," and she once expressed the wish to have a white baby. Conversely, she marketed a whole line of **beauty** products that capitalized on her blackness, including "Bakerskin," a cosmetic replacement for silk stockings.

More important, Baker was a member of France's League against Racism and Antisemitism; her husband at this time, Jean Lion, was Jewish, and Baker often compared the plight of blacks and Jews. She went on to become a Resistance fighter and was awarded the Legion of Honor for her work as an undercover agent in World War II. A tireless supporter of rights for blacks in the United States, she was named Most Outstanding Woman of the Year in 1951 by the National Association for the Advancement of Colored People (NAACP), with 100,000 people showing up to honor her. Baker was an active participant in the **civil rights movement**, having marched with Dr. Martin Luther King in 1963, when he made his famous "I Have a Dream" speech (which Baker actually criticized for not *demanding* rights for blacks). Further, she absolutely refused to perform for segregated audiences.

In 1931, Baker authored a book titled *My Blood in Your Veins*, which told the story of Joan, a young, poor black woman who falls in **love** with a wealthy white man. Coincidentally, both are hospitalized at the same time, he for an almost fatal accident. Secretly, Joan offers her blood for a transfusion that saves his life. But when his white fiancée finds out, she calls him a "white negro" and leaves him; he then commits suicide. Baker had hoped not only to see the published work a success but also to play the role of Joan in a film version of the work. Neither happened, since, as Baker lamented, no one wanted to hear the story of mixed blood. Ultimately, however, this mixing of blood to the point of ending race difference was what Baker most desired. Moreover, she wished for the harmonious coexistence of all races, classes, sexes, and religions and undertook, near age forty, to create this world by adopting twelve children of various races and creeds; she called them her Rainbow Tribe and herself the Universal Mother. With her fourth husband, Jo Bouillon, Baker created Les Milandes, a complex including a fifty-room chateau, and the surrounding village and farms. Baker employed everyone in the vicinity and generated revenues by turning Les Milandes into a tourist attraction, including "Jorama," a wax museum filled with scenes from Baker's life. In fact, one might say that Baker's life history is a history of performing her life, which she acted and reenacted in at least four memoirs and various stage and television productions. Sadly, Les Milandes literally broke her, the endeavor proving too onerous financially (her marriage also failed in the process). Determined to maintain her independence and to support her twelve children, Baker took to the stage to perform yet again the story of her life. She died in Paris, after playing herself in the very successful *Joséphine*, a revue feting her fifty years in the business.

Work By

Joséphine. Written with Jo Bouillon. Trans. Mariana Fitzpatrick. New York: Harper and Row, 1977.

Works About

Baker, Jean-Claude, and Chris Chase. *Josephine: The Hungry Heart*. New York: Random House, 1993.

Chilcoat, Michelle. "Civility, Marriage, and the Impossible French Citizen: From *Ourika* to *Zouzou* and *Princesse Tam Tam*." *Colby Quarterly* 37.2 (2001): 125–144.

Dayal, Samir. "Blackness as Symptom: Josephine Baker and European Identity." *Blackening Europe: The African American Presence*. Ed. Heike Raphael-Hernandez. New York: Routledge, 2004. 35–52.

Gates, Henry Louis, Jr., and Karen Dalton. *Josephine Baker and La Revue Negre: Paul Colin's Lithographs of Le Tumulte Noir in Paris, 1927*. New York: Harry N. Abrams, 1998.

Hammond, Bryan, and Patrick O'Conner. *Josephine Baker*. London: Jonathan Cape, 1988.

Haney, Lynn. *Naked at the Feast: A Biography of Josephine Baker*. New York: Dodd Mead, 1981.

Kalinak, Kathryn. "Disciplining Josephine Baker: Gender, Race, and the Limits of Disciplinarity." *Music and Cinema*. Ed. James Buhler, Caryl Finn, and David Neumeyer. Hanover, NH: Wesleyan University Press, 2000. 316–335.

Kirkby, John Abraham. *In Search of Josephine Baker*. London: Minerva Press, 2002.

Kraut, Anthea. "Between Primitivism and Diaspora: The Dance Performances of Josephine Baker, Zora Neale Hurston, and Katherine Dunham." *Theater Journal* 55.3 (2003): 433–450.

Martin, Wendy. " 'Remembering the Jungle': Josephine Baker and Modernist Parody." *Prehistories of the Future: The Primitivist Project and the Culture of Modernism*. Ed. Elazar Barkan and Ronald Bush. Stanford, CA: Stanford University Press, 1995. 310–325.

Papich, Stephen. *Remembering Josephine: A Biography of Josephine Baker*. New York: Bobbs-Merrill, 1976.

Rose, Phyllis. *Jazz Cleopatra: Josephine Baker in Her Times*. New York: Doubleday, 1989.

Wood, Ian. *The Josephine Baker Story*. London: Sanctuary Publishing, 2000.

Michelle Chilcoat

BALDWIN, JAMES (1924–1987)

A feminist approach to the works of James Baldwin reveals female characters ranging from victims to self-assertive and confident achievers. Regarding the former, in *The Devil Finds Work* (1975), Baldwin objects to the portrayal of black women in **films** such as *The Birth of a Nation* (1915) and *Guess Who's Coming to Dinner* (1967). In both these films, Baldwin argues, an African American maid is overly loyal to her white employers and objects to other African Americans who are portrayed as uppity. Such characters as these maids, claims Baldwin, demonstrate their weakness, become "more white than black," and serve to protect their white mistress from any possible harm that might be caused by dangerous African American men. Baldwin's own works, though, contain their share of relatively weak women, regardless of their **race**. One such character is Mrs. Alice Hunt from *If Beale Street Could Talk* (1974), whose weakness stems from her concern of keeping up bourgeois appearances, so much so that she is shameful in her condemnation of Tish's unplanned pregnancy. Mr. Hunt, recognizing his wife's poor behavior, slugs her to the ground. (Due to Mr. Hunt's being one of the "good" characters and his wife being one of the "bad," the novel tempts the reader to regard Mr. Hunt's violent act as appropriate behavior between a husband and wife.) Another example is Leona from *Another Country* (1962), who is so morally weak that she refuses to abandon her boyfriend, even after he begins raping her. She only leaves him after the intervention of one of his own friends, and even then, she claims to **love** and feel sorry for her boyfriend. Eventually she suffers a breakdown, is found wandering the street half-naked, and is taken back to Georgia. Another weak character, despite her career ambitions, is Ida from *Another Country*. She continually blames herself and berates others for her brother's untimely **death**. Having depended on her brother to get her out of their unfulfilling environment, Ida feels cheated when he dies, and at the end of the novel, her state is ambiguous. Finally, one of the saddest characters is Amy in *Just Above My Head* (1979), who allows her daughter, a child minister, to manage the entire **family**. By bequeathing this power to her daughter (and thereby emerging as a weak mother), Amy's physical problems go untreated, and she eventually dies in a hospital.

If not inherently weak, then some of Baldwin's female characters make questionable choices. Usually these choices involve an unquestionable support for men, despite their foibles. Mrs. Proudhammer in *Tell Me How Long the Train's Been Gone* (1968) puts up with her husband, manages the family's finances, and feeds her family. Her source of happiness, though, depends upon her husband's mood: She is happy when her husband is happy. In the same novel, Barbara arranges her career as a successful actress so that Leo's place in it will never be jeopardized. In *If Beale Street Could Talk*, Tish idealistically stands by her man Fonny, even though he is incarcerated and she is unmarried, pregnant with his child.

Just the same, within Baldwin's output reside numerous female characters of considerable strength. For example, although the artist Jane in *Another Country* is self-absorbed, moody, and a heavy drinker, she is a woman of considerable force. Jane causes much harm, but her strength is such that for quite a while her boyfriend cannot find his own strength to leave her. Another character possessing much power is the actress Bunny from *Tell Me How Long the Train's Been Gone*. Professional and congenial, this white actress calls her fellow actor Leo, an African American, back onto stage to bow with her and to receive the accolades of the audience.

Some of Baldwin's other characters convey their strength through their occupations. One example is Hilda from *Tell Me How Long the Train's Been*

Gone. Having saved money from working as a cook in private houses, Hilda invests it in her own restaurant. A hardworking African American woman, Hilda seems to have no business partners and sends almost all her earnings back to Trinidad. Another successful business owner is Madame Clothilde from *Giovanni's Room* (1956), a shrewd Frenchwoman who knows both how to manage her customers and also how to operate her place of business.

Baldwin's female characters often react when oppressed by male characters. For instance, in "The Man Child" (1965), Jamie's beautiful wife runs away from her unappreciative and ultimately murderous husband. In "The Rockpile" (1965), Elizabeth does not allow her husband to discipline one child for the wrongdoings of another. Usually the long-suffering wife, Deborah in *Go Tell It on the Mountain* (1953) finally confronts her husband about his illegitimate son, claiming that if he had owned up to his adultery, then she would have raised his son as her own. Cass from *Another Country* tells her husband about her affair (and physically suffers for doing so). Florence from *Just Above My Head* confronts Joel that he needs to regain control of his household (to be the man of the house) and therefore not to allow his young daughter to be the boss. *Giovanni's Room*'s Hella claims to be traditional, wanting a husband and a family. Just the same, when she realizes the truth of her fiancé's **sexuality**, she leaves him and does not look (or wave) back at him as she departs.

Several characters reveal their strength by protecting men from the oppression represented by the police, especially when racism seems to motivate the policemen's actions. Three such characters appear in *Tell Me How Long the Train's Been Gone.* Early in the novel, Mildred attempts to hide Caleb from the police. Later, Madeleine is indignant and enraged when the police unfairly bring in Leo, Caleb's younger brother, for questioning. Finally, Lola berates the police officers for their actions. Another example of a protecting female character appears in *If Beale Street Could Talk*, where an anonymous Italian woman protects Fonnie from a racist police officer.

Within Baldwin's works, the most common method by far for female characters to obtain and to demonstrate power is to be active within a church environment. Some characters are themselves ministers or evangelists, such as Praying Mother Washington (*Go Tell It on the Mountain*), Sister Margaret Alexander (*The Amen Corner* [1968]), Julia (*Just Above My Head*), and Sister McCandless and Sister Daniels of "The Outing" (1951). When within the confines of the church, enjoying considerable power, female characters usually make much use of their chastity. For example, Sister McCandless testifies that even at her advanced age, she is still a virgin. A similar character is Sister Moore, from *The Amen Corner.* Both characters use their virginity to their benefits, cementing their respective positions within their respective churches.

On the other hand, some of Baldwin's strongest characters are not chaste at all and are instead sexually adventurous. In *Giovanni's Room*, Sue allows herself a brief sexual fling with David, although she is fully aware that he is not in love with her. She has no emotional expectations of him. When David refuses her postcoital suggestion to have dinner together, she does not fall apart, sobbing; throughout the entire brief encounter, she maintains her composure. A more complex example of a sexually adventurous character is Cass from *Another Country*, who realizes that her marriage to Richard is not fulfilling and then commences an affair with Eric. When their affair comes to an end, she does not attempt to hang on to him; she lets him go. Probably the most complex example of such a character is Esther from *Go Tell It on the Mountain*; she asserts that life is for living. Esther is willing to pay after death for any sins that she might commit while on the earth. When she gets pregnant by Gabriel, who is married, she realizes that she does not want to be with him, considering him weak. She bravely refuses to marry anyone to cover up her pregnancy. Although Esther does die young, she resolutely never paints herself as a victim.

To be fully competent mothers is yet another way that Baldwin's female characters demonstrate strength. Such characters reinforce the importance of the family unit. In "Previous Condition" (1948), Peter's mother consoles her son when he is victim of racial slur, while in "This Morning, This Evening" (1960), Harriet seeks to learn how to protect her husband and her son as they prepare to immigrate to America. In *Go Tell It on the Mountain*, Elizabeth refuses to bow to societal standards by regretting bearing her illegitimate son. In *Another Country*, Cass claims that her husband and children are her life and does much to promote their well-being. She fits her life around her husband's life and career and does not make her husband try to fit his life around hers. Sharon Rivers in *If Beale Street Could Talk* becomes a take-charge mother who will inform the rest of the family about her daughter's pregnancy. Sharon bravely (and as some critics have noted, unbelievably) leaves America for San Juan, successfully hunting Victoria Rodgers, the woman who has unfairly accused Sharon's future son-in-law of **rape**. Florence in *Just Above My Head* is the voice of reason, advocating that African Americans need to focus on living their lives and raising their families.

Perhaps only one of Baldwin's creations finds much strength from bitterness. Florence from *Go Tell It on the Mountain* is a character whose strength stems from her resentment of her hypocritical brother, Gabriel, who is awarded all the advantages that she feels would have been hers, had he never been born. When Florence's white master proposes that she become his concubine, she instead sets off alone for New York. She leaves for the railroad station, disregarding the attempts of her mother and brother to convince her to stay. In her older years, Florence confronts Gabriel with a thirty-year-old letter from his first wife that questions the parentage of a local illegitimate child. In addition, Florence defends Elizabeth, Gabriel's second wife, against Gabriel's unfounded accusations of her bad parenting. It is her aversion to her brother (as well as the need to protect Elizabeth) that motivates Florence.

A common theme in Baldwin's writings, both the essays and the fiction, are women who overcome adversity. Sometimes these women overcome the limitations of race and racial expectations. In *The Devil Finds Work*, Baldwin praises actress Sylvia Sidney (1910–1999) because she was at the time the only American film actress who reminded him of an African American woman, by which Baldwin means that Sidney reminded him of reality. Sidney, a Polish New Yorker perhaps best known for her comic role in *Beetlejuice* (1988), is invoked several times in *Tell Me How Long the Train's Been Gone*. In the essay "Color" (1962), Baldwin notes the social difficulties of African American women who allow their hair to resume its natural texture. Rarely are such women admired. Such women, for daring to not mimic the hairstyles of white women, are looked upon with nervousness. The novels contain several examples of women who battle the breakdown of the family. In *Just Above My Head*, Julia asserts her desire to live her life—and not merely as a victim of incest. Martha from the same novel leaves her girlhood behind her, escaping a dead-end relationship for a much more promising one. In *Giovanni's Room*, David's landlady survives not only the death of two sons but also the loss of all of her and her husband's money. Yet she perseveres.

Works By

Collected Essays. Ed. Toni Morrison. New York: Library of America, 1998.
Early Novels & Stories. Ed. Toni Morrison. New York: Library of America, 1998.

Works About

Bell, Roseann P., Bettye J. Parker, and Beverly Guy-Sheftall, eds. *Sturdy Black Bridges: Visions of Black Women in Literature.* Garden City, NY: Doubleday, 1979.
Harris, Trudier. *Black Women in the Fiction of James Baldwin.* Knoxville: University of Tennessee Press, 1985.
O'Daniel, Therman B., ed. *James Baldwin: A Critical Evaluation.* Washington, DC: Howard University Press, 1977.

William S. Hampl

BAMBARA, TONI CADE (1939–1995)

Born in Harlem on March 25, 1939, and named for her father's employer Milton Mirkin, Miltona Mirkin Cade began, at around age six, to be called Toni and selected the surname Bambara in 1970 while pregnant with her daughter Karma Bene. One of two children born to Helen Brent Henderson Cade and Walter Cade II, Bambara was raised by her mother after her father left the **family** in her childhood. Early biographical details surrounding Bambara are often disputed, though some certainties exist. Among them is the importance of her mother's insistence that both Bambara and her brother Walter be self-reliant as well as the centrality of a female role model to her life.

The encouragement for self-discipline brought structure to her early life and led her to seek knowledge from family, friends, and neighbors. Her **fiction** evinces the stored folk knowledge she gained in her upbringing and a great sense of loyalty to her **community**. Educated in English and theater arts at Queens College and City College in New York, Bambara began her literary career during her senior year with the publication of the short story "Sweet Town" in the January 1959 issue of *Vendome*. During the 1960s, Bambara finished her master's degree and began her university teaching career, focusing time on community education components, all the while remaining involved in activist groups and actively writing stories and essays.

Her most often overlooked work is the 1970 *The Black Woman: An Anthology*, to which she both contributed a preface and three essays and edited as well. The first of its kind, *The Black Woman* featured work from **Nikki Giovanni**, **Paule Marshall**, the near-unknown **Alice Walker**, **Sherley Anne Williams**, and **Audre Lorde**. In addition to being a showcase for emergent and established writers, *The Black Woman* contained essays discussing black women's roles in society, the family, and the community. Like her preface, Bambara's essay "On the Issue of Roles," an excerpt from her larger, autobiographical work *The Scattered Sopranoes*, forthrightly confronts the challenges before the black women at the commencement of a post–civil rights decade. Witnessing the burgeoning feminist enterprise, Bambara questions the validity of white women as experts for experiences particular to African American women. Her work on *The Black Woman* anticipates both Mary Helen Washington's *Black-eyed Susans* (1990) and the essays of Barbara Christian.

Bambara followed *The Black Woman* with *Tales and Stories for Black Folks* (1971), an anthology aimed at middle and high school students to encourage reading and acquisition of personal stories. The anthology featured fiction from Bambara as well as **Langston Hughes**, Albert Murray, Alice Walker, **Ernest Gaines**, and others. Also included were classic fairy tales rewritten from an African American perspective, including "The Three Little Panthers," which Bambara cowrote with Geneva Powell. In her introduction to the collection, Bambara anticipates the later critical focus on orality in African American writing, saying that "it is equally important for young folks to learn how to listen, to be proud of our oral tradition, our elders who tell their tales in the kitchen. For they are truth." While her first two works filled a need for collections of African American writing, her own short stories published over the previous decade were not widely available. Aware that the then-editor at Random House **Toni Morrison** was looking for African American authors to publish, Bambara approached her with what would become Bambara's first book of her own work.

In 1972, Bambara published the first collection of her own short fiction, *Gorilla, My Love*. In addition to previously published work, including "Sweet Town," the book contained several new stories as well. Of that collection, "My Man Bovanne" became the most often anthologized. The story of Miss Hazel and the kindness she extends to the neighborhood blind man Bovanne encapsulates many of the themes Bambara would develop throughout her career. Castigated by her children, Elo, Joe Lee, and Task, as inappropriately dressed and ill-behaved for the social function at which they gather, Miss Hazel responds with an independent and self-assured manner. While her ideas, like her speech patterns, do not match those of her more progressive children, Miss Hazel nonetheless sees a particular responsibility to Bovanne who, because of his age and handicap, is relegated to outside of the community. By juxtaposing the urban dialect of Miss Hazel with the proper English of her children, Bambara offers a meditation on the changing role of activism within a community and the marginalizing effects the younger generation has upon the elders. Aware that she will find nothing but criticism from her children and skewed glances from those in attendance, Miss Hazel leaves to take Bovanne home with her for an evening free of the confining nature of a new sense of activism.

With *Gorilla, My Love*, Bambara shows that she is unabashedly an African American writer who clings to a verbal, rhetorical tradition. There is no explanation in this, or any of her works, of the slang or colloquialisms used. Instead, one is thrust into fictional worlds where actions exist alongside signs of the richness of African American culture. Her writing style has matured; in *The Sea Birds Are Still Alive* in 1977, a gritty realism appears. For example, in "The Long Night" the single woman living alone in a dangerous area must hide in the bathtub she was bathing in when unknown men break into her apartment. By chance, her life is spared; Bambara confronts the changing reality of neighborhoods and the rise of urban crime and **violence**. Likewise, in "The Organizer's Wife," Virginia imbues the support and frustration involved in the sacrifice of **identity** for the sake of the cause. In the renaissance of African American women writing in the 1970s and 1980s, Bambara has remained in the foreground.

With the publication of her first novel, ***The Salt Eaters***, in 1980, Bambara further extended her writings on the place of African American women. Centered on Velma Henry's **healing**, *The Salt Eaters* celebrates the idea of wholeness within the female tradition by contrasting it with its opposite, fragmentation. Pulled away from her family by her many responsibilities to the community, Velma Henry must decide to embrace the idea of wellness in order to once again become whole and function within her community. She does so in full knowledge of the difficulties the future holds. With the appearance of *The Salt Eaters*, critical commentary on Bambara's work began to flourish. Of note is Eleanor W. Traylor's essay "Music as Theme: The Jazz Mode in the Works of Toni Cade Bambara" in Mari Evans's anthology *Black Women Writers (1950–1980): A Critical Evaluation*. Traylor, a former colleague of Bambara's, wrote what Bambara felt was the finest critical evaluation of her efforts as a writer.

Following publication of *The Salt Eaters*, Bambara turned her attention to **film**. In addition to several filmic adaptations, including a screenplay of Toni Morrison's 1983 novel ***Tar Baby***, Bambara's most well known film work remains the documentary *The Bombing on Osage Avenue* (1986), which chronicled the deadly bombings by West Philadelphia police of the headquarters of the African American activist group MOVE, and her work on *W.E.B. Du Bois: A Biography in Four Voices* (1995) with **Amiri Baraka**, Thulani Davis, and Wesley Brown. Her contributions to African American film remain on par with those of Marlon Riggs, while her critical insights on Spike Lee place him into a context noticeably absent from contemporary film theory.

In 1995 Bambara died from complications of colon cancer. She left several works unfinished, but thanks to the editorial direction of Toni Morrison, two additional works have been published. The 1996 collection *Deep Sightings and Rescue Missions* contains, in addition to Bambara's most candid and open interview ("How She Came by Her Name: An Interview with Louis Massiah"), essays on African American culture, film, and writing, as well as six previously unpublished short stories. The short fiction marks a subtle change in style for Bambara as she considers the widening consequence of multiculturalism upon African Americans. In "The War of the Wall," an African American neighborhood is perplexed and dismayed by a seemingly inhospitable artist who has been sent to their neighborhood to paint a mural. Over the course of the story, one realizes that the artist is a Jewish woman who, rather than being rude as originally thought, is instead following the customs of her faith. Regardless, the residents continue, to a lesser degree, their initial skepticism until the ending where the mural is revealed and no further details are offered. Read either as a boon to the locals or a disappointment, the mural's very ambiguity echoes the apparent growing uncertainty of where African Americans fit within a multiethnic America.

Those Bones Are Not My Child (1999), a novel of historical fiction, represents the mature work of Bambara. During the research for and writing of the novel, Bambara was threatened and heckled. Composed over a period of twelve years, Bambara's story explores the Spencer family's search for their missing son Sundiata (Sonny) and their attempt to reconstruct their lives when he was found injured and confused nearly one year later. Set against the backdrop of the Atlanta child abductions and murders of the early 1980s, the book powerfully confronts racially motivated crimes. Both far-reaching and myopic—the wide response of neighbors, authorities, and citizens contrasts the narrow focus of Sonny's mother Mazala Rawls Spencer in her experience of life following his disappearance—the novel blends public and private emotions in the wake of a missing child report. Difficult, discomforting, at times diabolic, *Those Bones* polarizes the manner in which racial difference exists and illumines the government agencies' improper handling of a horrifying case. More linear in form than *The Salt Eaters*, *Those Bones* more profoundly explores the consequences of omission and marginality using children as a means to raise awareness.

An awareness of issues and culture informs all of Bambara's multimedia work. From her early lessons on the importance of individuality through her lifetime of work devoted to her African American community, Bambara created a fictional world to mirror her own indefatigable idealism. By surmounting the obstacles they encounter, Bambara's female characters teach a lesson in resiliency tinged with humor and compassion. In her documentary works, Bambara's sensitivity to the stories told reinforced her identity as a writer and teller of tales. Finally, in her essays, Toni Cade Bambara showed that her major themes were more than literary preoccupations; they offered a systematic approach for invigoration of and loyalty to her community. Upon her untimely death in 1995, Bambara bequeathed a formidable legacy to contemporary African American women writers.

Works By

The Black Woman: An Anthology. Ed. Toni Cade Bambara. New York: Signet, 1970.
Deep Sightings and Rescue Missions: Fiction, Essays, and Conversations. Ed. Toni Morrison. New York: Pantheon Books, 1996.
Gorilla, My Love. New York: Random House, 1972.
The Salt Eaters. New York: Random House, 1980.
The Sea Birds Are Still Alive: Stories. New York: Random House, 1977.
Tales and Stories for Black Folks. Ed. Toni Cade Bambara. New York: Zenith, 1971.
Those Bones Are Not My Child. New York: Pantheon Books, 1999.

Works About

Butler-Evans, Elliott. *Race, Gender, and Desire: Narrative Strategies in the Fiction of Toni Cade Bambara, Toni Morrison, and Alice Walker.* Philadelphia: Temple University Press, 1989.
Traylor, Eleanor W. "Music as Theme: The Jazz Mode in the Works of Toni Cade Bambara." *Black Women Writers (1950–1980): A Critical Evaluation.* Ed. Mari Evans. New York: Anchor Books, 1984.

F. Gregory Stewart

BARAKA, AMIRI (1934–   )

Everett LeRoi Jones was born in Newark, New Jersey, in October 1934, to working middle-class parents Coyette (known as Coyt) LeRoi and Anna Lois Jones, a postal service employee and a social worker. His only sibling, Kimako Baraka (born Sandra Elaine Jones), an actor and activist, was raped and murdered in 1983. Baraka's numerous children by several mothers include Kellie and Lisa Jones (with Hettie Cohen Jones), Dominique Cespedes (with Diane di Prima), and Obalaji, Ras, Amiri Jr., Ahi, and Shani Baraka (with Amina Baraka, formerly Sylvia Richardson), and possibly another two daughters, Maria and Sarah Jones, whose mother is not easily identified. Another child died unborn with its mother due to serious complications in late pregnancy. His youngest child, Shani Baraka, was murdered in August 2003.

Jones's early life was typically middle-class Newark, among what he later would call the black bourgeoisie, graduating with honors from high school and starting undergraduate study at Rutgers University. He transferred to

Howard University, a predominantly black school in Washington, D.C., where he soon changed the spelling and pronunciation of his name to LeRoi. This act of naming is perhaps the first explicit moment in his self-conscious construction of **identity**. After that, during a time when he began exploring Greenwich Village on visits back North, he also flunked out of his pre-med program at Howard. Jones realized he wanted an intellectual life but had yet to determine what form such a life would take. Somewhat surprisingly, he then enlisted in the air force, where his catholic and eclectic reading habits, such as *Partisan Review*, generated sufficient official concern that he was undesirably discharged in 1957. After he discarded life in the academy and the military, Jones decided to try living in bohemia and moved into the Village.

A long chapter ("The Village") of his **autobiography** is devoted to the Beat years he spent there. For Jones and many others, it was a time and place of enormous ferment in a compressed population of artists of all kinds. He was influenced by the music of Ornette Coleman, John Coltrane, Theophilus Monk, and Sun Ra, by the **poetry** and friendship of Allen Ginsberg, Frank O'Hara, and Charles Olson, the kind and gentle encouragement of **Langston Hughes**. Jones identifies **James Baldwin** as "the last great black arts figure who related to Europe as center" (*Autobiography* 129). In the dynamic and organic American literary scene, Jones learned from the major and minor Beat, New York School, and Black Mountain School writers, all of whom he knew—especially learning from Charles Olson, who "had the broader sword" (158) and whose seminal work *Projective Verse* Jones published.

Jones went to the Village to cultivate his intellectual life and to nurture his own literary ambitions. To that end, he worked as shipping manager at *Record Changer*, a **jazz** magazine, where he met his first wife, Hettie Cohen, with whom he established and edited the avant-garde magazine *Yugen* from 1958 to 1963; together, they established Totem Press in 1958. He also founded and ran another underground publication with Diane di Prima. The *Floating Bear* flourished from 1961 to 1969, with Jones involved only for the first two years. In these magazines, the work of emerging writers who are now considered major forces in twentieth-century American poetry first appeared. Di Prima and Jones also cofounded the New York Poets' Theatre in 1961. He self-published his first book of poetry in 1961, and his important study *Blues People: Negro Music in White America* appeared in 1963 as part of his practice of jazz and **blues** cultural criticism.

Poetry, **drama**, and music were central creative and intellectual occupations for Jones during this period, and his years in Greenwich Village are considered by many his most important creatively. His theater work garnered the most attention initially. His play *Dutchman* opened off-Broadway at the Cherry Lane Theatre in 1964 and won an Obie Award. Collectively, his dramatic writing "scared, angered, and inspired both blacks and whites" (Watts 65). The overt anger politics of his provocative plays came at a time when growing impatience with the **civil rights movement** was on the verge of creating a rift between those who continued to believe in nonviolent means to effect change and those who began to espouse **violence** as a necessary strategy. Subsequently, Jones took his radical voice, which became explicitly anti-Semitic, and began to advocate violence against whites, out of Greenwich Village—abandoning his white wife and mixed-race daughters—and into Harlem. He did not embrace **Black Nationalism** until after the assassination of **Malcolm X** in 1965, when he began to identify and align himself with the articulation and development of a black cultural **community**.

He established the Black Arts Repertory Theatre (BART) in Harlem in 1965, and later Spirit House in Newark in 1967, and became a leading proponent of the **Black Arts Movement**, also investigating Yoruba religious practice, philosophically attached to the idea of a self-consciously black art leading to the emergence of black nationhood. But as his writing became more propagandistic and polemical, critics have condemned it for a correlative weakening of its artfulness and for its varied racially based assertions that substituted for cultural analysis and argument. BART failed to flourish, and Jones stayed in Harlem less than a year, returning to his suburban origins in Newark, but as a changed man. He became ideologically enamored of Maulana Karenga's Kawaida, an activist essentialist Pan-African philosophy. Jones once again used the strategy of self-naming in 1967 as an expression of identity and transformed himself into Imamu (Spiritual Leader) Amiri (Prince) Baraka (Blessed), later dropping the title Imamu. As his influence grew and his ideology narrowed, Baraka began more frequently to frame his racial commentary in terms of sex and **sexuality**.

For Baraka and black Nationalists, heterosexual **black masculinity** was a necessary part of the revolutionary persona (Watts 233) and included (as did Kawaida) the subjugation of black women even though those women might be publicly extolled for their virtues. It was a period during which feminism was seen, by black men and even among women, as a potentially divisive racial topic. In other words, black women who expressed feminism could be perceived as traitors because in order to disrupt white power, black power needed to present a unified front and could not tolerate such an examination of gender issues. Ironically, this attitude, justified as important to the cause of black community, was of course harmful to black communities. Baraka's virulently sexist essay, "American Sexual Reference: Black Male," originally published in *Cavalier Magazine* (January 1966), advocated the black **rape** of white women as a politically legitimate act, stressing the objectification of white women as property held by white men.

Therefore, black-male-on-white-female rape was a politically motivated property crime, thus adding a racial element to a misogynistic attitude extant since the Middle Ages. In Baraka's thinking, the white woman served as a location for racial struggle rather than a person entitled to rights and respect. Further modifying the medieval foundation of the **myth** of woman's rape fantasy, Baraka suggests that the event would be a pleasurable sexual experience for a white woman whose previous encounters, confined to white men he portrayed in homophobic terms, would be weighed in the balance and found wanting. Hence the political prowess exhibited in the act could somehow be rationalized as furthering the cause of Black Nationalism. Baraka's uninhibited racism and sexism plumbed the depths of misogyny before he experienced yet another political transformation. After almost twenty years of grappling with his identity in terms of intellectualism, racism, and the black bourgeoisie, Baraka's attention turned to capitalism as a root cause of black oppression and necessarily as an extension of that logically to its role in the oppression of women. Retreating from Kawaida and Black Nationalism in the mid-1970s, he turned his political attentions to Marxism.

This decision, to which he has remained attached for almost thirty years, is responsible for the rehabilitation of his antiwoman stance. His antiwhite and anti-Semitic attitudes remain and in fact are responsible for his dismissal from the post of New Jersey Poet Laureate in the aftermath of a poem he wrote questioning Jewish involvement in the terrorist events of September 11, 2001. Some of his children have followed their father's example in terms of being politically active and vocal through their artistic product. Baraka is the author and editor of over seventy-five publications, of poetry, drama, and social essays. During his Black Nationalist period, he was founder and chair of the Congress of African People, organizer of the National Black Political Convention, and chair of the Committee for a Unified Newark. He is professor emeritus of the State University of New York, Stony Brook, where he taught Africana studies until his retirement in 1996, and he also has taught at several other prestigious universities. He has held fellowships from the Guggenheim Foundation and the National Endowment for the Arts, won the PEN/Faulkner Award, and the Langston Hughes Award. Baraka was elected to the American Academy of Arts and Letters in 2001. He is without doubt the primary force in the development of community-based arts projects and is the most influential figure of the Black Arts Movement.

See also Sanchez, Sonia

Works By

The Autobiography of LeRoi Jones. New York: Freundlich Books, 1984. Rev. ed.

The Autobiography of LeRoi Jones/Amiri Baraka. Chicago: Lawrence Hill Books, 1997.

Black Art. Newark, NJ: Jihad, 1966.

Blues People: Negro Music in White America. New York: Morrow, 1963.

The Essence of Reparations. Philipsburg, St. Martin, Caribbean: House of Nehesi, 2003.

The Fiction of LeRoi Jones/Amiri Baraka. Chicago: Lawrence Hill Books, 2000.

Funk Lore: New Poems, 1984–1995. Ed. Paul Vangelisti. Los Angeles: Littoral Books, 1996.

The LeRoi Jones/Amiri Baraka Reader. Ed. and Introd. William J. Harris. New York: Thunder's Mouth Press, 1991.

Preface to a Twenty Volume Suicide Note. New York: Totem Press/Corinth Books, 1961.

Selected Plays and Prose of Amiri Baraka/LeRoi Jones. New York: Morrow, 1979.

Transbluesency: The Selected Poems of Amiri Baraka, 1961–1995. New York: Marsilio, 1995.

Works About

Elam, Harry J., Jr. *Taking It to the Streets: The Social Protest Theater of Luis Valdez and Amiri Baraka.* Ann Arbor: University of Michigan Press, 1997.

Gwynne, James B., ed. *Amiri Baraka: The Kaleidoscopic Torch.* New York: Steppingstone Press, 1985.

Jones, Hettie. *How I Became Hettie Jones.* New York: E. P. Dutton, 1990.

Lacey, Henry C. *To Raise, Destroy and Create: The Poetry, Drama and Fiction of Imamu Amiri Baraka (LeRoi Jones).* Albany, NY: Whitston Publishing, 2001.

Watts, Jerry Gafio. *Amiri Baraka: The Politics and Art of a Black Intellectual.* New York: New York University Press, 2001.

Woodard, Komozi. *A Nation within a Nation: Amiri Baraka (LeRoi Jones) and Black Power Politics.* Chapel Hill: University of North Carolina Press, 1999.

A. Mary Murphy

BEAUTY

"Mirror, mirror on the wall, who's the *fairest* one of all?" As African American women and girls look into the mirror of American culture, what they see reflected back are Snow *White* images of beauty. Mass-produced images from Dick and Jane elementary school readers, classic fairy tales and **literature** to popular media have worked to reinforce Caucasian standards of beauty with faces that are fair, rosy cheeked, blue-eyed, delicate featured, bodies that are rail-thin and emaciated, and hair that is long, straight, wispy, and silky soft. While African American men do not have to fit into a socially accepted ideal of male aesthetics, African American women are presented with white standards of beauty on a daily basis and are taught from childhood that in order to be successful and loved, they should recreate themselves into the dominant white beauty aesthetic. In **J. California Cooper**'s "Vanity," Vanity is lured into the white culture's self-absorption with perfect beauty, which ultimately leads to ruin. Vanity combs her "luxuriant" hair so that it could be a "cape of beauty for others to enjoy." But Vanity buys into the mythology of white beauty encapsulated in the vision of movie stars, and her obsession with that beauty frames her isolation and eventual demise. **Toni Morrison**'s first novel, *The Bluest Eye*, explores white beauty standards and their devastating effect on one small black child, Pecola, who learns that because she is black, she will never be beautiful, never be loved, never be worthy. Pecola dreams of having blue eyes because she believes that only people with blue eyes are beautiful, and only beautiful people are loved. Her belief is dangerously reinforced by her **family** and peers, most of whom are victims of the white beauty **myth** themselves. For Pecola, having blue eyes is the only thing that will validate her humanity.

One of the profound liberating effects of the rise in black feminist literature is the ability of African American women writers to reconstruct the beauty norm for black females outside the dominant controlling images of white beauty standards. African American feminist literature is richly textured with images of full black lips, beautiful dancing dark eyes, proud nose, lush mahogany-rich skin, soft, sexy, strong melodious voices, and a lively myriad of hairstyles that express the exquisite splendor of African American women. African American feminist literature presents positive images of the black female **body** that function to unite African American women in a discourse that neutralizes white standards of beauty. Black feminist writers dissipate and fracture the white gaze that looks upon the black female as *not* white, and therefore *not* beautiful, and instead present ideal images of beautiful, desirable black women.

In **Alice Walker**'s *The Color Purple*, Celie's appreciation for and awakening of her own **sexuality** starts when she admires the captivating beauty of Shug Avery's body and her lovely "black plum nipples" and long graceful limbs. Shug introduces Celie to her sexuality and the magic button of Celie's femaleness. Harpo explains to Celie that he likes Sofia because of her "bright skin": It shines with life and vitality. **Zora Neale Hurston** describes the modern woman's connection to the pulsing beauty of Africa in "How It Feels to Be Colored Me," when the **jazz** music she listens to transports her to the jungle, where, in her imagination, she dances; face painted red and yellow, body painted blue, graceful body moving rhythmically, wildly, freely celebrating her femininity and sexuality. In Toni Morrison's *Tar Baby*, Jadine, who is a model and a product of white beauty standards, is awestruck by the "unphotographable" beauty of an African woman in a yellow dress, whose eyes are so darkly beautiful they have no lashes. In Imani Constance Johnson-Burnett's "The Dream and Lettie Byrd's Charm," when Yasmine sleeps, her mother, aunts, and grandmother visit her and remind her that she will grow and change, her womanhood a reaffirmation of and testament to the ideal beauty of her **ancestors**. As Yasmine studies her reflection in the mirror, she sees reflected back the softness and strength of her mother and father, delicately blended to create her feminine beauty—a beauty she believes is rooted in her hair.

African American women's hair has unfortunately been the most affected victim of white beauty standards. White biases about black women's hair reinforce Western perceptions that only straight silky hair is beautiful. Hair straightening products that are rigorously marketed to African American women strongly reinforce the belief that African American hair cannot be beautiful unless it looks white. Even white women who have naturally curly or kinky hair spend hundreds of dollars to straighten it in order to look less black. In Bridgitt M. Davis's "Bianca," the smell Bianca hates most in the world is burning hair: "cooked like catfish in melted grease" as her mother used hot curlers and combs to straighten her hair. Bianca finds out her daddy is not her real daddy as she sits in her mother's beauty parlor chair having her hair straightened. For Bianca, her artificially straightened hair symbolizes her prepackaged American **identity**, and she heads for Paris, France, where she can experience the "blues and oranges and greens of the world" instead of being restricted to a black or white mold. **Carolivia Herron**'s *Nappy Hair* is a lively affirmation of black female beauty that is especially important for young black girls who are inundated with white culture's consistent demonization of kinky or nappy hair. Brenda is taught to be proud of her nappy hair and all it represents. Herron's tale counters the persistent white myth that nappy hair is bad hair and somehow ungodly. Instead, God tells Brenda that "one nap [from your] head is the only perfect circle in nature," an affirmation of black female beauty that gives *Nappy Hair* a special power to endow young African American girls with pride in their own natural beauty.

No one captures the luminous beauty of the African American woman better than **Maya Angelou**. Her **poetry** and prose are filled with images of the lyrically radiant beauty of black men and women, though like a lot of young African American girls, Angelou also desired to "wake up out of [her] black ugly dream" and have "real hair" that was long, blonde, and silky soft as she describes in her **autobiography** *I Know Why the Caged Bird Sings*. Much of Angelou's poetry describes the compelling richness of African American female beauty in all its forms. In her "Mothering Blackness," the images of blackness are uplifting and comforting, beautiful "mothering blackness" and "black arms waiting" for the child whose tears leave "icicle gold plains" on her "rich brown face." Angelou's "Black Ode" celebrates "beauty [as] a thunder" and laughter "black and streaming." In "Sepia Fashion Show" Angelou comments on young black girls' desire for high-society fashion and beauty: "Their hair, pomaded, faces jaded/bones protruding, hip-wise" then reminds them that they got their knees "at Miss Ann's Scrubbing." For Angelou, beauty is much more than outward appearance. It encompasses all the things that make up woman. In her "Phenomenal Woman" Angelou describes her own beauty in "The stride of my step / The curl of my lips," and she is, as are all African American women, "Phenomenally / Phenomenal woman."

African American feminist writers celebrate and reaffirm their beauty and strength for each other through what Zora Neale Hurston describes in ***Their Eyes Were Watching God*** as "words walking without masters"—words free of white standards and criticisms and, instead, words by black women writers who privilege the resplendent beauty and sexuality of African American women.

Works About

Banks, Ingrid. *Hair Matters: Beauty, Power, and Black Women's Consciousness.* New York: New York University Press, 2000.

Birch, Eva Lennox. *Black American Women's Writing: A Quilt of Many Colors.* New York: Harvester Wheatsheaf, 1994.

Brand, Peg Zeglin, ed. *Beauty Matters.* Bloomington: Indiana University Press, 2000.

Lester, Neal A. "Nappy Edges and Goldy Lockes: African-American Daughters and the Politics of Hair." *Lion and the Unicorn* 24.2 (April 2000): 201–224.

Rooks, Noliwe M. *Hair Raising: Beauty, Culture, and African American Women.* New Brunswick, NJ: Rutgers University Press, 1996.

Debbie Clare Olson

BEHIND THE SCENES, OR, THIRTY YEARS A SLAVE, AND FOUR YEARS IN THE WHITE HOUSE

Behind the Scenes, the title of **Elizabeth Keckley**'s postbellum **slave narrative** published in 1868, suggests the contrast between the public view and private reality of her experiences in **slavery** and in the political world of the nation's capital. On the title page, the author describes herself as "Formerly a slave, but more recently modiste, and friend to Mrs. Abraham Lincoln," emphasizing the Reconstruction narrative that follows as an American success story. The term *modiste* implies that she was more than a dressmaker; she was a fashion adviser and designer for the elite.

Keckley devotes the first part of the book to her experiences as slave to the Burwell family of Dinwiddie, Virginia, from her early years as nursery maid to her **work** as a dressmaker in St. Louis, supporting both her own **family** and her master's. After the author's successful effort to buy her own and her son's **freedom** for $1,200 in 1855, the middle section shows Keckley establishing a growing business in Washington, D.C., as modiste to the upper echelon of political wives, notably the wife of Jefferson Davis and the wife of President Lincoln. Established in the inner circle of the White House family, Keckley concludes her book by recounting her experiences as confidante of Mary Lincoln, from the president's assassination to the "Old Clothes Scandal," defending her controversial role in helping the widow sell some of her wardrobe to pay off her enormous debt. Although questions have arisen over whether it was ghostwritten, abolitionist James Redpath most likely only edited the book, though he certainly was responsible, along with the publisher, for reprinting her letters from Mary Lincoln without permission. Those who knew Keckley testified to the long hours of hard work she put in on the book.

Like the antebellum slave narratives, *Behind the Scenes* underscores the wrongness of chattel slavery that deprived slaves of their human rights. Keckley depicts slavery as a crucible that tempered the soul and produced heroism in slaves through suffering. Keckley's postbellum slave narrative modifies the genre to accommodate female experience, just as **Harriet Jacobs**'s *Incidents in the Life of a Slave Girl*, which had appeared earlier, added a female perspective to the antebellum slave narrative. Told from childhood that she was worthless, the author wrote to show how she struggled to overcome her position as dehumanized slave, subject to the sexual harrassment of white men and the cruelty of white mistresses, to achieve her own dreams of economic independence and social status as a dressmaker employing twenty women. Although *Behind the Scenes* ends with the author's earnest attempts to set the record straight about her friend and client Mrs. Lincoln, it does not record the conclusion to her story. Keckley died alone and destitute, limited in the end by **race** and gender, a black woman who proved she had value yet still could not triumph in a world of white male privilege.

Works About

Andrews, William L. "The Changing Moral Discourse of Nineteenth-Century African American Women's Autobiography: Harriet Jacobs and Elizabeth Keckley." *De/colonizing the Subject: The Politics of Gender in Women's Autobiography.* Ed. Sidonie Smith and Julia Watson. Minneapolis: University of Minnesota Press, 1992. 225–241.

Fleischner, Jennifer. *Mastering Slavery: Memory, Family, and Identity in Women's Slave Narratives.* New York: New York University Press, 1996.

Foster, Frances Smith. "Autobiography after Emancipation: The Example of Elizabeth Keckley." *Multicultural Autobiography: American Lives.* Ed. James Robert Payne. Knoxville: University of Tennessee Press, 1992.

——. *Written by Herself: Literary Production by African American Women, 1746–1892.* Bloomington: Indiana University Press, 1993.

Beth L. Lueck

BELOVED

Toni Morrison's fifth novel, *Beloved* (1987), based on the true story of Margaret Garner, is set in the outskirts of Cincinnati, Ohio, in the 1870s. Much that happens at 124 Bluestone, however, depends on events two decades earlier at Sweet Home, the Kentucky plantation that was neither sweet nor **home** for Sethe, the novel's protagonist. Morrison's most acclaimed novel and winner of the 1988 Pulitzer Prize for **Fiction**, *Beloved* explores the complexity of a too-deep mother-**love**, the psychological scars forged in a brutal slave system, the necessity of **community**, and the difficult path of self-forgiveness. On a larger level, the text is a discussion about individual, communal, and cultural humanity.

Sethe's murder of her crawling-already baby, not recounted until midway through the novel, highlights the psychological trauma of a mother who believes her primary duty is to protect her children from what she knows is evil: **slavery**. Having escaped from Sweet Home, giving birth to her fourth child in the process, Sethe enjoys twenty-eight days of **freedom** before Schoolteacher comes to reclaim her. As she gathers her four children in her arms and runs toward the shed, her only thought is to send them all, finally, outside the reach of slave owners. In an America ruled by the Fugitive Slave Act, the only refuge she can imagine is **death**. She succeeds in killing only one of her children–her oldest girl—by running a saw across her neck. In the bloody aftermath, Schoolteacher writes them off as a loss. Although Sethe thus succeeds in ensuring freedom for herself and her remaining three children, their lives are all circumscribed by this act of **violence** as the baby's spirit returns to haunt 124 Bluestone.

Unable to live longer with the ghost of their sister, Sethe's sons Howard and Buglar run off in their early teens to join the war. In guilt over her failure to prevent her granddaughter's murder, and worn out finally from a life too filled with loss, Baby Suggs, Sethe's mother-in-law and once the strong, maternal spiritual center of the community, withdraws to her bed to contemplate something harmless: color. Denver, the girl born in a broken boat on the banks of the Ohio River, is left with a ghost for a sister and the fear that whatever made her mother once kill might make her do it again.

The awkward peace Sethe and Denver forge with the ghost is disrupted by Paul D, the last of the Sweet Home men and the embodiment of a strong, sensitive **black masculinity**. After being sold as slave labor for the war and spending days sleeping in a box in a Georgia prison, subject to sexual abuse from the white prison guards, Paul D, his heart secure in a rusted tin, turns his feet finally toward Sethe. Paul D does two things upon his arrival: exorcise the ghost and have sex with Sethe. He, Sethe, and Denver form a tentative **family**, a union prefigured in their hand-holding shadows on the way home from the carnival. This newly (re)constructed family, however, is shattered by the ghost who returns, now physically embodied. When Sethe sees the young woman sitting against a tree stump in the front yard, she has the irrepressible urge to urinate in a scene suggestive of a woman's water breaking during labor. Sethe takes the girl in without question, unwilling to turn a young black woman into the street. The stranger, who can barely speak, walk, or stay awake, calls herself Beloved, the only word Sethe had inscribed on her daughter's pink tombstone. Documenting the rampant sexual abuse of black women by white men even in northern states, the stonecutter trades seven letters for ten minutes of Sethe's "time," allowing his son to watch as he has sex with her. Accepting the sexual exploitation as an unalterable fact of her world, Sethe primarily regrets not having asked for seven more: Dearly Beloved, the only words she heard the preacher say at her daughter's funeral.

Denver is the first to understand that Beloved is the ghost of her dead sister, whose blood she once drank along with her mother's milk. Beloved gains strength quickly and soon moves Paul D out of Sethe's bed and into the cold house. Against his will, he has sex with her, but her irresistible demand for intimacy is less about sex than it is about the raw exchange of some life force that she lacks. In an attempt to confess to Sethe, Paul D finds himself instead asking her to have his baby. Sethe rejects the idea, unwilling to accept once more the boundless loss of self she equates with **motherhood**.

When Stamp Paid shows Paul D a newspaper article describing Sethe's trial, Paul D's compassion temporarily fails him, and he reminds Sethe that she has two legs, not four. His distinction between animal and human behavior echoes an earlier moment in the text when Sethe overhears Schoolteacher and his two nephews comparing her "human characteristics" with her "animal" ones. Sethe rejects Paul D's oversimplification of her act, just as the text rejects his implicit assignation of blame to Sethe alone. If the infanticide is indeed the act of an animal rather than the ultimate sacrifice of a mother, the slave system is culpable: Sethe's psychological response to Schoolteacher's approach is specifically linked to her mistreatment at Sweet Home, an abuse Sethe understands as particularly threatening to mother-hood.

The slaves of Sweet Home had planned an escape, but something went awry. After her husband Halle fails to meet them at the predetermined spot, the six-months-pregnant Sethe sends her three children on in care of a group bound North. When she returns to look for Halle, she is violated by School-teacher's nephews in a way worse than sexual **rape**: Schoolteacher calmly takes notes as one nephew holds Sethe down and the other drinks her breast milk. What Sethe only learns much later, after Paul D comes to 124 Blue-stone, is that Halle was above in the loft, watching. Halle's inability to protect his wife–the effective erasure of his masculinity–drives him to madness. Paul D, himself caught, chained, and with a bit in his mouth, sees the mentally broken Halle at the butter churn, butter and clabber smeared across his face. A psychologically scarred Sethe tells the sympathetic but dying Mrs. Garner of her violation and is promptly and violently whipped by Schoolteacher, her round stomach placed in a hole to protect the fetus. Even more determined to get her milk to her baby girl, the beaten, bloody, pregnant Sethe runs on her own. For Paul D, however, neither her account of what happened nor the devotion that drove her forward to reach her children mediates Sethe's act.

Shortly after Paul D leaves her, Sethe realizes Beloved's **identity**. Overjoyed that she no longer has to remember all the things that haunt her, relieved that her baby girl was not even mad, Sethe puts down her sword, as Baby Suggs had instructed her, and picks up a pair of ice skates. Sethe loses her job as a restaurant cook and the threesome–beribboned, candy-fed, and dressed in carnival-colored cloth–speed through Sethe's meager life savings. At first content in this isolated female space, Denver eventually recognizes that she is an interloper. The energy that sustains 124 Bluestone, the force that helps Beloved hold her flesh together, is a circuit between Sethe and the embodiment of her guilt. Unable to forgive herself, Sethe begins a futile attempt to explain. The more Sethe offers of herself, however, the more Beloved demands: Be-loved's life force expands as Sethe, consumed by her own psychological trauma, contracts. Denver sees the shift in the relationship and begins to fear for her mother's life. Hunger and fear finally motivate Denver to step off the edge of her world in search of help.

Although the women of the community still cannot understand Sethe's act, they understand their own complicity: a smoldering, unarticulated jealousy over Baby Suggs's bounty spurred them to an apathy that failed to warn Sethe of Schoolteacher's approach. After Sethe was released from prison, their guilt turned to a self-righteousness answered by Sethe's scornful pride. But when Denver reaches out for help, the women of the community finally begin the **healing**. They leave food in the yard of 124 Bluestone. However, it is Ella, the woman who brought Sethe to Baby Suggs's door, who finally motivates the women to decisive action. Kept as a sex slave for father and son, Ella had given birth to a white-skinned baby whom she refused to nurse. It is in part the **memory** of this rejected child who died five days later that allows Ella to feel compassion for Sethe: Anything dead cannot be suffered to cross back into the land of the living. Metaphorically, Ella rejects the paralysis caused by allowing the past—which for the black community includes the dehumanizing system of slavery—to define the present.

At novel's end, thirty women converge on the house from one direction while Mr. Bodwin—a white man sympathetic to the plight of African Americans—approaches from the other. As the women begin to sing, making a sound from the beginning of time, Sethe and a naked, belly-swollen Beloved emerge from the house. In the women's song, Sethe is reminded of the Clearing, where Baby Suggs called her community to celebrate itself; in the white man approaching in the wagon, Sethe sees Schoolteacher. This psychological reenactment allows Sethe to redirect her rage upon the oppressor rather than to further victimize the oppressed. Thus, she turns the ice pick in her hand outward toward the white man, rather than inward toward the flesh and spirit of her daughters. As a consequence, Beloved disappears, explodes, or runs off, depending, that is, on whom you ask.

Beloved, as Denver tells Paul D, was more than just her sister's ghost. In the novel she comes to symbolize not only Sethe's guilt but also the misery of the 60 million or more the book is dedicated to, the people who made—or died during—the **Middle Passage**. She is the crime born of slavery, the pain born of loss, the trauma born of separation. She is the tragedy of the broken slave family, and the separation of mother from child, husband from wife, sister from sister. Born in hope and hatred, desire and despair, love and loss, she is an angry, jealous, sorrowful pain. But in the end, she gives way to hope, healing, and the possibility of promise. Denver exits the text a young, employed woman, no longer psychologically dependent upon her mother and a member of the black community. Paul D returns to Sethe, bathing her body and soothing her recovering spirit. He reminds Sethe that she, not her children, is her best thing, and the novel closes with Sethe, who had for two decades defined herself only as mother, beginning to understand what her "me" could be.

Works About

Abel, Elizabeth, Barbara Christian, and Helene Moglen, eds. *Female Subjects in Black and White: Race, Psychoanalysis, Feminism*. Berkeley: University of California Press, 1997.

Change, Shu-li. "Daughterly Haunting and Historical Traumas: Toni Morrison's *Beloved* and Jamaica Kincaid's *The Autobiography of My Mother*." *Concentric: Literary and Cultural Studies* 30.2 (2004): 105–127.

Cullinan, Colleen Carpenter. "A Maternal Discourse of Redemption: Speech and Suffering in Morrison's *Beloved*." *Religion and Literature* 34.2 (Summer 2002): 77–104.

Fleming, Kathryn R. "Exorcising Institutionalized Ghosts and Redefining Female Identity in Mariama Bâ's *So Long a Letter* and Toni Morrison's *Beloved*." *Emerging Perspectives on Mariama Bâ: Postcolonialism, Feminism, and Postmodernism*. Ed. Ada Uzoamaka Azodo. Trenton, NJ: Africa World, 2003. 205–226.

Jeremiah, Emily. "Murderous Mothers: Adrienne Rich's *Of Woman Born* and Toni Morrison's *Beloved*." *Motherhood to Mothering: The Legacy of Adrienne Rich's "Of Woman Born."* Ed. Andrea O'Reilly. Albany: State University of New York Press, 2004. 59–71.

Kang, Nancy. "To Love and Be Loved: Considering Black Masculinity and the Misandric Impulse in Toni Morrison's *Beloved*." *Callaloo* 26.3 (Summer 2003): 836–854.

Kanthak, John F. "Feminisms in Motion: Pushing the 'Wild Zone' Thesis into the Fourth Dimension." *LIT: Literature Interpretation Theory* 14.2 (2003): 149–163.

Schapiro, Barbara. "The Bonds of Love and the Boundaries of Self in Toni Morrison's *Beloved*." *Contemporary Literature* 32.2 (Summer 1991): 194–210.

Spearey, Susan. "Substantiating Discourses of Emergence: Corporeality, Spectrality, and Postmodern Historiography in Toni Morrison's *Beloved*." *Body Matters: Feminism, Textuality, Corporeality*. Ed. Avril Horner and Angela Keane. Manchester, England: Manchester University Press, 2000. 170–182.

Watson, Reginald. "The Power of the 'Milk' and Motherhood: Images of Deconstruction in Toni Morrison's *Beloved* and Alice Walker's *The Third Life of Grange Copeland*." *CLA Journal* 48.2 (2004): 156–182.

Wyatt, Jean. "Giving Body to the Word: The Maternal Symbolic in Toni Morrison's *Beloved*." *PMLA: Publication of the Modern Language Association of America* 108.3 (May 1993): 474–488.

Julie Cary Nerad

BENNETT, GWENDOLYN B. (1902–1981)

Born in 1902 in Giddings, Texas, Gwendolyn Bennett was the daughter of teachers who eventually moved to Nevada to work on an Indian reservation. When Bennett was five years old, the **family** moved to Washington, D.C., so that her father could study law. It was here that life became less stable when her parents divorced and her mother was awarded custody. Her father, unhappy with the decision, kidnapped Bennett and lived a nomadic life with her until finally settling in Brooklyn, New York.

In Brooklyn, Bennett's creative life came alive as she joined her high school's literary and **drama** societies, won the school's art contest, and wrote her class's graduation speech and the lyrics to their graduation song. Her talents and intellect earned her the opportunity to study fine arts at Columbia University and the Pratt Institute, from which she graduated in 1924. She received a scholarship from Delta Sigma Theta Sorority to study art in Paris for a year after graduation.

Upon returning to the United States, Bennett became actively involved in the **Harlem Renaissance**, which was then in full swing. Already working as an art teacher at Howard University, she also worked diligently on her **poetry** and short **fiction**, making the years between 1923 and 1928 her most productive, creatively. Bennett had at least twenty-two poems and several pieces of artwork published in journals such as *Crisis, Opportunity, Fire!!, Palms,* and *Gypsy.* Unfortunately, however, she never had her poetry published as a single collection.

In 1926, Bennett began working for *Opportunity* as the assistant editor and columnist of "The Ebony Flute," a column that provided the social and literary happenings of prominent artists. She worked at the magazine for two years until her husband's medical practice forced them to move to Florida. Bennett quickly became unhappy, longing for the stimulation of New York. Unfortunately, by the time they returned, the Great Depression had greatly depleted the movement.

After her husband's death, she supported herself by working with **community**-based government art projects and at several schools. Suspicion of communist activities forced her out of these last positions, and she ended up collecting and selling antiques in Pennsylvania.

Bennett's art is best known for the focus she places on the **beauty** of black people. Perhaps her most well known poem, "To Usward," acknowledges the diversity in the black experience and celebrates the unity of the black **race**. Her poem "Heritage" (written prior to **Countee Cullen**'s poem of the same name) uses natural imagery to remind readers of the majesty of the African past. She is careful to emphasize the importance of black femininity to that past by drawing Negro girls against the backdrop of the scenery. She does this again in "To a Dark Girl," which speaks specifically to black womanhood, calling for recognition of the beauty of black feminine grace and struggle.

While few scholars have chosen Bennett as a subject for thorough study, her focus on racial pride and gender consciousness proves her to be a woman who deserves such attention.

Works About

Griffin, Farah J., and Cheryl J. Fish, eds. *A Stranger in the Village: Two Centuries of African-American Travel Writing.* Boston: Beacon Press, 1998.

Hine, Darlene Clark, ed. *Black Women in America.* New York: Carlson Press, 1993.

Miller, Nina. *Making Love Modern: The Intimate Public Worlds of New York's Literary Women.* New York: Oxford University Press, 1999.

RaShell R. Smith-Spears

BETSEY BROWN

Betsey Brown (1985), written by **Ntozake Shange**, is a story about the coming of age of a young girl in the midst of the racial turmoil in the 1950s. At a time when African Americans had difficulty defining a place in society and often felt like second-class citizens, the portrait of the Brown **family** is positive and reinforcing for the upkeep of ancient African traditions. The story confronts the confusion and understanding of a young girl growing up and attempting to create an **identity** of her own while still having an image that is family oriented. In the end, Betsey discovers a way to combine these two aspects of her life and define herself without having to abandon one or the other.

The family is not without problems. There is resistance between Jane and Greer, the mother and father of the family. Greer demands that his children have authority concerning their black heritage and demands they protest and take an active role in making their situation better. On the other hand, Jane wishes that her children could simply learn to blend in so as not to be recipients of racial hate or confrontation. This theme is revisited throughout the novel—the choice between blending in or being outspoken about personal social positions.

However, Betsey is still dealing with defining herself as a woman who is allowed to have **freedom** in her life. She does not seem to be overcome with defining herself according to her **race** in society. The Brown family creates a positive understanding of what it means to be African American, and therefore the children seem not to be plagued with doubt or fear about what they can or cannot do with their lives. They have confidence and understanding about who they are because of the methods Greer takes to educate them about their ancestry and break down the untrue **stereotypes** that appear in society. For example, Greer uses African drumbeats and call and response to wake the kids up in the morning. Not a day passes when he does not manage to teach the children something new about Africa and, essentially, about themselves.

The Brown family is under a new kind of stress in 1959 because of the forced integration of schools and the smoothing over of racism in society. Although the newly enforced laws claim that racism is over and that there is equality for all, regardless of color, racism was still prevalent and affected the lives of many African Americans. The novel follows the Brown family through this hard time and especially documents what it might have been like to be growing up a black woman during this period.

Work About

Kent, Assunta. "The Rich Multiplicity of *Betsey Brown*." *Journal of Dramatic Theory and Criticism* 7.1 (Fall 1992): 151–161.

Fayme Perry

BIRTHA, BECKY (1948–   )

Few can rival the unique ambiance found in the richly textured simplicity of Becky Birtha's **poetry** and short stories. Birtha's writings reflect her unique insight into the reticular nuances of interracial relationships between women. Birtha was born in Hampton, Virginia, and spent her childhood in Philadelphia. Birtha is named after her great-grandmother, who was a slave, and Birtha's writings reflect her distinctive personal diversity: She is African American, Irish, Cherokee, and Choctaw, a lesbian, a feminist, and a Quaker.

Birtha attended the State University of New York at Buffalo, earning a B.S. degree in children's studies in 1973. In 1984 she received her M.F.A. in creative writing from Vermont College. In 1985 Birtha received an Individual Fellowship in Literature from the Pennsylvania Council on the Arts, and in 1988 she received a Creative Writing Fellowship Grant from the National Endowment for the Arts. In 1989 Birtha's short story "The Saints and Sinners Run" was adapted for the stage and performed by the Rose and Swan Theatre Company, Media, Pennsylvania. In 1993 she was awarded a Pew Fellowship of the Arts. Birtha's poems and stories are widely anthologized.

Birtha's first published work was *For Nights Like This One: Stories of Loving Women* (1983), a charming collection of shorts stories that presents same-sex romance in a genuine way that is a testament to the infectiousness of the human spirit and the efficacy of believing in **love**. *For Nights Like This One* explores lesbian relationships in a remarkably unremarkable way that accentuates lesbian women's experiences in love as fully human—and not something socially deviant or mysterious. Birtha creates characters that are inhabited with vitality and joy, anger and pain, love and sacrifice. Their stories speak to the broader experience of being a woman and the search for love and acceptance that is common to all people. Birtha's second collection of short stories, *Lovers' Choice* (1987), continues the theme of celebration of the complexity and diversity of women's relationships with women. The compelling blend of grace and compassion in Birtha's characters cuts short the notion that same-sex love cannot be an adequate expression of *affaire d'amour*. Many of Birtha's stories in *Lovers' Choice* also offer a unique view of white women by black women through the struggles of lesbian interracial relationships. Birtha's first poetry collection, *The Forbidden Poems* (1991), offers a resplendent array of images that offer an affirmation of the forces of love and hope in the face of social intolerance and criticism. Birtha's poetry uses the soft and subtle power of metaphor to express her belief in a world of tolerance and acceptance as in "How It Happened." Most of all, Birtha's poetry and short stories are about women—women whose lyrical experiences of love function to foster hope within us all.

Works By

The Forbidden Poems. Seattle: Seal Press, 1991.

For Nights Like This One: Stories of Loving Women. San Francisco: Frog in the Well, 1983.
Literature by Black Women: A List of Books. Comp. Becky Birtha. Philadelphia: Privately printed, 1983.
Lovers' Choice. Seattle: Seal Press, 1987.

Works About

Carbado, Devon W., Dwight A. McBride, and Donald Weise, eds. *Black Like Us: A Century of Lesbian, Gay and Bisexual African American Fiction.* San Francisco: Cleis Press, 2002.
Cruikshank, Margaret, ed. *Lesbian Studies: Present and Future.* Old Westbury, NY: Feminist Press, 1982.

Debbie Clare Olson

BLACK ARTS MOVEMENT

The Black Arts Movement (BAM) was a collective attempt among African American writers, musicians, visual artists, activists, and cultural critics to articulate a specifically black art. This project entailed the definition of a black aesthetic as the underlying impetus of their work. Although such a definition could never be fully codified, most participants agreed that a work created in the spirit of a black aesthetic endeavored both to raise its audience's awareness of social inequalities and to valorize African and African American cultural practices. The BAM shared the idea of a black aesthetic with the Black Power movement, a concurrent drive to further the social rights of black people through black Nationalist organizations such as the Black Panther Party and the Nation of Islam; activists like Stokely Carmichael urged artists to advance Black Power principles in their work. As a creative movement, the BAM was seen by some commentators as the inheritor of **Harlem Renaissance** efforts to promote black art; others conceptualized its purpose more pointedly as the responsibility to succeed in cultivating a space for black creativity where Harlem Renaissance artists had failed. In any case, BAM supporters, unlike their 1920s predecessors, understood art and politics as inextricably linked. Many artists used black nationalist or separatist themes as a way of highlighting this relationship.

The BAM spanned roughly the years 1965 to 1976. Several critics cite LeRoi Jones/**Amiri Baraka**'s February 1965 decision to leave his Greenwich Village life for literary activist projects in Harlem as the movement's true beginning; some have labeled his 1969 **poetry** collection *Black Magic* as one of the BAM's first "official" publications. However, several black women writers made life-changing decisions during the same period that suggest other possible opening moments for the movement. **Gwendolyn Brooks** attended the Second Black Writers' Conference at Fisk University in 1967, a conference that brought many BAM writers together for the first time; the ideas of the poets she met there radically altered the style and themes of her poetry. **Nikki Giovanni** graduated from Fisk University in the winter of 1967 and organized Cincinnati's first Black Arts Festival that summer. **Sonia Sanchez** published her first book of poetry, *Home Coming*, in 1969. BAM activities were also inspired by historical events and situations. The 1950s **civil rights movement** had gained ground for African Americans, but substantial social change was still needed. In 1961, several Mississippi "**freedom** riders" were pulled off the buses they were riding to protest segregation and severely beaten. President John F. Kennedy was assassinated on November 22, 1963. **Malcolm X** was assassinated on February 21, 1965, at a rally. Writers like Brooks, Giovanni, and Sanchez were motivated by these events and others to argue for the worth of black achievement.

BAM creativity was grounded in a desire to define new approaches to African American expression. In **literature**, these new expressive strategies translated into innovative formal techniques, a use of African cultural references, and emphasis upon the term *black* as a replacement for *Negro*. Writers sometimes celebrated their heritage by choosing African names to replace their "slave names." The proliferation of literature that explored African American experience also prompted BAM teachers to reconfigure their notions of education. Psychologist Nathan Hare worked with Sonia Sanchez to establish the first Black Studies Department at San Francisco State University in 1969; poet **Sarah Webster Fabio** supported their efforts from her post at Oakland's Merritt College. Sanchez also taught the very first college seminar on literature by African American women writers that year, a course at the University of Pittsburgh titled "The Black Woman."

Prose writers formed a vanguard to BAM productions, but their longer pieces did not lend themselves as easily to political argument as did poetry and **drama**. The Harlem Writers Guild, established in 1950, counted among its 1960s members **Maya Angelou**, **Rosa Guy**, and **Sarah Elizabeth Wright**. Their work, primarily **fiction**, received acclaim without being considered revolutionary. **Toni Cade Bambara** is another fiction writer, not associated with the Harlem Writers Guild, whose work in the 1960s and 1970s grew out of contemporary social struggles. **Adrienne Kennedy**, the author of such plays as *Funnyhouse of a Negro* (1969) and *An Evening with Dead Essex* (1973), explores in her work the violent racial tensions that have fractured the United States. Umbra, a Manhattan-based collective of black poets and fiction writers that included Calvin Hernton, Tom Dent, **Ishmael Reed**, and Brenda Walcott, paved the way for other BAM organizations through its focus on radical political statements, its innovative art, and the publication of *Umbra Magazine*. Both individual writers and groups like Umbra established structural experimentation and rhetorical boldness as central characteristics of BAM writing.

Poets comprised the largest group of BAM writers for several reasons. Poetry could be easily performed; its formal malleability encompassed both experimental writing and vernacular expressions; its metrical patterns were aligned with the repeated rhythms of political exhortations; and its relatively short length meant that poets could self-publish. Many poets also wrote articles, plays, short stories, novels, and books for children, yet their investment in the movement's capacity for widespread public communication often encouraged them to publish poetry first. Sonia Sanchez produced seven poetry publications between 1969 and 1974, including *Ima Talken Bout the Nation of Islam* (1971), *Liberation Poem* (1970), and *A Blues Book for Blue Black Magical Women* (1974), all of which consider the role that black women play in defining a black aesthetic. The linguistic abbreviations, erratic use of capitalization, and nonstandard spacing characteristic of Sanchez's work in the 1970s are common to many BAM writers. Nikki Giovanni published *Black Feeling, Black Talk* and *Black Judgment* in the late 1960s; her poems in these two volumes lament the **death** of leaders like Martin Luther King, Jr., and demand retribution for crimes committed against African Americans. Giovanni is also known for her "Poem of Angela Yvonne Davis," a poem honoring activist and cultural critic **Angela Davis**.

The women poets of the BAM raised issues that were not always in the forefront of the movement's political concerns. **Audre Lorde**, a writer associated briefly with the Harlem Writers Guild, came into prominence on the BAM scene in 1968 when she published her first book of poetry, *The First Cities*, taught at Mississippi's historically black Tougaloo College for six weeks, and found her lifelong romantic partner. Lorde's personal life intersected with her professional activities in a way that some other BAM writers' did not: She was a lesbian who explored issues of **sexuality** in her work at a time when many of her contemporaries openly expressed homophobic sentiments. **June Jordan** began her teaching career in 1966 and published her first poetry collection, *Who Look at Me*, in 1969. Her work is notable for its investigation of **race** relations and the processes by which American society complicates black people's sense of **identity**. **Carolyn Rodgers** studied poetry in workshops with Gwendolyn Brooks and the Organization of Black American Culture (OBAC). Her work reflects the militant themes and rhetoric of Black Power, but she tempers her promotion of Black Nationalism with a feminist politics that calls into question Black Power beliefs in female subservience. Rodgers uses the linguistic abbreviations common to BAM poetry in order to illustrate how language serves as a tool for political manipulation. The social themes that define the poetry of Lorde, Jordan, Rodgers, and their contemporaries also appear in the work of two poets from an earlier generation who were still active during the BAM, **Margaret Walker** and Gwendolyn Brooks. Brooks published *In the Mecca* (1968) and *Riot* (1969) a few years after her attendance at the Fisk Writers' Conference; these poems' interrogation of urban social conditions reflects the period's turbulence. Walker's *Prophets for a New Day* (1970), her third book of poetry, condemns specific instances of racial violence.

The efforts of independent publishers and editors who compiled anthologies of BAM work helped to sustain the movement's momentum. The *Journal of Black Poetry* and *Black Scholar* were both published out of San Francisco's Bay

Area; *Negro Digest* (later *Black World*), edited by Hoyt Fuller, came out of Chicago. Don L. Lee/Haki Madhubuti's Third World Press in Chicago and Dudley Randall's Broadside Press in Detroit also provided opportunities for African American writers to publicize their work and meet others with similar interests. Broadside Press in particular supplied invaluable support for the careers of Nikki Giovanni and Sonia Sanchez. Giovanni published three books, one tape featuring a reading of her poetry, one broadside, and twenty-four anthologized poems during her time with Broadside. Sanchez produced four books, three tapes, two broadsides, and fourteen anthologized poems during the same period. Both poets also participated in hundreds of readings, conferences, and other activities. Giovanni formed her own press, Nik-Tom, Ltd., in 1970; Sanchez established 5X Publishing Co. in 1971. Among the anthologies that featured work by BAM poets like Giovanni and Sanchez were Amiri Baraka and Larry Neal's *Black Fire: An Anthology of Afro-American Writing* (1968) and Stephen Henderson's *Understanding the New Black Poetry: Black Speech and Black Music as Poetic References* (1972). *Black Fire* also contained essays that attempted to quantify the emerging characteristics of the BAM, as did Addison Gayle's *The Black Aesthetic* (1971) and Floyd B. Barbour's *The Black Seventies* (1970). Most of the critics who contributed to these anthologies were men; however, Toni Cade Bambara's *The Black Woman: An Anthology* (1970) compiled the work of several prominent black women writers who sought to define the place of **black feminist** thought in the wake of BAM ideas.

The BAM included writers who were noted as much for their political activities as for their publications. Public political expressions often carried serious consequences. Angela Davis, a well-known member of the Communist Party, lost her teaching appointment and was imprisoned in 1970 after her involvement with Black Panther Party members. She contributed to *If They Come in the Morning: Voices of Resistance* (1971) during her incarceration. Sonia Sanchez was investigated by federal agents in the mid-1960s after she was accused of teaching subversive materials; she and some of her fellow BAM poets were regularly put under surveillance by the FBI, local police, and Michigan state police because of their supposedly illicit activities. The gradual dissolution of the BAM can be attributed in part to Internal Revenue Service (IRS), Counterintelligence Program (COINTELPRO), and FBI investigations, which undermined movement leadership and bred dissent among members. Some contemporary black feminists also felt that the BAM had long been marred by internal antagonisms. Michele Wallace, literary and cultural critic, wrote *Black Macho and the Myth of the Superwoman* in 1978 as a reflection on the gender politics of Black Power. She argued that black men's internalization of white American beliefs in their aggressive sexuality culminated in 1960s Black Power sentiments. Although her work garnered criticism from several quarters, she articulated the concern about male domination of the BAM that was shared by many women affiliated with its organizations.

The BAM resulted in positive gains overall for black women writers. The interest of writers like Sanchez, Giovanni, and **Jayne Cortez** in **blues** themes as a source of feminist expression defied the belief some BAM activists held in blues' resonance with the oppressive social conditions of **slavery**. Writers sought out the work of lesser-known authors for republication; **Alice Walker** reintroduced the novels and short stories of **Zora Neale Hurston** to the reading public in the 1970s. Several books that assessed the end of the BAM also appeared. Walker's *Meridian* (1976) narrates the experiences of a young black woman whose physical illness mirrors the social unrest she works to combat. **Ntozake Shange**'s choreopoem *for colored girls who have considered suicide/when the rainbow is enuf* (1976) comprises a series of monologues on black female experience narrated by seven anonymous women. When this work premiered on Broadway, its success was interpreted by many critics as a triumph for black women working in theater. Toni Cade Bambara's *The Salt Eaters* (1980) depicts a group of civil rights workers seeking a mythical source of **healing**. Such works both reflect on the social efforts of the preceding decades and pay tribute to the innovations of BAM participants.

See also Black Nationalism

Works About

Ford, Karen Jackson. *Gender and the Poetics of Excess: Moments of Brocade*. Jackson: University Press of Mississippi, 1997.

Hine, Darlene Clark, ed. *Black Women in America: An Historical Encyclopedia*. Brooklyn, NY: Carlson Publishing, 1993.

Salaam, Kalamu ya. "Black Arts Movement." *The Oxford Companion to African American Literature*. Ed. William L. Andrews, Frances Smith Foster, and Trudier Harris. New York: Oxford University Press, 1997.

Smith, David Lionel. "Black Arts Movement." *Encyclopedia of African-American Culture and History, Volume I*. Ed. Jack Salzman, David Lionel Smith, and Cornel West. New York: Simon and Schuster Macmillan, 1996.

Thompson, Julius E. *Dudley Randall, Broadside Press, and the Black Arts Movement in Detroit, 1960–1995*. Jefferson, NC: McFarland, 1999.

Jennifer Denise Ryan

BLACK FEMINISM

The black feminist movement developed in response to the experience of black women in black liberation movements, which include the **civil rights movement**, the Black Nationalist Movement, the Black Panther movement, and others, and in the women's movement. Black women often found themselves facing sexual oppression within black liberation movements and racial oppression within the women's movement. White feminists often refused to see themselves as racist, projecting an antiracist attitude that was not reflected in either their ideology or practice. Although the black feminist movement was realized in the 1970s, the foundation had long since been developing.

As far back as the **slave narratives**, African American women have been asserting their desire for sexual as well as racial equality. This assertion was perhaps best exhibited by **Sojourner Truth** in her "Ar'n't I a Woman" speech. Born in Ulster County, New York, and identified as "Isabella," Truth experienced the hardships of **slavery** before gaining her **freedom** with the passing of the 1827 New York law. In 1843, Isabella assumed the name Sojourner Truth and worked with prominent figures like **Frederick Douglass** and William Lloyd Garrison in antislavery activities. In 1851 Truth attended the Women's Rights Convention in Akron, Ohio, and both the reception she received there and the speech she ultimately gave reflect the multiple oppression that black women have had to cope with historically. Upon her arrival at the convention, Truth was met with antagonism from white participants who were against her participation in the convention. While some white males were opposed to Truth's "gender," some white female participants feared that Truth's inclusion into the convention would minimize the focus on gender by bringing the **race** question forward. Many of these women were concerned that their supporters would turn from the women's movement if they saw it as a support system for the antislavery movement. Truth was eventually able to give her speech, and in it she established not only her humanity but her desire to have both her race and her gender acknowledged. Truth's positioning would be echoed later in the 1970s by black women who still felt that their gender and race ideals were being marginalized. Truth in effect set the foundation for the black feminism of the 1970s when black women were calling for the recognition of their multiple sites of oppression.

Sojourner Truth in many ways set the tone for black women's writing that followed. **Harriet Jacobs**'s *Incidents in the Life of a Slave Girl* while following the genre of the slave narrative also emphasized the significance that gender played in the life of the enslaved. Jacobs acknowledged that slavery was hard for black men, but she went on to suggest that it was much harder for black women whose **sexuality** was often used against them. With this emphasis on sexual abuse, Jacobs highlighted an aspect of the slave experience that was often minimized in the male slave narrative. Thus the foundation of black feminism was being developed, and from the onset, the questioning of sexual oppression was paralleled by a questioning of racial oppression. In her 1892 piece "Womanhood a Vital Element in the Regeneration and Progress of Race," **Anna Julia Cooper** clearly weaves together issues of race and sexuality. Cooper establishes to the leaders of her time the important roles that women can and should play in uplifting the race. "Womanhood a Vital Element" puts forth the idea that women can be leaders of the race both inside and outside of the church. The piece establishes the significance of a woman's status within a culture or **community**. Cooper acknowledges that the sign of a civilized community was in the status of its women. If the black race wanted to be uplifted, women should and must play a vital role in the struggle.

What Cooper was struggling against, and what women of the 1970s would struggle against, was the emphasis placed on black manhood in black liberation movements. Scholars have long suggested that the greatest travesty of American slavery was the systematic theft of African American manhood. Thus for many black leaders racial uplift was equated with recuperating black manhood. At the turn of the century, Booker T. Washington and W.E.B. Du Bois were central figures within the African American community. In the literary pieces written by both leaders, much emphasis is placed on retrieving, developing, and pushing forward African American manhood. This emphasis on uplifting the race through a reassertion of black manhood limited the roles that women could play in race uplift, literary movements, and day-to-day living. Part of the agenda of black feminism, which was established by Anna Julia Cooper, is to acknowledge the strength of black women and their ability to be leaders in the black community.

Prior to the 1970s, black women were central figures in the racial progress and development of the black community. Unfortunately, due to the emphasis on manhood, much of their work was left unacknowledged until recently. During the **Harlem Renaissance**, African American women were central to the literary movement. It was in their homes that writers gathered to share and develop their work. African American women at this time served as journal editors as well as writers. Women's writing during this time was provocative and progressive but unappreciated. The greatest strength of this work was its incorporation of both gender and race issues, and this is perhaps one reason why these women went unrecognized. From early on, women activists and writers such as Truth and Cooper insisted on including discussions about gender and sexuality into ongoing debate of the race question. During the Harlem Renaissance, **Jessie Redmon Fauset**'s *Plum Bun* was critiqued by Du Bois and other scholars who took the subtitle of the novel, "A Novel without a Plot," literally. These scholars saw the novel as a text that did not contribute to the ever-present goal of race uplift. Ironically, Fauset, in *Plum Bun*, succeeds in not only addressing the race question; she links that discussion to a conversation about the Cult of True Womanhood. Fauset posits race and gender as interwoven characteristics that for the African American woman writer cannot be separated. The novel successfully highlights the problems that black women have faced and continue to face in the women's liberation movement. Many who were integral in the feminist movement were middle-class white women who were not overly concerned with issues of race and **class**. They were solely concerned with gaining sexual equality with men. Fauset's novel demonstrates that this narrow focus did not fully address the needs of black women, who also had issues pertaining to race and class that could not be ignored.

The black feminist movement recognizes that women of color are oppressed on multiple levels and that change cannot come by fighting singular forms of oppression; this movement focused on addressing all forms of oppression and developing political theory for advancing the status of women. The black feminist movement developed out of the concerns established by early writers like Truth, Jacobs, Cooper, and Fauset; the organization saw that it was essential to confront race, gender, and class issues at the same time. In 1973 the National Black Feminist Organization was developed. The group acknowledges in their statement of purpose that as black women they want to define for themselves who they are; these women were in part concerned with the image or **stereotypes** of black womanhood that were being put forth by both the male-dominated black liberation movement and by the women's movement. The organization hoped to lend a strong political voice to the already established women's movement and to establish to the black liberation movement the need to acknowledge that only half the race could not be uplifted. The women who developed this organization also wanted to ascertain that as feminists they were not "selling out" or dividing the race. It was important that leaders in the black community understand that as a part of the race black women were impacted by racism, but even within their own community, issues of sexism pervaded.

In 1977 black feminist ideology was further advanced with a statement from the **Combahee River Collective**, a group of black feminists who had been meeting since 1974. Like the organizers of the National Black Feminist Organization, the collective acknowledged that all forms of oppression were linked, and they presented black feminism as the political movement to fight the many and simultaneous oppressions faced by women of color. The collective asserted the need for autonomy and established the importance of **identity** politics, confirming that their political voice must come from their own identity and experiences. They asserted that while it was impossible to separate race from class from sexual oppression, their experience as black people necessitated solidarity around their race. Black feminists recognized that their political and personal lives were interwoven and desired to develop theory that addressed this point of intersection.

What was perhaps most critical about the collective's statement was its discussion of the organizational problems that black feminists faced. The biggest problem that the collective highlighted was the lack of access to power and resources. The statement alludes to Michele Wallace's positing of black women as a group in a state of isolation. Fundamentally, these women acknowledge that freedom for black women would come when there was freedom for everyone, as black women's freedom called for the destruction of all systems of oppression.

The 1970s saw an increase in the number of black women writers whose works were being published. This was a significant step for the black feminist movement, as it provided a place for their concerns to be addressed. Black women used their **poetry**, stories, and novels to address the issues that had historically been impacting upon them. With the publication of her 1973 novel *Sula*, **Toni Morrison** opened the door for black women to address the question of black female sexuality that had been left unanswered for years. Black female sexuality had been a taboo subject for so long, stemming back to the stereotypes that developed about black women during slavery. Black women were stereotyped as overly sexual beings, and often when a black woman was raped by a white master or plantation owner, the victim was blamed. Early American **literature** is full of accounts of white men being "overpowered" by the sexuality of African American women and who could not help themselves but to rape them. This stereotype helped to establish some of the tension that existed between white women and their black counterparts. In writing their slave narratives, most women were seeking financial stability as well as hoping to cast attention on the system of slavery. And for the most part, the men and women who were part of the abolition movement and who lent their support to these early writers were also linked to religious organizations. In order to receive the support they needed, black women writers were often forced to downplay the instances of sexual abuse they were certain to have experienced during slavery. After the Civil War and with the turn of the century, the pressures of the Cult of True Womanhood also had an impact on the way that black women's sexuality was written about. In fact, literary black females became asexual. This writing of black female characters combatted the images that came out of slavery of black women as **Jezebels**.

With her groundbreaking novel *Sula*, Toni Morrison allowed the black female character to be empowered by her sexuality. Sula is a character that is aware of the centrality of both her race and gender in defining her identity. She is not bound by the patriarchy of the American society in which she lives; she makes her own rules and defines her own space and place in American society. Most important, Sula helps to empower the community around her. Morrison demonstrates the effectiveness of the black female to uplift and transform her community.

Alice Walker has also played a critical role in the black feminist movement. It was Walker who coined the term **womanism** to place emphasis on the self-determination of black women, to show appreciation for all aspects of womanhood, and to advocate for the commitment to the survival of both men and women. Walker's literary works, including *The Color Purple* and *Possessing the Secret of Joy*, highlight the struggles of women of color globally.

Black feminist theory has opened up a space for black women to address the personal within the political. **Maya Angelou**'s *I Know Why the Caged Bird Sings* established a new genre of expression as autobiographical fiction became a medium for women of color to bring attention to how their personal lives have been impacted by larger social and political systems. This form of writing can be linked to the newly coined term *faction* wherein writers take factual events and write about them in a fictional context. Toni Morrison's *Beloved* is perhaps the best-known example of this writing form. *Beloved* highlights the way that the American system of slavery continues to impact American society, both black and white, and how the roles of African American women today are tied to the systematic abuses they received during slavery.

African American men, such as Michael Awkward, have also played a role in the black feminist movement. Awkward, in "A Black Man's Place in Black Feminist Criticism," explores the role that black men play and have played in the subjugation of women.

See also Autobiography; Black Nationalism

Works About

Carby, Hazel. *Reconstructing Womanhood*. New York: Oxford University Press, 1987.

Christian, Barbara. *Black Feminist Criticism: Perspectives on Black Women Writers*. New York: Pergamon, 1985.

Collins, Patricia Hill. *Black Feminist Thought*. New York: Routledge, 1991.

Davies, Carol Boyce. *Black Women, Writing and Identity: Migrations of the Subject*. New York: Routledge, 1996.

Giddings, Paula. *When and Where I Enter: The Impact of Black Women on Race and Sex in America*. New York: Bantam Books, 1984.

hooks, bell. *Feminist Theory from Margin to Center*. Boston: South End Press, 1984.

James, Joy, and T. Denean Sharpley-Whiting, eds. *The Black Feminist Reader*. Malden, MA: Blackwell Press, 2000.

Wall, Cheryl. *Changing Our Words: Essays on Criticism, Theory, and Writing by Black Women*. New Brunswick, NJ: Rutgers University Press, 1989.

Josie Brown-Rose

BLACK FEMINIST CRITICISM

Although its particular manifestations are quite diverse, black feminist criticism generally refers to politically informed analyses of literary and cultural representations produced by or about black women. Black feminist criticism became a recognizable intellectual approach during the 1970s when black women responded to their lack of representation in the male-dominated **civil rights movement** and the white-dominated women's movement. As greater numbers of black women began to write essays and form groups to raise consciousness and intervene in politics, those in academic circles attended to the way African American women have been represented (or misrepresented) in **literature** and worked to build a literary tradition of empowerment.

Black feminist criticism has been visible since at least the end of the nineteenth century, however. Even before the Civil War, some black women were involved in literary circles. The 1890s gave rise to a number of African American women's clubs and, in 1896, the National Association of Colored Women. Such organizations led to an African American women's newspaper called *Woman's Era*; to a number of conferences addressing the relationship between literature and racial politics, such as the 1895 National Conference of Colored Women featuring **Victoria Earle Matthews**'s the "Value of Race Literature"; and to publications examining the possible roles of black literature. Among these were **Anna Julia Cooper**'s *A Voice from the South* (1892) and **Gertrude Mossell**'s *The Work of the Afro-American Woman* (1894). Both texts argue for the inclusion of African American women in discussions of either an American or an African American heritage, and they also insist that artistic self-representation is a vital ingredient for the improvement of racial conditions. Such work was continued in the early twentieth century when **Alice Moore Dunbar-Nelson** included the works of women activists in a volume she edited (*Masterpieces of Negro Eloquence: The Best Speeches Delivered by the Negro from the Days of Slavery to the Present Time*, 1914) and the monthly journal *Woman's Voice* began to be published (1919).

From the days of the **Harlem Renaissance** to the **Black Arts Movement**, most of the critical attention given to gendered aspects of literary representations came from writers who also produced creative works. Such authors as **Jessie Redmon Fauset, Zora Neale Hurston**, and **Margaret Walker** considered African American expressive traditions in general terms as well as the particular concerns facing black women and the place of black women's literature. Hurston's anthropological recording of black **folklore** has been contextualized by scholars such as **Alice Walker** in terms of its womanist implications, and it is at times understood as a prefiguring of the cultural studies emphasis among contemporary black feminists such as bell hooks and Michele Wallace. Black feminist literary criticism was not widespread during the Harlem Renaissance or the eras following it, however, and it did not begin to gain momentum until the mid-1970s.

A number of publications signaled the beginning of black feminist criticism. In 1974, an issue of the popular black journal *Black World* included an article by Mary Helen Washington titled "Black Women Image Makers," an essay by **June Jordan** about Zora Neale Hurston and **Richard Wright**, a review of Zora Neale Hurston's work, and a review of a television version of an **Ernest Gaines** novel that focused on a woman. This amount of attention to black women was striking at the time. Then Alice Walker's "In Search of Our Mothers' Gardens" (1974) was published in the feminist magazine *Ms.* Here, Walker uses the term "**womanism**" rather than "**black feminism**" as a way of valuing black roots and an inclusive politics; that is, womanism is about improving conditions for women *and* men while addressing the concerns of women of color, lesbians, and others who are often excluded from feminism. Walker also champions the recovery of a black female creative heritage, suggesting that not only literature but also more everyday artistic expressions be included in such a tradition. The **poetry** of **Phillis Wheatley**, the **quilting** of countless anonymous black women, and the gardens of Walker's own mother are thus considered as valuable and inspirational manifestations of an indomitable creative spirit. Barbara Smith's "Toward a Black Feminist Criticism" (1977) is also often heralded as the beginning of a new wave of black feminist writing. Smith's essay calls for analyses of the interlocking oppressions of gender, **race**, **class**, and sexual orientation, with attention to black lesbian writers and recognition of a distinct tradition of writing by black women. Smith's emphasis on the combined effects of various types of oppression has continued to be a premise in black feminist criticism, often termed "double jeopardy," "multiple jeopardy," or "simultaneity of oppressions." Much feminist work by scholars such as Hortense Spillers and Mae Henderson continues to analyze the way systems of capitalism, patriarchy, racism, and heterosexism build upon one another. Early anthologies that explored issues of black feminist criticism include *This Bridge Called My Back: Writings by Radical Women of Color* (edited by Gloria Anzaldúa and Cherrie Moraga, 1981), *All the Women Are White, All the Blacks Are Men, but Some of Us Are Brave* (edited by Gloria Hull, Patricia Bell Scott, and Barbara Smith, 1982), and *Home Girls: A Black Feminist Anthology* (edited by Barbara Smith, 1983). The first of these brought issues of black feminism into conversation with the perspectives of Latinos and other women of color. All three anthologies attended to lesbian concerns and worked to address the racism in the women's movement.

Much early black feminist criticism worked both to disrupt **stereotypes** common in literary representations of black women and to restore African American women's writing that had all but disappeared. bell hooks's *Ain't I a Woman* (1981) notes the tendency of black women to remain invisible, even during times when white women and black men were fighting to express the concerns of "women" or "blacks." In English departments, this invisibility meant that attention was given to women writers such as Virginia Woolf or black protest writers such as Richard Wright and **Ralph Ellison**, but African American women's writing continued to be ignored. Deborah McDowell thus inaugurated the Black Women Writers series for Beacon Press that included new editions of such works as Jessie Redmon Fauset's ***Plum Bun*** (1929) and **Nella Larsen**'s ***Quicksand*** (1928) and ***Passing*** (1929). Henry Louis Gates acted as general editor for the **Schomburg Library of Nineteenth-Century Black Women Writers** (1988), an important series that included volumes by thirty authors who had received little critical attention. Other scholars, including Alice Walker, Barbara Smith, Hazel Carby, Barbara Christian, Claudia Tate, Mary Helen Washington, Valerie Smith, Hortense Spillers, and Mae Henderson, have continued to reprint writings by black women and/or encourage scholarship on black women writers, including **autobiographies**, **slave narratives**, and novels of the Harlem Renaissance. When drawing together themes and motifs among various generations of black women writers, critics have focused on such issues as silence and voice, **family** and **community**, and personal and social empowerment. Even as black feminist critics have worked to build a heritage of black women's writing, however, they have also participated in conversations problematizing notions of canon and tradition, both of which tend to rely on separations between "literary" and "popular" writing while privileging some texts and excluding others. Hazel Carby, for example, goes beyond ideas of a "tradition" in *Reconstructing Womanhood: The Emergence of the Afro-American Woman Novelist* (1987) by noting the many discontinuities in writings by black women and setting forth a black feminist criticism that is multiple and contextualized.

Black feminist criticism has also been important in responding to the rise of contemporary publications by black women, especially during the 1970s and following. Until this time, most feminist presses and journals focused exclusive attention on writing by white women, while publishing venues controlled by black or white men similarly avoided writing by black women. In 1979, however, an issue of the *Black Scholar* criticized **Ntozake Shange**'s play *for colored girls who have considered suicide/when the rainbow is enuf* and

Michele Wallace's *Black Macho and the Myth of the Superwoman*. An ongoing controversy began as critics discussed the negative portrayal of black men in texts written by black women, including not only those by Shange and Wallace but also Alice Walker's ***The Color Purple*** (both the novel and the **film** version) and some of the novels of **Toni Morrison** and **Gayl Jones**. Many black males believed that negative characterizations of African American men reinforced stereotypes associating black men with violent behavior and sexual aggression, turned attention to problems internal to the black community so that larger issues of racism became easier to ignore, and created a spectacle of black conflict for the enjoyment of white audiences. Many black feminist critics defended writing that portrayed abusive men by recentering the focus on women and women's experiences, refuting a standard for literature that included an idealized picture of the black family, and examining the fuller contexts of male portrayal, which often included change or redemption of some form.

Scholars have extended analyses of contemporary black women's creative writing to go beyond issues of black male portrayal. Some of the writers whose careers have been bolstered through critical attention include **Maya Angelou**, **Audre Lorde**, Toni Morrison, **Toni Cade Bambara**, **Gloria Naylor**, **Terry McMillan**, June Jordan, **Sherley Anne Williams**, **Lucille Clifton**, **Nikki Giovanni**, and **Sonia Sanchez**. Many of these creative writers also write critical commentary on the works of their peers, and they have published their reviews and analyses not only in literary academic journals but also in general interest magazines. The increased publications of contemporary black women has also increased attention to earlier black writers as feminist critics such as Deborah McDowell and Dianne Sadoff have connected contemporary writing with earlier black women's literature.

During the 1980s, as black feminist criticism gained momentum, a number of attempts were made to define the movement and articulate its relationship to poststructuralism, the predominant literary theory at the time. On the one hand, writers worked to refine the definition of black feminist criticism as presented in Barbara Smith's "Toward a Black Feminist Criticism." Deborah McDowell's "New Directions for Black Feminist Criticism" (1980), for example, suggests that black feminist criticism attend to the context of textual production and reception rather than focus on common themes in black women's writing, while Hazel Carby's " 'Woman's Era': Rethinking Black Feminist Theory" (1987) attempts to move beyond an assumption of an essential black female **identity** that would be expressed in African American women's literature. In the course of such writing, the question of who can actually be considered a black feminist critic regularly arises (Must it be a black person? Must it be a woman?), and the usual response is that black feminist criticism needs to be governed by the voices of African American women, but both women and men of other races and ethnicities may contribute scholarship that is mindful of the context and complexities involved in addressing black women's texts.

In the same time period, black feminist critics Barbara Christian and Joyce A. Joyce argued that poststructural theories were problematic for black criticism in general as well as black feminist criticism in particular. Christian's "The Race for Theory" (1987) asserts the importance of specific literary analyses informed by attention to race, class, and gender, opposing such a practice to the jargon-filled language and abstract observations that she associates with poststructuralism. Joyce's "The Black Canon: Reconstructing Black American Literary Criticism" (1987) was printed in *New Literary History* along with rebuttal essays by Henry Louis Gates, Jr., and Houston Baker. Joyce argues that a commitment to poststructuralism compromises and depoliticizes African American criticism due to its inaccessibility and its use of theories from white men, but as Gates and Baker respond, the debate appears to be a divide between male theory and female practice. Although Christian's and Joyce's essays have garnered a great deal of attention, most black feminist critics have not been completely opposed to theory but instead call for a politically useful poststructuralism. While poststructuralism may be problematic in its questioning of stable identities and canons at a time when African American women were beginning to assert their identities and form a canon, many critics have used poststructural theories to question dominant assumptions, understand relationships between "center" and "margin," and attend to issues of difference and hybridity.

By the 1990s, black feminist criticism had made such a strong impact on English departments that most scholars considered, in varying degrees, issues of difference and became more likely to set their claims within specific historical contexts and showed self-conscious awareness of their own ideological positioning. The influence of black feminist criticism spread beyond literature departments as well, as scholars in disciplines such as sociology and **history** began to consider black women and other minorities more carefully. The growth of black feminist criticism also both enabled and was enabled by the critical concerns of other women of color, both within the United States and across the globe. Issues of postcolonial conditions and global economics began to have a bearing on black feminist criticism, and many cross-cultural studies placed black women's writing in relationship to lesbian writing, Chicana writing, and African writing. Black feminist criticism also contributed to an understanding of **whiteness** as a racially inflected rather than "neutral" position, as theorized, for example, in Toni Morrison's *Playing in the Dark: Whiteness and the Literary Imagination* (1992). A number of books and anthologies appeared in the 1990s that marked the widespread significance of black feminist criticism and displayed the interest and involvement of black men, white women, and women of other ethnicities. These include Houston Baker's *Workings of the Spirit: The Poetics of Afro-American Women's Writing* (1991), an anthology of black feminist criticism edited by Henry Louis Gates, Jr. (1990), and *Female Subjects in Black and White: Race, Psychoanalysis, Feminism* (edited by Elizabeth Abel, Barbara Christian, and Helene Moglen, 1997). Many African American women scholars have also increasingly adopted critical approaches such as psychoanalysis, ecocriticism, New Historicism, cultural materialism, queer theory, and cultural studies when considering texts and power relations. The rise of cultural studies has been particularly fertile ground for black feminist critics, for it focuses attention on popular, contemporary texts, including films and other nonliterary cultural expressions, in order to think about the political implications of various representational practices. In black feminist criticism, literary studies have often been combined with attention to music, painting, **spirituality**, or other black arts, particularly quilting, the **blues**, and **jazz**. Studies of **sexuality** and the black woman's **body** have also been central to the development of black feminist criticism, theorized by such scholars as Evelyn Hammonds. As the influence of black feminism has grown and contributed to the development of race and gender studies, however, many African American women scholars caution against a simplistic association of black women with the body, the material realm, and activism, while either white women or white or black men represent the intellectual and theoretical position. Such oppositions, even when appearing to be radical by including black women, tend to reinforce gendered and racialized hierarchies.

At this point, no single black feminist criticism exists. Instead, texts by and about African American women are analyzed in a number of ways, often attending to issues of not only race and gender but also economics and sexuality, two of the earliest concerns of black feminist critics. The roots of black feminist criticism are also continued in the ongoing attempts to link academic work with cultural practices outside the university setting. While black feminism has become firmly entrenched in English departments, its impact is generally less visible in other cultural realms, so many black feminist critics are working to solidify connections between their scholarship and political issues of import, often by maintaining ties to black communities. Throughout its history, black feminist criticism's strength has been not only its ability to challenge the invisibility of black women and build a heritage of black women's writing but also its encouragement of serious and self-reflexive discussion about how critics talk about literature and to what ends.

See also Black Masculinity; Combahee River Collective; Kitchen Table: Women of Color Press; Lesbianism

Works About

Christian, Barbara. *Black Feminist Criticism: Perspectives on Black Women Writers.* New York: Pergamon Press, 1985.

Gates, Henry Louis, Jr., ed. *Reading Black, Reading Feminist: A Critical Anthology.* New York: Meridian, 1990.

Guy-Sheftall, Beverly, ed. *Words of Fire: An Anthology of African-American Feminist Thought.* New York: New Press, 1995.

Hull, Gloria, Patricia Bell Scott, and Barbara Smith, eds. *All the Women Are White, All the Blacks Are Men, but Some of Us Are Brave: Black Women's Studies.* Old Westbury, NY: Feminist Press, 1982.

McDowell, Deborah. *"The Changing Same": Black Women's Literature, Criticism, and Theory.* Bloomington: Indiana University Press, 1995.

Smith, Barbara, ed. *Home Girls: An Anthology of Black Feminist Criticism*. New York: Kitchen Table: Women of Color Press, 1983.

Wall, Cheryl A., ed. *Changing Our Own Words: Essays on Criticism, Theory, and Writing by Black Women*. New Brunswick, NJ: Rutgers University Press, 1989.

Laurie McMillan

BLACK MASCULINITY

It would be impossible to discuss contemporary black masculinity without first addressing the fact that African American men are considered by most to be in crisis. A recent study has shown that public schools actually track black boys as criminals, creating what they fear by keeping them alienated and in the margins (Ferguson 2). Another cause may be law enforcement agencies, which many hold responsible for criminalizing all black men through racial profiling, police brutality, and racist court procedures. These practices demoralize many, murder others, and create a national environment of fear (Neal 13). The young black man is the easiest scapegoat and primary target for multiple sins and the owner of the face seen drawn in shadowy figures on the evening news almost every night.

The dominant white culture of America has been taught to live in fear of black men. Black men are the Other; they are victims or thugs or simply made invisible. Robert Staples addresses the three main **stereotypes** that persist about black men: the "sexual superstud, the athlete, and the rapacious criminal" (1). And then there is the "bling bling" commodity culture promoted by many young black male artists today. The promise of the civil rights era has given way to economic relapses. Politicized artists from the Black Power movement have been overthrown by an easy materialism backed by "violence and aggression" (Boyd 133). However, black men themselves are the ones who have the most to fear. Their very survival is threatened by "higher rates of heart disease, hyper-tension, infant mortality, mental disorders, psychiatric hospitalization, homicide, unemployment, suspension from school, imprisonment, and morbidity and low life expectancy" than any other demographic in the United States (Majors 16). **John Edgar Wideman** calls the problems of black men a "*national* shame affecting us all" (27).

And yet this bleak portrait of crisis does not paint an accurate picture of black men in America. Stereotypes persist and obstacles are great, but there is no monolithic black man (Belton 4). The majority of black men are not the admired or condemned celebrity athletes whose faces appear regularly on commercials and in the news. Statistics about young black men in jail are staggering, but it is important to remember that 75 percent of black men never have anything to do with the criminal justice system (Ellis 11). And if the stereotype persists that black men are often emasculated by black women, the flip side, and more realistic version of this story, is that black men are "man enough" to have meaningful and functional relationships with powerful women (Westwood 56). To understand the causes of the stereotypes, to redress the apparent contradictions, and to get a more realistic picture of black masculinity today, a historical perspective is necessary.

Amiri Baraka may homogenize African cultures somewhat when he discusses the genesis of the African **family**, but his claim that capitalism and **slavery** forever affected African relationships is a necessary addendum to the discussion of black masculinity (199). Most African cultures were not as intent on the complete subjugation of women as their Western counterparts (Staples 8). For instance, the Igbo culture (found in Nigeria), which practiced polygyny and all but demanded healthy sons from wives, also promised more autonomy and gender flexibility for women than Eurocentric cultures. Igbo wives demanded respect and proper treatment from husbands through striking with co-wives; women could end their sexual and **domestic** duties to their husband through becoming a "female husband" and supporting another woman who could be a wife in their place; and daughters could take on the role of first son when no male children were born. Older women served on their own political council that advised the chief, and women were often cunning businesswomen who ensured their children's education through their sales at market. As Buchi Emecheta demonstrates in *The Joys of Motherhood*, (neo)colonial, and thus, capitalist, culture is what undermined the delicate balance between men and women in Igbo culture. The introduction of colonial powers in Africa undermined the communalism that had reigned previously, and of course, slavery and the slave trade further destroyed the black family and, necessarily, black masculinity.

In an American context, masculinity in general was (and is still) in flux, particularly during the nineteenth century. White men were struggling to define themselves in new contexts of urban life and industrialism. Many men, particularly upper- and middle-class men, sought to define their role through the strict definition of feminine roles. The "Cult of True Womanhood," enforced by women as well as men, promoted the ideals of domesticity, piety, submissiveness, and purity. Keeping women in their place, the private sphere, allowed men access to their own normative masculine role—having a job in the public sphere that was meaningful and that provided for the needs and protection of his family. If masculinity in America means being able to **work** and provide for and protect your family, it is obvious that black men (and many working-class and other poor men) rarely had access to these normative definitions.

Race exacerbates the complications of gender roles in the United States. If white women are dependent on men for their livelihood and definition, then black men and women are also dependent on white masculinity to define them and circumscribe the possibilities of their existence (Young 271). This was particularly true in antebellum America, when black (especially slave) women were seen as the "colonial Other" whose definition had to be "sexually licentious" in order to justify their economic exploitation (Young 282). If slave women survived **rape** and pregnancy by their masters only to see their children sold away from them, then slave men were forced to stand by as their wives, mothers, and daughters went through this dehumanizing process. Enslaved men, and to a lesser extent, free black men (even in the North) were dealt the "double blow" of watching African American women be used by white men, while being denied any contact with white women, commonplaces that symbolize black men's secondary status in society based on race (Bell 201).

Relationships between black men and women were necessarily structured differently than white men's relationships were with white women (or anyone else), and black men could not be dominant in the same way. Hazel Carby notes that black men have been systemically denied male privilege through the oppressions of slavery, colonialism, imperialism, and violent aggression (391). Just as black women were denied access to "true womanhood's" definition of women, black men were denied access to normative definitions of masculinity. While white women and men are both attempting to enforce an idea of femininity that adheres strictly to the ideals of "true womanhood," masculinity was somewhat up for grabs. White middle-class men were dealing with increasing competition and industrialization, the demand for more time with their families, and a lack of access to physical definitions of manhood. Black men and working-class men were struggling with middle-class ideals of masculinity while not having access to the same institutional privileges as white middle-class men.

While the reasons for this denial are horrendous, the effects are not always negative. It becomes quite clear in **Harriet Jacobs**'s *Incidents in the Life of a Slave Girl* that while black men are cut off from traditional white male definitions of "gentleman," this has a positive effect, which allows them to be open to different and more flexible forms of masculinity. Further, Jacobs shows us that southern white "gentlemen" and their limitations are clearly undesirable for any woman or society. The black men characterized in *Incidents* are shining examples of embattled manhood. Jacobs admits that for the slave being a good man (being able to protect a wife or children) is almost impossible, but time and again we are shown men who, even as slaves, rise far above their masters in her estimation of true manhood. Slavery dehumanizes all involved with the system, and in particular, it constructs slave men who are degraded, unable to be all they can be for themselves or their families. Jacobs recognizes that many slaves would never dream of trying to escape because "[i]t is difficult to persuade such that freedom could make them useful men, and enable them to protect their wives and children" (375). In spite of this prognosis, Jacobs tells us of men who live up to their full potential. James, the slave killed in the cotton gin, was full of "manliness and intelligence," and his crime was trying to escape (380). Young master Nicholas is deceitful and unfair to William, so William physically bests him and proves to be the better man (352–353). Characters like Jacobs's father, her Uncles Phil and Benjamin, and her son, among others, dare to be men and, as such, demonstrate that appropriate manhood is a matter of integrity, pride, and strength. These characteristics are open to any man, black or white, slave or free, but those who have more uncontested power have less access to a positive masculinity.

The hazards to masculinity and the black family during slavery still affect black men. Until the legacies of slavery, institutionalized racism and systemic economic exploitation, are fully dealt with and amended, black manhood, at least for some, will be in turmoil. The literary legacy of African American women can attest to the turmoil this wreaks on women's lives. In **Harriet E. Wilson**'s *Our Nig*, the one black man Frado meets marries her and abandons her. He is a fraudulent speaker, claiming to be an escaped slave speaking on the abolitionist circuit. His inability to find a decent job near their home leads him onto ships, long absences, and eventual **death**. Sadly, Harriet Jacobs's son is similarly forced onto a voyage to Australia, and she never hears from him again. More recently, **Ntozake Shange**'s *for colored girls who have considered suicide/when the rainbow is enuf* depicts a father more intent on destroying the mother of his children in a jealous rage than protecting his own progeny. **Alice Walker** received criticism for her portrayal in *The Color Purple* of abusive husbands and fathers in the rural South of the early twentieth century. When female authors note the effects black masculinity has on women, they are often attacked.

Despite the climate of fear and prejudice about black men in America—think of Susan Smith's tragic drowning of her children and her alibi, the black male carjacker—there is reason for much optimism. The tradition given to white men allows for men to be the absolute rulers of their households; it also allows for aggression and **violence** when their masculinity is at stake. But just because this is the role white men have been given, not all have embraced it. For the many black men who have never had access to this story of patriarchal privilege, there is even more hope. As many note, the privilege of maleness is more than canceled out in most cases by the oppression of race in America. Therefore, room for transformation of normative masculine roles may be much more possible for black men. Jacobs showed America that the true gentlemen in the South were slaves. **Zora Neale Hurston** explores a companionate, loving, and joyous union between Janie and Tea Cake in *Their Eyes Were Watching God*. And in **Toni Morrison**'s most recent novel, *Love*, we get a glimpse of the complications, possibilities, and **beauty** of black masculinity. Even though Bill Cosey is a wealthy tyrant who all but destroys his family and workers, and the book is primarily about the after-effects of his legacy of hate on the women in his life, we are also introduced to Sandler, a strong, dependable, and, importantly, flexible husband and father. Romen, a young man searching for his path in life, leads to the most promising possibilities. While he does not always make the right choices immediately, in the end he can be counted on to do the right and loving thing. Mutual respect between men and women, between people, is the necessary ingredient for **love**, and he finds it. Through African American feminist authors, descriptions and prescriptions for black masculinity go a long way to counteract the destructive stereotypes that still seem to rule our everyday world.

See also Civil Rights Movement

Works About

Baraka, Amiri. "The Black Family." *Speak My Name: Black Men on Masculinity and the American Dream.* Ed. Don Belton. Boston: Beacon Press, 1995. 197–202.

Bell, Derrick. "The Race-Charged Relationship of Black Men and Black Women." *Constructing Masculinity.* Ed. Maurice Berger, Brian Wallis, and Simon Watson. New York: Routledge, 1995. 193–210.

Belton, Don. "Introduction: Speak My Name." *Speak My Name: Black Men on Masculinity and the American Dream.* Ed. Don Belton. Boston: Beacon Press, 1995. 1–5.

Boyd, Todd. *Am I Black Enough for You? Popular Culture from the 'Hood and Beyond.* Bloomington: Indiana University Press, 1997.

Carby, Hazel V. "White Woman Listen!" *Theories of Race and Racism: A Reader.* Ed. Les Back and John Solomos. London: Routledge, 2000. 389–403.

Ellis, Trey. "How Does It Feel to Be a Problem?" *Speak My Name: Black Men on Masculinity and the American Dream.* Ed. Don Belton. Boston: Beacon Press, 1995. 9–11.

Ferguson, Ann Arnett. *Bad Boys: Public Schools in the Making of Black Masculinity.* Ann Arbor: University of Michigan Press, 2001.

Jacobs, Harriet. *Incidents in the Life of a Slave Girl.* 1861. *The Classic Slave Narratives.* Ed. Henry Louis Gates, Jr. New York: Mentor Books, 1987. 333–515.

Majors, Richard. "Cool Pose: Black Masculinity and Sports." *African Americans in Sport.* Ed. Gary A. Sailes. New Brunswick, NJ: Transaction Publishers, 1998. 15–22.

Neal, Mark Anthony. "Just Another 'Nigga': Reflections on Black Masculinity and Middle-Class Identity." *Not Guilty: Twelve Black Men Speak Out on Law, Justice, and Life.* Ed. Jabari Asim. New York: HarperCollins, 2001. 1–14.

Staples, Robert. *Black Masculinity: The Black Man's Role in American Society.* San Francisco: Black Scholar Press, 1982.

Westwood, Sallie. "Racism, Black Masculinity, and the Politics of Space." *Men, Masculinities and Social Theory.* Ed. Jeff Hearn and David Morgan. London: Unwin Hyman, 1990. 55–71.

Wideman, John Edgar. "The Night I Was Nobody." *Speak My Name: Black Men on Masculinity and the American Dream.* Ed. Don Belton. Boston: Beacon Press, 1995. 23–27.

Young, Lola. "Imperial Culture." *Theories of Race and Racism: A Reader.* Ed. Les Back and John Solomos. London: Routledge, 2000. 267–286.

Nicole Lynne Willey

BLACK NATIONALISM

Black Nationalism refers to African American sociopolitical theories, organizations, and actions that responded collectively and interactively to deep-seated institutional racism in the United States during the nineteenth and twentieth centuries and into the twenty-first century. Black Nationalism evolved in response to the fact that, as individuals and as a group, African Americans have seen their social, political, economic, and educational endeavors hindered by institutional racism. Its rationale relies on the belief that blacks should—instead of focusing on civil rights that have yet to be enjoyed or that prove to be insufficient—create institutions independent of whites, either within the United States or outside the United States. Developed as a response to a dominant white culture, Black Nationalism's organizational objectives, rhetoric, and activity depend on its proponents' ability to identify social and political techniques of subjugation and separatism. By strategically adapting its literary and activist responses to these techniques, Black Nationalism endeavors to oppose white supremacy. Although the term did not appear in an American dictionary until 1963, specific characteristics of Black Nationalist principles are evident in African American **literature** as early as the eighteenth century. In a 1774 letter to Samson Occom, **Phillis Wheatley** both supports and nuances his argument for the immediate bequest of African Americans' civil rights, which is the central issue encompassed in Black Nationalist thought.

Scholars disagree about how best to define Black Nationalism. Sometimes the term is defined as being rooted in the philosophies and mobilizing activities of the Black Power movement in the 1960s. African American studies discourse, however, tends to define Black Nationalism as a complex collection of theories responding in writing and action to racial oppression. In this definition, Black Nationalism is understood as responding to no single methodology for instituting racism; instead, it is a system of adjustments made as blacks' response to immediate modes of apparent oppression practiced within American institutions. Viewed from this perspective, Black Nationalism, by design, revises its strategies and goals to accommodate immediate redress, yet retains the belief that blacks are globally connected and therefore constitute a black nation.

Although most black political movements have traditionally been dominated by men, this statistical fact is misleading for two reasons. First, efforts to protect black women within Black Nationalist thought is demonstrated by the promotion of women as valued matriarchs of a black nation dependent on their well-being as producers of new generations. Second, **black feminist criticism** has always engaged Black Nationalism in specific ways. However, in many cases, their contributions foreground disparities between gender roles in shaping Black Nationalism and the black nation. By reexamining key words and phrases associated with its Black Nationalist rhetoric and approaching the discourse from the position of black female experiences and knowledge, black women have contributed yet another level to Black Nationalist thought. What this suggests is not an indifference to Black Nationalism, nor a manipulation of its terms and meanings. Rather, black feminist texts represent the different relationship experienced by black women within and without Black Nationalist thought. Therefore, black feminist **poetry**, **autobiography**, **fiction**,

historical fiction, nonfiction prose, and academic scholarship offer new viewpoints of Black Nationalism, its organization, and activity.

Antebellum literature written by **Harriet E. Wilson**, **Harriet Jacobs**, and **Maria Stewart** are examples of early contributions to Black Nationalist discourse. Each woman raises well-defined issues concerning the precarious position of black women's chastity during **slavery**. Their observations of and arguments for the protection of slave women from physical and sexual **violence** at the hands of white men are not only implicitly and explicitly made, but each woman is also an independent proponent of the significance of black women as matriarchs and mothers.

Embedded with morality and **Christianity**, Maria Stewart's 1831 publication of *Religion and the Pure Principles of Morality, the Sure Foundation on Which We Must Build* adamantly contends that America's foundation, propagandized as a place for **freedom** and liberty, is yet to be realized, as America enslaves African Americans based on the erroneous idea that they are inferior to whites. Although Phillis Wheatley's eighteenth-century poetry and prose addresses the virtue of slave women accessing Christian argument, she likens Africans to heathens in need of saving by gracious and Christian whites. Therefore, Stewart's works are the first written by a black woman abolitionist who denotes African Americans as "daughters" and "sons" of Africa, maintaining that black women deserve equal respect for their virtue as that received by their European counterparts. Stewart poses questions concerning the sexual autonomy of slave women and the continuous jeopardy of that virtue by licentious white men, suggesting that slave women's piety and resistance to **rape** and sexual coercion will be rewarded with freedom and morality. Additionally, like the black Jeremiad David Walker (1785–1830), with whom she was a close friend, Stewart implies that if Americans refused to free Africans and grant them equal rights, the wrath of God would be rendered upon them.

Harriet Jacobs's **slave narrative** *Incidents in the Life of a Slave Girl* is similar to Stewart's prose in that it presents an argument for black women's virtue by explicitly foregrounding the sexual and physical coercion and abuse routinely carried out against slave women on American plantations. Jacobs publicly scrutinizes such violations against slave women's sexual choices by offering her predominantly white readers a detailed account of her own. Her narrative is the first to specifically address the complexities of placage, an intricate system of coercion in which slave women or octoroons (biracial women) were coerced into sexual liaisons with white men, who, in exchange for sex, offered them freedom, protection, property, and education for their children. Jacobs faced the choice of remaining enslaved by a master, James Norcum, who harassed and threatened her with rape, or placage. She chose the latter and entered into a sexual liaison with the unmarried Tredwell Sawyer, who offered her protection. For Jacobs, choosing placage provided freedom for her and her children. Telling her life story makes the case for two of the most important characteristics of Black Nationalism: freedom for blacks and the value of the black matriarch's sexual autonomy.

Harriet Wilson accesses yet another literary genre, historical fiction, in her book ***Our Nig; or, Sketches from the Life of a Free Black*** (1859), which is the first novel published by an African American. In the text, Wilson presents the life story of the daughter of an unnamed black man and a white woman, Mag Smith. The child, Frado, is abandoned by her parents and left under the auspices of a white **family** determined to keep her in servitude, despite her free black status. *Our Nig* demonstrates specific principles of Black Nationalist thought in both its telling and title. First, it inscribes the Black Nationalist belief that although one may be biracial, if he or she descends from an African, it is that ethnic **identity** that supersedes all others; thus, *Our Nig* explores the antimiscegenation notions within Black Nationalist thought.

The Reconstruction era (1865–1910) was an extremely precarious time in the black experience, particularly for women. By 1870, Congress had enacted the Thirteenth, Fourteenth, and Fifteenth Amendments to the U.S. Constitution, which, respectively, ended slavery, protected all citizens equally, regardless of **race** and gender, and granted voting rights to black men. However, the amendments did not address suffrage. More important, the amendments were selectively and inconsistently enforced. Consequently, Black Nationalism modified its objectives and strategies to confront racist institutions and practices that were, in theory, but not in reality, outlawed by the three new amendments. Despite the Fourteenth Amendment, black women continued to be victimized and were forced to protect themselves not only from abuse but from the new economic adversities. However, they boldly faced these challenges, and within African American literature, they were able not only to incorporate the technical skills found in early American literature but to become self-empowered by relating their experiences as women. **Anna Julia Cooper**'s feminist text ***A Voice from the South***, published in 1892, speaks to black life in the **South** as well as to living under white supremacy. Cooper accesses **history**, **religion**, and ethics to foreground the inhumanity of whites against blacks and emphasizes the need for a nonsexist black leadership unafraid to vocalize and act upon such violations. Similarly, **Ida B. Wells-Barnett**, one of the most outspoken women of her time, composed texts focusing on the rights espoused and guaranteed in the Fourteenth Amendment, dedicating her life to the antilynching campaign she established. Wells-Barnett's activism included the publication of *Southern Horrors: Lynch Law in All its Phases* (1892), which investigates specific cases of lynching and rape committed against blacks. Through their literary crusades, Wells-Barnett and Cooper served as proponents for one of the most significant principles of Black Nationalism: the right to protect oneself from the American pogrom, mob lynchings, and rapes.

By 1900, African American literature and journalism began to proliferate. However, the **Harlem Renaissance** marked the first period in American literary history in which blacks could openly debate questions of racial identity. Notions of the black aesthetic, central to Black Nationalist thought, emerged. Although prose by black men such as W.E.B. Du Bois (1868–1963) and Alain Locke (1886–1954) expressed a Black Nationalist understanding of aesthetics and the rights of blacks, they were not acting or writing without the input of black women. The early twentieth century presented myriad opportunities for black women also to make a case for equality. Their prose, fiction, and poetry consider Black Nationalist principles, including black identity, economic self-reliance, education, and the importance of recognizing and maintaining black aesthetics.

What may have been the result of two centuries of forced miscegenation, a popular literary theme during the Harlem Renaissance was black identity, how to define it, and in some cases, determining its value and existence. Some writers, such as **Nella Larsen**, author of *Passing*, **Jean Toomer**, author of *Cane* (1923), and **Charles Waddell Chesnutt**, author of *The House behind the Cedars* (1900), had a stake in identifying themselves as more than **mulatto**, while others writers rejected their identified blackness as a disadvantage. **Zora Neale Hurston**'s short essay "How It Feels to Be Colored Me" (1925) not only honors her racial identity but also makes it clear that being African American is not a tragedy; thus she celebrates her identity by accessing **folklore** and black vernacular. Although there were different ideological understandings among Harlem Renaissance writers regarding racial identity, their paradigmatic bantering is not the most important feature about this era in African American literary history but rather the fact that, for the first time, blacks debated subject matters that directly affected their lives among and for themselves without mainstream interference or subjugation, thus moving away from the sentimental apologetic literature of their nineteenth-century forebears.

However, race was only one focus of early-twentieth-century African American literature. In addition, black women wrote about their triple identity that threatened to jeopardize their lives: race, gender, and **sexuality**. In 1925, Elise Johnson McDougald (1885–1971) published her article "The Struggle of Negro Women for Sex and Race Emancipation" in Alain Locke's magazine *Survey Graphic*. Her article is the first prose to foreground the notion that as both African Americans and females black women are subjected to twice the amount of discrimination, not only from white America but also from men. However, this does not negate the impact of Frances Beale's 1970 publication "Double Jeopardy." **Angelina Weld Grimké** and **Alice Moore Dunbar-Nelson** took McDougald's observations one step further and, with skilled metaphorical poetics, added sexual preference to the list of discriminatory justifications to be contested. As lesbian women who were unable to openly admit their sexual choices, Grimke' and Dunbar-Nelson used poetry to express their feelings of isolation. Although homosexuality is not accepted within Black Nationalist doctrine, it is important to the principles of **black feminism** and is widely represented in prose and fiction by women such as **Audre Lorde**.

Notions of mass black emigration were popularized in the nineteenth century by David Walker, Martin Delaney (1812–1885), and Bishop Henry McNeal Turner (1834–1915); during the Harlem Renaissance the torch of Black Nationalism was carried by Marcus Garvey (1887–1940) and his second wife, Amy Jacques-Garvey (1896–1973). From 1924 to 1927 she served as the associate editor of the column for women titled "On Women and What They Think" in *Negro World*, a newspaper published by the Universal

Negro Improvement Organization (UNIA). A few years after Garvey's death in 1940, she continued his Pan-Africanist/Black Nationalist campaign by establishing the Africa Circle of the World in Jamaica and working as a contributing editor for the *African*, which was published in Harlem, New York, during the 1940s. Later in life, Jacques-Garvey began writing and successfully published *Garvey and Garvyism* (1963), *Black Power in America*, and *The Impact of Garvey in Africa and Jamaica*.

During the protest movement (1940–1959), Black Nationalism's notion that poverty was a result of racism was challenged by a Marxist-influenced socialism. Perhaps partly influenced by ideas of socialism, literature during this period did not view emigration as a viable solution to racism but, rather, saw labor movements as a potential alternative. Socialist influence on African American literature is recognizable in feminist texts that articulate the deprivation within the black experience. **Ann Petry**'s (1908–1997) ***The Street*** (1946) provides a fictional account of the social and political consequences for uneducated and poor African Americans, while Claudia Jones's (1915–1965) essay "An End to the Neglect of the Problems of Negro Women," published in *Political Affairs* in 1949, speaks to the racism black women historically defy using a Marxist analysis.

The politically and racially charged 1960s brought about the rise of the Black Power movement (1955–1980), whose rhetoric heavily influenced African American literature. The **Black Arts Movement** produced **jazz** and rhythm and **blues** (R&B) music compositions, poetry and spoken word, critical essays, dramatic plays and **film**, and fiction embedded with black power, pride, and nationalism. **Lorraine Hansberry**'s plays ***A Raisin in the Sun*** (1959) and *To Be Young, Gifted and Black* (published posthumously in 1969) encouraged blacks to face restrictive covenants head on and to be proud of their blackness. **Gwendolyn Brooks**, a writer and poet whose literary career spanned more than sixty years, used her personal life as a backdrop to the poetry, prose, and fiction she produced during her lifetime, including *A Street in Bronzeville*, her first book of poetry published in 1945.

Contemporary literature, including poetry, prose, drama, and fiction produced by women such as **Angela Davis**, **Octavia Butler**, **Gloria Naylor**, **Margaret Walker**, **Toni Morrison**, **Nikki Giovanni**, **Sonia Sanchez**, **Alice Walker**, and many others, not only foregrounds the discriminatory struggles that black women routinely face but also demonstrates the Black Nationalist principles begun with the simple eighteenth-century recognition that blackness is something beautiful, powerful, and worthy of protection and study.

See also Civil Rights Movement

Works About

Collins, Patricia Hill. *Black Feminist Thought: Knowledge, Consciousness, and the Politics of Empowerment*. 2nd ed. New York: Routledge, 2000.

Davis, Angela Y. *Women, Race, and Class*. New York: Vintage Books, 1981.

hooks, bell. *Feminist Theory: From Margin to Center.* 2nd ed. Cambridge, MA: South End Press, 2000.

Robinson, Dean E. *Black Nationalism in American Politics and Thought.* Cambridge, MA: Cambridge University Press, 2001.

Wyatt, Gail Elizabeth. *Stolen Women: Reclaiming Our Sexuality, Taking Back Our Lives.* New York: John Wiley and Sons, 1997.

Ellesia Ann Blaque

BLANCHE AMONG THE TALENTED TENTH

Barbara Neely's first novel, ***Blanche on the Lam***, focused on the racism and classism leveled against **domestic** workers, especially women of color. In *Blanche among the Talented Tenth* (1994), the second in her Blanche White mystery series, Neely makes clear that she plans to target more than the prejudices of whites toward blacks by turning her attention to the African American color hierarchy. The prejudice within some African American communities against those with darker skin tones is, she points out, an especially hurtful expression of the pervasive acceptance of a light/white standard of **beauty**.

The very dark Blanche has felt the weight of this prejudice all her life, but never so much as now, for the story opens with her on vacation at an exclusive seaside resort frequented by wealthy, light-skinned African Americans. The stares and ostracism of the upper-class clientele make Blanche acutely aware of how much her dark skin stands out in this crowd. Her occupation—she is a longtime domestic worker—would elicit even more prejudice if revealed. The novel's title plays on the phrase W.E.B. Du Bois used to describe the black elite in America, but here the elite are portrayed as anything but the force of racial uplift imagined by Du Bois.

Blanche resents and is hurt by the snobbery she encounters from African Americans; her primary concern, though, is that her children not buy into this color hierarchy, and she agonizes each time she sees the influence of a color-biased culture on them, especially on her image-conscious daughter. Blanche knows how much skin lighteners, hair straighteners, and fashion play in constructing the self-image of some African Americans, especially women. She hopes her own affirmations of the beauty of blackness will help her children resist cultural pressures to accept **whiteness** as their standard of beauty, just as she hopes her unapologetic career choice will help them to resist the classism behind so many social prejudices. She fears, though, that peer pressure will do more to shape their perceptions than her influence.

This novel also focuses on Blanche's **sexuality**, not what readers might expect of a novel about a nearing-fifty, heavyset African American domestic worker. There is a mystery to be solved in this book, and Blanche does plenty of sleuthing—or snooping—into a suspicious **death** being written off as accidental, but she is equally occupied with the attentions of a dashingly handsome man.

A third focus of this book is Blanche's **spirituality**. Not a churchgoer, Blanche has done a lot of reading and thinking about the best way to express her spiritual self. Her religious practices and beliefs are uniquely her own, but they owe much to African influence; communion with the **ancestors** is at the heart of Blanche's spiritual life.

Predictably, Blanche solves the mystery, but as usual, it is the sleuth herself who is the draw. In a genre with few African American protagonists, especially women, a black female detective stands out. To encounter such a sassy, savvy, feminist black woman sleuth is a real treat.

See also Blanche Cleans Up; Blanche Passes Go; Detective Fiction

Work About

Steinberg, Sybil S. Review of *Blanche among the Talented Tenth. Publishers Weekly* 241.29 (1994): 238.

Grace McEntee

BLANCHE CLEANS UP

Blanche Cleans Up (1998) is the third book in the Blanche White mystery series by **Barbara Neely**. In this novel, as usual, Blanche's strong opinions on selected social issues are the heart of the story. There is a difference here, though; the issues in Neely's previous two mysteries were race centered, but here the author turns her attention to social problems that go well beyond racial concerns (while still making clear that each issue has its racial dimension). What remains a constant in each of her novels, though, is Neely's agenda to use mass-market fiction as a vehicle for social commentary.

The story line begins when Blanche, a housekeeper-cook, once more becomes embroiled in the doings of her white employers. A mysteriously incriminating videotape stolen from the politically ambitious husband and the murder of two persons likely to know something about the tape send Blanche into snoop mode. She quickly learns of his unhappy wife's extramarital affairs, but the **family**'s darker secrets are harder to unearth. Homophobia, lead poisoning, and a complex of sexual issues (including masochism and pedophilia) weave through the story. Issues concerning **sexuality** are addressed not just in Blanche's white environment but also in her **home**, as the usually unflappable Blanche agonizes over how to handle her just-hit-puberty children and her just-got-pregnant teenage niece.

Set in Boston and its environs, the novel also looks at problems that plague largely black urban communities such as Roxbury, where Blanche and her family now live. Neely makes clear that homophobia, political corruption, teen pregnancy, and environmental hazards are problems that transcend racial concerns, but she also points out that each can have a racial dimension. For example, Blanche is quick to see connections between racism and homophobia, and she is abashed to realize that even she is prone to stereotyping homosexuals. Meanwhile, she is keenly aware that politicians court and manipulate black constituents while ignoring social problems like lead poisoning that have a disproportionate impact on black communities (Blanche learns as the story progresses that lead-infused housing may be implicated in a child's turn toward violence). And she comes to see how the pregnancy of her smart, college-bound niece could have psychological roots in the girl's fear of failure in the white world outside the inner city.

Blanche Cleans Up, like its predecessors, offers a strong, feminist African American presence in a mass-market detective novel, filling a near-void in this genre. As is usual with Neely's mysteries, it is Blanche's personality, her astute reading of the social scene, and her in-your-face commentary that keep fans coming back for more.

See also Blanche among the Talented Tenth; *Blanche on the Lam*; *Blanche Passes Go*; Detective Fiction

Works About

DeCandido, GraceAnne A. Review of *Blanche Cleans Up*. *Booklist* 94.14 (1998): 1206.

DiNizo, Alice. Review of *Blanche Cleans Up*. *Library Journal* 123.5 (1998): 95.

Herbert, Rosemary. "A Tidy Look at Domestic Deceit." *The Boston Herald*, April 19, 1998, 077.

Turner, Patricia. "Housekeeper Negotiates Two Worlds While Sweeping Up a Murder." *San Francisco Chronicle*, March 22, 1998, 5.

Grace McEntee

BLANCHE ON THE LAM

Blanche on the Lam (1992) marked the debut of **Barbara Neely**'s feisty protagonist Blanche White in a book that won multiple first-novel awards, including the Agatha, Macavity, and Anthony. Neely opens her story with a courtroom scene where Blanche, a heavyset dark-skinned **domestic** worker, is appearing (not for the first time) on charges of check bouncing. Neely uses this scene to immediately begin infusing her story with social commentary, as Blanche muses on the fact that her bounced checks have all resulted from white employers failing to pay her on time. Blanche's awareness of the law's lack of concern for her ill treatment at the hands of her employers sets the stage for the many pointed observations that follow about what it is like to be an African American in a racist society.

The novel's plot is set in motion when Blanche is handed down a prison sentence rather than the expected fine, which she was prepared to pay. Unable to face jail, Blanche bolts when she has a chance. Once on the lam, she drops out of sight by taking a job as a live-in maid/cook for a wealthy white couple. As Blanche settles into the familiar routine of catering to the needs of an upper-class white **family**, she clues readers in on what it is like to be financially dependent on people who treat you as if you are not there or who relate to you only in patronizing or other demeaning ways. Blanche explains white employer/black "help" relationships in terms of **race** and **class** politics that go back to **slavery** times.

Blanche does not simply see herself as a victim, however, for she knows she is heir to another practice handed down from her slave **ancestors**—the ability to exploit what few sources of power her position of servitude offers her. Luckily, she is very good at manipulating circumstances for her own ends, because Blanche's instincts tell her that she has taken refuge with a family hiding secrets—secrets that spell danger for her unless she gets to the bottom of them. Blanche relies on her employers' belief in racial **stereotypes** to conceal her savvy understanding of the family dynamics she witnesses and to hide her snoopings into their affairs.

Because of her looks and her profession, the stereotype most easy for Blanche to assume is that of the **Mammy** or **Aunt Jemima**. Neely has daringly made Blanche outwardly conform to the Mammy stereotype as a way to deconstruct this icon of black womanhood. Blanche understands the popular conception of this stereotype and avoids arousing her employers' suspicions about her investigation by allowing them to believe that she fits the image—that she is content in her life of servitude, as fond of her "white family" as of her own kin, genuinely respects her white employers, and is blissfully unaware of the disrespectful treatment she receives at their hands.

Blanche's views about the racial origins of power and class relationships become complicated, however, once she meets Mumsfield, an adult nephew of her employers who lives with the family. Mumsfield's mild form of Down's syndrome has cast him in much the same position as Blanche in the power relationships of this family, Blanche realizes with a jolt. He, too, is treated condescendingly, and his capacity for understanding and wisdom go unnoticed by all but her.

Although Blanche occasionally resorts to acting the part of the Mammy before her employers, readers always recognize this as trickster behavior not at all at odds with her usual assertive, sassy, perceptive, self-confident, and humorous demeanor. And as in most **detective fiction**, all turns out well, thanks to Blanche's intelligent deductions and courageous actions. The story ends, significantly, with Blanche rejecting a chance to earn a lot of money playing a Mammy role—and she is surprised that this rejection comes at some emotional cost. Asked to become Mumsfield's caregiver, Blanche hesitates, for she genuinely likes the young man and the two of them are in instinctive accord with one another. But quickly Blanche puts aside the temptation, for to accept would be to put Mumsfield's needs above those of her family. Her children's needs will best be met if they move north—a move many of her ancestors have made before her.

Because Mumsfield is such a sympathetic character, and because he and Blanche seem to have a special relationship, readers might easily expect or want Blanche to accept the offer to stay in his life. Blanche's dismissal of Mumsfield's needs helps such readers see how easy it is to unquestioningly accept assumptions about the service-oriented nature of blacks (and the self-sacrificial nature of women) at the heart of a powerful white construction of black womanhood. Here, and throughout the story, Neely also makes clear the emotional strength black women must call on daily to combat negative stereotypes that work to strip them of dignity, self-esteem, and confidence. Blanche's no-nonsense, in-your-face attitude, her sophisticated analyses of the world she lives in, and her habit of speaking her mind are humorous, but ultimately very serious, weapons in this struggle.

See also Blanche among the Talented Tenth; Blanche Cleans Up; Blanche Passes Go

Works About

Bailey, Frankie Y. "Blanche on the Lam; or, The Invisible Woman Speaks." *Diversity and Detective Fiction.* Ed. Kathleen Gregory Klein. Bowling Green, OH: Popular Press, 1999.

Hathaway, Rosemary V. "The Signifyin(g) Detective: Barbara Neely's Blanche White, Undercover in Plain Sight." *Critique* 46.4 (2005): 320–332.

Herbert, Rosemary. "An Interview with Barbara Neely." *Harvard Review* 5 (1993): 107–116.

Grace McEntee

BLANCHE PASSES GO

In this fourth Blanche White mystery novel, *Blanche Passes Go* (2000), author **Barbara Neely** takes her most feminist stance yet as she illustrates the impact of **domestic violence** and **rape** on the lives of women. Readers used to the feisty, in-your-face protagonist of the earlier novels see here a Blanche more vulnerable than they are used to. When Blanche moves back **home** to Farleigh, North Carolina, she is pulled back into **memories** she has tried hard to repress—memories of being raped by a white employer years earlier. Blanche's assertive demeanor usually hides the psychological damage of this assault, but she knows that true emotional healing has never been effected.

In Farleigh, Blanche's best friend Ardell has opened a catering business and wants Blanche to be her partner, a tempting offer she must balance against the independence the cleaning profession allows her. Blanche also notes with concern how being a boss has changed Ardell's personality and values; cost-effectiveness and profit have become her new lens for looking at the world.

Meanwhile, Blanche begins a romantic relationship. The strands of the story merge as Blanche realizes how much of her life is still being shaped by her rape. She wants to fall in **love** with Thelvin, but love and trust feel like dangerous vulnerabilities. And she finds herself making assumptions about Thelvin based on the fact that he is *a* man rather than on what she has seen of him as a particular man, an unfair perspective she knows has roots in her assault years ago.

Then Blanche sees her rapist for the first time in years and realizes that as a caterer she might come in contact with him at any time. She comes undone. Seeing Blanche cringe, suffer physical sickness, emotional cowardice, and psychological distress is a potent reminder to readers of the effect rape can have on even strong, self-assured women. When Blanche becomes suspicious that the woman living across the street is abused, her emotional turmoil increases. She grapples with her moral responsibility in the face of this situation: Should she take some form of action? How can she respond and still stay safe?

Throughout the story Blanche agonizes over how to achieve psychological **healing**. She finally admits that she must quit merely reacting and start acting. When offered a job investigating the rapist's sister (is her upcoming marriage a gold-digging scam?), she becomes proactive at last, taking this as an opportunity to learn more about her assailant and to find a way to come to terms with her rape—perhaps even confront the rapist.

Along the way there is a murder to be solved—another crime against a woman—and Blanche's sleuthing uncovers the murderer. The book's end brings resolutions to the various strands of the story, but what readers are likely to remember longest is Blanche's personal struggle to reclaim her trust in men and her self-confidence in an environment that evokes her worst memories.

See also Blanche among the Talented Tenth; Blanche Cleans Up; Blanche on the Lam

Works About

Herbert, Rosemary. "Cleaning House—Domestic Worker—Detective Blanche White Tackles Social Issues in Latest Mystery by Barbara Neely." *The Boston Herald*, August 7, 2000, 029.

——. "Rewriting the Rules—Mystery Author Barbara Neely Breaks New Ground with Genre-Bending Domestic Worker—Sleuth." *The Boston Herald*, August 28, 2000, 031.

Hunt, Sharita. Review of *Blanche Passes Go. Black Issues Book Review* 2.6 (2000): 22.

Phillips, Kathy. Review of *Blanche Passes Go. Women's Review of Books* 17.10/11 (2000): 42.

Grace McEntee

BLOODCHILD AND OTHER STORIES

Octavia Butler's single book of short stories, *Bloodchild and Other Stories* (1995), is a slim volume consisting of five short stories and two essays. The essays are autobiographical; in the second Butler muses on the significance of writing and reading, especially science fiction, for an African American. Of the short stories, the two that have garnered the most attention are the title story "Bloodchild" and "Speech Sounds."

"Bloodchild" describes the complex relationship between Terrans (humans) and the insectlike Tilc, a relationship that has evolved over generations from the Tilc using Terrans as mere hosts for their eggs to a complicated familial social network. Since the Tilc need Terrans in order to survive as a species, the emotional ties between the two species are difficult to read: How much of their affection is real? How much a product of need? The story takes place on the day the Terran Gan will be implanted with eggs from T'Gatoi, a Tilc who has been his lifelong friend and second mother. Butler's decision to make her prospective human host male instead of female gives new resonance to the social construction of defining women by their capacity to bear young.

Each story in this collection is accompanied by an afterword. Following "Bloodchild," Butler comments that this story is meant to explore the complexities of choosing to become pregnant. Both **love** and a sense of obligation motivate Gan, but his maleness and his last-minute revulsion at the alien nature of being a host to insect eggs complicate readers' responses to the decision he must make. As in her **Xenogenesis trilogy**, Butler suggests here that familiarity breeds not contempt but acceptance. "Bloodchild" received both Hugo and Nebula Awards.

In "Speech Sounds," another Hugo Award winner, Butler creates a world where a strange pathology has damaged people's ability to communicate. Some cannot speak, others can no longer make sense of verbal language they hear, others have forgotten how to read or write. Some cannot read even basic **body** language. **Memory** problems abound. Many people did not survive the plague; many others became so frustrated they committed suicide, so angered they turned to murder, or so dysfunctional they could not survive. Protagonist Valerie Rye sadly thinks of herself as now living in a world that seems populated with chimpanzees as she watches people grunting and gesturing, usually futilely, in attempts to make themselves understood. Like many of Butler's works, this one depicts a bizarre world that nonetheless asks readers to contemplate what it means to be human.

The stories that round out this volume, "The Evening and the Morning and the Night," "Near of Kin," and "Crossover," each depict psychically scarred women trying to come to terms with their **identities**. Like other stories in this volume and many of Butler's novels, they show this author's fascination with how disease can affect our sense of selfhood and how it can be used to examine the human condition. Likewise, these stories show Butler's strategy of using unusual sexual arrangements in the interest of exploring the human capacity for love and tolerance. Like her longer fiction, Butler's stories are original and provocative.

See also Kindred; Parable Series; Patternist Series

Works About

Helford, Elyce Rae. " 'Would You Really Rather Die than Bear My Young?': The Construction of Gender, Race, and Species in Octavia E. Butler's 'Bloodchild.' " *African American Review* 28.2 (1994): 259–271.

Scheer-Schazier, Brigitte. "Loving Insects Can Be Dangerous: Assessing the Cost of Life in Octavia Estelle Butler's Novella 'Bloodchild' (1984)." *Biotechnological and Medical Themes in Science Fiction.* Ed. Domna Pastourmatzi. Thessaloniki, Greece: University Studio, 2002.

Grace McEntee

BLUES

Because of its persistent and variously influential role in African American life, the blues defies precise definition and categorization. Whether a musical form, broader aesthetic framework, stylistic element, or underlying mood that inspires them, the blues ranks as one of the most formative artistic forms in African American expressive culture. Though endlessly adapted, certain characteristics of blues music remain distinctive. A secular form of lyric verse steeped in southern black folk tradition, the blues is sung by a single performer who adopts a specific persona and witnesses to painful misfortune or personal loss, often caused or exacerbated by adverse economic, racial, or sexual conditions. Plaintive, sad, hopeful, tragicomic, witty, bawdy, condemnatory, triumphant, or a combination of these, the blues expresses the troubles or desires of either the blues performer or his/her sympathetic audience. Blues lyrics marshal culturally resonant allusions, emotionally evocative imagery, and playful double entendres. Its music employs raw vocal intonation, elastic phrasing, the distinctively mournful "blue note" (the flattened 3rd, 5th, or 7th note in standard scales), and a formal structure rooted in repetition, improvisation, and call and response patterns. Depending on how it is played and how one interprets it, the blues may fluctuate between solitary witnessing and communal expression, endless despondency and emergent hope, control of life and its impossibility, signs of weakness and strength.

The origins of the blues are at least as nebulous as its definition. Antecedents of the blues range from West African rhythmic texturing and complex syncopations, the **work** songs and **spirituals** forged under **slavery**, field hollers of the post-Emancipation period, and ragtime and vaudeville music. This amalgamation demonstrates the uniquely American character of the blues' emergence and to the devastating social conditions that inspired it. When and where these influences ultimately converged to form the blues is still unclear, although blues and **jazz** composer W. C. Handy, who heard blues songs as early as 1890 in Mississippi, composed the first written blues song, "Memphis Blues," in 1912 and standardized the traditional twelve-bar, three-line stanza with an AAB scheme. The blues developed in the rural **South** as talented workers and, later, musicians and traveling bands migrated across the region. Even the coarse, gritty texture of this early folk or country blues (with sparse instrumental accompaniment) had its geographical variants, namely, the popularly recognized Mississippi Delta (exemplified by Charley Patton and Robert

Johnson), East Texas (Leadbelly and Blind Lemon Jeffers), and Piedmont blues (Josh White).

As musicians and shows spread, so too did the influence and appeal of the blues. The Great Migration created a surge of southern musicians and audiences in the urban North, in conjunction with changes in the recording industry, that radically transformed the blues in the 1920s. The rise of the black-targeted "race record," sparked by Mamie Smith's acclaimed recording of "Crazy Blues" in 1920, laid the groundwork for the classic blues' huge success. Greatly influenced by ragtime and tent-show performances, the classic (vaudeville) blues, unlike the male-dominated folk blues, almost exclusively featured female singers, including Gertrude "Ma" Rainey, Bessie Smith, Ethel Waters, Ida Cox, and Alberta Hunter. These recordings in turn became blueprints for emerging musicians in both city and country, and the performers became the musical forbearers of singers like Etta James, **Billie Holiday**, and Nina Simone. This wave of popularity was followed by a move toward increased instrumentalization, electric amplification, and the discernable urban sophistication found in 1930s and 1940s Memphis, Chicago, and Detroit (Muddy Waters and B. B. King). Post–World War II urban blues were also increasingly influenced by jazz, whose roots were themselves shaped by early blues forms. The blues also inspired more "polished" popular offshoots like boogie woogie, swing, and rhythm and blues.

The blues song and its performance reflect a general ethos or worldview, captured in **Ralph Ellison**'s definition of the blues: "an impulse to keep the painful details . . . of a brutal experience alive in one's aching consciousness, to finger its jagged grain, and to transcend it . . . by squeezing from it a near-tragic, near-comic lyricism" (5). For many, the blues represents a profound underlying resilience and triumphant life force. According to **Amiri Baraka**, the emergence of the blues marks the achievement of a fully black American **identity**. Houston A. Baker, Jr., presents the blues as the defining "phylogenetic recapitulation . . . of species experience" (5). Others resist using the blues paradigm to define African American culture, citing among other things opposition to the blues by members of the black church and middle **class**.

This blues ethos underwrites a broader blues aesthetic featured in African American visual art and **literature**. Modernist interests in folk culture led to formal experimentation with the blues structure and ethos evident in texts by Sterling Brown, **Langston Hughes**, **Zora Neale Hurston**, and **Richard Wright** and the artwork of Romare Bearden. More contemporary works by **James Baldwin**, Amiri Baraka, Robert Hayden, **Toni Cade Bambara**, **Gayl Jones**, **Sherley Anne Williams**, **Alice Walker**, and **Harryette Mullen** pay tribute to classic blues women and their songs. The presence of these figures in black women's texts indicates their continued deep symbolic value. Female blues characters repeatedly facilitate explorations of defiant black female independence, **lesbianism** or bisexuality, and patriarchal constraints over women.

Black feminist critics have turned to the blues, and its frank sexual content, to help frame analyses of **sexuality**, gender relations, and black **domestic** space. Hazel Carby argues that women's blues construct sensuous, sexually autonomous female subjects, in contrast to the desexed, middle-class self-representations of black women at the turn of the century. **Angela Davis** also regards the blues as a powerful, consciousness-raising cultural force that articulates a protofeminist, working-class political consciousness and exemplifies the politicization of the personal. But Ann duCille challenges the exclusionary politics of authenticity often marshaled by invoking the blues and questions the realism of the liberated blues-songstress archetype. Despite disagreements about the blues' meaning and function, most would agree with Lawrence Levine that the significance of the blues art form is its "insist[ence] upon the meaningfulness of black lives," which are "worth taking note of and sharing in song" (269–270).

See also Poetry

Works About

Baker, Houston A., Jr. *Blues, Ideology, and Afro-American Literature: A Vernacular Theory.* Chicago: University of Chicago Press, 1984.

Baraka, Amiri (Leroi Jones). *Blues People: Negro Music in White America.* New York: William Morrow, 1963.

Carby, Hazel. " 'It Jus Be's That Way Sometime': The Sexual Politics of Women's Blues." *Unequal Sisters: A Multicultural Reader in U.S. Women's History.* Ed. Ellen Carol Du Bois and Vicki L. Ruiz. New York: Routledge, 1990. 746–758.

Davis, Angela Y. *Blues Legacies and Black Feminism: Gertrude "Ma" Rainey, Bessie Smith, and Billie Holiday.* New York: Pantheon, 1998.

duCille, Ann. "Blues Notes on Black Sexuality: Sex and the Texts of Jessie Fauset and Nella Larsen." *Journal of the History of Sexuality* 3.3 (1993): 418–444.

Ellison, Ralph. *Shadow and Act.* New York: Vintage, 1964.

Harrison, Daphne Duval. *Black Pearls: Blues Queens of the 1920s.* New Brunswick, NJ: Rutgers University Press, 1988.

Jahn, Janheinz. *Neo-African Literature: A History of Black Writing.* New York: Grove Press, 1969.

Jones, Gayl. *Liberating Voices: Oral Tradition in African American Literature.* New York: Penguin, 1991.

Levine, Lawrence W. *Black Culture and Black Consciousness: Afro-American Folk Thought from Slavery to Freedom.* Oxford: Oxford University Press, 1977.

Murray, Albert. *Stomping the Blues.* New York: Vintage, 1982.

Tracy, Steven C. *Langston Hughes and the Blues.* Urbana: University of Illinois Press, 1988.

Wall, Cheryl A. *Women of the Harlem Renaissance.* Bloomington: Indiana University Press, 1995.

Williams, Sherley Anne. "The Blues Roots of Contemporary Afro-American Poetry." *Afro-American Literature: The Reconstruction of Instruction.* Ed. Dexter Fisher and Robert B. Stepto. New York: MLA, 1979. 72–87.

Stéphane Robolin

BLUEST EYE, THE

Toni Morrison's first novel, *The Bluest Eye* (1970), is set in Lorain, Ohio, in 1941. Framed within the discourse of women's "secret" communal knowledge, the story relates the psychological damage of racism upon the most vulnerable member of U.S. culture, a young black girl. Eleven-year-old Pecola Breedlove longs for the blue eyes of the little blonde girls hailed as icons of **beauty**. The image of Shirley Temple painted on a little girl's teacup or Mary Jane emblazoned on a candy wrapper makes Pecola see herself through the cultural lens that constructs her ugliness. If only she were pretty—an achievement reached through the blue eyes that mark **whiteness**—then, she believes, people would **love** her.

Another casualty of American racism, Pecola's mother Pauline is crippled not only by her slightly deformed foot but also by the ideals of physical beauty and romantic love that mature for her in the darkened space of the movie theater where she escapes from the loneliness of her small **domestic** sphere. As she watches the embraces of idealized white movie stars, her hair piled in imitation of Jean Harlow's, Pauline loses a front tooth, cementing the physical difference more broadly marked upon her black **body**. She ultimately finds an alternative escape in her domestic **work** for a white **family** that values her cleanliness and her relentless dedication, two characteristics she no longer shares with her own family that she sees as poor, ugly, and broken.

Pecola's father, Cholly, has his own psychological scars: Two white men discover him as a young teen having sex with a girl in a field. Instead of hating the white men, he despises the girl for witnessing his shame. This enduring shame, and the anger it engenders, is redirected toward his wife; the two regularly exchange physical and verbal abuse. Cholly's crisis comes when, frustrated and intoxicated, he sees his daughter reenact a physical movement that reminds him of a young Pauline. The tenderness that wells up inside him turns to an irrepressible sexual urge, and he violently rapes her. Thus, *The Bluest Eye*, like later Morrison novels, turns on an act of physical and/or psychological **violence** precipitated by self-doubt and a feeling of loss or emptiness created by a racist, sexist, and classist world. However, because these violent acts (including **rape**, murder, infanticide, and child abuse) often function as attempts to gain some lost thing, the victims embodying an unbearable absence, the perpetrators often conflate violence with love. Tenderness prompts Cholly to cover his violated daughter with a quilt; hatred of his shame—directed again toward the female body—prevents him from lifting her from the floor.

When Pauline finds Pecola on the kitchen floor, the traditional domestic space of the female, she beats her daughter rather than offering a sympathetic embrace. The pregnant Pecola also finds little compassion from the "respectable" neighborhood women. Indeed, the only kind adults in Pecola's life are three prostitutes who live in the apartment above her and hate with a proud authority (almost) all men. Marked as ruined by the **community**, Miss Marie, China, and Poland accept Pecola as she is, without judgment, just as they accept each other. Their celebration of black female **sexuality** leads to a certain **freedom**, even if it does not protect from pain or suffering.

Claudia and Frieda, Pecola's girlfriends, are also sympathetic to her plight. The primary narrator of the novel, Claudia stands in distinct contrast to Pecola and Pauline. Rather than coveting the blue-eyed, blonde-haired white baby dolls that she receives every Christmas without asking or wanting, Claudia harbors a desire to dismember them, a scenario that gets played out in **Maya Angelou**'s *I Know Why the Caged Bird Sings* (1970). Young enough to believe that real babies come from when a man loves you and to be slightly jealous when her sister Frieda is groped by the family's male lodger, Claudia is at least old enough to know that Pecola deserves compassion. The sisters plant marigold seeds, solemnized with prayer and magic words, in hope that Pecola's baby will survive. The marigolds, however, do not grow, and the premature baby dies, the embodiment of Pecola's sterile, loveless world.

But Pecola's wish for blue eyes comes true. At least Pecola believes so, after visiting the town's mystic Soaphead Church. The neighbors avoid Pecola because she is pregnant with her father's child, but she believes their aloofness stems from jealousy over her very blue eyes. By novel's end, Pecola has created a second personality, a friend who admires her new eyes. Claudia, whose voice closes the novel, cannot see Pecola's blue eyes but does finally understand that Pecola is "all the beauty of the world." Claudia thus rejects the white **stereotype** of beauty and celebrates her own embodied **identity** as a young black woman.

See also Black Masculinity

Works About

Bump, Jeromo. "Family Systems Therapy and Narrative in Toni Morrison's *The Bluest Eye*." *Reading the Family Dance: Family Systems Therapy and Literary Study.* Ed. John V. Knapp and Kenneth Womack. Newark: University of Delaware Press, 2003. 151–170.

Cheng, Anne Anlin. "Wounded Beauty: An Exploratory Essay on Race, Feminism, and the Aesthetic Question." *Tulsa Studies in Women's Literature* 19.2 (Fall 2000): 191–217.

Dickerson, Vanessa D. "The Naked Father in Toni Morrison's *The Bluest Eye*." *Refiguring the Father: New Feminist Readings of Patriarchy.* Ed. Patricia Yaeger and Beth Kowaleski-Wallace. Carbondale: Southern Illinois University Press, 1989. 108–127.

——. "Summoning SomeBody: The Flesh Made Word in Toni Morrison's Fiction." *Recovering the Black Female Body: Self-Representations by African American Women.* Ed. Michael Bennett and Vanessa D. Dickerson. New Brunswick, NJ: Rutgers University Press, 2001. 195–216.

Gourdine, Angeletta K. M. "Colored Reading; or, Interpretation and the Raciogendered Body." *Reading Sites: Social Difference and Reader Response.* Ed.

Patrocinio P. Schweickart and Elizabeth A. Flynn. New York: Modern Language Association of America, 2004. 60–82.

Hooper, Lita. "A Black Feminist Critique of *The Bride Price* and *The Bluest Eye*." *Journal of African Children's and Youth Literature* 6 (1994–1995): 74–81.

Kuenz, Jane. "*The Bluest Eye*: Notes on History, Community, and Black Female Subjectivity." *African American Review* 27.3 (Fall 1993): 421–431.

Miner, Madonne M. "Lady No Longer Sings the Blues: Rape, Madness, and Silence in *The Bluest Eye*." *Conjuring: Black Women, Fiction, and Literary Tradition*. Ed. Marjorie Pryse and Hortense Spillers. Bloomington: Indiana University Press, 1985. 176–191.

Potter, Georga. "Forced Domination: Intersections of Sex, Race and Power in *Light in August* and *The Bluest Eye*." *Proteus: A Journal of Ideas* 21.2 (2004): 43–48.

Julie Cary Nerad

BODY

The body is a site of intersections, a place where **violence**, **healing**, oppression, and empowerment are expressed. It is likewise a screen onto which cultural values are projected. Images and representations of the black body resonate throughout African American **literature** and signal, often simultaneously, ancient strength and authority, disempowerment, and the reclamation of power. According to Louis V. Zakbar's collection *Hymns to Isis in Her Temple at Philae* (1988), Egyptians revered the goddess as all powerful; her body created, nourished, and destroyed. However, her very **identity**, as well as sites of worship devoted to her, transformed and almost disappeared during the emergence of monotheistic religions, Judaism and **Christianity**. Ancient attempts to annihilate the black goddess were portents of colonization and **slavery** forced upon Africans almost 1,500 years later. The horrific, systematic degrading of the African body into the mechanized, animalized slave body reverberates throughout Western culture and in popular depictions of black women as the embodiment of sexual promiscuity. This **stereotype** promoted early-nineteenth-century representations of South African Saartjie Baartman (Sarah Bartmann), the so-called Hottentot Venus, whose body was showcased for the pleasure and curiosity of European audiences and whose genitalia became a subject of intense scientific inquiry for those attempting to prove the superiority of the Caucasian race.

Many African American women in the 1920s, however, notably **Josephine Baker** and the female **blues** singers, including Bessie Smith, Ma Rainey, and **Billie Holiday**, reclaimed their bodies as conduits of self-expression and carved successful, powerful public roles for themselves. The complexity of the black female body's evolution in **history** and culture is a poignant subject for many African American writers who illustrate that the black body serves, paradoxically, as a site of oppression and empowerment.

Violence against women is the most obvious form of oppression in African American literature. In *Their Eyes Were Watching God*, **Zora Neale Hurston** depicts a legacy of violence toward black women, first through Nanny's impregnation by her slave master and then in Leafy's **rape** by the local schoolteacher, an incident from which Leafy never recovers and of which Janie is the product. Janie's life, too, is haunted by looming violence—emotional and physical—and in her marriage with Tea Cake, domestic violence becomes an expression of his control, which Hurston represents troublingly as an act of **love** and devotion. However, in her short story "Sweat," Hurston presents intraracial domestic violence as utterly destructive and doubly dangerous because it prevents Delia, who is a washerwoman for whites, from addressing systems of racial inequality, thereby preventing her from improving her status.

This same theme appears in **Alice Walker**'s *The Color Purple*, where intraracial violence constantly threatens to destroy Celie. Her rape and impregnation by her stepfather and the constant physical abuse by her husband are symbolic of the dangers of patriarchal society in which men "own" women. The rapes of Pecola in **Toni Morrison**'s *The Bluest Eye* and Maya in **Maya Angelou**'s *I Know Why the Caged Bird Sings* also illustrate the young black woman's struggle within intersections of domination of which racism is one component along with gender, **class**, and **sexuality**.

Similarly, in his poem "Mulatto," **Langston Hughes** makes clear the double-edged oppression African American women face in interracial violence: first as a black woman in a white society that does not acknowledge her rights over her own body and second as a member of the female sex, thought to exist only to service and appease men. In this poem, a white man rapes the young **mulatto** boy's mother against a fence; she is literally trapped at the intersections of so many levels of violence and oppression that her fate seems inescapable. Like the narrator in Hughes's poem, **Gayl Jones**'s *Corregidora* heroine Ursa, a blues singer who weaves her **family**'s painful history into song, is overwhelmed with loathing for the white slave master who fathered, raped, and dehumanized her grandmother and mother. Jones's novel traces Ursa's attempts to understand her family's story and to overcome the psychic damage caused by that past.

The continual oppression of blacks by white society becomes the impetus for violence against women in **Richard Wright**'s *Native Son*. Bigger's fear and anxiety of the all-encompassing power of white society leads him to act out his own feelings of suffocation by smothering the white socialite Mary Dalton by accident, an event that causes more intense terror and leads him to burn her corpse in the furnace. When his plan of escape spirals out of control, Bigger attempts to reclaim his threatened autonomy by asserting sexual dominance over his black girlfriend Bessie. However, raping Bessie does not strip her of all power; Bigger fears she can still expose him. The only way Bigger can completely conquer Bessie is to kill her.

The depiction of murder as control is perhaps most disturbing in **Nella Larsen**'s novel *Passing*, in which a childhood friend, Clare, becomes the adult object of Irene Redfield's hatred and jealousy. Irene's abhorrence and fear of the beautiful Clare culminates in Clare's destruction when Clare falls out of a sixth-story window to her **death**. While Larsen does not directly reveal whether Irene pushed her or Clare committed suicide, Clare's death is indicative of racial or color-focused tensions within the black **community**. Clare's death is complicated by her status as a mulatta who has successfully passed in white society, and her story is similar to the **myth** of the tragic mulatto who is torn between black and white society and who is ultimately destroyed due to this seeming irreconcilable conflict.

The objectification of the black female body often leads to violence. Larsen's *Quicksand* features another mulatto character, Helga Crane, who, in an effort to obtain the lifestyle she desires, aligns herself with the Dahls, her extended white family in Copenhagen. The Dahls provide Helga with every lovely trinket she wishes, but it comes at a price: She must perform the role of the exotic savage for the Danish socialites, much like the "Hottentot Venus." The artist Axel Olsen also wants to capture Helga and further objectifies her by demanding that she sit for a portrait, a form of confinement. Larsen presents the lionlike Olsen's pursuit of a sexual relationship with Helga as a hunt, suggesting that if he succeeds, Helga will be consumed and therefore destroyed. When Helga refuses his advances, she is the victim of a searing verbal assault that leaves her reeling. Olsen's final punishment is the painting itself, which leaves all members of the household unsettled and makes Helga appear, in the words of the maid, "wicked."

In *The Street*, **Ann Petry** presents analogous intimidation via her protagonist Lutie Johnson, who, to her detriment, becomes the sexual object of many men. William Jones, the super of her building, has rape fantasies about Lutie, and even after discovering that she has been "marked" for someone else to own, he attempts to violate her. Failing in his attempt, he develops a plan to hurt her as deeply as possible by ruining her son, Bub. Junto, the powerful white owner of the local juke joint, also desires to possess Lutie. Like Jones, he acts as a voyeur, constantly watching and monitoring her. Junto simultaneously empowers and oppresses Lutie by allowing her to be the singer in his club. Lutie sees the spotlight as an opportunity to escape the street; however, she must serve as a sexual object and a source of entertainment to do so. Boots, who carries out Junto's dirty work, also sees Lutie as sexual prey and, at Junto's command, stalls and ruins Lutie's strategy for escape. When Boots attempts to rape Lutie, she recognizes him as all the forces that have prevented her success, and usurping phallic power via a candlestick, she murders him and leaves the city.

Petry's assertion of Lutie's power at the end of *The Street* is indicative of another trend in African American literature: using the black female body as a sign of empowerment. In the essay "Uses of the Erotic: The Erotic as Power," **Audre Lorde** also acknowledges women's internal creative energy and inspires women to reconnect with this force in order to empower themselves through self-expression and union with other women to facilitate activism and social change. bell hooks also calls black women to battle against negative and oppressive depictions of them. In "Selling Hot Pussy: Representations of Black

Female Sexuality in the Cultural Marketplace," hooks reads **Nikki Giovanni**'s "Woman Poem" as a call to oppressors to acknowledge and rectify their actions but also indicates that empowerment must be accomplished by black women's actively creating and recovering positive representations of their bodies and womanhood.

Throughout the twentieth and twenty-first centuries, African American women authors have successfully developed a stunning tradition of literature that portrays black women as highly capable of overcoming their oppressors. Hurston, Walker, and Angelou in the texts cited above enable their characters to overcome their situations and lead fulfilled and thriving lives. For Walker and Angelou, **motherhood** becomes the redemptive feature of Celie's and Maya's lives. Through their children, they are metaphorically reborn and revitalized. **Gwendolyn Brooks**'s *Maud Martha* also presents motherhood as an anodyne to the pain of living in a racist society, and in her poem "Sadie and Maud," motherhood is crucial to a full and therefore hard and complicated life. For Petry's Lutie Johnson, motherhood is the catalyst that sparks her desire to break away from the oppressive "street." And to Lorde, being a mother entails pleasurable and infinite connection to her child, her creation, in "Now That I Am Forever with Child."

Motherhood, however, is a contentious subject for many African American women. W.E.B. Du Bois, in "The Damnation of Women," argues that society's conventions restrict women's ability to achieve their best because they are cemented into the role of mother. Larsen's *Quicksand* and *Passing* display intense anxiety about motherhood and depict it as entrapping and inhibiting. For Morrison's Pecola, pregnancy ostracizes her from black society. Jones's Ursa fears she cannot carry on her family's story by "making generations" due to her infertility. **Rita Dove**'s poems "Mother Love," "Daystar," and "Motherhood" illustrate the complexity of the role of the black mother: the fear, limitations, and willing selflessness it inspires.

The most poignant imagery of the reclamation of power through the body is evident in the centrality of healing to African American women's literary texts. In answer to the themes of violence explored above, many women writers use scar imagery to illustrate the inescapable presence of a wound as well as the body's power to recover from and thrive despite it. The best example of this is the tree scar on Sethe's back in Toni Morrison's *Beloved.* The scar results from a whipping Sethe endured as punishment for revealing to Mrs. Garner that the schoolteacher's nephews had forcefully taken her breast milk. Whipping in this novel and countless **slave narratives** (or **freedom** narratives) represents one of the consequences a black woman faces if she challenges white male authority. However, the wound is healed, and the process of healing becomes a central theme in the novel, concluding with Sethe's need to address her guilt and responsibility for the baby girl she murdered in an attempt to spare her the horrors of slavery. The women in **Edwidge Danticat**'s *Breath, Eyes, Memory* also have to confront a history of violence beginning with the rape of Martine— an act of violence that serves as an emblem of political violence in 1930s Haiti. Sophie Caco, the product of this rape, bears her mother's burden both psychologically and physically, as her face is repeatedly associated with the face of her mother's attacker. Her mother's insistent "testing" to learn whether Sophie's hymen is still intact causes intense sexual trauma that leads Sophie to inflict an extremely painful self-deflowering that mirrors her mother's rape. Both experiences prevent her from having a fulfilling love life and a positive body image. However, Sophie begins to heal herself by returning to her native village, where she revisits the site of her mother's trauma and beats back the sugar cane that symbolizes violent phallic power.

Toni Cade Bambara also explores the healing process in *The Salt Eaters*. Velma Henry, a feminist and civil rights activist who attempts suicide because she is exhausted and frustrated by the seemingly unwinnable and endless battle against oppression, develops a relationship with Minnie Ransom, the local healer, who facilitates Velma's psychological and bodily recovery. Bambara skillfully links Velma's recovery with the community, extending the need for healing beyond the personal to politics and the environment. Similar to Minnie, **Gloria Naylor**'s healer Miranda in *Mama Day* channels supernatural forces through her body in order to help, heal, and punish people in the Willow Springs community. Women's power is at the heart of the community from the myth of the great conjure woman who aided and protected the island in its infancy to Sapphira Wade, the formidable, shrewd mother-of-all, whose sacrifices freed her children and their descendants. Miranda's healing ability is put to the test when her greatniece Cocoa is the target of a deadly curse. Miranda calls on her sister Abigail's prayer and Cocoa's husband's mortal sacrifice to revitalize Cocoa so that she can carry on her family's powerful female legacy.

While the healing process forces us to recognize the limits of the body, the celebration of the body's physical possibilities is also fundamental to recovering authority in African American women's writing. For example, **Lucille Clifton** acknowledges the strength and ability of her body in "homage to my hips" and links the potency and ferocity of the black Hindu goddess Kali to women's potential power in "Kali." Strength and, more specifically, the ability to overcome hardship are central to **Ntozake Shange**'s choreopoem *for colored girls who have considered suicide/when the rainbow is enuf.* Shange's dramatic work is intensely connected with the body in dialogue, dance, and song, as seven female performers, each representative of a color of the rainbow, weave stories of the pain of initiation into womanhood with declarations of triumph and perseverance, ending with a communal song of internal empowerment about finding god in themselves and loving her fiercely. Similarly, Bambara's story "Raymond's Run" is a bildungsroman in which the brash preadolescent Hazel Parker's ability to be the fastest runner in her school is linked to achievement and self-esteem. Running also inspires friendship between Hazel and her competitor Gretchen, suggesting that friendly rivalry and genuine commitment to a shared interest facilitate unity among women. Unity is essential to self-realization in **Paule Marshall**'s *Praisesong for the Widow* in which Avey (Avatara) Johnson's reunification with her heritage and the self that she has lost in her assimilation into mainstream white American culture can only be achieved through the cleansing and recognition of her body and the performance of her natal nation's dance in the Beg Pardon ritual. Like Avey, the avatar of culture and ritual, African American literature contains the **beauty** and pain of the black experience and the importance of acknowledging and remembering our origins through the body.

See also Black Arts Movement; Conjuring; Folklore; *Hottentot Venus: A Novel*; Lesbianism; Middle Passage; Passing; Race; Work

Works About

Bennett, Michael, and Vanessa Dickerson, eds. *Recovering the Black Female Body: Self-Representations by African American Women.* New Brunswick, NJ: Rutgers University Press, 2001.

Conboy, Katie, Nadia Medina, and Sarah Stanbury, eds. *Writing on the Body: Female Embodiment and Feminist Theory.* New York: Columbia University Press, 1997.

Henderson, Carol E. *Scarring the Black Body: Race and Representation in African American Literature.* Columbia: University of Missouri Press, 2002.

Wallace-Sanders, Kimberly, ed. *Skin Deep, Spirit Strong: The Black Female Body in American Culture.* Ann Arbor: University of Michigan Press, 2002.

Jessica Labbé

BONDWOMAN'S NARRATIVE, THE

The Bondwoman's Narrative (c. 1850s) is acknowledged as the first novel written by an African American woman. In the tradition of bildungsroman, popular in the nineteenth century, the book tells the story of a young woman who grows to maturity through America's institution of **slavery. Hannah Crafts**, the purported author, claims to be a **mulatta**, light enough to **pass** for white yet a person whose **identity** and sympathies are clearly with the enslaved.

Early on, the main character, who seems to also be the narrator, shows a resilience that establishes her strength. "The life of a slave is not a good one," she says, "but I had formed a resolution to look on the bright side of things, to be industrious, cheerful, and true-hearted, to do some good though in a humble way, and to win some love if I could." The statement locates her character as central, not only to her personal survival but to the preservation of the **race**. Crafts represents the continuation of the culture through spirit more than gender. Moreover, the qualities cited transcend the bounds of womanhood and color.

The protagonist escapes from masters in Virginia and North Carolina to eventually gain her **freedom**. At the same time, readers might be surprised to hear a voice that found ways to resist the oppressive influences around her from the beginning. The intensity of the prose is amplified by editor Henry Louis Gates, Jr.'s textual annotations and the appendixes that reveal the quest for the manuscript's authentication.

On the mend from a hip replacement operation near the start of 2001, Gates, W.E.B. Du Bois Professor of the Humanities and chair of Afro-American studies at Harvard University, thumbed through an auction catalog from New York's Swann Galleries. The upcoming sale of a handwritten manuscript caught his eye. Gates, who authenticated and edited a volume on **Harriett E. Wilson**'s 1859 novel *Our Nig; or, Sketches from the Life of a Free Black*, was intrigued that Lot 30, the 301 pages bound in cloth, was said to be a "fiction-alized biography" from the 1850s. The entry explained that the literary work was signed by the author, Hannah Crafts, an escaped slave. Gates was in-trigued by the idea of such an early work written by a black person and was prodded to believe the claim because the advertisement said the book came from the collection of Dorothy Porter, a noted African American historian and librarian at Howard University's Moorland-Spingarn Research Center.

The Swann catalog offered almost 400 pieces—first editions, manuscripts, documents, posters, photographs, and memorabilia—in the annual Black His-tory Month sale of African American collectibles. The author and scholar writes that his habit is to give the magazine a thorough read, even when he chooses not to buy something for his personal collection or the university. Gates, with the help of historian Richard Newman, who brokered the deal, purchased Lot 30 on the first bid for $8,500 on February 15, 2001.

Gates concedes that he wondered about the investment. Many of the pub-lishers he consulted would not commit money to produce an unauthenticated text. The assertions of Porter and others were no guarantee as to its unique nature. His past research taught him that writers in the mid-nineteenth century often published under pseudonyms or as poseurs. Women sometimes pre-tended to be men. Whites sometimes claimed to write as blacks.

Gates risked a lot on Porter's decision to buy the book for $85 from Emily Driscoll, a New York City dealer, in 1948. He knew the woman was serious and meticulous in her work. He wrote as she did that the author would gain no benefit from the pretense of blackness.

Gates became even more convinced the book was a real find when he read the work. The professor writes that he was certain that no white author would write as a protagonist in a sentimental novel about slaves. He also said it is not likely a non–African American would develop a story that referred to so many black characters, nor describe them as people with so much depth. Also, he maintained that someone outside the slave experience was not likely to include "so very many counterintuitive observations" on slavery.

After he bought *The Bondwoman's Narrative*, Gates contacted Warner Books as the potential publisher. Then he had to prove that the text was real. Time Warner, the parent company, pushed him on the issue of authenticity. The corporation got burned in the past on fake diaries attributed to Adolf Hitler and Jack the Ripper.

He copied the bound pages onto microfilm and sought the advice of Harvard College Library's manuscript curator. He writes that she concluded that "in its physical form, the manuscript is typically mid-nineteenth century, perhaps dating from the 1850s or 1860s." At her suggestion, he checked the quality of the paper with Craigen W. Bowen, the Philip and Lynn Strauss Conservator of Works of Art and Paper at Harvard's art museum. With his assurance, they conjectured that the novel was written between 1855 and 1860. Wyatt Houston Day, who appraised the document for the Swann Galleries, said he concurred. The paper, writing style, and ink all point to the 1850s.

Lawrence Kirshbaum, the Time Warner Books Group chairman, suggested Gates show the work to rare manuscript dealer Kenneth Rendell. He helped to expose the Hitler and Ripper diaries as frauds. Rendell looked into his microscope and identified the manuscript as a first draft, or "composing copy," etched with "iron-gall ink" widely used before 1860.

Joe Nickell, the author of more than a dozen works that include the 1996 *Detecting Forgeries: Forensic Investigation of Documents* and *Pen, Ink and Evidence: A Study of Writing and Materials for the Penman, Collector, and Document Detective* (1990), provided such a thorough, well-written breakdown on the manuscript that Gates decided to include the authentication report as part of the text.

With the aid of census records from the Library of Congress and the Family History Library of the Church of Jesus Christ of Latter-day Saints in Salt Lake City, Utah, background on Hannah Crafts and the manuscript emerged.

Nickell's report cites the novel's reference to "an equestrian statue of (Andrew) Jackson" in Washington, D.C., as evidence that the piece could not have been written before 1853. He also notes that the author's failure to mention the Civil War indicates the book must have been written before the attack on Fort Sumter in 1860. The report says Crafts was "a relatively young, African-American woman who was deeply religious and had obvious literary skills, although eccentric punctuation and occasional misspellings suggest someone who struggled to become educated."

Nickell pegged the handwriting as a style popular between 1840 and 1865 called "round hand." She wrote more for legibility than speed, the report says, and was right-handed. He also noted that the ink seemed to be iron-gall. He wrote that if she had been a middle-class white woman of the period, the writing likely would be more elegant and diminutive.

His report shows quite a bit of evidence that Crafts was a self-taught reader and writer. In specific, he remarks that the use of multisyllable words such as *magnanimity* and *vicissitudes* and frequent misspellings bear out the testimony of the novel's main character that she worked hard to make the transition from an illiterate slave girl to a schoolteacher.

Readers often hold a happy ending to be suspect these days. The author presents, as a matter of coincidence, that she gains freedom surrounded by her mother, husband, and friends. When the novel was written, a good end to such a story would have been a requisite. For one thing, the positive resolution fits the protagonist's expressed hopes and upbeat personality. Although unstated, it seems the narrative exists more to convey the message that a better life is possible than to document the pain and evil of slavery.

Also, nineteenth-century readers might not have accepted a future devoid of possibility.

Works About

Buncombe, Andrew. "Story of Black Slave's Escape to Freedom." *London Independent*, December 10, 2001, 13.

Carter, Zakia. Review of *The Bondwoman's Narrative*. *Black Issues Book Review* 4.3 (May–June 2002): 39.

Gates, Henry Louis, and Hollis Robbins, eds. *In Search of Hannah Crafts: Critical Essays on "The Bondwoman's Narrative."* New York: Basic Books, 2004.

"Henry Louis Gates Donates Slave Novel to Yale University." *Black Issues in Higher Education* 20.9 (June 19, 2003): 12.

Jabari, Asim. "From Experience to Eloquence: *The Bondwoman's Narrative.*" *New Crisis*, May 1, 2002, 50–51.

Minzesheimer, Bob. "Novel May Be First by Escaped Female Slave." *Chicago Sun Times*, March 28, 2002, 32.

Segal, Ronald. "The First in Line, *Bondwoman's Narrative.*" *Spectator*, July 13, 2003, 36.

Vincent F. A. Golphin

BONNER, MARITA (1899–1971)

Marita Odette Bonner is known today not only for her prolificacy as a short-story writer during the **Harlem Renaissance** but also for presaging the radicalism of the 1960s in her dramatic work and for addressing gender issues by depicting women's lives in her short fiction.

Born in Boston, Massachusetts, the third of four children to Joseph and Mary Anne Bonner, Marita Bonner attended Brookline High School, where she excelled in music and German and wrote for the high school magazine. She enrolled at Radcliffe in 1918 as an English and comparative literature major. There she joined a number of musical clubs, twice winning the Radcliffe song competition, studied creative writing under Professor Charles Townsend Copeland, and founded the Radcliffe chapter of Delta Sigma Theta, an African American sorority. Graduating in 1920, Bonner taught at Bluefield Colored Institute in Virginia from 1922 to 1924 and at Armstrong High School in Washington, D.C., from 1924 to 1930.

In Washington, D.C., Bonner met and married William Occomy, who held an M.B.A. from Boston University. They moved to Chicago, where they raised their three children. Although Bonner's writing career thrived for a time in the 1920s and 1930s with publication of her short stories, she eventually ceased literary activities. She began teaching again in the 1940s, retiring in 1963. She died in 1971 at the age of seventy-three from smoke inhalation complications after her apartment caught fire.

Among Bonner's earliest publications, three plays remain her most widely known dramatic works: *The Pot Maker: A Play to Be Read* (1927), *The Purple Flower* (1928), and *Exit, an Illusion: A One-Act Play* (1929). Singled out by critics as notable because of its experimental form, *The Purple Flower* allegorically portrays the treatment of oppressed African Americans and shows a futuristic vision of seeing the African American predicament as global and connected to other oppressed people throughout the world. Through a surrealistic style, the play called for social and political revolution long before other writers dared to. Additionally, unlike the works of other African American women playwrights of the Harlem Renaissance, neither *The Purple Flower* nor Bonner's other plays deal with issues connected specifically with women's lives.

It was in her numerous short stories, however, where Bonner did focus on women's lives. Written primarily in the late 1920s and 1930s, Bonner's **fiction** often depicts lower-class female characters from southern towns or Chicago's working class, unlike her own middle-class upbringing. Cited by Judith Musser as a "proletariat writer," Bonner employs realism in her short stories by portraying living conditions of families and exposing problems faced by working-class African American women, particularly single mothers, either through divorce, desertion, or by never having married. As breadwinners, these women hold a variety of occupations. They vary from eighteen-year-olds to eighty-year-old grandmothers. Most of Bonner's short stories take place on her fictional Frye Street, which resembles a lower-class, ethnically mixed Chicago neighborhood.

Works By

Exit, an Illusion: A One-Act Play. *Crisis* 36 (October 1929): 335–336, 352. Reprinted in *Black Female Playwrights*. Ed. Kathy A. Perkins. Bloomington: Indiana University Press, 1990. 200–205.

Frye Street and Environs: The Collected Works of Marita Bonner. Ed. Joyce Flynn and Joyce O. Stricklin. Boston: Beacon, 1987.

"On Being Young, a Woman, and Colored." *Crisis* 31 (December 1925): 63–65.

The Pot-Maker: A Play to Be Read. *Opportunity* 5 (February 1927): 43–46.

The Purple Flower. *Crisis* 35 (January 1928): 202–207. Reprinted in *Black Female Playwrights*. Ed. Kathy A. Perkins. Bloomington: Indiana University Press, 1990. 191–199.

"The Young Blood Hungers." *Crisis* 35 (May 1928): 151, 172.

Works About

Hatch, James V. "The Harlem Renaissance." *A History of African American Theatre*. By Errol G. Hill and James V. Hatch. Cambridge: Cambridge University Press, 2003. 223–225.

Musser, Judith A. "'The Blood Will Flow Back to You': The Reactionary Proletarian Fiction of Marita Bonner." *Canadian Review of American Studies* 32.1 (2002): 53–79.

Roses, Lorraine Elena. "Marita Bonner: In Search of Other Mothers' Gardens." *Black American Literature Forum* 21 (1987): 165–183.

Wall, Cheryl A. *Women of the Harlem Renaissance.* Bloomington: Indiana University Press, 1995.

Sherry Engle

BOYD, CANDY DAWSON (1946–)

A professor of education and author of **fiction** for middle-grade children, Candy Boyd was born and raised in an African American **community** in Chicago, part of a dynamic, loving **family**. She read avidly but never found the faces of her family or the stories of her **ancestors** in her library books. In high school, she became an activist, joining with others, black and white, to combat blockbusting practices by realtors in the area around the school. She continued her activism at Northeastern Illinois State University, focusing on the **civil rights movement** as she pursued the dream of an acting career. Finding racism an obstacle to that goal, she quit school and worked as a field organizer with the Southern Christian Leadership Conference for one year. Returning to college, she earned a teaching degree and worked as an elementary school teacher in her old neighborhood and then in multicultural neighborhoods in Berkeley, California. She says she never saw her students' ethnicities reflected in realistic fiction about children whose culture was an inherent part of them, yet who underwent ordinary, sometimes life-changing experiences within their families, schools, and communities. She was also interested in writing about the way children cope with the decisions adults make. She completed her doctorate in education at St. Mary's College of California, eventually becoming its first tenured African American professor.

Her first published novel was *Circle of Gold* (1984), a Coretta Scott King Honor book in which a young girl tries to earn money to buy an expensive gift for her widowed mother, who works long and hard to support her two children. *Breadsticks and Blessing Places* (1985) drew on her experiences of surviving the **death** of a childhood friend, dealing honestly and perceptively with children's grief. *Charlie Pippin* (1987) is a bright, entrepreneurial eleven-year-old who is puzzled by her stern father's reluctance to discuss his participation in the Vietnam War, though she knows it shattered his dreams. An inadvertent rebel in school, she becomes deeply engaged in a social studies project on the war and discovers a clipping about her father's heroism and the death of his two close friends. During the project, she stands up to a male team member who expects her to take the notes because she is a girl and who is condescending though not well informed. Charlie's mother is always negotiating between her strong husband and equally strong daughter. Eventually, she and her father understand each other better, and she uses her business skills to help another school group organize a fund-raiser for a relief agency dealing with hunger in Africa. Though there are moments of great family tension, the family is a source of loving strength.

Two related novels, *Fall Secrets* (1994) and *A Different Beat* (1996), deal with the often-neglected subject of skin color prejudice within the African American community. Her picture book, *Daddy, Daddy, Be There* (1995) is an impassioned plea for fathers to be present for their children.

Works By

Breadsticks and Blessing Places. New York: Macmillan, 1985.
Charlie Pippin. New York: Macmillan, 1987.
Circle of Gold. New York: Scholastic, 1984.
Daddy, Daddy, Be There. New York: Philomel, 1995.
Fall Secrets. New York: Puffin Books, 1994.

Works About

Children's Literature Review. Vol. 50. Detroit: Gale Research, 1999. 1–8.
Holtze, Sally Holmes, ed. *Seventh Book of Junior Authors and Illustrators.* New York: H. W. Wilson, 1996.
Kutenplon, Deborah, and Ellen Olmstead. *Young Adult Fiction by African American Writers, 1968–1993: A Critical and Annotated Guide.* New York: Garland, 1996. 4–16.
Something about the Author. Vol. 78. Detroit: Gale Research, 1994. 23–25.

Susan L. Golden

BOYD, MELBA (1950–   )

Melba Joyce Boyd was born in Detroit, Michigan, to John P. and Dorothy Boyd. She received her B.A. from Western Michigan University in 1971 and her M.A. in 1972. In 1979 she was awarded the D.Arts from the University of Michigan. Her professional career has been multifaceted; she is known as an educator, a filmmaker, a poet, an editor, and a writer.

Boyd's credentials as an educator are extensive. She has been a high school English teacher; at the university level, she has taught English, black studies, Africana studies, and women's studies. She has lectured at many colleges and universities in the United States and abroad, including Columbia University, the University of Notre Dame, the University of Pennsylvania, the University of Houston, Mississippi State University, the University of Hanover, the University of Osnabruck, the University of Colorado, Sinte Gleska College, and Grinnell College. In 1983–1984, she was a senior Fulbright lecturer at the University of Bremen, Germany. At this time, she is professor of Africana studies at Wayne State University.

In 1995, Boyd produced and directed *The Black Unicorn: Dudley Randall and the Broadside Press,* a documentary on the life of Randall and the impact the press had on American **literature**. The press was born when Randall published two of his poems, "Ballad of Birmingham" and "Dressed All in Pink," as broadsides.

Boyd explained to a reporter from the *Detroit Free Press* that the establishment of the Broadside Press "opened up the literary canon, and... mainstream publishers began publishing poetry and black writers and other minority writers." As Randall's friend and protégée', Boyd worked at the press as editor and was named Randall's authorized biographer. In 2003, she published *Wrestling with the Muse: Dudley Randall and the Broadside Press.* In the book, Boyd credits Randall as a feminist and a literary visionary as well as a major inspiration in her own artistic development. The biography has received praise for its impressive scholarship and Boyd's sophisticated and accessible writing style.

As a poet, Boyd is inspired by her interests in African American **history**, in human oppression, and in countering self-interest and materialism. Her poems create their own distinctive **beauty**, imposing dignity on often ugly and painful subject matter.

Boyd's honors and awards include, among others, the Literature Award from the Michigan chapter of the National Conference of Artists in 1978; the Wayne State University President's Affirmative Action Award in 1995; an award from the Ann Arbor chapter of Links, Inc. for literary contributions to African American Culture in 1995; and an award from the **Frances E. W. Harper** Literary Society for outstanding achievements in the literary arts in 1996.

See also Black Feminism

Works By

Cat Eyes and Dead Wood. Detroit: Fallen Angel Press, 1978.
Discarded Legacy: Politics and Poetics in the Life of Frances E. W. Harper. Detroit: Wayne State University Press, 1994.
Letters to Che. Detroit: Ridgeway Press, 1996.
Song for Maya. Detroit: Broadside Press, 1983.
Thirteen Frozen Flamingoes. Bremen, Germany: Die Certel, 1984.
Wrestling with the Muse: Dudley Randall and the Broadside Press. New York: Columbia University Press, 2003.

Works About

Bacon, Margaret. Review of *Discarded Legacy. African American Review* 30 (Fall 1996): 485–486.
Foster, Frances Smith. Review of *Discarded Legacy. Black Scholar* 25.4 (November–December 1995): 54–55.

Anne Mangum

BRADLEY, DAVID (1950–)

An analysis of David Bradley's two novels reveals strong female characters and an appreciation of the societal role women play. Interviews with Bradley suggest, however, that it was his father's side of his **family**—his father, uncles, and male cousins—that influenced his art and gave rise to many of the stories and characters present in his novels. Bradley was born in 1950 in Bedford, Pennsylvania, to the Reverend David H. Bradley and Harriette M. Jackson Bradley. Although Bradley enjoyed hearing his father's sermons, and although he greatly enjoyed the trips he made with his father down **South** to revival meetings, he did not become a minister, the first time a male Bradley had declined to enter the profession since before the Civil War. Bradley's father, forty-five years old when his son was born, felt no calling to the ministry but entered it because there were so few professional options open to blacks of his generation. Bradley Sr. would rather have been a historian, much like John Washington, protagonist of his son's second novel *The Chaneysville Incident* (1981). That fact, coupled with a rural upbringing, led to the worldviews Bradley later put forth in his two novels.

After graduating from high school in Bedford in 1968, Bradley was named a Benjamin Franklin Scholar, a National Achievement Scholar, and a Presidential Scholar and attended the University of Pennsylvania. It was while he was a freshman that he heard the kernel of the story that would become *The Chaneysville Incident*. Knowing that David Bradley, Sr., was an amateur historian, Bedford officials approached him to write the **history** of African Americans in the county for its bicentennial celebration. Bradley Sr. wanted nothing to do with the project and recommended his son, who also refused to participate. Harriette Bradley eventually accepted the project. After visiting the county courthouses and many local cemeteries, she discovered an old gravesite on the property of a white man named Lester Iames. Her research determined that thirteen slaves attempting to flee north on the **Underground Railroad** were trapped at this location and chose to die rather than to be sent back down South. Soon after his mother's call, Bradley wrote a short story about the event. Years later, this story evolved into *The Chaneysville Incident*, a novel that won the PEN/Faulkner Award in 1982 and earned Bradley a position of prominence not only in African American literary studies but also in American letters.

Bradley felt excluded from student life at the University of Pennsylvania. The university had begun to accept and embrace its black students, but the majority of these students came from urban areas. As the son of a rural preacher, Bradley felt out of place. Rather than spend much time associating with his fellow students in their popular hangouts, Bradley began to frequent the bars of South Street. The people he met there became the basis for his first novel, *South Street* (1975), which he began in a writing workshop. Bradley graduated in 1972 summa cum laude and went to graduate school on a Thouron Scholarship to the University of London Institute of United States Studies. *South Street* was published after his return. Although Bradley has not published a novel since *The Chaneysville Incident*, he is purportedly at work on a nonfiction book about racism and its roots in America, which he claims can be traced back to the writings of Benjamin Franklin and Thomas Jefferson.

In *South Street*, Bradley explores the concept of what it means to be a black male in Philadelphia in the 1970s. While his female characters are strong and well defined, they ultimately serve as foils to the men in the novel. The sisters Leslie and Vanessa, for example, see their lives only in terms of the sexual pleasure they can give to men. Although Leslie seems to have a voracious sexual appetite that gives her power, in reality she feels so lost without a man that she willingly accepts Leroy Briggs's brutal treatment of her. Vanessa, an ex-prostitute whom Briggs pays not to **work**, seems independent and full of self-respect until she meets Adlai Stevenson Brown, a middle-class man who has come to live on South Street. When faced with someone she perceives to be smarter and stronger than herself, Vanessa becomes full of self-doubt. Big Betsy, an aging prostitute who unsuccessfully attempts to find customers on South Street, likewise views herself in terms of what men think of her. Her self-worth has been reduced to the possible in terms of men: As long as new men enter Lightnin' Ed's, the bar where she passes most of her evenings, Big Betsy clings to the hope that she may yet again regain her prowess as a woman.

The men of South Street similarly define themselves in relation to women, although at times this definition is fulfilled through the absence of women. Jake, the resident wino, claims that he gave women up years ago because they distracted him from his mission of staying steadily drunk. Leo, the proprietor of Lightnin' Ed's, eschews any mention of romantic entanglements with women and becomes highly embarrassed when Big Betsy hints at his own **sexuality** or lack thereof. Rayburn and Leroy Briggs, Leslie's husband and lover, both crave and fear Leslie's abundant desire. Rayburn mourns her desertion and attempts to redeem his self-worth by bedding a wealthy white woman. Leroy shamefacedly hides when Leslie's antics exhaust him and later threatens her life by forcing her to perform sex acts with what he considers to be the ultimate phallic symbol of his power: his fully loaded gun. The Reverend Peter Sloan, pastor of the Abundant Life Church, views bedding his female parishioners as a way to confirm his power. Not content to deliver sermons and count his riches, the Reverend feels that he will not be the perfect man unless he can prove his sexual worth to the women in his church.

It is Bradley's inclusion of Adlai Stevenson Brown, the novel's central character and catalyst for its action, that renegotiates the balance of sexual power on South Street. As feminist critic Cathy Brigham notes, much of the novel's action hinges on female pleasure and desire. It is not until Brown meets and befriends Vanessa that he understands what it means to be empathetic. Through their relationship, Vanessa learns that she is more than property to be bought and sold. Even Leroy Briggs, who still desires Vanessa despite the fact that he is bedding her sister, is changed by the relationship. Just as Vanessa and Brown consummate their relationship in a mutually satisfactory way, Briggs enters the apartment intending to kill his rival. When Briggs realizes that Brown has managed to satisfy Vanessa, something he was never able to accomplish, he slinks away in disgrace. He realizes that perhaps there is more to relationships than exchange and bargaining for power.

Similarly, John Washington's relationship with Judith in *The Chaneysville Incident* results in a growing understanding that maleness need not be defined by an exclusion of empathy and kindness. Washington is a history professor who becomes obsessed with finding out why and how his father died. He firmly believes that only the facts about his father's life, and about any historical event, can lead to the truth. Empathy and imagination, he believes, lie in the domain of women and do not belong as a part of serious scholarship. What Washington comes to discover, however, is that these so-called women's weaknesses are essential to recapture the past and even to discover the truth.

When Moses Washington dies mysteriously in an accident, his best friend Jack Crawley becomes a father figure for young John. According to Old Jack, Moses claimed that John needed his tutelage in how to be a man because John had "a lot of woman" in him. Old Jack teaches John how to hunt, how to drink whiskey, and how to tell stories. He also discourages his young protégé from entering into romantic entanglements with women, whom he considers dangerous. As John matures and embarks on his quest to discover the meaning of his father's **death**, and therefore his life as well, he eschews anything he finds illogical or emotional, in other words, anything he defines as feminine.

This separation between male and female seems to parallel the separation between the races in the novel. When John receives the call that his brother Bill has been killed in Vietnam, he vents the rage he feels at the white establishment in town that he blames for Bill's death on the white girl he has been dating. He returns from the funeral, goes to see the girl, and rapes her. Although he claims to feel guilty for his actions, he later tells Judith that he still believes he did nothing wrong in blaming the girl for his anger simply because she was white.

Years after the novel's publication, in his interview with Kay Bonetti, Bradley professed shock that feminist critics neglected to mention the **rape** and John's casual reference of it to Judith. In his view, only a psychiatrist such as Judith could continue to **love** a man despite his cold treatment of her and his callous mention of such a heinous act. If the rape illustrates both John's chauvinism and his hatred of white people and Judith's desperate need to be loved, it also demonstrates how much John's worldview changes by the end of the novel. When Judith compels John to tell her the story of his father's life and death, she also forces him to fill in the historical gaps that his imagination has not been able to supply. This process of telling the story and recreating the past allows John to recognize and value the complexity of racial relations, sexual difference, and human nature. The hole that Moses Washington left in John's life has finally been filled.

Judith not only helps to heal John's emotional wounds and the intellectual inability to continue with his work, but she also helps to heal him physically. Throughout the novel, disturbing dreams that manifest themselves physically in the feeling of a penetrating coldness plague John. As a result of the icy feeling that grips him whenever he falls asleep, and which continues should he have one of his terrifying nightmares, John is unable to sleep. The only cure for this affliction, besides trying to stay awake at all costs, is whiskey. After Old Jack's funeral, which as critic Martin Gliserman notes occurs at the exact center of the novel, John is finally able to fall asleep with Judith.

The ice inside him begins to melt as Judith slowly draws the story of his family history out of him. By the end of the novel, when John finally reconstructs what happened to his great-grandfather and the other twelve slaves at Chaneysville, it is clear that the coldness is gone forever and that John is cured: the male and female, black and white, dichotomies that formally ruled his life have become both more complex and less threatening.

Works By

The Chaneysville Incident. New York: Harper and Row, 1981.
South Street. New York: Grossman Publishers, 1975.

Works About

Blake, Susan L. "The Business of Writing: An Interview with David Bradley." *Callaloo* 7.2 (1984): 19–39.
Bonetti, Kay. "An Interview with David Bradley." *Missouri Review* 13.3 (1992): 69–88.
Brigham, Cathy. "Identity, Masculinity, and Desire in David Bradley's Fiction." *Contemporary Literature* 36.2 (1995): 289–316.
Egan, Philip J. "Unraveling Misogyny and Forging the New Self: Mother, Lover, and Storyteller in *The Chaneysville Incident.*" *Papers on Language and Literature* 33.3 (1997): 265–287.
Gliserman, Martin J. "*The Chaneysville Incident* by David Bradley: The Belly of the Text." *Pyschoanalysis, Language and the Body of the Text.* Gainesville: University Press of Florida, 1996. 150–169.

Elizabeth Ely Tolman

BREATH, EYES, MEMORY

Women populate **Edwidge Danticat**'s works. Men tend to be peripheral: shadowy figures to avoid, emotionally remote, or distanced by authority. In *Breath, Eyes, Memory* (1994), Sophie grows up in Haiti under the loving care of her Tante Atie and Grandmother Ifé. Though they are all "daughters of the land," they also live in a place where nightmares are passed on "like heirlooms." When Sophie was still small, her mother Martine escaped her Haitian nightmares, begun when she was raped in a cane field, but now supports her daughter's education and improved living conditions from New York.

Ifé's daughters Martine and Atie had been quite surprised to learn their limits as young Haitian women, yet Ifé emphasizes to Sophie the importance of female bonds, reminding her that her mother remains her best friend. But sent to New York herself at twelve years old, Sophie finds a woman who hardly looks as though she has left the cane fields and only reluctantly joins her mother's weary and troubled existence. (The **rape** still returns to Martine in nightmares.) Over the next years, Sophie strives instinctively to connect with her mother, as well as her aunt and grandmother, but her desires are thwarted by Martine, who resists her daughter's own maturation and thereby her inclusion in the circle of Haitian women. Most difficult to the mother-daughter relationship, she forces a distance between herself and Sophie, as well as Sophie and other men, by physically testing for evidence of her daughter's virginity.

Very early in the novel, this circle of Haitian women of various generations appears to break apart. Not only have Sophie and Martine relocated to New York, but Martine later rejects her eighteen-year-old daughter, angrily relinquishing her to Joseph, Sophie's older boyfriend, after Sophie's purposeful act of violently breaking her own hymen with a pestle; but Sophie has finally rejected her mother's testing, deciding what will and will not enter her **body**. However, despite problematic relationships and the ocean's separation, the mothers and daughters of this **family** are bound to one another, a kinship emphasized structurally when Danticat sets the bulk of the novel in Haiti, where all the women reunite. Sophie, now married though scarred by the pain of sexual intercourse, returns with daughter Brigitte. Only in Haiti does Sophie learn through Atie that both her aunt and her mother were regularly tested as girls, as she was.

Martine and Sophie each come to realize that they are sexual beings, and upon their return to New York, they begin their mother-daughter relationship again through Martine's surprise pregnancy. But Martine has never had control over her body. Even more difficult, she is unable to connect with her violent past. Martine commits suicide, unable to bear a child whose face she sees as too reflective of the man who raped her more than twenty years ago.

After her mother's **death**, Sophie reempowers Martine through dressing her in a red funeral dress and then returning to Haiti to vent her rage at her mother's rape site. Sophie will also come to gain strength herself as a daughter of Haiti, by belonging to those who have been tested. But Sophie is not all knowing; she can only speak from the **violence**, not of the violence. Danticat demonstrates that in order to recapture the Haitian landscape and the body, each must be redefined. In the end, both homeland and the circle of womanhood complete the individual.

Works About

Francis, Donette A. "'Silences Too Horrific to Disturb': Writing Sexual Histories in Edwidge Danticatt's *Breath, Eyes, Memory*." *Research in African Literatures* 35.2 (2004): 75–90.

Mardorossian, Carine M. "From Literature of Exile to Migrant Literature." *Modern Language Studies* 32.2 (2002): 15–33.

Samway, Patrick. "A Homeward Journey: Edwidge Danticat's Fictional Landscapes, Mindscapes, Genescapes, and Signscapes in *Breath, Eyes, Memory*." *Mississippi Quarterly: The Journal of Southern Cultures* 57.1 (2003–2004): 75–83.

Thomas, Katherine M. "Memories of Home: Edwidge Danticat's *Breath, Eyes, Memory.*" *Kentucky Philological Review* 18 (2004): 35–40.

Lisa Muir

BROOKS, GWENDOLYN (1917–2000)

Born in 1917 at her maternal grandmother's house in Topeka, Kansas, Gwendolyn Brooks was raised in Chicago, Illinois, by her parents, David Brooks and Keziah Wims Brooks. She and her younger brother, Raymond, were sheltered by their mother, leading the already shy Gwendolyn to become increasingly reserved around her peers through childhood and adolescence. Brooks's mother espoused "middle-class" values; thus, despite the family's poverty, Brooks remembers being perceived as "stuck up." Such hurtful rejections were exacerbated by frequent reminders of the devaluation of her dark skin and untamable hair. With her parents' encouragement, she took refuge in books and in the poems she began writing at seven years old.

Family and **home** were always central for Brooks. Her deep enjoyment of the family's holiday rituals was offset by unhappiness caused by her parents' depression-era financial quarrels. Her mother's demanding standards motivated Brooks, however, who recalls her mother's conviction that Brooks would be "the lady **Paul Laurence Dunbar**" as an early source of her commitment to **poetry**. Her mother pushed the teenaged Brooks to share her work with writers **James Weldon Johnson** and **Langston Hughes**, both of whom offered significant advice and encouragement. Hughes, in particular, remained a generous mentor into Brooks's adulthood.

Brooks began to teach herself prosody by reading the Romantic poets assigned in classes, including Wordsworth, Keats, and Byron, and the modernist poets Johnson recommended, like Hughes and **Countee Cullen**, as well as T. S. Eliot, Ezra Pound, and e.e. cummings. Brooks concentrated on traditional forms like ballads, sonnets, and quatrains, while experimenting with enjambment and syntax. By the time of her graduation from Englewood High School, she was contributing **poetry** regularly to the *Chicago Defender*, the city's black newspaper.

Her next two years were spent at Wilson Junior College, from which she graduated in 1937. The racial and economic climate of that time compelled Brooks to accept employment as a **domestic** in the homes of wealthy whites and as assistant to the fraudulent "spiritual adviser" of the poor residents of the tenement called the Mecca Building—experiences she drew upon in later writing. Though Brooks found her employment conditions demeaning, she derived intellectual and social sustenance during this period from participation in the National Association for the Advancement of Colored People (NAACP) Youth Council, where she interacted with ambitious achievers like **Margaret Taylor Goss Burroughs** and John H. Johnson, publisher of *Ebony* magazine. In Youth Council, Brooks also met Henry L. Blakely II, whom she married in 1939. Their son, also named Henry, was born in the fall of 1940.

For years, the Blakelys moved from one cramped kitchenette apartment to another, unable to obtain the kind of single-family home in which Brooks had grown up, as the growing number of blacks in Chicago intensified problems of residential segregation and employment discrimination. Nonetheless, despite the disruptions and challenges of near-poverty, she continued to practice her craft, snatching time away from household chores and child care for writing. Significantly, in 1941 Inez Cunningham Stark began a poetry workshop for blacks on the South Side. Stark—a wealthy, white Chicagoan and member of the board of *Poetry* magazine—brought to the workshop a strictly modernist poetics and a ruthless, yet constructive critical sensibility. Other participants who remained important to Brooks included Blakely, Burroughs, Edward Bland, and **Margaret Esse Danner**. Langston Hughes, who visited the group, was quite impressed by the quality of their writing. Here Brooks embraced the aesthetics that have characterized her mature writing, especially an emphasis on linguistic compression.

Brooks began to win poetry awards, leading to the publication of her first book, *A Street in Bronzeville* (1945), by Harper and Row, which published all her books through the mid-1960s. **Richard Wright**, who read the draft manuscript at Harper's request, commended Brooks's portrayal of African American life in Chicago. The collection's scope was subsequently broadened from neighborhood scenes to include a sequence of antiwar sonnets written primarily from the perspective of young soldiers. The book was acclaimed as an accomplished debut from a talented poet, though often in terms that suggested such merits were unexpected in a "Negro" woman. Reviewers stressed the poems' "universality," apparently to assure white readers—Brooks's primary audience—that their focus on blacks would not be alienating. These poems feature the alliteration, rhyme, tightly controlled lines, and intricate syntax that typify Brooks's poetics. They also establish themes to which Brooks returned throughout her literary career: the impact of white **beauty** standards on African Americans, especially dark-skinned black women; the challenge of creating a rewarding life in impoverished and racist conditions; and the importance of according everyone basic human dignity. Poems notable for their moving depiction of black women's concerns, in particular, include "the mother," which portrays the emotional aftermath of economically motivated abortions, and "The Ballad of Pearl Mae Lee," which explores the rage of a dark-skinned woman rejected in favor of a white woman.

The book's critical success did not change Brooks's material circumstances significantly. Tellingly, she often recounted that she was sitting in the dark when she received word in 1950 that she had become the first African American to win a Pulitzer Prize; she and her husband had been unable to pay the electric bill. Notwithstanding its prize-winning status, *Annie Allen* (1949), her second poetry collection, received somewhat mixed reviews. Praise for its technical virtuosity and emotional intensity was matched by criticism of its ornate diction and stylistic excess. The collection's eponymous heroine faces domestic challenges caused or complicated by her **identity** as a poor, dark-skinned African American woman. Annie hopes to model her life on fairy tales, which she learns are doubly out of reach for her. Especially in its long centerpiece poem, "The Anniad," *Annie Allen* turns a critical eye upon the limitations patriarchal gender norms and racist beauty standards impose upon black women.

Receiving the award opened opportunities for Brooks to review for local and national newspapers and journals, including Chicago's *Daily News* and *Sun-Times*, the *New York Herald Tribune*, and *Negro Digest*. However, **race** and gender prejudices, combined with her possession of only a two-year degree, precluded her from obtaining other advantages that typically attended such distinction. More than a decade passed before Brooks was invited to teach a college-level poetry workshop; in 1963, she received and accepted Columbia College's invitation and later taught as well at Elmhurst College, Northeastern Illinois State College, University of Wisconsin at Madison, and City College of New York, before finally withdrawing from teaching in 1971.

Following the 1951 birth of her daughter Nora, Brooks began working on her only published novel: the heavily autobiographical *Maud Martha* (1953). Brooks turned to **fiction** in hopes of earning enough money finally to purchase a home—a goal that, with her parents' help, materialized in the small South Side house where she lived until her **death**. As with her previous works, Brooks carefully negotiated her editor's resistance to more direct critiques of white racism, arguing successfully to retain a chapter that emerged from her experiences as a domestic worker, despite her editor's concern that the white employer was portrayed two dimensionally. Brooks's story follows an ordinary black girl's maturation within the race, gender, and **class** confines of Chicago from 1917 through the conclusion of World War II. The critical reception was positive but highly gendered; *Maud Martha*'s so-called delightfulness paled in comparison to the perceived powerfulness of the first novels released contemporaneously by **Ralph Ellison** and **James Baldwin**. Recently, feminist critics have demonstrated the novel's importance to the African American tradition, drawing attention to the nuanced analysis of the limitations upon Maud Martha's possibilities for growth lodged in Brooks's minimalist, impressionistic prose.

Soon thereafter, she produced a collection of children's poetry, *Bronzeville Boys and Girls* (1956), and then devoted herself simultaneously to a second novel and a new collection of poems. Though the would-be novel never saw print, its material—the lives of the residents of the Mecca Building—would find a compelling voice and publication later as the title poem of her book *In the Mecca* (1968). The collection of poems written during this period, *The Bean Eaters* (1960), was dedicated to Brooks's father, who died in 1959. It reflected Brooks's awareness of the changing racial climate in the United States, in poems responding to the 1955 lynching of Emmett Till and the 1957 desegregation of Little Rock, Arkansas, schools. Critics disapprovingly perceived of the poems in this collection as more overtly politicized than Brooks's previous work. Brooks herself saw these poems, like the new work appearing in her 1963 *Selected Poems*, as evidence that the oft-discussed 1967 "turning point" in her poetics was not as dramatic a shift as critics have claimed.

In the spring of 1967, Brooks and her friend Danner participated in the Second Fisk University Writers' Conference in Nashville, Tennessee. Brooks enjoyed a warm reception but was amazed by the young black audience's energetic response to **Amiri Baraka**'s work. From this point forward, Brooks began associating with young poets in the **Black Arts Movement**—particularly Haki Madhubuti (Don L. Lee) and Walter Bradford, who became like sons to her—and absorbing tenets of the "black aesthetic" that would remain critical to her work, long after she had distanced herself from that label. She found personal and artistic affirmation in the movement's assertion that "black is beautiful" and embraced the challenge of writing poems as a black person, about blacks, and to a black audience. She published her work thereafter only with black presses, including Dudley Randall's Broadside Press, Madhubuti's Third World Press, and her own The David Company.

The difficulties of working with financially struggling presses were perhaps less disruptive than those of integrating her new priorities with her exacting poetics. Striving to produce poems that would be accessible and interesting to less-educated African Americans, without giving up her distinctive voice, Brooks did not create as prolifically or with as much satisfaction for many years thereafter. Her next collections—such as *Family Pictures* (1970), *Beckonings* (1975), and *Primer for Blacks* (1980)—were quite slim. Interviews during this period convey her frustration about her creative output; in them, she also appears disconcerted by the observation of feminist critics that her poems no longer featured women and women's concerns as prevalently. While Brooks privileged the fight for racial equality over black women's struggle for gender equity, the decline in focus on women in her poetry was arguably an unintended side effect of the black aesthetic's male-centered politics. Toward the end of her career, trips to Kenya, Russia, and Ghana, along with increased awareness of the South African antiapartheid struggle, promoted a more global focus on blacks in Brooks's poetry, as evident in *The Near-Johannesburg Boy and Other Poems* (1986) and *Gottschalk and the Grande Tarantelle* (1988), with which she was particularly pleased.

Despite and because of the contradictory impulses informing Brooks's work, she and her writing have been widely influential for several generations of African American poets. She is admired and beloved for her generous investment of time and money into encouraging young urban poets. Brooks used her position as Consultant in Poetry to the Library of Congress from 1985 to 1986 and her life appointment as Poet Laureate of Illinois (beginning 1968) for this purpose, holding readings and sponsoring contests for personally funded prizes, among other activities. The state and the black poetic **community** have honored her contributions in a variety of ways, including renaming an Illinois junior high school for her and establishing the Gwendolyn Brooks Center at Chicago State University. Brooks's other awards include two Guggenheims, the 1994 National Endowment for the Humanities Jefferson Lectureship, and numerous honorary degrees.

Brooks's idiosyncratic **autobiographies**, *Report from Part One* (1972) and *Report from Part Two* (1996), provide invaluable insight into the life and mind of a writer whose career was shaped by the interaction between an insistence on artistic excellence, on one hand, and a commitment to exposing and countering racial, gendered, and economic injustice through poetry, on the other. They stand with her brilliant oeuvre of poetry and fiction to establish her as one of the most significant African American women writers of the twentieth century.

See also Protest Tradition

Works By

Annie Allen. New York: Harper, 1949.
The Bean Eaters. New York: Harper, 1960.
Beckonings. Detroit: Broadside Press, 1975.
Blacks. Chicago: David Company, 1987.
Bronzeville Boys and Girls. New York: Harper, 1956.
Family Pictures. Detroit: Broadside Press, 1970.
Gottschalk and the Grande Tarantelle. Chicago: David Company, 1988.
In the Mecca. New York: Harper, 1968.
Maud Martha. New York: Harper, 1953.
The Near-Johannesburg Boy and Other Poems. Chicago: David Company, 1986.
Report from Part One. Detroit: Broadside Press, 1972.
Selected Poems. New York: Harper, 1963.
A Street in Bronzeville. New York: Harper, 1945.
Winnie. Chicago: David Company, 1988.

Works About

Burr, Zofia. *Of Women, Poetry, and Power: Strategies of Address in Dickinson, Miles, Brooks, Lorde, and Angelou.* Urbana: University of Illinois Press, 2002.
Gayles, Gloria Wade, ed. *Conversations with Gwendolyn Brooks.* Jackson: University Press of Mississippi, 2003.
Kent, George E. *A Life of Gwendolyn Brooks.* Lexington: University Press of Kentucky, 1990.
Melhem, D. H. *Gwendolyn Brooks: Poetry & the Heroic Voice.* Lexington: University Press of Kentucky, 1987.
Mootry, Maria K., and Gary Smith, eds. *A Life Distilled: Gwendolyn Brooks, Her Poetry and Fiction.* Urbana: University of Illinois Press, 1987.
Shaw, Harry B. *Gwendolyn Brooks.* Boston: Twayne, 1980.
Wright, Steven Caldwell, ed. *On Gwendolyn Brooks: Reliant Contemplation.* Ann Arbor: University of Michigan Press, 1996.

Evie Shockley

BROTHERS AND SISTERS

Brothers and Sisters (1994) by **Bebe Moore Campbell** is set against the backdrop of the 1991 Los Angeles riots that followed the brutal beating by white officers of an African American male, Rodney King. While the city burns and racial tensions smolder, Esther Jackson, an aspiring banker and operations manager in a branch of Angel City Bank, struggles to come to terms with the racial tensions played out in her own personal and corporate life. When Esther's coworker, a white woman named Mallory, accuses their African American supervisor, Humphrey Boone, of sexual harassment, Esther struggles with questions of loyalty and friendship. To unite with a white woman and believe, without substantial evidence, that Humphrey is a sexual predator is to substantiate the notion that all black men are lecherous and all white women are harmless victims. Esther knows that this is not true, and while she questions Mallory's accusations, she comes to realize how both African American and white women are pawns in a larger game, one that corporate America wages against aspiring women regardless of **race**. If Esther believes Mallory's allegation against Humphrey, then she feels she must betray her race. However, if she denies Mallory completely, she is betraying the bond that links women by virtue of gender. Such is Esther's bind, and, as Campbell suggests, the ties that link women to women and women to men calls into question what does make us "brothers and sisters."

Central to Campbell's second work of **fiction** is the quest to locate oneself in an ongoing narrative of survival and success. While the novel largely focuses around Esther, it also considers how black men are vulnerable to abuse. When money goes missing from certain bank accounts, charges are leveled against Humphrey, who is innocent of allegations of fraud, financial and otherwise, that are leveled against him. It is a white coworker, Kirk, initially held above suspicion because of his gender and race, who is the culprit in the mismanagement and theft of funds. After she is unceremoniously dismissed from the bank, as is Humphrey, Esther must risk future prospects and her career to see justice served and Kirk rightfully named as a white-collar thief. That she does so with the help of Mallory is a testimony to her strength and her integrity, as well as the bond between two women who know they must do what is right. By the novel's close, Esther realizes that it is not race and gender that separates or unites men and women but the belief that justice must be served and certain individuals held accountable for wrongdoing that links people together. If, as Campbell suggests, justice was not served in the case of Rodney King, then it can be met in the lives of individuals with the resolve to address trespass with dignity and fortitude. To see justice served, Esther, Mallory, and Humphrey must agree to cast aside their suspicions of one another, make amends with the fears, real and imagined, that they harbor against one another, and acknowledge the ways in which they have harmed one another and been harmed.

Brothers and Sisters is a novel that celebrates friendships, particularly those forged between women of different races who are initially suspect of one another. Individually and collectively, Esther and Mallory must face issues such as sexual harassment, gender discrimination, glass ceilings in the corporate workforce, and questions of race and privilege. Their friendship and its evolution are set against the background of themes such as affirmative action, black-on-black racism, white-on-black racism, and greed and envy. Ultimately, the novel argues for the idea that to sustain friendship cultural and racial differences must be acknowledged; otherwise, misapprehension cannot be overridden.

Works About

Gleick, Elizabeth. "To Live and Die and Do Your Banking in L.A." Review of *Brothers and Sisters*. *New York Times Book Review*, October 16, 1994, 18.

Newkirk, Pamela. "Expert, Unexpectedly." Review of *Brothers and Sisters*. *New York Times*, November 15, 1995, C1.

Winter, Kari. Review of *Brothers and Sisters*. *African American Review* 31.2 (Summer 1997): 369–372.

Jennifer Driscoll

BROUGHTON, VIRGINIA W. (?–1934)

No one was more influential in uniting Tennessee women in Baptist missionary work than Virginia Broughton. Broughton was a driving force behind the success of Tennessee's Bible Band in the 1880s and 1890s, a powerful women's missionary movement that met staunch opposition from male members of the church who feared the rising power of these women's groups. Broughton's exceptional speaking skill and literary verve helped her achieve success in her quest to better educate and emancipate women from the patriarchal restrictions that hindered their desire to be equal partners in missionary endeavors. Broughton urged women to put God first and answer the call to do His **work**, which she describes in her first publication, *Women's Work, as Gleaned from the Women of the Bible, and Bible Women of Modern Times* (1904), a work that explores, and argues for, the validity of women's spiritual contribution to the **community** based on biblical passages. She also wrote for numerous periodicals associated with the black Baptist church.

Broughton was born to emancipated parents sometime before the Civil War and went to private school as a child. She attended Fisk University, the oldest university in Nashville, Tennessee, and one of the earliest African American colleges. Broughton was part of the first graduating class of 1875. After graduation, she took a teaching position in the Memphis public school system, where she taught successfully for twelve years. She married John Broughton, a Memphis lawyer active in Republican politics.

Broughton's missionary journey began when her friend Joanna Moore, a white missionary with the American Baptist Home Mission Society and founder of the Fireside Schools, invited her to a women's only missionary meeting. Soon after, Broughton, along with Moore and other women, formed Bible Bands (black women's Bible study groups) that became very popular. In 1888, Broughton was asked to lead the Memphis station of Bible Bands to help raise funds for the Baptist Bible and Normal Institute, where Broughton taught for years. Broughton became a full-time missionary in 1892, as well as continuing to teach, and the Bible Bands enjoyed enormous success under her leadership. The Bible Bands grew throughout the **South** and developed into a powerful movement that helped to assert women's rights within the Baptist church and championed a female interpretation of scripture.

Broughton applied a unique feminist approach to her missionary work, which she outlines in her spiritual **autobiography** *Twenty Year's Experience of a Missionary* (1907). The work, written in the third person, is a significant addition to black women's spiritual narratives, particularly as Broughton examines the numerous places in the Bible that offer support for women's involvement in missionary work. She was skilled at the political maneuvering necessary when dealing with the all-male church councils and was well educated in the Bible, an education she used frequently when up against male resistance to the Bible Bands. She was firm in her resolve to advocate for more female involvement in missionary work and encouraged women, white and black, to answer God's call to service. Broughton's discursive command and her no-nonsense approach evinced the strength of women in the South and their quest for racial and gender equality.

Works By

Twenty Year's Experience of a Missionary. Chicago: Pony Press, 1907.
Women's Work, as Gleaned from the Women of the Bible, and Bible Women of Modern Times. Nashville, TN: National Baptist Publishing Board, 1904.

Works About

Higginbotham, Evelyn Brooks. *Righteous Discontent: The Women's Movement in the Black Baptist Church, 1880–1920*. Cambridge, MA: Harvard University Press, 1993.
Houchins, Sue E. Introduction to *The Schomburg Library of Nineteenth-Century Black Women Writers*. New York: Oxford University Press, 1988.

Debbie Clare Olson

BROWN, HALLIE Q. (1850–1949)

The daughter of former slaves Thomas Arthur Brown and Frances Jane Scroggins, Hallie Quinn Brown grew up free in Pittsburgh. Her father, who had purchased his **freedom** in 1834, was a noted black businessman who had ties to the **Underground Railroad**. Because of her mother's failing health, the family moved to Chatham, Ontario, in 1864, and there her elocutionary powers first attracted attention. The family moved again a few years later, this time to Wilberforce, Ohio, so that Brown and her youngest brother could attend Wilberforce College.

Brown took her bachelor's degree in 1873. Over the next decade, she taught in schools in South Carolina, Mississippi, and Ohio; she also lectured extensively and toured with the Wilberforce Concert Company, singing and raising money for her alma mater. Her first book, *Bits and Odds: A Choice Selection of Recitations for School, Lyceum, and Parlor Entertainments*, which grew directly out of her lecturing, was published in 1884. The following year, she was named dean of Allen University in Columbia, South Carolina (a university affiliated with the African Methodist Episcopal Church). During her two years with Allen, she also attended the Chautauqua Lecture School. From 1888 until 1892, she taught in the Dayton, Ohio, public schools before accepting the position of Dean of Women at Booker T. Washington's Tuskegee Institute, which she held until late 1893.

Wilberforce offered her a professorship in elocution, but she chose instead to travel to Europe. There, her lectures, which considered both American black life and temperance, were immensely popular—earning her membership in the Royal Geographical Society, roles at the 1895 Woman's Christian Temperance Union and the 1897 International Congress of Women, and presentations to Queen Victoria. On her return to the United States, she continued to lecture across the nation and became active in the "club movement" among African American women. Wilberforce renewed its offer in 1906, and she taught there intermittently for the rest of her life. Her teaching, though, was limited because the university recognized both her national fame and her fund-raising potential (the latter led to another trip to Europe, specifically for Wilberforce, in 1910).

In 1920, Brown won the presidency of the National Association of Colored Women, and during the next four years, she helped the organization initiate both a scholarship fund and efforts to preserve **Frederick Douglass**'s Washington, D.C., **home**. She was also active in the Republican Party and addressed the Republican National Convention in 1924. While this period saw the publication of a selection of short works, Brown's key literary achievement was her *Homespun Heroines and Other Women of Distinction* (1926). *Homespun Heroines*, a collection of biographies of sixty African American women edited by Brown (who also, notably, wrote twenty-one of the essays), is important for its emphasis on black women, who were often given limited (and sometimes no) coverage in other biographical collections on African Americans but also as a collaborative project *by* black women (over two dozen contributed essays). In later life, Brown continued teaching, lecturing, and writing.

Works By

Bits and Odds: A Choice Selection of Recitations for School, Lyceum, and Parlor Entertainments. Xenia, OH: Chew Printers, 1884.

Elocution and Physical Culture. Wilberforce, OH: Homewood Cottage, 1940.

Homespun Heroines and Other Women of Distinction. Xenia, OH: Aldine Publishing Company, 1926.

Works About

Burkett, Randall K. Introduction to *Homespun Heroines and Other Women of Distinction.* New York: Oxford University Press, 1988. xxvii–xxxv.

Wesley, Charles H. "Hallie Q. Brown." *Notable American Women.* Ed. Edward T. Jones. Cambridge, MA: Harvard University Press, 1971. 1:253–254.

Eric Gardner

BROWN, LINDA BEATRICE (1939–)

Although she was born in Ohio, Linda Beatrice Brown has become a southerner by choice, having lived in Greensboro, North Carolina, since 1970. Brown's first publication was **poetry**, but since 1984 she has been writing and publishing **fiction** and nonfiction prose. Brown's background in poetry, however, marks her prose, which relies on poetic language and metaphor for much of its power. Her themes focus on significant events in the lives of twentieth-century black women and on women's struggles for **identity** and spiritual wholeness.

Born in 1939 to social worker Raymond R. Brown and artist Edith Player Brown, Linda Beatrice Brown was educated at Bennett College in Greensboro, North Carolina, where she received a B.A. degree. She earned her M.A. from Case Western Reserve University and a Ph.D. from Union Graduate School. Her first marriage to Harold E. Bragg ended in divorce in 1962, after they had two children, Willa B. Bragg and Christopher P. Bragg. Her career has combined college-level teaching with writing and lecturing. From 1970 to 1986, she was an instructor in English at the University of North Carolina at Greensboro; from 1986 to 1992, she was an assistant professor of English at Guilford College; and since 1992, she has held the Willa B. Player Chair in Humanities at Bennett College in Greensboro.

Brown's first major publication was the book of poetry *A Love Song to Black Men,* published in 1974. All of the poems are short, but they convey volumes with the denseness of their images that sing of women as real people who bear heavy burdens, that sing of women and men who are trying to emerge from the shadows of racism into their full **beauty** and being, and that sing of the endurance of **family** relationships and of hope. Brown has said that poetry is the language of the young and that fiction requires more maturity for full expression. Her fiction emerges from her maturity but maintains the language and imagery of her poetry.

Brown's first novel, ***Rainbow Roun Mah Shoulder***, was published in 1984, after winning first prize from the North Carolina Coalition for the Arts in that same year. Focusing on the life of Rebecca Florice Letenielle from 1915 to 1954, the novel's sweep casts light on the struggles of black women to find and keep jobs, on racist practices such as lynching and Jim Crow discrimination, and on the shelter and hope provided within the grounds of a historically black college. Against this background, Florice, as she becomes known, struggles against the gift of **healing** that her hands contain. Finally she comes to accept it and to reconcile it with traditional Christian values and is comfortable with the sense of light that seems to place the rainbow that she had heard about in an old song in New Orleans around her shoulders. The novel's overriding message is that **love** wins over fear and that acceptance of one's gifts is required for peace of mind and soul.

This same message eventually emerges from Brown's second novel, *Crossing Over Jordan*, published in 1995, but the scope is broader and the story more complex. *Crossing Over Jordan* traces the lives of four generations of women, focusing on the final two generations. The foremother is Georgia, born a slave who must bear her white master's children even after the end of the Civil War. One of these children is Sadie, the next woman we learn about. She marries Jacob Temple, a black minister, and bears four children. The two girls become main characters, Story and her sister Bertricia, known as Bertie or Baby Sister. Story Temple Greene emerges as the novel's main character, determined to be a credit to her family and to succeed in a hostile world. Story's daughter Hermine becomes the fourth generation. Through all four of these generations we see the struggles of women to deal first with their men, both their black husbands and the white men who take advantage of their powerless position, and then with a broader world that gives them only grudging credit. Set in a frame that takes place in a future 2012, the story slowly moves through the generations, focusing primarily on Story's life from the 1920s forward and on Hermine's life from the 1950s forward. The central metaphor of crossing over Jordan, drawn from the biblical story of Moses and from the **spiritual** Brown quotes as part of the novel's frontispiece, promises **home** and salvation, a destination Hermine eventually achieves through hard-won love and forgiveness.

Most recently, Brown has published *The Long Walk: The Story of the Presidency of Willa B. Player at Bennett College* (1998). Commissioned when Brown began her professorship at Bennett, this **history** serves as a commemoration of the work her maternal aunt, Willa B. Player, did to guide the historically black college through the turbulent period of the early 1960s when the **civil rights movement** was bringing integration to the **South**. Brown opens *The Long Walk* with a history of Bennett College as background to the achievements of Willa B. Player. The publication of *The Long Walk* in 1998 marked the 125th anniversary of Bennett College, founded under the auspices of the Methodist church. Originally coeducational, Bennett was reorganized as a women's college in 1926 and strove to provide a quality education to train young black women for positions of leadership in their communities and in the broader society. Brown wishes, in addition to writing the history of Player's presidency at Bennett, to present Player as a valuable role model for young black women.

Player's presidency was remarkable in that she was the first woman president of Bennett and the first African American woman president of a four-year liberal arts college. Brown defines Player's leadership as one of service and of principled vision. During Player's presidency, Bennett experienced positive growth and was admitted to the Southern Association of Colleges and Schools. Brown based her research on a combination of oral history, gleaned from interviews with faculty, staff, students, and alumnae of Bennett as well as with Dr. Player herself, and of archival research. Brown's history is important as a personal testimony to Dr. Player and as a document of the struggle for survival of a historically black college. The title refers literally to the pathway from the president's home to the administration building at Bennett, a path that the president walked daily and that students and faculty walked at graduation and other ceremonial occasions. Figuratively, the long walk is from **slavery** to **freedom**, from ignorance to education, from shadows to achievement. *The Long Walk* is, therefore, a testimonial to the power of education, to the struggle for black freedom, and to the achievements of one person as a role model for others.

Brown's personal connection to Bennett College continues as a focal part of her life as she works in the classroom to encourage young women to follow in her aunt's steps to achieve for themselves. On February 23, 2003, Brown delivered the first of the Willa B. Player Faculty Lectures as part of Bennett President Johnetta Cole's efforts to follow in Player's footsteps and continue to enhance intellectual development opportunities for Bennett students. Like her aunt, Linda Beatrice Brown stands as an example for other women of intellectual and artistic achievement possible in the contemporary world if commitment and determination are part of the mix.

Brown's tribute to her aunt Willa B. Player can also stand as a statement of her own goals as an educator and author. Brown stresses Player's commitment to a vision of the possibilities generated by the empowerment of others. Personal empowerment is also a theme central to Brown's fiction as she portrays black women battling personal demons in an effort to find positive lives for themselves and for their descendants. Florice Letenielle battles against her gift of healing and against her own passions to come to an acceptance of her gifts and of her role as godmother to Ronnie Johnstone. Similarly, the women in the Temple family struggle to emerge from dependence to autonomy and personal freedom. Brown's message is that self-empowerment is not easy, but with spiritual commitment, determination, concern for future generations, and the willingness to accept help from others, it is possible.

See also Motherhood; Myth, Use of; Violence

Works By

Crossing Over Jordan. New York: Ballantine Books, 1995.
The Long Walk: The Story of the Presidency of Willa B. Player at Bennett College. Danville, VA: McCain Printing Company, 1998.

A Love Song to Black Men. [Poetry by Linda Brown Bragg.] Detroit: Broadside
   Press, 1974.
Rainbow Roun Mah Shoulder. 1984. New York: Ballantine Books, 1989.

Works About

Reisman, Rosemary M. Canfield. "Linda Beatrice Brown." *Contemporary South-*
   ern Writers. Ed. Roger Matuz. Detroit: St. James Press, 1999. 56–57.
Weil, Eric. "Inner Lights and Inner Lives: The Gospel According to Linda
   Beatrice Brown" [interview]. *North Carolina Literary Review* 1.1 (Summer
   1992): 106–114.

Harriette C. Buchanan

BROWN, WILLIAM WELLS (c. 1814–1884)

William Wells Brown was one of seven children born to an enslaved woman,
Elizabeth. They were owned by a Dr. John Young, a near relative of Brown's
white father, George Higgins–hence Brown's original name, William Higgins.
In 1816 the Youngs relocated from their farm near Lexington, Kentucky, to
Saint Charles County, Missouri. As Brown grew, he labored primarily as a
house servant or as a medical assistant to his master, although he also experienced fieldwork. However, his **family** connection did not excuse him from
the **violence** of **slavery**. Indeed, it incited the wrath of Mrs. Young, who chafed
at Brown's striking familial resemblance, and his occasionally being mistaken
for a white family member. While Young had apparently made a promise to his
relative, Brown's father, not to sell the boy, he did eventually find a way to
remove him from the family, hiring him out to a succession of owners, including the editor of the *St. Louis Times*, Elijah P. Lovejoy, who would give
Brown his first rudimentary education. To further distance him from the white
family, William (a family name) was renamed Sanford, an unlikely first name
for a white boy.

   When, at around age fourteen, Brown was hired to a violent and drunken
innkeeper in St. Louis, he made his first attempted escape. This unsuccessful
attempt was followed by severe punishment, but a respite came when Brown
was then hired as a servant on a steamer in 1830. There he first heard a Fourth
of July oration and realized the mobility of his white countrymen. Others
realized his intelligence and industry, and while Young refused to sell him, he
did hire him out to a slave trader, Walker, who regularly traveled to the New
Orleans slave market. This experience of the worst practices of the slave trade
provided Brown with much material for his later abolitionist writings.

   By 1832 Young was experiencing substantial financial difficulties and resolved to sell Brown. Brown and his mother tried to escape; after eleven days,
they were recaptured, she to be sold to New Orleans and away from Brown
forever, following the fate of the sister with whom he had been raised. He was

sold to a tailor, Samuel Willi, who again hired Brown out before selling him to Enoch Price, a steamboat owner. Brown used the opportunity his travel afforded him to finally escape on New Year's Day of 1834 in Cincinnati, Ohio. There he was assisted by the Quaker Wells Brown, whose name he took in gratitude. The year 1834 proved productive in other ways: Brown married Elizabeth Schooner, and while their first daughter died in 1835, their second, Clarissa, was born later that year. At the end of the summer of 1836, Brown moved his family to Buffalo, New York, in order to gain greater opportunities for employment and a closer connection to African American communities and organizations. There he formed a temperance society that at one point boasted the majority of the city's black population among its membership, participated in the **Underground Railroad**, and devoted himself to advancing his education.

In 1840 Brown toured Cuba and Haiti, gathering material for later work. Returning to the United States, he continued in his efforts to undermine slavery; in 1842 alone, Brown was credited with assisting over sixty slaves to freedom. By 1843 he was a popular lecturer with the New York Slavery Society, affiliated with the Garrisonian movement, and attending the National Convention of Colored Citizens with **Frederick Douglass**. In 1847 Brown moved to Boston to lecture for the Massachusetts Anti-Slavery Society. Separated from his wife (who would die in 1851), he lodged his daughters (Josephine was born in 1836) with the white abolitionist Johnson family of New Bedford, who had once sheltered Douglass and his wife. That same year Brown published his *Narrative of William W. Brown*, which proved enormously popular in the United States and Britain, going through multiple printings in a relatively short period of time. He followed this with *The Antislavery Harp* (1848), a collection of songs that included an account of Thomas Jefferson's rumored sale of his daughter. This account would become the basis of Brown's first novel, *Clotel* (1853), in which several generations of a near-white family of women would be repeatedly sold for the sexual pleasure of white men, echoing the likely fate of Brown's much-beloved sister.

In 1849 Brown was sufficiently respected to be elected a delegate of the American Peace Society to Paris's International Peace Conference. His popularity in Britain may have informed his move to London the same year, where he was employed as a journalist and lecturer. When the passage of the Fugitive Slave Law in 1850 made his return dangerous, he sent for his daughters to join him. This decision afforded him their company but also protected them. As the children of a fugitive from slavery, they might legally be claimed as property by whoever held title to Brown, despite their mother's status as a free woman, as the chaotic enforcement of the Fugitive Slave Law made it increasingly difficult to prove claims to northern freedom. Brown was more aware than most of their fate, should this happen. In her biography of her father, Josephine recounts they first attended a seminary in Calais, France, and then the Home and Colonial School in London, a teacher training institute, making them economically self-sufficient, should the need arise.

Brown used the opportunities Europe afforded him as a professional writer. His anti-slavery lectures and accounts of his travels were published as *Three Years in Europe* (1852) and *Clotel* in 1853, and in 1855, *The American Fugitive*, a revised version of *Three Years*, appeared. This flurry of publications made Brown the first African American author of a travel narrative, as well as the first to publish a novel. Both allowed him to mount critiques of the "peculiar institution," his travel narratives by recounting his treatment in and experiences of different lands; his novel by appealing to the sympathetic hearts of his readers. While *Clotel* borrows from a short story by white abolitionist Lydia Maria Child for some of the action, it is nevertheless original for the way it weaves together various writing styles to mount a multileveled argument that slavery hurts families, particularly women, by allowing male power and greed to go unchecked.

His sojourn in England was more than just professionally productive; it was also personally liberating in more than one way: Brown's British friends, as a tribute, negotiated his purchase and emancipation in 1854 for $300, a token fee, and he returned home later that year. From 1856 to 1857 Brown toured the northeastern states, reading from his play *Experience, or How to Give a Northern Man a Backbone*. While no copies of this, the first play written by an African American, have survived, the second, Brown's *The Escape, or A Leap for Freedom*, fared better, thanks to its publication in 1858.

In 1860 Brown again married, this time to Annie Elizabeth Gray (1838–1902), of Cambridegeport, Massachusetts. Of an age with his daughters, she was of a well-connected **mulatto** family and shared his interest in activism. Settling in Boston, Brown was a member of the city's Colored Civic Committee. With the outbreak of the Civil War, Brown served as a recruiter for the famed all-black 54th Massachusetts Regiment, alongside Douglass. Not content with his fame as an author and success as an agitator, during the war Brown turned his attention to the medicine with which he had assisted Young and then, in England, studied with a well-known physician. By the end of the war, despite no formal medical education, Brown had added the appellation of M.D. to his name, a not uncommon practice of the time.

With slavery over, Brown was able to devote more time to his other political cause, namely, temperance. As a member of both the Order of the Sons of Temperance and the Independent Order of Good Templars, Brown promoted his belief that alcohol destroyed families and impeded the moral, intellectual, and social advancement of African Americans. When the primarily African American John Brown Division of the Sons of Temperance was formed in Boston, Brown was named its leader. Brown's new wife shared his devotion to this cause and was herself elected as its leader in 1867. Throughout the 1860s and 1870s they remained the division's most active members. Given Brown's firm beliefs, it is no surprise that he ran as a temperance candidate in elections for alderman, governor, and senator, albeit without success.

For Brown, this cause and racial uplift were inseparable, as was evident in his leadership of the National Association for the Organization of Night

Schools and the Spread of Temperance Among the Freed People of the South. His work with this organization resulted in the distribution of over 9,000 educational texts; however, it also returned him to his birthplace of Kentucky, resulting in his being captured by members of the Ku Klux Klan. With characteristic ingenuity Brown escaped and continued his activism. Though ambivalent in his relation to the racial politics of the national temperance organizations, he remained committed to the cause more generally and his local **community** in particular. This included his sponsoring of a temperance essay competition for Boston's black youth that was won by a young **Pauline Hopkins**, apparently a crucial event in her decision to become an author.

Brown did not neglect his writing during the war and Reconstruction periods. In 1862 he published the groundbreaking historical work *The Black Man: His Antecedents, His Genius, and His Achievements*, in 1867, a second history, *The Negro in the American Revolution*, and in 1873, *The Rising Son*. The last included sketches of prominent African American men and women, including **Frances E. W. Harper**, Fanny M. Jackson, **Phillis Wheatley**, Harriet Tubman, and Edmonia Lewis. His final book, *My Southern Home*, both a memoir and a critique of the post-Reconstruction **South**, appeared in 1880. That same year the census reported that Brown, a physician, headed a Boston household that included his wife, her younger sister Henrietta, Henrietta's husband, Thomas S. Calvin, a tailor, and one servant. No record of his daughters has been found after 1856, though they may have remained abroad. Four years later, Brown died in his Chelsea **home**, in a suburb of Boston. He is buried in Cambridge Cemetery in an unmarked plot shared with his mother-in-law.

Works By

The American Fugitive in Europe: Sketches of People and Places Abroad. Boston: J. P. Jewett, 1855.

The Anti-Slavery Harp: A Collection of Songs for Anti-Slavery Meetings. Boston: Bela Marsh, 1848.

The Anti-Southern Lecturer. London: Partridge & Oakey, 1862.

The Black Man: His Antecedents, His Genius, and His Achievements. Boston: R. F. Walcutt, 1862.

Clotel; or, The President's Daughter: A Narrative of Slave Life in the United States. London: Partridge and Oakey, 1853.

The Escape, or A Leap for Freedom. Boston: R. F. Walcutt, 1858.

A Lecture Delivered Before the Female Anti-Slavery Society of Salem, at Lyceum Hall, November 14, 1847. Boston: Anti-Slavery Society, 1847.

Memoir of William Wells Brown, an American Bondsman. Written by Himself. Boston: Anti-Slavery Office, 1859.

My Southern Home; or, The South and Its People. Boston: Brown, 1880.

Narrative of William W. Brown, a Fugitive Slave, Written by Himself. Boston: Anti-Slavery Society, 1847.

The Negro in the American Rebellion: His Heroism and His Fidelity. Boston: Lee and Shepard, 1867.

The Rising Sun; or, The Antecedents and Advancements of the Colored Race. Boston: A. G. Brown, 1873.

St. Domingo: Its Revolutions and Its Patriots. Boston: Bela Marsh, 1855.

Three Years in Europe; or, Places I Have Seen and People I Have Met. London: Gilpin, 1852.

Works About

Brown, Josephine. *Biography of an American Bondsman, by His Daughter.* Boston: R. F. Walcutt, 1856.

Carter, Linda M. "William Wells Brown." *African American Autobiographers: A Sourcebook.* Ed. Emmanuel S. Nelson. Westport, CT: Greenwood Press, 2002. 56–60.

Farrison, W. Edward. *William Wells Brown: Author and Reformer.* Chicago: University of Chicago Press, 1969.

Heermance, Noel J. *William Wells Brown and Clotelle, a Portrait of the Artist in the First Negro Novel.* Hamden, CT: Archon, 1969.

Jennifer Harris

BROWN GIRL, BROWNSTONES

In **Paule Marshall**'s first novel, *Brown Girl, Brownstones* (1959), the protagonist, American-born Selina Boyce, grows up in a Caribbean immigrant **community** in New York and struggles to integrate the heritage of her **family** with their new life in America. Many of the tensions Selina encounters, including family responsibilities, integration of the American dream of consumption, and racial and ethnic identification, begin in this text and develop throughout Marshall's other stories.

Brown Girl, Brownstones follows as Selina experiences childhood and young adulthood within her tight-knit and ethnically defined community. She constantly negotiates her relationship with her mother, Silla, and her father, Deighton, each of whom has different approaches to life in their new **home** of America. Silla incorporates the values of the larger Caribbean immigrant community, focusing on the material. Silla's main goal throughout the text is to place a downpayment on the brownstone in which they live. Deighton rejects this dream, instead focusing his attention on his past in Barbados, where he wishes to return. In a key scene, Silla threatens to sell Deighton's land in Barbados and use the money to buy the brownstone.

Selina travels between her parents' extreme perspectives, trying to find her own life in this new land. She rejects the conformity she sees her community experience as they delve into a world of materialism, but she also fails to fully embrace her Barbadian heritage, as she never lived there. In the end, the daughter symbolically accepts and rejects her parents' viewpoints by tossing a silver bracelet into the air; by ridding herself of this Caribbean ornament while at the same time keeping another bangle in her possession, Selina opens a space to look both forward and backward to define herself in America.

Scholars understand this novel as one of balancing extremes. Silla represents American materialism in her quest for financial savings and property ownership. The close-knit Caribbean immigrant community teaches these values, especially through the influential Association of Barbadian Homeowners and Businessmen. Their unwavering concentration on material acquisition dictates the proper way for immigrants to integrate into American life; when Deighton fails to adopt values of property ownership, he is denigrated by the community. With Silla symbolically representing American individualism, and Deighton embodying heritage and community, Selina must balance the two in order to find wholeness for herself. Her journey illustrates the downfalls of both living in the past and conforming to expectations of materialism. Many critics praise Marshall's story for its unwillingness to side with either past or future, Caribbean or American, communalism or individualism, and its insistence that hope is located in the space of an immigrant daughter struggling to find a new, balanced way of life.

Marshall's life echoes many of the struggles in *Brown Girl, Brownstones*. As portrayed in the novel with Silla and her female community, Marshall traces the influence of her mother's friends talking in the kitchen with her own growth as an artist. In both Selina's and Marshall's lives, we see that the integration of Caribbean heritage and American opportunity can produce artful and honest, and thus **healing**, expression.

Works About

Buma, Pascal P. "Paule Marshall's *Brown Girl, Brownstones*: A Nexus between the Caribbean and the African-American Bildungsroman." *CLA Journal* 44.3 (2001): 303–316.

Japtok, Martin. "Paule Marshall's *Brown Girl, Brownstones*: Reconciling Ethnicity and Individualism." *African American Review* 32.2 (1998): 305–315.

Jones, Gavin. " 'The Sea Ain't Got No Back Door': The Problems of Black Consciousness in Paule Marshall's *Brown Girl, Brownstones*." *African American Review* 32.4 (1998): 597–606.

Nair, Supriya. "Homing Instincts: Immigrant Nostalgia and Gender Politics in *Brown Girl, Brownstones*." *Caribbean Romances: The Politics of Regional Representation*. Ed. Belinda J. Edmondson. Charlottesville: University Press of Virginia, 1999. 183–198.

Orr, Lisa. " 'Cotton Patch Strumpets' and Masculine Women: Performing Classed Genders." *Race, Gender and Class* 7.1 (2000): 23–42.

Sherrard, Cherene. "The 'Colonizing' Mother Figure in Paule Marshall's *Brown Girl, Brownstones* and Jamaica Kincaid's *The Autobiography of My*

Mother." *MaComère: Journal of the Association of Caribbean Women Writers and Scholars* 2 (1999): 125–133.

Laura Baker Shearer

BURROUGHS, MARGARET TAYLOR GOSS (1917–)

Artist, activist, educator, museum curator, writer, and poet Margaret T. G. Burroughs was born on November 17, 1917, in the all-black town of St. Rose, Louisiana. She is the youngest of three daughters born to Christopher and Octavia Taylor. Her father was an agriculturalist, and her mother worked as a **domestic** in the homes of whites. Not only was her mother a maid to white families in the next county, but she was also teacher to the black children in St. Rose. Desiring a better life for their family and fearing the violently aggressive actions of the Ku Klux Klan, Christopher and Octavia moved their family to Chicago, Illinois.

From her experience as a child in the Chicago Public School System, Burroughs became acutely aware that the achievements of blacks were ignored in the classroom and erased in textbooks. In her 2003 **autobiography** *Life with Margaret*, Burroughs reasons that although she did moderately well academically, her grades and self-esteem suffered because nothing in the classroom or in books resembled "her people." At Englewood High School, the interlocking issues of **race**, **class**, and especially gender complicated Margaret's academic and personal journey. She dozed off in class until the teacher mentioned something specifically about black people and was only fully alert when the accomplishments or failures of black women were discussed. This attempt at black erasure fueled Burroughs's artwork, and her **poetry** and paintings address social issues, particularly the concerns of black women.

Burroughs firmly believed that the arts were one way of educating and highlighting the achievements of black men and women. At seventeen, she began a long and enduring close friendship with famed actor/singer Paul Robeson, and it was through this friendship that Burroughs's activism and resistance were further cultivated. She decided to work within the system and became a teacher after graduating from Chicago Teacher's College. Later, she earned a B.A. in art education and an M.F.A. from the Art Institute of Chicago. As a teacher, Burroughs was often confronted and castigated by the administration and peers for her progressive ideas concerning education and her open defiance of rules she deemed unfair. Her refusal to be defined by societal constraints and expectations led to one of her most radical decisions— embracing her natural **beauty** as a black woman. Before the Black Power movement of the 1970s, she decided to throw away her straightening comb and curling irons. She wore her hair in its natural "kinky" state, much to the dismay of the school administration and her students.

In her personal life, Burroughs defied cultural convention and proposed to her first husband, Bernard Goss. The couple had one daughter, Gayle, and divorced shortly after her birth. Years later she married "the love of her life," Charles Gordon Burroughs. In 1961, the couple founded the Ebony Museum of Negro History—now known as the DuSable Museum. The DuSable Museum boasts an extensive collection of African and African American artifacts and is the first of its kind.

Works By

Africa, My Africa. Chicago: DuSable Museum Press, 1970.
Did You Feed My Cow?: Street Games, Chants, and Rhymes. New York: Follet Publishing, 1969.
Life with Margaret. Chicago: In Time Publishing, 2003.
What Shall I Tell My Children Who Are Black? Chicago: M.A.A.H. Press, 1968.

Works About

Stewart, Jeffery C. *1001 Things Everyone Should Know About African American History*. New York: Main Street Books, 1997.
Waller, James, and Douglas Brinkley. *Prejudice across America*. Oxford: University Press of Mississippi, 2000.

Karen Arnett Chachere

BURTON, ANNIE LOUISE (1858?–?)

Annie Louise Burton was born in Alabama in the 1850s; her mother was a household slave, and her father was the white owner of a nearby plantation. Her mother escaped **slavery** after being whipped by her owners, and she returned to retrieve her children only after the end of the Civil War. After her mother's death, Burton cared for her youngest siblings while earning money in **domestic work**. She eventually made her way to New England, where she worked in a variety of jobs, but she returned to the **South** to take over care of her young nephew after the **death** of her sister. Working once again in New England in 1888, she met and married Samuel H. Burton.

The greatest resource regarding Burton's life is her sole literary work, the **autobiography** *Memories of Childhood's Slavery Days*. Begun while Burton was enrolled in night school and published in 1909, the autobiography is structured unconventionally; it begins with Burton's early **memories** of plantation life during the Civil War, chronicles her experiences as an adult in the years following the war, and then returns to her experiences as a child immediately following Emancipation. In addition to including personal reminiscences, the autobiography also contains an essay Burton wrote about Abraham Lincoln, another essay titled "The Race Question in America" by the progressive Christian minister P. Thomas Stanford, and sections containing Burton's favorite poems and hymns. This unusual, pieced-together structure of the narrative has the effect of a collage or a quilt, in contrast to the more common linear structure feminist critics have noted in autobiographies of American males.

Memories of Childhood's Slavery Days has been criticized for its idealization of slavery. While Burton does begin her autobiography by describing her youth as "happy" and "care-free," the work is not composed only of happy reminiscences of childhood; it also addresses the violent, exploitative, and individually damaging effects of slavery. Early in the narrative, for example, she notes the whipping of slaves, including herself, and she further emphasizes institutionalized **violence** against blacks when she explains how a slave from a nearby plantation was hanged for a murder he did not commit. Burton recognizes the destructive power of slavery on the slave **family**, acknowledging how regularly families are torn apart when slaves are sold. Furthermore, she obliquely addresses white male sexual exploitation of enslaved women and the consequences of that exploitation when she discusses her own father's refusal to acknowledge her.

Despite the antebellum focus of the autobiography's title, the narrative is largely concerned with the subject of work during and after Reconstruction, especially Burton's own succession of jobs as a domestic worker, a restaurateur, and a lodging-house keeper. Burton's writing is especially important for her detailed catalog of jobs available to black women in the late nineteenth century, her complex and highly personal evaluation of the institution of slavery, and her unconventional approach to autobiographical composition.

See also Slave Narrative

Work By

Memories of Childhood's Slavery Days. Boston: Ross, 1909.

Work About

Andrews, William L. Introduction to *Six Women's Slave Narratives.* New York: Oxford University Press, 1988. xxix–xli.

Linda Joyce Brown

BUSH-BANKS, OLIVIA WARD (1869–1944)

Olivia Ward Bush-Banks was a writer, teacher, proponent of the arts, and advocate for minority concerns. She was born in 1869 in Sag Harbor, New York, to parents of African American and Montauk Indian descent. Throughout her life, she remained an ardent supporter of her dual ethnic heritage, championing causes that sought to further the artistic and cultural **identity** of both African Americans and Native Americans. For many years, Bush-Banks acted as Montauk tribal historian, zealously trying to preserve the tribe's Native Indian identity that was being threatened by a governmental legal decision that sought to declare the tribe extinct. And during the first half of the twentieth century, Bush-Banks stood as a vigorous proponent of the New Negro movement and the avant-garde in the arts.

Bush-Banks, one of three children born to Abraham and Elizabeth Ward, was raised by her aunt after her mother's death before Bush-Banks reached her first birthday. Bush-Banks's formal education ended in secondary school in Providence, Rhode Island; however, it was in high school that she first formed an interest in the arts, particularly in behavioral acting at the Dodge School of Dramatics. Bush-Banks later taught this **drama** technique in schools and studios in Chicago and New York.

Bush-Banks married twice, although neither marriage was long-lived. With her first husband, Frank Bush, came two children: Rosa Olivia and Marie. She later married Anthony Banks.

As a single parent with limited means, Bush-Banks traveled between Providence and Boston for work at a variety of endeavors. She contributed to the *Colored American Magazine* between 1900 and 1904. Later she acted as the literary editor of Boston's *Citizen* journal. In Boston in 1914 she became the assistant drama director for the Robert Gould Shaw Community House. She was also an activist in the Federation of Women's Club.

Between the late 1920s and the early 1940s, Bush-Banks lived in Chicago and in New York, where she was established the Bush-Banks School of Expression to teach drama and public speaking. In Chicago, she taught acting in the city's public school system and was also involved with Chicago's Lincoln Center. From 1936 to 1939 in New York she wrote an arts column for the *Westchester Record-Courier* and worked under the Works Progress Administration (WPA) Community Drama Unit, where she taught drama at the Abyssinia Community Center. She encouraged other artists like **Langston Hughes** and Richmond Barthé through her zeal for artistic excellence, organizing dramatic presentations, readings, and musical recitals.

Little of Bush-Banks's writing was published during her lifetime. Her first volume, *Original Poems* (1899), follows conventional literary styles of the turn of the century. *Driftwood* (1913), a more substantial and inventive work, includes twenty-five poems and two prose works. Her **poetry** received praise from **Paul Laurence Dunbar**, Ella Wheeler Wilcox, and other artists. As a minor dramatist, Bush-Banks produced such ethnically conscious plays as *Indian Trails; or, Trail of the Montauk* (1920), performed at Booker T. Washington High School in Norfolk, Virginia. Other unpublished plays include several religious dramatic pieces performed at churches. Much of Bush-Banks's unpublished work has been assembled by Bernice F. Guillaume, the author's great-granddaughter, in *The Collected Works of Olivia Ward Bush-Banks* (1991).

Bush-Banks is recognized not only for her poetry, drama, and essays but also for her activist consciousness centered on her ethnic heritage and other minority voices in the arts. Her writing, transformed in style and subject from the more polite neoclassism to the rough edge of realism, represents the literary and cultural changes in the United States between the late nineteenth century and World War II. Along with Langston Hughes, **Claude McKay**, and other artists of the **Harlem Renaissance**, Bush-Banks is remembered as a protest poet who affirmed both the past and the future.

Works By

The Collected Works of Olivia Ward Bush-Banks. Ed. Bernice F. Guillaume. New York: Oxford University Press, 1991.
Driftwood. 1913. digilib.nypl.org/dynaweb/digs-p/wwm97246@Generic_Book TextView/1;pt=106.
Original Poems. Providence, RI: Louis A. Basinet Press, 1899. digital.library .upennn.edu/women/bush/poems/original-poems.

Works About

Shockley, Ann Allen. *Afro-American Women Writers 1746–1933: An Anthology and Critical Guide.* Boston: G. K. Hall, 1988.
Smith, Jessie Carney, ed. *Notable Black American Women, Book II.* Detroit: Gale Research, 1996.

Michael D. Sollars

BUTLER, OCTAVIA (1947–2006)

Octavia Butler, America's only nationally recognized female African American science **fiction** novelist, was a self-proclaimed feminist who liked to cast strong black women as protagonists of her imaginative stories. She grew up in an era when science fiction seldom included African American characters and seldom cast women in lead roles. Butler has helped to correct both omissions.

Butler was born and raised in Pasadena, California. Her father died when she was quite young; she was reared by her mother (who instilled in her daughter a **love** of reading) in a strict Baptist environment. Shy, bookish, and self-conscious about her height, Butler felt like an outsider during her school years; one result is her special sympathy for characters who do not quite fit in—a type she often depicts in her fiction. By the time she was ten, Butler was writing stories, inspired, she liked to say, by *Devil Girl from Mars* (1954), a movie so bad she knew she could do better.

Butler attended Pasadena City College and California State University at Los Angeles and took writing classes at the University of California at Los Angeles at night. For several years, she worked a variety of temp jobs in order to have time to write fiction. (Her depiction in ***Kindred*** of Dana's struggles to make ends meet while she writes and sends off manuscripts draws on her own experiences.) Eventually Butler began to meet supportive mentors, first at the Writers Guild of America and then at the Clarion Science Fiction Writers Workshop, which she attended in 1970. She especially credited Sid Stebel, Harlan Ellison, and Theodore Sturgeon (she took classes from the latter two) with teaching her the nuts and bolts of preparing a manuscript for publication and for encouraging her to keep writing.

Butler's first manuscripts to sell were two short stories she worked on at the Clarion Workshop. It was not until 1976, however, that she sold her first novel, *Patternmaster*. Over the following years, she published the other volumes that, with *Patternmaster*, make up her **Patternist series**: *Mind of My Mind* (1977), *Survivor* (1978), *Wild Seed* (1980), and the more loosely related *Clay's Ark* (1984). These books describe the rise of a society of telepaths and explore the consequences of possessing extreme power. In the midst of writing this series, Butler published her sole stand-alone novel *Kindred* (1979), about a young African American woman from the 1970s who is pulled into the early 1800s, where she must learn to survive **slavery**. In this work Butler explores the psychology of slavery and what it takes to resist becoming mentally enslaved when your **body** belongs to another.

Critics by now recognized that Butler's work was adding a new dimension to the science fiction genre. Although many of her motifs are familiar—apocalyptic settings, time travel, first contacts—she gives original twists to her stories, often by casting a black woman as her protagonist. The need for ethnic tolerance is one of Butler's recurring themes, as is her warning against reliance on patriarchal social structures to solve problems. In the mid-1980s Butler's talent was recognized when she was awarded back-to-back Hugo Awards, in 1984 for her story "Speech Sounds" and in 1985 for her novella "Bloodchild," which also won Nebula and Locus Awards. Both of these works are included in her collection ***Bloodchild and Other Stories*** (1995).

In the late 1980s, Butler wrote her **Xenogenesis trilogy** (*Dawn*, 1987; *Adulthood Rites*, 1988; *Imago*, 1989), a postapocalyptic/alien encounter saga that examines resistance to adaptation and to cultural tolerance. In 1989 this trilogy came out under a single cover in a work titled *Lilith's Brood*.

In the mid-1990s Butler published the first novel of a new series, *Parable of the Sower* (1993), followed a few years later by *Parable of the Talents* (1998). These books are the story of Lauren Olamina's response to an apocalyptic United States. Lauren brings together an ethnically diverse group of victims; together they strive to build a social order that will ensure not just their personal survival but also the survival of the human race. Lauren also creates a new religion, Earthseed, to provide others with the vision needed to carry out her bold plan. More books in the **Parable series** are planned for future publication. *Parable of the Sower* was a Nebula Award finalist; *Parable of the Talents* was a Nebula winner.

In 1995, Butler won her most prestigious honor—a so-called genius grant of $250,000 from the John D. and Catherine T. MacArthur Foundation. These grants are awarded to creative thinkers who have broken new ground in their fields, as a way to encourage their continued productivity. Butler's contributions to **literature** include her efforts to make science fiction a site that includes strong female protagonists and African American characters in lead roles, an important contribution to a genre that historically offered only token representation to blacks and women. Butler is credited with breaking through both color and gender barriers in this genre of popular fiction.

Butler's fiction is also significant for the themes she explores. Her novels often look at issues particularly relevant to African American social **history**, such as the consequences of prejudice or the effects of enslavement, but they rarely explicitly focus on the black experience. Rather, they show how **race** issues fit into a larger picture of species survival. Butler reminds readers that racial prejudice can have many guises, that extreme power tempts the empowered to enslave others, and that recent attempts to ensure racial equality are extremely vulnerable to reversal. Until we find better solutions to our social problems, her works suggest, the survival of our species is at risk.

Works By

Adulthood Rites: Xenogenesis. New York: Warner Books, 1988.
"Amnesty." *Callaloo* 27.3 (2004): 597–615.
Bloodchild and Other Stories. New York: Four Walls Eight Windows, 1995.
Clay's Ark. New York: St. Martin's Press, 1984.
Dawn: Xengenesis. New York: Warner Books, 1987.
Fledgling. New York: Seven Stories Press, 2005.
Imago. New York: Warner Books, 1989.
Kindred. Garden City, NY: Doubleday, 1979.
Lilith's Brood. New York: Warner Books, 1989.
Mind of My Mind. Garden City, NY: Doubleday, 1977.
Parable of the Sower. New York: Four Walls Eight Windows, 1993.
Parable of the Talents. New York: Seven Stories Press, 1998.
Patternmaster. Garden City, NY: Doubleday, 1976.
Survivor. Garden City, NY: Doubleday, 1978.
Wild Seed. Garden City, NY: Doubleday, 1980.

Works About

Birns, Nicholas. "Octavia Butler: Fashioning Alien Constructs." *Twayne Companion to Contemporary Literature in English.* Vol. 1. Ed. R.H.W. Dillard and Amanda Cockrell. New York: Twayne, 2002.
Dunning, Stefanie K. "Octavia Butler." *American Writers: A Collection of Literary Biographies.* Supplement XIII: Edward Abbey to William Jay Smith. Ed. Jay Parini. New York: Scribner's, 2003.
Keating, AnaLouise. "Octavia Butler." *Contemporary African American Novelists: A Bio-Bibliographical Critical Sourcebook.* Ed. Emmanuel S. Nelson. Westport, CT: Greenwood Press, 1999.

Mehaffy, Marilyn, and AnaLouise Keating. "'Radio Imagination': Octavia Butler on the Poetics of Narrative Embodiment." *MELUS* 26.1 (2001): 45–76.

Grace McEntee

BY THE LIGHT OF MY FATHER'S SMILE

By the Light of My Father's Smile (1998), **Alice Walker**'s first novel after a six-year break, tells the story of two sisters, Susannah and Magdalena, who grew up in Mexico. Their parents go to Mexico to study a mixed African American and Indian tribe called the Mundo under the pretext of being missionaries spreading **Christianity**. They could not secure the funding as anthropologists. The father begins to absorb the Christian teachings and punishes Magdalena for her sexual relationship with a Mexican boy, Manuelito. Using the belt Manuelito gave Magdalena, the father beats Magdalena behind the locked bedroom door while Susannah watches through the keyhole. This action forces his daughters and wife to deny him the very affection he needs to sustain himself to study the Mundo. Though the wife eventually forgives him, the daughters, particularly Magdalena, cannot.

Like Alice Walker's *The Color Purple* and *The Temple of My Familiar*, this novel covers many decades to fully develop and tell the story. Both Magdalena's adolescent lover Manuelito and her father die and must complete two tasks, according to the Mundo traditions, before they can rest: guide someone back to the path that is lost and host a ceremony to reconcile with eternity. The father must make peace with his daughters, as Manuelito must do with a Vietnamese woman. Susannah has become a novelist and freely explores her **sexuality** with a succession of lovers. Magdalena has become an academic who uses food to obese proportions as a balm for her pains. Magdalena and Manuelito briefly encounter to rekindle their desire; this is quickly followed with his **death** by bus and hers by food. The novel ends with the death of Susannah observed by the spirit herself and the spirit of Magdalena. They witness at the funeral the burning of Susannah's **body** and all her literary works.

Similar to *Possessing the Secret of Joy*, the novel allows the dead to speak and pay tribute to the living. In this novel, Walker playfully uses names of characters to symbolize their significance in the tale. Like Walker's *The Color Purple* and *Possessing the Secret of Joy*, the plot begins with a childhood trauma that connects and separates two sisters. Also, readers encounter missionaries or anthropologists who set out to study and convert another culture and fail. Most blatant is the same-sex relationship between Susannah and her lover, Pauline, which represents the closeness and distance between sisters or women that develops due to a negative patriarchal occurrence. Walker describes this novel as a celebration of sexuality.

See also Womanism

Works About

Byrd, Rudolph P. Review of *By the Light of My Father's Smile*. *African American Review* 33.4 (Winter 1999): 719–722.

Fulton, Jean C. "*By The Light of My Father's Smile*: Alice Walker's 1998 Novel." *Magill Book Reviews*, February 1, 2000.

Laura Madeline Wiseman

 C

CAINES, JEANNETTE (1938–)

Jeannette Franklin Caines was born and raised in Harlem, New York City. She checked out *Call Me Charley* (1945) by pioneer black children's author Jesse Jackson when she was in the fourth grade and became an avid reader. As an adult, she worked in the children's department of Harper and Row, publishers, for twenty-five years. During her life in New York City, she belonged to many professional organizations including the Council of 100 Black Women as well as the Council on Adoptable Children, and she served on the board of directors of the Salvation Army. She moved to Charlottesville, Virginia, in the late 1980s, where she opened a short-lived bookstore and where she still resides. In 2004, she was awarded a Lifetime Achievement Award from the Virginia Center for the Book. Caines wanted to write for children to portray black families with warm and loving interactions among the generations, as they both enjoy everyday life and sometimes face difficult situations.

Caines's picture book *Abby* (1973), illustrated by Steven Kellogg, was one of the first books to deal with adoption for young children. Kevin, older brother to Abby, who is adopted, initially feels too busy to read the baby book Abby requests about her arrival in the **family** but then realizes she needs reassurance to feel she has a permanent place in her loving family, and he even decides he wants to take her to school for show-and-tell. Kevin is a sympathetic male character, and this engaging book remains on many school and public library reading lists. Her next book, *Daddy* (1977), was an early picture book portraying the warm, steady relationship a little girl has with her father, who is divorced from her mother. Daddy is shown to be reliable and fun, and although he has another woman in his life, the importance of his relationship with his daughter is clear.

Just Us Women (1982), illustrated by Pat Cummings, is a joyous paean to the fun and **freedom** of a road trip a little girl takes with her aunt. In this perennially popular story, they confidently plan their trip to North Carolina, a repeat of last year's visit, and tell about the fun they will have stopping wherever they please to shop at flea markets, walk in the rain, buy peaches from a roadside stand, or even have breakfast at night. Pictures show an envious man and boy watching their preparations, and a family group of a man and several women shaking their fingers and frowning while the caption says nobody will be there to admonish them about being in a hurry or not stopping another time. Their great affection for one another is clear from the ebullient pictures and short, rhythmic text. Another popular Caines book is *I Need a Lunch Box* (1988) in which a younger boy, whose sister is starting school, wants a lunchbox like hers. Told he does not need one yet, he is sad, but his insightful father understands his longing and gives him one.

Works By

Abby. New York: Harper and Row, 1973.
Chilly Stomach. New York: HarperCollins, 1986.
Daddy. New York: Harper and Row, 1977.
I Need a Lunch Box. New York: HarperCollins, 1988.
Just Us Women. New York: Harper and Row, 1982.
Window Wishing. New York: Harper and Row, 1982.

Works About

Children's Literature Review. Vol. 24. Detroit: Gale Research, 1991. 61–64.
"Facetime—Alligators' [*sic*] Author: No Blues for This Cowgirl." *Hook* (Charlottesville, VA), March 25, 2004.
Murphy, Barbara Thrash. *Black Authors and Illustrators of Books for Children and Young Adults: a Biographical Dictionary*. 3rd edition. New York: Garland Publishing, 1999.
Something about the Author. Vol. 78. Detroit: Gale Research, 1994. 23–25.

Susan L. Golden

CAMPBELL, BEBE MOORE (1950–)

The majority of Bebe Moore Campbell's works focus on African American women who are struggling to reach self-fulfillment in their careers while wrestling with relationships with **family** and **community** members. These women wage personal battles against racial injustices as well as certain atrocities that reside in our collective conscience: **slavery**, the Jim Crow laws, the senseless killing of Emmett Till, and the Los Angeles riots of the early 1990s that followed the **death** of Rodney King. Wounds of the past both near and far inform Campbell's subjects, and her female protagonists must encounter, on their own terms, hardship—historical, social, communal, and personal. With its attendant histories, the past has a way of creeping into Campbell's significant literary achievement; making sense of an archaic world is as much a part of Campbell's **fiction** as it is her life.

Born in 1950 in the racially segregated **South** of Pasquotank, North Carolina, Campbell is the only child of Doris and George Moore. Campbell's mother, a high achiever, earned two master's degrees (one in sociology and the other in social work), while her father, a hardworking man who labored as a county farm agent until he suffered a car accident that left him a paraplegic when Campbell was just ten months old, lacked his wife's educational achievements but never his daughter's adoration or respect. The two divorced early on, and their parting left Campbell spending the school year with her mother in Philadelphia and summers and vacations with her father. Summers and holidays found her witnessing the racial segregation of the South, and the fall and winter left her bearing testimony to the equally damaging but less overt racism of the North. A careful observer of human relationships, Campbell brings her assessments of racial tensions and the further injustice of bias based on gender and notions of masculinity and femininity to bear on her written works. Much like her mother, Campbell is a woman bent on turning these observations into an opportunity for intervention. Whereas her mother, a social worker in Philadelphia's Department of Welfare, intervened in the social infrastructure of her day, as a writer Campbell engages injustice, particularly the bind that strong, successful African American women experience in their inter- and intrapersonal relationships, in literary form.

Campbell's ambitions took root at an early age. While living with her mother in Philadelphia, in 1964 she enrolled in the Philadelphia High School for Girls, an academy for aspiring women. After graduation in 1968, Campbell attended the University of Pittsburgh and completed a bachelor's degree in elementary education. Her formal teaching career began in 1972 and lasted five years, ending when she enrolled in a writing class presided over by well-recognized African American writer **Toni Cade Bambara**. This tutorial altered Campbell dramatically and led to a writing career that began in 1976. Ten years after she began submitting and seeing her works to print in newspapers and magazines such as *Essence*, the *Washington Post*, and *Black Enterprise*, her first book, *Successful Women, Angry Men: Backlash in the Two-Career Marriage* (1986), was published. In this work of nonfiction, Campbell interviews 100 couples to explore the difficulties that men and women have establishing themselves in the workforce while seeking an egalitarian relationship within the **home**.

In 1977, when Campbell was living in Washington, D.C., and struggling to establish herself as a writer, her beloved father suffered another car accident, this time fatal. The loss eventually led Campbell to write a memoir, *Sweet Summer: Growing Up with and without My Dad* (1990). Campbell's memoir is as much a heartfelt portrait to the father who had a pronounced influence on her life as a young child of divorce as it is a testimony to the importance of black men in the lives of their daughters. Within this text, as well as her first one and the subsequent fiction that followed, Campbell engages themes that characterize her as an important writer and chronicler not just of African American women's experiences but of women's collective experiences: the search for acceptance and **love** in an egalitarian relationship, the difficulty in defining oneself within a socioeconomic and geographic space that devalues certain female intellects while privileging others, the quest for voice, and the need to establish oneself in a historical and political climate that has been routinely unkind to women, particularly African American women.

Despite the loss of her father, in her own life Campbell has found much to celebrate. After an early marriage that resulted in divorce but whose union produced a daughter, Maia, she later married Ellis Gordon, Jr., a banker and father of a son, and moved to Los Angeles, where they currently reside. Since the early 1990s she has written four works of fiction and has been praised for her adept ability to create complicated female protagonists that must first heal themselves as members of a disenfranchised **class** before they can reach any resolution in their interpersonal, communal, and corporate lives.

While **history** plays a significant role in Campbell's fiction, she is not a historical writer; history is merely the backdrop. As a young observer, she knew the story of Emmett Till, a teenager murdered in 1955 by two whites for supposedly making a lewd remark to a white woman. (The two whites were later acquitted, despite the fact that one openly boasted about the slaying.) This murder informs her first work of fiction, *Your Blues Ain't Like Mine* (1992), which reached the *New York Times* bestseller list within two weeks. Similarly, the acquittal of two police officers after the brutal beating of Rodney King informs the work that follows, **Brothers and Sisters** (1994). In **Singing in the Comeback Choir** (1998) Campbell's focus again turns to racial tension and, now, urban gentrification. Personal accomplishment and achievement, as it is in all Campbell's fiction, is played against the fear that another's success, particularly an African American woman's success, will be met with fear and loathing, perhaps even **violence**. In her latest work, **What You Owe Me** (2001), this fear is located in the friendship between two women, one African American and the other a Jewish immigrant, who do not so much betray one another as they are betrayed by the racism and xenophobia that surround them in post–World War II California.

In tackling themes such as history's maltreatment of women, both as bodies and intellects, the inheritance of a racist past as it informs contemporary relationships, men's trespasses against women and their retaliation in kind, and the importance of community to the **healing** process, Campbell has received the following accolades: A National Association of Negro Business and Professional Women's Literature Award, the 1994 NAACP (National Association for the Advancement of Colored People) Image Award, a National

Endowment for the Arts Literature Grant, and the University of Pittsburgh's Distinguished Black Alumna Award. As of yet there are no full-length texts devoted to the life and literary accomplishments of Bebe Moore Campbell. Her work now awaits the scholarly inquiry that it deservedly merits.

Works By

Brothers and Sisters. New York: Putnam, 1994.
Singing in the Comeback Choir. New York: Putnam, 1998.
Successful Women, Angry Men: Backlash in the Two-Career Marriage. New York: Random House, 1986.
Sweet Summer: Growing Up with and without My Dad. New York: Putnam, 1990.
What You Owe Me. New York: Putnam, 2001.
Your Blues Ain't Like Mine. New York: Putnam, 1992.

Works About

Campbell, Jane. "An Interview with Bebe Moore Campbell." *Callaloo* 22.4 (1999): 954–972.
Chambers, Veronica. "Bebe Moore Campbell and Joyce Carol Oates: An Interview." *New York Times Magazine*, December 25, 1994, 6.
Oates, Joyce Carol. "Which Counts More, Gender or Race?" *New York Times Magazine*, December 28, 1994, 16–22.
Satz, Martha. "I Hope I Can Teach a Little Bit: An Interview with Bebe Moore Campbell." *Southwest Review* 81.2 (Spring 1996): 195.

Jennifer Driscoll

CANCER JOURNALS, THE

An account of the author's own battle with breast disease, *The Cancer Journals* (1980) by **Audre Lorde** was named Gay Book of the Year by the American Library Association. In 1997, a new edition appeared with a section of tributes by **Jewelle Gomez**, **Ann Allen Shockley**, and several other feminists. Lorde had presented the first chapter, "The Transformation of Silence into Language and Action," as part of the Lesbian and Literature panel for the Modern Language Association's 1977 conference in Chicago, two months after her biopsy for a benign breast tumor. The speech subsequently appeared in the feminist journal *Sinister Wisdom*, along with a second chapter, "Breast Cancer: A Black Lesbian Feminist Experience." To form *The Cancer Journals*, Lorde added an introduction and a third chapter, "Breast Cancer: Power vs. Prosthesis," which opens with her discovery of a malignant lump in her right breast during a monthly self-examination on Labor Day of 1978. In a prefatory note, Lorde thanks "all the women who shared their strength" during the difficult period described in the slim volume. She cites several friends by name, among them her partner Frances Clayton and the feminist writers **Michelle Cliff** and Adrienne Rich.

The 1980 Spinsters Ink edition of *The Cancer Journals* includes a book-cover tribute from **Alice Walker**, who says every woman should read Lorde's "words of **love** and wisdom and courage." Lorde herself emphasizes the power of the written word in effecting change. "As women we were raised to fear," she states; and she admits that the task of writing *The Cancer Journals* forced her to relive the terror surrounding her mastectomy. For months, she was unable to write **poetry**; diary entries about her two biopsies, her cancer operation, and her recovery formed a nucleus for *The Cancer Journals*. The book has become a familiar text in the field of disability studies, fulfilling Lorde's hope that her record of personal struggle would be useful to other women.

Lorde compares the "pain of separation" from her breast to the "pain of separating from my mother," but she also emphasizes the possibilities for "self-**healing**" in the aftermath of serious illness. Appropriately, *The Cancer Journals* evokes the image of the Amazon, a heroic female figure who appears throughout Lorde's works. Criticizing the social pressures that force many cancer patients to adopt the "mask of prosthesis" or to undergo reconstructive surgery, Lorde envisions a troop of single-breasted women storming Congress to protest carcinogenic cattle feed and other health threats. She similarly targets dangerous products of modern culture in "The American Cancer Society or There Is More Than One Way to Skin a Coon," a satiric poem from her 1974 book *New York Head Shop and Museum*.

The long title essay in Lorde's 1988 *Burst of Light* collection should be read in conjunction with *The Cancer Journals*. Weaving together diary entries from 1984 through 1987, "Burst of Light" describes the metastasis of her breast cancer into the liver cancer that eventually caused her **death** in 1992. Lorde wrote several of the diary segments in Europe, where she frequently taught, lectured, and underwent homeopathic therapy. Orlanda Women's Press in Berlin published a German translation of *The Cancer Journals*. Interviewed by Orlanda editor Dagmar Schultz, Lorde described breast cancer as a "feminist concern," even for the "twenty-one-year-old feminist who doesn't know it is."

See also Autobiography; Black Feminism; Body; Lesbianism; *Zami: A New Spelling of My Name*

Works About

Alexander, Elizabeth. " 'Coming Out Blackened and Whole': Fragmentation and Reintegration in Audre Lorde's *Zami* and *The Cancer Journals*." *American Literary History* 6.4 (Winter 1994): 695–715.

Herndl, Diane Price. "Reconstructing the Posthuman Feminist Body Twenty Years after Audre Lorde's *Cancer Journals*." *Disability Studies: Enabling the Humanities*. Ed. Sharon L. Snyder, Brenda Jo Brueggemann, and Rosemarie Garland-Thomson. New York: Modern Language Association of America, 2002. 144–155.

Major, William. "Audre Lorde's *The Cancer Journals*: Autopathography as Resistance." *Mosaic: A Journal for the Interdisciplinary Study of Literature* 35.2 (June 2002): 39–56.

Perreault, Jeanne. " 'That the Pain Not Be Wasted': Audre Lorde and the Written Self." *A/B: Auto/Biography Studies* 4.1 (Fall 1988): 1–16.

Schultz, Dagmar. "Audre Lorde on Her Cancer Illness." *Conversations with Audre Lorde*. Ed. Joan Wylie Hall. Jackson: University Press of Mississippi, 2004. 132–141.

Joan Wylie Hall

CARTIER, XAM WILSON (1949–)

Xam Cartier is an artist, dancer, and writer in whose work issues of **identity**, **family**, creativity, and the personal and social liberation of women are explored. Cartier's distinctive lyrical writing style is characterized by the use of a **jazz** music motif and elements of jazz performance style rendered in prose.

Cartier was born in 1949 in St. Louis, where she was raised as the only child of a postal worker and a guidance counselor. Cartier attended Catholic school and earned a B.A. in English from the University of Missouri at Columbia. She moved to San Francisco in the mid-1970s and worked with a local ABC radio affiliate. Later, she became a producer with an ABC television affiliate. Cartier worked as a legal secretary while writing her first novel, *Be-Bop, Re-Bop* (1987). Subsequently, Cartier became a writer-in-residence at Wayne State University and Oberlin College.

Cartier's two novels both have protagonists who are creative, intelligent, and highly individualistic African American women. Her work presents women who possess and express rich and creative inner worlds. Both narratives are nonlinear and exemplify a spirit of improvisation characteristic of modern jazz. This improvisational characteristic serves to liberate the texts from prescriptive narrative forms. This liberation from form also serves to highlight the personal liberation of Cartier's female characters through jazz.

Cartier's prose style makes use of vernacular speech and rhythmic patterns in language. Cartier employs word-play, sly wit, and puns in her creative use of language. The story lines of her texts are interwoven with interludes of fantasy that also invoke the melodic departures in improvisational jazz.

Be-Bop, Re-Bop, Cartier's first novel, has an unnamed woman as its protagonist who is searching for identity and self-fulfillment. The protagonist is alienated from her family of origin as she strives to become self-referencing and to begin to define "family" from within her own worldview. The character uses jazz music and family relationships shaped through the mutual experience of jazz to make sense of her life. *Be-Bop, Re-Bop* explores the social experience of **motherhood** and femaleness in an urban environment and the various difficulties, struggles, and indignities of material poverty that women suffer.

Muse-Echo Blues (1991), Cartier's second novel, has as its protagonist a composer/pianist named Kat and her historical, Jazz Age counterpart Kitty. Time and space are traversed throughout the narrative as Kat attempts to overcome composer's block by having consort with jazz musicians of the past such as **Billie Holiday**, Lester Young, and Sarah Vaughn, via her counterpart Kitty. Kitty attempts to resolve personal and relationship issues as both women simultaneously struggle to thrive in their respective environments with the powerful, mediating force of jazz.

Literary critics have compared Cartier's work to that of **Ishmael Reed** because of its postmodern sensibility that also invokes elements of the black aesthetic. Cartier herself has been influenced by **Amiri Baraka** and has noted his *Blues People* (1963) as especially significant. Cartier has also described the **literature** of **Richard Wright** and Chester Himes to have impacted her work.

Works By

Be-Bop, Re-Bop. New York: Available Press, 1987.
Muse-Echo Blues. New York: Harmony Books, 1991.

Works About

Peterson, V. R. "Xam Cartier: Writing Rhythms." *Essence* (June 1992): 54.
Smith, Valerie. "Dancing to Daddy's Favorite Jam." *New York Times*, December 13, 1987, 12.
Waller, Rayfield Allen. " 'Sheets of Sound': A Woman's Bop Prosody." *Black American Literature Forum* 24 (Winter 1990): 791–802.

Kimberly Black-Parker

CAUCASIA

Danzy Senna's debut novel *Caucasia* (1998) centers on Birdie and Cole, daughters of a black father and a white "blue-blooded" mother who are activists in the **civil rights movement** in Boston in the 1970s. The sisters share a bond that is highlighted by their creation of a private language, Elemeno. Elemeno speakers are described as chameleons; the girls' mixed **race** causes them to create fictional identities to more easily navigate their polarized environment. Despite their sisterly bond, however, their race complicates their relationship and ultimately leads to their separation. Birdie appears white like her mother, whereas Cole appears black like her father, and this is the basis for much internal and external conflict.

While the girls are originally home-schooled because of their mother's fear of racism, they are eventually placed in a Black Power school, Nkrumah, where Cole fits in easily and Birdie encounters racism. Racial prejudices are embraced by the **family**: Birdie's father is distant from her and makes attempts at racial IQ testing on the girls; Cole's mother does not know how to do her hair; their maternal grandmother favors Birdie over Cole; and their father's black girlfriend favors Cole over Birdie. When the parents decide to separate, they split the children according to color: Cole moves to Brazil with her father and his girlfriend, where he hopes to find greater racial equality than in America, and Birdie is left behind with her mother. When Birdie's mother flees with Birdie, the two spend four years on the road, one of which is spent in a women's commune, where her mother has a lesbian affair. They eventually end up in New Hampshire, where Birdie's ambiguous coloring allows her to "pass" for Jewish as Jessie Goldman and where her mother returns to relationships with men.

The novel is narrated by Birdie, and it is her **identity** that propels the story. Birdie is not so much concerned with growing up female in a male-centered society but rather with growing up mixed in what seems to be a divided world of only white or black. When a young white girl is kidnapped, Birdie is made to feel at risk, because she is taught that only white girls are desired, and while she does not see herself as white, others do. Throughout, Birdie resolves that she will be reunited with her sister, and it is their bond that highlights the significance of their shared gender in the development of identity.

Birdie and Cole's names are symbolic. Their father theorizes that American **mulattos** are the canaries of coal mines, sent to gauge how poisonous the environment is. He believes his children are the first generation of canaries to survive. *Caucasia* may be read as Senna's canary, sent into the literary world to see if a book about young girls of mixed race can survive in a white male world. *Caucasia* not only has survived; it has received much critical acclaim.

See also Passing

Works About

Boudreau, Brenda. "Letting the Body Speak: 'Becoming' White in *Caucasia*." *Modern Language Studies* 32.1 (Spring 2002): 59–70.

Harrison-Kahan, Lori. "Passing for White, Passing for Jewish: Mixed Race Identity in Danzy Senna and Rebecca Walker." *MELUS* 30.1 (Spring 2005): 19–48.

Hunter, Michele. "Revisiting the Third Space: Reading Danzy Senna's *Caucasia*." *Literature and Racial Ambiguity*. Ed. Teresa Hubel and Neil Brooks. Amsterdam: Rodopi, 2002. 297–316.

Millian Arias, Claudia M. "An Interview with Danzy Senna." *Callaloo* 25.2 (Spring 2005): 447–452.

Deirdre Fagan

CHASE-RIBOUD, BARBARA (1939–   )

In a review of a work on Barbara DeWayne Chase-Riboud's sculpture, Wayne Anderson writes that her artwork opens "eyes to see more in primitive art than its primitiveness–and more primitiveness in today's societies than one is wont to admit" (110). The observation also provides a good insight into her **poetry** and **fiction**.

The sixty-seven-year-old visual and literary award winner adapts the elements of her resume–woman, African American, artist, international traveler, and thinker–to probe the tender underside of contemporary consciousness. Her novels and poems force discussions about **race**, racism, gender, sexism, and other human boundaries. Her descriptive prose and insightful dialogue compel readers to move beyond traditional assumptions in **history** and human relations. Readers are in effect forced to think about the *holes* in what is often portrayed as knowledge or **beauty**.

Chase-Riboud seeks to create the kind of epiphany she experienced during her first visit to Egypt during the early 1970s. After artistic studies in the United States and Europe, she discovered a new aesthetic, that many of the notions about the universality of Western concepts of art and beauty excluded a grasp of African and other non-European cultures. The author's novels often juxtapose the ideas and actions of people of European ancestry with those of African, especially women. An average reader might wonder whose culture is more primitive.

Chase-Riboud was born to Charles Edward and Vivian May West in 1939 Philadelphia, when the United States and Europe were about to enter a war that changed the dynamics of political and economic power on the planet. Racial segregation was strong then, even in a major northern metropolis, but after the war in 1945, blacks gained small victories in civil rights. By the mid-1950s, the social climate in Philadelphia improved enough so that Chase-Riboud's early talent for visual art could be nurtured.

In her elementary school years, music, art, and **literature** were already a fascination. She played the piano, sculpted, and wrote poetry before and during high school. After graduation, Chase-Riboud went to Temple University. In 1957, she earned a fine arts degree (B.F.A.) from the university's Tyler Art School.

Her career path seemed set, and as many times since, awards opened Chase-Riboud's paths toward greater achievement and opportunities. She received a John Hay Whitney Fellowship that same year to study art in Rome.

The international exposure took her global. She showed work throughout Europe, the Middle East, Africa, and the United States on a regular basis for the next twenty years. Rome also led her to expand her vision and grasp of sculpture. Upon her return to the United States, the experience pushed her toward graduate studies at Yale, where she earned a masters (M.F.A.) in 1960.

Chase-Riboud has said several times in interviews that she is not an expatriate, but after Yale, the sculptor decided to live in Paris. She continues to live in the city of light and Rome, which reflects a trend found in her writing to blur the human-drawn lines between nations and cultures.

Another motivation for her settling in Paris was her 1960 marriage to Marc Edward Riboud, a photojournalist. The now-divorced couple has two children. In 1981, she married Sergio Tosi.

Chase-Riboud credits the end of her first marriage as the spur for her writing career. *From Memphis to Peking*, published in 1974, was her first book. The poetry collection muses on the author's real-life experiences in Egypt and Communist China. A second collection, *Portait of a Nude Woman as Cleopatra* (1987), won the 1989 Carl Sandburg Prize for best American poet. The lengthy narrative poem imagines a dialogue between Marc Antony and Cleopatra about a Rembrandt portrait of a nude.

Chase-Riboud does not separate her visual art from the literary. Both are rooted in a passion to make the public rethink issues of race and gender. Her first novel, **Sally Hemings** (1979), is an account of a three-decade romantic relationship between Thomas Jefferson and his slave Sally Hemings. The book drew controversy and praise enough to establish her credentials as a novelist and garnered the Janet Heidinger Kafka Prize for the best book by an American woman in 1979.

A second saga, *Valide: A Novel of the Harem* (1986), is about the 1741 kidnap of a Creole woman by Algerian pirates. They sell her as a slave to Sultan Abdulhamid I, which marks her entry into the harem world in Topkapi palace in Istanbul. The vivid glimpse into the self-indulgent and treacherous sexual and political pecadillos of the eighteenth-century Ottoman Empire follows the woman through the harem ranks. When her son becomes sultan, she is made valide, the highest position for a woman in the kingdom.

Echo of Lions, a third novel, published in 1989, was inspired by the true nineteenth-century struggle of Joseph Cinque and the African slaves freed aboard the *Amistad*. Chase-Riboud later sued Steven Spielberg, whom she claimed used her book as the basis for his 1997 film. The suit over *Amistad*, as the movie was called, was settled for an undisclosed amount out of court.

A sequel to *Sally Hemings*, based on the real life of Harriet Hemings, one of the children Jefferson is thought to have fathered, was titled *The President's Daughter*. The 1995 novel tells how Harriet on her twenty-first birthday, in 1822, leaves Monticello for New York. Her light skin gives her the **freedom** to pass as white. The protagonist becomes an archetypal tragic **mulatta**. She is tortured by the fear her lie might be discovered. At the same time, her psyche is torn by the pain of living between two races. What seems an option for liberation soon becomes a noose that tightens as she journeys to London, Paris, and Florence.

Chase-Riboud's latest novel, **Hottentot Venus: A Novel** (2003), reveals the bizarre tale of Sarah Baartman, a South African woman whom French scientists dissected and displayed as "proof" that Africans were the missing link in the Great Chain of Life. The narrative prods the reader to consider the depth of human cruelty and economic exploitation. In the end, as with most of her works, the reader might wonder where to find civilization.

Works By

Echo of Lions. New York: HarperCollins, 1989.
Hottentot Venus: A Novel. New York: Doubleday, 2003.
Portrait of a Nude Woman as Cleopatra. New York: HarperCollins, 1987.
Sally Hemings: A Novel. New York: Penguin, 1979.

Works About

Anderson, Wayne. "Looking at Sculpture Darkly: The Sculpture of Barbara Chase-Riboud." *Art Journal* 59.3 (Autumn 2000): 110–112.
Cohen, Roger. "Judge Says Copyright Covers Writer's Ideas of a Jefferson Affair." *New York Times,* August 15, 1991, C13.
"Review of *Sally Hemings.*" *New York Times,* October 28, 1979, 14.
Trescott, Jacqueline. "The Hemings Affair: The Black Novelist and Jefferson's Mistress." *Washington Post,* June 15, 1979, B1.

Vincent F. A. Golphin

CHESNUTT, CHARLES WADDELL (1858–1932)

It is due to the determination of two free black women that we owe the existence of Charles Waddell Chesnutt and his writings. In 1856, Chloe Sampson and Ann Chesnutt joined an exodus from Fayetteville, North Carolina, to Cleveland, Ohio, fleeing the increasingly unstable slaveholding **South.** Sampson was attended by her daughter, Ann Maria (c. 1832–1871), whose father is believed to be white slaveholder Henry E. Sampson. In turn, Chesnutt was accompanied by her son, Andrew Jackson Chesnutt (1833–1920), one of seven children conceived with Waddell Cade, a prosperous white tobacco farmer who supported the **family.** The journey made a match, and Ann Maria and Andrew were married on July 27, 1857, in Cleveland.

Ann Maria exemplified the commitment to education and civil rights that would prevail in her family. In the South she had been whipped for violating laws that outlawed the educating of enslaved blacks. Andrew, in turn, exemplified the **work** ethic and ambition his famous son would inherit. Following the Civil War, in which Andrew served as a teamster, the family returned to Fayetteville, where he immediately opened up a grocery, assisted by his father, then becoming a county commissioner and justice of the peace. Not surprisingly, the family participated in the establishment of the Howard School, which Chesnutt would attend.

With the death of Ann Maria in 1871, it was necessary that Chesnutt begin teaching in order to continue his education and assist in supporting his five younger siblings. By 1872 he was teaching in various rural areas of North Carolina and had also seen his first short story in print in a Fayetteville paper. However, while this period marked the end of Chesnutt's formal education, he continued his studies of piano, organ, and foreign languages independently. His experience and ambition no doubt facilitated his return to Fayetteville in 1877, first as an instructor, then as first assistant vice principal in the State Colored Normal School. The following year he married fellow teacher Susan Perry, daughter of prosperous barber Edward Perry.

By 1881 Chesnutt was the father of two daughters (Ethel, born 1879, and Helen, born 1881) and principal of the Normal school. Yet he remained ambitious, writing in his journal: "I want fame; I want money; I want to raise my children in a different rank of life from that which I spring from." Studying accounting on the side, in 1883 he resigned his position to become a financial columnist for the *New York Mail and Express* and employee of the famed Dow, Jones and Company. While his New York residence was short-lived, it facilitated his return to Cleveland as an employee of the Nickel Plate Railroad Company. In 1884 his family and new son, Edwin, born the year before, joined him there.

Interestingly Chesnutt's desire for financial security and advancement is matched in this era by his development and success as a writer. Simultaneously studying law and writing for *Family Fiction Magazine*, in 1887 Chesnutt passed the state bar exam, secured a job in the offices of Henderson, Kline, and Tolles, and saw his dialect short story, "The Goophered Grapevine," published in the *Atlantic Monthly*. The following year, he opened his own legal practice and again graced the magazine's pages—the first African American to do so—with "Po' Sandy." For Chesnutt, literary success and financial success were not inseparable: Both were facilitated by his residence in the North, and both enabled him to challenge racism. However, in later years he would be critiqued by other authors for what they saw as his bourgeois lifestyle, ignoring the ways in which he had struggled to achieve such security for himself and his family.

As a writer of "local color realism" in dialect form, Chesnutt proved popular with editors and readers of the *Atlantic Monthly*, securing his literary reputation. However, editors remained unaware of Chesnutt's **race** until 1891, when he informed them, and then chose to keep the fact from their readers. By this time Houghton Mifflin had already approached Chesnutt about a short story collection, and many of his *Atlantic Monthly* publications of the 1890s, a period of significant literary productivity for Chesnutt, were published in 1899 as *The Conjure Woman*. This was followed the same year by *The Wife of His Youth and Other Stories of the Color Line* and, in 1900, by the novel *The House behind the Cedars*, enabling Chesnutt to become a full-time writer in time for the birth of his fourth child, Dorothy, in 1901.

The House behind the Cedars followed the lead of two earlier, unpublished Chesnutt manuscripts, *Mandy Oxendine* and *Rena Walden* (which Chesnutt revised into his first novel). As the titles suggest, at the center of these tales are strong female characters. Hindered by the racial designations that determine their economic and educational opportunities, heroines in both attempt to "pass" as white in order to advance themselves. While *Mandy Oxendine* is uneven in quality, it is notable for the ways in which it complicates the trope of the tragic **mulatta**, presenting a resilient and pragmatic heroine who defies sentimental **stereotypes**. This exploration of the nuanced negotiations of color, caste, and racism, and the ways in which they determine character in conventionally unanticipated ways, is the most consistent of Chesnutt's thematic concerns.

Unfortunately, many readers did not respond as well to Chesnutt's writings on racial inequality as they had to his earlier dialect stories. When sales figures for *The Marrow of Tradition*, published in 1901 and concerning a North Caroline race riot, were less than Chesnutt expected, he returned to balancing his legal practice and his writing career. Likewise, the editorial revisions demanded to make the novel *The Colonel's Dream* (1905) less controversial were distasteful to Chesnutt. Nonetheless, the reviews of his novels, as well as his presence at Mark Twain's seventieth birthday party in 1905, suggest his acceptance as a talented writer by other American luminaries. No doubt Chesnutt's inability to secure production or publication of his play (*Mrs. Darcy's Children*) and publication of the novels *The Rainbow Chasers*, *Paul Marchand*, and *The Quarry* influenced his decision to concentrate on shorter works and political activism. Notably, Chesnutt led the protest that would result in the famously racist film *The Birth of a Nation* (1915) being banned in Ohio.

By the second decade of the twentieth century, Chesnutt could claim that he had achieved the desire he articulated in 1881 for fame, money, and success for his children. Chesnutt himself was president of the Cleveland Council of Sociology and a member of the Cleveland Chamber of Commerce, the National Arts Club, and the Rowfant Club (a respected literary organization) and had received an honorary degree from Wilberforce University. All four of his children had graduated from university, Edwin from Harvard, and Helen and Ethel from Smith. All followed their father's lead as educators. Ethel and Edwin both taught at Tuskegee, Edwin then completing a degree in dentistry. Helen and Dorothy both taught in the Cleveland public school system. Helen, who would write a biography of her father, also taught at Western Reserve University, followed by a master's from Columbia, while Dorothy pursued graduate work at the University of Chicago. That all of his daughters had such opportunities speaks to the commitment to female education in Chesnutt's family, evident both in the naming of the Ann Chesnutt Middle School in Fayetteville after his sister, as well as the careers of numerous other female family members in the field.

While Chesnutt's publications were scant through the 1910s and 1920s, his reputation was on the rise. In 1924 famed African American **film** director Oscar Micheaux adapted *The House behind the Cedars*, while in 1927 *The Conjure Woman* was reissued. In 1928, the same year he testified before the U.S. Senate about matters of integration, he was recognized with the National Association for the Advancement of Colored People (NAACP) Spingarn Medal for his "pioneer work as a literary artist depicting the life and struggle of Americans of Negro descent, and for his long and useful career as scholar, worker, and freeman of one of America's greatest cities" (*Postscript* 176). This solidified Chesnutt's productive relationship with the organization and its magazine, the *Crisis*. In 1932, the same year Micheaux released a second adaptation of Chesnutt's work, titled *Veiled Aristocrats*, the author died at his home in Cleveland. Despite the NAACP's assessment of his contributions, only in the late twentieth century have readers been finally able to appreciate the true scope of Chesnutt's oeuvre and complexity of his thinking. This is a result of the publication of his novels previously deemed unprintable, due to their political content, as well as his journals and letters. Other unpublished manuscripts deposited in the Chesnutt Collection, Fisk University Library Special Collections, await publication.

Works By

Charles W. Chesnutt: Stories, Novels, and Essays. New York: Library of America, 1992.
Collected Stories of Charles W. Chesnutt. New York: Signet, 1992.
The Colonel's Dream. New York: Doubleday Page, 1905.
The Conjure Woman. Boston: Houghton Mifflin, 1899.
The Conjure Woman and Other Conjure Tales. Durham, NC: Duke University Press, 1993.
The House behind the Cedars. Boston: Houghton Mifflin, 1900.
The Journals of Charles Chesnutt. Durham: Duke University Press, 1993.
Mandy Oxendine. Urbana: University of Illinois Press, 1997.
The Marrow of Tradition. Boston: Houghton Mifflin, 1901.
Paul Marchand, Free Man of Color. Jackson: University Press of Mississippi, 1998.
To Be an Author: Letters of Charles W. Chesnutt, 1889–1905. Princeton, NJ: Princeton University Press, 1997.
The Wife of His Youth and Other Stories of the Color Line. Boston: Houghton Mifflin, 1899.

Works About

Andrews, William L. *The Literary Career of Charles W. Chesnutt.* Baton Rouge: Louisiana State University Press, 1980.
Charles Chesnutt Digital Archive. faculty.berea.edu/browners/chesnutt/.
Chesnutt, Helen M. *Charles Waddell Chesnutt, Pioneer of the Color Line.* Chapel Hill: University of North Carolina Press, 1952.
Ellison, Curtis W., and E. W. Metcalf, Jr. *Charles W. Chesnutt: A Reference Guide.* Boston: G. K. Hall, 1977.
Heermance, J. Noel. *Charles W. Chesnutt: America's First Great Black Novelist.* Hamden, CT: Archon Books, 1974.
Keller, Frances Richardson. *An American Crusade: The Life of Charles Waddell Chesnutt.* Provo, UT: Brigham Young University Press, 1978.
Postscript: The Crisis 35 (August 1928): 176.
Render, Sylvia Lyons. *Charles W. Chesnutt.* Boston: Twayne Publishers, 1980.
Thompson, Cliff. *Charles Chesnutt.* New York: Chelsea House, 1992.

Jennifer Harris

CHILDREN'S AND YOUNG ADULT LITERATURE

Women authors and illustrators and representation of the lives and experiences of girls and women have always been a large and important, if not equal, part of African American **literature** for young people. Since the 1960s, children's literature has been studied and taught as two distinct but overlapping categories: children's literature as meant for pre- and elementary school children, and young adult literature designed for readers approximately ten through eighteen years of age. However, preadolescents often read young adult titles, and people of all ages enjoy illustrated texts and fairy or folk tales. Just as there are no fixed boundaries regarding the age of the audience, young readers are multiracial and multicultural. Critics and educators have come to define African American children's and young adult literature as a body of **work** produced by African American authors and illustrators that appeals to a wide variety of readers. A feminist overview of this body of work cannot make such clear-cut distinctions based on gender; African American men as well as women have offered accurate and empowering representations of girls and women in the books they write for children and young adults, in which females of all ages survive, even under the most oppressive and discriminatory conditions, and emerge as heroines who conquer conflicts and emerge triumphant. However, just as African Americans are still underrepresented in the wider field of children's literature, African American women are still a minority in children's publishing, and school curricula rarely include their work. This entry will therefore focus on women's contributions, even as it discusses how girls and women are represented in African American children's and young adult literature by women and men.

The genre of children's literature emerged as a distinct and independent form only in the late eighteenth century, although young people from all cultures have always appropriated oral and written narrative for their entertainment. Literature for young people grew as a broad generic category in England and the United States through the nineteenth century and encompasses a wide range of work, including acknowledged classics of world literature, picture books and easy-to-read stories, **poetry**, novels and short **fiction**, and the lullabies, fairy tales, fables, folk songs, and folk narratives from oral tradition. African American children's and young adult literature began to be written in the late 1880s. Because literature for children and young adults has typically been seen as a "lesser" genre of literary or artistic endeavor, or simply as part of the **domestic** sphere, it has also been seen as an appropriate genre for women to write in. Many classic books for young people were written by women, such as Louisa May Alcott's *Little Women,* and the first African American to contribute to the genre was a woman; **Amelia E. Johnson** printed a number of religious tracts for children through the 1880s, including an eight-page magazine, *The Joy.* She later published novels such as *Clarence and Corinne; or, God's Way* (1890), which were overtly religious and didactic and featured male and female characters who did not transgress gender roles and restrictions and were often white. Also published in the early era of African American children's literature, poet **Paul Laurence Dunbar**'s *Little Brown Baby* (1895) is a germinal text in the genre. A collection of dialect poems that celebrate African American folk culture, *Little Brown Baby* was meant to delight girls and boys even as it shows African American people and culture in a positive light. Other early pieces have only recently been recovered, among them Leila A. Pendleton's *An Alphabet for Negro Children* (n.d.).

After the turn of the century the development of an educated African American middle **class** demanded and could support this growing body of literature for its youth. Recognizing the urgent need for characters black children could respect and emulate, W.E.B. Du Bois, the only black founder of the National Association for the Advancement of Colored People (NAACP), experimented with "Children's Numbers," an annual issue of the NAACP's the *Crisis* (1919–1926), which he edited. These issues were so successful that, in 1920, Du Bois, along with business manager Augustus Granville Dill and literary editor **Jessie Redmon Fauset**, established the *Brownies' Book* (1920–1921). Aimed at children aged six to sixteen, the magazine incorporated a variety of popular forms, such as fiction, folk and fairy tales, poetry, **drama**, biography, and photography and illustrations by African American artists and offered nonreligious, nondidactic entertainment that infused black youth with a sense of self-worth and impressed upon them the importance of education.

Du Bois and Dill pioneered another important form of African American literature for young people, biographies of African Americans for children and young adults, and women were the more prominent writers of these works. Elizabeth Ross Haynes's *Unsung Heroes* (1921) and Julia Henderson's *A Child's Story of Dunbar* (1921) are important early works in this genre. Haynes published twenty-two biographies, and many of them introduced children to African Americans rarely depicted in their school texts, figures that are now well known, such as **Frederick Douglass** and Harriet Tubman. Ellen Tarry (1906–   ) also published biographies, among them *Young Jim: The Early Years of James Weldon Johnson* (1967) and *Pierre Toussaint: Apostle of Old New York* (1981) as well as picture books and her **autobiography**, *The Third Door* (1955). Born in Alabama, Tarry moved to New York in 1929 and formed associations with many of the people who figured prominently in the **Harlem Renaissance**, most notably Johnson, **Claude McKay**, **Langston Hughes**, and **Countee Cullen**. These men made significant contributions to African American children's and young adult literature; for example, Hughes's *The Dream Keeper* (1932) is a classic collection of poetry for children, as is *Golden Slippers* (1941), an anthology of poetry by Dunbar, Cullen, Hughes, and Johnson edited by Arna Bontemps. However, their work overshadows that by their female contemporaries, critically and in the classroom, out of all proportion, and Tarry is rarely mentioned in comparison to her male counterparts. Bontemps created an extensive body of work, including biography, fiction, and poetry that helped African American children's literature gain widespread acceptance and offered children positive African American role models. Carter G. Woodson followed Bontemps in publishing biographies of notable African Americans and later founded the Associated Press, which continues today. A contemporary of Woodson and Bontemps, playwright Shirley Lola Graham Du Bois (1896–1977) receives little critical attention, but her biographies of African Americans for young adults are important contributions to the field, including *There Once Was a Slave: The Heroic Story of Frederick Douglass* (1947), *Booker T. Washington, Educator of Hand, Head, and Heart* (1955), and *The Story of Phillis Wheatley: The Poetess of the American Revolution* (1949).

Through its development, librarians, classroom teachers, and postsecondary educators and administrators have worked to ensure that African American children's and young adult literature flourishes. During her thirty-seven-year career with the New York City Public Library as a children's/young adult librarian, storyteller, and administrator, Augusta Baker (1911–1998) added appropriate books to the Library's collections, encouraged authors and illustrators, and worked with publishers to get this literature produced and distributed. The first black librarian to hold an administrative position in the Library, by 1961 Baker was in charge of children's policies and programs in all eighty-two branches. Widely influential, she worked with schools and **community** groups, was a consultant for the television program *Sesame Street*, and taught courses on storytelling and children's literature. Following Baker, African Americans Glyndon Greer and Mabel McKissack, members of the American Library Association, established the Coretta Scott King Award for African American authors and illustrators of books for children and young adults in 1969. Also in the late 1960s, the Council on Interracial Books for Children began holding contests in order to identify and support promising young artists. These awards have garnered wide professional and public recognition for many of their winners; for example, the first winner of the Council Award, Kristin Hunter's (**Kristin Hunter Lattany**) *The Soul Brothers and Sister Lou* (1969), sold over a million copies.

As it became an established genre through the 1940s into the 1960s, African American children's and young adult literature reflected contemporary social and cultural consciousness. Early texts, such as Jesse Jackson's *Call Me Charley* (1945) and Lorenz Bell Graham's *South Town* (1958), offered an integrationist approach to racial difference and the problems of bigotry. These novels tried to instill in all children a social conscience that afforded awareness and tolerance of racial difference without taking into account social and cultural, and often gendered, difference. Since the late 1960s, African American children's literature is most often "culturally conscious," with its focus on African American perspective and setting. Over the last thirty years, dozens of African American writers have gained wide popularity through a variety of works that present the range of African American experiences. They entertain and educate even as they offer historically accurate portrayals of African American lives, female and male, and a tradition of resistance to racism and discrimination. Today, African American children's and young adult literature addresses the concerns of feminism, including perceptions of gender and **sexuality**, in illustrated texts for young children that offer a visual schemata that will inform **identity** formation and in texts for older readers that provide rich literary material for exploring the issues and dilemmas of human experience.

Illustrated texts have the ability to offer visually positive gender and cultural role models, and African American children's literature is particularly reliant on the ability of illustrations to depict girls and women as individuals; many women authors and artists have gained prominence in the field. Writer **Eloise Greenfield** recognizes the importance of pictures by stipulating that her work be illustrated by African American artists. Some authors depict the African roots of African American culture and identity even as they show females as empowered individuals, such as Muriel Feelings with her Swahili abcediary and counting book *Jambo Means Hello* (1974) and *Moja Means One* (1971), illustrated by Tom Feelings; Verna Aardema's editions of African fables, such as *Why Mosquitoes Buzz in People's Ears* (1976), illustrated by Leo and Diane Dillon; and John Steptoe's African Cinderella story, *Mufaro's Beautiful Daughters* (1988). African motifs empower African American girls and women and help tell their stories in Carole Byard's illustrations for **Camille Yarbrough**'s *Cornrows* (1979), and Faith Ringgold's African-inspired quilts and tankas (fabric sculptures) are predominant in her *Tar Beach* (1991) and *Dinner at Aunt Connie's House* (1993). In this latter book, Ringgold relies on the African American **history** that informs many picture books, as her young protagonist imagines historical figures such as Harriet Tubman and Mary McLeod Bethune coming to dinner with her extended family. Illustrated children's books provide readers of all ages with positive images of African American females and the rich diversity of their history and culture and offer girls a literary experience that can aid in understanding and interpreting life experience.

Similarly, an awareness of literature by African American female authors and with African American girls and women in prominent and empowered roles is vital for both male and female young adults. The portrayal of female roles in adolescent fiction is important because it provides an environment for young adults to see the results of decisions made by characters and to evaluate their ideas and behaviors. How girls and women interact in those fictional situations can shape thinking by reinforcing **stereotypes** or by promoting alternative views. Key issues in young adult literature, issues that are often ignored in books that feature male protagonists, are girls' acceptance of their bodies' changes and growth patterns and themes of relationships with those of the same sex and of the opposite sex and with parents. Because ethnographic settings—religious, cultural, racial—affect the development of identity, the African American adolescent female must be able to find role models and affirmation in young adult literature, while others should be able to understand the uniqueness of her situation. African American young adult fiction has grown into a vast and widely popular body of work since the 1960s, and a good deal of that work offers positive and empowering role models for girls and young women. Two of the most popular and best known writers of young adult fiction are African American women. **Mildred D. Taylor** and **Virginia Hamilton** have written some of the most compelling female protagonists in the genre. Taylor's Logan family series follows the growth and maturity of Cassie Logan in *Song of the Trees* (1975), *Roll of Thunder, Hear My Cry* (1976), *Let the Circle Be Unbroken* (1981), and *The Road to Memphis* (1990). Set in segregated rural Mississippi, these historical novels tell the story of this brave and appealing character from a female and African American perspective. Hamilton offers several unique adolescent black heroines in the stories of Teresa in *Sweet Whispers, Brother Rush* (1982), Sheema in *A Little Love* (1984), Talley in *A White Romance* (1987), and the interracial Buhlaire Simms in *Plain City* (1993). Other writers deal with themes about and alongside race, such as **Rosa Guy**'s exploration of a lesbian relationship between two black teenagers in *Ruby* (1976), Sharon Bell Mathis's *Listen for the Fig Tree* (1973) about the experience of a blind girl, or **Joyce Carol Thomas**'s short stories representing the African American teenager in the midst of various ethnic groups in *A Gathering of Flowers* (1990). Thomas's earlier works *Marked by Fire* (1982) and *Water Girl* (1986) trace the stories of Abby and Amber, respectively, as they struggle to find themselves as young black women. Guy depicts a different black American tradition with her Caribbean young adult heroine in *My Love, My Love; or, The Peasant Girl* (1985). Others who have dealt with lives of African American females include **Alice Childress**'s *A Short Walk* (1981) and *Rainbow Jordan* (1982); Jacqueline Woodson's examination of interracial friendships and incest in *I Hadn't Meant to Tell You This* (1994); and Walter Dean Myers, who presents the story of Didi in *Motown and Didi: A Love Story* (1984), one of his many Harlem novels. African American children's and young adult literature performs essential functions in the growth and development of its female readers, and its benefits can go far past simply making visible the formerly absent African American girl or woman. It can enable them to define themselves as empowered females in terms of their cultural and their national heritage, and its importance to the wider projects of African American feminism cannot be overemphasized.

Works About

Baker, Augusta. "The Changing Image of the Black in Children's Literature." *Horn Book* 51 (February 1975): 79–88.

Harris, Violet J. "African American Children's Literature: The First One Hundred Years." *Journal of Negro Education* 59.4 (1990): 540–555.

Johnson-Feelings, Dianne. *The Best of "The Brownies' Book."* New York: Oxford University Press, 1996.

Monseau, Virginia, and Gary Salvner. *Reading Their World: The Young Adult Novel in the Classroom.* Portsmouth, NH: Boynton/Cook, 1992.

Park, Carole A. "Goodby Black Sambo: Black Writers Forge New Images in Children's Literature." *Ebony* (November 1972): 60–70.

Roethler, Jacque. "Reading in Color: Children's Book Illustrations and Identity Formation for Black Children in the United States." *African American Review* 32.1 (1998): 95–105.

Rollock, Barbara. *Black Authors and Illustrators of Children's Books.* New York: Garland, 1988.

Sims, Rudine. *Shadow and Substance: Afro-American Experience in Contemporary Children's Fiction.* Urbana, IL: National Council of Teachers of English, 1982.

Tolson, Nancy. "Making Books Available: The Role of Early Libraries, Librarians, and Booksellers in the Promotion of African American Children's Literature." *African American Review* 32.1 (1998): 9–16.

Whaley, Liz, and Liz Dodge. *Weaving in the Women Transforming the High School English Curriculum.* Portsmouth, NH: Boynton/Cook, 1993.

Roxanne Harde

CHILDRESS, ALICE (1916–1994)

Alice Childress was born in Charleston, South Carolina, on October 12, 1916. Her time in this city of such historical and cultural significance to African Americans was limited to less than a decade, however, as her parents' marriage dissolved in 1925. Childress moved at this time with her mother Florence to Harlem, yet another bastion of racial significance. Mother and daughter moved in with Childress's maternal grandmother, Eliza Campbell White. Living in a female-run household during her adolescent years surely helped to mold Childress into the confident playwright, actress, and novelist that she was to become. There was no doubt in Childress's mind, as she grew to adulthood, that a woman could take care of herself financially and emotionally and be successful in any endeavor into which she threw her passions. Indeed, such a way of life surely seemed natural to Childress as she matured.

Childress found not only the natural strength of women in her **home**; she also found a personalized education in the arts as her grandmother made specific efforts to expose the young woman to the cultural and artistic offerings of New York City. Childress's grandmother was also adamant about fostering the spiritual life of her granddaughter, taking her to church services regularly and exposing her to the trials that accompanied the lives of the poorest of the poor. In this way Eliza White weaved into Childress's consciousness the idea that human beings had certain duties to help one another, especially those less fortunate. Even though life was not luxurious at the home in which Childress was growing up, she was raised to realize that there is always someone in greater need than one's self and that that person must indeed be aided. Childress took these lessons of the poor with her and often used themes of the struggling poor in her written works.

Childress's mother and grandmother also encouraged the young woman's voracious appetite for books. Despite all of the intellectual stimulation she had received at home—or perhaps *because* of just that—Childress dropped out of high school before entering her senior year. It was also at this time that both

Childress's mother and grandmother died, leaving Childress to completely take over the orchestration of her own life much sooner than she had anticipated this would happen. Still, the two older women had prepared Alice Childress for independence and for continued intellectual growth. Surely, despite her grief, Childress must have been confident that she could proudly and without hesitation follow in the footsteps of these two important women. Sometime during this point in Childress's life, she married the actor Alvin Childress. It is known with certainty that Childress gave birth to her only child, a daughter named Jean, in 1935. Because of Childress's own efforts to keep such information secret, it is not known with certainty when Alice and Alvin Childress married and consequently divorced, although the divorce occurred fairly early in Jean's life. Childress remarried, to the musician Nathan Woodard, in 1957.

Childress began an acting and theater career before she began her writing career. In 1943 she began acting for the American Negro Theater in Harlem. It was also for this company that she wrote her first play, a one-act piece titled *Florence*, in 1949. Remarkably, this play was written overnight when Childress took up what she saw as a challenge presented by fellow actors—including Sydney Poitier—at the American Negro Theater. The actors had argued that it was impossible to write a good play in one night. What Childress presented to them the next morning was not only a good play but also a springboard to her writing career. *Florence*'s central themes of racism, sexism, and economic disadvantage became critical themes to all of the work that was to follow from Childress's pen. In this first play Childress presents the reader/audience with the mother of Florence, an African American woman trying to make it in the acting world. In a conversation with the white Mrs. Carter, whom Florence's mother had perceived would be willing to help Florence's acting career, the mother is accosted with both racism and sexism, which leads her to an almost physically angry moment but also to the realization that she must urge on her daughter's dreams. It is surely no mistake that this first play of Childress's contains both autobiographical elements and feminist elements. Childress's life to this point had been a struggle, but it had also been incredibly buoyed by the unquenchably fiery spirits of her mother and grandmother.

Despite Childress's passion for her work and her moderate success, she still found herself in need of other jobs to assist in supporting both herself and her daughter. She toiled at a variety of menial jobs during this period of her life, including **domestic work**. Much of this work experience became of thematic importance to her future writing, including the 1956 work *Like One of the Family . . . Conversations from a Domestic's Life*, which Childress dedicated to her grandmother. This nondramatic work consists of a series of conversational vignettes told by Mildred, an African American domestic worker employed by a white **family**, to her friend Marge. Each vignette or conversation is light and rhythmic in tone but quite serious in the social themes revealed and dissected. Childress's Mildred is an independent woman, despite her economic station in life. She is a proud woman who insists on being treated as a human being and who insists on cherishing her own basic sense of self-worth.

Childress is careful to fashion Mildred as much of a feminist both philosophically and practically as were in actuality the women who raised Childress herself.

The year before *Like One of the Family* appeared, Childress's play *Trouble in Mind* was produced, although it did not find its way to publication until 1971. *Trouble in Mind* deals head on with racism in the theater. The premise of this play revolves around a white producer putting on a play about lynching that contains stereotypical depictions of its black characters. Although all of the black actors become increasingly incensed with the portrayals, it is the veteran actor Wiletta Mayer who eventually takes the lead in protesting the racist treatment by refusing to continue the farce. Wiletta begins by trying to placate the other actors, urging them to do what they must for the theater. Eventually she experiences a transformation and sees that she must be a leader in the movement against racism. Once again, Childress focuses on a woman character as the strong character and as the one willing to fight for what is just. It takes little imagination to hypothesize as to why it took so long to get the play published.

Trouble in Mind is certainly not the only controversial piece that Childress penned. The play *Wedding Band* was written in 1966 and first performed at the University of Michigan. This play did not have a major production, however, until 1972, when it was "introduced" at the New York Shakespeare Festival. The play was not published until 1973. *Wedding Band* delves into the world of interracial **love** and marriage, an issue that was absolutely controversial in the 1960s and continued to be a heated topic throughout much of the rest of the twentieth century. *Wedding Band* introduces the audience/reader to the white Herman and the black Julia, who live together as husband and wife even though they are forbidden to legally marry in their home state of South Carolina. It is Julia who rises up most against the racism tainting her and Herman's relationship, and it is Julia who urges Herman to be morally stronger. It is also Julia who tries to transcend the bonds of racism by caring for the extremely racist mother of Herman when she falls ill. Julia survives Herman, upon whose **death** the reader/audience becomes painfully aware of the legal ramifications for Julia, who is for all practical purposes a widow without any of the sustaining benefits. While the theme of interracial relationships is foremost in this play, Childress's signature feminism also surfaces here as the character Julia represents so many facets of the strong woman fighting against so many social odds.

Another controversial play of Childress's, *Wine in the Wilderness*, was produced in 1969. This play takes Childress's controversies to another level, in that she deals with socioeconomic prejudices among African Americans themselves. Again we have a strong woman character, only this time the strong woman is perhaps an unlikely version of strength. Tomorrow Marie Fields, nicknamed Tommy, is a down-to-earth African American woman of the 1960s who not only respects her roots and her elders but also delights in an almost childlike way in the comfort she feels in her own skin. Unlike the other characters in the play, who are much better educated and who fancy themselves a better **class** than she, Tommy represents reality. While the other characters set about using Tommy as an actual model to help the artist Bill complete a work representative of the many faces of the **race**, Tommy is indeed the true face of the race, although the others are too caught up in their own importance and in their estimation of themselves as better human beings than is Tommy to notice what truths she represents. To her credit, Tommy, as undereducated as she is, is the only character to truly do credit to the race. While there are elements of sexism as well as classism evident in this play, Childress also cunningly brings out the problems that some women create for each other. The other woman in the play, Cynthia, is highly educated; in fact, she is a social worker, who should know better than to perpetuate social **stereotypes**. Cynthia does finally realize what she is doing by the end of the play, but it is the earth-mother-type Tommy who shows the most grace and strength in the play. One senses that Childress has a deep respect for the "common woman" and that she wishes to uplift that woman to her rightful place in the world.

Childress worked also in the genre of **fiction**, writing three novels for adolescents and one novel for adults. Her first two young adult novels, *A Hero Ain't Nothin' but a Sandwich* (1973) and *Rainbow Jordan* (1981), deal with African American teenage boys struggling with what life has dealt them; namely, both Benjie of *A Hero* and Rainbow of the second novel live in single-parent households, with their biological fathers missing. While Childress could have used these novels to further her use of strong women characters, she instead tends to make the mothers in these two novels ineffectual. Both mothers leave their sons turning to others for love, guidance, and support. To her credit, Childress does represent the character to whom Rainbow turns for such things as a foster mother, but it still remains interesting to note the change in feminist approach to her **literature** with these two novels.

Childress uses more ineffective parents in her third and final young adult novel, *Those Other People*, published in 1989. Here, however, the main character, Jonathon, finds difficulties with his parents because of his homosexuality. Clearly, Childress's focus in this novel is quite different from that in her other young adult novels. It may be that her intent in all three novels was to focus specifically on how adults in general fail children, perhaps in the hopes of awakening a sense of accountability in parents, especially in parents of at-risk children. If this was indeed the author's intention, then these novels also naturally have a place in the feminist themes of Childress's work overall.

Childress's only adult novel, published in 1979, is *A Short Walk*. Here the author's feminist themes definitely shine through. Racism and sexism become central struggles for the main character, Cora, who, in her abbreviated life through the first four decades of the twentieth century, lives with all of the racial and gender tensions that these decades so insistently dealt out. Cora is the quintessential twentieth-century black woman, struggling to be her own person and to embrace all that she feels is her due as a human being. Though her mother dies giving birth to Cora, Cora is blessed with a circle of women who help her form her own inner strength throughout her life.

Childress rounded out her adult canon with the 1987 play *Moms: A Praise Play for a Black Comedienne*. Childress wrote this musical in collaboration with her husband, Nathan Woodard, as a tribute to Jackie "Moms" Mabley. In the last years of her life, Childress worked on, but never published, the story of her maternal great-grandmother, Ani Campbell, who was abandoned as an infant and adopted and raised by a white woman. It seems fitting that Childress would have ended her work by drawing once again upon the facts of the lives of the women in her own family, the women who had taught her to be a strong and independent woman herself.

Both Childress's personal and professional lives were richly satisfying. She traveled extensively, she won awards, she lectured on her craft and her ideals, she had the good fortune to enjoy her family, and she had the talent to leave behind a canon of work that will allow her to live on indefinitely. Childress was intent on illustrating the problems that black women particularly faced in contemporary life; she was equally intent on celebrating the strength of black women in most of her writings.

Childress died of cancer on August 14, 1994, in New York City, four years after her daughter also died of cancer.

See also Children's and Young Adult Literature; Drama

Works By

The African Garden. Black Scenes. Ed. Alice Childress. Garden City, NY: Doubleday, 1971. 137–145.

Florence: A One Act Drama. Masses and Mainstream 3 (October 1950): 34–47.

A Hero Ain't Nothin' but a Sandwich. New York: Coward, McCann, and Geoghegan, 1973.

Let's Hear It for the Queen. New York: Coward, McCann, and Geoghegan, 1976.

Like One of the Family . . . Conversations from a Domestic's Life. Brooklyn: Independence, 1956; Boston: Beacon Press, 1986.

Mojo: A Black Love Story. Black World 20 (April 1971): 54–82.

Moms: A Praise Play for a Black Comedienne. New York: Flora Roberts, 1993.

Rainbow Jordan. New York: Coward, McCann, and Geoghegan, 1981.

A Short Walk. New York: Coward, McCann, and Geoghegan, 1979.

String. New York: Dramatists Play Service, 1969.

Those Other People. New York: G. P. Putnam's Sons, 1989.

Trouble in Mind: A Comedy-Drama in Two Acts. Black Theater: A Twentieth Century Collection of the Work of Its Best Playwrights. Ed. Lindsay Patterson. New York: Dodd, Mead, 1971. 135–174.

Wedding Band: A Love/Hate Story in Black and White. New York: Samuel French, 1973.

When the Rattlesnake Sounds. New York: Coward, McCann, and Geoghegan, 1975.

Wine in the Wilderness: A Comedy-Drama. Plays by and about Women. Ed. Victoria Sullivan and James Hatch. New York: Vintage, 1973. 379–421.

The World on a Hill. Plays to Remember. Ed. Henry B. Maloney. Toronto: Macmillan, 1970. 103–125.

Works About

Brown-Guillory, Elizabeth. *Their Place on the Stage: Black Women Playwrights in America.* Westport, CT: Greenwood Press, 1988.

Buck, Claire, ed. *The Bloomsbury Guide to Women's Literature.* New York: Prentice Hall, 1992.

Jennings, LaVinia Delois. *Alice Childress.* New York: Twayne, 1995.

Smith, Karen Patricia. *African-American Voices in Young Adult Literature.* Metuchen, NJ: Scarecrow Press, 1994.

Terry D. Novak

CHINABERRY TREE, THE

Jessie Redmon Fauset's third novel, *The Chinaberry Tree: A Novel of American Life*, first published by Stokes in 1931, is set within the middle-class black **community** of Red Brook, a quintessential New Jersey "small town." One-third of the way into the novel, it becomes obvious that the main character, Melissa Paul, is embarking upon a doomed relationship with a local man, the politically and socially conservative Malory Forten. Wrongly, Melissa believes that her parents were married. Actually, she was fathered by Malory's father, who had an affair with Melissa's mother. If consummated, the relationship between Malory and his half sister would be incestuous.

The narrator manipulates the reader, heightening anxiety: Will the couple marry and perpetuate the ultimate sexual taboo? Or will they find out the painful truth beforehand? We wait until the day of their planned elopement to find out. Allusive of ancient Greek tragedy, the novel's tension rises; with self-conscious, theatrical language, the narrator asks: Will *The Chinaberry Tree* end in tragedy or in comedy? Men are held responsible for the cruelties that flourish in Red Brook. Melissa's mother was not an enthusiastic participant in the adulterous relationship with Sylvester Forten; the man simply "wouldn't leave Judy [Melissa's mother] alone." Men are possessive and greedy, keen for sexual "hunting" and for female deference. Melissa's cousin, Laurentine Strange, is shunned because she is illegitimate, the product of a relationship between a black woman and an irresponsible, married white man, Colonel Halloway. Men seek to transform women into commodities; one particularly aggressive youth, Harry Robbins, would "do anything to possess" Melissa. Even the novel's ultimate hero, Asshur Lane, has a hectoring propensity to patronize women, telling Melissa, endlessly, that "you must be good."

In addition to the problems caused by males with wandering eyes, Fauset's characters must also deal with "this nonsense about color." Although the novel conveys disgust at the second-class status of blacks—a system of oppression symbolized by a bizarre restaurant incident, when Malory and Melissa are not allowed the full choice of desserts—the novel is more preoccupied with **class** differences between African Americans. Some blacks are left behind by those who progress to be doctors and successful dressmakers. One young black woman, Pelasgie Stede, profoundly resents having to serve better-off blacks; her only pleasure is to gossip about the misfortunes of the middle-class blacks, resenting them more than whites. One such misfortune is a public fight between Robbins and Lane over Melissa. A racist newspaper editor sees the fight and plans to report it, to cause embarrassment for the Strange **family**. Only a sort of bribe from a businessman who is courting Laurentine prevents him from running the story. But blacks can be bribed, too. The Stranges' old black gardener, Stede, always asserts, amusingly, that he never asks for food, but he hints that he wants food with evident imploring. Tipping Stede results in "ample and satisfactory rewards"—good service. Red Brook, then, is not a community but a gathering of self-interested individuals. When the network of mutual back scratching breaks down, or when male urges work to fracture marital unions, it is the female characters who suffer.

See also Comedy: American Style; Plum Bun

Works About

Feeney, Joseph J. "Greek Tragic Patterns in a Black Novel: Jessie Fauset's *The Chinaberry Tree*." *College Language Association Journal* 18 (1974): 211–215.

Gale, Zona. Foreword to *The Chinaberry Tree: A Novel of American Life*, by Jessie Redmon Fauset. College Park: McGrath Publishing, 1969. vii–viii.

Knopf, Marcy Jane. Foreword to *"The Chinaberry Tree" and Selected Writings*, by Jessie Redmon Fauset. Boston: Northeastern University Press, 1995. ix–xxix.

Lupton, Mary Jane. "Bad Blood in Jersey: Jessie Fauset's *The Chinaberry Tree*." *CLA Journal* 27.4 (1984): 383–392.

Sylvander, Carolyn Wedin. *Jessie Redmon Fauset: Black American Writer*. Troy, NY: Whitston, 1981. 193–229.

Kevin De Ornellas

CHOSEN PLACE, THE TIMELESS PEOPLE, THE

Paule Marshall's second novel, *The Chosen Place, the Timeless People* (1969), has been lauded as one of the most significant novels by a black women in the twentieth century. Critics such as Hortense Spillers and Barbara Christian find the novel's examination of oppressed peoples in Western culture to be both artful and culturally regenerative. Through the intersection of three main characters from three different ethnic backgrounds, Marshall reveals how facing and integrating an oppressive past into the present offers the only available hope for a restorative future.

Set in the fictional West Indian island of Bourne, *The Chosen Place* uses geography as a major actor on its characters. Bournehills, a district within Bourne, becomes the "chosen place," and the **community** of Bournehills represents the "timeless people." Marshall uses the tight-knit native community to represent cultural tradition and heritage lacking to her main characters Merle, Saul, and Harriet. Each character encounters the place and people with their own life struggles, and each meets a different end as a result of their experience.

Merle Kinbona symbolizes the most hopeful character in the story. Black, educated, and well traveled, Merle returns to Bourne facing a failed marriage to an African man and a troubled sense of herself. She meets white Jewish American anthropologist Saul Amron, who wants to help the Bournehills community. Harriet, Saul's wife, represents the mainstream white culture and thus the larger oppressive society.

As each character interacts with the inhabitants of Bournehills, each is confronted with a living **memory** of **slavery** and oppression embodied in the people and the place itself. Merle ultimately learns the importance of confronting her heritage in order to both heal herself and help her people; the end sees her traveling to Africa to find and repair her fractured **family**. Saul also finds **healing** by facing the oppressive **history** of Jewish people but does not find as clear a resolve as Merle. Critics tie this inconclusiveness to his status as a white, although Jewish, man, thus linking him to the dominant and oppressive culture. Harriet's status as a white woman without minority affiliation leads her to face her heritage of **violence** and domination. As a result, she finds little solace in the past and ultimately commits suicide.

The Chosen Place, the Timeless People is an expansive novel exploring the personal, social, cultural, and historical implications of slavery and domination. Unlike her other well-known novels, ***Brown Girl, Brownstones*** and ***Praisesong for the Widow***, Marshall's second novel extends beyond one protagonist to three main characters plus a larger island community. She locates regenerative hope in the integration of the past into the present and places female characters squarely in positions of power for healing. She links personal wholeness with social healing and continues to emphasize the role cultural memory plays in individual and social unity.

See also Ancestor, Use of

Works About

Christian, Barbara. *Black Women Novelists: The Development of a Tradition, 1892–1976*. Westport, CT: Greenwood Press, 1980.

——. "Trajectories of Self-Definition: Placing Contemporary Afro-American Women's Fiction." *Conjuring: Black Women, Fiction, and Literary Tradition*. Ed. Marjorie Pryse and Hortense J. Spillers. Bloomington: Indiana University Press, 1985. 233–248.

DeLamotte, Eugenia. "Women, Silence, and History in *The Chosen Place, the Timeless People*." *Callaloo* 16.1 (1993): 227–242.

LeSeur, Geta. "'Read Your History, Man': Bridging Racism, Paternalism, and Privilege in Paule Marshall's *The Chosen Place, the Timeless People*." *CLA Journal* 44.1 (2000): 88–110.

Meyer, Adam. "Memory and Identity for Black, White, and Jew in Paule Marshall's *The Chosen Place, the Timeless People*." *MELUS* 20.3 (1995): 99–120.

Olmstead, Jane. "The Pull to Memory and the Language of Place in Paule Marshall's *The Chosen Place, the Timeless People* and *Praisesong for the Widow*." *African American Review* 31.2 (1997): 249–267.

Schenck, Mary Jane. "Ceremonies of Reconciliation: Paule Marshall's *The Chosen Place, the Timeless People*." *MELUS* 19.4 (1994): 48–60.

Spillers, Hortense J. "Chosen Place, Timeless People: Some Figurations on the New World." *Conjuring: Black Women, Fiction, and Literary Tradition*. Ed. Marjorie Pryse and Hortense J. Spillers. Bloomington: Indiana University Press, 1985. 151–175.

Verge, Shane Trudell. "Revolutionary Vision: Black Women Writers, Black Nationalist Ideology, and Interracial Sexuality." *Meridians: Feminism, Race, Transnationalism* 2.2 (2002): 101–125.

Laura Baker Shearer

CHRISTIANITY

Feminist literary engagements with Christianity explore the vibrant belief systems of African American women and their communities of faith. While black Christian women are often associated with intense religious fervor and self-sacrifice in American popular culture, gynocentric representations seek to uncover the deeper complexities of "church mothers" and "preacher's wives." An overwhelming number of texts in genres ranging from **spirituals** and **slave narratives** to **protest tradition literature** and speculative **fiction** further accentuate black women's efforts to assert themselves within male-dominated ecclesiastic institutions and racially prejudiced scriptural interpretations. Indeed, the church functions not only as a transcendent source of hope and liberation but as a site of worldly contestation in literature. Central to African American feminist renderings of faith *and* doubt are the woman's ability to claim her own religious **identity**, to associate freely with a fellowship of believers, and to testify in her own voice of her personal relationship with God.

Christian beliefs and practices are a vital component of eighteenth- and nineteenth-century black women's writing. **Phillis Wheatley**'s collection *Poems on Various Subjects, Religious and Moral* (1773) reflects the strong influence of her Puritan upbringing as a slave in New England. Replete with Christian allusions and classical imagery, Wheatley's odes and funeral elegies emphasize Calvinist doctrines of election and grace as preached by Rev. George Whitefield, the English Methodist evangelist of the First Great Awakening (1720–1750).

Several of Wheatley's poems such as "On Being Brought from Africa to America" and "To the University of Cambridge, in New England" have been criticized by African American literary scholars for suggesting that the conversion of Africans to Christianity was a beneficial consequence of **slavery**. Yet recent critics have highlighted the subversive nuances in Wheatley's brief writing career. The poet's reference to Exodus in her letter to Samson Occom, for instance, casts slave owners as Egyptians, while aligning African slaves with the chosen people of Israel. Such a framework provides readers with a new perspective on Wheatley's lyrical reflections on "Egyptian gloom" and the "sable race" awaiting earthly deliverance.

The ambiguities of Wheatley's verse call attention to the multifaceted role that Christianity has played in African American **history** and culture. Biblical concepts such as the "curse" of Ham in Genesis 9:25 and Paul's epistle to the Ephesians were narrowly interpreted by white clergy during the colonial and antebellum eras to indicate that people of African descent were intended by God to be enslaved and, therefore, should obey their "earthly masters" (Eph. 6:5). Yet the same Bible that was used by proslavery advocates as an instrument of racial oppression and patriarchal domination was also embraced by African American women as a source of hope. The Second Great Awakening (1800–1840), with its emphasis on the experiential elements of conversion and revivalism, saw an overwhelming number of African American slaves and free people convert to Christianity, particularly through Baptist and Methodist denominations that initially supported the antislavery cause.

It is the spirituals, or "Sorrow Songs," of these early black Christians that constitute one of the formative "texts" of African American religious expression. With the spirituals, slaves offered their own interpretations of biblical scripture through West African rhythms, harmonies, and antiphonal "call and response" patterns. The collective anonymity of these songs, with their improvised lyrics and revisions, further demonstrates the edifying creativity of slave **religion**. While no one can claim whether or not the voices that composed "Been in the Storm So Long" or "Run, Mary, Run" belonged to women, religious songs such as these initiated the pioneering strains of Christian sisterhood that would sustain black women in their struggle not only to survive slavery but, in some cases, to work actively for its abolition.

Likewise, the concept of Christian egalitarianism was a widespread theme in slave narratives and abolitionist pamphlets that condemned the hypocritical action (and inaction) of white Americans who supported the enslavement of human beings. While **Frederick Douglass**, Josiah Henson, David Walker, and others incorporate faith-based critiques in their narratives, **Harriet Jacobs**'s **autobiography** *Incidents in the Life of a Slave Girl* (1861) explores the nuances of a black female slave's efforts to uphold her own religious moral standards and protect her children from a life of servitude.

Jacobs, writing under the pseudonym Linda Brent, speaks forthrightly about her master's mental cruelty and his relentless attempts to sexually abuse her. The slaveholder's harassment intensifies, she notes, after he joins an Episcopal church. Jacobs rejects his proslavery religious ideology in her narrative, but she is also very careful to distinguish her beliefs from her beloved grandmother's rigid ideas about virtue. Where her grandmother regards her efforts to escape as an abdication of her obligations as a good Christian mother, Jacobs boldly asserts that discontent with slavery is more in keeping with Jesus Christ's liberating ministry. Such a theology leads the author of *Incidents* to praise a number of women, black and white, from southern as well as northern states, whose activity on behalf of abolition reflects true Christian benevolence in Jacobs's view.

In the North, independent black churches began to develop as early as 1794 with the formation of the African Methodist Episcopal (AME) Church in Philadelphia. While the challenge for black men to become ordained ministers was difficult, it was nearly impossible for black women preachers to be recognized as such. The autobiographies and conversion narratives of feminist evangelists such as **Jarena Lee**, **Zilpha Elaw**, Amanda Berry Smith, **Rebecca Cox Jackson**, and **Julia A. J. Foote** offer critical glimpses into the increasingly codified hierarchies of power within black religious institutions.

The Life and Religious Experience of Jarena Lee (1836) vividly describes the free-born northern woman's personal struggle against sin and her conflicts with AME church leaders who prohibited her from preaching. After waiting eight years to be given permission to speak before her fellow congregants, Lee interrupted a visiting minister's sermon on Jonah with an exhortation in which she compared herself with the Old Testament prophet who ran away from his calling. Afterward, with the support of AME bishop Richard Allen, Lee began her work as an official—though not licensed—itinerant preacher.

Likewise, the words of evangelist **Sojourner Truth** underscore the social and political implications of male-centered readings of the gospel, particularly when such readings were used to deny women full citizenship rights. Truth put forth her own biblical exegesis in a speech to the Women's Rights Convention in 1851 when she pointed out that Christ was not born of man but of God and a woman. Convinced that their actions were sanctioned by God, Lee, Truth, and other black female exhorters put the authority of the scriptures before the laws of man.

Frances E. W. Harper combines women-centered religious beliefs with late-nineteenth-century racial uplift ideology in her essays, **poetry**, and novels. Grounded in Christian morality, her writing addresses issues such as suffrage, education, temperance, and the responsibility of the black middle **class** after Emancipation. One of her earlier poems, "Ethiopia" (1853), invokes the "Ethiopian Prophecy" of Psalm 68, a verse frequently interpreted by African Americans to signify the redemptive mission of the African race. Written after the Civil War, another poem, "Moses: A Story of the Nile" (1869), revisits the story of Exodus within the context of the abolition of slavery.

The same year that Harper published her well-known novel ***Iola Leroy*** (1892), fellow women's rights activist and educator **Anna Julia Cooper** published ***A Voice from the South***. This compilation of political essays and speeches casts the collective potential of African Americans in the language of spiritual awakening. In the essay "Womanhood a Vital Element in Regeneration and Progress of a Race," Cooper emphasizes the importance of Christian women as a civilizing force within society. Prefiguring twentieth-century literary works such as **Pauline Hopkins**'s novel *Contending Forces* (1900) and **Jessie Redmon Fauset**'s *There Is Confusion* (1924), Cooper's essays call upon black women, in particular, to take a more dynamic role in providing social, political, and religious guidance to their communities.

While the feminist religious discourse of racial uplift extends well into the twentieth century, Christianity acquires new dimension in the imaginative works of the **Harlem Renaissance**, the Great Migration, **Black Nationalism**, **womanism**, and contemporary fiction. In keeping with W.E.B. Du Bois's celebration of the preacher in *The Souls of Black Folk* (1903), literary renderings of the church after 1900 often focus on the **sermon tradition** and the leadership of black male clergy. Such is the case with texts such as **James Weldon Johnson**'s *God's Trombones: Seven Negro Sermons in Verse* (1927), **Zora Neale Hurston**'s novel *Jonah's Gourd Vine* (1934), and **Richard Wright**'s short story "Fire and Cloud" (1938). Just as common, however, are fictional works that explore the lives of churchwomen. The institutional silencing of mothers, wives, sisters, and daughters is countered in these texts by the overwhelming bodily presence of women in sacred spaces and by women-centered extra-ecclesial activities and auxiliary groups.

Nella Larsen's novel ***Quicksand*** (1928) offers a gendered perspective of Christianity from four different pews: a black southern college, an urban chapel, a storefront revival, and a rural southern church. The narrative's main focus is on the educated New Negro woman's quest for identity and sexual freedom in the 1920s. Yet Larsen often conceptualizes the social anxieties of protagonist Helga Crane through her inability to find a satisfying church "home." Issues of **race**, **class**, **sexuality**, and religion converge in the tragic ending of this Harlem Renaissance novel. An unsatisfying marriage to an Alabama preacher draws Helga into a domestic quagmire, and in her misery, she renounces God and the black church.

Zora Neale Hurston frequently incorporates religion into her representations of black folk life in the **South**. While most of her characters are avowed Christians, heroines like Janie from ***Their Eyes Were Watching God*** (1937) nurture religious identities that subvert societal norms. In other instances, characters from Hattie Tyson in *Jonah's Gourd Vine* to Docia Boger's mother in the short story "Black Death" (1995) employ **conjuring**, "root work," and other non-Christian practices as alternative modes of empowerment within black communities. Hurston's literary works are supported by the research assembled in ***Mules and Men*** (1935) and *The Sanctified Church*—a collection of folktales, sermons, and spiritual autobiographies gathered by Hurston in the 1930s. *The Sanctified Church* anticipates stories such as **Gloria Naylor**'s ***Mama Day*** (1989) and the character Baby Suggs in **Toni Morrison**'s ***Beloved*** (1987) by depicting the formidable power of holy women like Mother Catherine, a preacher whose matrifocal religion combines Christianity with African-influenced beliefs.

African Americans who fled the South during the Great Migration of World War I and again in the 1940s and 1950s brought their distinctive forms of worship to the urban North. The primary setting for **James Baldwin**'s semi-autobiographical novel *Go Tell It on the Mountain* (1953) is a Pentecostal storefront church made up of southern migrants who have relocated to Harlem. While the spiritual conversion of adolescent protagonist John Grimes is central to the story, Baldwin demonstrates the complex ways in which John's identity as a black Christian male is explicitly and implicitly shaped by his spiritual elders. Indeed, the novel explores the turbulent religious heritage of John's mother and aunt in rich detail. Baldwin scrutinizes the faith that these women maintained in spite of the religious doctrines and social customs that sought to stifle their independent spirit.

After the publication of his first novel, Baldwin began writing *The Amen Corner*, a play first performed in 1955. The drama follows the life of storefront preacher Sister Margaret Alexander and her struggle to maintain her power as a religious leader in the face of domestic strife. The manner in which Sister Margaret wields Christian authority in her home has been described as tyrannical at times, much like Mama Lena Younger from **Lorraine Hansberry**'s drama *A Raisin in the Sun* (1959). Recent critics have taken a closer look at the ways in which the fiercely protective Christian **love** of these matriarchs can operate as a dangerous and debilitating force in black families, even as it is claims to hold them together.

Criticisms of Christianity become more combative with the advent of the **Black Arts Movement** during the 1960s. As the faith-based activism of the **civil rights movement** transformed into the assertive nationalism of Black Power, poets like **June Jordan** and **Nikki Giovanni** condemned the oppressive image of God and other divine beings as white and male. Particularly fascinating in this regard is the poetry of Chicago-born **Carolyn Rodgers**. She began her career with an imaginative tirade against her mother's self-righteous morality in "Jesus Was Crucified, or It Must Be Deep" (1969) but offered contrition after her own religious conversion in later poems such as "and when the revolution came" and "how i got ovah II/It Is Deep II" (1975).

The work of **Alice Walker** highlights female characters whose forthright criticisms of the Christian church act as signposts of their own spiritual transformation. This is especially true in early works such as the short story "Roselily" (1973) and the novels *Meridian* (1976) and the Pulitzer Prize–winning *The Color Purple* (1982). In *The Color Purple*, Celie expresses her feelings about the anxiety and shame of physical, psychological, and sexual abuse in diarylike "letters" to God. Although Celie is a devoted churchgoer, her intimate relationship with **blues** singer Shug Avery forces her to reconsider her beliefs about God and the patriarchal religious **community** that labels her race and gender as inferior.

Walker, along with Carolyn Rodgers, makes a distinction between her critique of oppressive Christian doctrine and her high esteem for the racial wisdom and strength of black churchwomen. Indeed, Walker describes her agenda in works like *The Color Purple* as womanist. As explained in her collection *In Search of Our Mothers' Gardens: Womanist Prose* (1983), the term characterizes feminists of color who cherish women's creativity, emotional flexibility, and strength. Walker's understanding of womanism is not necessarily Christian, yet it is grounded in a sense of spiritual wholeness and connectivity with all of humanity. In the last two decades, black Christian womanist theologians have adopted Walker's gynocentric concept as a way to distinguish their interpretation of the Bible and their focus on black women's religious heritage.

Recent works of African American literature engage Christianity through experimental forms and genres. **Octavia Butler**'s speculative novels *Parable of the Sower* (1993) and *Parable of the Talents* (1998), use Christian stories to frame a multicultural community's fight to survive in a dystopian future. Butler's black heroine in the **Parable series** is the daughter of a minister who creates "Earthseed"—a belief system that embraces the idea that God is manifested through change. Likewise, contemporary women's fiction places a strong emphasis on the distinctive religious culture of African Americans, particularly in stories such as ***Baby of the Family*** (1989) by **Tina McElroy Ansa** that concentrate on black **family** life in the South. The popularity of inspirational themes in current fiction is further indicated by developments such as BET Books' "New Spirit" black Christian fiction and romance imprint. The female protagonists in "New Spirit" novels, including Jacqueline Thomas's *The Prodigal Husband* (2002) and Angela Benson's *Awakening Mercy* (2002), emphasize the power of Christian faith, forgiveness, and reconciliation in overcoming personal struggle.

Works About

Bassard, Katherine Clay. *Spiritual Interrogations: Culture, Gender, and Community in Early African American Women's Writing*. Princeton, NJ: Princeton University Press, 1999.

Cannon, Katie Geneva. *Katie's Canon: Womanism and the Soul of the Black Community*. New York: Continuum, 1995.

Gilkes, Cheryl T. *"If It Wasn't for the Women...": Black Women's Experience and Women's Culture in Church and Community*. Maryknoll, NY: Orbis Books, 2001.

Harris, Trudier. *Saints, Sinners, Saviors: Strong Black Women in African American Literature*. New York: Palgrave, 2001.

Higginbotham, Evelyn Brooks. *Righteous Discontent: The Woman's Movement in the Black Baptist Church, 1880–1920*. Cambridge, MA: Harvard University Press, 1993.

Qiana J. Whitted

CIVIL RIGHTS MOVEMENT

There is not a large body of imaginative **literature** that takes the civil rights movement as its subject. **Alice Walker**'s *Meridian* (1973) and **Toni Cade Bambara**'s *The Salt Eaters* (1980) center on women who were movement workers. Walker and Bambara also wrote short stories with characters involved in or influenced by civil rights activism. Thulani Davis's *1959* (1992) explores a young girl's coming of age just as the movement arrives in her Virginia town. Some novels are inspired by or evoke specific events in the movement, such as **Bebe Moore Campbell**'s *Your Blues Ain't Like Mine* (1992) and **Toni Morrison**'s *Song of Solomon* (1977). Anthony Grooms's recent and powerful novel *Bombingham* (2001), set in the summer and city of the Sixteenth Street Church bombing that killed four young girls, suggests that African American writers will continue to revisit the movement for their subject matter. In the meantime, however, the dominant genre of civil rights movement literature is the memoir or personal **autobiography**. Through autobiographical accounts (as well as oral narrative and biography), we learn of the women who organized boycotts, desegregated schools, participated in sit-ins, marched in demonstrations, taught in **freedom** schools, and assisted local residents in registering to vote. From the Montgomery bus boycott to the Black Power movement of the 1960s, women played important roles in the fight for civil rights, and in some of those roles, their participation surpassed that of African American men.

African American women have always been involved in the struggle for freedom, and the civil rights movement was no exception. The traditionally heralded "opening" to the movement was the Montgomery bus boycott. The two recognizable figures from that event are **Rosa Parks**, the woman who was arrested for refusing to give up her bus seat, and the new young minister in town, Martin Luther King, Jr. Although King is generally seen as the architect of the boycott and the leader of the movement itself, it was actually women who organized, initiated, and carried out the boycott.

As an active member in and secretary for the National Association for the Advancement of Colored People (NAACP), Parks was well aware of the ramifications involved in challenging segregation laws. The roots of Parks's act of civil disobedience also came from her training at the Highlander Folk School, a school for social activists that was founded in the depression. The Monteagle, Tennessee, school was a model of interracial and progressive activism. In the fall of 1955, Parks attended a workshop on leadership directed by Septima Clark, one of the "mothers" of the movement who was a lifelong activist and trained many civil rights workers. Clark had been born in 1878 in South Carolina and became active in the NAACP as a young woman. In Charleston, Clark was involved in a successful petition drive to allow black teachers to **work** in the public schools and then pressed further for equal pay. She had a career as a teacher herself until she was fired for her political activities. In the 1950s, Clark was introduced to the Highlander Folk School and began attending and teaching workshops, often bringing others with her. Three months after Rosa Parks attended Clark's leadership workshop, the Montgomery bus boycott began.

When Parks was arrested, E. D. Nixon, head of the NAACP, and local ministers met to discuss how they could uses Parks's arrest to test segregation laws. In the meantime, the Women's Political Council, an organization of professional black women, sprang into action, and its president, Jo Ann Robinson, spent all night at Alabama State College mimeographing 35,000 handbills urging African Americans to stay off the buses on the following Monday. The flyers were distributed through black neighborhoods and networks during the weekend, and on Monday morning—and for many mornings after—empty buses drove through the city. Women also played a central role in maintaining the boycott for thirteen months. **Domestic** workers were a large part of the bus-riding population, and their willingness to walk to work, organize and ride in carpools, make arrangements with their white female employers for transportation, and attend mass meetings after a long day of work contributed greatly to the success of the boycott.

In addition to initiating legal challenges to segregation in public transportation, NAACP activism concentrated on school desegregation cases as well. Another early confrontation in the civil rights movement took place in Little Rock, Arkansas, in 1957 where nine black teenagers (six of whom were female) desegregated all-white Central High School. Daisy Bates, president of the Arkansas NAACP, was instrumental in leading the legal challenge to segregation and was adviser to the Little Rock Nine. Like Parks, Bates had long defied discrimination in both her personal and professional life. She and her husband owned the *Arkansas State Press*, which spoke out against police brutality, economic exploitation, and legal injustice.

While longtime activists and established organizations coordinated the battles fought at the dawn of the movement, the young people who were coming of age during those events stepped forward as college students. In the early months of 1960, student activism manifested itself in cities throughout the **South** in the form of sit-ins, boycotts, and demonstrations. **Anne Moody**, a student first at Natchez Junior College and later at Tougaloo College, worked with many civil rights organizations and participated in the sit-ins at Woolworth lunch counters. She tells of her civil rights activities in her powerful memoir *Coming of Age in Mississippi* (1968). At Fisk University in Nashville, Diane Nash attended workshops conducted by nonviolent theorist and activist James Lawson. As part of the Nashville Student Movement, Nash organized and participated in sit-ins and other nonviolent direct action that protested segregation in Nashville. After three months of student activism, 2,500 students and **community** members marched on City Hall in April 1960. Nash took the opportunity to ask Mayor Ben West if he personally felt that discrimination was wrong. Forced to respond to a question of ethics, the mayor agreed that discrimination was morally wrong. The morning newspapers reported the mayor's reply as support of desegregation, and relieved business leaders saw the opportunity to end the boycotts and sit-ins. As a consequence of the students' actions and Nash's probing questions, the Nashville lunch counters were soon serving their black patrons.

When college students began organizing sit-ins, it was Ella Jo Baker of the Southern Christian Leadership Conference (SCLC) who recognized their potential and called for a conference to bring the young people together. In

April 1960, the Student Nonviolent Coordinating Committee (SNCC) was born. Guided by Baker, the students created an organization that employed nonviolent direct action, grassroots organizing, and nonhierarchical leadership. Baker was a tremendous shaping influence on the student organization and was responsible for insisting that it remain independent of other civil rights organizations. Like Septima Clark, Baker had been involved in personal and collective resistance to oppression her entire life. She held numerous leadership roles in the NAACP throughout the 1930s and 1940s before resigning as its national director of branches in 1946. Baker criticized the organization's leadership for emphasizing membership numbers rather than participatory activities. A desire to see black people more directly involved in the fight for equality led to Baker's involvement in the Southern Christian Leadership Conference during the late 1950s. In 1957, Baker set up the SCLC's first office in Atlanta and traveled throughout the South during the group's first voter registration program. She repeatedly emphasized the need for group leadership and local organizing, putting her in conflict with those in the organization who upheld a hierarchical male ministerial leadership. It was Baker who advised SNCC to remain independent of other groups, who modeled egalitarian and group-based leadership, and who nurtured the students' empowerment through participatory democracy.

When SNCC arrived in Ruleville, Mississippi, in August 1962, Fannie Lou Hamer, a forty-four-year-old sharecropper, was among the first to attend meetings and attempt to register to vote. Although it was not Hamer's first act of resistance, it was the start of her political life. Hamer became a field secretary for SNCC, devoting her life to grassroots organizing and the fight for political and economic justice. She was cochair of the Mississippi Democratic Freedom Party (MDFP), which was formed to give black residents a political voice and to challenge the legitimacy of the all-white Mississippi delegation. The MDFP traveled to the 1964 Democratic Convention in Atlantic City, where Hamer rose to national prominence through her nationally televised, unforgettable testimony about the atrocities committed in Mississippi's attempts to keep black people disenfranchised.

The autobiographies and biographies that tell women's movement stories are among the most compelling, inspiring, and memorable texts in American literature. The leaders and activists mentioned here are only a few of the legion of women who fought for civil rights in large and small ways throughout the **history** of black people in America. While the conventional narrative of the civil rights movement represents it as a series of key events engendered by the charismatic and motivating male leaders, particularly ministers, a more accurate representation of the movement is emerging. Some of the most exciting research on the civil rights movement is directly focusing on the participation of women. Current scholarship suggests that the grassroots organizing tradition was the underlying foundation for the movement's successes; as the memoirs, oral narratives, and biographies confirm, at the heart of that organizing tradition were the movement's women.

Works About

Bates, Daisy. *The Long Shadow of Little Rock: A Memoir*. 1962. Fayetteville: University of Arkansas Press, 1987.

Beals, Melba Pattillo. *Warriors Don't Cry: A Searing Memoir of the Battle to Integrate Little Rock's Central High*. New York: Washington Square Press, 1994.

Clark, Septima Poinsette. *Ready from Within: Septima Clark and the Civil Rights Movement*. Navarro, CA: Wild Trees Press, 1986.

Crawford, Vicky L., Jacqueline Anne Rouse, and Barbara Woods, eds. *Women in the Civil Rights Movement: Trailblazers and Torchbearers, 1941–1965*. Bloomington: Indiana University Press, 1993.

Grant, Joanne. *Ella Baker: Freedom Bound*. New York: John Wiley and Sons, 1998.

Lee, Chana Kai. *For Freedom's Sake: The Life of Fannie Lou Hamer*. Urbana: University of Illinois Press, 1999.

Ling, Peter J., and Sharon Monteith. *Gender in the Civil Rights Movement*. New York: Garland, 1999.

Mills, Kay. *This Little Light of Mine: The Life of Fannie Lou Hamer*. New York: Penguin, 1993.

Moody, Anne. *Coming of Age in Mississippi*. 1968. New York: Laurel Books, 1997.

Parks, Rosa. *Rosa Parks: My Story*. New York: Dial, 1992.

Payne, Charles M. *I've Got the Light of Freedom: The Organizing Tradition and the Mississippi Freedom Struggle*. Berkeley: University of California Press, 1995.

Robinson, Jo Ann Gibson. *The Montgomery Bus Boycott and the Women Who Started It*. Knoxville: University of Tennessee Press, 1987.

Robnett, Belinda. *How Long? How Long? African American Women in the Struggle for Civil Rights*. New York: Oxford University Press, 1997.

Janelle Collins

CLAIR, MAXINE (1939–   )

For a woman who has spent most of her life *not* writing, Maxine Clair's literary achievements are remarkable. An award-winning poet, short-story writer, and novelist, she did not start writing until her forties, when she resigned her position as chief technologist at Children's Hospital National Medical Center in Washington, D.C. By this point, Clair, the mother of four, had divorced her husband. The pain of divorce inspired her to write. Seeking guidance, she mailed her poems to **Toni Morrison**, then an editor at Random House. Morrison advised that if she was serious about writing, Clair should read more **poetry**. Clair agreed and soon was publishing her work.

Clair's decision to write full-time came in 1980, during a long, soul-searching Caribbean vacation paid for by her IRS refund. Upon her return, she submitted all the poems she had ever written—six of them in total—to a free workshop at George Washington University. Soon after, while working part-time as a medical technologist, she earned her Masters of Fine Arts from American University and began teaching courses there. In 1988 her poetry collection *Coping with Gravity* was published, followed in 1992 by her **fiction** chapbook *October Brown*, which won Baltimore's Artscape Prize for Maryland Writers. In 1994, the interrelated story collection *Rattlebone* was published to rave reviews and won numerous awards, including the Chicago Tribune Heartland Prize for fiction and the American Library Association's Black Caucus Award. She wrote her most recent book, a 2001 finalist for the Hurston-Wright Legacy Award titled *October Suite*, on a Guggenheim Fellowship. Currently, Clair is a professor at George Washington University.

Both *Rattlebone* and *October Suite* are set mainly in Kansas during the 1950s, in a town like Clair's childhood **home**, where she grew up as one of nine children born to Lucy and Robert Smith. In this manner, she shares much with Irene, the young protagonist of *Rattlebone*, who, with her **family**, interacts in small, vivid, occasionally secret ways with the **community** at large. Like Irene, Clair formed close relationships with teachers—characters she revisits in her fiction. Intrigued by the fact that only single women were hired to teach in 1940s Kansas, she created the character of October Brown—an unmarried, much-gossiped-about schoolteacher who pursues an affair with Irene's father, James, in *Rattlebone*. The consequences of this affair are developed in *October Suite*, which chronicles October's choices to have James's baby and give it to her sister.

With an ear to the cadences of neighborhood life, Clair writes about choices that are sometimes discordant, sometimes harmonious to families, communities, perhaps even readers. Above all, Clair's characters, like the author herself, follow their own rhythms.

Works By

Coping with Gravity. Washington, D.C.: Washington Writers' Publishing House, 1988.
October Brown. Baltimore: Time Printers, 1992.
October Suite. New York: Random House, 2001.
Rattlebone. New York: Farrar, Straus, Giroux, 1994.

Works About

Liston, Richard. "Re-educating Maxine: Maxine Clair's Mid-life Crisis Liberated Her." *Weekly Journal*, April 13, 1995, 12.
Schneider, Bart. "'October Suite': Flings Fall Apart." *New York Times Book Review*, November 11, 2001, 31.
Streitfeld, David. "The Stories They Can Tell; For Two D.C. Writers, the First Time Just May Be the Charm." *Washington Post*, July 6, 1994, B1.

Rebecca Meacham

CLARKE, CHERYL (1947–   )

Born in Washington, D.C., Cheryl Lynn Clarke received a B.A. from Howard University and attended graduate school at Rutgers University (where she has worked since 1969), earning an M.A. (1974), an M.S.W. (1980) and a Ph.D. (2000). She has been Rutgers' director of Diverse Community Affairs and Lesbian-Gay Concerns since 1992. She lives in Jersey City.

Activist, poet, critic, and scholar, for the last thirty years Clarke has been weaving together a black lesbian feminist **identity**. Early exposure to the **civil rights movement** and the works of **James Baldwin** politicized her reading. In the 1970s Clarke participated in feminist collectives that enlightened her as to the importance of writing. Barbara Smith, **Pat Parker**, and **Audre Lorde** were mentors and comrades. She was active in the defense of Assata Shakur. Her early story, "Women of Summer" (1977), set in the grim days when the Federal Bureau of Investigation (FBI) had infiltrated Black Power, describes the escape of lesbian outlaws to an older, rural tradition of sanctuary and self-defense. She has been a member of the *CONDITIONS* editorial collective (1981–1990) and of the Board of New York Women against Rape (1985–1988); a founding member of the New Jersey Women and AIDS Network (1987–1990); a board member of the City University of New York's Center for Lesbian and Gay Studies; and chair of the Board of the Astraea National Lesbian Foundation (2000–2003).

Clarke's **poetry** supplies an integrative force in a life committed to complex values. Her four volumes of verse revolve around the lives of black women, lesbian desire, oppression, and communities of resistance. *Narratives* (1982) consists of poems in which individual black women speak about their lives in blunt words, reminiscent of **blues** lyrics. Clarke has given numerous readings. *Narratives*, in some ways similar to the monologues in **Ntozake Shange**'s *for colored girls*, was also well received when performed on stage and on tour. *Living as a Lesbian* (1986) is far more insistently personal and sexual. Its explicit descriptions of lesbian desire made vague "poetic" erotica instantly obsolete, and gay and lesbian critics frequently cite this volume as a groundbreaking work. In "wearing my cap backwards," Clarke chants as a bad, butch witch but is also confident enough to include strict forms. Some poems address public figures, including, for instance, Indira Ghandi and Vanessa Williams. *Humid Pitch* (1989) continues Clarke's explorations of the lives of intersecting communities; notably, it contains a seventy-one-page poem "based loosely" on a relationship between Ma Rainey and Bessie Smith. Other poems present historical voices or deal with childhood memories, Catholic school, and uneasy alliances with gay men. Nominated for a Lambda Book Award, *Experimental Love* (1993) begins with the lush invocation of "A Great Angel" ("oh my soul,/ Oh my moon and coal black sea"), which highlights the sustained range of Clarke's poetic moods and ambitions. There are, again, witty dyke poems, erotic anthems, political prose/poem journals, and (increasingly personal) elegies, all written from a deep involvement in black **literature** and music. **Jewelle Gomez** writes that Clarke "is the progeny Walt

Whitman might have imagined," a writer who "has painted a truly American landscape." Clarke's poems appear in many anthologies; her manuscript-in-progress is called *Corridors of Nostalgia*.

Clarke lists "being a poet" with her other "subversive identities," and her influential activist essays balance her sometimes more vulnerable poetic voice. She has fearlessly criticized her own communities. "Lesbianism: An Act of Resistance" (1981) presents a rejoinder to the sexism of the **Black Arts Movement**, in particular, aiming to "kill" "the homophobic father...Amiri Baraka," and arguing for a politics based on choice rather than color. In "The Failure to Transform: Homophobia in the Black Community" (1983), Clarke acknowledges the homophobic national context, attacks the denigration and/or absence of lesbians and gay men in works by black intellectuals, and describes a black working-class tradition of tolerance. Her conference speeches, essays, and reviews have been published in a wide variety of black, gay, and feminist journals. Her review of **Sapphire**'s *Push*, essays in **memory** of Pat Parker and Audre Lorde, and her elegies for **Toni Cade Bambara** and Jewel Terri have a deep authenticity conferred only by shared experience over time. Clarke finished a dissertation analyzing the impact of poetry by black women on the black arts and feminist movements long after she was a well-known writer herself. (One scholarly essay published from that project considers "transferences and confluences," another, the work of **Gwendolyn Brooks**.) Clarke's dissertation ends with a chapter on the birth of black lesbian feminist poetry: the ground where her career began.

Clarke has often revisited but not greatly revised her early values. In 1995, she advised students not to settle for less than changing "the power dynamic of sexual politics in this culture" ("Being Pro-Gay" 99). Looking back in 2000, she wrote, "I don't give up *Black* for 'African-American,'...*lesbian* for queer;...I don't give up *feminist*, which is a doppleganger for lesbian and always gives me a way to move" ("Lesbianism, 2000" 233). Although photographs of Clarke document her progression from a frowning outsider to poised author, they continue to radiate intelligence and energy. She clearly enjoys her ironic cameo appearance in Cheryl Dunye's **film** *The Watermelon Woman* (1997). Militant, but undogmatic, she has had the courage to inhabit publicly all of her identities and created literature that both defines and bridges difference(s).

See also Black Feminism; Black Feminist Criticism; Kitchen Table: Women of Color Press; Lesbianism; Protest Tradition; Sexuality

Works By

"After Mecca": Women Poets and the Black Arts Movement. New Brunswick, NJ: Rutgers University Press, 2005.
"Being Pro-Gay and Pro-Lesbian in Straight Institutions." *Lesbians of Color: Social and Human Services.* Ed. Hilda Hidalgo. New York: Haworth Press, 1995. 95–100.

The Days of Good Looks: Prose and Poetry, 1980–2005. New York: Carroll and Graf, 2006.

Experimental Love: Poems. Ithaca, NY: Firebrand Books, 1993.

"The Failure to Transform: Homophobia in the Black Community." *Home Girls: A Black Feminist Anthology.* Ed. Barbara Smith. Latham, NY: Kitchen Table: Women of Color Press, 1983. 197–208. Reprint, New Brunswick, NJ: Rutgers University Press, 2000. 190–201.

Humid Pitch: Narrative Poetry by Cheryl Clarke. Ithaca, NY: Firebrand Books, 1989.

"Lesbianism: An Act of Resistance." *This Bridge Called My Back: Writings by Radical Women of Color.* Ed. Cherríe Moraga and Gloria Anzaldúa. Waterstown, MA: Persephone Press, 1981. 128–137. Reprint, *Words of Fire: An Anthology of African-American Feminist Thought.* Ed. Beverly Guy-Shaftall. New York: New Press, 1995. 242–251.

"Lesbianism, 2000." *This Bridge We Call Home: Radical Vision for Transformation.* Ed. Gloria Anzaldúa and AnaLouise Keating. New York: Routledge, 2002. 232–239.

Living as a Lesbian: Poetry. Ithaca, NY: Firebrand Books, 1986.

"Living the Texts Out: Lesbians and the Uses of Black Women's Traditions." *Theorizing Black Feminisms: The Visionary Pragmatism of Black Women.* Ed. Stanlie M. James and Abena P. A. Busia. London: Routledge, 1993. 214–227.

Narratives: Poems in the Traditions of Black Women. New Brunswick, NJ: Sisters Press, 1982. Rev. ed. Illus. Gaia [Gay Belnap]. Brooklyn: Kitchen Table: Women of Color Press, 1983.

"Women of Summer." *Home Girls: A Black Feminist Anthology.* Ed. Barbara Smith. Latham, NY: Kitchen Table: Women of Color Press, 1983. Reprint, rev. ed. New Brunswick, NJ: Rutgers University Press, 2000. 222–245.

Works About

Campbell, Jane. Review of *Humid Pitch,* by Cheryl Clarke. *Belles Lettres* 6.1 (Fall 1990): 53.

Cohen, Cathy J., and Tamara Jones. "Fighting Homophobia versus Challenging Heterosexism: 'The Failure to Transform' Revisited." *Dangerous Liaisons: Blacks, Gays and the Struggle for Equality.* Ed. Eric Brandt. New York: New Press, 1999. 80–101.

Gomez, Jewelle. Icons. "The Body Electric: Jewelle Gomez on Cheryl Clarke's Frank, Unsentimental Verse." *Lambda Book Report* 10.9 (April 2002): 15. June 7, 2004. Proquest: Gender Watch. OhioLINK, Blackmore Library, Capital University, Columbus, OH.

Holland, Walter. "Gay and Lesbian Poetry in These Times." *Lambda Book Report* 10.9 (April 2002): 6. May 24, 2004. Proquest: Gender Watch. OhioLINK, Blackmore Library, Capital University, Columbus, OH.

Jewell, Terri. Review of *Experimental Love: Poetry. Lambda Book Report* 4.2 (December 1993): 47. May 24, 2004. Proquest: Gender Watch. Ohio-LINK, Blackmore Library, Capital University, Columbus, OH.

Parkerson, Michelle. Review of *Narratives*. *Off Our Backs* 13.4 (April 1983): 17. May 24, 2004. Proquest: Gender Watch. OhioLINK, Blackmore Library, Capital University, Columbus, OH.

Reid-Pharr, Robert F. "Living as a Lesbian." *Sister and Brother: Lesbians and Gay Men Write about Their Lives Together*. Ed. Joan Nestle and John Preston. San Francisco: HarperCollins, 1994. 297–306.

Susan Nash

CLASS

Until recently, there were few scholarly analyses of class relations within the black **community** and how the black class structure fit into American society as a whole, and consequently the clearest insight into African American class relations was to be discovered through literary representations. Authors such as **Charles Waddell Chesnutt**, **James Weldon Johnson**, **Angelina Weld Grimké**, **Jessie Redmon Fauset**, **Nella Larsen**, **Dorothy West**, and **Lorraine Hansberry** chronicle in their works of **literature** the intricacies of African American class dynamics, including models of the black class structure and the characteristics defining class position and the relationship between the existence of the so-called aristocrats of color and the development of the upwardly mobile group of black people who gained access to a lifestyle commensurate with that of the white American middle class.

Some scholars take issue with the applicability of the term *class* to the system of stratified social relations in existence prior to the massive influx of southern black people into northern cities, commonly termed the Great Migration of 1915–1920. Using principles of categorization established by Marxist and Weberian economic theory, this position contends that the black aristocrats or elites who maintained social precedence in the black community prior to 1915 should be considered a status group rather than a legitimate class, if class is defined strictly as a function of how an individual is positioned with relation to the means of production of goods in a capitalistic society. Those who own the major manufacturing and financial enterprises and employ workers constitute the upper class, while those workers who depend on the members of the upper class for wages belong to the working class. The middle class, then, is itself composed of those educated professionals who operate outside of this wage labor system, such as doctors, lawyers, or teachers, as well as "white-collar" workers within the system—managers and officeworkers who are not themselves engaged in manual labor. The black elite group in existence from the antebellum period through Reconstruction up until the first decade or so of the twentieth century did not qualify as a middle or upper class in terms of this general structure. Instead, this elite set drew its members from an incongruous cross section of occupations and income levels, where standards for inclusion were based on traceable, distinguished ancestry, movement within exclusive social circles, taste, cultivation, and gentility. Charles Chesnutt's Blue Vein

Society, clearly delineated in his 1900 collection *The Wife of His Youth and Other Stories of the Color Line*, is the best textual representation of this status elite and its foibles.

A changing of the guard, so to speak, occurred during the early decades of the twentieth century, at which point the aristocratic status group had been completely displaced from the pinnacle of black society throughout the nation by the rising black middle class. The coalescence of this upstart class, however, was in large part dependent on the resources of the status group that preceded it. Many entrants into the middle class were sons of the status elite educated into white-collar professions with money earned by fathers who were caterers, railroad porters, hostlers, barbers, or **domestic** servants for wealthy white families. Those who were not born into the elite group often married elite women in order to secure their own status within the upper echelon of black society. This class further distinguishes itself from its antecedent status group because unlike the black aristocrats who depended primarily on white patronage for the prosperity they enjoyed, the black middle class was able to establish itself mainly due to its ability to serve the black populace often neglected by white professionals.

The black doctors, dentists, teachers, real estate and insurance agents, ministers, undertakers, editor/journalists, and entrepreneurs who formed the burgeoning middle class are abundantly in evidence in the fictive urban settings of the novels penned by Fauset, Larsen, and West. Although many critics have registered discomfort with the so-called middle-class bias endemic in their novels, their depictions are among the few extant close descriptions of early black middle-class **home** life. The women proved to be remarkably astute cultural observers, encoding the transition in the black community from aristocratic status group to middle-class upward mobility in perfect accordance with retrospective analyses of the phenomenon.

The head of the Marshall **family** in Fauset's *There Is Confusion* (1924) is the former slave Joel Marshall, a successful New York caterer to wealthy white clients; he sends his sons to Harvard and persistently discourages their becoming involved in the service-oriented business that financed their expensive educations. Instead, his elder son becomes a Harlem real estate agent, and his younger son leads a racial uplift organization. Similarly, Larsen centers her 1929 novel *Passing* on Irene Westover Redfield, the college-bred wife of a doctor who returns to her college-bred father's home in Chicago for a visit and consequently reenters a whirlwind of upscale social activities, including teas, resort weekends, and card and dinner parties. Then, in *The Living Is Easy* (1948), Dorothy West focuses on Cleo Judson, a southern-born social climber who marries a produce wholesaler for his money but cultivates friendships among the impoverished, yet genteel, faded aristocracy in order to maneuver her way into upper-crust Boston black society.

By most standards, the characters enumerated above would assuredly have been counted within the upper class, with the possible exception of Cleo Judson, who because of her lack of cultural capital might be more appropriately classified as an upper-middle-class woman aspiring to secure a position in the upper class. Relative status and public perception in the post–World War I era provide the basis for the division of the northern, urban black community into three basic classes: lower, middle, and upper. The lower class represents the largest, composed largely of recent migrants from the **South** with low incomes, low-status occupations, and "low" standards of living. The middle class differs from the lower class less in terms of economic well-being than in terms of values, goals, and manner of living. The middle class ranges from the lower middle, still struggling to effect a complete dissociation from the lower class, to the upper middle, perpetually attempting to elevate their status into the upper class. The upper class is then defined principally by way of a cultural barometer that rewards those who successfully accumulate the critical markers of achievement: college degrees, professional success, conspicuous consumption, and cultural refinement. As opposed to the "wealthy leisure class" characterization of upper-class white people, members of the black upper class were compelled to work in order to maintain their social position, essentially corresponding in lifestyle and level of prosperity to the white middle class and even sharing its fundamentally conservative values, family form, and social agenda.

Class advancement for African Americans typically elicited reactionary charges of assimilationism. While black novelists generally advocate racial consciousness in the sense of developing sincere pride in and commitment to advancing the collective interests of the **race**, passive resignation to a second-class social rank is universally excoriated. While individual writers explore various forms of resistance to racial hierarchy, all rely on the repudiation of "lower-class" behavioral models and servile demeanors. They avoid the semantic dissension inherent in using the "upper, middle, lower" classification system by employing alternative terms to describe the relative status of the characters in their novels. Fauset uses phrases like "the better class of colored people," "colored society," and "colored ladies," while black characters of lesser station speak of "them real hinckty culled folks." Larsen is more subtle, occasionally deploying such referents as "Negro society," "Negro circles," and "people of consequence," but preferring to describe personal attributes, such as religious affiliation, education, taste, or habits, to signal social status. West refers to "the nicer colored people," "these self-styled better Negroes," "the genteel poor," and the "Old Colored Families."

Despite the critical resistance to representations of this early black elite class, its treatment in **fiction** is an indispensable contribution to African American social and cultural **history**, as well as the literary tradition. The invisibility of black intellectuals and professionals is a problematic misrepresentation in texts like the popular white writer Fannie Hurst's *Imitation of Life* (1933), in which the central character Bea Pullman considers the entire black community of Atlantic City, New Jersey, nothing more than a pool of potential domestic laborers; she expresses frustration that despite a black population of 9,000, she still has difficulty finding good help. However, texts centered on the black upper class critique the pretension and elitism pervading it, and they seek to promote a black American aesthetic that unifies the cultural practices of the rural South with those of the urban North.

Black regional dissimilarity surfaces in different forms in the novels, though the South is universally represented as an environment in desperate need of reform and its black inhabitants as a population in desperate need of regeneration. In West's *The Living Is Easy*, fifteen-year-old Cleo Jericho is sent North with an elderly white lady who travels to the Jerichos' backwoods community seeking a more temperate climate to relieve a terminal ailment. The concerned dowager entreats Cleo's parents to deliver their beautiful young daughter out of the sultry, morally depraved South. Cleo eventually settles in Boston with another elderly lady who welcomes Cleo's arrival because she expects the absolute devotion of black servants to their white employers she has read about in accounts of southern race relations. This romanticized vision of black servility and fidelity is denounced through Cleo's contempt for black people who appear to reinforce the racialist convictions. The stark distinction Cleo, who herself worked in service before her marriage, draws between herself and the domestic servants she encounters becomes clear through a platitude concerning the correlation of etiquette and class mobility she pretends to address to her daughter Judy but truly means for a maid who makes the mistake of presuming to be familiar with her.

During the early-twentieth-century time frame encompassed by such novels as *The Living Is Easy*, many married black women were compelled to find employment as domestics, abandoning their own homes to care for the households of wealthier people. The upscale characters Larsen depicts all have black female servants, though Larsen never delves into the personal lives of the hired help. Fauset's *There Is Confusion* briefly investigates the private concerns of Myrtle, the teenaged daughter of Essie, a domestic in the Marshall household. Myrtle resolves to finish high school despite the discouragement of her white classmates who assert the futility of her efforts since the diploma will afford her no advantage in finding **work**. Though the resolution of Myrtle's dilemma is immaterial to the predominant concerns of the novel, the attention to it demonstrates Fauset's consciousness of the difficulty involved in transcending class stratification. However, Joel Marshall's transmutation of his experience in domestic service into a lucrative catering enterprise does reinforce Fauset's conviction that it could indeed be accomplished. Rather, Essie's preoccupation with Myrtle's problems and Joanna's distracted, rather dismissive, response to the confidence illustrate the difficulty faced by female domestics whose lives are so fully consumed by the needs of their employers that they have little time to devote to the needs of their own families.

Historically, domestic work was forced on black women when their husbands did not earn enough to support their families alone, and there were few occupational alternatives open to the women, especially after World War I, when millions of discharged soldiers returned home to reclaim their abandoned positions in the American workforce. The resultant competition for a scarcity of employment opportunities, exacerbated by racial prejudice, pushed postwar black women out of the jobs they had finally acquired as a result of upwardly mobile white women securing better ones. Black women were barred from office, retail, and factory work; fictional characters able to obtain such jobs are compelled to pass for white to do so. The dearth of opportunities available to black women to advance their own economic prospects made them largely dependent on marriage and **motherhood** to access a comfortable lifestyle and elevated class standing.

See also Blanche among the Talented Tenth; *Chinaberry Tree, The*; Kelley-Hawkins, Emma Dunham; Passing; *Plum Bun*; *Quicksand*; *Raisin in the Sun, A*; *Wedding, The*

Works About

Billingsley, Andrew. *Black Families in White America*. Englewood Cliffs, NJ: Prentice-Hall, 1968.

Drake, St. Clair, and Horace R. Cayton. *Black Metropolis: A Study of Negro Life in a Northern City*. New York: Harcourt, Brace, 1945.

Frazier, E. Franklin. "The New Negro Middle Class." *On Race Relations: Selected Writings*. Chicago: University of Chicago Press, 1968.

Giddings, Paula. *When and Where I Enter: The Impact of Black Women on Race and Sex in America*. New York: Bantam Books, 1984.

Jones, Jacqueline. *The Dispossessed: America's Underclasses from the Civil War to the Present*. New York: Basic Books, 1992.

Shaw, Stephanie J. *What a Woman Ought to Be and to Do: Black Professional Women Workers during the Jim Crow Era*. Chicago: University of Chicago Press, 1996.

Licia Morrow Calloway

CLEAGE, PEARL (1948–   )

The blossoming consciousness of poet, essayist, novelist, and playwright Pearl Michelle Cleage began at an early age. Born on December 7, 1948, in Springfield, Massachusetts, to Rev. Albert B. and Doris Cleage, she grew up in Detroit, Michigan. Her father, a political activist, was the founder of the Pan-African Orthodox Christian Church and in 1962 ran for governor of Michigan on the Freedom Ticket. Later he embraced **Black Nationalism** and changed his name to Jaramoji Abebe Agyemen. Her more sedate mother was an elementary school teacher. Cleage's parents believed it was equally important to maintain an atmosphere that fostered an appreciation and knowledge of black culture and academics.

Pearl and her older sister were expected to excel academically and were introduced to controversial ideologies in an attempt to expand their intellectualism. According to Cleage, it was not unusual to find the works of **Langston Hughes**, Simone de Beauvoir, and **Richard Wright** strewn around the Cleage home. In addition, the Cleage parents cultivated an appreciation in their children for the performing arts. Some of Cleage's fondest memories include evenings spent at the theater, enjoying plays and dance ensembles.

After graduating from Northwestern High School in 1966, the academically gifted Cleage studied playwriting from 1966 to 1969 at Howard University in

Washington, D.C. She left Howard University to marry Atlanta politician Michael L. Lomax, with whom she has a daughter, Deignan Cleage Lomax. After leaving Howard University, her quest for knowledge led to further study at Yale University in 1969 and the University of the West Indies in 1971. After moving to Georgia in 1971, Cleage earned her B.A. from Spelman, a historically black female college. Years later she returned to Spelman as a professor and Distinguished Playwright in Residence. Cleage attended graduate school at Atlanta University. She currently resides with her second husband, writer Zaron W. Burnett, in Atlanta.

As a young wife and mother Cleage held a variety of jobs in Atlanta. At the Martin Luther King Memorial, she worked in the Archival Library. Next, Cleage became the on-air personality of *Black Viewpoints*, a local television show, and later hosted, produced, and wrote scripts for *Ebony Beat Journal*. While her career flourished, she continually questioned societal expectations concerning the role of women. Working as the director of communications for Atlanta's first black mayor, Maynard Jackson, Cleage began to feel that she was neglecting certain aspects of her personal life, for example, being a "good" wife and mother. At this time in her life, she admits to questioning whether she was performing as others expected, which eventually led to feelings of incompetence and eventually depression. In retrospect, Cleage concedes that at the time she was unable to recognize that the anxieties she experienced in her younger years concerning the **home** versus a career had little to do with her own defectiveness and more to do with a bigger problem—sexism.

This realization provided Cleage with many issues to write about in her large repertoire of works. A female associate of her husband's introduced Cleage to the feminist movement. The two women immersed themselves in feminist readings. The interlocking issues of **race** and gender always informed Cleage's feminist readings and writings. In a 1996 interview, Cleage recalls her introduction to the feminist movement as a pivotal moment in her life, because it explained so many feelings that she had as a woman. While she supports the feminist movement, Cleage believes that until it addresses the racism and classism that exist within, its gains will be marginal, and thus she aligns herself with the more encompassing womanist movement.

While she is extremely vocal about the racist division within feminism, her works seek to unify the fragmented sectors of the movement by speaking out against common issues that all women face, regardless of race or **class**. Although her essay collection *Mad at Miles: A Black Woman's Guide to Truth* (1990) focuses on **violence** committed against black women, there is a strong message for all women concerning **love** relationships that are sometimes violent. Cleage is unafraid to confront and express her disappointment with **jazz** icon Miles Davis for the physical assault on his wife at the time, actress Cicely Tyson. She urges readers to shun Davis because he publicly boasted about his abuse of Tyson.

Unabashed by criticism concerning her stance, Cleage later protested vehemently against basketball superstar Earvin "Magic" Johnson's use of the word *floozies* to describe his female sexual conquests in her essay "Fatal

Floozies" (1993). *Deals with the Devil and Other Reasons to Riot* (1993) is a personal collection of essays directed at the black **community**. In *Deals*, Cleage gives the reader her stance on controversial issues such as Spike Lee's *Malcolm X*, the **film** *Driving Miss Daisy*, and the Anita Hill–Clarence Thomas hearings. Cleage is forthright in her criticism of both Hill and Thomas, whom she refers to as "Uncle Thomas." Unwilling to allow her womanist views to cloud her opinion of Hill, Cleage is not convinced that Hill deserves the title "Shero" for bringing light to the issue of Thomas's alleged sexual harassment. Instead, she argues that as an officer of the court Attorney Hill was morally and legally obliged to report his behavior a long time ago.

Even though the black community has touted the brilliance of Cleage for some time, recently she was exposed to a larger, more racially diverse audience. Her first book of **fiction**, *What Looks Like Crazy on an Ordinary Day* (1998), became one of the reading selections of Oprah Winfrey's book club. The book was so well received that Cleage published a sequel titled *I Wish I Had a Red Dress* (2001). Often called "a master storyteller" for her rich blend of truth and her stirring portrayal of black life and black womanhood in racist and sexist America, Cleage has recently published a third novel, *Some Things I Never Thought I'd Do* (2003).

Works By

Deals with the Devil and Other Reasons to Riot. New York: Ballantine, 1993.
Mad at Miles: A Black Woman's Guide to Truth. Southfield, MI: Cleage Group, 1990.
What Looks Like Crazy on an Ordinary Day. New York: Avon, 1998.

Works About

Bennett, Suzanne, and Jane T. Peterson. "Pearl Cleage." *Women Playwrights of Diversity: A Bio-Bibliographical Sourcebook.* Westport, CT: Greenwood Press, 1997. 90–92.
Giles, Freda Scott. "The Motion of Herstory: Three Plays by Pearl Cleage." *African American Review* 31 (1995): 709–711.
Paige, Linda R. "Pearl Cleage." *Significant Contemporary American Feminists: A Biographical Sourcebook.* Ed. Jennifer Scanlon. Westport, CT: Greenwood Press, 1999. 66–72.

Karen Arnett Chachere

CLIFF, MICHELLE (1946–)

Toni Morrison has described Michelle Cliff's writing as "full of razors, blossoms and clarity." The seeming contradiction inherent in this metaphor is one of the defining features of Cliff's work. Drawing on paradoxical experiences of colonialism and diasporization, Cliff articulates a more complex understanding of **identity**, one that emphasizes the syncretism that develops out of the interaction of **race**, **class**, gender, and **sexuality**.

Born in Kingston, Jamaica, in 1946, Cliff immigrated to the United States with her parents at the age of three. Although the **family** returned to Jamaica when she was ten, Cliff would eventually leave the island again, this time for London to attend Wagner College, from which she graduated in 1969. Over the next few years, Cliff would move frequently back and forth between Jamaica, the United States, and the United Kingdom. She received her M.Phil in Art History from the Warburg Institute at the University of London in 1974. Writing her thesis, a study of Italian Renaissance intellectualism, caused her to reconsider the benefits of her colonialist education. Inspired by the anticolonialist movements of the 1960s and 1970s, as well as the burgeoning women's movement, Cliff began to search for alternatives to post-Enlightenment knowledge, specifically the conceptions of identity that did not devalue its African and feminine aspects.

Because of her complex life **history** as a light-skinned black lesbian woman, Cliff came to realize that identity was incredibly complex. She began to search for ways to use writing to reflect and comment on that complexity. Her first piece of writing was *The Winner Names the Age, a Collection of Writing by Lillian Smith* (1978). An early feminist, Cliff would continue to explore the ramifications inherent in this more complex articulation of these radical ideas about identity and history in a collection of **poetry** and prose titled *Claiming an Identity They Taught Me to Despise*. Published in 1980, the text mixes together poetry and prose in a fragmentary, yet lyrical, fashion. The essays and prose poems in this collection frequently engage notions of history and **memory**.

Cliff continued her experimentation with alternative generic forms in her first novel, *Abeng*, published in 1984. In this semiautobiographical novel, the protagonist Clare Savage, a light-skinned Jamaican girl, tries to come to self-knowledge in a world that denies and denigrates her existence as an African and a woman at every turn. The novel, like the earlier collection, engaged with many of the themes Cliff would go on to explore in further detail and from different perspectives in her future work in novels such as *No Telephone to Heaven* (1987), a continuation of Clare's story begun in *Abeng*, this time highlighting the connections between self-identity and activism, and her next novel, *Free Enterprise* (1993), which begins with John Brown's raid at Harper's Ferry and traces abolitionist Mary Anne Pleasant's relationship with a Jamaican woman named Annie and their efforts to resist **slavery** and sexism.

Recovering the unknown stories of those at society's margins, as well as claiming one's voice and identity and rewriting history, Cliff argues, is necessary for resistance, in particular resistance to colonialist and sexist thinking.

Works By

Abeng. New York: Crossing Press, 1984.
Bodies of Water. New York: Methuen/Dutton, 1990.

Claiming an Identity They Taught Me to Despise. New York: Persephone Press, 1980.

Free Enterprise. New York: Dutton, 1993.

"History as Fiction, Fiction as History." *Ploughshares* 20 (Fall 1994): 2–3.

The Land of Look Behind. New York: Firebrand Books, 1985.

No Telephone to Heaven. New York: Dutton, 1987.

The Store of a Million Items. New York: Houghton Mifflin, 1998.

Trace Elements. Forthcoming.

The Winner Names the Age, a Collection of Writing by Lillian Smith. New York: Norton, 1978.

Works About

Chancy, Myriam J. A. "Exile and Resistance: Retelling History as a Revolutionary Act in the Writings of Michelle Cliff and Marie Chauvet." *Journal of Caribbean Studies* 9.3 (Winter 1993–Spring 1994): 266–292.

Ilomonen, Kaisa. "Rethinking the Past, Rewriting History: Counter-narratives in Michelle Cliff's *Abeng.*" *Atlantic Literary Review* 3.2 (April–June 2002): 110–129.

Nicole N. Aljoe

CLIFTON, LUCILLE (1936–)

Lucille Clifton was born in Depew, New York, on June 27, 1936, to Thelma Moore and Samuel Sayles, Sr. Clifton, like her mother and her first daughter, was born with six fingers on each hand. Clifton takes this trait, once thought to be the sign of witchery, and glorifies it in several of her later poems as a means of communicating what she sees as a potent and magical female power in her **family**. Her extra digits, as well as her daughter's, were removed at birth, and Clifton mourns their loss and the magical power she imagines them possessing. Even in their absence, however, this physical feature is just one of the many details of Clifton's life that imbues her work with a deep female sense of magic and power.

Both of Lucille Clifton's parents migrated from the rural **South** (her mother from Georgia, and her father from Virginia) to find **work** in the industrial North. Her father worked in steel mills, while her mother worked in a laundry. Although neither parent earned beyond an elementary school education, Clifton received many lessons from them that would later prove to be the fulcrum of her literary and artistic career. Clifton's mother was herself a poet. When Clifton was a little girl, she remembers watching her mother burn her poems because her father would not allow her to publish them. Her father's mercurial nature, however, is tempered in Clifton's **memory** and poetic rendering of him because of his ability to remember and retell stories of his great-grandmother Caroline.

As a child, Clifton recalls sitting at her kitchen table while her mother braided her hair, listening to her father tell stories of Caroline's capture by slave traders from Dahomey, West Africa, in 1830. When her great-great-grandmother arrived in New Orleans at the age of eight, she was forced on a journey to Virginia, entirely on foot. It was in Virginia that Clifton's roots in this country were established. Her father was born there and was raised by Caroline. Clifton returns to Virginia in her **poetry** as a space where she locates her own connection to her African past and this female **ancestor**. From this direct link to African roots, Clifton draws much inspiration for her poetry and **identity** as a black woman. Through Caroline, Clifton knows of the tradition of Dahomey women as strong, warrior leaders.

Clifton attended Howard University from 1953 to 1955 on a scholarship. She was the first in her family and in her church to attend college. In 1955, she left Howard to attend Fredonia State Teacher's College (now State University of New York at Fredonia), where she ultimately decided to leave the world of institutionalized education altogether to pursue her life as a poet. By 1958, Clifton met and married Fred Clifton; shortly thereafter, the couple moved from New York to Maryland, where they raised their six children.

While she was writing her first collection of poetry, the African American **community** was deeply involved in a struggle for equality that involved protests, riots, revolutionary movements, and some of the most inspirational and controversial art and **literature** that the country had ever seen. With regard to this era, known as the **Black Arts Movement**, Clifton says with a laugh that she was pregnant for most of it. While her physical absence from larger cities and elite college campuses left her outside of the major activity of these movements, Clifton's work clearly reflects the decade's focus on black pride and activism. Her work especially draws attention to the black feminist concerns of **freedom** for black women from both racism and sexism, family and community welfare, as well as the reversal of white patriarchy's influence on black men. Clifton has suggested in interviews that the vast majority of black people in American were not physically a part of the major **drama** of this movement but had been brought up in traditions, like hers, that took great pride in blackness, the power of community, the power of women-centered families. In other words, the message of the 1960s for Clifton was a message she had been hearing since she first heard about her great-great-grandmother Caroline.

In the body of Clifton's work, themes of feminism manifest not only in her discussion and celebration of strong women but in her inclusion of strong men as well. Her work is truly an example of womanist thought, as defined by **Alice Walker** in its ability to explain the power of women as the life force through which strong men, sons, husbands, daughters, and communities are made. In her children's books, Clifton communicates themes of cultural pride and dignity in rich African and African American histories and traditions. Other major themes that describe her work in general include the vital importance of storytelling and the duality and complexity of life experiences.

Clifton is the only poet ever to have two books chosen as finalists for the Pulitzer Prize in the same year. Other honors include an Emmy Award from the American Academy of Television Arts and Sciences, two fellowships from the National Endowment for the Arts, the Shelley Memorial Prize from the Poetry Society of America, the Charity Randall citation, and a Lannan Literary Award. She was also a National Book Award finalist in 1996 for *The Terrible Stories*. In 1999, she was appointed a chancellor of the Academy of American Poets and elected a fellow in the Literature of the American Academy of Arts and Sciences. Clifton also served as the Poet Laureate of Maryland in 1979. In 1980, she received honorary doctorate degrees from Goucher College and the University of Maryland. Clifton continues to tirelessly give readings, work as an activist in education, and teach poetry. She is currently a Distinguished Professor of Humanities at St. Mary's College in Maryland.

In her first collection of poems, *Good Times* (1969), Clifton focuses on hope against losing cherished things like **love**, happiness, family, and memories. The poem "miss rosie" commemorates a homeless woman who wanders the streets. Clifton, however, makes her a heroic figure by seeing her as a person upon whose shoulders and suffering other black women's success was built. In this and other poems in the collection, Clifton reminds the reader of the strength and perseverance of black women (including her ancestors) and the importance of not forgetting the sacrifices of those who came before. The poem from which the collection's title was taken, "good times," points to the strength of men in the African American community, specifically her father's ability to support his family and let them know the joy and celebration of community.

Her next collection of poetry, *Good News about the Earth* (1972), focuses on nature and the female **body** and black pride in general. The poem "the way it was" describes Clifton's negotiation of herself as a black woman and her own attempts to contain her body and behave like a nice, quiet white girl when she was growing up. Clifton also situates herself as teller and bearer of stories in poems about African American leaders **Malcolm X**, Eldridge Cleaver, and **Angela Davis**. In the final section of the collection she retells stories of people in the Old Testament as something sensual, mortal, and woman centered.

Clifton's next collection of poems is titled *An Ordinary Woman* (1974). The first half of the collection, "sisters," begins with a poem about black witches and their defiance of ordinary, white existence. This sisterhood poem is followed by poems to and about specific women to whom she feels deep and meaningful female connections, including her sister, her girlfriends, Harriet Tubman, her grandmother, poet Adrienne Rich, Sally Hemings, as well as her sons and her daughters. In this section, Clifton also introduces "Kali," the black goddess. The collection's second half, "i agree with the leaves," returns to this goddess and Clifton's struggle to incorporate and calm the dark nature of Kali's force into her own identity as a woman.

In *Two-Headed Woman* (1980), Clifton continues to explore her strong sense of self as a woman. She celebrates her female ancestors and Dahomey strength in poems like "lucy and her girls," which trace this lineage as some force of nature. Other poems honor the poet's body and take pride in features that define her as a black woman, as in "homage to my hair" and "homage to my hips." The final section, "the light that came to lucille clifton," celebrates her identity as a poet and a woman and glorifies the sources of her inspiration.

Clifton followed this collection of poetry with a prose piece that continues to explore the lives of her ancestors. In *Generations: A Memoir* (1976), which was edited by **Toni Morrison**, Clifton begins with a dedication to her father Samuel Sayles. The narrative is divided into the genealogy of Clifton's family: "caroline and son," "lucy," "gene," "samuel," and "thelma." Each section is punctuated by a photograph of the family member and a line from Walt Whitman's *Song of Myself* (1855). Much of this narrative is written in Samuel's voice, telling a young Lucille the stories Caroline told him. These memories are interrupted by Clifton's telling of her father's **death** and her family's journey to New York for the funeral, which she parallels to Caroline's journey from New Orleans to Virginia. As a whole, the stories communicate Clifton's belief in unity and continuity of family, love, and hope; the photographs and words and the memories they trigger hold the lines of family together. The narrative begins and ends with stories of women, as if to punctuate and shore up the entire family's identity with this female strength.

In *Next: New Poems* (1987), Clifton shifts from speaking to ancestors and people close to her to speaking from the voices of people after their death. She speaks for Crazy Horse, for Thelma Sayles, for her recently deceased husband Fred Clifton, and from her own near-death experience with leukemia. Clifton also presses beyond geographical, cultural, and chronological boundaries in her exploration of seemingly disparate notions of Asia, Native American cultures, Japanese internment camps, and karma. This collection takes on more global themes than her other collections and at the same time focuses on issues of American identity and memory. Although this text is broader in scope, Clifton is never far from her focus on feminine power; several poems in this collection revolve around the magical nature of young girls.

In *The Book of Light* (1993), Clifton's poetry reflects her own hungry desire to keep climbing past her age of sixty. She again recalls and celebrates her family as a source of strength in poems about her daughters, her husband, her father, and her mother. In two poems about the 1985 bombing of the Afrocentric group MOVE in Philadelphia, Clifton pays homage to one of the group's brave survivors, Ramona Africa. In the final section of the collection, Clifton explores biblical and mythological figures such as Sarah, Naomi, Ruth, and Leda to retell the stories through their own female voices.

In *The Terrible Stories* (1996), Clifton gives human female strength and qualities to a fox. The fox poems explore the animal's ability to voice terrible, previously untold stories. Some of the specific stories that Clifton focuses on are of her breast cancer diagnosis and lumpectomy; Clifton links her ability to survive this experience to her strength as a Dahomey woman. In one of her breast cancer poems, Clifton speaks directly to other black women who know this fear and the reality of breast cancer statistics within this community. Her mother's strength and wisdom is again emphasized in "what did she know when did she know it" as Clifton wonders how her mother's wisdom was acquired and from what strong and powerful source it grew.

In *Quilting: Poems, 1987–1990* (1991), Clifton draws on an artistic form (the quilt) that has historically been used in the African American community as a means to preserve histories and family legacies. Quilts have also been used to ensure physical survival by providing warmth, as well as signals and maps of the **Underground Railroad**. Sections of the text share names of various **quilting** patterns and work to mend together stories in the same way a quilt does. Also in this collection, poems about Adam and Eve retell the story of the first words spoken, giving more agency to Eve. Other poems compare menstruation and its force and magic to the world's rivers. Clifton continues to tap into feminine life forces in "poem to my uterus" and "to my last period."

Blessing the Boats: New and Selected Poems, 1988–2000 (2000) contains excerpts from earlier collections, as well as a section of new poetry. These new poems focus partly on her own despair at the world and the people in it and her recent experiences with kidney failure and cancer. In an attempt to retell history from her own perspective, Clifton describes a lynching photograph and the roles of the women spectators, a recent lynching in Jasper, Texas, as well as her own Aunt Timmie's role in deconstructing the **myth** of America. In this, her most recent collection to date, Clifton ultimately returns to narratives of hope, rebirth, and waiting for an ultimately unknowable future.

The whole of her work explores how life can be both joyous and tragic, both blithe and burdensome, both mundane and extraordinary. This image of complete wholeness in her expression of universal and personal histories is created through an economy (but not simplicity) of language that says as much about the world through what she does not say as through what is explicitly stated. In her rendering of a more complete story and **history** of herself and her world, Clifton responds to a tenet of **black feminism** in her remark that she wants to write stories for academics, students, and literary critics as much as she wants to write them for folks like her Aunt Timmie.

Works By

Blessing the Boats: New and Selected Poems, 1988–2000. Rochester, NY: BOA Editions, 2000.

The Book of Light. Port Townsend, WA: Copper Canyon, 1993.

Generations: A Memoir. New York: Random House, 1976.

Good News about the Earth. New York: Random House, 1972.

Good Times. New York: Random House, 1969.
Good Woman: Poems and a Memoir, 1969–1980. Brockport, NY: BOA Editions, 1987. (Reprints first 4 volumes of poetry and *Generations*)
Next: New Poems. Brockport, NY: BOA Editions, 1987.
An Ordinary Woman. New York: Random House, 1974.
Quilting: Poems, 1987–1990. Brockport, NY: BOA Editions, 1991.
The Terrible Stories. Brockport, NY: BOA Editions, 1996.
Two-Headed Woman. Amherst: University of Massachusetts Press, 1980.

Works About

Glaser, Michael. "I'd Like Not to Be a Stranger in the World." *Antioch Review* 58.3 (Summer 2000): 310–329.
Holladay, Hilary. "Black Names in White Spaces: Lucille Clifton's South." *Southern Literary Journal* 34.2 (Spring 2002): 120–154.
———. "Song of Herself: Lucille Clifton's Poems about Womanhood." *The Furious Flowering of African American Poetry.* Ed. Joanne Gabbin. Charlottesville: University Press of Virginia, 1999. 281–297.
Kallet, Marilyn. "Doing What You Will Do: An Interview with Lucille Clifton." 1998. *Sleeping with One Eye Open: Women Writers and the Art of Survival.* Ed. Marilyn Kallet and Judith Ortiz Cofer. Athens: University of Georgia Press, 1999. 80–85.
Lazer, Hank. "Blackness Blessed: The Writings of Lucille Clifton." *Southern Review* 25.3 (Summer 1989): 760–770.
Madhubuti, Haki. "Lucille Clifton: Warm Water, Greased Legs, and Dangerous Poetry." *Black Women Writers (1950–1980): A Critical Evaluation.* Ed. Mari Evans. New York: Anchor Press/Double Day, 1984. 150–161.
Mance, Ajuan Maria. "Re-locating the Black Female Subject: The Landscape of the Body in the Poems of Lucille Clifton." *Recovering the Black Female Body: Self Representations by African American Women.* Ed. Michael Bennet and Vanessa D. Dickerson. New Brunswick, NJ: Rutgers University Press, 2001. 123–140.
McClusky, Audrey T. "Tell the Good News: A View of the Works of Lucille Clifton." *Black Women Writers (1950–1980): A Critical Evaluation.* Ed. Mari Evans. New York: Anchor Press/Double Day, 1984. 139–149.
Rowell, Charles. "An Interview with Lucille Clifton." *Callaloo* 22.1 (Winter 1999): 56–72.
Rushing, Andrea Benton. "Lucille Clifton: A Changing Voice for Changing Times." *Coming to Light: American Women Poets in the Twentieth Century.* Ed. Diane Wood Middlebrook and Marilyn Yalom. Ann Arbor: University of Michigan Press, 1985. 214–222.
Wall, Cheryl. "Sifting Legacies in Lucille Clifton's *Generations*." *Contemporary Literature* 40.4 (Winter 1999): 552–575.

Keely A. Byars-Nichols

COLEMAN, WANDA (1946–   )

A recipient of the Lenore Marshall Prize, Wanda Coleman is an acclaimed poet, novelist, and performance artist, deeply concerned with the issue of racism and the lives of inner-city Los Angeles. Coleman grew up in the Watts district of Los Angeles and was involved in a number of social organizations set up in 1965's post-Watts rebellion. She has also worked as a medical secretary, a magazine editor, a journalist, and a scriptwriter. She is the first African American to receive an Emmy for television writing. Her poems have been frequently anthologized, and she has received fellowships from the National Endowment for the Arts and the Guggenheim Foundation for her **poetry**.

Coleman's persistent portrayal of urban, dispossessed African American women highlights the often marginalized struggles that they have against anonymity, poverty, racism, sexism, and **violence**. Characterized as demotic, idiosyncratic, at once celebratory and embittered, Coleman's poems are not always easy to read. Like many **blues** lyrics, her writing is consistently direct and stark, but she has also been noted for the wide range in tone. Invoking an unforgettably pungent lyricism, Coleman captures the striking iconography of urban southern California: Bondi Beach, the all-night diner and laundromat, Griffith Park, Hollywood, the "Chevy graveyard."

Bathwater Wine (1998), which won the Lenore Marshall Prize, is a collection of poems documenting a black woman's transformations through passion and rage. Evocative of themes of **Gwendolyn Brooks**, the collection begins in the working-class South Central of the poet's childhood. The poet's father is a ring-damaged former boxer working the numbers and other hustles by day and employed as a "maintenance engineer" in an office building by night. His overshadowing presence sets off the isolation of the girl's childhood in the intricate social systems of elementary and junior high school. Here her poems acutely render her overarching theme, the intimacies of everyday life, weaving traditional poetic tradition together with fragments of popular culture.

Works By

African Sleeping Sickness: Stories & Poems. Santa Rosa, CA: Black Sparrow Press, 1990.

Bathwater Wine. Santa Rosa, CA: Black Sparrow Press, 1998.

The Dicksboro Hotel. Tarzana, CA: Ambrosia Press, 1989.

Hand Dance. Santa Rosa, CA: Black Sparrow Press, 1993.

Heavy Daughter Blues: Poems & Stories 1968–1986. Santa Rosa, CA: Black Sparrow Press, 1988.

Imagoes. Santa Rosa, CA: Black Sparrow Press, 1983.

Love-ins with Nietzsche: A Memoir. Fresno, CA: Wake Up Heavy Press, 2000.

Mad Dog Black Lady. Santa Rosa, CA: Black Sparrow Press, 1979.

Mambo Hips & Make Believe: A Novel. Santa Rosa, CA: Black Sparrow Press, 1999.

Mercurochrome: New Poems. Santa Rosa, CA: Black Sparrow Press, 2001.

Native in a Strange Land: Trials & Tremors. Santa Rosa, CA: Black Sparrow Press, 1996.

Ostinato Vamps. Pittsburgh: University of Pittsburgh Press, 2003.

A War of Eyes & Other Stories. Santa Rosa, CA: Black Sparrow Press, 1988.

Works About

Comer, Krista. "Revising Western Criticism through Wanda Coleman." *Western American Literature* 33.4 (Winter 1999): 357–383.

MacPhee, Graham. "Lines of Descent: Frank O'Hara, Wanda Coleman and the Recollection of Tradition." *Other Americans, Other Americas: The Politics and Poetics of Multiculturalism.* Ed. Magdalena J. Zaborowska. Oxford: Aarhus University Press, 1998. 104–118.

Rei Magosaki

COLLINS, JULIA C. (?–1865)

Julia C. Collins, a schoolteacher from Williamsport, Pennsylvania, authored *The Curse of Caste; or The Slave Bride* (1865), the first serialized novel by an African American woman. *The Curse of Caste* appeared in the *Christian Recorder*, a weekly newspaper published in Philadelphia by the African Methodist Episcopal Church, from February 25 to September 23, 1865. On the verge of completion, the novel lapsed after publication of chapter 31. Collins's **death** from tuberculosis on November 25, 1865, left *The Curse of Caste* unfinished.

Little is known of Collins other than what she wrote and what a few others wrote about her in the *Christian Recorder*. For almost a year before the appearance of her novel, Collins contributed short essays to the *Recorder* that reveal her commitment to originality of thought and self-culture, while also offering practical advice on how to be an effective and nurturing teacher and how young women of color should prepare themselves for matrimony. Early in 1865, probably in response to the looming defeat of the Confederacy and **slavery**, Collins forecast "the seemingly invincible destiny of our people" to be "a nation that shall shine forth as a star on the breast of time, and be gathered into the brilliant galaxy of great nations!" (1). Her own brand of African American cultural nationalism soon found expression in the act of writing a novel.

Although the *Recorder* published two notices of her death, little information about Collins's life, other than that her husband was named Stephen C. Collins, was included in these testimonies to her character. What can be ascertained, however, is that Collins was a respected, articulate, and relatively well educated black woman who felt a strong sense of inner calling to become what she almost certainly felt she was—the first African American woman novelist. Although **Harriet E. Wilson**'s novel *Our Nig* was published in

1859, making *The Curse of Caste* the second novel published by an African American woman in the United States, it is extremely unlikely that Collins knew of Wilson or read her self-published novel.

The Curse of Caste focuses on the lives of a beautiful mixed-race mother and daughter whose opportunities for fulfillment through **love** and marriage are threatened by slavery and caste. Since slavery had not yet been abolished in the United States when Collins launched *The Curse of Caste*, the author's decision to make her maternal heroine, Lina Tracy, a slave whose husband must purchase her in order to free and then marry her, was timely. Collins not only depicts this marriage but allows it to flourish in the United States instead of moving it abroad, as would become conventional in later "tragic **mulatta**" **fiction**. After Lina's death, her daughter Claire, ignorant of her mother and of her own racial heritage, must discover her **identity**, her **family**, and her future. Although slavery does not menace Claire in the latter chapters of Collins's novel, the "curse of caste" does, particularly with regard to the young heroine's marital prospects. What Collins held in suspense for the unwritten ending of *The Curse of Caste* was whether Claire's climactic moment of self-discovery as well as her own chance to become a bride would be overshadowed by "the curse of caste." Nevertheless, the thirty-one surviving chapters of *The Curse of Caste* show that its author was determined to imagine a fictional United States in which slavery and caste existed but could not totally deny to deserving African American women the **freedom** to marry and pursue a fulfilling **domestic** life, even if such choices challenged the color line.

Works By

The Curse of Caste: or, The Slave Bride. Christian Recorder, running weekly from 5.8 (February 25, 1865) to 5.38 (September 23, 1865).
"Life Is Earnest." *Christian Recorder* 5.1 (January 7, 1865): 1.

William L. Andrews

COLLINS, KATHLEEN (1942–1988)

Kathleen Conway Collins Prettyman was born on March 18, 1942, in New Jersey. Collins graduated from Skidmore College with a Bachelor of Arts degree in philosophy and **religion**. She also studied French and cinema at the graduate level in France (Middlebury Graduate School of French). She enjoyed a range of professional experiences from editor, writer, filmmaker, and producer to educator and mother of two, Nina and Emilio. Collins spent the early part of her career working as a **film** editor. Later, she became a professor in the Theatre Arts Department at City College in New York, where she taught a number of courses until her **death**.

Arguably, her greatest contribution is her **work** in the film industry during a time when black women filmmakers were rare. Exercising authority over her art, Collins chose not to create films in Hollywood. As an independent filmmaker and a black woman, Collins faced many obstacles. After writing a script titled *Women, Sisters, and Friends* in 1971, she found it impossible to secure funding for production. Unrelenting, she directed the film *The Cruz Brothers and Miss Malloy* (1980), an adaptation of one of Henry Roth's works, *The Cruz Brothers*, from *The Cruze Chronicle: A Novel of Adventure and Close Calls*, with very little money. The film earned Collins first prize at the Sinking Creek Film Festival. In 1982, she managed to collect enough money to produce *Losing Ground*, the first feature film written, directed, and produced by an African American woman. The film starred Kathleen's good friend, Seret Scott, who would go on to perform in several other films by Collins. In *Losing Ground*, a comedic **drama**, Scott plays the protagonist, Sara Rogers, a professor of philosophy, so immersed in research and scholarship, she finds it difficult to inhabit ecstasy. *Losing Ground* received the First Feature award at the Portuguese International Film Festival, while Collins's second play, *The Brothers* (1982), earned her a National Endowment of the Arts Playwriting grant. *The Brothers* also received recognition as one of the best plays of 1982, according to the Audelco Society. The same year the Theatre Communications Group chose it as one of the twelve outstanding plays. Other plays by Collins include *In the Midnight Hour* (1981), *Remembrance* (1985), and *Only the Sky is Free*, about Bessie Coleman, the first African American aviatrix.

Collins was a daring writer. Her texts are significant in that they provide images of people of color, particularly women, rarely seen in popular film (i.e., middle-class black women). Collins's films challenge **stereotypes** and explore the interlocking oppressions of **race**, **class**, and gender.

Collins died in 1988, several years after she was diagnosed with cancer. She left behind work in a number of genres: stage plays (i.e., *Waiting for Jane*), short stories, screenplays (i.e., *Conversations with Julie*, *Madame Flor and Love*, and *Summer Diary*), and a novel, *Black and White Imagery*. At the time of her death, Collins was working on the film, *Gouldtown: A Mulatto Settlement*, and a novel, *Lollie: A Suburban Tale*. Today, African American filmmakers (and writers in general) continue to marvel at and be influenced by Kathleen Collins's work.

Works By

The Brothers. 9 Plays by Black Women. Ed. Margaret B. Wilkerson. New York: New American Library, 1986. 293–346.

Losing Ground. Screenplays of the African American Experience. Ed. Phyllis Rauch Klotman. Bloomington: Indiana University Press, 1991. 122–185.

Work About

Gibson-Hudson, Gloria J. "The Cultural Significance of Music to the Black Independent Filmmaker." Ph.D. diss. Indiana University, 1986.

KaaVonia Hinton-Johnson

COLOR PURPLE, THE

The Color Purple, the Pulitzer Prize–winning novel by **Alice Walker** published in 1982, chronicles the life of an African American girl, Celie, growing up in the Deep **South**. As Celie's mother becomes sick after multiple childbirths and refuses sex with her husband, Celie's stepfather begins raping Celie, resulting in two pregnancies. He gives the children, Adam and Olivia, to a missionary couple who later go to Africa. Celie is then married off to physically abusive Mr. ——, a man whose wife recently died, leaving him to raise their children. However, Mr. —— is in **love** with the **blues** singer Shug Avery. Strong-willed Sofia marries Mr. ——'s son, who attempts to break her as Mr. —— has done to Celie. Consequently, Sofia leaves him and is eventually imprisoned for striking a white man. Celie meets and falls in love with Shug, who through intimacy shows her the love that gives her strength. Meanwhile, Celie's sister Nettie meets up with the missionaries who have adopted Celie's two children and joins them on their move to Africa. Throughout the years Nettie writes Celie at Christmas and Easter, despite Mr. ——'s promise to keep them apart permanently. Eventually, with the help of Shug, Celie finds Nettie's letters that Mr. —— had hidden, leaves Mr. ——, starts her own pants business, and is reunited with her sister.

The Color Purple is described as a feminist novel about an abused and uneducated black woman's struggle for empowerment. The novel was praised for the depth of its female characters and for its eloquent use of black English vernacular. Though some critics attacked Walker's depiction of Mr. ——, just as they did of Grange Copeland in *The Third Life of Grange Copeland*, these critics often overlooked the transformation male characters go through as they move from an abusive individual to one more certain of his connection to the world. Many themes are explored in critical inquiries of the text such as **religion**, **sexuality**, **slavery**, education, sisterhood, patriarchy, epistolary conventions, clothing, fairy tales, African American folk culture and tradition, gender, and **race**. Ultimately, this novel brought much-needed national recognition of the literary works of African American women. Walker develops some of the characters in this novel in her later books *Possessing the Secret of Joy* and *The Temple of My Familiar*.

See also By the Light of My Father's Smile; *In Search of Our Mothers' Gardens: Womanist Prose*; Womanism

Works About

Alice Walker and The Color Purple: Inside a Modern American Classic. A BBC Production. London: BBC, 1986; Princeton, NJ, 1998.

Banks, Erma Davis, and Keith Byerman. *Alice Walker: An Annotated Bibliography 1968–1986.* New York: Garland, 1989. 85–113.

Gates, Henry Louis, Jr., and K. A. Appiah, eds. *Alice Walker: Critical Perspectives Past and Present.* New York: Amistad, 1993. 16–21.

Lauret, Maria. *Alice Walker*. New York: St. Martin's Press, 2000. 90–120.
Winchell, Donna Haisty. *Alice Walker*. New York: Twayne Publishers, 1992.
    85–99.

Laura Madeline Wiseman

COMBAHEE RIVER COLLECTIVE

One of the earliest and most vocal groups to express a vision of radical **black feminism** was the Combahee River Collective. This Boston-based organization rooted itself in an **identity** politics and worked to address the simultaneous and intertwined oppressions of sexism, racism, classism, and heterosexism that affect black women and the communities to which they belong.

The Collective was an offshoot of the National Black Feminist Organization (NBFO), which held its initial conference in New York in 1973. The Boston chapter called itself the Combahee River Collective, a name taken from the river where Harriet Tubman headed the only military action led by a black woman. The Collective first met in Roxbury, Massachusetts, in January 1974, and it broke from the national organization in 1975. Among its members were Beverly Smith, Barbara Smith, Gloria Hull, Margo Okizawa Rey, and **Cheryl Clarke**. Although the Collective was first formed because the needs of black women were not being addressed either in the white-dominated feminist movement or in the male-based **civil rights movement**, the Collective's mission soon came to be additionally characterized by a strong lesbian politics and socialist perspective.

The Collective was responsible for two important publications. "The Combahee River Collective Black Feminist Statement" was widely distributed in 1977 and has since been reprinted. It discusses the roots of black feminism, the basic assumptions on which the Collective based its politics, challenges and possibilities of a black feminist movement, and issues central to black feminism. A second pamphlet—"Twelve Black Women: Why Did They Die?"—was published in 1979 in response to a series of murders of black women in the Boston area.

Although the Combahee River Collective is most often cited today on the basis of its publications, it also took a politically active stance on a number of issues. Consciousness raising was its most important function, especially in the early years. It defined itself as a study group that would also publish and distribute black feminist writing. A number of retreats were held to bring black feminists together, beginning in 1977. At the same time, members of the Collective worked with other groups on a number of issues, including the opposition of sterilization abuse, **violence** against women, and racism in the women's movement, and the formation of coalitions to support reproductive **freedom**, black women's art, and women in prison. The Collective is still recognized for its work and its revolutionary visions.

See also Black Feminist Criticism

Works By

"A Black Feminist Statement." Combahee River Collective, Boston, 1977.
"Twelve Black Women: Why Did They Die?" Combahee River Collective, Boston, 1979.

Works About

Harris, Duchess. "'All of Who I Am in the Same Place': The Combahee River Collective." *Womanist Theory and Research* 3.1 (1999): 1–26. December 14, 2003. www.uga.edu/~womanist/harris3.1.
Smith, Barbara. "Combahee River Collective." *Black Women in America: An Historical Encyclopedia.* Vol. 1. Ed. Darlene Clark Hine. Brooklyn, NY: Carlson, 1993. 269–270.

Laurie McMillan

COMEDY: AMERICAN STYLE

The first novel by **Jessie Redmon Fauset**, *There Is Confusion*, told of the effects of racial and sexual discrimination on several generations of light-skinned, middle-class African Americans; Fauset's other novels *Plum Bun* and *The Chinaberry Tree* focus on a smaller number of (mainly female) in-dividuals. Fauset's fourth and final novel, *Comedy: American Style*, first pub-lished in 1933, combines these techniques. *Comedy* describes a Philadelphia **family history** that crosses several generations, but separate sections are dedicated to portraits of individuals.

Fauset structures the novel in a quasi-theatrical manner. The first two sections are designated as "The Plot" and "The Characters"; the final section is called "Curtain." The other three sections are "Acts" dedicated to one character's story. "Teresa's Act" narrates the coming of age of Teresa Cary, a **mulatta** who, from an early age, is told not to associate with dark-skinned friends. Her mother, the light-skinned Olivia Cary, has been scarred by racist incidents from childhood, incidents that have convinced her that her family's black heritage must be hidden. Intelligent and insightful, Teresa resents the "sham" of "**passing**," realizing that her neighbors see the Carys as "colored people trying to be white." After a white youth molests her, Teresa falls in **love** with the black-skinned Henry Bates. The couple plans to elope, but her mother discovers the plot. Olivia's bile horrifies Bates, but believing in racial integrity, he rejects Teresa when she suggests, in desperation, that he could exploit his Spanish-speaking capacities to pass as Mexican. Teresa's thwarted romantic life is compounded when she visits Europe, marrying, hastily, a Frenchman who turns out to be stingy, too close to his mother, unambitious, and racist.

Teresa's life's tragedy is followed by that of her young brother, Oliver, who breaks Olivia's heart when he is born because he is dark. He grows up bereft of maternal affection. One grotesque episode summarizes the hideousness of Olivia's contempt for her wrong-colored son. When Olivia's friends visit, Oliver pretends to be the butler. Only when concealing his true **identity**, performing as the stock Negro servant, does Oliver gain approval from Olivia. Eventually, Oliver discovers the reason for his mother's coldness, and he kills himself.

Phebe Grant is a light-skinned friend of Teresa's. Olivia despises her because her mother is black and had not been married to Phebe's long-gone (white) father. Like Teresa, Phebe suffers romantically because of color-based prejudice. She falls for the dark-colored Nicholas, but he tells her that he fears for their safety; a black man partnered with a white girl is an easy target for white racists' **violence**. The most profound tragedy, however, belongs to the least sympathetic character: Olivia. Responsible for Oliver's suicide and for her other children's romantic miseries, she is ostracized by her husband, Dr. Christopher Cary. The novel concludes with a bleak description of Olivia's empty, lonely life. Quashing her African heritage has backfired. As with all of Fauset's characters who fail to repent for their wrong-headed passing, she suffers for not following the Shakespearean maxim "To thy own self be true."

Works About

Davis, Thadious M. Introduction to *Comedy: American Style*, by Jessie Redmon Fauset. New York: G. K. Hall, 1994.

Lewis, Vashti Crutcher. "Mulatto Hegemony in the Novels of Jessie Redmon Fauset." *College Literature Association Journal* 35.4 (1992): 375–386.

Lupton, Mary Jane. "Black Women and Survival in *Comedy: American Style* and *Their Eyes Were Watching God*." *Zora Neale Hurston Forum* 1.1 (1986): 38–44.

Sylvander, Carolyn Wedin. *Jessie Redmon Fauset: Black American Writer*. Troy, NY: Whitston, 1981. 193–229.

Kevin De Ornellas

COMMUNITY

Like-minded and close-knit, the positive idea of community remains good; the pejorative connotations of community become restrictive and closed. Traditionally in the African American use of the word, *community* centers around the idea of the **ancestor** and finds its strength in **memory**. Likewise, a shared mythos often cements African American communities in a manner respective of **history**; out of the collective memory of **slavery**, communities cohere. Nebulous and paradoxical as an idea, community in African American women's **literature** remains at once inclusive and exclusive, local and universal, peaceful and militant, simple and complex.

To speak of the African American community in a limited manner akin to the sociopolitical Moynihan Report of 1965, *The Negro Family and the Case for National Action*, results in **stereotypes** and cultural misrepresentations. The nuclear **family** so representative of the white middle **class** becomes grotesquely rendered in the broken homes of a popular, fragmented idea of African American community. Starting at the individual household, one discovers the means of assessing the interactions that define community in its strictest sense. Beyond that, through the values, mores, and customs operating in a given arena, an individual makes connections to a larger, more substantial group of like-minded people. The individuality that characterizes communities manifests the profound inspiration from which authors write their stories, poems, and novels. By reaching out to local communities, one strikes toward the universal and better understands the dynamics shaping community. In the same way the definition of African American feminism changes over time to include womanist and lesbian ideas, the idea of community necessarily shifts in order to respond to cultural change. Communities, by their nature, change in design and population; the inclusive becomes exclusive, while wholeness becomes fragmented.

One may argue that the peculiar institution of slavery began the fragmentation of community that African American writers have since attempted to reassemble. Slavery offered no cohesive community; families torn apart often found no reunion, while the reality of communal gatherings was more forced and expected than arrived at freely. In **Audre Lorde**'s 1984 essay collection *Sister Outsider*, she enumerates further divisions continuing to split rather than bring together African Americans. Citing the black male's oppression of women, the misunderstanding of **lesbianism**, and the ongoing prejudices of whites, Lorde reaffirms the outsider as reality to community's ideal. Lorde and others show the often hierarchical side of community.

Neither does community necessarily remain cohesive when class lines are crossed. In *Our Kind of People: Inside America's Black Upper Class*, Lawrence Otis Graham shows the restrictive bonds of the African American elite that pervade government and industry in America. Graham's work makes sharp distinctions between the lower and middle classes aside the upper class. **Jessie Redmon Fauset**'s *There Is Confusion* reverses that by showing the hardships of the ambitious middle-class African Americans striving against discrimination to rise above the normal standards of the time. Similarly, **Ann Petry**'s *The Street* offers Lutie Johnson's belief that money can be a panacea to all of her problems. She finds, of course, that money does not alleviate her problems, and rather than being included into her community, she becomes exiled.

Like class, color also proves divisive within the black community, a gradient of privilege by which lighter-skinned African Americans gain advances denied to those with dark skin. Even before Madame C. J. Walker brought it to the forefront of African American culture, an obsession with light skin has pervaded the African American imagination; **Zora Neale Hurston** described one such character as "color struck." Pecola Breedlove in **Toni Morrison**'s *The Bluest Eye* cannot compete against the "high-yellow" Maureen Peal. While Pecola identifies with a blonde-haired, blue-eyed white ideal of **beauty**, one sees discrimination from other African Americans at the darkness of her skin. Similarly, Clare Kendry's decision to pass in **Nella Larsen**'s *Passing* shows the sacrifices to community one makes in such a decision. By willingly excising herself from the African American community she grew up in, Clare finds an insatiable longing to rejoin that community, one her husband, unaware of her racial background, despises.

On another level, in the absence of community one finds a better definition of it as an ideal. **Sherley Anne Williams**'s Dessa Rose strives to unite all of those she loves in **freedom**, while **Nikki Giovanni**, in "Adulthood," offers a litany of all of the **violence** and triviality separating the speaker from a true sense of community. The need to belong thrusts Frado in **Harriet E. Wilson**'s *Our Nig; or, Sketches from the Life of a Free Black* into a search for community that she never realizes. When Cleo in **Dorothy West**'s *The Living Is Easy* tries to arrange a permanent reunion with her sisters, she learns that community cannot be forced. The iron-fisted rule by the men of Ruby, Oklahoma, in Morrison's *Paradise* also fails to result in true community due to their rejections of outsiders. In all of these examples, community is more of a goal than a reality. Though all find that community is something to aspire toward, the various paths taken offer little opportunity to create a true sense of belonging.

Often, the most striking examples of true community are found among the lower or more rural classes. **Paule Marshall**'s *Praisesong for the Widow* shows Avey Johnson's introduction into community during the Carriacou Excursion in Grenada. There she must put aside her usual high-class notions of behavior and surrender to the experience. In so doing, she becomes aware of the presence of community that is genuine rather than forced. Like Indigo's community of healers in **Ntozake Shange**'s *Sassafrass, Cypress, & Indigo*, Avey witnesses and participates in a sense of *communitas* where judgment is suspended for the sake of a commonality and equality. In that state, Avey can see clearly the importance of her past and understand the deep wound her great aunt Cuney felt upon expulsion from the church for dancing.

In **Alice Childress**'s *Like One of the Family*, the distancing effect Mildred uses when she rejects being one of the family to those for whom she works clearly makes known that her community is outside of that family. Yet one sees that Mildred does have a community to call her own. Ultimately, with the influence of memory, one might see that true community is limited by time. As in **Gloria Naylor**'s *Bailey's Café*, community is there when it is needed but grows into a genuine sense of something special through the aid of memory. The "good old days" that memory harkens toward, though finite and in the past, reveal a transitory sense of community not necessarily large but satisfying, much like the scene on the porch where Pheoby listens to Janie's story in ***Their Eyes Were Watching God***. Community exists, but generalizations must be avoided in order to see the intricate forms it can take. At its best, community is the all-embracing, welcoming, and strong metaphor writers cling to; yet beyond a polished surface, community can be back-biting, judgmental, and wholly antithetical to its definition. Over the course of a century, African American women writers have worked to deconstruct its very nature in order to suggest, in their writing, a healthy and sound approach to community.

Works About

Griffin, Farah Jasmine. *"Who Set You Flowin'"*: *The African American Migration Narrative*. New York: Oxford University Press, 1995.
Manning, Carol S., ed. *The Female Tradition in Southern Literature*. Urbana: University of Illinois Press, 1993.
Page, Philip. *Reclaiming Community in Contemporary African American Fiction*. Jackson: University Press of Mississippi, 1999.

F. Gregory Stewart

CONJURING

Conjuring is a folk practice that stems from African religious beliefs. In many West African **religions**, spiritual forces are believed to participate in dynamic interactions with the human and material world, and certain humans, following particular ritualistic practices, are believed to be able to manipulate these spiritual forces and therefore to affect events in the natural world. West African conjurers, who serve the function of doctors, diviners, and intercessors with the dead, are central figures in African religions and have both sacred and secular manifestations. Enslaved Africans brought these religious beliefs to the Americas, where they became separated from their original religious cosmologies, syncretically merged with elements of European and Native American beliefs, and acquired new rituals and purposes. While in Africa most conjurers are trained and sanctioned by the religious **community**, in the Americas most conjurers have worked independently, apprenticing with a practitioner of conjure but receiving no communally recognized position. Nonetheless, they are important cultural figures who act as healers, mediate interpersonal conflicts, and provide African Americans with a folk source of social agency.

Conjuring goes by a variety of names, including juju, mojo, hoodoo, rootwork, goopher, and gris-gris. Conjurers might be called hoodoo doctors, two-heads, rootworkers, or simply conjure men or women. The ability to conjure is open to members of both sexes and has historically allowed African American women a culturally empowered position within the community. As the name *two-head* suggests, conjurers are thought to have second sight, to be able to foretell the future, read the causes behind events, and commune with the dead. Conjurers are thought to act as intermediaries between the living and their **ancestors**. Some conjurers show these abilities from birth, and being born with a caul over one's head is considered a sign of conjuring potential. Most conjurers keep to themselves to heighten their status and allow few initiates to see how they perform their conjuring rituals. To study conjure as an anthropologist, **Zora Neale Hurston** apprenticed with a number of conjure men and women throughout the **South** and published a fascinating account of the rituals she learned in *Mules and Men*.

In addition to Hurston, other folklorists and anthropologists, including Alan Dundes, Harry Hyatt, and John Roberts, have collected and analyzed thousands of folktales concerning conjure within the African American community. These conjure tales tell of ghosts and haunts, of lovers seeking retribution when wronged, of people healed and others made ill through conjure potions, of people gaining luck through the use of "hands," of prophecies foretold and fulfilled. In these tales, the person who is ill or who has been wronged approaches the conjurer for help, and the first act of the conjurer is to validate the supplicant's perspective as valid. Conjure practice does not, in other words, include any sort of investigation into the objective state of events, though some acts of conjure may be performed to discover whether a lover is philandering, for instance, but only if that is what has been requested. Conjurers therefore perform an important function for the African American community; in a country where the legal system has often ignored or discredited complaints from African Americans, conjure practitioners regularly validate and **work** to remedy their experiences of being wronged. As John Roberts has suggested in *From Trickster to Badman*, this function of conjure practice served a particularly important role during **slavery**; by using conjure to deal with internal disputes in the slave community, enslaved African Americans retained control over their own affairs to a greater extent than more overt aggression would have allowed them, and they gained a means of exerting power and influence over their surroundings.

Many **slave narratives** depict conjure as a potential means of protection from the dangers of slave life, though most slave narrators struggle with whether to acknowledge their belief in it to their white abolitionist audiences. Notably, **Frederick Douglass** discusses the role of conjure in the turning point of his narrative—his fight with the slave master Covey. Just before this fight, a fellow slave, Sandy, has given him a root to keep in his pocket for protection. When at first Covey does not whip him, and later attempts to beat him but is unsuccessful, Douglass leaves the reader to decide the root's efficacy. **William Wells Brown** and **Harriet Jacobs** also discuss the use of conjure in their narratives and claim some belief in it. There is, importantly, a competing tradition of tales debunking conjure as mere tricks and hoaxes, and Henry Bibb's narrative offers a number of these instances. Two competing forces have traditionally been in conflict with widespread conjure belief: **Christianity**, which teaches that conjure is heresy, since it claims to offer access to the supernatural outside of sanctioned religion, and science, which teaches that conjure is mere superstition.

Religious scholars, particularly Theophus Smith, have studied the ways in which African Americans have syncretically practiced Christianity itself as a form of conjure, using the Bible as a source of ritual incantation that offers material for performative enactment, for conjuring or calling forth a liberating God. In this light, many of the **spirituals**, the abolitionist orations of Henry Highland Garnet, David Walker, and **Sojourner Truth**, as well as the beliefs underpinning the revolts of Nat Turner and Denmark Vesey, for instance, can be understood as within the conjure tradition.

Since the slave narratives, African American writers have frequently depicted conjure in their novels, and conjure's emphasis on the performative power of words (in the act of conjuring, words are often repeated ritualistically or written a magic number of times and then buried) has particularly interested writers. **Charles Waddell Chesnutt**'s conjure stories depict this power in a number of ways. In the tale "Mars Jeems's Nightmare," for instance, the master's use of language to change reality—to designate one as "slave," for instance—is countered by the conjure woman Aunt Peggy, who uses her own powerful words and rituals to transform the master into a slave. The narrator of this tale, Uncle Julius, tells it to his own employer, John, who has recently fired Julius's nephew, and the effect of Julius's words is that John rehires the nephew. Thus the words of the conjure story itself act as a kind of conjure, redressing a wrong and providing agency for the African American characters in the story.

Conjure is also often used as a motif to stand for African American "roots" more generally and therefore as a sign of authenticity or rejection of an assimilated perspective. In *My Bondage and My Freedom*, Douglass enhances his description of Sandy, the rootworker, claiming that he spoke in an African language and specifically putting the root in opposition to the books in which Douglass has formerly placed his faith. Throughout this text, Douglass gives voice to the African Americans who influenced his life to a far greater extent than he does in the earlier *Narrative of the Life of Frederick Douglass*. In Arna Bontemps's historical novel *Black Thunder*, Gabriel's rebellion against slavery in 1800 fails partly because Gabriel does not place enough faith in conjure, so that he does not read the stars correctly or protect himself with a conjure hand. More recently, **Gloria Naylor**, in **Mama Day**, and **Toni Morrison**, in many of her novels, have depicted the ways in which younger African Americans have first rejected conjure as superstition, only to have to relearn it from an older mentor in order to develop a fulfilling life.

Since the 1980s, literary critics have been particularly interested in the literary uses of conjure by African American women. The 1985 publication of *Conjuring: Black Women, Fiction, and Literary Tradition* opened the door for critics to consider a link between conjurers, as symbols of empowerment and active control over the environment, with narrative forms that broke from the realist and naturalist traditions. In the introduction to *Conjuring*, Marjorie Pryse traces depictions of conjure women in **literature** by Chesnutt, Hurston, and **Alice Walker** and argues that each not only represents conjure characters but uses conjure symbolically to gain narrative authority. Literary conjure, particularly for African American women, Pryse argues, offers a powerful means of self-definition and a way of rejecting the narratives of environmental determinism that realism and naturalism produce. Conjure's emphasis on the unseen, on the possibility of sudden transformations or reversals, counters realism's emphasis on the visible, the common, and the likely, which tend to highlight and perhaps maintain the status quo.

See also Folklore; Healing; Myth, Use of; Womanist Conjure

Works About

Baker, Houston. *Workings of the Spirit: The Poetics of Afro-American Women's Writing.* Chicago: University of Chicago Press, 1991.

Brown, David H. "Conjure/Doctors: An Exploration of Black Discourse in America, Antebellum to 1940." *Folklore Forum* 23 (1990): 3–46.

Dundes, Alan, ed. *Mother Wit from the Laughing Barrel: Readings in the Interpretation of Afro-American Folklore.* Englewood Cliffs, NJ: Prentice Hall, 1972.

Hurston, Zora Neale. *Mules and Men.* 1935. New York: Harper Perennial, 1990.

Hyatt, Harry M. *Hoodoo, Conjuration, Witchcraft, Rootwork.* Hannibal, MO: Western Publisher, 1970.

Morrison, Toni. "Rootedness: The Ancestor as Foundation." *Black Women Writers (1950–1980): A Critical Evaluation.* Ed. Mari Evans. New York: Doubleday, 1984. 339–345.

Pryse, Marjorie, and Hortense J. Spillers, eds. *Conjuring: Black Women, Fiction, and Literary Tradition.* Bloomington: Indiana University Press, 1985.

Roberts, John. *From Trickster to Badman: The Black Folk Hero in Slavery and Freedom.* Philadelphia: University of Pennsylvania Press, 1989.

Smith, Theophus. *Conjuring Culture: Biblical Formations of Black America.* New York: Oxford University Press, 1994.

Suzanne Lane

CONTENDING FORCES

Pauline Hopkins's first novel, *Contending Forces* (1900), illustrates the blurring of the color line at the beginning of the twentieth century and asserts that black women did not deserve the sexual stigmas that both white and black societies placed on them. Though a black press published *Contending Forces*, Hopkins nevertheless relied on a white audience—specifically white women—to ensure her work was a commercial success. The novel's sentimental form appealed to these readers, and she used this genre to draw them into the text's deeper levels of social commentary and protest.

The novel's plot is divided into an antebellum section and a postbellum section. The former, set in the 1780s, follows Charles Montfort and his

family after they relocate from Bermuda to America. When Grace, Montfort's wife, arrives in North Carolina with her family, the local people are taken with her looks and charms. However, the evil Anson Pollack and Hank Davis suspect her family lines may contain black blood. Armed with this rumor and fueled both by a fear that Charles will emancipate his slaves as well as a burning jealousy for the Montfort fortune, the two men and their "committee on public safety" steal the Montfort plantation, kill Charles, and place Grace and her two sons, Charles and Jesse, into **slavery**. Grace is thus transformed, in the eyes of society, into a black woman. Hopkins completes this transformation with Grace's brutal beating at the hands of Bill Sampson and Hank Davis. By putting Grace on the whipping post, Hopkins evokes white women's sympathies and attempts to make them question whether this ruthless white patriarchal power could be turned against them. Unwilling to submit to Pollack, Grace takes her own life, while Charles and Jesse later escape to England and New England, respectively.

Jesse's descendants then become the focus of the postbellum section of the novel. His grandchildren, Will and Dora, live with their mother, Ma Smith, who runs a Boston boarding house. Two of their boarders also become key characters: the beautiful, mysterious, and very light-skinned Sappho Clark and the unscrupulous John Langley, Dora's fiancé. Sappho disappears after John threatens to reveal her tragic past—as a girl, she was raped by her white uncle and bore a child as a result—and attempts to blackmail her in order to take her as his mistress. Langley seeks to win Sappho Clark just as his granduncle Pollack had sought to win Grace Montfort—by discrediting her rather than courting her honorably. Will, who is in **love** with Sappho, tries desperately to find her. He learns of John's plot through a letter Sappho leaves for him, and he then tells Dora, who casts off John and eventually marries a promising schoolmaster. A discouraged Will soon leaves the country.

Throughout the novel is Hopkins's biting, and often ironic, direct address to challenge sternly the equation of **race** and sexual purity. As part of this challenge, the text asserts not only that the color line remains ambiguous but also that pervasive white ideologies that question the purity of black women are neither fair nor truthful.

Works About

Berg, Allison. "Reconstructing Motherhood: Pauline Hopkins' *Contending Forces*." *Studies in American Fiction* 24.2 (1996): 131–150.

McCoy, Beth. "Rumors of Grace: White Masculinity in Pauline Hopkins's *Contending Forces*." *African American Review* 37.4 (2003): 569–581.

Nerad, Julie Cary. "'So Strangely Interwoven': The Property of Inheritance, Race, and Sexual Morality in Pauline E. Hopkins' *Contending Forces*." *African American Review* 35.3 (2001): 357–373.

Somerville, Siobhan. "Passing Through the Closet in Pauline E. Hopkins' *Contending Forces*." *American Literature* 69.1 (1997): 139–166.

Watkins, Patricia D. "Rape, Lynching, Law and *Contending Forces*: Pauline Hopkins–Forerunner of Critical Race Theorists." *CLA Journal* 46.4 (2003): 521–542.

Jennifer Larson

COOPER, ANNA JULIA (1858–1964)

Owing to her vibrant social activism, prominent role within a budding black elite, and unwavering commitment to African American higher education, Anna Julia Cooper may be identified as one of the preeminent black female intellectuals during the late nineteenth and early twentieth centuries. Moreover, in her most famous work *A Voice from the South* (1892), Cooper emerges as one of the first black feminists. A leading spokeswoman at the 1893 World's Congress of Representative Women and the 1900 Pan-African Congress, she also remained active within the black women's club movement.

Cooper was born on August 10, 1858, in Raleigh, North Carolina, to her slave mother, Hannah Stanley, and George Washington Haywood, her mother's white master. Awarded a scholarship to attend St. Augustine's Normal and Collegiate Institute in 1868, young Annie Haywood also worked as a student tutor. Shortly after graduation she married George A. C. Cooper on June 21, 1877. With her husband already employed as a Greek instructor at St. Augustine's, she took a position there as well. Widowed two years later at the age of twenty-one, Cooper never remarried, a decision that later exposed her to scandalous–albeit unfounded–charges of impropriety. Cooper did foster two orphaned children and in 1915 became the legal guardian of her brother's five grandchildren.

A lifelong educator dedicated to promoting equal educational opportunities for black men *and* women, Cooper taught at her Raleigh alma mater until 1881, when she enrolled at Oberlin College in Ohio. Receiving her A.B. in 1884, she planned to resume lecturing at St. Augustine's; however, a disagreement regarding her position delayed her return, and she instead taught at Wilberforce College. Accepting a faculty appointment at St. Augustine's the following year, Cooper taught Latin, Greek, and mathematics courses. In 1887, primarily due to the strength of her teaching, Oberlin awarded her a master's degree.

Moving that same year to Washington, D.C., Cooper took a position at the renowned M Street (later Dunbar High) School. During her tenure as principal (1902–1906), the school became the focus of an intense educational debate between proponents of Booker T. Washington's industrial training model and advocates of a college preparatory model. Despite pressure to implement an industrial program, Cooper continued promoting a classical curriculum that prepared students to enter well-known, esteemed universities.

Following this controversy her contract was not renewed, and she was forced to teach briefly at Lincoln Institute in Missouri before returning to the M Street School in 1910.

A rigorous academic throughout her life, Cooper pursued doctoral studies at Columbia University (1914–1917) and the University of Paris (Sorbonne), where she received her Ph.D. in 1925. Even after her ostensible retirement, she assumed the presidency of Frelinghuysen University in Washington, D.C., in 1930. Upon her death on February 27, 1964, she had—for the better part of a century—worked tirelessly not only to fashion and participate in a thriving African American intellectual **community** but also to demonstrate the crucial roles black women should play within such communities. Indeed, through her own extraordinary example Anna Julia Cooper enacted their heretofore-latent possibilities.

Works By

L'Attitude de la France a L'Egard de L'Esclavage Pendant la Revolution. Ph.D. diss., University of Paris, 1925. Trans. Frances Richardson Keller as *Slavery and the French Revolutionists (1788–1805).* Lewiston, NY: Mellen Press, 1988.

Le Pèlerinage de Charlemagne: Voyage a Jerusalem et a Constantinople. Ed. Anna Julia Cooper. Paris: A. Lahure, 1925.

Personal Recollections of the Grimké Family and the Life and Writings of Charlotte Forten Grimké. N.p., 1951.

The Third Step. Cooper Papers, Moorland-Springarn Research Center, Howard University. N.d. (1945–1950/51?).

A Voice from the South. Xenia, OH: Aldine Printing House, 1892.

Works About

Baker-Fletcher, Karen. *A Singing Something: Womanist Reflections on Anna Julia Cooper.* New York: Crossroad, 1994.

Carby, Hazel. *Reconstructing Womanhood: The Emergence of the Afro-American Woman Novelist.* New York: Oxford University Press, 1987.

Gabel, Leona C. *From Slavery to the Sorbonne and Beyond: The Life and Writings of Anna J. Cooper.* Northampton, MA: Smith College History Department, 1982.

Hutchinson, Louise Daniel. *Anna J. Cooper: A Voice from the South.* Washington, DC: Smithsonian Press, 1981.

Johnson, Karen A. *Uplifting the Women and the Race: The Educational Philosophies and Social Activism of Anna Julia Cooper and Nannie Helen Burroughs.* New York: Garland, 2000.

Lemert, Charles, and Esme Bahn, eds. *The Voice of Anna Julia Cooper.* New York: Rowman and Littlefield, 1998.

Mary Alice Kirkpatrick

COOPER, J. CALIFORNIA (?–   )

J(oan) California Cooper was born in Berkeley, California, to Joseph C. and Maxine Rosemary Cooper. She attended a technical high school and a number of colleges. She has one daughter, Paris A. Williams.

Cooper first garnered attention as a playwright. She has written seventeen plays and was named Black Playwright of the Year in 1978 for *Strangers*. Cooper has won a number of awards—Literary Lion Award and James Baldwin Award, both from the American Library Association, 1988, and the American Book Award, 1989, for **Homemade Love**. She also received the National Book Club Conference Author of Distinction Award in 2004.

It was as a result of her **work** in the theater that she attracted the attention of **Alice Walker**, who encouraged Cooper to write **fiction**. Because of Cooper's use of vernacular, her narrative style has been compared to **Zora Neale Hurston** and Walker. Like Janie in Hurston's **Their Eyes Were Watching God** and Celie in Walker's **The Color Purple**, Cooper's characters speak in black dialect. At the same time, however, Cooper also emphasizes the need to learn standard English in order to become successful. This message is most evident in the novel **In Search of Satisfaction**, published in 1994, in which the character Hosanna is advised to learn to speak better because it can make a difference in life. Cooper's characters also value education and crave knowledge, and they recognize that both are necessary elements in order for them to succeed in the white man's world. While Hosanna sadly thinks about school and dreams of an education, poverty forces her to seek a job; however, her job becomes her education as she vows to learn as many skills as she can. Similarly, in Cooper's first novel, **Family**, published in 1991, Always recognizes that knowledge is power, and she learns anything that she can. Her master's land thrives as a result of her knowledge, but Always knows that she can use her skills to improve her life as well.

Cooper uses the first-person narrator, so the reader feels intimately involved with the characters. While Cooper's narrators are both male and female, there is a feminist pattern in the work: There is a strong emphasis on the ability of women to empower one another. Cooper's first collection of short stories is titled *A Piece of Mine* and was published in 1984. This collection of twelve stories is dedicated to Cooper's "female **ancestors**." She describes them as women who have "struggled to survive, which is the only reason I am here." Certainly, the theme of survival is a prevalent one in the collection, which is primarily told by older and wiser first-person narrators. The stories focus on women who become empowered and seek revenge upon the abusive men in their lives. In the collection of ten stories in *Some Love, Some Pain, Sometime*, published in 1995, Cooper, in a folksy, conversational style, again explores the lives of black women who are trying to improve their lives. Some of the characters are older women who finally find their dream, either in the form of a loving man or a house.

Much of her work is set in rural communities and focuses on the lives of poor to middle-class black people, generally women. Some of her characters are drawn to city life, but they come to value the simplicity and authenticity of life in the country after they have experienced the corruption of the city. For example, in *Homemade Love*, published in 1986 and Cooper's second short-story collection, the man in "Living" leaves his wife and their country life, which he perceives as being old and worn, for the big city. He quickly learns that the city is not all that he imagined and returns **home** within three days with a greater appreciation for his life in the country.

Many of her characters are seeking modest versions of the American dream. In *In Search of Satisfaction*, the characters want to escape their impoverished lives after **slavery** has been abolished. For example, Joel and Ruth struggle to own their own home and dream of sending their son, Lincoln, to college. In *Homemade Love*, the characters in "Without Love" find that they can own a home that is full of the **love** of children and grandchildren, but Cooper's message is that work is necessary to achieve this success.

Some of her characters are admirable, but others are not. Some are simply nosy neighbors, such as "The Watcher," who is too concerned about her neighbors' lives to notice her own troubled **family**. Others are completely consumed by greed and material wealth, such as the wealthy, white, and powerful Befoes in *In Search of Satisfaction*; they are worth millions but take advantage of their town's poorest inhabitants. On the other hand, many more, such as Joel and Ruth, cannot escape poverty and meet with much disappointment in life. At the same time, however, it is often the impoverished characters that recognize the value of the family. Although Ruth and Joel's children are sad as individuals, they are happy being together as a family. It is through the help of friends and family that many of Cooper's characters learn important life lessons that lead them to happiness.

Cooper identifies herself as a student of the Bible, and **religion** is a significant element in her writing; in fact, much of her work can be considered morality tales that teach lessons with a strong moral message. This is most apparent in *In Search of Satisfaction* in which the roles of good and evil and God and Satan are examined. Cooper conveys the idea that life is difficult and there is much evil in the world, but we must do the right thing and follow the Ten Commandments.

Another theme in Cooper's work is the impact of slavery on the lives of blacks. *Family* consists of four tales that deal with the tragedy, hope, and survival of a black family as a result of slavery. The narrator, Clora, like her mother and her grandmother, kills herself to escape the horrors of slavery. She tries to poison her children as well, but they survive. Before her own **death**, Clora's mother warns her twelve-year-old daughter about what lies ahead for a slave girl on the verge of womanhood. Shortly after, Clora is raped by her master's son and gives birth to her first child at thirteen. Clora cries for the future of her newborn daughter whose life has been decided for her because she was born into slavery. Characters such as Yin in *In Search of Satisfaction* hope to give birth to boys because they know that life is too hard for a girl, especially a black girl in a white man's world. In much of her work, such as the collection *Homemade Love*, characters express their hatred for white people but often come to recognize that not all whites are evil. For example, in "Happiness Does Not Come in Colors," the narrator learns that love, like happiness, "does not come in colors."

Cooper's style is simple, but she has much to say, and she frequently uses humor to convey her messages about love, hate, family, and religion.

Works By

Family. New York: Doubleday, 1991.
The Future Has a Past. New York: Doubleday, 2000.
Homemade Love. New York: St. Martin's Press, 1986.
In Search of Satisfaction. New York: Doubleday, 1994.
The Matter Is Life. New York: Doubleday, 1991.
A Piece of Mine. Navarro, CA: Wild Tress Press, 1984.
Some Love, Some Pain, Sometime. New York: Doubleday, 1995.
Some Soul to Keep. New York: St. Martin's Press, 1987.
The Wake of the Wind. New York: Doubleday, 1998.

Works About

Oliver, S. S. "J. California Cooper: From Paper Dolls to Paperbacks." *Essence* (May 1991): 52.
Weaver, James. "Rehabilitative Storytelling: The Narrator-Narratee Relationship in J. California Cooper's *Family.*" *MELUS* 30.1 (2005): 109–136.
Winterson, Jeannette. "Lightning and Loss." *Times Literary Supplement,* August 22, 1986, 921.

Diane Todd Bucci

COPPIN, FANNY JACKSON (1837–1913)

The first African American woman to serve as principal of an American educational institute, Fanny Jackson Coppin was a dedicated and influential educational reformer. Born a slave, Jackson's **freedom** was bought by her aunt, Sarah Orr Clark, to whom she ultimately dedicated her **autobiography** *Reminiscences of School Life and Hints on Teaching. Reminiscences,* written near the end of her life, tells of her own life experiences as well as those of a number of teachers and students with whom she worked.

Soon after her aunt purchased her freedom, Jackson found work as a **domestic** servant in Massachusetts and Rhode Island, and with the help of generous employers, she eventually received an education through private tutoring and formal schooling. After graduating from Rhode Island Normal School, Jackson entered Oberlin College in Ohio, the first college in the United States to admit women and among the first to admit blacks. At Oberlin she studied English, mathematics, and classics, and she began teaching in the college's Preparatory Department. Her courses were popular among the students, despite the faculty's concern that some students might object to having an African American woman as a teacher.

While at Oberlin, Jackson was recruited by Philadelphia's Institute for Colored Youth, a high school and teacher training institute opened by the Society of Friends in 1837. She began **work** there as the principal of the Ladies Department after earning her baccalaureate degree in 1865, and she was promoted to principal of the entire Institute in 1869. The Institute offered a classical education for black youth—including courses in Greek, Latin, and mathematics—and under Jackson's directorship, the Institute also began to offer industrial training, predating the industrial programs offered by the Tuskegee Institute. Jackson, however, did not view industrial training as a substitute for classical higher education but as a supplement to it.

Jackson was especially concerned with the education and professional development of young women. While living in Philadelphia, she organized the Women's Exchange and Girls' Home, which provided both housing and instruction to working women and students. She also found ways to explicitly express her feminism by speaking publicly on black women's **history** and intellectual potential and by publishing a regular newspaper column in which she reported the professional and intellectual achievements of notable women and encouraged women to attend school, pursue careers, and open their own businesses.

In 1881, Fanny Jackson married Levi J. Coppin, a bishop in the African Methodist Episcopal Church. She continued to administer the Institute for Colored Youth until 1902, even when her husband was transferred to Baltimore. In 1902, she accompanied her husband on missionary **work** to South Africa, where she developed domestic training and temperance projects, working primarily with poor women.

Fanny Jackson Coppin died in 1913. Coppin State College in Baltimore, Maryland (originally called Fanny Jackson Coppin Normal School) is named for her.

See also Black Feminism; Slavery

Work By

Reminiscences of School Life and Hints on Teaching. Philadelphia: A.M.E. Book Concern, 1913.

Works About

Coppin, Levi J. *Unwritten History.* Philadelphia: A.M.E. Book Concern, 1919.
Haley, Shelley P. Introduction to *Reminiscences of School Life and Hints on Teaching,* by Fanny Jackson Coppin. 1913. New York: Hall, 1995. xv–xxvii.
Perkins, Linda Marie. *Fanny Jackson Coppin and the Institute for Colored Youth, 1865–1902.* New York: Garland, 1987.

——. "Fanny Jackson Coppin (1837–1913): Educator, Civic and Religious Activist, Feminist." *Notable Black American Women.* Ed. Jessie Carney Smith. Detroit: Gale, 1992. 224–228.

——. "Fanny Marion Jackson Coppin." *Women Educators in the United States, 1820–1993: A Bio-Bibliographic Sourcebook.* Ed. Maxine Schwartz Seller. Westport, CT: Greenwood Press, 1994. 168–176.

——. "Heed Life's Demands: The Educational Philosophy of Fanny Jackson Coppin." *Journal of Negro Education* 51.3 (1982): 181–190.

——. "Quaker Beneficence and Black Control: The Institute for Colored Youth 1852–1903." *New Perspectives on Black Educational History.* Ed. Vincent P. Franklin and James D. Anderson. Boston: Hall, 1978. 19–43.

Peterson, Elizabeth A. "Fanny Coppin, Mary Shadd Cary, and Charlotte Grimké: Three African American Women Who Made a Difference." *Freedom Road: Adult Education of African Americans.* 1996. Rev. ed. Ed. Elizabeth A. Peterson. Melbourne, FL: Krieger, 2002. 164+.

Smith, Eric Ledell. "To Teach My People: Fanny Jackson Coppin and Philadelphia's Institute for Colored Youth." *Pennsylvania Heritage* 29.1 (2003): 6–11.

Linda Joyce Brown

CORREGIDORA

Main character and **blues** singer Ursa Corregidora loses her womb in the opening pages of **Gayl Jones**'s brilliant and disturbing novel *Corregidora* (1976), after her husband accidentally pushes her down some stairs when he is drunk and jealous. Ursa's husband, Mutt, wants her to stop singing so he can support her but also so that he can prevent other men from watching her; Ursa refuses because her singing is as much self-expression and art as it is a job. This loss is symbolic of what women can lose in the struggle with men for self-determination and ownership of their own bodies. The loss for Ursa, however, has greater significance as well, since she has been raised to "make generations"—to produce descendants that will exist as evidence of the brutal enslavement and **rape** of her maternal **ancestors** by the Portuguese planter Corregidora. Ursa's childhood is filled with her grandmother's and great-grandmother's stories about the way Corregidora kept them as prostitutes and slept with both, fathering Ursa's grandmother and mother, and these stories, too, threaten to deny Ursa her own **identity** as anything but the evidence of oppression. In this context, the loss of her womb can be understood as an ironic and painful emancipation from the mandate to reproduce that legacy.

In many other ways as well, the contexts of sexual, racial, and historical oppression overlap, entwine, and conflict. Before Mutt assaults Ursa, he has threatened to auction her off on stage to the highest bidder, as if she were both prostitute and slave. He speaks about her **body** as if he owns it, forcing her to say that her vagina is his, forcing her to have sex with him when she does not want to, and refusing to have sex with her when she does want to.

This intersection of racial and gender oppression is also highlighted through the subplot of Ursa's neighbor, Cat, who leaves her husband because she refuses to be cast in a lowly role as a **domestic** worker in a white woman's kitchen, only to come **home** to be a sexual object in her husband's bed.

Cat's rejection of subservience to both men and white employers (she becomes a self-employed hairdresser) offers one empowering response to this oppression, and another is offered through the story of a slave who cut off her master's penis when he tried to rape her. But despite these examples, Ursa is hampered by the one-sided nature of the stories she has been told since her childhood. She is oppressed both by the legacy of **slavery** that is passed on through her grandmothers' stories of Corregidora and by the silences. What is omitted from these stories are her mother's personal memories of her relationship with Ursa's father and the act of resistance her great-grandmother performed before escaping from slavery. Only when she recovers these can Ursa discover her own means of empowerment.

Works About

Allen, Donia Elizabeth. "The Role of the Blues in Gayl Jones's *Corregidora*." *Callaloo* 25 (2002): 257–273.

Goldberg, Elizabeth Swanson. "Living the Legacy: Pain, Desire, and Narrative Time in Jones's *Corregidora*." *Callaloo* 26 (2003): 446–472.

Munoz-Cabrera, Patricia. "(Em)Bodying the Flesh: Mythmaking and the Female Body in Gayl Jones's *Song for Anninho* and *Corregidora*." *PALARA* 1 (1997): 106–116.

Rushdy, Ashraf. " 'Relate Sexual to Historical': Race, Resistance, and Desire in Gayl Jones's *Corregidora*." *African American Review* 34 (2000): 273–297.

Tate, Claudia. "*Corregidora*, Ursa's Blues Medley." *Black American Literature Forum* 13.4 (1979): 139–141.

Suzanne Lane

CORTEZ, JAYNE (1936–)

Jayne Cortez is a noted and prolific poet, visual artist, performance artist, filmmaker, and teacher. She has often been called a "**jazz** poet" whose work commonly embraces themes of social justice and empowerment of people of color worldwide.

Cortez was born on May 10, 1936, in Fort Huachuca, Arizona. Her early life was spent as part of a military **family**; her father was in the army. The family moved briefly to San Diego, then to Los Angeles and Watts, where she grew up.

Cortez received sustained and extensive exposure to jazz music during her youth. She attended Manual Arts High School and later Compton Junior College, where she received training in the visual arts of painting and drawing.

She cofounded and served as director of the Watts Repertory Theater from 1964 to 1970. She has traveled extensively, particularly to African and Latin American countries, gaining experiences that often find expression in her work. Cortez has been self-published at times in her career and founded Bola Press in 1972. Along with Ghanaian writer Ama Ata Aidoo, Cortez helped to establish the Organization of Women Writers of Africa (OWWA).

Cortez has had many other successful personal collaborations. She married jazz legend Ornette Coleman in 1954 and then later divorced him in 1964; they have one son, Dernardo, who is an accomplished musician with whom Cortez has often performed. Cortez married sculptor Melvin Edwards in 1975; Edwards has created illustrations for some of her books.

Cortez has received many awards throughout her long, fruitful career. In 1979, she received a National Endowment for the Arts Fellowship; two New York Foundation for the Arts Awards in 1973 and 1981; an award from the Afrikan Poetry Theatre in 1994; and a Fannie Lou Hamer Award in 1994.

Cortez's work and personal expression merge art, music, **poetry**, orature, performance, and painting into a single form. Her work has been described as "fusion." Many critics have commented that her poetry skillfully incorporates jazz and **blues** structures. Cortez frequently performs her work; she has had her own jazz ensemble. Critics have also described her poetry as "surreal"— Cortez uses dreams and explorations of the subconscious in her work—and visceral in her word choice and use of language.

Thematically, Cortez's work explores the psychology of the African American experience and social justice. In her early works, such as *Pissstained Stairs and the Monkey Man's Wares* (1969) and *Scarifications* (1973), Cortez explores issues of social protest and Pan-Africanism and expresses solidarity with the experiences of the urban poor. In her later works, such as *Coagulations* (1984), she embraces a human rights stance that actively confronts militarism, globalization, and environmental degradation. Cortez has also addressed **rape** and the abuse of women in her poetry as well as celebrated many women who have inspired her, such as Bessie Smith, Fannie Lou Hamer, and **Billie Holiday**.

Cortez has many inspirations for her work: Ella Fitzgerald, Billie Holiday, Charlie Parker, Thelonius Monk, Lena Horne. Cortez has noted the influence of many poets including **Amiri Baraka**, **Langston Hughes**, Aimé Césaire, **Gwendolyn Brooks**, **Margaret Walker**, and Pablo Neruda.

Works By

Coagulations: New and Selected Poems. New York: Thunder's Mouth Press, 1984.
Festivals and Funerals. New York: Cortez, 1971.
Firespitter: Poems. New York: Bola Press, 1982.
Jazz Fan Looks Back. Brooklyn, NY: Hanging Loose Press, 2002.
Mouth on Paper. New York: Bola Press, 1977.
Pissstained Stairs and the Monkey Man's Wares. New York: Phrase Text, 1969.
Poetic Magnetic. New York: Bola Press, 1991.

Scarifications. New York: Cortez, 1973.

Somewhere in Advance of Nowhere. New York: Serpent's Tail, 1996.

Works About

Brown, Fahamisha Patricia. "Jayne Cortez." *American Women Writers.* Vol 5: Supplement. Ed. Carol Hurd Green and Mary Grimley Mason. New York: Continuum, 1994. 233–234.

Lavazzi, Tom. "Cortez, Jayne." *Encyclopedia of World Literature in the 20th Century.* 3rd ed. Detroit: St. James Press, 1999. 537–538.

Melham, D. H. "A MELUS Profile and Interview: Jayne Cortez." *MELUS* 21.1 (Spring 1996): 71.

Kimberly Black-Parker

COWDERY, MAE (1909–1953)

Mae Virginia Cowdery, appelled by anthologist William Stanley Braithwaite as a "fugitive poet," had a brief but noteworthy literary career. An only child, she was born into the middle **class** in Philadelphia in 1909. She received her secondary education at the Philadelphia High School for Girls, a school that catered to scholastically talented students. During Cowdery's senior year, three of her poems were accepted for publication in the 1927 spring issue of *Black Opals*, a Philadelphia-based monthly publication that attempted to rival W.E.B. Du Bois's *Crisis* magazine. That same year, Cowdery received the Krigwa Poem Prize for "Longings," which was published in Harlem's most successful magazine, *Crisis.* After high school, Cowdery studied at Pratt Institute in New York to pursue fashion design but did not graduate. Beyond her sporadic trail of publications, little biographical information is available on Cowdery. Between 1927 and 1930, Cowdery's **poetry** appeared in *Crisis, Opportunity, Unity,* and *Carolina* magazines as well as in three anthologies. In 1928 Cowdery also published the one-act play *Lai-Li* in *Black Opals.* Between 1931 and 1935, there is no record that Cowdery published, but in 1936, she completed *We Lift Our Voices,* a volume of poetry.

Fellow Philadelphian Alain Locke and poet **Langston Hughes** befriended Cowdery, but even with such well-respected allies, and even as one of the only **Harlem Renaissance** women poets to publish a full-length book of poetry, she remains on the margins of the Harlem Renaissance canon. The only available image of Cowdery is a photo that appeared in the magazine *Crisis* in 1927. Pushing the boundaries of 1920s gender expectations, the photograph shows her with short, cropped hair, wearing a suit and bowtie. Evoked in this snapshot and unambiguously projected is the butch lesbian persona. But the butch psyche is articulated not simply in the image of Cowdery but also in her poetry. (By *butch* I refer to the sexually masculine persona that has historically been a part of lesbian culture.)

"Longings" is a sensual poem full of feminine images with a subtext that hints at the strong **lesbianism** theme that will come to characterize her later work. In this poem, Cowdery approaches blackness, like lesbian **sexuality**, obliquely and through metaphor. Her narrator is dark skinned and achieves a metaphoric orgasm with the stanza that reads "To plunge– / My brown body."

Cowdery's poem "Dusk" was published in Charles Johnson's collection *Ebony and Topaz* in 1927 and continues with a celebration of blackness, lesbian desire, and eroticism. It echoes a theme we find in many black writers of the time–that the true self can be embraced only in the shadows or at nighttime. Though Cowdery's female images of sensuality and sexuality are cloaked and ambiguous in "Longings" and "Dusk," she embraces them fully in her later work. In "Insatiate," Cowdery's most unapologetic and brazenly lesbian poem, she laughs at the foibles of jealously and desire.

Cowdery took her own life at age forty-three, and much of her work still remains in critical obscurity. Yet through her embodied metaphors and disruptive choice of poetic personae, Cowdery allows the reader to hear the voice of the early-twentieth-century American butch lesbian.

Work By

We Lift Our Voices and Other Poems. Introduction by William Stanley Braithwaite. Philadelphia: Alpress, 1936.

Works About

Honey, Maureen, ed. *Shadowed Dreams: Women's Poetry of the Harlem Renaissance.* New Brunswick, NJ: Rutgers University Press, 1989.
Jubilee, Vincent. "Philadelphia Afro-American Literary Circle and the Harlem Renaissance." Ph.D. diss., University of Pennsylvania, 1980. Abstract in *Dissertation Abstracts International*, 41.1112A (1980).
Patton, Venetria K., and Maureen Honey. *Double-Take: A Revisionist Harlem Renaissance Anthology.* New Brunswick, NJ: Rutgers University Press, 2001.
Roses, Lorraine E., and Ruth E. Randolph, eds. *Harlem's Glory: Black Women Writing 1900–1950.* Cambridge, MA: Harvard University Press, 1996.

Lorna J. Raven Wheeler

CRAFT, ELLEN (1826–1891) AND WILLIAM (1824–1900)

Unlike the majority of those born into American **slavery**, Ellen and William Craft documented their lives for posterity in *Running a Thousand Miles for Freedom* (1860), a **slave narrative** that they published jointly in England. Ellen was born on a large plantation in the town of Clinton, Georgia, to a **mulatto** called Maria and her white owner, Colonel James P. Smith. When Smith's daughter Eliza married Robert Collins, a prosperous doctor and businessman, her father's wedding present was the eleven-year-old Ellen. She was forced to leave her mother and accompany the newlyweds to Macon, a growing cotton production and transportation center in the middle of the state.

By her early twenties, Ellen had met and fallen in **love** with William Craft, an enslaved carpenter and the "property" of a Macon banker. In December 1848, the couple initiated a bold escape to the North. Ellen, who could easily pass for white, boarded the first-class compartment of a train disguised as the sickly gentleman planter Mr. Johnson, whose black valet William escorted "him" to medical treatments in Philadelphia.

Although fugitives frequently fled bondage dressed as members of the opposite gender, Ellen's successful camouflage incited notoriety and controversy—extending to her staunchest white supporters—about whether African **identity** diminished or even negated an enslaved woman's femininity. Reports in the northern newspapers of Ellen's **domestic** life in Boston, the national base for antislavery reform where the Crafts settled, spoke back to such conceptions of **race** by proclaiming how she epitomized **whiteness** and **motherhood**. They described her as a reticent and retiring wife, an excellent and industrious seamstress, and a devout Christian mother whose desire to marry—and to bear children that no southern man or woman owned—superseded any scruples she might possess about unsexing herself in trousers.

Ellen herself actively reinforced such conventional gender roles when she participated in public abolitionist gatherings. Following the carefully choreographed lectures of his male contemporaries **Frederick Douglass** and **William Wells Brown**, William would present a stirring oral account of their escape. In contrast, Ellen waited and, on cue from William, acknowledged the applause by standing, speaking briefly, and then returning to her seat on the podium. She certainly would have been aware of social taboos that prohibited respectable women from speaking before mixed-gender or promiscuous audiences. Although she was never coy about expressing her opinions directly and firmly in society as well as private correspondence, this staging partnership distinguishes her from **Sojourner Truth**, **Maria Stewart**, and other African American women who stood alone behind podium and pulpit in the years before the Civil War.

The Fugitive Slave Act of 1850, which gave judicial support to slaveholders' efforts to return escaped blacks to bondage, forced the Crafts to seek safer, more hospitable domicile in England. When their owners commissioned agents to retrieve the now-famous pair, irate Bostonians rallied against them and, led by the biracial Vigilance Committee, chased away the bounty hunters. Sequestered in separate houses for their own security, the couple became virtual prisoners in the most free of the nominal Free States. Fleeing overland through Maine to Halifax, Nova Scotia, they boarded a Liverpool-bound ship and rang in the following year as British residents.

Ellen and William lived in Great Britain for nearly two decades, primarily in the London suburb of Hammersmith. Ellen refined her public persona as a conventional woman who revolved around **home** and **family**, even though the challenging realities of a fugitive slave often contradicted this image. While William traveled to West Africa for long stints to educate and bring **Christianity** to the youth, and to cultivate cotton crops that would undermine the southern plantation economy, Ellen managed their household for extensive periods as a single parent. They bore five children: Charles, William, Brougham, Alfred, and Ellen. However, rumors circulated by the southern press that Ellen wanted to return to slavery impugned her character. In addition, two white Bostonians, Theodore Parker and James Freeman Clarke, would recall conversations where she reputedly confessed to having had a child before she met William. Even though she may have been a victim of **rape**, even though the child reputedly died because of a cruel mistress, Ellen most certainly would not have registered as virtuous by Victorian standards of morality. The prospect of such a shaming story fouling the ears of sympathizers and detractors alike must have magnified the pressures both Crafts faced to walk a straight-laced, pious path.

In 1870 they returned to Georgia. An initial attempt to open a school was foiled by night riders, who burned the building to cinders. On land purchased with funds raised by northern benefactors, they next instituted a cooperative farm and school for newly freed slaves in Ways Station, near Savannah, where decades before they had disembarked the Macon train and boarded a steamer toward **freedom**. The abolitionist Lydia Maria Child had published their story in a primer for the southern black **community** called *The Freedmen's Book* (1865, 1866), so it seemed only fitting that they actually launch their own educational institution. Ellen thus joined the ranks of African American women like **Charlotte Forten (Grimké)**, a minority among the masses of white schoolmarms educating the freedmen. Yet both she and William lacked the **class** privilege and freeborn status that even Forten claimed.

Unfortunately, this second project ended in financial ruin and scandal. In their final years, the Crafts joined their daughter in Charleston, South Carolina, a former port for the slave trade where, as "Mr. Johnson," Ellen had once rested as they escaped in the rooms of a posh hotel where human beings were sold at street level.

While the Crafts' written legacy is *Running a Thousand Miles*, William's first-person voice dominates. We can only speculate about portions Ellen may have contributed and the stylistic and editorial suggestions she may have made. Yet her courage in particular has inspired the work of many women writers, from Harriet Beecher Stowe's *Uncle Tom's Cabin* (1852), **Hannah Crafts**'s *The Bondwoman's Narrative* (c. 1855), and Lydia Maria Childs's *The Stars and Stripes* (1858), to **Georgia Douglas Johnson**'s *William and Ellen Craft* (1926), to the performances of Marcia Estabrook's Character Educational Theatre and Gertrude Jeanette's Hadley Players of Harlem, New York. Both Ellen and William are remembered as heroes for all seasons.

See also Passing

Work By

Running a Thousand Miles for Freedom; or, the Escape of William and Ellen Craft from Slavery. Introduction by Barbara McCaskill. Athens: University of Georgia Press, 1999.

Works About

Barrett, Lindon. "Hand-Writing: Legibility and the White Body in *Running a Thousand Miles for Freedom.*" *American Literature* 69.2 (June 1997): 315–336.

Blackett, Richard J. M. "The Odyssey of William and Ellen Craft." *Beating Against the Barriers: Biographical Essays on Nineteenth-Century Afro-American History.* Baton Rouge: Louisiana State University Press, 1986. 87–137.

Brusky, Sarah. "The Travels of William and Ellen Craft: Race and Travel Literature in the 19th Century." *Prospects: An Annual of American Cultural Studies* 25 (2000): 177–192.

Foreman, Gabrielle P. "Who's Your Mama?: 'White' Mulatta Genealogies, Early Photography, and Anti-Passing Narratives of Slavery and Freedom." *American Literary History* 14.3 (Fall 2002): 505–539.

Heglar, Charles J. *Rethinking the Slave Narrative: Marriage and the Narratives of Henry Bibb and Ellen Craft.* Westport, CT: Greenwood Press, 2001.

McCaskill, Barbara. "Ellen Craft–The Fugitive as Text and Artifact." *African American Review* 28.4 (Winter 1994): 509–529.

Sterling, Dorothy. "Ellen Craft: The Valiant Journey." *Black Foremothers: Three Lives.* 2nd ed. Old Westbury, NY: Feminist Press, 1988. 3–59.

Weinauer, Ellen M. "'A Most Respectable Looking Gentleman': Passing, Possession, and Transgression in *Running a Thousand Miles for Freedom.*" *Passing and the Fiction of Identity.* Ed. Elaine K. Ginsberg. Durham, NC: Duke University Press, 1996. 37–56.

Barbara McCaskill

CRAFTS, HANNAH (1830?–1880?)

Hannah Crafts is an enigma. The runaway slave who finally made a life in New Jersey is said to be the first black woman novelist. Yet, as the *American Heritage Dictionary* sums *enigma*, the woman is a puzzle, ambiguous, and inexplicable. Her true **identity** remains a boggle to literary researchers. Her authorship role in the novel *The Bondwoman's Narrative* is ambiguous. Lastly, how she garnered the skills to produce such a work remains largely inexplicable. What is left is speculation. Nonetheless, readers will experience the psychological development of a woman from a child who self-concedes her insignificance to a woman who shows her strength through accomplishment, compassion, and ingenuity.

Readers will not find a lot of information on the author in what is billed as an 1850s fictionalized **autobiography**. The manuscript, resurrected from the shelves of New York's Swann Galleries auction house by Harvard professor Henry Louis Gates, Jr., is largely written in the first person, but there are times when the writer seems not to be the narrator. Those who have the tenacity to plow through the Warner Books–produced *New York Times* best-seller, edited by Gates, will find about all of the extant biographical information about Crafts.

She appears to be a self-taught writer who sampled liberally from classic novels such as Charlotte Brontë's *Jane Eyre* (1847), Sir Walter Scott's *Rob Roy* (1817), and Charles Dickens's *Bleak House* (1852–1853). Researchers say those books were included in the library of her third master, North Carolina politician, landowner, and author John Hill Wheeler. Scholars also cite as influences Shakespeare's tragedies, Byron, **Phillis Wheatley**, biographer Felicia Hemans, and the Bible.

Historical document expert Joe Nickell, one of the scholars who helped authenticate the manuscript, ties Wheeler to Crafts because the novel describes the mid-1850s U.S. minister to Nicaragua in a manner similar to the way he presents himself in his diaries. Crafts refers to the slaveholder as "Wh——r," early in the novel. Later, she uses the full name. Also, Wheeler was born and raised and owned land in Murfreesboro, in Lincoln County, North Carolina, which is mentioned in the narrative.

"I am neither clever, nor learned, nor talented," Crafts begins her self-description in the novel. "When a child they used to scold and find fault with me because they said I was dull and stupid." The narrator concludes that what she really had was a "silent unobtrusive way of observing things and events." Readers gain evidence of that perceptiveness as the manuscript continues.

Crafts says she was "not brought up by anybody in particular." The author emerges as a blank slate, which is typical in **slave narratives**. The problem is that the lack of information hides her time and place of birth. If, as some researchers suspect, the author was in her twenties during the 1850s, Hannah Crafts's birth can be fixed in the 1830s.

"The birds of the air, or the beasts of the field are not freer from moral culture than I was," she writes. From those vague images throughout the novel develops the tale of a woman who grows up on a Virginia plantation called Lindendale, owned by the Cosgroves, is sold to a **family** named Henry, who in turn sell her to the Wheelers of North Carolina, and from whom she escapes to New Jersey. In the end, as the narrative states and as experts believe, Crafts becomes the teacher in a black school and is the wife of a Methodist minister. In the end, the writer states that her husband sits nearby as she writes.

Crafts tends to speak about the places she works and her escape adventures through women. Readers will learn more about Mrs. Henry and Mrs. Wheeler than their husbands. Those who grew used to novels where male slaves take the lead in the control of plantation life or escapes will see those activities through women's eyes. Even when Crafts, during the successful escape attempt, disguises herself as a white man, she is urged by the black Aunt Hetty to move toward **freedom** within her own gender—as a white woman.

Gates notes that many of the names and places referenced in the book correspond to nineteenth-century places and people. Three Cosgroves are mentioned in the 1850 census. Henry was a Presbyterian minister in Stafford County, Virginia. Also, Milton, a small village mentioned during one of Hannah's attempts to escape, existed near Tyler's Mill in Charles City County, Virginia.

The novel frequently refers to Jane Johnson, who escaped John Wheeler's bondage in 1855. The case gained notoriety because William Passamore, one of the abolitionists who aided her, was sued. Researchers believe Crafts was bought to replace her. Gates and others estimate that she also escaped from Wheeler between late March and early May 1857. If so, it is supposed that the real Hannah Crafts might be Hannah Vincent, who appears in 1870 and 1880 New Jersey census records as the wife of Thomas Vincent.

Gates credits the late Howard University scholar Dorothy Porter with piquing his interest in the verification of the author's racial identity. She asserted that the author was a runaway slave because the narrator identifies herself as a black with "white" looks. According to Gates, Porter said there would be no reason for a white author to try to disguise herself as African American. Also, Porter backs the narrator's claim based on the sensitive way the work represents black characters.

In his hunt for the real Crafts, Gates began with federal census records. "No Hannah Crafts are listed in the entire U.S. Federal census between 1860 and 1880," he writes. The researcher found a Hannah *Craft*. Gates said the name was popular in the mid-nineteenth century, but all of the women were white.

He found a black Hannah *Kraft* who lived in Baltimore County, Maryland, in 1880. The woman was married to Wesley Kraft. The woman was born in Virginia, as was the story's narrator. Gates thought the protagonist's nuptial with a Methodist minister might have been a play on the real-life husband's name. The Rev. John Wesley was a Methodist founder. Gates was disappointed.

A copy of the census record from the Mormon Family History Library in Salt Lake City showed Hannah Kraft was thirty in 1880. That makes the person too young. They believed the book was written between 1855 and 1861. Also, Kraft could neither read nor write.

Gates turned to the 72,000 records of deposits into the Freedman's Bank, which are also available from the Mormon library. He found a Maria H. Crafts, who opened an account in 1874, whose complexion was listed as "white." Gates returned to census records and found twenty-three *Mary* H. Crafts in the 1880 list who were described as black. Six were described as **mulatto**. One was born in 1840s Virginia. She was a decade older than the researchers expected, but as a teacher, the woman could also be a writer. Gates's search continued.

The protagonist begins as the property of the De Vincent family. Gates checked whether she used that last name after the escape from **slavery**. He found a Hannah Ann Vincent in Burlington, New Jersey, in 1850. The twenty-two-year-old, mixed-blood woman, according to the census, lived with a forty-seven-year-old black woman, Mary Roberts. Gates thought this was a dead-end lead but revived her as a possibility after a check of Joseph H. Morgan's 1887 *History of the New Jersey Conference of the A.M.E. Church.* A Hannah Vincent is listed as a stewardess, treasurer, and teacher at Burlington's Bethel African Methodist Episcopal (AME) Church.

Despite all that remains unknown about the author, Hannah Crafts's novel provides chilling insight into the life of an antebellum slave. Experts say the book breaks many of the **stereotypes** present in other recollections of the time. Crafts's story does not present a system of exploitation that offered the enslaved a pleasant life. At the same time, there are some lighter moments. In the end, the author's life and work show that slaves' persistence and patience were key in their ability to maintain and fulfill their hopes.

Work By

The Bondwoman's Narrative: A Novel. Ed. Henry Louis Gates. New York: Warner Books, 2003.

Works About

Buncombe, Andrew. "Story of Black Slave's Escape to Freedom." *London Independent,* December 10, 2001, 13.

Carter, Zakia. Review of *The Bondwoman's Narrative. Black Issues Book Review* 4.3 (May–June 2002): 39.

Gates, Henry Louis, and Hollis Robbins, eds. *In Search of Hannah Crafts: Critical Essays on The Bondwoman's Narrative.* New York: Basic Books, 2004.

"Henry Louis Gates Donates Slave Novel to Yale University." *Black Issues in Higher Education* 20.9 (June 19, 2003): 12.

Jabari, Asim. "From Experience to Eloquence: *The Bondwoman's Narrative.*" *New Crisis,* May 1, 2002, 50–51.

Minzesheimer, Bob. "Novel May Be First by Escaped Female Slave." *Chicago Sun Times,* March 28, 2002, 32.

Segal, Ronald. "The First in Line, *Bondwoman's Narrative.*" *Spectator,* July 13, 2003, 36.

Vincent F. A. Golphin

CROSSING OVER JORDAN

Linda Beatrice Brown's second novel, *Crossing Over Jordan* (1995), tells the story of four generations of African American women, focusing on the last two of those generations. The story is of the struggle from **slavery** to **freedom**, from oppression to independence.

The novel opens with a prologue that tells an African creation **myth** about the Longmother Spirit and her gifts of **memory** and words to generations of Africans and African Americans. The epilogue returns to the Longmother with images of undoing clothing and lives to take the fragments and reweave them into stories to pass to future generations. Within the frame formed by this mythic prologue and epilogue is another frame story set in a future 2012 that features two elderly women, Hermine Greene and her Aunt Story, who bicker and argue during their final days together. The narrative is divided into chapters, each beginning in the 2012 frame, then going back to pick up the thread that begins in 1873 with the story of Georgia McCloud, mother to Sadie and grandmother to Story, and continues across the chapters to 1974.

Sadie marries the abusive Reverend Jacob Temple. Story resents her mother's weakness and fears and loves her domineering father. Story's younger sister, Bertricia, also known as Bertie, or Baby Sister, is the spoiled baby of the **family** whom Story resents. Story hardens herself in her resolve to achieve education and a respected position in her **community**. She intervenes in Bertie's **love** life, stealing her boyfriend Herman Greene and indirectly causing Bertie's **death**. Story marries Herman and bears a daughter, Hermine. After Herman's death, Story returns to Hattenfield, North Carolina, where she grew up, establishing the **fiction** that Hermine is her orphaned niece. By sheer determination, Story gains a college education and becomes a respected teacher in her community but shuts Hermine out of her life for fear that she will lose herself in **motherhood**.

Hermine struggles with her educational goals, her sexual **identity**, and civil rights and student activism of the early 1960s. After spending much of her adult life in California, Hermine returns to North Carolina in 1987 to care for Story. Through the family photo album and inquiries from Herman's family, Hermine finally learns, in the last 2012 segment, that Story is her mother. She confronts Story, who grudgingly admits the truth. While Story never comes to terms with the lies she has lived to achieve her position, Hermine is able, finally, to reconcile herself to her **history** and to figuratively cross over Jordan to reach a kind of peace with her mother, her history, and herself.

Crossing Over Jordan, with its use of myth and its intense story of the struggles of several generations of women, showcases Brown's poetic skills and her commitment to the theme of the struggles of black women to liberate themselves from the oppression of history and society to become their own persons.

See also Civil Rights Movement; Sexuality

Works About

DeLombard, Jeannine. Review of *Crossing Over Jordan*. *New York Times Book Review* 100 (February 19, 1995): 21.

Pearl, Nancy. Review of *Crossing Over Jordan*. *Library Journal* 120.3 (February 15, 1995): 1059.

Review of *Crossing Over Jordan*. *Publishers Weekly* 242.4 (January 23, 1995): 61.

Ruff, Patricia Elam. Review of *Crossing Over Jordan*. *Emerge* 6.7 (May 1995): 58–60.

Harriette C. Buchanan

CULLEN, COUNTEE (1903–1946)

One of the most acclaimed poets of his time, Countee (pronounced count-tay) Cullen was born Countee LeRoy Porter in Louisville, Kentucky, though some sources claim it was New York, New York, or Baltimore, Maryland. His early life is unclear, but it is thought that he was raised by his paternal grandmother until her **death** when he was nine. In 1918, when he was fifteen, he was unofficially adopted by the Reverend and Mrs. Frederick A. Cullen. Frederick Cullen was the prominent pastor of Salem Methodist Episcopal Church in Harlem and later became the president for the Harlem chapter of the National Association for the Advancement of Colored People (NAACP). The Reverend Cullen's political activity and religious leadership in Harlem pulled Countee physically as well ideologically into the **Harlem Renaissance**, the flowering of black artistry in the twentieth century.

While Cullen was exposed to black leaders of his age, his formal education took place in predominantly white schools such as the De Witt Clinton High School in Manhattan, where his academic achievements led him to become vice president of his class and editor of the school newspaper as well as winning prizes for his speeches and **poetry**. While attending New York University (NYU), he won a number of poetry contests, in particular, winning the Witter Bynner Contest for undergraduate poetry sponsored by *Poetry* magazine. In 1925, he graduated Phi Beta Kappa from NYU, and *Color*, his first book of poetry, was published. *Color* contains some of his best-known poems: "Heritage," "Incident," and "Yet Do I Marvel."

The third poem is perhaps his most widely referred to because in it Cullen marvels at God's creation of a poet who is black but whom God calls to art anyway. This poem has often been seen as a cry of despair from a poet struggling to be who he is in a time and place that often tried to prevent him from doing just that, but it can also be seen as a declaration, a loud affirmation, of the black poet's work. God calls the black writer to art just as white writers have been called. While the theme of the poem is clearly current with the political and artistic milieu of his day, the style of "Yet Do I Marvel" is a traditional sonnet. This suggests a central concern for the reading of Cullen's poetry. While many writers of the Harlem Renaissance were experimenting with new rhythms and forms, all of Cullen's poems show a clear influence of the traditional white European style of poetry. Though he was a prominent writer during this time, his popularity was not universal. Some critics preferred a less rigid, less traditional style for the "new" poetry being written. Unlike **Langston Hughes** and others who were experimenting with poetic form and voice, Cullen's major poetic influences were the English Romantics, particularly John Keats. Like Keats, Cullen seemed to believe that art should be transcendent; it should take us out of our time and place and be universal for all people. This ideal was clearly not shared by many other writers of the Harlem Renaissance, many of whom were more interested in creating an art that spoke about a people's experience within the particular place of the United States.

Cullen has often been critiqued for not writing more about **race** or protest, and much has been made of his stated desire to write a race-neutral poetry. However, a close examination of his poetry reveals that he wrote many poems about what it meant to be black in the United States during the early part of the twentieth century, but he did so using traditional poetic forms and with Greek, Roman, and European allusions. Cullen did write poems about the racial injustices of the day, but he placed those thematic concerns within the confines of a white European poetic tradition embodied by Keats and the other Romantics.

In 1926, he earned a master's degree from Harvard University and began working as an assistant editor for the magazine *Opportunity*. His column, called "The Dark Tower," helped make him more prominent in literary circles by his criticism and promotion of other writers. He published three books over the next three years: *The Ballad of the Brown Girl* (1927), *Copper Sun* (1927), and *The Black Christ, and Other Poems* (1929). In the title poem of *The Black Christ*, Cullen uses the analogy of the lynching of a black man to Christ's crucifixion, revealing that the poet was far from indifferent to the causes of his day and that he was moved to write his own particular kind of protest poetry.

The year 1929 was monumental in Cullen's life. He published *The Black Christ, and Other Poems* and married the daughter of W.E.B. Du Bois in a lavish ceremony celebrated by what seemed to be all of Harlem, and he was awarded a Guggenheim Fellowship to France. But his marriage ended in 1930, in part because of his close relationships with men, particularly his friend Harold Jackman. Though he married again in 1940, there are veiled references to homosexual desire in some of his poetry.

In the 1930s, his poetic flow slowed down, but he continued to write steadily for the rest of his life: writing children's books, collaborating on several plays, and penning a somewhat unsuccessful satirical novel about life in Harlem. He began teaching in 1934 in New York City and died at the age of forty-three of uremic poisoning. Though he is not as well known now as other writers of the time who experimented with rhythmic forms, Cullen's lyrical poems, though sometimes derivative of the tradition he emulated, express his desire to write the fullest expression of poetic beauty while grappling with the demands of being a poet and a black man in America.

Works By

The Ballad of the Brown Girl: An Old Ballad Retold. New York: Harper, 1927.

The Black Christ, and Other Poems. 1929. Ann Arbor, MI: University Microfilms, 1973.

Caroling Dusk: An Anthology of Verse by Negro Poets. Ed. Countee Cullen. 1927. New York: Harper, 1974.

Color. 1925. New York: Arno Press, 1969.

Copper Sun. New York: Harper, 1927.

The Lost Zoo (A Rhyme for the Young, but Not Too Young). 1940, 1969. New York: Burdett, 1992.

The Medea, and Some Poems. New York: Harper, 1935.

My Lives and How I Lost Them. 1942. Chicago: Follett, 1971. (Juvenile.)

My Soul's High Song: The Collected Writings of Countee, Voice of the Harlem Renaissance. Ed. Gerald Early. New York: Doubleday, 1991.

One Way to Heaven. 1932. New York: AMS Press, 1975. (Novel.)

On These I Stand: An Anthology of the Best Poems of Countee Cullen. New York: Harper, 1947.

St. Louis Woman Black. Theatre. Ed. Lindsay Patterson. New York: Dodd, 1971. (Play with Arna Bontemps.)

Works About

Anderson, Jervis. "Review of *My Soul's High Song: The Collected Writings of Countee Cullen, Voice of the Harlem Renaissance.*" *New Republic,* April 8, 1991, 27–36.

Baker, Houston A., Jr. *A Many-Colored Coat of Dreams: The Poetry of Countee Cullen.* Detroit: Broadside Press, 1974.

Bontemps, Arna, ed. *The Harlem Renaissance Remembered.* New York: Dodd, Mead, 1972.

Bronz, Stephen H. *Roots of Racial Consciousness; The 1920's: Three Harlem Renaissance Authors.* New York: Libra, 1964.

Davis, Arthur P. *From the Dark Tower: Afro-American Writers, 1900–1960.* Washington, DC: Howard University Press, 1974.

Emanuel, James A., and Theodore L. Gross, eds. *Dark Symphony: Negro Literature in America.* New York: Free Press, 1968. 172–187.

Ferguson, Blanche E. *Countee Cullen and the Negro Renaissance.* New York: Dodd, 1966.

Lewis, David Levering. *When Harlem Was in Vogue.* New York: Vintage Books, 1982.

Perry, Margaret. *A Bio-Bibliography of Countee P. Cullen, 1903–1946.* Westport, CT: Greenwood Press, 1971.

Powers, Peter. " 'The Singing Man Who Must Be Reckoned With': Private Desire and Public Responsibility in the Poetry of Countee Cullen." *African American Review* 34 (2000): 661+.

Shucard, Alan. *Countee Cullen.* Boston: Twayne, 1984.

Amy Sparks Kolker

CUNEY-HARE, MAUD (1874–1936)

Just two generations removed from **slavery** in Galveston, Texas, Maud Cuney-Hare rose to artistic distinction in an impressive variety of media and should be recognized as a pioneer in the field of ethnomusicology. She was an accomplished concert pianist who entered Boston's exclusive New England Conservatory of Music in 1890, despite the opposition of several of her classmates; Maud Cuney was one of just two students of African descent in the school. While in Boston she met and befriended the influential scholar and **race** leader W.E.B. Du Bois, then a student at Harvard University. Du Bois later proved instrumental in securing the publication of Cuney-Hare's first literary effort, a biography of her father, the prominent post-Reconstruction politician Norris Wright Cuney, in 1913. Cuney-Hare also compiled a volume of **poetry**; composed, collected, arranged, and delivered lecture recitals about black American music; wrote and produced an original play; and in 1927 founded and began the general directorship of Boston's Allied Arts Centre, an educational facility and performing arts venue showcasing visual art, music, and theater.

Cuney-Hare's paternal grandfather was Philip Cuney, a reasonably prosperous white planter who eventually manumitted his longtime slave housekeeper/mistress Adeline Stuart, along with their eight children, and also provided for the education of Maud's father, Norris Wright, and his seven siblings. Cuney-Hare's mother, Adelina Dowdie Cuney, was also the child of an interracial liaison between a slaveholder and his chattel property. A vocalist who periodically performed at public events, Adelina Cuney fostered her daughter's musical inclination. Following her study at the Conservatory, she returned to Texas, where she taught music successively at the Texas Deaf, Dumb, and Blind Institute for Colored Youths, at the settlement program of the Institutional Church of Chicago, and at Prairie View State College. A productive scholar, she contributed to periodicals such as the *Christian Science Monitor*, *Musical Quarterly*, *Musical America*, and *Musical Observer*. She also worked with Du Bois's National Association for the Advancement of Colored People (NAACP) journal *Crisis*, as the editor of a regular column on music and the arts.

Cuney-Hare's collection of poems *The Message of the Trees* appeared in 1918. She published a compilation of Creole songs in 1921 and staged her original play, *Antar of Araby*, with the Allied Arts Players in 1926. The work that has earned the greatest distinction for her, *Negro Musicians and Their Music*, was published just months after Cuney-Hare's **death** on February 13, 1936. The product of extensive travels throughout Mexico, the Caribbean, and the United States during which she collected songs and researched materials, the seminal text traces the roots of the black musical tradition from the continent of Africa and explores the common influences permeating the African diaspora. Containing biographical accounts of working artists as well as their illustrious precursors, the book is an invaluable resource in the study of the **history** of black music.

Though she married William Parker Hare and permanently relocated to Boston, where she became an active clubwoman and avid proponent of the arts, Maud Cuney-Hare is buried beside her parents in Galveston.

Works By

Antar of Araby. Plays and Pageants from the Life of the Negro. Ed. Willis Richardson. Washington, DC: Associated Publishers, 1930.

The Message of the Trees; an Anthology of Leaves and Branches. Boston: Cornhill Company, 1918.

Negro Musicians and Their Music. Washington, DC: Associated Publishers, 1936.

Norris Wright Cuney: A Tribune of the Black People. New York: Crisis Publishing Company, 1913.

Six Creole Folk-Songs: Six Songs for Medium Voice with Piano Accompaniment/ [arranged] by Maud Cuney Hare. New York: C. Fischer, 1921.

Works About

Hales, Douglas. *A Southern Family in White & Black: The Cuneys of Texas.* College Station: Texas A&M University Press, 2003.

Hunter, Tera W. Introduction to *Norris Wright Cuney: A Tribune of the Black People,* by Maud Cuney-Hare. New York: G. K. Hall, 1995.

Love, Josephine Harreld. Introduction to *Negro Musicians and Their Music,* by Maud Cuney-Hare. New York: G. K. Hall, 1996.

Licia Morrow Calloway

 **D**

DANNER, MARGARET ESSE (1915–1988)

Margaret Esse Danner was a powerful force in the Chicago/Detroit literary movements of the 1960s, helping to foster the next generation of African American women writers through her work at various cultural centers and colleges. She should be situated as a key transitional figure in the African American poetic tradition between poets of the previous generation such as **Margaret Walker** or **Gwendolyn Brooks** and **Sonia Sanchez** or **Lucille Clifton** of the next wave. Today Danner is best known for achieving precise visual imagery and evoking African themes and **history** in her verse.

Danner's parents, Caleb and Naomi Esse, moved from Kentucky to Chicago, where Danner attended Englewood High School. Danner won a prize in eighth grade for her poem "The Violin." She attended Loyola and the Midwestern Writers Conference at Northwestern, where she received second place in their **poetry** workshop. She became an editorial assistant at the influential *Poetry* magazine in 1951, moving up to assistant editor in 1956. She was the first African American to hold this position at that national magazine. Danner was awarded a John Hay Whitney Fellowship in 1951 and used the award money to travel to Senegal in 1966. She held poet-in-residence positions at Wayne State University in Detroit (1961), Virginia Union University in Richmond (1968–1969), and LeMoyne Owens College in Memphis (1970–1975). The poet also helped found Detroit's Boone Cultural Arts Center in 1962.

Danner was married twice (Cornell Strickland and Otto Cunningham). With her first husband, Danner had a daughter, Naomi, named after the poet's mother. Her grandson Sterling Washington, Jr., is the source for her series of "Muffin" poems: "Muffin, His Baba and the Boneman" and "Inheritance for Muffin," among others. Danner published five collections of poetry from 1960 to 1976. The last one, *The Down of a Thistle*, is dedicated to Robert Hayden, another member of the Baha'i faith. Her use of Africa as an inspiration can be found in works such as "This Is an African Worm" and "Far from Africa: Four Poems." Danner's literary friendship with Dudley Randall produced the 1966 *Poem Counterpoem*, a work that includes ten poems by each poet engaged in a dialogue on facing pages. Her generous encouragement of young talent is evident in her two edited collections, *Brass Horse* (1968) and *Regroup* (1969). Danner was a model for poetic craftsmanship as well as a mentor for the next generation of poets.

Works By

The Down of a Thistle: Selected Poems, Prose Poems, and Songs. Waukesha, WI: Country Beautiful, 1976.

Impressions of African Art Forms in the Poetry of Margaret Danner. Detroit: Broadside Press, 1960.

Iron Lace. Millbrook, NY: Kriya Press, 1968.

Poem Counterpoem. Detroit: Broadside Press, 1966.

To Flower: Poems. Nashville, TN: Hemphill Press, 1963.

Works About

Aldridge, June M. "Margaret Esse Danner." *Dictionary of Literary Biography* 41 (1988): 84–89.

Stetson, Erlene. "Dialectic Voices in the Poetry of Margaret Esse Danner." *Black American Poets Between Worlds, 1940–1960.* Ed. R. Baxter Miller. Knoxville: University of Tennessee Press, 1986. 93–103.

Ann Beebe

DANTICAT, EDWIDGE (1969–)

Born in Port-au-Prince, Edwidge Danticat lived her first twelve years in Haiti. Unable to find **work** in his native country, her father André immigrated to the United States when his daughter was two years old. Once in New York he worked in a glass factory and for a car wash before becoming a taxi driver. Danticat's mother Rose immigrated when Edwidge was four and became a textile worker. Danticat remembers clinging to her mother, with others having to remove her physically, when she realized that her mother was to leave Haiti without her. Edwidge and her younger brother Eliab went to live with their father's brother and wife in Bel Air, a poor section of Port-au-Prince.

At twelve Danticat joined her parents in Brooklyn. By then she had two new brothers. Danticat's formal education had been in French, though the family spoke Haitian Creole at **home**. While she learned English quickly and remained proud of all three languages, once in the United States she withdrew as schoolmates taunted her as a boat person. Danticat felt a loss of **identity** in being between countries, simultaneously feeling a loss of her childhood in Haiti and like a young child in New York learning to function. Yet immigration and its changes would provide much material for the **fiction** she would write.

Danticat had kept journals in Haiti, sewing together pieces of paper to create a book. After receiving the Madeline books, she rewrote them, creating instead a Haitian heroine. In her very first short story she wrote about a girl who is visited by an assemblage of women each night. These visions would become part of the unstable Marie's experience in "Between the Pool and the Gardenias" in *Krik? Krak!* Once in the United States, Danticat continued to keep journals, written in fragmented Creole, French, and English. Mirroring Danticat's own uncomfortable entry into the English-speaking world, this fragmented presentation, representing those unused to, or uncomfortable with, speaking has become a powerful quality of Danticat's characters. That Danticat writes and publishes in English is something she attributes more to timing, the fact that she arrived in the United States as an adolescent, rather than to any conscious choice. At twelve she had still been learning French in school, not to the point of a literary facility with the language; and Creole, spoken at home but not taught in Haitian schools, was therefore not a written language for Danticat.

Proud of her origins, Danticat arrived in New York already possessing a love of storytelling, having heard folktales and family stories throughout her childhood in Haiti. She was used to the Haitian call-and-response technique of storytelling—the storyteller calling out "Krik?" and the listeners responding "Krak!"—having learned the power of storytelling through her aunt's grandmother. Children around her used to vie to comb the older woman's hair, into which she braided coins. Danticat later wove the importance of hair and heirs and women and wisdom together into the epilogue of *Krik? Krak!* where a young Haitian girl, very much like Danticat must have been, defends her desire to write in a country that devalues a woman's experience, especially in text, while simultaneously learning the importance of the myriad generations of women whose spirits run through her blood. In the United States, Danticat would find solace in books and was influenced by black writers such as **James Baldwin**, **Richard Wright**, **Alice Walker**, and **Paule Marshall**, feeling they wrote of her experience, too. Thus, for Danticat, reading and writing became a way to understand her new world once in Brooklyn.

Danticat was the first female Haitian American author to write in English and publish through a major publishing house. While the foreign nature of many ethnic female authors is promoted in the United States—as long as their works are without the more cumbersome aspect of translation—Danticat's works can be seen as forming a bridge between literatures. As though choosing from an archival largesse, she blurs the divide between American and so-called foreign literature with her presentation of engrossing, intimate testimonials from a heretofore silenced **history**. Danticat's characters speak of suffering and even occasionally of prevailing. And to give voice to the lost, especially those female, is arguably Danticat's most crucial aim, an end she achieves expertly since the reader of her works can feel not only that her characters might have lived but that they must have lived.

Danticat graduated from Barnard College in 1990 and then earned a Master of Fine Arts from Brown University in 1993. She sold her novel ***Breath, Eyes, Memory*** to Soho Press while still a graduate student. The work had actually originated in high school as an article about leaving Haiti for a New York teen newspaper, yet she calls its emotions autobiographical rather than its plot. Expanded, the story would become her graduate thesis. Published in 1994, *Breath, Eyes, Memory* tells the story of a Haitian girl who at twelve joins her mother in New York, but Danticat also wanted to examine the lives and relationships of ordinary people as they cope with a dictatorship or with post-dictatorship. As a child, Danticat had formed strong bonds with her caretaker aunt and uncle in Haiti after her parents' emigration and at twelve felt torn when reunited with her **family** in New York. The novel explores the broken relationship between mother Martine and daughter Sophie, a relationship arrested because of the need to immigrate separately to the United States. However, Haiti later becomes as much a location of reunification for the women as it is a place of horror and anger. The testing for female virginity that Danticat writes about in the novel was seen by some Haitian Americans as an insulting outing of a cultural practice and garnered Danticat hate mail.

In the nine stories of *Krik? Krak!*, a short-story collection published in 1995 and a finalist for the National Book Award in the same year, Danticat allows women to speak of the emotional rather than political Haitian experience. Her female characters gain strength and identity through the persistent spirit of previous generations of women, the vast majority of whom they never met. The separate stories typify the fragmented nature of the Haitian experience, but the connections between the women are revealed in surprisingly profound ways. ***The Farming of Bones*** centers on Rafael Leonidas Trujillo Molino's 1937 murder of 15,000 to 20,000 Haitians on Dominican soil at the border between the two countries. Here, as in all of Danticat's fiction, the bonds between women are more important than those between men, but in this novel, in which Amabelle searches for her lover Sebastien until coming to accept that he was slaughtered by Trujillo's forces, Danticat portrays real **love** between a man and a woman. Yet the critical relationship of the novel is again between two women, the Dominican-born and wealthy Valencia and the Haitian-born and poor Amabelle. While Amabelle and Sebastien never reunite, the women are able to meet decades after Trujillo's slaughter, but each comes to the cheerless realization that their political and emotional loyalties have long prevented any reconciliation. Amabelle instead regains her identity in the decades following the massacre through substitute mother-daughter relationships with the mothers of Sebastien and Yves, Sebastien's friend.

Public history has long displaced the personal narrative, yet those who live within a history have a great desire to fill in the gaps that traditional and sanctioned history has left out. Only recently recognized as a reliable genre, **autobiography**, even autobiographical fiction, allows the nameless and forgotten of history to speak to those who never were there. All of Danticat's works, fiction and nonfiction (she has also edited, singly and with others, collections of Haitian voices), emphasize that **memory** is what has been forgotten in the public telling of history, for history never records the victim's horror. These memories of horror keep victims isolated, unable to speak of a lived experience in history's distinct separation between the personal and the sanctioned. However, Danticat does not present her works as any sort of truth of experience, for ironically victims may only keep a measure of sanity through explicit failures in memory, something almost all of Danticat's female characters exhibit on some level in order to survive and continue.

Danticat writes of one of the most underrepresented cultures in the world and yet emphasizes that she does not speak for all Haitians. Instead, her telling of the Haitian experience through separate stories allows a measure of acceptance by individual victims themselves. Danticat's stories underscore that no history can be fully understood until told, though details will come only in pieces. Her non-Western circular approach to storytelling allows characters to chronicle their stories, thereby destabilizing the traditional notions of the immigrant and highlighting their enduring strength instead. Danticat shows the female Haitian experience as incomplete without the recognition of Haiti's horrors. Despite the **violence** of the Haitian homeland, it is only through the acknowledgment of that violence that one is completed.

Danticat has won numerous awards, including a *Granta* Regional Award for the Best Young American Novelists and a Pushcart Prize, and has taught creative writing at New York University and the University of Miami. Most recently, she has worked for the National Coalition for Haitian Rights on a three-year grant from the Lila Acheson Wallace Foundation.

Works By

Breath, Eyes, Memory. New York: Soho, 1994.
The Dew Breaker. New York: Knopf, 2004.
The Farming of Bones. New York: Soho, 1998.
Krik? Krak! New York: Soho, 1995.

Works About

Alexandre, Sandy, and Ravi Y. Howard. "My Turn in the Fire: A Conversation with Edwidge Danticat." *Transition: An International Review* 12.3 (2002): 110–128.
Anglesey, Zoë. "The Voice of the Storytellers: An Interview with Edwidge Danticat." *MultiCultural Review* 7.3 (1998): 36–39.
Horn, Jessica. "Edwidge Danticat: An Intimate Reader." *Meridians: Feminism, Race, Transnationalism* 1.2 (2001): 19–25.

Lyons, Bonnie. "An Interview with Edwidge Danticat." *Contemporary Literature* 44.2 (2003): 183–198.

Shea, Renée H. "The Dangerous Job of Edwidge Danticat: An Interview." *Callaloo* 19.2 (1996): 382–389.

——. "Edwidge Danticat." *Belles Lettres* 10.3 (1995): 12–15.

Wachtel, Eleanor. "A Conversation with Edwidge Danticat." *Brick* 65–66 (2000): 106–119.

Lisa Muir

DAUGHTERS

In *Daughters* (1991), **Paule Marshall**'s fourth novel, women are envisioned as not only the hope for a regenerative future but also as the source of political upheaval and power. Whereas much of Marshall's writing locates personal and cultural **healing** in the self-discovery of a female character, *Daughters* takes this idea one step further, into the decidedly political realm. The female characters in *Daughters* certainly experience enlightenment through their encounters with the past, but more important to this novel, their female **ancestors** inspire political activism. Through a small circle of interconnected women, political change occurs in both the United States and a Caribbean island.

Ursa McKensie is the novel's protagonist. She stands in a long line of political activists from the fictional island of Triunion, including her mother Estelle and island legend, **freedom** fighter Congo Jane. As the story begins, Ursa is an educated and successful woman working in the New York and New Jersey areas. She receives a message from her mother in Triunion, asking her to return to the island to aid in her father's election campaign. Ursa's father, Primus, began his political career with positive intentions, sincerely wanting to help the impoverished inhabitants of Triunion. More recently, however, he becomes manipulated by corporate interests; Estelle's concern for Primus's politics causes her to enlist her daughter's help. Once Ursa recognizes the decline of her father's good intentions toward the Triunion **community**, she schemes to affect his eventual defeat.

Daughters uses constellations and celestial imagery to connect present characters such as Ursa to her ancestral roots. Signifying one of the stars in the Little Dipper, Ursa defines herself in relation to her father and potentially her grandmother's status as "Ursa Major." The celestial references also tie the modern American woman Ursa has become to her past, both her childhood memories as well as her more distant cultural heritage.

Daughters presents an interplay of voices and generations as it interchanges temporal and geographical locations. Telling several stories at once, Marshall develops the many characters from Triunion's early **history**, including freedom-fighting Congo Jane, through Ursa's parents' meeting and marriage, into the present life of Ursa herself. The sections also vary physical settings between Triunion and New York. Marshall's narrative technique further develops her larger literary themes of integrating the past and the present, the African and the American.

Significantly, the title refers to the potential for political change through the heirs of Congo Jane. Estelle and Ursa embody the daughters of political radicalism that is both effective in its ability to change the course of the Triunion election and striking in its feminine core. Unlike much African American literature, Marshall locates political upheaval rather than strictly personal or individual change in the figure of a woman. Through female connection across generations, Marshall gives black women power beyond themselves; in *Daughters*, women enact external, political, and national change for the betterment of black people.

Works About

Ferguson, Moira. "Of Bears and Bearings: Paule Marshall's Diverse *Daughters*." *MELUS* 24.1 (1999): 177–195.
James, Cynthia. "Gender and Hemispheric Shifts in the Caribbean Narrative in English at the Close of the 20th Century: A Study of Paule Marshall's *Daughters* and Erna Brodber's *Louisiana*." *Jouvert: A Journal of Postcolonial Studies* 5.3 (2001). http://social.chass.ncsu.edu/jouvert/vsi3/cyja.htm.
Pettis, Joyce. "Legacies of Community and History in Paule Marshall's *Daughters*." *Studies in the Literary Imagination* 26.2 (1993): 89–99.

Laura Baker Shearer

DAVENPORT, DORIS (1949–   )

Through her **work** as a poet, doris davenport has made her mark on African American literature, but her essays and her work as a teacher, lesbian-feminist activist, and performance artist are significant as well. Informing almost all her work are davenport's feminist politics and her refusal to be pigeonholed by labels.

Davenport's first several collections of **poetry**, including *it's like this* (1980), *eat thunder & drink rain* (1982), and *VOODOO CHILE/slight return* (1991) were all self-published, partly because, as davenport herself has said, even small niche presses, including black and lesbian presses, did not see her work as being ideologically appropriate for them. Within all three books, davenport explores a range of topics from **love** poems and revenge poems for lovers and ex-lovers, to women's **spirituality**, to short imagistic poems capturing glimpses of nature, and especially, to forthright, defiant poems addressing the conflicts within feminist circles in the 1980s. For example, titles like "a statement in self-defense / regarding that shit about my negativity," "for sistuhs & others who object to my plain statements of fact, mixed metaphors, sick humor, and etc.– LISTEN," and "DOGMATIC DYKES" reflect davenport's refusal to accept a "party line" of any sort of politics. In "for sistuhs" she rejects straight women who object to any critique of males that conflicts with their "adulation" of men; in "DOGMATIC DYKES" she equally rejects lesbians who insist on only one way of being lesbian. Such poems reveal davenport's stature as a true individualist.

More recently, davenport has drawn on her northeast Georgia **home** for inspiration. Even the early volumes contain poems that pay homage to the place from which she comes, but her 1995 collection, *Soque Street Poems*, is focused completely on the small Georgia towns such as Gainesville, where she was born, and Cornelia, where she grew up. A recent essay, "All This, and Honeysuckles Too" (1998), shows davenport staking a claim to her "Affrilachian" **identity** (Frank X Walker's term for southern Appalachian African Americans). The essay is a lyrical celebration of her southern homeplace, one in which both **memory** and the present figure prominently.

Equally important is davenport's work as a scholar. Her 1981 essay "The Pathology of Racism: A Conversation with Third World Wimmin" unabashedly takes white women to task for their racism and calls for women of color to give up almost exclusively the desire for unity with white women and instead focus their attentions where they should be: on one another. "Black Lesbians in Academia: Visible Invisibility" (1982) was one of the first explorations of what it means to be an out black lesbian in an academic **community**.

Davenport earned her B.A. from Paine College in Augusta, Georgia, her M.A. in English from the State University of New York at Buffalo, and her Ph.D. in English from the University of Southern California. She has taught at a variety of schools; currently, she is an assistant professor of English at Stillman College in Tuscaloosa, Alabama. She is also in demand as a performance artist and lecturer.

Works By

"All This, and Honeysuckles Too." *Bloodroot: Reflections on Place by Appalachian Women Writers.* Ed. Joyce Dyer. Lexington: University Press of Kentucky, 1998. 88–97.

"Black Lesbians in Academia: Visible Invisibility." *Lesbian Studies: Into the Twenty-first Century.* Ed. Bonnie Zimmerman and Toni McNaron. New York: Feminist Press at the City University of New York, 1982. 9–11.

"Claiming Another Identity: Wimmin's Spirituality." *Day Tonight/Night Today* 3 (1981): 15–18.

eat thunder & drink rain. Los Angeles: Self-published, 1982. Iowa City: Iowa City Women's Press, 1982.

it's like this. Los Angeles: Self-published, 1980.

"Music in Poetry: if you can't feel it/you can't fake it." *Mid-American Review* 10.2 (1990): 57–64.

"The Pathology of Racism: A Conversation with Third World Wimmin." *This Bridge Called My Back: Writings by Radical Women of Color.* Ed. Cherríe Moraga and Gloria Anzaldúa. Watertown, MA: Persephone Press, 1981. 85–90.

"Pedagogy &/of Ethnic Literature: The Agony and the Ecstasy." *MELUS* 16.2 (1989–1990): 51–62.

"A Signifying Short Story." *Azalea* 3.3 (1980): 25.

Soque Street Poems. Sautee-Nacoochie, GA: Sautee-Nacoochie Community Association, 1995.

VOODOO CHILE/slight return. Charlotte, NC: Soque Street Press, 1991.

Works About

Miller, James A. "Coming Home to Affrilachia: The Poems of doris davenport." *Her Words: Diverse Voices in Contemporary Appalachian Women's Poetry.* Ed. Felicia Mitchel. Knoxville: University of Tennessee Press, 2002. 96–106.

Montgomery, Helena Louise. "Doris Davenport (1949–)." *Contemporary Lesbian Writers of the United States: A Bio-Bibliographical Critical Sourcebook.* Westport, CT: Greenwood Press, 1993. 155–159.

Christina G. Bucher

DAVIS, ANGELA (1944–)

Born to schoolteachers B. Frank and Sally E. Davis in Birmingham, Alabama, Angela Yvonne Davis grew up during the **civil rights movement** as witness to the injustice that she would spend her life fighting against. A writer, speaker, and political activist, Davis was introduced early to communism—her parents had friends who were Party members—and she has maintained close ties to this cause and its proponents ever since. She received a scholarship to Brandeis University and spent a year at the Sorbonne before graduating and traveling to Germany to study philosophy at Goethe University. In 1968, she earned her master's degree from the University of California, San Diego, and she worked with her mentor, political philosopher Herbert Marcuse, for her doctoral studies.

Since her youth, Davis has been involved in political activism, joining several groups in California such as the Black Communists and the black liberation movement. She joined the Communist Party in 1968 and soon after the Black Panthers. A year later she began teaching philosophy at the University of California at Los Angeles (UCLA) as an assistant professor, but her political activism was threatening to the establishment, and she was dismissed, though her reviews had all been positive ones. She was reinstated after a court order required it, but the university refused to renew her contract in 1970, and a further attempt by the Philosophy Department to reinstate her in 1972 failed. Undaunted, Davis continued to take an active role in demonstrations and protests against the repression of minorities by the American socioeconomic system, a system that seemed to encourage police **violence** against young black men in particular.

In fact, one of the main arguments used by UCLA's Board of Regents in not rehiring Davis was her activism on behalf of the "Soledad Brothers," three black inmates accused of murdering a white guard at Soledad Prison. Davis, along with other political activists of the day, believed the three men had been falsely accused, and Davis began making speeches about the plight of the Soledad Brothers as well as about prison conditions for prisoners of color.

Davis struck up a mail correspondence with one of the Soledad Brothers, George Jackson. Soon after, Jonathon Jackson, George's biological brother, began to do security work for Davis, as she had begun receiving **death** threats. In August 1970, Jonathon Jackson took guns legally registered to Davis and used them while attempting to help a man on trial escape from the courthouse. When Jackson came into the courtroom, he gave weapons to three prisoners who were there as witnesses for the defense. Once Jackson and the three prisoners took their five hostages to a waiting van, the police opened fire, killing four people, including the judge in the case, two of the prisoners, and Jackson himself.

Because weapons registered in Davis's name were used during the crime, Davis was charged as an accomplice to murder, kidnapping, and conspiracy. She went into hiding, evading police for up to two months and was one of only three women up to that time to have ever been named to the Federal Bureau of Investigation's "Ten Most Wanted" list. Many people sympathized with Davis, and there were reports of people taping signs to windows claiming safe passage for their "sister" Angela in their homes. Davis was eventually caught and spent almost seventeen months in jail before her bail was paid by a sympathetic white farmer five days before her trial began. During those months, a massive campaign of both national and international support welled up among the black **community**, liberals, the Communist Party, and activists of all sorts. Her supporters created a defense fund that Davis insisted be called the National United Committee to Free Angela Davis and All Political Prisoners. Even during this difficult time, Davis was able to see her experiences as part of a greater experience; she recognized not just how the justice system often failed people of color but how it often brutalized them.

After her acquittal on all charges, Davis continued her work on behalf of prisoners of color, whom she sees as being political prisoners caught up within the system because of their **race**. The book *If They Come in the Morning: Voices of Resistance* (1971) collects her early essays on the subjects of her belief in communist theory, her views on race and oppression in the United States, and her activism on behalf of those political prisoners who, she argues, are pioneering the fight against oppression. After her trial ended, Davis used the momentum to help create another organization, the National Alliance against Racist and Political Repression. She also published her **autobiography** in 1974. In it, she describes her life as a political one, describing the connection she sees between black liberation and the ideals of the Communist Party. Davis puts the fight for black liberation into the larger struggle of the proletariat against the oppression of the capitalistic system, which prevents the working class from rising up. Her autobiography is not just the story of a life but a story of the struggle to overcome oppression itself.

Davis's book *Women, Race, and Class* (1982) continues to examine the struggle to overcome, but this book explores the role of gender in historical terms by examining how the different paths taken by white and black women during the nineteenth century led to an estrangement between the races within the women's liberation movement during the 1970s and later. Davis continues the exploration of gender, race, and **class** in her book *Women, Culture, and Politics*, published in 1989, that collected the speeches she made during the middle years of the 1980s. Her later books analyze many facets of American culture as it concerns class and race. She has examined violence against women within the framework of racism in 1988's *Violence against Women and the Ongoing Challenge to Racism*. She continues her activism on behalf of political prisoners such as Mumia Abu Jamal and Leonard Pelletier.

For many years, she taught at San Francisco State University and became a well-known public speaker both nationally and internationally. She has become a prominent member of the American Communist Party and ran as the vice presidential candidate on the Party's 1980 and 1984 tickets. In 1992 she began teaching at the University of California at Santa Cruz where she was appointed to the Presidential Chair in 1995. Today, she continues her **work** as a political activist, persistently raising her voice to be heard as she works for the liberation of those who remain oppressed.

Works By

Angela Davis: An Autobiography. New York: Random House, 1974.
The Angela Davis Reader. Ed. Joy James. Cambridge, MA: Blackwell, 1998.
Are Prisons Obsolete? New York: Seven Stories Press, 2003.
Beyond the Frame: Women of Color and Visual Representation. New York: Palgrave Macmillan, 2005.
Blues Legacies and Black Feminism: Gertrude "Ma" Rainey, Bessie Smith, and Billie Holiday. New York: Pantheon Books, 1998.
If They Come in the Morning: Voices of Resistance. New York: Third Press, 1971.
The Prison Industrial Complex. Oakland, CA: AK Audio, 2003. (CD-ROM.)
Violence against Women and the Ongoing Challenge to Racism. New York: Kitchen Table Press, 1988.
Women, Culture, and Politics. New York: Random House, 1989.
Women, Race, and Class. New York: Random House, 1982.

Works About

Abbot, Diane. "Revolution by Other Means." *New Statesman* 114 (1987): 16–17.
Angela Davis: Civil Rights Leader. Langhorne, PA: Chelsea House, 2004.
Aptheker, Bettina. *The Morning Breaks: The Trial of Angela Davis.* New York: International, 1975.
Ashman, Charles R. *The People vs. Angela Davis.* New York: Pinnacle Books, 1972.

Bhavani, Kum Kum. "Complexity, Activism, Optimism: An Interview with Angela Y. Davis." *Feminist Review* 31 (1989): 66–81.

Nadelson, Regina. *Who Is Angela Davis? The Biography of a Revolutionary.* New York: David McKay, 1973.

Timothy, Mary. *Jury Woman: The Story of the Trial of Angela Y. Davis.* Volcano, CA: Volcano Press, 1976.

Amy Sparks Kolker

DAWN. See Xenogenesis Trilogy

DAY LATE AND A DOLLAR SHORT, A

Terry McMillan's fifth novel, *A Day Late and a Dollar Short* (2001), opens with the novel's narrator, Viola Price, who is in the hospital after suffering a severe asthma attack. She is unable to speak because she is connected to a respirator, and readers are invited into her consciousness and are able to hear her thoughts. Through Viola, readers learn about the importance of self-empowerment and personal growth. A divorced mother with four children, Viola tells the story of the **family**'s conflicts and their celebrations.

Paris, the eldest daughter, is a world-renowned chef and a single parent of a teenaged son. While her life appears easy, she suffers the pains of loneliness and the dangers that come with prescription drug addiction.

Charlotte, the second born, spends most of her relationship with Violet in conflict. Still living in Chicago, Charlotte sees herself as an island unto herself where she celebrates the fact that she is self-reliant. Unfortunately, her self-perceived independence is the very thing that threatens her relationship with her husband and child and also her relationship with her siblings.

Lewis, the third of the Price children, struggles with demons from his past. Once married to Donneta, Lewis cannot seem to move beyond the memories of his embattled marriage. He is unable to recognize that his trouble with relationships began early in his life when he was sexually abused by his older cousins. Without the insight into the connections between his early traumas and his present state, Lewis self-medicates with drugs, alcohol, and women. Moreover, not only is Lewis's life colored by his early abuse, but Lewis, described by his mother as a genius, is unable to complete anything, especially high school, in order to be a more productive citizen. Instead, Lewis's contribution to society is related to the criminal activities that continually land him in jail.

Janelle, the youngest of the Price children, struggles with naiveté and low self-esteem. After divorcing her daughter's father, Janelle has an affair with a much older married man named George. Eventually George leaves his wife and marries Janelle and becomes Shanice's stepfather. Unfortunately, however, it is soon discovered that George has been molesting Shanice, thus the reason for her strange behaviors such as pulling out her hair.

Cecil, Viola's ex-husband and the father of her children, plays a major role in the narrative as he struggles with Viola's resentment toward him for leaving their marriage and getting into a relationship with a much younger woman, Brenda. Although Brenda has three children from a previous relationship, she and Cecil have a child together.

McMillan's fifth novel brings readers back to the discussion of what it means to come of age as an African American. Through Viola, readers learn lessons about the importance of family connections, self-love, and self-empowerment. With Viola representing feminist viewpoints of survival and growth, readers watch as Viola teaches her family about **love**, hope, and forgiveness.

Works About

Acker, Jennifer. "A Day Late and a Dollar Short (Books)." *The Antioch Review* 60.1 (2002): 159.

Maryles, Daisy. "Another Day, Another Dollar." *Publishers Weekly* 248.5 (2001): 22.

Catherine Ross-Stroud

DEATH

Death is a pervasive presence in black literature, partly as a result of inhuman sufferings during **slavery** and lynching laws in the post–Civil War eighteenth century. Among early African American writers, **Lucy Terry** (1724–1821) was the first black woman to write **poetry**. Her only surviving poem, "Bars Flight," is a vivid account of a gruesome fight and the death of several men in a bar fight. Two other writers from this period are **Phillis Wheatley** (1753–1784) and **Jarena Lee** (1783–?). Lee's only contribution to literary **history** is her spiritual **autobiography** published in 1836. Wheatley's poetry is primarily religious and spiritual.

Nineteenth-century writers dealt with the issues of slavery, abolitionism, and post–Civil War racial tensions. **Frederick Douglass** (1818–1895) was born into slavery and later won his **freedom**. He was a leader of the abolitionist movement in the years before the Civil War. His autobiography *Life and Times of Frederick Douglass* (1884) deals briefly with the death of his mother. His description of the deathbed scene of the slave overseer in this autobiography is very poignant.

Frances E. W. Harper (1825–1911) was an important poet, **fiction** writer, abolitionist, and philosopher of the nineteenth century. In her writing, she seeks collective justice as opposed to individual justice. Harper's *Iola Leroy* (1892) is a classic of nineteenth-century African American women's fiction. Death is featured prominently in her poetry. Examples of this are poems such as "A Little Child Shall Lead Them," "Death of the Old Sea King," "The Night of Death," and "Songs for the People."

Charles Waddell Chesnutt's (1858–1932) novel *The Marrow of Tradition* (1901) is based on the Wilmington, North Carolina, **race** riot of 1898. It tells a complex tale of racial injustice, lynching, and social complications following the Civil War. Lynching, of course, is inevitably tied to the topic of death. His narrative is laced with metaphors of death.

The period from the end of World War I through the middle of the 1930s Great Depression is known as the **Harlem Renaissance**. During this period, a group of talented African American writers produced a great body of literature filled with racial consciousness and racial integration. Many writers exhibited an acute awareness of their dual **identity** as an American and a Negro. **Paul Laurence Dunbar** (1872–1906) is major poet of this era. His poem "When Dey, 'Listed Colored Soldiers" is about the loss of a loved one during war. It is about pride as well as sadness. Death appears in many of his poems mostly as a welcome, sometimes a reluctant visitor, for example, "Dead," "A Death Song," "The Right to Die," and "Paradox."

Jessie Redmon Fauset (1882–1961) explored the theme of personal and racial achievement in her works such as ***There Is Confusion*** (1924) and ***Plum Bun*** (1929). Her poems "Oblivion," "Dead Fires," and "La Vie C'est la Vie" touch upon the death theme in various forms.

Sterling Brown's (1901–1989) *Memphis Blues* (1932) displays an innocent indifference to death. Brown created a humorous character called Slim Greer and wrote a series of satiric poems about him. He is using this character to try and reclaim a sense of black humanity, as witnessed in "Slim Greer in Hell." In another poem, "Sharecroppers," the black hero pays the ultimate price for his loyalty to the union, a kind of interracial brotherhood. He is shot and killed by his boss.

Death in its most graphic and brutal form is depicted by **Langston Hughes** (1902–1967) in his *Three Songs about Lynching* (1936). His poem "The Negro Speaks of Rivers" has a quality of deathlessness about it. Another poem, "Night Funeral in Harlem," describes the funeral of a young boy. In an essay titled "Bop," Hughes traces the source of the soulful quality in **blues** music to the beatings that blacks had suffered.

James Weldon Johnson (1871–1938) is the creator of the black national anthem "Lift Every Voice and Sing." He describes death as a kindly creature who relieves a mother from her painful sickness and takes her to God's **home** in his poem "Go Down, Death." He urges her **family** not to weep. Another well-known poem, "White Witch," is a ballad to a witch who lures away young men and threatens to kill them. It is a metaphor for the black and white sexual relations of the time period when lynching was prevalent.

In his poem "If We Must Die," **Claude McKay** (1890–1948) gives public voice to black men as a group. He builds a contrast between man and beast in this heroic sonnet to the black male, in an attempt to build a powerful racial identity. In another poem, "The Lynching," McKay describes the lynching of a black man whose **body** is already burned to char. He juxtaposes the unnatural and the natural and death/night against life/day to create a powerful image of lynching. In another poem, "White City," a deep hatred for the city's callousness is what keeps the speaker alive. Other poems such as "Birds of Prey," "Futility," and "The Night-Fire" all have this element of darkness: "darkly death," as he calls it.

Contemporary black authors were born in a free world. They are one step removed from the dark history of slavery and lynching. Perhaps this fact accounts for the deeper and more spiritual treatment of death in modern black writing. The horror of the immediacy is gone, but a lingering fear and dissatisfaction with the injustices remain.

Richard Wright's (1908–1960) novel *Native Son* (1940) tells the story of a young black man whose life is turned upside down after he kills a young white woman in a moment of panic and confusion. It is a story of inner-city life. It explores what it means to be a black youth in contemporary America. Another one of his novels, *Black Boy* (1945), is an autobiographical account of growing up in the Jim Crow **South** during the early part of the twentieth century. In *Uncle Tom's Children* (1938), Wright brings postslavery black characters to life.

Perhaps the most definitive poem about untimely deaths of young black men is **Gwendolyn Brooks**'s (1917–2000) "We Real Cool."

Rita Dove's (1952–) poem "Parsley" is a meditation on a death sentence. It is based on a historical event that took place in the Dominican Republic in 1937. Rafael Trujillo, the dictator at the time, executed 20,000 Haitian black workers who worked in the sugarcane fields. Trujillo ordered them to pronounce the word *perejil*, Spanish for parsley. The ones who could not roll the "r" correctly were executed. The first half of the poem is written from the point of view of the victims, but then Dove gets inside the head of the dictator in the second half and conjures up his rationale for the killings.

Many of **Toni Morrison**'s (1931–) novels deal with violent death including death by suicide. There is an abundance of self-destruction in her novels. In the opening scene of ***Song of Solomon*** (1977), Robert Smith leaps from the top of Mercy Hospital to his death. In ***Jazz*** (1992), Violet's mother drowns herself in the well. In Morrison's novel ***Beloved*** (1987), Sethe, an escaped slave, commits the most brutal and horrific act of killing her infant daughter. She does this in order to keep her daughter from being enslaved. In *Song of Solomon*, one of the main characters, Pilate, murders a man. Pilate in turn is accidentally killed during the attempted murder of her son. In *Jazz*, Joe kills his lover Dorcas. In ***Sula*** (1973), Eva Peace kills her son to spare him lifelong sorrow and suffering. In spite of all the beatings, **rapes**, murders, deaths, and suicides, Morrison's narratives always tell the story of an individual and not a **stereotype**. The stories are never clichéd or melodramatic. She also explores moral ambiguity in society through her characters' actions.

Ernest Gaines (1933–) has skillfully engaged the theme of death in his novel *A Lesson before Dying* (1993). A young black man named Jefferson reluctantly gets involved in a shootout at a liquor store. The two other men involved are killed, along with the white storeowner. Jefferson, the only survivor, is accused of murder. He is condemned to death. His godmother persuades Grant, a young university-educated man, to teach Jefferson. She wants Jefferson to die like a man, with pride in his heritage. Death is a constant presence in *A Lesson before Dying*. Another Gaines novel, *A Gathering of Old Men* (1983), is set on a Louisiana sugarcane plantation in the 1970s. It depicts the racial tensions that arise over the death of a Cajun farmer at the hands of a black man.

Sonia Sanchez's (1934–) *Does Your House Have Lions* (1997) is a rhyme novel chronicling her brother's death from AIDS (acquired immunodeficiency syndrome). It deals with the family's estrangement and ultimate reconciliation. This is one of few African American novels dealing with slow and natural death as opposed to violent and sudden death.

Toni Cade Bambara's (1939–1995) novel *Those Bones Are Not My Child* (1999) deals with the topic of child murders at the hands of strangers. In the early 1980s more than forty black children were murdered in Atlanta, their bodies found strangled, beaten, and sexually assaulted. This novel is based on a true crime. It is a story of a struggling single mother whose twelve-year-old son is reported missing during that time period. The novel focuses on the search for the child without any support from the police or the politicians.

The Women of Brewster Place (1982) by **Gloria Naylor** (1950–) chronicles the communal strength of seven black women occupants of ramshackle rented houses on a street that is walled off from the rest of the town. The novel is not so much about racism as it is about sexism. The tone of the novel is unmistakably feminist. Deaths occur frequently and are predictably violent. The most ambiguous and problematic is the death of Ben who is killed by his friend, Lorraine, in the chapter titled "The Two." Another character, Ciel, has to deal with the death of her daughter by electrocution and also an abortion, essentially signifying the death of her **motherhood**.

Death in African American literature is often violent and unjust. This fact is nowhere more poignantly stated than in the collection of short stories by black female writers titled *Black-Eyed Susans/Midnight Birds* (1990), edited by Mary Helen Washington. One short story from this collection, "Requiem for Willie Lee" by Frenchy Hodges (1940–), portrays a young black boy in his early twenties. Willie Lee leads a life of **violence** and crime. His whole existence is based on physical and psychological violence. In the same collection, "Remember Him an Outlaw" by **Alexis De Veaux** appears. It is a story about a kind-hearted, alcoholic, innocent man who is wrongfully accused and killed. His nephew Richie uses Uncle Willie as a sacrificial lamb, as if Willie's life were dispensable. Death is, indeed, an enduring theme in African American literature.

Works About

Cheatwood, Kiarri T.-H. "Fire-Casting an Eternal De-Fascination with Death: Writing about the South, and the Responsible Necessity of Reading and Knowing Black South Writing in the Quest for Afrikan World Salvation and Restitution." *African American Review* 27 (Summer 1993): 301–313.

Holloway, Karla F. C. *Passed On: African American Mourning Stories: A Memorial.* Durham, NC: Duke University Press, 2002.

Janmohamed, Abdul R. *The Death-Bound-Subject: Richard Wright's Archaeology of Death.* Durham, NC: Duke University Press, 2005.

Wardi, Anissa Janine. *Death and the Arc of Mourning in African American Literature.* Gainesville: University Press of Florida, 2003.

Pratibha Kelapure

DELANEY, LUCY A. (c. 1830–c. 1890s)

Author of an **autobiography**, *From the Darkness Cometh the Light; or, Struggles for Freedom* (c. 1891), Lucy Ann Berry Delaney was born into **slavery** in St. Louis, Missouri. Her mother, Polly Crocket Berry, had been born free, but while living with Mr. and Mrs. Andrew Posey in Illinois as a child, she was kidnapped and transported to St. Louis. She was sold in slavery to Thomas Botts and, a year later, to Major Taylor Berry. At the Berry home, Polly, who worked primarily as a seamstress, met another slave, and with the consent of Major Berry and his wife Fanny, the couple was married and had two daughters. When Berry was killed in a duel, Fanny remarried Robert Walsh, a lawyer and judge, who, upon her **death**, sold Delaney's father to a plantation near Vicksburg, Mississippi.

The sale of Delaney's father prompted his wife and daughters to vow to escape slavery by any means necessary. While accompanying Mary Berry Cox and her husband on their honeymoon trip, Delaney's sister, Nancy, acted on that pledge and fled to Toronto, where she resided for the remainder of her life. Three weeks after she was sold and separated from Delaney, Polly also attempted to escape but was soon arrested in Chicago and returned to St. Louis. After her return, she successfully sued for her **freedom** on the basis that she had been born free and, on September 8, 1842, petitioned the court for her daughter's liberation as well. Delaney spent seventeen months in jail until the case was resolved in court, which she recounts in specific detail in her autobiography, until, with the aid of Judge Edward Bates, she was awarded her freedom on February 8, 1844.

After her emancipation, Delaney married Frederick Turner in 1845 and moved to Quincy, Illinois. Turner was killed in a steamboat explosion shortly afterward, and Delaney returned to St. Louis and met and wed Zachariah Delaney. The couple was married for forty-two years and had four children, all of whom died early. After her mother's death, she began a "long and persistent search" for her father, and when she located him, both he and Nancy traveled to St. Louis for "a most joyful reunion."

Delaney remained active in the cause of racial uplift throughout her life. In addition to publishing her autobiography, which Deborah Garfield maintains focuses on "the liberating feats of slave-**motherhood**" and, thereby, situates Delaney within the context of other "celebrants of African American maternalism," including **Harriet Jacobs**, **Sojourner Truth**, and **Toni Morrison**, she was elected president of the Female Union, the first African American women's society, and the Daughters of Zion. She also served as matron of Siloam Court and Grand Court of Missouri and as "Past Grand Chief Preceptress" of the Daughters of the Tabernacle and Knights of Tabor and was a member of Colonel Shaw Woman's Relief Corps. Of her life, Delaney says, in *From the Darkness Cometh the Light*, that "[c]onsidering the limited advantages offered [her], [she] made the best use of [her] time" and that her numerous hardships and successes should help "settl[e] the problem" in American's minds of whether "the negro race [can] succeed, proportionately, as well as the whites, if given the same chance and an equal start."

Work By

From the Darkness Cometh the Light; or, Struggles for Freedom. St. Louis, MO: J. T. Smith, c. 1891.

Works About

Barrett, Lindon. "Self-Knowledge, Law, and African American Autobiography: Lucy A. Delaney's *From the Darkness Cometh the Light.*" *The Culture of Autobiography: Constructions of Self-Representation.* Ed. Robert Folkenflik. Stanford, CA: Stanford University Press, 1993. 104–124.

Garfield, Deborah. "Lucy A. Delaney." *The Concise Oxford Companion to African American Literature.* Ed. William L. Andrews et al. New York: Oxford University Press, 2001. 102.

Kara L. Mollis

DELANY SISTERS

Sarah Louise "Sadie" Delany (1889–1999) and her sister Annie Elizabeth "Bessie" Delany (1891–1995) achieved fame in 1993, when they were 104 and 102, with the phenomenal success of their first book, *Having Our Say: The Delany Sisters' First 100 Years*. Their say included commentary about the **history** of the twentieth century from the perspective of black women who had struggled to achieve professional status in a time when few blacks and fewer women were welcome in professional circles. First recognized for their remarkable age, the sisters gained popular acclaim for their positive attitudes, notable achievements as professional women, and enduring **love** for each other and their **family**.

Sadie and Bessie Delany grew up in Raleigh, North Carolina, the second and third of ten children born to Henry Beard Delany and Nannie James Logan Delany, the chief administrators of St. Augustine's College. Born a slave, Henry Delany encouraged his children to pursue higher education with the consequence that theirs became one of the most prominent families in Harlem and New York during the first third of the twentieth century. After early **work** teaching in black schools in the rural **South**, both Sadie and Bessie left North Carolina to attend Columbia University, where Sadie earned a master's degree in teaching and Bessie earned a doctor of dentistry degree. Sadie became the first African American woman to teach high school **home** economics in the New York Public School System, and Bessie became the second African American woman licensed to practice dentistry in New York.

Their autobiographical memoir *Having Our Say* records the struggles and successes of the family and of the two sisters. Sadie and Bessie tell of their dismay at the coming of Jim Crow laws during their childhood in Raleigh. They also tell of their determination to succeed in professions at a time when women had to decide between public work and having a family.

When Amy Hill Hearth interviewed them for a 1991 article in the *New York Times*, the Delany sisters' wit and charm captured the public imagination. A pattern, successfully repeated over three books, was established, with Hearth recording and arranging the sisters' stories and thus preserving a valuable oral history. Both Sadie and Bessie coauthored both the first and the second books, *The Delany Sisters' Book of Everyday Wisdom* (1994), and Sadie authored *On My Own at 107: Reflections on Life without Bessie* (1997). With both hardcover and paperback editions of *Having Our Say* reaching the bestseller list, a successful play based on the Delanys' story was first staged in 1995, with a **film** produced as a CBS movie in 1999. Hearth has also published a children's book based on their childhood, *The Delany Sisters Reach High* (2002).

Bessie died at 104 in 1995, followed in 1999 by Sadie at 109. The Delany sisters were remarkable women, choosing to be professionals when most women married and remaining optimistic during years of Jim Crow segregation and oppression.

Works By

The Delany Sisters' Book of Everyday Wisdom. New York: Kodansha, 1994.
Having Our Say: The Delany Sisters' First 100 Years. New York: Kodansha, 1993.
On My Own at 107: Reflections on Life without Bessie. San Francisco: Harper, 1997.

Works About

Hearth, Amy Hill. *The Delany Sisters Reach High.* Illus. Tim Ladwig. Nashville, TN: Abingdon Press, 2002.
Mason, M. S. "Delany Sisters' Victory over Tears and Years." *The Christian Science Monitor* 91.98 (April 16, 1999): 17.
Nicastro, Nicholas. "Kodansha Pays Homage to Ladies Who've Lived a Lot." *Publishers Weekly* 240.24 (June 14, 1993): 31–33.
Rosen, Marjorie. "Free Spirits: The Sisters Delany Have Been Ahead of Their Time for a Century." *People Weekly* 40.21 (November 22, 1993): 97–100.

Ryan, Michael. "Their Story, Our History: 'Having Our Say,' about the Struggles of Bessie and Sadie Delany—Produced for TV by Camille Cosby—Airs Tonight on CBS." *Parade*, April 18, 1999, 12–15.

Harriette C. Buchanan

DERRICOTTE, TOI (1941–)

Toi Derricotte was born Antoinette Webster in Michigan in 1941. She is the author of one memoir, titled *The Black Notebooks* (1997), and four books of **poetry**: *The Empress of the Death House* (1978), *Natural Birth* (1983), *Captivity* (1990), and *Tender* (1997). Derricotte's work has received recognition in the form of two fellowships from the National Endowment for the Arts; the United Black Artists, USA, Inc. Distinguished Pioneering of the Arts Award; the Lucille Medwick Memorial Award from the Poetry Society of America; a Pushcart Prize; the Folger Shakespeare Library Poetry Book Award; and most recently, the Guggenheim Fellowship. Derricotte is professor of English at the University of Pittsburgh. With Cornelius Eady, she is the cofounder of Cave Canem, a workshop for black poets.

Derricotte's works reflect her commitment to exposing painful and often hidden stories about shame, sex, and anger within the context of **family**, **race**, and **class**. Each of her books confronts head-on a different subject that is considered taboo. The speaker in her poetry and prose leads readers through these stories in a voice that is often doubtful and self-critical but also courageous, empowered, and at times, joyful. In *The Empress of the Death House*, Derricotte portrays a complex world to which the speaker both belongs and feels distant. She says that with this book she desired to uncover silences around "anger and sex." *Natural Birth* tells her story of giving birth to her son in a "home for unwed mothers." In addition to chronicling the birth and the conversations among women in the **home**, this book also records the shame and fear surrounding that experience. In *Captivity*, Derricotte's pen turns to themes of servitude and confinement within the black middle class against the backdrop of a black working-class **community**. *Tender* continues to link personal struggles (such as abuse within the family) to historical struggles (such as the legacy of and responses to **slavery**). As the book's title poem implies, Derricotte's focus is on "the tenderest meat," which comes from "houses where you hear the least squealing."

In *The Black Notebooks*, Derricotte explores her experiences as a "white-appearing Black person" from childhood to adulthood. She writes about experiencing race from many complicated positions: that of desiring for communion with black people while desiring to escape the hatred often directed toward black people, that of being experienced as a threat to many communities and of experiencing oneself as an Other, and that of understanding the need to tell these stories while fearing that telling them will not make things better. In addition to writing these stories, she writes about what it means to write them.

Derricotte's critical engagement with questions of power and equality in intimate settings and her commitment to telling untold stories are present throughout her writings. One can read these feminist concerns through each of her books, as well as through her publications in feminist publications such as *Homegirls: A Black Feminist Anthology* and the journal *Feminist Studies*. Of her own work, Derricotte writes: "Truthtelling in my art is a way to separate my 'self' from what I have been taught to believe about my 'self,' the degrading stereotypes about black females in our society" (Gabbin and Riha).

Works By

The Black Notebooks: An Interior Journey. New York: W. W. Norton, 1997.
Captivity. Pittsburgh: University of Pittsburgh Press, 1997.
The Empress of the Death House. East Lansing, MI: Lotus Press, 1978.
Natural Birth. Freedom, CA: Crossing Press, 1983.
Tender. Pittsburgh: University of Pittsburgh Press, 1996.

Works About

Gabbin, Joanne, and Donna Shafer Riha, eds. "Toi Derricotte." *Furious Flower Facilitator's Guide*. www.newsreel.org/guides/furious.htm.
Hernton, Calvin. "Black Woman Poets." *The Sexual Mountain and Black Women Writers*. New York: Anchor Books, 1987. 119–155.
Lee, Don. "Toi Derricotte, Contributor Spotlight." *Ploughshares* (Spring 1996): 208–211.
Rowell, Charles H. "Beyond Our Lives: An Interview with Toi Derricotte." *Callaloo* 14.3 (Summer 1991): 654–664.

Mendi Lewis Obadike

DESSA ROSE

Sherley Anne Williams's *Dessa Rose* (1986) is a historical novel that explores the **history** of African American resistance in the antebellum **South**. While other novels in the **neo-slave narrative** tradition document what Ashraf H. A. Rushdy calls the "dailiness" of **slavery**, such as **Margaret Walker**'s *Jubilee* (1966), or the repercussions that a slave past has in the present, such as **Gayl Jones**'s *Corregidora* (1975) and **Octavia Butler**'s *Kindred* (1979), *Dessa Rose* considers resistance as an integral part of the African American experience.

Another innovative aspect of this novel is Williams's use of shifts in point of view. The world of the novel is represented by a number of perspectives. This approach exposes the distortion of African American history and the cultural constructs of **race** that define and condition the relationships between blacks and whites in the text. In the first section of the narrative, point of view shifts between Dessa, the condemned pregnant slave, and the white amanuensis who attempts to record the story of her insurgence on a slave coffle. The discrepancies between the black woman's oral history and its reconstruction in the white man's written record is thus emphasized. Williams dramatizes the misrepresentation of African American history by exposing the differences between the fragmented pieces of information Dessa chooses to relate to the white man and his journal entries. The loss of the black female's history is further highlighted by the white man's inability to understand both Dessa's experience and the language through which she expresses herself. However, if Nehemiah fills in the gaps with his own words, distorting Dessa's narrative, her vernacular functions as a site of resistance. The black vernacular, the humming, the vacant smiles, and the silences with which Dessa resists the white man's questioning illustrate that, for Williams, the act of resistance becomes synonymous not only with survival but also with keeping a part of oneself to which the hegemonic others do not have access. In this way the writer also pays a tribute to the **slave narrative** tradition, illustrating the willful silences left in the ex-slaves' texts.

The first part of the novel, significantly titled "The Darky," seems to be dominated by Nehemiah's views on Dessa. However, if the novel's prologue had signaled that this is Dessa's narrative, her dreams and recollections of her lover, **family**, and friends, which sometimes are italicized and extend to several pages, disrupt the white man's narrative and claim space in the text for the black woman's expression.

In the second section of the novel titled "The Wench," the narrative alternates between two points of view, Dessa's and that of the white woman whose farm becomes an accidental safe harbor for fugitive slaves. Williams uses this device effectively to explore preconceived notions of blackness and **whiteness** and furthermore to racialize the latter. Looking at the white woman through Dessa's eyes, the white **body** becomes the locus of strangeness and unattractiveness conventionally identified with the black skin and physiognomy, dislocating whiteness as an archetype for the familiar and appealing. Placing her characters in atypical circumstances, Williams creates for them an unfamiliar realm in which they are forced to look beyond skin color and socially assigned roles. In this section, **motherhood** is the critical issue through which boundaries between blacks and whites are redefined. Rufel nurses Dessa's baby, not only reversing the role of the black **Mammy** but also destabilizing the slave/mistress relationship by acknowledging the infant's humanity and refusing to see him as chattel. The child was hungry, and Rufel could and did feed him.

Nevertheless, the simplicity of this gesture, which defies all Dessa knew about white women, further exacerbates the contradictory nature of the black woman's feelings in relation to Rufel. Williams also explores the theme of motherhood and the figure of the black Mammy in order to unsettle the white female character's preconceived notions of African American **identity**. Through her brief but tempestuous exchanges with Dessa, Rufel is forced to acknowledge that she hardly knew the woman she called "Mammy" and in whom she confided and implicitly trusted. Rufel has to come to terms with the fact that all she knew about Mammy was what both herself and her family imposed on their slave's identity—a fabricated name, date of birth, and history. Rufel's memories of Mammy and the contours of the familiar face become somewhat indistinct, compelling Rufel to inquire about the woman she became accustomed to thinking of as an extension of herself.

In the third and final major section of the novel, Williams abandons the variable viewpoint in favor of a first-person narrative. The title of this section, "The Negress," which, as Dessa's future lover explains to her, is French for "Black woman," announces both her rebirth and her newly found voice. In the first-person narrative, Dessa asserts control over her history and validates African American oral tradition by adopting storytelling as a legitimate means of revising and recording the past. The silenced attempts to insert African American history in the white record signaled by Dessa's italicized dreams and memories of the previous sections of the novel fade away. Dessa becomes the creator of her own text, ungirding the silenced black female—her second rebellious act.

Dessa's text is rooted in the **blues** tradition of call and response. The telling and retelling of her story to her son so that he can tell it as if her memories were his ensures not only that the familial history is passed on to the following generations but also that Dessa's individual experience finds meaning in the shared history of African Americans. In the tradition of call and response the past becomes a regenerative force by way of cultural practice. In this way, reimaging the African American past by rooting it in the oral tradition that has kept it alive, Williams uses the blues language to subvert the hegemonic discourses that attempted to silence the black woman's history.

See also Historical Fiction

Works About

Beaulieu, Elizabeth Ann. *Black Women Writers and the American Neo-Slave Narrative: Femininity Unfettered.* Westport, CT: Greenwood Press, 1999. 29–55.

Dawson, Emma Waters. "Psychic Rage and Response: The Enslaved and the Enslaver in Sherley Anne Williams's *Dessa Rose*." *Arms Akimbo: Africana Women in Contemporary Literature.* Ed. Janice Lee Liddell and Yakini Belinda Kemp. Gainesville: University Press of Florida, 1999. 17–31.

Henderson, Mae G. "The Stories of O(Dessa): Stories of Complicity and Resistance." *Female Subjects in Black and White: Race, Psychoanalysis, Feminism.* Ed. Elizabeth Abel, Barbara Christian, and Helene Moglen. Berkeley: University of California Press, 1997. 285–306.

McDowell, Deborah E. "Negotiating between Tenses: Witnessing Slavery after Freedom—*Dessa Rose*." *Slavery and the Literary Imagination: Selected Papers from the English Institute, 1987.* Ed. Deborah E. McDowell and Arnold Rampersad. Baltimore, MD: Johns Hopkins University Press, 1989. 144–163.

Rushdy, Ashraf H. A. "Reading Mammy: The Subject of Relation in Sherley Anne Williams' *Dessa Rose*." *African American Review* 27.3 (Fall 1993): 365–389.

Ana Nunes

DETECTIVE FICTION

The archetypal detective is of white Anglo-Saxon ethnic origin and male. He is a man whose superior mental capabilities make him a paragon of intelligence and rationality. At the opposite end of the scale are nonwhites and females, who are often cast as incapacitated by their **race** and gender. In traditional detective fiction, they appear in secondary and/or stereotyped roles. Sally Munt observes, "Black man, because of his construction as nonthinking, non-rational, and non-literate, cannot deliver the denotation 'detective' easily" (85). The same holds true for members of other ethnic groups and for women.

However, black characters turned up early on in the genre. They were created by white and African American authors alike, and they fit popular **stereotypes**. Writers took advantage of racial clichés to meet readers' expectations. The depiction of blacks was shaped by Eurocentric images of "the Other" and—as Frankie Bailey notes—restricted to variations of the slave or the slum dweller. Woman's role was, on the whole, confined to that of victim or vamp. Creating a nonwhite and female detective—who is independent of male guidance and protection and who herself is successful in a male profession—seemed to be a double violation of the genre's conventions. But eventually black, female, and feminist detectives began to appear.

African Americans have been writing detective fiction almost from its beginnings in the nineteenth century. Their first experiments with the genre reach back to **Pauline Hopkins** (1856–1930). "Talma Gordon" (1900) deals with miscegenation and covers the theme of the "tragic **mulatto**" torn between cultures. Hopkins also makes use of the locked-room device, established by Edgar Allan Poe in "The Murders in the Rue Morgue" (1841). As Poe rose to fame as the "father" of the detective story, so Hopkins can be claimed as the "mother" of African American detective **fiction**. Among her heirs are Rudolph Fisher (1897–1934; author of *The Conjure-Man Dies: A Mystery Tale of Dark Harlem*, 1932, the first detective novel by an African American, featuring black characters and set in the black **community**), George Schuyler (1895–1977; author of thrillers serialized in the 1930s), Chester Himes (1909–1984; famous for his "Harlem **domestic** novels" about black detectives Grave Digger Jones and Coffin Ed Johnson), Hugh Allison (1908–1974; his "Corollary," 1948, was the first short story by an African American published in *Ellery Queen's Mystery Magazine*), Walter Mosley (1952–   ; famous for his hard-boiled series about black private eye Easy

Rawlins, who first appeared in *Devil in a Blue Dress*, 1990), Gar Anthony Haywood (1954– ; author of three novels featuring L.A. private investigator Aaron Gunner, first investigating in *Fear of the Dark*, 1987), and more recently, many female African American writers.

Since the post–World War I "Golden Age" of the detective novel, women have been prolific in the genre. It was not until the 1970s, however, that feminist crime writing emerged. Much contemporary detective fiction by and about women—whether they regard themselves as feminists or not—challenges traditional role scripts and power conceptions. It undermines binary oppositions between male and female, white and nonwhite, good and evil. It gives visibility and voice to authors and protagonists who are not male and/or of Anglo-American descent. It reflects an appreciation of diversity, whether it is cultural, religious, political, or sexual. In 1977 Marcia Muller (1944–) broke new ground with the introduction of Sharon McCone in *Edwin of the Iron Shoes*. Sharon is considered the first female hard-boiled private eye. With her toughness and independence, she served as a model for later female and ethnic sleuths. "Tough girls" like Grafton's Kinsey Millhone and Paretsky's V. I. Warshawski soon got distinguished African American colleagues, created by African American women. The first detective novel by and about an African American woman is Dolores Komo's *Clio Browne, Private Investigator* (1988), featuring black private eye Clio Browne, the owner of a St. Louis detective agency. Komo tries to provide a believable picture of middle-class blacks, but her aspirations fall victim to the genre's conventions. Other novels, however, stretch the genre's boundaries and reveal a strong interest in the confluence of black **identity** with the detective genre. The simultaneous appearance and success of Nikki Baker's *In the Game* (1991), Eleanor Taylor Bland's *Dead Time* (1992), and **Barbara Neely**'s ***Blanche on the Lam*** (1992)—all introducing female African American serial sleuths—testify to an interest of authors and readers in the compatibility of race, **class**, and gender issues with detective fiction. These authors employ and modify the genre's conventions to explore African American identity, color consciousness, racism, and **sexuality**. For them, the established form functions as a tool for expressing a social critique of mainstream attitudes toward race, class, and gender.

Eleanor Taylor Bland's (1944–) series depicts police officer Marti MacAlister, who had quit her job with the Chicago police to get away from her husband's **death** and moved to cozy Lincoln Prairie, Illinois, where she encounters as much **violence** as in the city. Marti is teamed up with Vik Jessenovik, a white cop with outdated attitudes about women and racial minorities. Throughout the series, which starts with *Dead Time* (1992), Marti is confronted with social problems affecting women: domestic violence, abuse, abortion, poverty.

Barbara Neely (1941–) subverts the genre's formula in that she substitutes the classical detective with Blanche White, a strong and witty cleaning woman. Blanche is highly successful because she relies on her intuition and a tight-knit female network to solve murders at her employers' homes. Nikki

Baker's (1962–) series starts with *In the Game* (1991). It is set in Chicago and features black investment banker Virginia Kelly. Baker and others use the detective formula to highlight problems that homosexuals face in society. Penny Micklebury's series about lesbian cop Gianna Maglione and her lover Mimi Patterson, who make their debut in *Keeping Secrets* (1994), also explores issues of importance to racial and sexual minorities. Micklebury's second series starts with *One Must Wait* (1998) and introduces black criminal defense attorney Carole Ann Gibson.

The protagonist in Valerie Wilson Wesley's (1947–) series is Tamara Hayle, who makes her living as a private investigator in Newark, New Jersey. Like many female authors, Wesley enriches the linear detective plot with nonlinear issues: **family** affairs, mother-child bonding, community ties, female networking, women's aspirations, and perceptions. Tamara is a divorced mother struggling to make ends meet for herself and her son. In *When Death Comes Stealing* (1994) she has already been five years in the business, and she is said to be able to handle anything from disappearances to homicide. According to the genre's conventions, the investigator has to be an uninvolved outsider. Wesley's series, however, implies that only someone whose sympathies lie with African Americans can be successful in the quest for truth. Tamara relies on her connections in the black community, and her being an African American woman becomes an essential factor for her investigations.

Feminist writer **Rosa Guy** (1925–) introduces a black male investigator, Imamu Jones. *The Disappearance* (1979) and *New Guys around the Block* (1983) are infused with a critique of racism. Less-known African American writers of detective fiction are Nora DeLoach (*Mama Saves a Victim*, 1997), Grace Edwards (*If I Should Die*, 1997), Terris McMahan Grimes (*Somebody Else's Child*, 1996), and Chassie West (*Sunrise*, 1994). Aya de León (1967–), an Afro-Latina, writes stories about Oakland, California, detective Madeline Moore ("Tell Me Moore," 1995).

African American writers have always used and subverted the traditional detective formula. The appearance of Fisher's *The Conjure-Man Dies* in 1932 already indicated an interest in the confluence of the genre with an exploration of matters of identity and of social and political issues. Contemporary black women writers have followed this lead. By simultaneously employing and subverting established detective formulas, they have demonstrated that the genre can be an effective device for discussing problems of race, class, and gender. They have shown that it is possible to establish a clearly defined female *and* African American point of view within the framework of the genre. And many of them have created a pointedly feminist perspective. In an attempt to do more than simply entertain, they have included substantial social, cultural, and political information in their plots. Thus, detective fiction—traditionally supposed to be male dominated, linear, straightforward, apolitical, and restricted to its basic formula—has assumed the function of a social document.

See also Blanche among the Talented Tenth; Blanche Cleans Up; Blanche Passes Go

Works About

Bailey, Frankie Y. *Out of the Woodpile: Black Characters in Crime and Detective Fiction.* Westport, CT: Greenwood Press, 1991.

Klein, Kathleen Gregory. *The Woman Detective: Gender and Genre.* Urbana: University of Illinois Press, 1988.

Munt, Sally R. *Murder by the Book? Feminism and the Crime Novel.* New York: Routledge, 1994.

Reddy, Maureen T. *Sisters in Crime: Feminism and the Crime Novel.* New York: Continuum, 1988.

Soitos, Stephen F. *The Blues Detective: A Study of African American Detective Fiction.* Amherst: University of Massachusetts Press, 1996.

Woods, Paula L., ed. *Spooks, Spies & Private Eyes: An Anthology of Black Mystery, Crime and Suspense Fiction of the 20th Century.* New York: Bantam, 1995.

Katrin Fischer

DE VEAUX, ALEXIS (1948–)

Alexis De Veaux is a poet, playwright, and novelist who teaches in the Department of Women's Studies at the University at Buffalo, where she received her M.A. and Ph.D. in American studies. She has also served as **poetry** editor for the popular magazine *Essence*. In addition to her work as a professor, De Veaux has also been involved in local **community** activism in Buffalo.

A prolific writer, De Veaux has published a novel, *Spirits in the Street* (1974), as well as two award-winning children's books, *Na-Ni* (1973) and *An Enchanted Hair Tale* (1987), in addition to numerous poems and short stories. A playwright of growing esteem, De Veaux's plays include *Circles* (1972), *Tapestry* (1986), *A Season to Unravel* (1979), and *Don't Explain: A Song of Billie Holiday* (1980).

De Veaux has also worked as a guest lecturer in Africa, Europe, Japan, and the Caribbean. In 1990, De Veaux was one of the first international journalists to interview Nelson Mandela upon his release from prison. On that occasion, she was granted an exclusive interview with both Nelson and Winnie Mandela.

De Veaux maintains that contemporary literatures are agents of social change that play a crucial part in diverse struggles for self-determination. Her work is particularly interested in the relationship between **literature** and **history**, especially the myriad ways in which women of color construct visions of history while engaging literary forms. As a writer immersed in this process herself, De Veaux openly seeks to challenge the dominant paradigms of the disciplines in which she teaches.

For De Veaux, writing occurs within particular social and political moments, so she approaches women's studies from the perspective of someone living a cultural life within those specific moments. She brings this experiential perspective to her scholarship and describes her work as empirical rather than primarily based on theory.

Among De Veaux's most significant work is the first biography of **Audre Lorde**: *Warrior Poet: A Biography of Audre Lorde* (2004). This monumental work, which took ten years to complete, draws out the complex intersections of those concerns shared by both De Veaux and Lorde, the development of a passionate and powerful artistic voice, and the ongoing struggle for social justice. Reflecting De Veaux's commitments, her biography of Lorde is not simply a literary biography but an expression of an artist's battles against multilayered oppressions.

Throughout her varied works, De Veaux, like other African American lesbian writers such as Lorde and **Pat Parker**, has contested hegemonic and essentialized notions of **race**, gender, and **sexuality**. For De Veaux, as for writers like Parker, black women both contest and construct **identity** as part of collective struggle and community building. Significantly, De Veaux asserts that contemporary black women in the United States are part of a conscious community of black women extending throughout U.S. history. De Veaux cites her mentors as the community of black women writers, both historical and contemporary, who have, in her view, allowed her to understand the great variety of voices in which she can speak as a black woman writer. In doing so, she not only draws attention to a literary community of black women who have taught and/or learned from each other over generations but also points to a largely neglected history that still has much to teach.

Works By

Don't Explain: A Song of Billie Holiday. New York: Harper and Row, 1980.
Na-Ni. New York: HarperCollins, 1973.
Spirits in the Street. New York: Anchor, 1974.
Warrior Poet: A Biography of Audre Lorde. New York: Norton, 2004.

Works About

Splawn, P. Jane. "Re-imaging the Black Woman's Body in Alexis De Veaux's *The Tapestry*." *Modern Drama* 40 (1997): 514–525.
Tate, Claudia. "Alexis De Veaux." *Black Women Writers at Work*. New York: Continuum, 1983. 49–59.

J. Shantz

DEW BREAKER, THE

As she does in ***Krik? Krak!*** (1995) **Edwidge Danticat** weds the genres of short story and novel in *The Dew Breaker* (2004), but in this work she gives voice to evil, to a *ton ton Macoute*, a henchman of the Duvalier regime. In "The Book of the Dead," the first of nine stories, daughter Ka, named for the good angel of ancient Egyptian mythology, is a sculptor who has carved her father, a survivor of Haiti's prison system under the first Duvalier regime, naked and kneeling in his prison cell. Only when he destroys the sculpture does he reveal to Ka that he was a "hunter," not the "prey," and exposes his horrific personal **history** to his daughter. Ka learns that his scar, which he has hidden in photographs for thirty years, is not from a guard but a prisoner, a man he then shot and killed, "just like I killed many people." This dew breaker, a torturer named for going out before dawn to collect his victims, is never named. He is known only by roles: father to Ka, husband to Anne, barber to the public, landlord to a few, murderer of a harrowing number. While readers remain unsure of how much his wife must know, in possessing any knowledge of his past she and her daughter become kas, angels that mask this dew breaker's existence.

The following seven stories seem to break away from Ka and her father, the dew breaker, but they deal with Haiti's tortured and their connections, both direct and indirect, to him. Danticat questions why one man, any one man, could be given the power to destroy so many lives. Dany of "Night Talkers" believes his New York landlord, the barber, is the person who burned his **home**, blinded his aunt, and murdered his parents when he was a boy in Haiti. He searches for opportunities to murder him in retaliation, but he agonizes over the possibility of killing the wrong man, widowing the wrong woman, and making fatherless the wrong children, feelings he understands too well. On a visit to his now elderly aunt in Haiti, he meets Claude, who has lived both in Haiti and the United States as he has. Claude describes himself as a puzzle in need of assembly, but Claude, unlike many of the other emotionally tortured in Danticat's work, is a lucky palannit, one who can speak his nightmares out loud. Most cannot. Nadine, who has aborted a child because she cannot reconcile the life of her parents left in Haiti with her own in New York, stares at an "unrecognizable woman" in the mirror by the end of "Water Child." Even Ka, born in the United States, is affected by the puzzle of Haitian history. One Christmas Eve she believes she sees Emmanuel Constant, wanted for the murder of thousands of Haitians, sitting in a New York church pew. In "The Book of Miracles," Ka, here a younger version of herself than first met in "The Book of the Dead," has no idea survivors might too recognize her father, had he not lost eighty pounds and changed his name and place of origin. Perhaps most moving is "The Bridal Seamstress," the story of Aline, a naive journalist intern who comes to know Beatrice Saint Fort, a woman who sees the dew breaker on every New York street she has lived and continually moves in an attempt to escape him. Aline, finding the woman foolish at first, comes to realize that she will now write about people like Beatrice, those who are constantly "chasing fragments of themselves."

"The Dew Breaker," the ninth and final piece, returns to the main subject but also Anne, his wife. How could she have loved such a man? Connections only hinted at in previous stories are now unveiled, but without any sense of satisfying resolution. Instead, the origins of the nightmares are divulged, and readers are left to decide how much to forgive the dew breaker who has poisoned so many lives. While the dew breaker has not caused all the anguish in the characters' lives, he is emblematic of all those who did. Anne realizes she cannot "escape this dread anymore." Her strength comes from revising herself, knowing that despite those close to her disappearing without a trace, and despite living already thirty years in New York, she is continually moving toward the woman she "wanted to become." And she credits her American daughter, not anything Ka has said or done, just Ka's presence, for making this perspective possible after her Haitian past.

Works About

Eder, Richard. "Off the Island." Review of *The Dew Breaker*, by Edwidge Danticat. *New York Times*, March 21, 2004, 5.

Iyer, Pico. "When Life Is a Ghost Story." Review of *The Dew Breaker*, by Edwidge Danticat. *Time*, March 8, 2004, 79.

Kakutani, Michiko. "Books of the Times; Hiding from a Brutal Past Spent Shattering Lives in Haiti." Review of *The Dew Breaker*, by Edwidge Danticat. *New York Times*, March 10, 2004, 1.

Salij, Marta. "Evil Confronted." Review of *The Dew Breaker*, by Edwidge Danticat. *Detroit Free Press*, April 11, 2004, 4E.

Washington, Kate. "What Father Did for Duvalier." Review of *The Dew Breaker*, by Edwidge Danticat. *San Francisco Chronicle*, March 21, 2004, M-1.

Lisa Muir

DICKEY, ERIC JEROME (1961–)

Eric Jerome Dickey was born in Memphis, Tennessee, and attended the University of Memphis (formerly Memphis State). After graduating with a degree in computer system technology, Dickey moved in 1983 to Los Angeles, where he worked as a software developer in the aerospace industry. During his time in L.A., Dickey began to pursue alternative work as an actor and stand-up comedian, eventually becoming a regular on the local and national comedy circuits. When a downturn in the aerospace industry left him unemployed in the early 1990s, Dickey decided to develop the writing skills he had nurtured writing stand-up comedy scripts into a career as a writer.

Dickey began writing **poetry** and short stories, eventually joining the International Black Writers and Artists (IBWA), where his participation in development workshops led to a scholarship to attend Creative Writing classes at the University of California at Los Angeles. Dickey's first published work, the short story "Thirteen," appeared in the IBWA's 1994 anthology *River Crossing, Voices of the Diaspora*.

Since the release of *Sister, Sister* in 1996, Dickey has established himself as perhaps the foremost male author of popular African American **fiction** predominantly read by women. His books consistently reach number one on the

Blackboard bestseller list. Dickey is part of a small number of such writers, along with **E. Lynn Harris**, Omar Tyree, Colin Channer, and Michael Basdin. Among these writers Dickey is perhaps the most developed in terms of the attention he gives to women's feelings and desires within relationships. His works, despite the professional or middle-class context, are less focused on wealth and upward mobility than the works of his male colleagues.

His works pursue the intricacies of diverse relationships, and the pressures that influence those relationships, in big cities. Dickey emphasizes themes such as dishonesty, the lack of accountability, infidelity, and noncommunication that he sees as characterizing contemporary urban relationships. For Dickey, men and women play complex and nonstereotypical parts in these relationships. Dickey is not afraid to pursue the irresponsibility and selfishness of male characters, and he deals forthrightly and unflinchingly with issues such as infidelity, absentee fathers, and fathers' decisions to withhold child support in attempts to hurt mothers. *Cheaters* (1999) examines relationships among people seeking immediate gratification. Dickey portrays male characters exhibiting characteristics typically attributed to women, such as "codependence," in order to break down the gender specificity given to such behaviors.

Dickey has attempted, by creating different scenarios from book to book while still focusing on relationship themes, to challenge **stereotypes** about men and women or African Americans and white people. His work has ventured beyond the clichés and stereotypes of much romance writing to delve into complex characters with unexpected and atypical motivations. In addition, Dickey's works are perhaps unique among romance writings in the direct attention given to social and political issues.

In *Friends and Lovers* (1997), Dickey challenges the assumptions of readers and critics alike by basing the novel's central conflict around the decision by the heroine Shelby to have an abortion. In this work Dickey goes against the grain of much popular romance writing by refusing to portray Shelby as an immoral person or someone undeserving of the hero Tyrell's affections.

Dickey addresses other themes that remain controversial in American public discourse. In *Milk in My Coffee* (1998), Dickey explores the intricacies of multiracial relationships and the pressures these relationships experience, within both African American and white communities in the United States.

In *Liar's Game* (2000), Dickey addresses issues of prejudice within African American communities. In many of his other works he examines questions of solidarity and **community** conflict within African American communities and the socioeconomic pressures impacting communities and neighborhoods in an era of globalization. In many of his works, most notably *Thieves' Paradise* (2002), Dickey presents characters attempting to deal with the results of failing social systems in the United States in the contemporary context. Economic recession and layoffs, hunger, incarceration, and **domestic** abuse are addressed in Dickey's forthright style. Characters in recent works have reflected on changes in economics and politics in the post-9/11 world.

Unlike other popular romance writers, Dickey does not shy away from expressing these concerns in direct and even provocative language. In *Drive*

Me Crazy (2004), for example, Dickey accepts the assessment of many residents of Los Angeles in the wake of the Rodney King beating in referring to the Los Angeles Police Department as "Los Angeles's most notorious gang."

Works By

Cheaters. New York: Dutton, 1999.
Drive Me Crazy. New York: Dutton, 2004.
Friends and Lovers. New York: Signet, 1997.
Griots beneath the Baobab: Tales from Los Angeles. Los Angeles: Larod, 2002.
Liar's Game. New York: Dutton, 2000.
Milk in My Coffee. New York: Dutton, 1998.
Naughty or Nice. New York: Dutton, 2003.
The Other Woman. New York: Dutton, 2003.
Sister, Sister. New York: Signet, 1996.
Thieves' Paradise. New York: Dutton, 2002.

Works About

Blacstone, Tiffany. "Eric Jerome Dickey." *Essence* (July 2005): 111.
Masilak, Alison Joyner. "Novel Intensions: An Interview with Eric Jerome Dickey." *University of Memphis Magazine* (Winter 2002). www.memphis.edu/magazine/v20il/feat2.

J. Shantz

DISAPPEARING ACTS

Following the critical acclaim of her first novel, **Mama** (1987), **Terry McMillan** introduces readers to Zora Banks and Franklin Swift. In *Disappearing Acts* (1989), McMillan continues her discussion of the effects of dominant ideologies as they relate to Eurocentric constructs of the **family**. A narrative about Zora and Franklin's early romance and its tragic ending is the focal point of the novel. However, what readers are reminded of is a different perspective of racial and sexual oppression. While the novel takes place in Brooklyn, New York, the ideologies that follow gender and **race** are just as alive in urban Brooklyn as they are in *Mama*'s more rural Point Haven.

The connections between the rural and the urban are important in that these connections also link the discussion to both the past and the present. *Disappearing Acts* is an exploration of the legacy of **slavery** and how, if we ignore the historical importance of the past, we will be trapped in a destructive cycle of conflict and misfortune. In this novel, McMillan offers some strategies for countering race and gender oppression.

While Zora is a music teacher, a white-collar profession, and Franklin is a carpenter, a blue-color profession, their common bond is the struggle for the ideal of the patriarchal construct of family. In this sense, while Franklin feels pressure to provide for his family within a Eurocentric model of the husband's role as provider, Zora struggles with the same ideological construct, but her struggle is twofold: She recognizes Franklin's inability to assume the role as provider, but as his wife, she feels the pressure to patiently support Franklin's quest to become the breadwinner of the family.

Because Zora recognizes Franklin's inability to fulfill the socially constructed definition of **black masculinity**, readers are introduced to some of the often-overlooked methods that black women use to be supportive of their mates while at the same time acting behind the scenes by doing what it takes to help the family to survive. In this sense, *Disappearing Acts* is a discussion of the ways in which the **myth** of the castrating black woman as the cause of the breakup of the black family are largely ill informed. At the same time, McMillan points out the strengths of black women that have held families together. Furthermore, McMillan puts forth the narrative of Zora and Franklin as a way to call attention to the politics that continue to disenfranchise blacks in America. With these ideas in mind, however, McMillan does not leave readers with a bleak picture of the negative effects of racism. Instead, readers are pointed toward Zora's singing and Franklin's woodworking as arts that remind readers to continue to be creative in solving life's troubles, no matter the odds.

Works About

Sparks, Leah. Review of *Disappearing Acts*, by Terry McMillan. *Library Journal* 124.16 (1999): 149.

Review of *Disappearing Acts*, by Terry McMillan. *New York Times Book Review* 95 (1990): 22.

"Wesley Snipes & Sanaa Lathan Bring Terry McMillan's Love Story 'Disappearing Acts' To TV." *Jet* 99.1 (2000): 58.

Catherine Ross-Stroud

DOMESTIC

As perhaps the most notable type of **work** in which African American women have been employed throughout **history**, the position of the domestic has been both a complicated and intriguing role for black women workers. Throughout history, particularly before World War II, the domestic sphere was the primary space where black women could be employed. This position of the domestic is complex in that it signifies the often influential role these women played in their employers' and masters' families, serving as the **Mammy** or primary caregiver for the children. However, at the same time, while being a trusted member of the household and often gaining "insider" information in the way that these families functioned, domestics were still forced into long hours of labor, harsh working conditions, and limited opportunities. While it is true that many of these domestic workers possessed positions better than those of their peers working in fields, mills, or factories, these household workers were still subjected to often severe discrimination and abuse.

From the time they were young girls, African American women were trained to do the work required of the domestic sphere. Great time and energy were put into ensuring that these women could care for and nurture children, keep up the **home**, and cook the **family**'s meals, and often these young women were trained alongside their own mothers, which created a generational cycle of domestic workers. The role of the domestic was also difficult for African American women because, often, there was only one domestic worker per household. This meant that little sense of **community** or fellowship was present for these women because they were so frequently isolated from one another, with little contact with the outside world.

In the period before the Civil War, women slaves often worked as domestic workers within the homes of their owners, cooking meals, caring for children, and cleaning the house. In writings such as **Harriet Jacobs**'s *Incidents in the Life of a Slave Girl* (1861), one gains a sense of what the daily lives of these domestic workers were like. Jacobs's narrative tells of her years working in the home of Dr. James Norcom and the severe physical and sexual abuse she suffered at his hands.

The period after the Civil War represents a migration of domestic workers from the rural **South** to urban centers such as Washington, Philadelphia, Baltimore, Chicago, and New York. In this Great Migration, the stories of now "freed" women make clear the great gender, racial, and socioeconomic disparities that still existed in their positions within wealthy, white families. As early as the 1870s, African Americans moved north in search of better lives and escape from the rampant discrimination present in the agrarian South. And from 1910 to 1920, this migration increased dramatically, with between 300,000 and 1,000,000 blacks moving north, many of whom became domestic workers.

Literature that represents the position of the domestic was fairly sparse after the time of the Civil War. There is Fannie Cook's *Mrs. Palmer's Honey* (1946) that details the social and political struggles of Honey Hoop, a domestic worker and eventual activist. There is also **Alice Childress**'s *Like One of the Family: Conversations from a Domestic's Life* (1956), where the author provides stories of African American female domestic workers in a way that shows the importance and diversity of these women and their working lives. Interestingly, some texts, such as **Alice Walker**'s *The Color Purple* (1982), demonstrate that domestics working in the homes of other African Americans were the victims of equally disturbing treatment. In this novel, for instance, Celie's position as Mr.'s wife is really more akin to that of a domestic worker than it is a partner in marriage. Additionally, even when working for middle- and upper-class black families who might not subject their domestics to such abuses, there were still significant socioeconomic and power disparities that proved complicated in their own ways.

In recent years, it seems there has been renewed interest in the role of the domestic. **Barbara Neely**, in her popular Blanche White mysteries, such as *Blanche on the Lam* (1993), *Blanche among the Talented Tenth* (1995), *Blanche Cleans Up* (1998), and *Blanche Passes Go* (2000), writes of an African American maid with a gift for solving mysteries. In Natasha Trethewey's collection of **poetry** *Domestic Work* (2000), the author uses photos of workers in the pre–civil rights era as inspiration for her poems, many of which focus on the domestic worker.

While black women working in domestic roles often had to contend with abuse, mistreatment, and other forms of discrimination, it is inaccurate to only view their domestic positions in these marginalized terms. As scholars such as Trudier Harris make clear, these women often possessed a great deal of unseen power and subversive influence. Inhabiting such important roles within wealthy, white families allowed these workers opportunities to influence their employers' families and societal views. This points to the complexity of the position of the domestic. While one can see the women in these roles suffered from many injustices due to their gender, **class**, and racial status, it is also clear that these women often held positions of power and influence within the homes in which they worked, even though this power was not always evident to their employers.

Works About

Clark-Lewis, Elizabeth. *Living In, Living Out: African American Domestics and the Great Migration.* Tokyo: Kodansha International, 1996.
———. *Living In, Living Out: African American Domestics in Washington, D.C., 1910–1940.* Washington: Smithsonian Institution Press, 1994.
Harris, Trudier. *From Mammies to Militants: Domestics in Black American Literature.* Philadelphia: Temple University Press, 1982.
Rollins, Judith. *Between Women: Domestics and Their Employers.* Philadelphia: Temple University Press, 1985.

Lisa A. Kirby

DOUGLASS, FREDERICK (1818–1895)

Douglass is well known as an antislavery activist, journalist, diplomat, and autobiographer. What is less well known is the fact that Douglass was also a tireless crusader for equal rights for women. This should come as no surprise; after all, women played a significant role in Douglass's life.

Frederick Augustus Washington Bailey was born on Holme Hill farm, near Tuckahoe Creek in Talbot County on Maryland's eastern shore. His mother was Harriet Bailey, and his father was an unknown white man. There are suggestions that his father might have been his master, Captain Aaron Anthony. He was raised by his grandmother, Betsey Bailey, and rarely saw his mother, who worked as a fieldhand. When he was about six years old, young

Frederick was taken to live on the Lloyd plantation near the Wye River. Although his grandmother had brought him to the plantation, she returned to the Holme farm, leaving Douglass in the care of "Aunt Katy," a cousin of his mother. As he details in his first **autobiography**, as a child, Douglass's **work** as a slave was relatively light. He writes that he was "introduced" to the **violence** and horror of **slavery** after witnessing his aunt receiving an extremely violent beating from her master. This vision not only initiated him into the horrors of slavery but also made clear the double victimization of slave women.

In 1827, Douglass was sent to Baltimore, Maryland, to live with Hugh and Sophia Auld. The Aulds were related to his master Aaron Anthony by marriage (Anthony's daughter, Lucretia, was married to Thomas Auld, Hugh's brother). While in Baltimore, Sophia Auld began to teach young Frederick to read. Her husband objected to her endeavors, explaining that teaching Douglass to read would spoil him for slavery. While in Baltimore, Douglass was a companion to the Aulds' young son, Tommy, and he also worked as an errand boy and general assistant to Auld in his shipbuilding concern. Although Sophia Auld stopped teaching him, Frederick eventually taught himself how to read and write using Tommy's old books. In 1833 after a disagreement between Hugh and Thomas Auld, Thomas demanded that Douglass be returned to Maryland. While back in Maryland, Douglass organized a Bible study group for the slaves on the Lloyd plantation and began to teach some slaves to read and write. After Thomas Auld discovered that Douglass had been teaching slaves to read, he decided to discipline him by renting him out for a year as a fieldhand to Edward Covey, a man known for his ability to "break" unruly slaves.

Covey proved to be a ruthless and sadistic master, subjecting Douglass to many beatings and abuse. One day after a particularly brutal beating, when he had collapsed from heat exhaustion, Douglass ran away from Covey and returned to Thomas Auld. Thomas Auld refused his requests to hire him out to anyone else and forced him to return to Covey. When Douglass returned, Covey was determined to beat him again, this time for running away and complaining to his master. Douglass refused to submit to Covey's unfair punishment, and what had been a war of words between the two turned into a vicious physical confrontation. Covey was unable to gain the upper hand and after the fight never again whipped Douglass. In December 1834, Douglass left Covey's farm for good and returned to the Lloyd plantation. While at the Lloyd plantation, he organized another Bible study group and also taught a small group of slaves to read and write.

In April 1836, Douglass and five other slaves planned to run away to **freedom**. Unfortunately, their escape plan was discovered. Although he and four other slaves were caught, they were not sold south but rather were jailed in Easton and released to their masters after a week. Douglass was sent back to Baltimore to live and work for Hugh Auld. Thomas Auld promised Frederick that he would manumit him at age twenty-five, but only if he behaved himself and learned a trade while in Baltimore. Frederick began to train as a caulker and was hired out to work in several shipyards. Though forced to turn over the bulk of the money he earned to Hugh Auld, as an urban slave in Baltimore Douglass had considerably more freedom of movement than when he was on the Maryland plantation and came into contact with free blacks. He joined the "East Baltimore Mental Improvement Society," a discussion group whose members were free black men. Through this group he met Anna Murray, a free black woman who worked as a housekeeper in Baltimore.

The year 1838 proved to be a pivotal year for Douglass. He became engaged to Murray and moved out of the Auld household into his own lodgings. His taste of relative freedom of movement, however, came to a quick end after Hugh Auld found out that Douglass had attended a church meeting without first asking Auld's permission. Afraid that he would be sold, Douglass put his plan of escape into action. Murray sold one of her feather beds to help Douglass finance his escape, and he purchased free papers from a retired sailor. Then, masquerading as a free black, Douglass was able to escape to New York. Murray joined him in New York, and on September 15, the Reverend J. C. Pennington married the two.

They left New York for New Bedford, Massachusetts, where Douglass could find work in a shipyard. It was at this time that he decided to take the last name of Douglass, after the Scottish Lord named in the Sir Walter Scott poem *The Lady of the Lake*. Due to racism on the docks, he was forced to leave his work as a caulker and became a laborer. While in New Bedford, he came into contact with free blacks and whites involved in the abolitionist movement. He also began to subscribe to William Lloyd Garrison's antislavery newspaper, the *Liberator*. In 1841, Douglass attended a meeting of the Bristol County Anti-Slavery Society and spoke at the meeting, sharing his experiences as a former slave with the audience. His speech was so well received that he was invited to become a paid general agent or speaker for the Massachusetts Anti-Slavery Society. He traveled around New England and the Northeast, giving speeches describing his life as a slave, while withholding details that might positively identify him.

At Garrison's urging, he began to write his autobiography. *Narrative of the Life of Frederick Douglass, an American Slave, Written by Himself* was published in 1845 by the American Anti-Slavery Society. Worried that the narrative might have endanged his freedom, Douglass left for an extended speaking tour of the United Kingdom. Hugh Auld purchased Douglass from Thomas Auld for $100 and vowed to capture Douglass as soon as he returned to the United States. In an endeavor to secure his freedom, two of Douglass's new British friends, the abolitionists Anna and Ellen Richardson, negotiated with Hugh Auld. Auld eventually agreed to free Douglass for approximately $700. Some abolitionists criticized Douglass and the Richardsons for their course of action, arguing that the purchase acknowledged the right to buy and sell human beings. Douglass defended his decision in a letter to the *Liberator*.

Douglass finally returned to the United States in 1847. Using money he raised in England, he decided to publish a newspaper called *North Star*, in

Rochester, New York. The paper's manifesto was "Right is of no Sex—Truth is no Color—God is the father of us all, and we are all brethren." He eventually moved his **family** to Rochester and began to shelter slaves escaping to Canada on the **Underground Railroad**.

As editor of the *North Star*, Douglass wrote several editorials and articles supportive of women's rights. For Douglass, the rights of women and the rights of blacks were intertwined. He recognized that the plight of women was similar to that of African Americans. His support of women's rights might also have stemmed from friendships he cultivated as a speaker for the American Abolitionists Society, such as Susan B. Anthony, Elizabeth Cady Stanton, and others. He saw that some of the strongest supporters of rights for African Americans were women. Indeed, Douglass was one of the few male nineteenth-century public figures to vociferously support women's rights. In 1848, Douglass was invited to attend and speak at the first Women's Rights Convention in Seneca Falls, New York. At the convention, he seconded the motion to support female suffrage, and his explicit support was instrumental in its passage. At the first national women's conference in 1850, Douglass signed the Declaration of Sentiments, which would become the movement's manifesto. Douglass would continue to support women's rights and to speak at most of the Women's Rights Conventions over the next twenty-one years.

In 1851, Douglass publicly disagreed with Garrison's interpretation of the Constitution as a document that supported slavery. Douglass felt the Constitution should be interpreted as an antislavery document because it enshrined and was founded on the notion of freedom. Garrison believed that the Constitution sanctioned slavery, and as a result, abolitionists should work toward exempting themselves from the Union. The estrangement with Garrison would continue and eventually cause Douglass to leave the American Anti-Slavery Society in 1854, when he then joined the Radical Abolitionist Party.

In 1855, Douglass published a second autobiography, *My Bondage and My Freedom*. In addition to detailing the horrors of slavery he had described in the 1845 narrative, Douglass also depicted the racism he encountered in the North and within the abolitionist movement. Douglass continued to lecture extensively. In 1856, John Brown visited Douglass in Rochester. When Brown's raid on Harper's Ferry failed and he was captured, a letter from Douglass was found among Brown's papers. An arrest warrant was issued for Douglass, and as a result, he had to flee from the United States. After a short sojourn in Canada, Douglass left for England, where he began another speaking tour, eventually returning to the United States months later in the spring of 1860.

When the Civil War erupted in 1861, Douglass continued to speak out and advocate rights for blacks. On January 1, 1863, he spoke in Boston at a celebration for passage of the final Emancipation Proclamation. He also became a recruiting agent for the 54th Massachusetts Infantry, the first all-black regiment.

Later that year, he attended the thirtieth anniversary meeting of the American Anti-Slavery Society, where he argued that the work of abolitionism was not done and the society should not be disbanded, as Garrison had proposed.

At a meeting of the American Equal Rights Association in 1868, Douglass argued that it was more important for black men to receive the right to vote than white women. Susan B. Anthony and Elizabeth Cady Stanton vehemently disagreed, insisting that women and blacks should receive the right to vote together.

Douglass moved with his family to Washington, D.C., after Ulysses S. Grant invited Douglass to become a member of his administration (assistant secretary to the commission investigating annexing Hispaniola). In 1874, he was named president of the Freedman's Bank and attempted to reorganize it. Unfortunately, the mismanagement of the bank prior to Douglass's tenure was so severe that the bank had to be closed. President Hayes eventually appointed Douglass U.S. marshal for the District of Columbia in 1877.

In 1882, Douglass published a new version of his autobiography, *The Life and Times of Frederick Douglass*. It sold few copies. In this same year, his wife died. In 1884 Douglass married Helen Pitts, a women's rights activist who worked in the record office with Douglass when he was demoted to recorder of deeds. Douglass's marriage to this white woman was denounced in the press by friends and foes alike. In order to escape the firestorm, they left the United States for an extensive tour of Europe and Egypt in 1886–1887.

In 1889, Douglass was appointed consul general to Haiti. He would eventually resign in 1891 after being continually undermined by the U.S. government. On February 20, 1895, after addressing a meeting of the National Council of Women in Washington, D.C., Douglass collapsed from heart failure at home. At his funeral, Susan B. Anthony read a eulogy written by Elizabeth Cady Stanton.

Works By

The Heroic Slave. Autographs for Freedom. Ed. Julia Griffiths. Boston: John P. Jewett and Co., 1853. 174–239.

The Life and Times of Frederick Douglass: Written by Himself. Boston: De Wolfe and Fisk Co., 1892.

My Bondage and My Freedom. New York: Miller, Orton and Mulligan, 1855.

Narrative of the Life of Frederick Douglass, an American Slave, Written by Himself. Boston: Anti-Slavery Office, 1845.

Works About

Andrews, William L., ed. *Critical Essays on Frederick Douglass*. Boston: G. K. Hall, 1991.

——, ed. *The Oxford Frederick Douglass Reader*. New York: Oxford University Press, 1996.

Foner, Philip S., ed. *Frederick Douglass on Women's Rights.* Westport, CT: Greenwood Press, 1977.

Nicole N. Aljoe

DOVE, RITA (1952–)

When Rita Dove was a young girl, she never thought that she would become a writer. Though she loved to read and write as a child, the thought of making a living writing did not occur to her until she was a senior in high school. Her teacher invited her to attend John Ciardi's book signing of his translation of Dante's *Divine Comedy*, and the experience made writers more real to her. Writers, Dove realized, could create in private and then share their creative inventions with the world. For the first time, she felt a connection between the author, the text, and herself, a feeling she lacked previously since many of the works she read as a child were authored by dead white men. Though as a child Dove did not see herself as a writer, she loved learning about language and would use her weekly assigned spelling words to create prose work she titled "Chaos." In fourth grade, Dove wrote the poem "The Rabbit with the Droopy Ear." She did not plan the solution to the rabbit's droopy ear or devise a plot for "Chaos." In both cases, Dove let the words shape the events of the work, a trait that she continues to use throughout her career.

Dove was born in Akron, Ohio, on August 28, 1952, to Elvira Hord Dove and Ray Dove. Ray Dove would become the first black research chemist in the rubber industry for Goodyear Tire and Rubber Company after attending the University of Akron. However, he did not obtain this post for many years and had to settle for being an elevator operator, where he was passed over by the very white students he tutored in chemistry. Eventually, management was changed, and he was hired as a chemist. Elvira Dove came from a well-educated **family**, and she received a full scholarship at Howard University. Her parents, though, decided that she was too young, at sixteen, to go away to college and sent her to secretarial school instead. Education became very important in the Dove household for Rita Dove and her two younger sisters and one older brother. For the young Rita Dove, each book became an exciting adventure, and learning brought good grades and praise from her family. By the time she was finishing high school in 1970, she was chosen as a presidential scholar, 1 of only 100 students in the United States, and was invited to the White House.

The emphasis on education put on Rita Dove by her parents not only earned her national recognition from the White House, but her academic success helped her fund college as well. She was named a National Achievement Scholar by Miami University in Oxford, Ohio, in the fall of 1970. Surprisingly, Dove's major was prelaw. While growing up, Dove was influenced by the popular media and wished to be a lawyer's or doctor's wife.

Now, however, she felt that she could obtain such a profession. Many of the adults surrounding Dove expected as much. Dove changed her major four times as a freshman and started her sophomore year as an English major. While enrolled in an advanced English composition class, creative writing instructor Milton White replaced Dove's regular instructor. It was in this class that Dove became inspired to be a writer. By her junior year, Dove decided that she wanted to be a poet. Dove's parents supported her decision to become a poet, and in 1973, she graduated summa cum laude, Phi Beta Kappa, and Phi Kappa Phi, with a Bachelor of Arts degree in English.

Dove continued her education and began publishing her work in the mid-1970s. After graduation, Dove became a Fulbright scholar and attended the University of Tübingen in West Germany for two semesters. There she studied European literature, and her discussions with classmates would foster one of her major concerns throughout her writing. **History**, particularly American history, always left out the common and oppressed peoples' struggle and heroics. Dove's new view of history would be represented throughout her **poetry** and other writing. In 1975, she returned to the United States and enrolled in the University of Iowa's Writer's Workshop program, where she was the only black women among her peers. Though competition was vehement among the students, she felt that her **race** helped in this respect. As a black woman, she was an outsider; therefore, she was left out of what she calls the "pecking order." She was the only student who published a poem in *The American Poetry Anthology* that year, a precursor to her eventual fame as a poet.

In 1976, Dove met her future husband, German novelist Fred Viebahn, who was invited as a Fulbright fellow to Iowa for the International Writing Program. Through their support of each other, both were able to continue writing, and Dove began **work** on what would later become published collections of her work. When she first met her future husband, Dove agreed to translate any German texts into English that Viebahn may use. In 1977, Dove received her Master of Fine Arts degree. She soon decided that she wished to be a freelance writer and move to Berlin. However, her plans were delayed when Viebahn was offered a visiting professorship at Oberlin College, which was near Dove's childhood home in Akron. Though Dove undertook many activities during Viebahn's two years at Oberlin, she also completed most of the poems that were included in her first published book, *The Yellow House on the Corner* (1980). She also worked on some prose writing that would later become part of a collection titled *Fifth Sunday* (1985).

After Dove married Viebahn in 1979, her husband was invited to Jerusalem for three months, and it was during this time that Dove sent out *The Yellow House on the Corner* to publishers. The manuscript was accepted in November of that year by Carnegie-Mellon University Press and published in 1980. What would become characteristic of Dove's writing first appears bluntly in the title of *The Yellow House on the Corner*, a concern with space and the impression space has on people's lives. For Dove, a poem can be a "house of sound" that impresses upon the reader, as well as Dove, the possibility of building a **home** in a place where she or he is too frightened to go. Dove's own backyard and the back door figure prominently in much of her writing. In "Adolescence III," the backyard can be a frightening place of confrontation, where one is enclosed and exposed, a place of growth and stagnation, as well as a place of security and loss. In "Geometry," another poem included in her first collection, the back door becomes symbolic as "the door of childhood" for Dove. The back door also provides a place of growth for the child; it is protected and enclosed, but it offers a view of the larger world. This notion of space, in various examples, continues throughout Dove's work.

Shortly after Dove's first collection was accepted for publication, she and her husband moved to Germany, where they hoped to work as freelance writers. During the cold German winter, Dove would write a series of short stories in a friend's unheated apartment; however, she also created a series of poems in the apartment she shared with her husband that would eventually become her second collection of poetry, *Museum* (1983). Though she planned to stay in Germany much longer, Dove noticed that her ability to create poems in English was beginning to suffer. The more she spoke German, the harder it was for her to create English poems according to her standards. After one year, the couple decided to move back to America, and Dove accepted an offer from Arizona State University as a tenure-track assistant professor of creative writing in 1981.

Two major events occurred in 1983; Dove published her second collection of poetry, and her daughter was born. Dove's focus on the home space continues in *Museum*. Such an example is found in "A Father Out Walking on the Lawn," where the speaker of the poem is outside the house and yard, looking into the interior. For this collection, Dove focuses on the space in between exterior and interior. She believes that the movement between inside to outside, similar to opening a door, is effortless. It is this moment of suspension for the poet and the reader that signifies the essence of the poem, one that Dove claims is the moment of possibility or of irresponsibility for the reader. In other words, one must go out into the world, and such movement into the exterior space is fraught with danger, yet it has possibilities also.

When Dove's daughter, Aviva Chantal Tamu Dove-Viebahn, was born, Dove would find that despite the hardships and rewards of child rearing her desire to create was ever present. In 1985, Dove dedicated her collection of short stories, published by the Callaloo Fiction Series at the University of Kentucky in Lexington, titled *Fifth Sunday* to her daughter. The very title of this work suggests the significance of a "fifth Sunday," which seldom occurs, indicating that these stories have special significance.

When Dove was in Germany, she wrote about five or six poems about her grandfather's youth and thought that these would work well by themselves. While she was a writer-in-residence at Tuskegee Institute in Alabama for the summer of 1981, she wrote several more poems about her grandfather. She now revised these and sent them to the *Ohio Review*, where they were published as the chapbook "Mandolin." The poems about her grandfather expanded, especially after Dove was awarded a Guggenheim Fellowship for the

1983–1984 academic year, allowing her the **freedom** to focus on her writing. One night while Dove looked over a poem from *Museum* titled "Dusting," Dove recognized that the solarium in the poem was her grandmother's, and the woman who was trying to remember her lover's name was, in fact, her grandmother. Dove felt that her grandmother, through the poem, spoke to her, asking to have her story told. At that moment, the poetry collection *Thomas and Beulah* was born.

Thomas and Beulah, published by Carnegie-Mellon in 1986, charts the lives of Dove's grandparents in the context of larger history that entailed the migration of blacks from the **South** to the North, several wars, and the **civil rights movement**, among other social events that affected blacks. Though *Thomas and Beulah* is not about a place, Dove asserts that the grandmother and grandfather function as one unit that is "defined" and "confined" to a particular place, Akron, Ohio. For Dove, the poems took charge of themselves, and each fell into place within the collection. Dove won the Lavan Younger Poets Award and served as the president of the Associated Writing Programs. She also received the General Electric Foundation Award for Younger Writers. However, the most significant impact of Dove's success with *Thomas and Beulah* was realized in April 1987, when she became the second African American poet besides **Gwendolyn Brooks** to win the Pulitzer Prize.

Dove soon found herself with celebrity status; the next year she had little time to write as she appeared throughout the country for interviews, presentations, and book signings. However, she was approved for a sabbatical for the 1987–1988 academic year, so she and her family left the country in June and spent time on the Yugoslavian islands, the German island Amrum, Mexico City, and then Berlin in August. While in Berlin, Dove managed to write prolifically for four weeks and then returned to the United States in September. Dove later returned to Europe in the summer of 1988 as a resident at the Rockefeller Foundation's Study and Conference Center in Bellagio, Italy.

When returning to the United States, Dove moved first to Durham, North Carolina, where she was a Mellon fellow at the National Humanities Center for 1988–1989; she later joined the faculty at the University of Virginia. She also received several more awards, including the Ohio Governor's Award. W. W. Norton published Dove's next collection of poetry, *Grace Notes* (1989). These poems reflect the influence that music has in Dove's life. While in fourth grade, Dove learned how to play the violoncello and took private lessons at the Akron Conservatory for Music. Shortly thereafter she joined the Akron Youth Symphony and was even part of a **jazz** quintet. She also played with the Miami University orchestra and continues to study music.

Later on, when her husband was at Oberlin College, Dove switched to the viola da gamba, an early cousin of the cello. For Dove's fortieth birthday in 1992, Viebahn surprised her with a custom-made seventeenth-century replica of an English bass viol. The scrollpiece was carved by hand to resemble the head of a black woman from Albrecht Durer's 1521 drawing *The Negress*

Katharina. Music played the role of discovery for Dove, and she claims that learning music provided her with her first sense of epiphany, of things fitting together that would no doubt be a feature in her literary creations. In 1991, Dove received the Ohioana Award for *Grace Notes*, the Charles Frankel/National Humanities Medal, the Harvard University Phi Beta Kappa poetry award, and the Literary Lion citation from the New York Public Libraries.

In 1992, Pantheon Books published Dove's first novel, *Through the Ivory Gate.* Dove spent many years working on the novel. In fact, the novel was born during a 1979 trip to Dublin, Ireland. The heroine of the novel, Virginia, shares things in common with Dove. She lives in Arizona and plays the cello. Virginia also has a revelation about the musical phrasing she notices in the Bach suites that was also Dove's. Though the novel is not biographical, the **love** of music and the elements found in Dove's poetry are consistent. Again, the very title of the work, *Through the Ivory Gate*, suggests that Virginia must move through her existing place. Her place serves as a passage, a "transient space."

More of Dove's poetry appeared in 1993 in a volume titled *Selected Poems*, published by Vintage Press. In this same year, Dove began serving as Poet Laureate of the United States and Consultant in Poetry at the Library of Congress. She was the youngest person and the first African American to receive such an honor. She served in this post for two years. Dove was also named a Commonwealth Professor of English at the University of Virginia and was given the National Association for the Advancement of Colored People (NAACP) Great American Artist Award and received the Woman of the Year Award from *Glamour* magazine.

Dove's first play, *The Darker Face of the Earth*, was published by Story Line Press in 1994 and would eventually become more personal for Dove when she later revised the play for production in 1996. Dove began working on the play shortly after *The Yellow House on the Corner* was published. Like her first collection of poems, Dove had a concern for lost details of history, and she tries to fill in the past in order to humanize the experience and to learn more about personal **identity**. When revising the play, Dove had another "coming home" experience because she had to add emotions to each of her characters. Each character becomes part of her; they were no longer "mythic representations." Yet no character is simply bad or good in terms of the **slavery** system where each person is fighting for his or her own space.

The sense of history and the personal feelings and identities of the characters connect in the play. Dove felt W.E.B. Du Bois's notion of double consciousness in her past when she realized that her dream as a young black girl and white mainstream society's dream differed. Her parents were very traditional, yet they told her that she could be whatever she wanted. There were, however, few professional women that Dove could use as role models; nonetheless, she grew up believing her dream was possible, though she recognized the obstacles she faced. This kind of realization, the understanding that what one is told may only be one version of the truth, would connect

Dove's personal and present life to the historical past and connect her own experience and identity to the play.

Dove also received many additional awards and honors that year, including the Distinguished Achievement medal from the Miami University Alumni Association, the Renaissance Forum Award for leadership in the literary arts from the Folger Library, and the Carl Sandburg Award from the International Platform Association.

Dove continued to be prolific in 1995, publishing a poetry collection, *Mother Love*, through W. W. Norton and a collection of essays, *The Poet's World*, published by the Library of Congress. The poems and essays move in a more personal direction and continue to universalize experiences often separated by race, gender, and **class**. Home and place are still important in these works. In 1996 she was honored with the Heinz Award in the Arts and Humanities and the Charles Frankel Prize/National Metal in the Humanities.

After a two-year respite, Dove published a song cycle, *Seven for Luck* (1998), through the Hal Leonard Corporation with John Williams, which was used by the Boston Symphony Orchestra at Tanglewood. The songs, which were originally from a group of poems called "Seven for Luck," engage the various stages of life that women go through and include adolescence, romance, love, pregnancy, disappointment, and renewal. This collection further connects Dove's musical interests with her poetic genius. Dove was also awarded the Levinson Prize from *Poetry* magazine at this time.

Dove published *On the Bus with Rosa Parks* in 1999. This collection of poems is largely about middle-age experience. Unlike many of her other collections, these poems were created over time and are less concentrated. Once again, the collection examines the personal, inner feelings of the self and connects those feelings to universal experience. Dove claims that the poems deal with the public and private parts of the self. This same year Dove was reappointed as special consultant in poetry for the Library of Congress and received the John Frederick Nims Translation Award from *Poetry* magazine. In 2001, Dove was honored with the Duke Ellington Lifetime Achievement Award. Over the span of her career, Dove has also been awarded numerous honorary doctorates. Her latest collection is the 2004 *American Smooth*.

One of Dove's most profound attributes is her willingness to get at history that is not told. In some respects, she is a controversial writer because she shows both the positive and negative characteristics of human nature, whether her characters are African American or white American. Dove's concept of how race shapes one's identity is, in some respects, in conflict with the **Black Arts Movement**. In her poetry, Dove seeks to uncover the limitations that any kind of movement can have on shaping one's identity, one's home, and one's personal/public life.

Works By

American Smooth. New York: Norton, 2004.
The Darker Face of the Earth. Ashland, OR: Story Line, 1994.

Fifth Sunday: Stories by Rita Dove. Lexington, KY: Callaloo, 1985.

Grace Notes. New York: Norton, 1989.

Mother Love. New York: Norton, 1995.

Museum. Pittsburgh: Carnegie-Mellon University Press, 1983.

On the Bus with Rosa Parks. New York: Norton, 1999.

The Poet's World. Washington, DC: Library of Congress, 1995.

Selected Poems. New York: Vintage, 1993.

Seven for Luck. Milwaukee, WI: Hal Leonard, 1998.

Thomas and Beulah. Pittsburgh: Carnegie-Mellon University Press, 1986.

Through the Ivory Gate. New York: Pantheon, 1992.

The Yellow House on the Corner. Pittsburgh: Carnegie-Mellon University Press, 1980.

Works About

Gabbon, Joanne V., ed. *The Furious Flowering of African American Poetry.* Charlottesville: University Press of Virginia, 1999.

Ingersoll, Earl, ed. *Conversations with Rita Dove.* Jackson: University Press of Mississippi, 2003.

Pereira, Malin. *Rita Dove's Cosmopolitanism.* Urbana: University of Illinois Press, 2003.

Reddy, Maureen T., Martha Roth, and Amy Sheldon, eds. *Mother Journeys: Feminists Write about Mothering.* Minneapolis, MN: Spinsters Ink, 1994.

Earl F. Yarington

DRAMA

Expanding the definition of drama beyond the play-text to consider oral traditions and ritual enactments as well as the theatrical activity in the culture at large, we can begin to widen the scope of what constitutes African American drama, particularly feminist drama. Performancelike drama involves the written and spoken word, gesture and image, text and **body**. It is a literary form and theatrical practice, an embodied way of knowing that employs "actors" and "audiences" ranging from the rhetorician and her listening audience to the performer and her theatergoing spectators. It includes oral literature and living art forms that bridge and merge disciplinary specific genres such as drama, dance, music, **folklore**, and the visual arts.

Why this emphasis on performance versus drama? The **history** of drama often relies on the circulation and survival of documented or printed plays. Moreover, ideas of what constitutes worthy drama rely on and reflect cultural ideologies, definitions of aesthetics, and hierarchies of art and representation. By turning our attention to performance as an object *and* lens of study, we begin to perceive the various continuities and connections between written and oral modes of expression—speeches and performance pieces, and rituals and ceremonies—that inform and shape African American women's performance creations.

Years before and after **William Wells Brown** wrote and performed *Escape, or a Leap to Freedom* (1858), the earliest documented play by an African American, the vernacular tradition functioned as the primary source of black expression that evoked theatrical and performative qualities. We might consider how **spirituals**, gospels, sermons, and folktales, to name a few genres within the vernacular tradition, employ voices, personae, and bodies to express and enact experience, messages, and lessons for specific audiences. As oral forms, these genres were invented for spoken performance in specific social and ritual contexts. As "actors," the orators or tellers relied on theatrical techniques such as movement, gesture, actions, intonation, and silences as well as literary conventions such as metaphor, imagery, characterization, narrative, and allusion to draw in and persuade their "audiences" as they engaged the performed word. Of course, each genre of the vernacular tradition is different and has its own specific oratorical forms. But as a whole, the vernacular tradition offers one site of performance in which African American women were participants and producers.

Public speeches and the activities related to demonstrations, town meetings, and yearly conventions associated with the abolitionist and feminist campaigns (the American Anti-Slavery Society in 1833, the Female Anti-Slavery Society in 1837), the Women's Rights and Suffrage campaigns in Seneca Falls (1848), and later the Woman's (Temperance) Crusade (1873–1874) invoked spectacle, theatrics, and social dramas as central tactics of the gatherings. **Maria Stewart**, who gave speeches on the topics of **slavery** and women's rights, is considered the first woman in U.S. history to speak publicly to an audience of men and women. On September 21, 1832, at the meeting of the New England Anti-Slavery Society, she called for an increase in the **work** toward educational and economic opportunity for young black women and men in Boston. Such lectures, including the more famous **Sojourner Truth**'s "Ar'n't I a Woman," delivered at the Women's Rights Convention in Akron, Ohio, in 1851, took on the valence of political sermons and employed the rhetorical and theatrical structure of the vernacular tradition.

Rethinking performance to include these public events is important because it constitutes and contributes to an evolving tradition that is not mutually exclusive of its specific sociopolitical contexts. Writing drama requires having access to resources including publications and theaters as sites of distribution and legitimization, if not site of encouragement from which to develop their craft. Moreover, to write drama requires an audience that is receptive to the material and content of the literature. As a public art, drama often works with or against public and ideological representations. The history of the black theater is one that exploited and restricted African American actors and the representation of black life to the popular amusement stage and vaudeville environs, which severely limited the spaces and opportunities for African American women dramatists. In addition, by the late nineteenth and early twentieth centuries, African American dramatists had to work against the predominant constructed images of minstrelsy, buffoonery, and low comedy; the white-produced minstrel shows employed **stereotypes** that posited African American women, for example, in the roles of "wench" or "**Mammy**."

The history and development of African American drama is very much connected to the performance history of African Americans on the stage and their struggle against these representations. The first dramas about black life to receive national acclaim, however, were by white male playwrights such as Ridgely Torrence and Eugene O'Neill. Even though their plays still reflected explicitly or implicitly racist attitudes and stereotypes, they commanded serious attention of white critics and public and exploded the roles available for black actors. Musical theater became one early site in which black artists began to transform perceptions of black actors on stage, and Bob Cole's *A Trip to Coontown* (1898) is considered the first show to be produced, directed, and managed by blacks. The first nonmusical play by a black playwright to reach Broadway, however, did not open until 1923: *The Chip Woman's Fortune* by Willis Richardson.

Plays by African American women dramatists, if produced, were staged in church and school auditoriums. **Angelina Weld Grimké**'s *Rachel* (1916) is considered the first play by an African American woman produced publicly. The Drama Committee of the National Association for the Advancement of Colored People (NAACP) produced this three-act **protest** drama in March 1916 in Washington, D.C., at the Myrtill Miner School. Subsequent performances occurred in New York at the Neighborhood Playhouse and in Cambridge, Massachusetts. The production of Grimké's play reflected a developing concerted effort among African American organizations to increase the visibility of "**race**" plays. In the early twentieth century, black theater groups emerged around the country: the Howard University Players in Washington, D.C., the Ethiopian Art Theater in Chicago, and the Lafayette Theater in New York (a product of the Federal Theater Project). In 1926 W.E.B. Du Bois organized the Krigwa Player' Little Negro Theatre in Harlem and published a manifesto that called for real black plays about, by, for, and near the African American **community** (a call that echoed the NAACP's call only a decade prior). Yet African American women's plays still appeared primarily in churches and schools.

African American women's drama did appear, however, in print. In response to Du Bois's call for an increase in "race drama," various black journals sponsored and supported contests for one-act plays. The *Crisis* and *Opportunity* magazines, for example, offered prizes for the best short plays about the black experience. The majority of the contributors and prizewinners of these contests were women who were writing feminist plays. Among the winners were **Zora Neale Hurston** for *Color Struck* and *Spears* (1925), Ruth Ada Gines-Shelton for *The Church Fight* (1925), **Georgia Douglas Johnson** for *Plumes* (1927), and **Marita Bonner** for *The Purple Flower* (1928). Yet even earlier women were writing and publishing feminist plays. Mary Burrill's *They That Sit in Darkness* (1919) was published in the *Birth Control*

Review's special issue (September 1919), "The Negro's Need for Birth Control as Seen by Themselves." Burrill's *Aftermath* (1919) appeared in the *Liberator*, a white, left-wing periodical.

The publication and circulation of these plays suggest that African American women's drama was alive and thriving even though it did not appear regularly on the stage. From protest plays to one-acts that address racial injustice, the rights of women to information about birth control, issues of miscegenation, church politics, and the achievements and contributions of African Americans to the community and nation, African American women emerged as an important force in the development of modern drama. These plays included a variety of dramatic genres that spanned the spectrum from tragedy, comedy, melodrama, drama of ideas, and moralities to surreal fantasies. While not all the stories or images are positive, most focus on the black woman's story and/or are told from her perspective. This treatment of black women characters distinguishes the work of African American women dramatists from that of their African American and white male counterparts.

Access, however, remained an issue that curtailed the exposure of this work in the literary and theatrical realms dominated by white authors and audiences. Between 1926 and 1959 only ten plays written by African American men were produced on Broadway. While the 1930s and 1940s saw an increase in venues for African American drama—the American Negro Theater was established in Harlem in 1940—it was not until mid-century that more and more black women dramatists received exposure on and off Broadway as legitimate and important contributors. One of the first black women to attract attention was **Alice Childress**, who, with her one-act play *Florence* (1950), cast the young black career woman in a hopeful light. Childress's *Trouble in Mind* (1955), a full-length play that focuses on a strong black female character, was produced off-Broadway and received an Obie Award. When **Lorraine Hansberry**'s ***A Raisin in the Sun*** opened on Broadway in 1959 and received numerous awards, suddenly black and white mainstream audiences began to give the long overdue attention to African American women characters and African American women dramatists.

The drama of the late 1950s to the 1970s grew out of the sociopolitical and cultural environments—the **civil rights movement**, the women's movement, the antiwar movement, and the **Black Nationalism** movement—that defined the period. Of course, not all black drama of this period aligned itself with these movements; however, the historical context is critical to understanding the artistic developments and the ways in which African American women playwrights negotiate the multiple intersections of gender, race, **class**, and **sexuality**. While much of the militant, masculine theater of **Amiri Baraka** (LeRoi Jones) and others of the **Black Arts Movement** were not feminist, women playwrights including Childress and Hansberry contributed to the black revolutionary theater by writing plays that foregrounded the idea of black mass liberation and strong female characters. Among the black revolutionary women playwrights, **Sonia Sanchez** and Martie Charles are most representative. Sanchez's one-act plays followed the method and form of agit-prop, which employed short plays, simplistic action, and direct language to convey a message in the most effective manner possible. This didactic tone is evident in Sanchez's *The Bronx Is Next* (1968) and *Sister Son/ji* (1969) as well as Charles's *Job Security* (1970), *Black Cycle* (1971), and *Jamimma* (1972).

Several playwrights broke with realism as a primary mode of representation. **Adrienne Kennedy**'s *Funnyhouse of a Negro* (1962) and *The Owl Answers* (1963) employ **poetry**, imagery, and metaphor to create disjoined yet intersecting layers of time, place, and consciousness. Kennedy's dramatic oeuvre is very much about the failure to locate embodied **identity** as the source of authenticity of experience, and she remains one of the most innovative African American playwrights in the twentieth century. With *for colored girls who have considered suicide/when the rainbow is enuf* (1976), **Ntozake Shange** developed a new dramatic genre she named the choreopoem, which merged music, dance, and poetry throughout its series of dramatic monologues. Originating as a series of seven poems, *for colored girls* presents monologues of seven female characters who create an account of black women's interconnected experiences of racial, gender, and class oppression and celebrate being both black and a woman. Shange's *for colored girls* was produced first off-off-Broadway at the Henry Street Settlement and then off-Broadway by the New York Shakespeare Festival at the Public Theater. Four months later the play was transferred to Broadway and opened at the Booth Theater on September 15, 1976.

Feminist drama in the last quarter of the twentieth century continues to express the multiple and fluid identities that construct and represent black experience. The drama of this period puts in conversation personal identities and cultural histories. Moreover, it highlights performance as a site of representation that constitutes and deconstructs identity simultaneously. As such, the drama of this period engages a relationship between a performance present and its historical past. Robbie McCauley's *Sally's Rape* (1990), Glenda Dickerson and Breena Clarke's *Re/Membering Aunt Jemima: A Menstrual Show* (1991), **Anna Deavere Smith**'s *Fires in the Mirror* (1991), and **Suzan-Lori Parks**'s *In the Blood* (2000), to name a very select few, rely on and recall the rich history of African American drama and performance from the solo orator to mainstream theatrical production.

See also Franklin, J. E.; *Topdog/Underdog*; *Venus*

Works About

Brown-Guillory, Elizabeth, ed. *Their Place on the Stage: Black Women Playwrights in America.* Westport, CT: Praeger, 1990.

Elam, Harry J., Jr., and David Krasner, eds. *African-American Performance and Theater History: A Critical Reader.* Oxford and New York: Oxford University Press, 2001.

Hill, Errol, and James Hatch, eds. *A History of African American Theatre.* New York: Cambridge University Press, 2003.

Hull, Gloria T., Patricia Bell Scott, and Barbara Smith, eds. *But Some of Us Are Brave: Black Women's Studies.* Old Westbury, NY: Feminist Press, 1982.

Keyssar, Helene. *The Curtain and the Veil: Strategies in Black Drama.* New York: B. Franklin, 1979.

Marsh-Lockett, Carol P., ed. *Black Women Playwrights: Visions on the American Stage.* New York: Garland, 1999.

Williams, Dana. *Contemporary African American Female Playwrights: An Annotated Bibliography.* Westport, CT: Greenwood Press, 1998.

Johanna Frank

DRUMGOOLD, KATE (1858–?)

Kate Drumgoold is known for her **autobiography** *A Slave Girl's Story*, and all that is known about her life comes from this book. Drumgoold apparently self-published *A Slave Girl's Story* in 1898 in Brooklyn, New York. The autobiography recounts Drumgoold's experiences growing up as a slave, as a young girl during the Civil War and its aftermath, and as an educator at the turn of the century.

Born in 1858 in Virginia, Drumgoold recounts a pivotal experience in her early life, the burning of her mother's house, after which she lived with her white owner, Bettie House. Drumgoold formed a close relationship with Mrs. House, her "white mother," who treated Drumgoold as a daughter and who was significant in grounding her in the religious life that would be so important to her. After House's death, Drumgoold returned to live with her own mother briefly; early in the Civil War, her mother was sold to finance a war proxy for her owner, John House. About 1864 or 1865, Drumgoold's mother returned to Virginia and began gathering up her scattered children in preparation for the move to the North. In 1865, the **family** moved to Brooklyn, assisted by Major Bailley, a northerner sent to Virginia to ensure that newly emancipated African Americans received their rights, and Drumgoold was baptized into the Washington Avenue Baptist Church in 1866.

From 1865 to 1878, Drumgoold embarked on her "twelve or thirteen years of service," working in various Brooklyn households full-time until she began school, then working summers in Saratoga Springs to finance her education. During that time she became ill with smallpox and had to return for a while to her mother. Her illness and its financial consequences forced her to delay her entry into college by three or four years, but in 1875 Drumgoold began attending Wayland Seminary in Washington, D.C.; in 1878, she left Washington, which did not suit her fragile heath, returning to **work** in Brooklyn so she might eventually return to school. From about 1881 to 1885, she attended school in the Blue Ridge, Alleghany Mountains at Harper's Ferry, and then in 1885 she began teaching in Woodstock, Shenandoah County. She moved briefly through two other schools before settling to teach for eleven years in Hinton, West Virginia.

In 1888 at a speech to a church in Talcott, Summers County, West Virginia, Drumgoold was asked to publish her narrative, but she refused, planning to publish the work from her home in Brooklyn; this episode suggests she had already done substantial work on the narrative at that time. In October 1895, after suffering continued ill health that eventually forced her to retire from teaching, Drumgoold returned home to Brooklyn, where she performed light household work for a number of families. The publication of *A Slave Girl's Story* in 1898 represents the last information available about her life, with the exception of one census document from June 1900, which reports a Kate C. Drumgold, a teacher, living in Brooklyn. A single black female aged forty-one, Drumgold was born in August 1858. Since several variations of her name exist in bibliographies citing her work (Drumgoold, Drumgold, Dormigold, and Dorrigold), it is difficult to assert with certainty that this record refers to her, but it seems probable.

Drumgoold's narrative highlights the contributions of women to her education and to her advancement as a teacher. She describes particularly the importance of her relationship with both her mother, a determined woman who restored her family after being sold away from them during the Civil War, and with her "white mother," a woman who treated Drumgoold kindly and tried to shield her from the experiences of **slavery**. A great deal of her autobiography recognizes the contributions of the many members of her **community** who supported her career; Drumgoold believed strongly that the advancement of the black **race** would take place with hard work, community support, education, and religious faith. In *A Slave Girl's Story*, Drumgoold resists racial prejudice and illness to present a portrait of a woman closely tied to her community and determined to contribute back to that community as an educator and a voice for social justice for African Americans.

Work By

A Slave Girl's Story. 1898. *Six Women's Slave Narratives*. Ed. William L. Andrews. Schomburg Library of Nineteenth-Century Black Women Writers. New York: Oxford University Press, 1988.

Works About

Carby, Hazel V. *Reconstructing Womanhood: The Emergence of the Afro-American Woman Novelist*. New York: Oxford University Press, 1987.

Fleischer, Jennifer. *Mastering Slavery: Memory, Family, and Identity in Women's Slave Narratives*. New York: New York University Press, 1996.

Gwin, Minrose C. *Black and White Women of the Old South: The Peculiar Sisterhood in American Literature*. Knoxville: University of Tennessee Press, 1985.

Lisa Hammond Rashley

DUNBAR, PAUL LAURENCE (1872–1906)

Paul Laurence Dunbar's literary cache includes short stories, novels, essays, and plays; however, this early African American writer is most often recognized as a poet. In fact, Dunbar is considered the first free black American who made his living as a writer, although the field of published literature had been entered earlier by the popular African American woman **Phillis Wheatley**. He was even given the title Poet Laureate of the Negro Race. He was born in Dayton, Ohio, during Reconstruction to parents who were former slaves. Dunbar's father, who escaped **slavery** and later fought in the Civil War, shared with his son his deep resentment of slavery's effects. His mother often told him stories in a humorous fashion about the slave life she had lived. The embittered feeling about experiences expressed by his father and the tales of plantation life shared by his mother served as major influences on Dunbar in his development of a black voice in literature.

During the late 1880s, Dunbar, the only African American in his class at Central High School, served as the school's newspaper editor and class poet and even edited, during this period, the *Tattler*, a newspaper primarily directed at the African American **community** and published by a classmate, Orville Wright. Dunbar accomplished a major feat when several of his poems, including "Our Martyred Soldiers" and "On the River," were published in the city's newspaper, the *Dayton Herald*, in 1888.

Benjamin Brawley, a Dunbar scholar, refers to the period from 1891 to 1896 as a critical turning point in the artist's literary life. During this time, Dr. James Newton Mathews, a man he met through a former teacher, asked Dunbar to read his original poem "Welcome Address to the Western Association of Writers" at the association's meeting in Dayton in 1892. As a result of this presentation, he received some exposure and in 1893, with the help of the United Church of the Brethren, he published his first book of **poetry**, *Oak and Ivy*.

The following year Dunbar went to Chicago to seek **work** at the first World's Fair. An introduction to **Frederick Douglass** resulted in Dunbar serving as an assistant to the famous abolitionist. In this position, Dunbar gained exposure and experience. Another of his newfound friends, Dr. H. A. Tobey, helped him publish his second book of poetry, *Majors and Minors* (1896). The book drew interest from the noted literary critic William Dean Howells. His assessment of Dunbar set the standards by which Dunbar has been judged even today.

From the early stages of his writing career, Dunbar was influenced by the Romantics, especially Shelley. As a result of this affinity, Dunbar produced a substantial amount of standard English verse including "The Colored Soldiers"(1895), "Frederick Douglass"(1895), and especially "Ode to Ethiopia"(1893). While Howells determined that Dunbar's work could be divided into two categories, "literary" and "dialect," he overwhelmingly critiqued and declared Dunbar to be an authentic African American writer of dialect. This assessment indelibly marked Dunbar as a writer of dialect only. In his dialectical poetry, Dunbar described stereotypical black plantation characters.

Such descriptions alienated blacks who just wanted to forget the past, but these images enticed whites to read and be entertained by such stories. In December 1896, Dunbar published *Lyrics of Lowly Life*, considered by some critics to be his finest work. Its success afforded Dunbar an opportunity to tour the United States and Europe, where he did readings and even collaborated with Samuel Coleridge Taylor to produce an operetta, *Dream Lovers* (1898), which was performed in London.

Dunbar met schoolteacher and poet Alice Moore in 1896, after reading her poetry, seeing a picture of her in a literary magazine, and corresponding with her through letters. When he returned from his European tour and secured a job in Washington, D.C., they married in 1898. Now married, Dunbar continued to support his mother financially, whose sacrifices he felt were responsible for his success. He and Alice Moore later separated, but she continued to carry his name.

In 1898, Dunbar published *Folks from Dixie*, a collection of short stories, illustrating his ability to write **fiction**. These stories contain characters, not all of whom are black but who all have some connection to the **South**. During that same year, his first novel, *The Uncalled*, was published. Ironically, the book deals with a white youth's conflict of decision about a career choice of the ministry. It is believed that this work actually details the struggle Dunbar had with his own career choices. *The Sport of the Gods* (1902) was Dunbar's final novel and probably his best effort in this genre. The book showcases the writer's only black protagonist and paints a very dire picture of the future for African Americans. A very successful musical work, *Clorindy* or "*The Origin of the Cakewalk*," was also produced in 1898 in collaboration with Will Marion Cook. Although the work was very well received, the press painted a negative portrayal of Dunbar as a degrading minstrel showman.

Themes around which Dunbar wrote his work included racial oppression of African Americans in all aspects of their lives, pride shown toward the inner strength and accomplishments of the **race**, and revolution against the brutality and corruption toward African Americans. In *We Wear the Mask* (1896), the poet, reflectively and with a bit of displeasure, admits his awareness of the many roles that African Americans must play in order to survive. In *The Old Cabin* published in *Lyrics of Sunshine and Shadow* (1905), Dunbar demonstrates a skillful production of rhythmical appeal. Additionally, he uses the elderly speaker of the poem to proclaim the tragic nature of slavery and what it does to those who are subjected to it. Dunbar's views on the plight of blacks were often published in newspapers across the country. The articles contained expressions that were both dignified and intelligently composed. The author strongly attempted to address the indignities and injustices suffered by African Americans at the turn of the twentieth century. However, this author is criticized, often by the African American community, because of the feeling that his literary work does not highlight issues of injustice substantially.

Several of Dunbar's poems continue to be favorites with readers. Among them are "When Malindy Sings"(1903)—a written recognition of his mother's **love** of singing; "Sympathy"(1899)—a metaphor for the pain of enslavement;

"The Corn'Stalk Fiddle" (1895)—a light, rhythmical rendition of party life under meager circumstances; "The Haunted Oak"(1903)—a denouncement of Ku Klux Klan activities and lynchings; "The Colored Soldiers"—a tribute to his father and black soldiers who died in the Civil War; "Frederick Douglass"—a memorial poem; and "Ode to Ethiopia"—recognition and praise of the black race and its expected productive destiny.

For a man whose literary life was severely handicapped generally by prejudice and specifically by illness, Dunbar produced a prolific amount of work across several genres. Dunbar died at his mother's home on February 9, 1906. His death was the result of a long battle with tuberculosis and alcoholism. He was only thirty-three years of age.

Works By

The Complete Poems of Paul Laurence Dunbar. New York: Dodd, Mead, and Co., 1913.
Folks from Dixie. New York: Dodd, Mead, and Co., 1898.
The Heart of Happy Hollow. New York: Dodd, Mead, and Co., 1904.
Howdy, Honey, Howdy. New York: Dodd, Mead, and Co., 1905.
In Old Plantation Days. New York: Dodd, Mead, and Co., 1903.
Lyrics of Lowly Life. New York: Dodd, Mead, and Co., 1896.
Lyrics of Sunshine and Shadow. New York: Dodd, Mead, and Co., 1905.
Majors and Minors: Poems. New York: Dodd, Mead, and Co., 1895.
Poems of Cabin and Field. New York: Dodd, Mead, and Co., 1899.
The Sport of Gods. New York: Dodd, Mead, and Co., 1902.
When Malindy Sings. New York: Dodd, Mead, and Co., 1904.

Works About

Braxton, Joanne M., ed. *The Collected Poetry of Paul Laurence Dunbar.* Charlottesville: University of Virginia Press, 1993.
Martin, Herbert Woodward, and Ronald Primeau, eds. *In His Own Voice.* Athens: Ohio University Press, 2002.
Redding, J. Saunders. "Negro Writing in America." *New Leader* 43 (May 16, 1960): 8.

Bettie Jackson Varner

DUNBAR-NELSON, ALICE MOORE (1875–1935)

A native of New Orleans, Louisiana, Alice Ruth Moore was born on July 19, 1875, to Joseph Moore, a Creole merchant marine, and Patricia Wright Moore, a seamstress of black and Native American blood. Fair enough to pass for white, Alice spent twenty-one years in the racially mixed Creole society of New Orleans. In 1896, she relocated to Medford, Massachusetts, with her sister, brother-in-law, and mother, and a year later she ended up in Brooklyn, New York. After her marriage and literary collaboration with renowned black poet **Paul Laurence Dunbar** ended in 1902, she left New York for Wilmington, Delaware.

After a second marriage, and a third to journalist Robert J. Nelson in 1916, Dunbar-Nelson's social and political activism was kindled. She coedited the *Wilmington Advocate*, a civil rights newspaper, and for over two decades she addressed issues that confronted blacks and women of her time. She was a field organizer for the woman's suffrage movement for the Middle Atlantic states, and she was later field representative for the Woman's Committee of the United States Council of National Defense in 1918 to further war **work** among black women.

In the 1920s and 1930s, Dunbar-Nelson was even more active. She served on the Republican State Committee of Delaware in 1920, and that same year, with women from the State Federation of Colored Women, she helped to found the Industrial School for Colored Girls, a facility for delinquent and homeless juvenile girls, where she worked as a teacher and parole officer in Marshalltown, Delaware, from 1924 to 1928. In 1924, she spearheaded the Democratic political campaign among black women from the party's New York City headquarters and published in the *Messenger* a two-part article on Delaware in "These 'Colored' United States." Between 1928 and 1931 she spent much of her energy and time traveling and speaking as the executive secretary of the American Friends Inter-Racial Peace Committee.

While Dunbar-Nelson's political and social activism thrived, and despite the fact that many of her manuscripts and typescripts were rejected when she explored themes of racism, the color line, and oppression, her writing flourished between 1895 and 1920. She published *Violets and Other Tales* (1885), *The Goodness of St. Rocque, and Other Stories* (1899), a one-act satire, *The Smart Set* (1900), and her most popular play, *Mine Eyes Have Seen* (1918), published by *Crisis*. She also wrote newspaper columns for the *Pittsburgh Courier* and the *Washington Eagle*. As an activist, short-fiction writer, journalist, poet, and dramatist, Dunbar-Nelson was genuinely dedicated to the cause of improving the conditions of blacks, and especially black women, whom she encouraged to become actively involved in politics and society.

Works By

"The Author's Evening at Home." *Smart Set* (September 1900): 105–106.
Love's Disguise. Unpublished drama, performed 1909–1916.
Mine Eyes Have Seen. Crisis 15 (April 1918): 271–275.

Works About

Bryan, Violet Harrington. "Creating and Re-creating the Myth of New Orleans: Grace King and Alice Dunbar-Nelson." *Publications of the Mississippi Philological Association* (1987): 185–196.

———. "Race and Gender in the Early Works of Alice Dunbar-Nelson." *Louisiana Women Writers: New Essays and a Comprehensive Bibliography*. Ed. Dorothy H. Brown and Barbara C. Ewell. Baton Rouge: Louisiana State University Press, 1992. 122–138.

Hull, Gloria T. "Alice Dunbar-Nelson (1875–1935)." *Color, Sex, and Poetry: Three Women Writers of the Harlem Renaissance*. Bloomington: Indiana University Press, 1987. 33–104.

———. *The Works of Alice Dunbar-Nelson*. Vol. 3. Ed. Gloria T. Hull. New York: Oxford University Press, 1988.

Ijeoma, Charmaine N. "Alice Dunbar-Nelson: A Biography." *Collections* 10 (2000): 25–54.

Shafer, Yvonne. "Alice Moore Dunbar-Nelson (1875–1935)." *American Women Playwrights, 1900–1950*. New York: Peter Lang, 1995. 383–387.

Whitlow, Roger. "Alice Dunbar-Nelson: New Orleans Writer." *Regionalism and the Female Imagination: A Collection of Essays*. Ed. Emily Toth. New York: Human Sciences Press, 1985. 109–125.

Williams, Ora. "Alice Moore Dunbar-Nelson." *Dictionary of Literary Biography. Afro-American Writers before the Harlem Renaissance*. Vol. 50. Ed. Trudier Harris and Thadious M. Davis. Detroit: Gale, 1986. 225–233.

Loretta G. Woodard

DUST TRACKS ON A ROAD

Zora Neale Hurston published her **autobiography**, *Dust Tracks on a Road*, in 1942, and while it won the Anisfield-Wolf Book Award for its contribution to **race** relations, many felt that Hurston was less then candid about many of the facts of her life and were disappointed that she barely discussed her own **literature**. However, two points must be noted regarding this memoir: First, Hurston did not want to write an autobiography at this point in her life, stating that she still had much living to do; second, Hurston biographer Robert Hemenway suggests that her publishers indicated that this text would be the first of a series of autobiographical narratives, making it reasonable to assume, at least in Hurston's eyes, that *Dust Tracks* was the first installment of her life story.

Regardless of the situation under which the memoir was published, *Dust Tracks* remains a powerful glimpse into Hurston's life because in it she shares vivid accounts of her **memories** as an imaginative young black girl of the **South**, rich and detailed descriptions of her ethnographic fieldwork, and recollections of her friendships with two important women in her life, white novelist Fannie Hurst and black singer-actress Ethel Waters. While Hurston does offer guarded reflections on her romantic life as well, she makes it clear that she has chosen to keep private certain of her intimacies.

In establishing her parentage, Hurston indicates that her father, John Hurston, felt that God had played a dirty trick on him by giving him another daughter. This observation gives the reader an early indication that Hurston recognized the devaluation of females in her society. At the same time, this recognition, along with her mother's advice to "jump at de sun," only served to make Hurston more determined to celebrate her black womanness. She was routinely accused of being "impudent" and of having a "sassy" tongue, labels that have been applied to black females since **slavery** to indicate the difficulty (impossibility) of silencing the black woman. Hurston's father, grandmother, stepmother, and teachers often warned her that her impudent ways and her sassy tongue would get her in trouble or possibly lynched. After all, her father cautioned her, she "wasn't white" (meaning that the double negative of being black and female gave her no voice). While Hurston's mother also acknowledged that Zora Neale was impudent, she did so with pride.

Hurston writes that she knew she was special even as a child, believing that the moon, the symbol of womanness, followed her. She often sat on the gatepost in front of her house in Eatonville, Florida, imagining the larger world that waited for her beyond the horizon and engaging, without fear or hesitation, the white folks that drove through town. She writes about a number of experiences in which she witnessed or suffered the attempts by others to silence the black woman's voice. The most poignant example occurs with the **death** of her mother, Lucy Ann Potts, when Hurston, as a young black girl, is pushed aside and silenced when she attempts to carry out her mother's last wishes.

Although Hurston notes in *Dust Tracks* a number of oppressive acts perpetrated against her because she is a black female—sexual harassment, accusations/expectations of wanton **sexuality**, attempts at silencing her—she remains strong in her determination to speak her mind and follow her convictions. In addressing the country's involvement in wartime activities, she finds an analogy and turns the focus on herself and on her own struggles when she states that she saw no need for "finger-nail warfare." In other words, when it came to battling for her place in the world, there would be no stereotypical "girly" fighting but out-and-out war. After all, the moon sat on her shoulder.

Works About

Boi, Paola. "Zora Neale Hurston's Autobiographic Fictive: Dark Tracks on the Canon of a Female Writer." *The Black Columbiad: Defining Moments in African American Literature and Culture.* Ed. Werner Sollors and Maria Diedrich. Cambridge, MA: Harvard University Press, 1994. 191–200.

Bordelon, Pamela. "New Tracks on *Dust Tracks.* Toward a Reassessment of the Life of Zora Neale Hurston." *African American Review* 31.1 (Spring 1997): 5–21.

Hemenway, Robert E. *Zora Neale Hurston: A Literary Biography.* Urbana: University of Illinois Press, 1977.

Rodriguez, Barbara. "On the Gatepost: Literal and Metaphorical Journeys in Zora Neale Hurston's *Dust Tracks on a Road.*" *Women, America, and Movement: Narratives of Relocation.* Ed. Susan L. Roberson. Columbia: University of Missouri Press, 1998. 235–257.

Johnnie M. Stover

 **E**

ELAW, ZILPHA (c. 1790–?)

Born around 1790 of free parents near Philadelphia, Zilpha Elaw was one of the best-known black women preachers of the nineteenth century. Like her sisters in the ministry, Elaw found scriptural validation of authority to preach. For example, on the title page of her **autobiography** *Memoirs of the Life, Religious Experience, Ministerial Travels and Labours of Mrs. Zilpha Elaw* (1846), Elaw quotes from 2 Corinthians 3:5, which asserts that "our sufficiency is of God." Elsewhere in her narrative she references Acts 5:29, which challenges Christians to obey God rather than man. These scriptures liberate women preachers from the limitations imposed on them by a male-dominated culture and religious tradition. Taking a clearly feminist stance on the role of women in the church, Elaw and other women preachers boldly affirmed their autonomy, insisting that their first duty was to God, not to men.

After her mother's **death**, Zilpha worked for a Quaker family from age twelve to age eighteen. During these early years, she was associated with the African Methodist Episcopal Church. She married Joseph Elaw in 1810 and fulfilled the **domestic** duties of a wife and mother. Her religious awakening occurred when camp meetings and outdoor revivals were popular in nineteenth-century America. Elaw's autobiography provides an extraordinarily vivid, detailed description of camp meetings. In one of those meetings in 1817, Elaw fell into a "trance of ecstasy" during which she became convinced that God had sanctified her soul. Emboldened by the sense of empowerment that sanctification confers upon believers, Elaw moved into the public sphere, a space from which women had been largely prohibited. She began to speak in public and offer prayers for others. At a later camp meeting, Elaw received a call to preach, which she reluctantly accepted on the urging of a group of Christian women supporters.

Although a few ministers in the Methodist Society of Burlington, New Jersey, endorsed her preaching ministry, the powerful male church leaders denied her petition for a license to preach. Some church leaders, male and female, viewed Elaw's spiritual self-reliance as nothing more than female waywardness, an unnatural deviation from the prescribed roles for women in the church. Nevertheless, the denial of a formal denominational sanction did not dampen Elaw's zeal to preach. She embarked upon her ministry fully persuaded that God's command to preach superseded man's injunctions to the contrary. Like Eldress **Rebecca Cox Jackson**, the black Shaker, Elaw was obedient to her inner voice.

Leaving her daughter with trusted friends, Elaw became a traveling evangelist, undertaking missions into the slave states in 1828. As a free black woman, Elaw risked her own **freedom** by traveling and preaching in the **South**. In 1840, Elaw extended her evangelical reach by traveling to London, where she preached for five years, despite the vocal opposition to women preachers that permeated British society in the nineteenth century. Elaw's insistence upon the right to travel extensively challenges the dictates of the male-inspired Cult of True Womanhood that governed the lives of women.

Elaw was also a visionary like Rebecca Jackson (and **Julia A. J. Foote**). Elaw's autobiography records some of her dreams and visions. For example, she writes of the time when she was milking a cow and saw a Christ-like figure standing before her with outstretched, welcoming arms. The cow sees the Christ-like figure and falls to its knees in reverence. One of Elaw's dreams reveals the "terrors of the day of judgment." In another vision, she observes five angels praising God.

Unfortunately, nothing is known about Elaw's life after 1845. Nevertheless, the feminist impulse underlies Elaw's successful resistance against male dominance in the **home** and in the church. By her example, Elaw offers women courage to pursue alternative roles in communities of faith and to accept the new birth of sanctification that eliminates gender distinctions and fosters a sense of being in touch with the will of God.

Work By

Memoirs of the Life, Religious Experience, Ministerial Travels and Labours of Mrs. Zilpha Elaw: An American Female of Colour in Sisters of the Spirit. Ed. William L. Andrews. Bloomington: Indiana University Press, 1986.

Works About

Andrews, William L. Introduction to *Sisters of the Spirit: Three Black Women's Autobiographies of the Nineteenth Century.* Bloomington: Indiana University Press, 1986. 1–22.

Riggs, Marcia Y., ed. *Can I Get a Witness?: Prophetic Religious Voices of African-American Women.* Maryknoll, NY: Orbis, 1997.

Elvin Holt

ELLISON, RALPH (1914–1994)

One of the most influential yet controversial writers of the twentieth century, Ralph Ellison has made an inestimable contribution to African American literature. Known primarily for his 1952 novel *Invisible Man*, Ellison continues to influence contemporary authors and critics. *Invisible Man* and his many essays, short stories, and second novel (*Juneteenth*) represent a small yet significant body of work by an author able to transcend the same color line that restricted his early life. His frequent interrogations of **race** in **literature** earned him advocate status for the African American **community** among whites, yet within his community many dissenting voices challenge the views and opinions advanced in his writing.

Born on March 1, 1914, in Oklahoma City, Oklahoma, Ralph Waldo Ellison had a literary inheritance thrust upon him by his father Lewis, an avid reader who believed that naming his son after the American poet Ralph Waldo Emerson would result in the promise of a literary career. Ellison's mother, however, would become the more influential parent following the accidental **death** of Lewis Ellison in 1917. Working as a maid for several families, Ida Milsap Ellison brought discarded record albums and books **home** to her son. Those albums and books created lifelong preoccupations of music and literature for Ellison, who learned early the importance of studying technique. Ellison played trumpet in high school under the tutelage of Zelia Breaux, who taught him musical theory, while at night Ellison would see **jazz** performances as various artists visited Oklahoma City.

Ellison's high school trumpeting won him a scholarship from the state of Oklahoma that he applied toward an education at the Tuskegee Institute in Alabama. In 1933 Ellison entered Tuskegee to study music in their new program. While there, Ellison worked in the library where he fed his voracious appetite for reading begun in high school. In reading the works of Joyce, Eliot, Faulkner, and Hemingway, Ellison found new worlds free from the confines of segregation he experienced in the **South**. Yet it would be to study art in New York City that sent Ellison North. Leaving behind Tuskegee in the summer following his junior year, Ellison's first sojourn to New York was interrupted in the winter of 1937 with news of an injury to his mother.

Ellison stayed in Dayton, Ohio, following his mother's funeral and worked with his brother Herbert to earn money for a return trip to New York. Using his nights for writing, Ellison produced his first published piece of writing for *New Challenge*. His review of Waters Edward Turpin's novel *These Low Grounds* (1937) thrust him into a critical arena he was never to leave. Returning to New York in 1938, Ellison made numerous influential contacts;

Duke Ellington, **Langston Hughes**, Alain Locke, and **Richard Wright** became acquaintances. Though the activities of the **Harlem Renaissance** were coming to a close, there remained a vibrant literary scene in New York, and Ellison found work at the Federal Writers Project recording oral histories while maintaining his own writing outside of **work**.

Today no complete edition of Ellison's short **fiction** exists, though one posthumous collection (*Flying Home and Other Stories* [1996]) includes the widest available selection. The 1939 publication of "Slick Gonna Learn" and the 1940 publication of "The Birthmark," Ellison's earliest published fiction, are segments of his first attempt at writing a novel. While the *Slick* novel, begun in Dayton, never came to fruition, Ellison's literary contributions clearly commenced in earnest with it. In 1944, Ellison published both "King of the Bingo Game" and "Flying Home"—his two most anthologized stories—and both anticipate the struggles of the protagonist in *Invisible Man*.

In "King of the Bingo Game," the unnamed protagonist goes to a local bingo hall in order to try his luck at winning a $36 jackpot. Unable to secure work and financially bereft, his mind returns constantly to his wife Laura and her unmet needs. Obsessively preoccupied with the demands of life in the city, he unexpectedly realizes that he has the winning card. In order to claim the jackpot, he must stop the prize wheel on its winning spot. He takes too much time, though, considering all of the options and mechanisms behind the operation of the wheel, and police come to remove him from the stage. The story ends with him beaten and bleeding behind the stage curtain and no closer to solving his fiscal dilemma. "King of the Bingo Game" offers an interesting commentary on racial division within the city. While the African American protagonist is offered equal opportunity to win in the luck of gambling, his behavior causes alarm in the officials who do not know his dire position. Further accentuating his outsider status is his revelation to the audience that he is from the South. Ellison imbues the character with the two most indicting **stereotypes** of the day by making him both backward and black. While one can see that the character's actions do not merit the treatment he gets, the story chronicles the climactic moments of one man's experience of desegregation over his lifetime, all the time mistakenly believing himself able to rise above his circumstances and win.

"Flying Home" tells the story of Todd, an airman for the Tuskegee unit who, while on a training flight, hits a bird and has to crash land the airplane. Ellison's use of literary symbolism in the story is effortless and profound and also anticipates *Invisible Man*. Death is all around Todd ("death," in German, translates as *tod*); however, he repeatedly transcends it. As a result, he is frequently in opposition to the other people he encounters. For instance, the moment he regains consciousness in the presence of Jefferson and Teddy, two African American men who see the plane go down, Todd sees he is not like them. They are sentenced to a life of labor, while Todd has created a greater responsibility for himself. Todd's prejudice, then, seems to be directed toward the role a black man is assigned in the community. Todd's place in the world is yet to be fully realized, though he senses its early manifestations in an episode from childhood where his mother admonishes him for wanting to fly planes.

By the time of the crash, the vehicle of his dream is the fuselage standing away from him in the field. Todd is so inextricably linked to the air in his own mind (and in the text) that he is not able to relate to the world around him, yet the tradition he finds himself a part of offers no future for him. When Todd is informed that the land his plane crashed on belongs to Dabney Graves, he again is confronted by images of death. In Graves's yard, Todd learns that he, like Jefferson and Teddy, is an outsider by virtue of the color of his skin. Blending the Western mythology of the Icarus story with the African American trickster tales told by Jefferson, Ellison incorporates the same focus he finds in music, for instance, that melds a classical tradition with the improvisation of jazz. Further, Todd, like the protagonist in "King of the Bingo Game," is assaulted by a white man (Graves), but his response is to laugh. Carried away by medics, Todd sees a crow transfigured in the sun into the form of a phoenix; the story offers a resilient ending to Ellison's homage to the Tuskegee airmen. Moving from a negative to a more positive ending, Ellison's two major short stories suggest an optimistic trajectory for African American fiction.

Noticeably absent from Ellison's stories are central female characters. The protagonist of "Bingo" remains concerned with the unseen Laura, while Todd recalls his mother's admonition to his childish dreams. Likewise, of principal objection by numerous critics is the stereotypical portrayal of women in 1952's *Invisible Man*. Claiming that women occupy no central roles whatsoever, contemporary critics fault Ellison for a omission that, when explored, does not hold; Ellison wrote from his experience as an African American male and focused on that role rather than one his own experience could not verify.

In 1946, one year after commencing work on his classic novel, he married Fanny McConnell fresh from a tour with the Merchant Marines. Ellison published *Invisible Man* and won the 1952 book award for his first novel. Told largely in retrospect by an unnamed protagonist, the story describes his life, from early childhood recollections of his grandfather, through his high school successes turned into exhibitions of racial division and **violence**, to his Tuskegee-like college experience, his affiliation with the communistlike Brotherhood, and his break from the group following the death of another of its members; it culminates in his confrontation of his own invisibility and lack of **identity**. The novel would become one of the most important works in the African American canon. Paradoxically enough, as a black bildungsroman, *Invisible Man* has an importance to African American women's literature that comes directly from its exalted place within the canon. While Henry Louis Gates, Jr., in *The Signifying Monkey*, contextualizes Ellison's conscious revision of Richard Wright's aesthetic, Michael Awkward, in *Inspiriting Influence*, argues for **Toni Morrison**'s revision of Ellison in ***The Bluest Eye***. Indeed, as Ellison's novel showed the importance of considering the consequences of being an African American male in the middle of twentieth-century civilization, African American women writing began to examine what roles black females occupied in America. Still, initial reception of *Invisible Man* and Ellison's subsequent 1964 essay collection *Shadow and Act* revealed a schism between those African Americans who praised Ellison for his contribution and those who faulted him for his lack of a racial militancy like Richard Wright's.

Ellison remained a staunch defender of the capacity for literature, ethnic or otherwise, to enlighten and inform readers. Meanwhile, he also saw the contributions of African Americans to American culture as vast and innumerable. This vision did not assuage those of Ellison's critics who continued to maintain that he was writing for white readership and consumption rather than for his own community—a charge that remains in the years following his death. Regardless, Ellison continued to write, and he began to accept academic appointments, the first in Rome at the American Academy in 1955. With the 1964 appearance of *Shadow and Act*, Ellison's various essays on music, literature, and American culture became widely available. His turn to collecting his essays indicated his growing frustration with his creative writing; and in an attempt to satisfy readers eager for his fiction, he published a collection of stories taken from his novel-in-progress *Juneteenth*. The Hickman stories, as they are collectively known today, remained the only glimpse of Ellison's second novel until its posthumous publication in 1999. Nearly 350 pages of that novel were lost in a house fire in November 1967. The extant novel, edited by Ellison's literary executor John F. Callahan, remains, like *Invisible Man*, concerned primarily with male protagonists (Senator Adam Sunraider and the Reverend Alonzo Hickman), though it offers an important furthering of Ellison's fictive vision.

Ellison also collected additional essays and in 1986 published *Going to the Territory*. Opening those essays, the reflective "The Little Man at Cheehaw Station" offers one of Ellison's finest considerations of critics and culture within America. In it, he recalls and elaborates on the capacity of words to create and disseminate information, but it is always left to the critic to test one's apprehension of that information. As a critic, Ellison worked tirelessly to show the incorporation and contribution of African Americans to literature, while as a writer, he focused on the need to explore the conditions of his present day in order to suggest the potential ways out of a prejudiced society. His mode was not the violence of Wright or the stridency of **James Baldwin** but of meditative contemplation toward possibility. Ellison died in 1994 at the age of eighty, leaving behind his wife of forty-eight years and a literary legacy unmatched by any African American male writer.

Works By

The Collected Essays of Ralph Ellison. Ed. John F. Callahan. New York: Modern Library, 1995.

Flying Home and Other Stories. Ed. John F. Callahan. New York: Random House, 1996.

Going to the Territory. New York: Random House, 1986.

Invisible Man. New York: Random House, 1952.
Juneteenth. Ed. John F. Callahan. New York: Random House, 1999.
Shadow and Act. New York: Random House, 1964.

Works About

Awkward, Michael. *Inspiring Influence.* New York: Columbia University Press, 1989.

Bentson, Kimberly W., ed. *Speaking for You: The Vision of Ralph Ellison.* Washington, DC: Howard University Press, 1987.

Bloom, Harold, ed. *Ralph Ellison: Modern Critical Views.* New York: Chelsea House Publications, 1986.

Butler, Robert J., ed. *The Critical Response to Ralph Ellison.* Westport, CT: Greenwood Press, 2000.

Gates, Henry Louis, Jr. *The Signifying Monkey.* New York: Oxford University Press, 1988.

Hersey, John, ed. *Ralph Ellison: A Collection of Critical Essays.* Englewood Cliffs, NJ: Prentice Hall, 1974.

Sylvander, Carolyn W. "Ralph Ellison's *Invisible Man* and Female Stereotypes." *Black American Literature Forum* 93 (1975): 77–79.

Tate, Claudia. "Notes on the Invisible Women in Ralph Ellison's *Invisible Man.*" *Speaking for You: The Vision of Ralph Ellison.* Ed. Kimberly Bentson. Washington, DC: Howard University Press, 1987. 163–172.

F. Gregory Stewart

EPISTOLARY NOVEL

The epistolary novel, a form that uses letters as the primary mode of narration, has become a powerful tool toward establishing female **identity** and self-empowerment in African American feminist **literature**. Although not common in African American literature, the epistolary form has been used to advantage in pivotal African American feminist novels such as **Alice Walker's** *The Color Purple* (1982) and **Sherley Anne Williams's** *Dessa Rose* (1986). Recording the experiences of women whose voices have been silenced by oppressive environments, the authors of both novels rely on the epistolary form to bring their stories to life.

A precursor of the modern novel, the epistolary novel first took shape within British and European American literature as a vehicle of sentimental and sensational **drama**. Reaching its zenith of popularity in the eighteenth century, the epistolary novel was viewed as a feminized genre, a natural conduit for women's literary voice. Women writers, often discouraged from entering public discourse, found the epistolary form appealing because it revealed the inner workings of the female mind, encouraged introspection, and allowed for a multiplicity of perspectives in the narrative.

Although few African American women writers in the nineteenth century turned to the epistolary form as an outlet for discourse, **Alice Moore Dunbar-Nelson**, in her novel *The Confessions of a Lazy Woman* (1899), employed a variation of the epistolary form. In this diarylike novel, accepted for publication but never making it to print, Dunbar-Nelson's female narrator records the foibles and eccentricities of her neighbors. It was not until the renaissance of African American female authors of the late twentieth century that a renewed interested in the epistolary form developed, as writers such as Alice Walker and Sherley Anne Williams used the epistolary form or variations of it as foundations for their groundbreaking novels.

Walker's Pulitzer Prize–winning *The Color Purple* (1982) is the first novel written by an African American woman to fit within the traditional definition of the epistolary novel. In ninety-four letters that cover the span of over thirty years between the two world wars, we hear and symbolically bear witness to the story of Celie, a young woman physically and psychologically battered in a series of abusive relationships with men. At the age of fourteen, Celie is raped and impregnated by a stepfather whom she believes is her father and later is bartered off in a loveless arranged marriage. Significantly, the first section of letters is addressed to God, whom she views as male, white, and conspicuously silent in her tribulations. The choice of God as the addressee of these letters signifies upon Celie's isolation from the human **community** surrounding her; it also speaks of the complicity of the male patriarchal system that stifles her voice and leaves no outlet for confession and introspection except a God graven in the image of her oppressors. It is only when Celie develops a support system of women around her, in particular through her relationship with the **blues** singer Shug Avery and her own sister Nettie, whom she had believed dead and whose letters had been withheld from Celie by her abusive husband, that Celie develops a positive self-image and is able to transition to addressing her letters to Nettie. The epistles that shape the novel thus become markers of Celie's psychological growth and development of a **womanist** or female-driven philosophy of life. In addition, through the letters Celie discovers a new system of gender equity and a burgeoning sexual identity that reflect her growing sense of independence and selfhood.

Dessa Rose, a novel written by Sherley Anne Williams, builds on the legacy of the epistolary form, signifying upon the authenticating documents written by whites often used to validate African Americans **slave narratives** and on William Styron's skewed account *The Confessions of Nat Turner* (1967). In the novel Adam Nehemiah, a white schoolteacher turned writer of proslavery guides, attempts to chronicle the heroine Dessa Rose's involvement in an unsuccessful uprising in a slave coffle. Nehemiah's journal entries serve as significant symbols of racist and sexist objectification as he dehumanizes Dessa despite his efforts to understand and analyze her psychological motivations. Yet at the end of the novel when Nehemiah tries to send Dessa back into **slavery** by using her own story recorded in his journal to indict her, Nehemiah fails to silence or invalidate Dessa's voice. Only Dessa herself can authenticate her story and her experience as an African American woman. Thus the fallen, invalidated pages of Nehemiah's journal serve as testimony of Dessa's triumph.

The impetus of a postmodern era has led to adaptations of the epistolary form to suit an increasingly heightened sense of political consciousness and the assertion of African American cultural identity. Trey Ellis's postmodernist novel *Platitudes* (1988) employs the epistolary form in an exchange of letters between Dewayne Wellington, a black male writer penning an experimental novel about a middle-class black youth; and Isshee Ayam, an African American feminist writer who critiques the work as lacking cultural authenticity and offers her own version. The letters between the two inextricably tie them together in a metafictional meditation of African American aesthetics and cultural authenticity. Significantly, Ellis, through the narratives of Dewayne and Isshee, parodies the overreliance of writers on the "platitudes" or the tropes and devices mastered by canonical black female writers such as Alice Walker and **Toni Morrison**. At question here is what defines authentic African American experience and whether we should rely on folk traditions and traditional tropes of African American literature or assert a new vision that privileges black middle-class values and cultural fluidity. As the two writers communicate through letters, they come to a middle ground that tempers artistic innovation with respect for cultural tradition and **history**. In the end, it is the epistolary novel that provides a gateway to new directions in African American literature and aesthetics.

Works About

Goldsmith, Elizabeth C. *Writing the Female Voice: Essays on Epistolary Literature.* Boston: Northeastern University Press, 1989.

Simon, Sunka. *Mail-Orders: The Fiction of Letters in Postmodern Culture.* Albany: State University of New York University Press, 2002.

Singer, Godfrey Frank. *The Epistolary Novel: Its Origins, Development, and Residuary Influence.* New York: Russell and Russell, 1963.

Valerie Frazier

EVANS, MARI (1923–)

Mari Evans was born in Toledo, Ohio, on July 16, 1923. Evans attended public schools in Ohio and then studied fashion design at the University of Toledo. In her essay "My Father's Passage" Evans credits her father as the most important influence on her life. He saved her first fourth-grade story, which had been printed in the school newspaper, and added a comment to it indicating his pride in her. Evans claims that she embarked on writing **poetry** unintentionally, as indicated by her initial choice to pursue a major in fashion design.

Evans has had a varied academic career, starting in 1969 when she spent a year as an instructor and writer-in-residence at Indiana University/Purdue. She has continued to teach at various universities, including Indiana University/Bloomington, Washington University in St. Louis, Cornell University, University of New York, and Northwestern University. In addition to her academic career, Evans worked for five years as producer, director, and writer of the television program *The Black Experience*, which aired on WTTV, Channel 4, in Indianapolis from 1968 to 1973.

Evans has published collections of poetry, plays, essays, and short **fiction** but is known primarily for her poetry. While mainly focusing on issues of **race** and ethnicity, many of her works have a feminist undertone. Her greatest contribution in furthering the **work** of women may be the volume she edited on black female writers: *Black Women Writers (1950–1980): A Critical Evaluation* (1984), a collection of writers and critics. The collection is an important addition to the scarce attention traditionally paid to black women writers; it challenged the literary canon's exclusion of black women authors.

Her first collection of poetry, *Where Is All the Music?* (1968), was not met with much critical acclaim. A major theme of the collection was the search of the individual, but it did set up Evans's focus on social issues, including feminism. Her next book, *I Am A Black Woman* (1970), was a collection of highly political poems that called for social change. The individual struggle of the individual black woman in *Where Is All the Music?* evolves into a collective struggle for all black women. The poems have often been referred to as **domestic** poems, and they are poems about the women of the black **community**, giving insight into the challenges of being black and of being a woman. *Nightstar: 1973–1978* (1981), Evans's third book of poetry, is considered one of her finest collections, showing a maturation of her themes and a marked improvement in her poetic technique. Her use of black idioms to communicate the authentic voice of the black community is a unique characteristic of her poetry.

Works By

Black Women Writers (1950–1980): A Critical Evaluation. Ed. Mari Evans. New York: Doubleday, 1984.

A Dark and Splendid Mass. New York: Harlem River Press, 1992.

Eyes. Musical adapted from Zora Neale Hurston's *Their Eyes Were Watching God*, first produced in New York at the Richard Allen Cultural Center, 1979. Produced in Cleveland at Karamu Theatre of the Performing Arts, March 1982.

I Am a Black Woman. New York: Morrow, 1970.

J. D. Garden. Chicago: Third World Press, 1974.

Nightstar: 1973–1978. Los Angeles: Center for African American Studies, University of California, 1981.

Rap Stories. Chicago: Third World Press, 1974.

River of My Song. Play first produced in Indianapolis, IN, at Lilly Theatre, May 1977. Produced in Chicago, at Northeastern Illinois University, Center for Inner City Studies, 1977.
Where Is All the Music? London: P. Breman, 1968.

Works About

Dorsey, David. "The Art of Mari Evans" in "Evans, Mari." Ed. Stephen E. Henderson. *Black Women Writers (1950–1980): A Critical Evaluation.* Ed. Mari Evans. Garden City, NY: Anchor-Doubleday, 1984. 170–189.

Edwards, Solomon. "Affirmation in the Works of Mari Evans" in "Evans, Mari." Ed. Stephen E. Henderson. *Black Women Writers (1950–1980): A Critical Evaluation.* Ed. Mari Evans. Garden City, NY: Anchor-Doubleday, 1984. 190–200.

Sedlack, Robert P. "Mari Evans: Consciousness and Craft." *College Language Association Journal* 15 (1972): 465–476.

Kyla Heflin

EVA'S MAN

Eva's Man (1977), **Gayl Jones**'s second novel, is a harsh but lyrical meditation on the possibilities of connection between men and women. The first-person narrator, Eva Medina Canada, is in jail after killing a man and biting off his penis, and her narration wanders through her **memories** of her relationships with men, including the neighbor boy who examined her with a Popsicle stick when she was five, her mother's lover who put her hand on his crotch when she was twelve, the man she stabbed when she was seventeen, her husband whom she abandoned, and the man she killed. Like **Toni Morrison**'s **Beloved**, *Eva's Man* is the backstory of a crime—the unreported, subjective perspective of a woman whom society has labeled "criminal" and "insane." Yet while we receive a first-person narration of these events, Eva is strangely silent during them, and after both the stabbing and the murder, she refuses to provide her own statements to the police or to respond fully to the psychiatrists' questions about her motives. The reader is therefore forced to piece together an interpretation from the interspersed memories.

What develops through the seemingly randomly interspersed memories is that, in Eva's mind, men do not see her as herself, differentiated, but instead fit her into preexisting categories, changing her name in the process from "Eva" to "Eve," which highlights their assumption that she was made for their pleasure, or from "Eva" to "evil," when she refuses to touch, rub, and please them. Societal pressures to conform to the Madonna/whore binary come in the form of both men's and women's explicit statements that women who do not want to be treated as whores ought to stay in the house, and indeed, in this novel, Eva's life is circumscribed by the variety of sexually predatory men who lurk directly outside the small apartment, on every street corner, on the bus, and in the workplace.

Readers might be tempted to view Eva's act of murder and castration as an attempt to reverse the gender roles, to be the sexual predator rather than the prey. Eva does view herself in terms of a story she has heard about another woman whose lovers die and who gains the reputation of a "queen bee"; she also views herself after the murder as Medusa. These two images of females who kill males are potential sources of empowerment, and Eva's desire to fend off men, live alone, and protect herself are strong. But the narration does not reduce to a simple or formulaic inversion; detectives, psychologists, and Eva's cell mate all offer potential interpretations that Eva rejects and complicates. Her memories are also filled with desire, and in her memory, the murder is also an act of **love**, the castration perhaps her final attempt to please him, to try the unnamed act he has asked her to perform. More complication stems from her potentially unreliable narration; she claims that she has trouble keeping things straight and worries that her memories lie. There is even some question in the text as to whether she has, in fact, bitten off the penis—she remembers doing it, but the psychiatrist claims that the police report states otherwise. Taken as a whole, the novel offers a grim and tragic account of gender relations, yet one in which complexity, nuance, and possibility for connection remain strong.

Works About

Basu, Biman. "Public and Private Discourses and the Black Female Subject: Gayl Jones's *Eva's Man*." *Callaloo* 19 (1996): 193–208.

Byerman, Keith. "Black Vortex: The Gothic Structure of *Eva's Man*." *MELUS* 7 (1980): 93–101.

Davison, Carol Margaret. " 'Love'em and Lynch'em': The Castration Motif in Gayl Jones's *Eva's Man*." *African American Review* 29 (1995): 393–410.

Wilcox, Janelle. "Resistant Silence, Resistant Subject: (Re)Reading Gayl Jones's *Eva's Man*." *Bodies of Writing, Bodies in Performance*. Ed. Thomas Foster et al. New York: New York University Press, 1996. 72–96.

Suzanne Lane

 **F**

FABIO, SARAH WEBSTER (1928–1979)

With the exception of **Sonia Sanchez**, **Nikki Giovanni**, and **Mari Evans**, women have largely been underrepresented in the scholarship on the **Black Arts Movement**. One glaring omission to most studies is that of Sarah Webster Fabio, who was a poet, educator, literary critic, devoted mother, and integral contributor to the black arts and black studies movements of the 1960s and 1970s. Born on January 20, 1928, in Nashville, Tennessee, to Mayme Storey and Thomas Jefferson Webster, Fabio demonstrated a prodigious intellectual ability at an early age.

In 1943, at the age of fifteen, Sarah graduated from high school and enrolled at Spelman College in Atlanta, Georgia. A year before completing her B.A. degree, however, she returned to Nashville to attend Fisk University, where she met Cyril Leslie Fabio, a dental student. After graduating in 1946, she married Fabio, who had enlisted in the military. Over the next seventeen years, she placed her career on hold in order to raise the couple's five children: Cyril Leslie III (1947), Thomas Albert (1948), Cheryl Elisa Louis (1949), Renee Angela (1955), and Ronald Eric (1956) as the **family** moved between Tennessee, Florida, Texas, Kansas, and Germany.

When the Fabios settled in California, where her husband established a dental practice, Sarah Fabio finally had an opportunity to complete graduate school. She attended San Francisco State College from 1963 to 1965, working on an M.A. in creative writing with a concentration in **poetry**. While a graduate student, she joined a Bay Area black writers' workshop where she met playwright Ed Bullins and poet **Amiri Baraka**. Upon receiving her M.A., she began teaching at Merritt Junior College in Oakland, California. With the support of Huey P. Newton, Bobby Seale, and other radical black students, Fabio organized a black studies program at Merritt, which she took to the University of California at Berkeley in 1968.

In addition to her progressive academic initiatives and continued care of her family, Sarah Fabio found time to become a prolific writer. Most definitely, Fabio's literary project was predicated on the desire to enlighten and elevate African Americans. Her first two collections of poetry were *Saga of the Black Man* (1968) and *A Mirror, a Soul: A Two-Part Volume of Poems* (1969). Fabio's **jazz**-inspired poems and academic articles were also published in journals such as *Negro Digest* and *Black World*, as well as the anthologies *The Poetry of the Negro, 1746–1970* (1970), *The Black Aesthetic* (1971), and *To Gwen with Love* (1971). By far, her most inspiring work is the seven-volume collection of poetry *The Rainbow Sign* (1973), published the year following her divorce from Cyril Fabio.

After teaching black literature at Oberlin College (1972–1974) and the University of Wisconsin, Madison (1974–1977), she was diagnosed with colon cancer. Despite her illness, Fabio continued to write, publishing her final collection of poems *Dark Symphony in Duet* shortly before her **death** in 1979. Although she has yet to receive the international recognition deserving of an artist-intellectual of her stature, Fabio's literary canon remains an example of the central role women played in the Black Arts Movement.

Works By

Dark Symphony in Duet: A Celebration of the Word; Seascapes, Love Poems, Tributes, Portraits, Black Talk, Africana. With Thomas Gayton. Seattle: Black Studies Program, University of Washington, 1979.

A Mirror, a Soul: A Two-Part Volume of Poems. San Francisco: J. Richardson Associates, 1969.

Race Results, U.S.A., 1966: White Right—A Favorite—Wins; Lurline—A Long Shot—Places; Black Power—A Long Shot—Shows; For Stokely Carmichael. Detroit: Broadside Press, 1967.

The Rainbow Signs: Seven Volumes of Poems. Oberlin, OH: New Media Workshop, 1973.

Saga of the Black Man. Oakland: Turn Over Book Store, 1968.

Works About

Bailey, Leoonead Pack, ed. and comp. *Broadside Authors and Artists: An Illustrated Biographical Directory.* Detroit: Broadside Press, 1974.

Contemporary Authors: A Bio-Bibliographical Guide to Current Writers in Fiction, General Nonfiction, Poetry, Journalism, Drama, Motion Pictures, Television, and Other Fields. Volumes 69–72. Detroit: Gale Research, 1978.

Page, James A., comp. *Selected Black American Authors: An Illustrated Bio-bibliography.* Boston: G. K. Hall and Co., 1977.

Rush, Theressa Gunnels, Carol Fairbanks Myers, and Esther Spring Arata. *Black American Writers Past and Present: A Biographical and Bibliographical Dictionary.* 2 vols. Metuchen, NJ: Scarecrow Press, 1975.

The Schomburg Center Guide to Black Literature. From the Eighteenth Century to the Present. Detroit: Gale Research, 1996.

Anthony J. Ratcliff

FAMILY

"I am because we are." This statement belies an ideology of the African **community** that speaks to their sense of connection and family. For Africans, family is not only significant; it is essential. This belief about the family is not restricted to the African nations alone but is germane to many around the world. Family is the cornerstone of society. It is the socializing unit that explains who we are and how we are to respond to our environments. For this reason, the family has been the subject of much study, much propaganda, and much manipulation. The black family, especially, has had to fight to maintain its stability in a society that is filled with racism, poverty, sexism, and fear.

Slavery has been especially harsh on the black family in America. It created an atmosphere in which individuals were not allowed to function in either a naturally or socially prescribed role. For instance, men and women were not given the legal right to marry. For slaveholders, this denial of rights was beneficial because they could validate their previous ideas of the immorality and inhumanity of black people and also mate slaves with whomever they wanted without disturbing their spiritual conscience. For the enslaved, this denial caused them to have to create different ways to solidify their marital bonds. One such way was to incorporate the African symbol of the broom as representative of the household into their ceremonies and "jump the broom."

It was the peculiar institution's way, also, to deny parental ties. The law stated that the children followed the status of the mother: If she were a slave, they were slaves. If she were free, they were free. Often, the mother was enslaved, forced to mate with someone who was not her husband, including the slave owners themselves. Not only did this law attempt to lower the morale of the black family, but it effectively excluded the black father from the destiny of his child.

It is commonly believed that the black family was destroyed on slavery's auction block. In truth, the majority of families were split apart at the selling of an estate after a slaveholder died. At other times when families were broken apart, there was an effort to keep the husband and wife together, leaving the children to be sold. However, slaveholders found it more profitable to keep families together, recognizing a correlation between positive family ties and a reduction in escape attempts.

This reluctance to physically break up families did not signal a respect for the black family unit. Numerous **slave narratives**, such as those by **Harriet Jacobs** and **William Wells Brown**, detail the ways in which the emotional bond between siblings, husband and wife, even parent and child were either ignored or attacked. The emotional life of black families was often considered by slaveholders (and sometimes nonslaveholders) to be lacking in the substance that white families possessed. This belief allowed them to overlook the emotional connection between black family members and to treat them in ways that were beneficial to whites but detrimental to blacks.

The black family did not overlook these connections, however. In the same way that the enslaved had to adapt to a new **religion** and created voodoo, and in the same way that they had to adapt to a new language and created a dialect of their own—in each instance retaining aspects of their original African culture—they adapted to the attack on their families and created new bonds. In their native culture, the family unit was an extended one, raising children, making decisions, and sharing responsibilities as a community. This value for community, represented in the extended family, did not end in slavery; it, in fact, helped the individual to survive. When the family bond was attacked, physically or emotionally, the enslaved would resolidify their family and community by forming fictive kinship ties, making them stronger as individuals and stronger as a community.

In spite of the hardships the black family faced during and after slavery, they were still expected to behave according to the mainstream's standards. To some extent, they expected it of themselves. These standards included maintaining the structure (husband, wife, and children) and the function of the nuclear family.

For the black man, this meant that he was to be the main, if not sole, provider for the family. He was to be the head of the household, making the family's decisions and demanding submission from his wife and children. Finally, he was expected to protect his house and **home**. These standards were challenging for him because, unlike his white counterparts, the black man was not as economically fortunate. He often discovered the difficulty in finding employment that could provide for a family or finding employment at all. He was also forced to suffer indignities in the greater society, being subjected to name-calling and other humiliations. Finally, the practice of lynching, which plagued the country for many generations after slavery's end, ensured that the black man knew his place: He was not to achieve too much, and he was not to assume that he could confront white masculinity, no matter what white men did to his person or his home. While these expectations were hard on black men who often lacked the legal authority and financial means of white fathers, they were especially difficult on black women.

During the ante- and postbellum years, both white and black women were considered to be the single most important influence on their families. This created pressure on white mothers to be the moral light for their husbands and children, but for black women, this pressure was doubly hard because while they were expected to be the moral light, they were often believed to be without morals. Black women were seen as the cause for the degradation of the black man and, ultimately, the black family. They were held to an impossible standard that called for them to be gentle and delicate, but the reality of their lives was that they had to **work** as much and as hard as their men. During slavery they were often required to meet the same quotas in the field as the men. After slavery, men were often denied jobs or had to leave home to seek them, and the women had to work as **domestics** to support the family. There was rarely the opportunity to develop the gentle sensibility that society said true women possessed.

Many writers, particularly female writers such as **Anna Julia Cooper** and **Pauline Hopkins**, criticized the image of black women and black **motherhood** that was accepted in the mainstream and even in the black community. In their works, they created truer pictures of the black woman, detailing the circumstances that she encountered in society that made her reality what it was. Even today, writers and scholars such as **Angela Davis**, Claudia Tate, and **Toni Morrison** are still battling the former image of the black woman as emasculating matriarch, as happy servant **Mammy**, and as loose Jezebel. There are also more recent images of the black woman as bitterly and overly independent and as welfare mothers, both reformulations of the same old images. Each character, however old or new, is still responsible for what the mainstream sees as the deficient black family.

In 1965, a great deal of controversy arose when white sociologist Daniel Patrick Moynihan published what is now known as the Moynihan Report. His research stated that there was a crisis in the black community that stemmed from the deterioration of the black family. He cited statistics and cases that demonstrated the rising level of illegitimate births in the black community and the increased level of dependence on governmental agencies for subsistence. A significant part of these problems was the growing number of female-headed households. This particular structure was problematic for Moynihan because it was incongruent with the structure of society at large, making it doubly difficult for the black family and its individual members to persevere.

Many were outraged by this report because they felt it blamed the victim and that Moynihan was not as concerned for the liberation of the black family as one needed to be when conducting research of this nature. Whether his critics' comments were valid or not, certainly he pointed to problems (which, incidentally, were discussed earlier in the 1930s by black sociologist E. Franklin Frazier) that continue to plague the black family.

The controversy surrounding Moynihan is not the only one to have affected the black family in the past forty years. Today there is a great deal of debate concerning single-parent, interracial, homosexual, and blended families. Perhaps as a result of the debate or as part of it, there is a push toward redefining the family. The idea of the nuclear family is no longer working for the larger society, and it has hardly ever worked for black people specifically. Now the focus is on the relationships between people, whether or not they are related. If there is a substantial bond between them, they can be considered family. This definition becomes especially pertinent in light of changing social relations: the increasing number of unmarried women who are choosing to adopt; the number of women who are choosing to have babies and maintain relationships with the fathers outside of matrimony; and the acceptance of homosexual couples who want to adopt or have babies of their own—to name a few.

Although the black family is plagued with problems and crisis, there is still an element of strength that is exemplified by its very existence. It has been attacked as a whole and through its individual members, yet it continues to survive.

See also Black Masculinity; Stereotypes

Works About

Bryant, Jacqueline K. *The Foremother Figure in Early Black Women's Literature: Clothed in My Right Mind.* New York: Garland, 1999.

Dixon, Chris. *Perfecting the Family: Antislavery Marriages in Nineteenth-Century America.* Amherst: University of Massachusetts Press, 1997.

Gutman, Herbert. *The Black Family in Slavery and Freedom, 1750–1925.* New York: Pantheon, 1976.

Staples, Robert, ed. *The Black Family: Essays and Studies.* Belmont, CA: Wadsworth, 1999.

Thompson, Aaron. "African American Families: Historically Resilient." *The African American Experience.* Ed. Arvah E. Strickland and Robert E. Weems, Jr. Westport, CT: Greenwood Press, 2001. 55–70.

RaShell R. Smith-Spears

FAMILY

Family, published in 1991 by **J. California Cooper**, is Cooper's first novel and is composed of four tales that deal with the tragedy, hope, and survival that a black **family** experiences as a result of **slavery**.

The narrator, Clora, is the child of a slave woman. Clora's grandmother and mother kill themselves to escape slavery. Just before her **death**, Clora's mother, well aware of the horrors of slavery, warns her twelve-year-old daughter of what lies ahead for a slave girl on the verge of womanhood. Indeed, Clora is raped by her master's son and gives birth to her first child at thirteen. Clora recognizes that she has become her mother, and she cries for the future of her newborn daughter whose life has been decided for her because she has been born into slavery. Ultimately, Clora gives birth to six children, but due to the hardships of slavery, only four survive. She also recognizes that death is the only means of escaping slavery and tries to poison herself and her children. Clora dies, but her children survive.

Clora's spirit, however, is able to follow the lives of her four remaining children: Always, Sun, Peach, and Plum. Sun, who is light-skinned, is taught by his master's daughter to read. Knowing that the ability to read empowers the slave, Sun transfers his knowledge to his siblings. Eventually, Sun makes his way north. Through his honesty and hard **work**, as well as the fact that he lives as a white man, Sun lives a successful life. Peach is sold into slavery, marries her master, and moves to Scotland. There she lives as a white woman, and her children are able to attend college, have careers, and marry well. Plum, unfortunately, dies a tragic death.

Most of the novel focuses on Always, who is impregnated by her master and has many children who are sold into slavery. When Always gives birth to a blue-eyed baby at the same time that her mistress gives birth to a baby, she switches the infants to ensure that her own son will not be sold and, instead, will live a life of privilege. Always, recognizing that knowledge is power, learns anything that she can. Her master's land thrives as a result of her knowledge, but Always knows that she can use her skills to improve her life as well. After the end of the Civil War, Always finds **love**, purchases land and a **home** of her own, and is a financial success.

The siblings come together at the end of the novel. Even those who have been living as white people recognize the importance of their black ancestry and want to reunite with their black brothers and sisters. The strength of the individual in overcoming adversity and the importance of the love of one's family as a means of surviving even the worst of circumstances are important themes in *Family*. Cooper's final reminder is that our blood "is mixed up," and we cannot know for certain who we are; in fact, our varying degrees of color mean that we are all related—we are all family.

See also Homemade Love; In Search of Satisfaction

Works About

Beaulieu, Elizabeth Ann. *Black Women Writers and the American Neo-Slave Narrative: Femininity Unfettered*. Westport, CT: Greenwood Press, 1990.

Oliver, Stephanie Stokes. "J. California Cooper: From Paper Dolls to Paperbacks." *Essence* (May 1991): 52.

Weaver, James. "Rehabilitative Storytelling: The Narrator-Narratee Relationship in J. California Cooper's *Family*." *MELUS* 30.1 (2005): 109–136.

Diane Todd Bucci

FARMING OF BONES, THE

In **Edwidge Danticat**'s *The Farming of Bones* (1998), Haitian-born Amabelle watches her parents drown in the Massacre River separating Haiti from the Dominican Republic. Amabelle grows up the companion of Valencia, a daughter of wealth and hence a young woman Amabelle refers to from the start as Senorita (and now Senora in the year since her marriage). However, Valencia's childhood friendship, begun in part since each was motherless, is further solidified when Amabelle helps deliver Valencia's twins, a robust girl and a weaker boy, at the novel's opening. The women's relationship notwithstanding, Valencia still worries her darker daughter will be mistaken for a Haitian. Yet Amabelle's attachment to the **family** (she affectionately calls Valencia's father Papi) will become her biggest obstacle to fleeing when Dominican forces are ordered to murder Haitians in 1937.

Valencia loses one of her twins, Rafael, named for the Generalissimo, and laments that he never clearly saw her face; yet this poignant moment is countered by the fact that her husband has struck and killed a Haitian cane worker with his car and, in his haste to see his new son, does not bother to check the man's condition. The lack of value placed on Haitian life is unmistakable. Years ago when Valencia and her father had encountered Amabelle at the river, her parents' burial place, she had firmly indicated with a pointed finger that she belonged to herself, yet Haitians in a Dominican world are clearly without destinies in Danticat's work. Thus Amabelle lives in a world of shadows, those without names and faces who vanish: first her parents and later her lover Sebastien and his sister, as well as an estimated 15,000 to 20,000 more who would die in the days following Rafael Leonidas Trujillo Molino's ordered mass murder of Haitians living in the Dominican Republic.

Once rumors of Trujillo's intentions become reality, the cane workers form a night-watchman brigade. Amabelle, her lover Sebastien, and his sister plan to meet at a church and escape together, but Sebastien and his sister are rounded up by Dominican forces before Amabelle can arrive. The bulk of the novel focuses on Amabelle's dangerous return to Haiti as well as her diminishing hope of finding Sebastien. Traveling with Yves, Sebastien's friend and fellow cane worker, the two join a small group traveling toward the river. Parsley (*parejil*), its importance having been emphasized in an early, moving passage, now becomes a weapon. Once in the river town, identified Haitians, including Amabelle and Yves, are beaten, their mouths stuffed with parsley by Dominican soldiers after failing to trill an *r* and precisely pronounce the *j*. Many will die. Part of Danticat's purpose is to give voice to nameless and faceless Haitians, which she does by allowing many in the ad hoc group of travelers Amabelle and Yves join, as well as patients in a makeshift hospital where a maimed Amabelle later recuperates, to offer testimonials of both their torture and their existence. More symbolically, Amabelle's **body** becomes a "marred testament."

Once in Haiti, Amabelle begins a kind of mother-daughter relationship with the mothers of Yves and Sebastien while living with Yves and his mother. Yves and Amabelle begin a strange new relationship, one that lasts at least twenty-four years; however, a sense of profound loss rather than **love** ties them together. Eventually finding mourning too hard, they use **work** as a consolation. Amabelle makes one trip back to her Dominican **home** years later, but the meeting with Valencia is a hollow one emotionally, despite Valencia's admission that she hid Haitians in 1937 in Amabelle's name. Amabelle instead receives her only real consolation from the river upon her return to Haiti. She realizes she is without **ancestors** and without heirs. All are ghosts.

Works About

Brice-Finch, Jacqueline. "Edwidge Danticat: Memories of Maäfa." *MaComère* 4 (2001): 146–154.

Ink, Lynn Chun. "Remaking Identity, Unmaking Nation: Historical Recovery and the Reconstruction of Community in *In the Time of Butterflies* and *The Farming of Bones*." *Callaloo* 27.3 (2004): 788–807.

Johnson, Kelli Lyon. "Both Sides of the Massacre: Collective Memory and Narrative on Hispaniola." *Mosaic* 36.2 (2003): 75–91.

Jurney, Florence Ramond. "Exile and Relation to the Mother/Land in Edwidge Danticat's *Breath, Eyes, Memory* and *The Farming of Bones*." *Revista/Review Interamericana* 31.1–4 (2001).

Larrier, Renée. "'Girl by the Shore': Gender and Testimony in Edwidge Danticat's *The Farming of Bones*." *Journal of Haitian Studies* 7.2 (2001): 50–60.

Shea, Renée H. "'The Hunger of Tell': Edwidge Danticat and *The Farming of Bones*." *MaComère* 2 (1999): 12–22.

Shemak, April. "Re-Membering Hispaniola: Edwidge Danticat's *The Farming of Bones*." *MFS* 48.1 (2002): 83–112.

Vega-González, Susana. "Sites of Memory, Sites of Mourning and History: Danticat's Insights into the Past." *Revista Alicantina de Estudios Ingleses* 17 (2004): 297–304.

Lisa Muir

FAUSET, JESSIE REDMON (1882–1961)

Jessie Redmon Fauset's work now receives considerable attention from scholars of black **literature** and of women's literature. Fauset, born in Camden County, New Jersey, was the youngest of the seven children of Redmon Fauset, an African Methodist Episcopal minister. When Jessie's mother, Annie Seamon Fauset, died, Fauset married again to a widow who already had three children. Fauset's new wife bore him three more children, giving him thirteen children to care for. Despite the grinding poverty of this very large **family**, Fauset raised two high-achieving individuals: anthropologist Arthur Huff Fauset (1899–1983) and his half sister Jessie Redmon Fauset. Jessie excelled at the renowned Girls' High School in Philadelphia. Administrators prevented this gifted black girl from entering Bryn Mawr. Instead, Fauset became a pioneering black student at Cornell University, where she graduated Phi Beta Kappa in 1905 after studying classical and modern languages. French was a forte for Fauset; she gained a master's in French from the University of Pennsylvania in 1919 and studied at the Sorbonne in Paris for six months in the mid-1920s.

After leaving Cornell, Fauset began teaching. She taught French and Latin at the all-black M Street High School in Washington, D.C. From 1912 onward, Fauset wrote **poetry** and fictional and nonfictional prose for publication. Most significantly, she submitted articles to *Crisis*, the National Association for the

Advancement of Colored People publication. Her work impressed the general editor of *Crisis*, W.E.B. Du Bois; he made her the journal's literary editor in 1919, which necessitated a move to New York. Fauset retained this editorship until resigning in 1926. Fauset also edited the *Brownie Book* during its two years of publication, 1920 and 1921. Her aim for that children's publication is typical: Fauset worked to encourage new African American writing, to celebrate the achievements of exemplary colored persons, and to raise the self-esteem and reputation of blacks. In a convincing polemic written for Allan Locke's 1925 *New Negro* collection, Fauset complained that in the theater black characters seemed always to be stereotyped as figures of trivial comedy. Such stereotyping was abhorrent because "no astute observer, looking at the Negro in modern American life, could find his condition even now a first aid to laughter." Fauset was preoccupied with the realities of life for black Americans, particularly black women. In her Harlem **home** of the 1920s, Fauset held literary meetings that developed fellow blacks' work; Fauset continually stressed that the black experience must be given a rounded portrayal, one determined by blacks themselves. Fauset's seriousness in fostering a black literary culture in Harlem goes some way to tempering clichés about noisy, "wild" Harlem. Fauset began teaching again in 1927. Staying in New York, she took a job at a junior school and then at de Witt Clinton High School, remaining until 1944. Fauset married Herbert Harris, an insurance broker, in 1929. Harris accepted the fact that his forty-seven-year-old wife would remain childless. After the 1933 publication of her fourth novel, Fauset's life got steadily quieter, although after 1944 she taught at Tuskegee and Hampton Institutes. An expected fifth novel never materialized. Harris died in 1958. The couple had lived in Montclair, New Jersey, for several years. Until her **death** from heart disease in 1961, Fauset lived with a stepbrother in Philadelphia, which, together with New York City, is one of the two main settings for her novels.

Fauset contributed to black culture through her **work** as an editor, poet, campaigner for black **history**, literary "midwife," teacher, and primarily, as a novelist. The novels—*There is Confusion, Plum Bun, The Chinaberry Tree*, and *Comedy: American Style*—were published between 1924 and 1933, receiving moderate critical acclaim and equally moderate sales. Fauset's readership has never been particularly large. Early white American reviewers sometimes took a patronizing tone, damning the novels with faint praise; a common comment was that the novels convey some curious information about the quirks of black folks' predicaments, but with an elaborate, over-ambitious literary pretension. The novels were published in England, too; the first three gained qualified appreciation in (albeit brief) reviews in the most significant British literary survey, the weekly *Times Literary Supplement*.

Interest in Fauset's work declined as interest in the **Harlem Renaissance** declined; her novels soon went out of print. There was a small revival of attention in the late 1960s, following the cultural impact of the **civil rights movement**. Her death merited a *New York Times* obituary (May 3, 1961), but it took a decade of campaigning for black cultural efficacy to alert white

America to the possibilities of "minor," "marginal" writers such as Fauset. As if marking the nation's vigor in reading black greats, reprints of Fauset's novels emerged but soon went out of print again. A more lasting rediscovery of Fauset has flourished since the late 1970s when feminist scholars began reading ignored women writers. Similarly, from the mid-1980s onward, academics augmented the traditional white "canon" by also privileging nonwhite literature. Fauset's legacy is ideal for scholars who critique the historical sidelining of a nonmale, nonwhite author of considerable talent. Scholarly articles on Fauset's works began to appear in the mid-1970s; interest continues to grow exponentially. Carolyn Wedin Sylvander published an outstanding book-length study of Fauset's work in 1981; a number of welcome monographs devoted wholly or partly to Fauset have appeared subsequently. Crucially, new editions of her novels were published—all are enhanced with affirming, vital introductions. The Marcy Jane Knopf–introduced *The Chinaberry Tree and Selected Writings* is particularly valuable for its inclusion of nonfictional pieces by Fauset, including the 1921 speech on black women's development that she delivered to the Pan-African Congress.

Fauset was once dismissively referred to as a black Jane Austen—a writer of harmless middle-class romances. Critics of Austen now regard Austen as an astute observer and challenger of **class** and gender-based assumptions. Similarly, critics of Fauset's novels now insist that Fauset did not write comfortable bourgeois **fiction**. There is too much **violence** in Fauset's novels for any of them to be read comfortably, and the female characters especially have an obvious sexual longing that is gritty and realistic. Fauset's black female characters suffer because of prejudices against them that are exercised in a personal, localized context and in the wider, legalized system of America's suppression of blacks. Fauset does not completely vilify the young black women who "pass" for white in her novels. Although Fauset insisted that African Americans should proclaim their black culture and **identity** proudly, the status of impoverished blacks is so demeaning that we sympathize with rather than excoriate the vulnerable characters who pretend to be white. The four novels are sprawling, complex entities, full of anxious studies of female **sexuality**, class division, family conflicts, and crude and subtle racism, so it is unproductive to simplify Fauset's message. However, one opinion of Fauset is clear: If people are suppressed, possibly talented people are left in enforced malaise, depriving society of their attributes. Racial and sexual demonization, then, is as practically wrong as it is morally wrong.

In his 1940 **autobiography** *The Big Sea*, **Langston Hughes** praised Fauset as one of the midwives of the Harlem Renaissance. Fauset assisted ably with the "birth" of much black culture of 1920s New York, but her own novels were passed over too swiftly by Hughes and others. Fauset's four novels have a sustained clarity of vision that makes them seminal reading for any student of black literature and/or women's literature and for any reader who enjoys articulate attacks on the manifestations of irrational prejudice. Above all, Fauset's novels should be read by anyone who enjoys what Fauset herself called a "good story."

Works By

The Chinaberry Tree: A Novel of American Life. New York: Frederick A. Stokes Co., 1931.

Comedy: American Style. New York: Frederick A. Stokes Co., 1933.

"The Gift of Laughter." *The New Negro.* Ed. Alain Locke. New York: Boni, 1925.

Plum Bun, A Novel without a Moral. New York: Frederick A. Stokes Co., 1929.

Selected Poems. www.nku.edu/~diesmanj/fauset.

Selected Prose. *The Chinaberry Tree and Selected Writings.* Ed. Marcy Jane Knopf. Boston: Northeastern University Press, 1995. 345–398.

There Is Confusion. New York: Boni and Liveright, 1924.

Works About

Allen, Carol. *Black Women Intellectuals: Strategies of Nation, Family, and Neighborhood.* New York: Garland, 1998. 47–76.

Calloway, Licia Morrow. *Black Family (Dys)Function in Novels by Jessie Fauset, Nella Larsen, and Fannie Hart.* New York: P. Lang, 2003.

duCille, Ann. *The Coupling Convention: Sex, Text, and Tradition in Black Women's Fiction.* New York: Oxford University Press, 1993. 86–190.

Jones, Sharon L. *Rereading the Harlem Renaissance: Race, Class and Gender in the Fiction of Jessie Fauset, Zora Neale Hurston, and Dorothy West.* Westport, CT: Greenwood Press, 2002.

Lutes, Jean Marie. "Making Up Race: Jessie Fauset, Nella Larsen, and the African American Cosmetics Industry." *Atlantic Quarterly* 58.1 (2002): 77–108.

McLendon, Jacquelyn Y. *The Politics of Color in the Fiction of Jessie Fauset and Nella Larsen.* Charlottesville: University Press of Virginia, 1995.

Schenck, Mary Jane. "Jessie Fauset: The Politics of Fulfillment vs. the Lost Generation." *South Atlantic Review* 66.1 (2001): 102–125.

Stetz, Margaret D. "Jessie Fauset's Fiction: Reconsidering Race and Revising Aestheticism." *Literature and Racial Ambiguity.* Ed. Teresa Hubel and Neil Brooks. Amsterdam: Rodopi, 2002. 253–270.

Sylvander, Carolyn Wedin. *Jessie Redmon Fauset, Black American Writer.* Troy, NY: Whitston Publishing, 1981.

Kevin De Ornellas

FERRELL, CAROLYN (1962–)

Born in Brooklyn and raised on Long Island, Carolyn Ferrell received a B.A. from Sarah Lawrence in 1984. Afterward, she lived in Germany for four years, combining study with performance as a professional violinist. While working on an M.A. from the City College of New York, she joined the New Renaissance writers, led by **Doris Jean Austin**, whose sense "of the questions writers must ask themselves" was crucial in Ferrell's development. A long list of grants and honors have marked her career as a student and writer; her first book, a short-story collection titled *Don't Erase Me* (1997), received the Zacharis Award and the *LA Times* Award for First Fiction. Married to Linwood Lewis, a psychologist, Ferrell currently teaches creative writing at Sarah Lawrence. She is a doctoral candidate at the City University of New York and is working on a novel about Long Island in the 1970s and 1980s.

Meri Nana-Ama Danquah describes her generation of black women writers, published since 1990: "We are biracial, bicultural, bisexual;...we are constantly insisting upon the recognition of our...complexity." Ferrell, like **Danzy Senna** and **Edwidge Danticat**, supplements **race** and gender with other dangerous categories; like **Sapphire**, she has worked in inner-city literacy programs. Many of her characters have a heartbreaking need for a language commensurate to their unspeakable experience. The protagonists of the stories set in the South Bronx inhabit marginalized niches but reach for their goals against terrible odds. Ferrell brilliantly constructs children and young adults whose thoughts are simultaneously innocent and experienced; she shows them forming themselves in a street argot tinted (and tainted) by the pervasive bromides of American culture.

Ferrell's protagonists touch many themes of contemporary **fiction**—hunger, imagination, the **family**, the **body**, ridicule, **sexuality**, **identity**, poverty, power—with fresh voices and sticky hands. In "Proper Library" (the most anthologized of her works, chosen for *The Best American Short Stories of the Century*), Lorrie cares for many children, suffers for being gay, and memorizes words, which weave a strange music through his short life. In "Don't Erase Me," Layla Jackson, knowing she has AIDS (acquired immunodeficiency syndrome), reverses her story's chronology as a remembrance for her children and a well of resistance for herself. The besieged heroine of "Tiger-Frame Spectacles" keeps a notebook celebrating "girl power" in the midst of a mean, misogynist culture. In "Can You Say My Name?" images from the **Middle Passage** weigh down Toya's plan to be a mother in the ninth grade.

James Baldwin, **Audre Lorde**, and **Rita Dove** have written about being African American in German cultures; clearly, having a German mother and an African American father has stretched Ferrell's own compass. Ferrell has called "Wonderful Teen" (a dystopic identity story in which a twelve-year-old, wanting to help her mother, realizes her irremediable difference) "my most autobiographical story." "Inside, a Fountain" shows an African American teenager, surrounded by her hostile German family and **history**, holding her own ground.

Works By

Don't Erase Me. Boston: Houghton Mifflin, 1997.
"Eating Confessions." *Callaloo* 40 (Summer 1989): 453–464.
"Linda Devine's Daughters." *Rise Up Singing: Black Women Writers on Motherhood.* Ed. Cecelie S. Berry. New York: Doubleday, 2004. 190–216.

"9/11 Victim's Identity Discovered Only through Investigation Led by Hairdresser." *110 Stories: New York Writes after September 11.* Ed. Ulrich Baer. New York: New York University Press, 2002. 93–96.
"Truth or Consequences." *Story* (Spring 1998): 70–78.

Works About

Danquah, Meri Nana-Ama. "The Incoming Wave: An Introduction." *Shaking the Tree: New Fiction and Memoirs by Black Women.* Ed. Meri Nan-Ama Danquah. New York: Norton, 2003. xiii–xxi.
Lee, Don. "Carolyn Ferrell, Zacharis Award." Postscripts. *Ploughshares* (Winter 1997–1998). www.pshares.org/issues/articles.cfm?prmarticleID=4392.
Naylor, Gloria. "Children of the Night." *Children of the Night: The Best Short Stories by Black Writers, 1967 to the Present.* Ed. Gloria Naylor. Boston: Little, Brown, 1995. 5–57.
Serle, Elizabeth. Review of *Don't Erase Me.* *Ploughshares* 23.2–3 (Fall 1997): 226–227. EBSCO, OhioLINK, Blackmore Library, Capital University, Columbus, OH, May 20, 2004.
Updike, John. Introduction to *The Best American Short Stories of the Century.* Ed. John Updike and Katrina Kenison. Boston: Houghton Mifflin, 1999. 1–6.
Whitemore, Katharine. "Books in Brief: Fiction and Poetry; Phrasemaker in the City." Review of *Don't Erase Me.* *New York Times on the Web,* September 14, 1997. query.nytimes.com.

Susan Nash

FICTION

Fiction is a form of storytelling written in prose or verse and created from an author's imagination. The word *fiction* comes from the Latin word *fictio,* which means "a fashioning or a making." Storytelling is as old as humanity, and in order to examine fiction in an African American context, one must acknowledge the roots of the African American literary legacy in preslave trade epics of the African continent where oral storytelling served as entertainment and historical, sociocultural documentary of origins, **myths**, and beliefs. In this way, the purpose of fiction in an African American context has not only been to entertain but to celebrate, document, and critically assess a **history** specific to the experiences and ever-changing pathos of African American people.

Fiction has appeared in various forms since the development of writing thousands of years ago. Since the 1700s, the main forms of fiction have been the novel and short story. The 1800s were formative years in African American literary and cultural history. In pre–Civil War United States, the majority of African Americans living in the United States were in bondage, as slaves. The law made it illegal for African Americans to learn reading and writing; however, a rich literary legacy was cultivated and maintained, even then. In 1988, the Schomburg Center, Henry Louis Gates, and Oxford University Press published the thirty-volume collection **Schomburg Library of Nineteenth-Century Black Women Writers** and made available works by such literary artists as **Alice Moore Dunbar-Nelson** and **Harriet E. Wilson**.

While all fiction contains elements that are partly or entirely imaginary, fiction does not necessarily differ much from reality. Harriet Wilson's fictional **autobiography** *Our Nig* (1859) is based on experiences and events both real and imagined. While pre–Civil War United States served as the landscape of Wilson's work, factual elements in fiction are always combined with the imaginary to create a piece of fiction. In this way, fiction differs from histories, biographies, and nonfiction that are created entirely from facts.

By the early part of the twentieth century, the New Negro movement was producing black literary artists such as novelist **Dorothy West**, whose work explored social construct and racial segregation. The New Negro movement later contributed to the birth of the **Harlem Renaissance** of the 1920s, and women writers such as **Zora Neale Hurston** and West were producing **literature** that explored the diversity of the African American experience in relation to skin color, economic **class**, gender, region, belief, and history at the turn of the century. With Hurston's *Their Eyes Were Watching God* (1937), readers were introduced to literature of a female focus and mind. Her protagonist, Janie, tells the revolutionary story of a woman unbound by social expectation and predefined notions of womanhood. Hurston's work was also revolutionary in that she included the cadence of oral tradition, dialect, and the spoken word in her writings. This inclusion of speechlike literature and story in published work further carved the space for oral tradition in U.S. American literature. This foundation would later inform the literary tradition and works of such writers as **Toni Morrison** and **Alice Walker**.

With the **civil rights movement**, the political climate of the United States shifted. African American literature by women made history with the **Black Arts Movement** of 1965–1975/1976. Among one of the milestones of this movement is the 1970 anthology, edited and published by fiction writer **Toni Cade Bambara**, titled *The Black Woman*. This publication marked the first major feminist anthology and featured the work of such fiction writers as Alice Walker and **Paule Marshall**. Also in 1970 Morrison published her first novel, *The Bluest Eye*, and cultivated mentor relationships with writers Toni Cade Bambara and **Gayl Jones**.

After the Black Arts Movement of the 1960s and 1970s, the **community** of black women writers expanded and solidified in very tangible ways. Toni Morrison had begun a professional editorial relationship with Gayl Jones to produce Jones's *Corregidora* (1975) and *Eva's Man* (1976). **Ntozake Shange** published her novel *Sassafrass, Cypress & Indigo* in 1982, and Caribbean-born **Jamaica Kincaid** published *Annie John* in 1983, contributing to a legacy of African American writings by women that broadened the scope of African American literature beyond the borders and territories of the

United States, to include the rest of the Americas. While Kincaid's works explore another experience of African immigration and migration, as well as colonialism, her works also explore themes common to the larger African American experience that frequently transcends nationality and birthplace. Her work explores **memory**, gender, power, oppression, language, **love**, **family**, and the history of **slavery** as it manifests itself in **body** and world. Haitian-born **Edwidge Danticat** continues in this same tradition with works such as *Breath, Eyes, Memory* (1994) and *The Farming of Bones* (1998).

By the late 1900s, many African American novelists produced literary works of myth and magical realism to reflect on the legacies of slavery, gender, racial prejudice, and the evolution of the nation. Novelist **Octavia Butler**, who was the first African American woman writer to gain acclaim as a major science fiction writer, had published her novel *Kindred*, and in 1995 she received a MacArthur Foundation "genius grant" for her literary works.

In 1983 Walker received the Pulitzer Prize for her novel *The Color Purple*. In 1988 Morrison received the Pulitzer Prize for *Beloved*. Both of these novels explored the pathos of black women in the context of slavery and oppression. Notably, Morrison's story is loosely based on the true story of Margaret Garner, a runaway slave and mother who, rather than see her children returned to slavery, killed one of her children and attempted to kill the others. This is an example of the blending of fact and fiction to create the fabric of African American women's literary fiction. In 1993, Toni Morrison was awarded the Nobel Prize for Literature, becoming the first African American to be awarded the prize.

An important phenomenon of African American women's fiction is its relationship with the cinematic world in the late 1900s. In the 1980s and 1990s, literary fiction by black women in the United States began to see a surge toward **film**, and both *The Color Purple* and *Beloved* were adapted to the big screen. Also included in this movement was the miniseries *The Women of Brewster Place* (1989), based on **Gloria Naylor**'s 1982 novel of the same title. Popular fiction writer **Terry McMillan** was also part of this movement, and her works *Waiting to Exhale* and *How Stella Got Her Groove Back* were made into films in the 1990s.

Black women writers continue to write and forge new literary works well into the twenty-first century. Among new works created at the century's turn are Pulitzer Prize–winning playwright **Suzan-Lori Parks**'s novel *Getting Mother's Body*, Gayl Jones's *Mosquito*, and collections by Mayra Santos-Febres and Shay Youngblood. Also noted for her contribution to African American letters is the Dominican-born writer Nelly Rosario, whose novel *Song of the Water Saints* won the 2002 Pen Open Book Award.

Works About

Brown, Sterling. *Negro Poetry and Drama, and the Negro in American Fiction.* 1937. Preface by Robert A. Bone. New York: Atheneum, 1969.

Bruce, Dickson D., Jr. *Black American Writing from the Nadir: The Evolution of a Literary Tradition, 1877–1915.* Baton Rouge: Louisiana State University Press, 1989.

Carby, Hazel. *Reconstructing Womanhood: The Emergence of the Afro-American Woman Novelist.* New York: Oxford University Press, 1987.

Christian, Barbara. *Black Feminist Criticism: Perspectives on Black Women Writers.* Berkeley: University of California Press, 1985.

———. *Black Women Novelists: The Development of a Tradition, 1892–1976.* Westport, CT: Greenwood Press, 1980.

Davies, Carole Boyce. *Black Women, Writing, and Identity: Migrations of the Subject.* New York: Routledge, 1994.

Gates, Henry Louis, Jr., ed. *Black Literature and Literary Theory.* New York: Methuen, 1984.

Holloway, Karla F. C. *Moorings and Metaphors: Figures of Culture and Gender in Black Women's Literature.* New Brunswick, NJ: Rutgers University Press, 1992.

Mitchell, Angelyn, ed. *Within the Circle: An Anthology of African American Literary Criticism from the Harlem Renaissance to the Present.* Durham, NC: Duke University Press, 1994.

Pryse, Marjorie, and Hortense J. Spillers. *Conjuring: Black Women, Fiction, and Literary Tradition.* Bloomington: Indiana University Press, 1985.

Stepto, Robert. *From Behind the Veil: A Study of Afro-American Narrative.* Urbana: University of Illinois Press, 1979.

Sundquist, Eric. *To Wake the Nations: Race in the Making of American Literature.* Cambridge, MA: Belknap Press of Harvard University Press, 1993.

Tate, Claudia. *Domestic Allegories of Political Desire: The Black Heroine's Text at the Turn of the Century.* New York: Oxford University Press, 1992.

Aracelis Girmay

FIELDS, JULIA (1938–   )

Julia Fields's promise as a poet remains unfulfilled. Born in 1938 in Alabama, Fields grew up on a farm as one of eight children. She received a B.S. from Knoxville College in Tennessee in 1961, spent two years studying abroad in Scotland, and received an M.A. in English from the Bread Loaf School at Middlebury College in Vermont in 1972. She has spent much of her professional career as an educator and counts poets **Georgia Douglas Johnson** and Robert Hayden among her greatest influences. **Langston Hughes** extolled Fields as one of the most promising writers emerging from the **South** during the height of the **Black Arts Movement**. However, since the 1970s her **poetry** and short **fiction** have received scant critical attention. Despite winning major library and literary magazine prizes and a National Council of the Arts Grant in 1968, her name is nearly absent from literary circles today except for a handful of obscure scholarly references to lost, southern black women writers.

Fields explores themes of social, political, and economic inequality between the sexes and races, but she departs markedly from her contemporaries. Rather than rely on overt, militant political expression in her work, Fields's poetic voice is fraught with subtlety. She relies on humor, nuance, and natural allegory to probe feminist and racial themes. Through references to the personal and reflective, Fields explores black people's **history**, **myth**, and legacy in light of the debilitating effects of racism, sexism, and poverty. The effects are most profoundly felt in their sense of loss and their search for a rightful place. These themes permeate Fields's work.

In a 1974 interview, Fields describes herself as working in isolation, and her poetry expresses separation from the perceived Eastern, aesthetic mainstream that dominated black cultural expression in the 1970s. Her themes are certainly not geographically limited to the South, but they resonate with southern sensibilities. She attacks the hypocrisy of northern integration and explores issues of racial and **class** ambiguity during a period of rapid social change. The influence of the South expresses itself most clearly in her deft exploration of the natural landscape and its connection to feminine creativity, **community**, and **spirituality**.

Through understatement, Fields articulates women's experiences to advocate women's strengths and to repudiate negative conceptions of black women. Dissatisfied with traditional negative assumptions, particularly of black women as sexually permissive and emasculating, Fields venerates black women's roles as mothers, teachers, and healers. For example, in her most critically acclaimed poem "High on the Hog," Fields demands recognition and reward for black women's abuse as slaves, sharecroppers, and menial laborers. She indicts male-centered **Black Nationalism** and rejects the pedestal existence offered as meager reward for the horrific struggles and ignored contributions of black women. Fields's poetry rejects the socially marginalized, morally denigrated, and politically limited spaces consigned to women in general and black women in particular. Her work allows women to gain a sense of themselves as creative, empowered, and spiritual beings.

Works By

East of Moonlight. Charleston, NC: Red Clay Books, 1973.
The Green Lion of Zion Street. New York: McElderry Books, 1988.
Poems. Millbrook, NY: Kriya Press, 1968.
Slow Coins. Washington, DC: Three Continents Press, 1981.
A Summoning, a Shining. Scotland Neck, NC: S.N., 1976.

Works About

Broussard, Mercedes. "Blake's Bard." *Callaloo* 1.1 (December 1976): 60–62.
Burger, Mary Williams. "Julia Fields." *Dictionary of Literary Biography.* Vol. 41, *Afro-American Poets since 1955.* Ed. T. Harris and T. M. Davis. Detroit: Gale Research Company, 1985. 123–131.

Hauke, Kathleen A. "Julia Fields." *Oxford Companion to African American Literature*. Ed. W. L. Andrews, F. S. Foster, and T. Harris. New York: Oxford University Press, 1997. 274–275.

Lee, Don L. *Dynamite Voices: Black Poets of the 1960s*. Detroit: Broadside Press, 1971. 63–65.

Redmond, Eugene. *Drumvoices: The Mission of Afro-American Poetry, a Critical History*. Garden City, NY: Anchor Press, 1976.

Shennette Garrett

FILM

Only ten years after the inception of the Academy Awards, the motion picture industry's public measurement of itself, a black person not only was nominated for the first time but also won the award: Hattie McDaniel received the Best Supporting Actress prize for her performance as Mammie in *Gone with the Wind* (1939). However, any optimism that this specific victory might be a sign that African Americans were being welcomed into the industry elite as full and equal participants was a misplaced optimism. It was another decade before another performance was even nominated, and twenty-five years passed before another black actor received the award. Sidney Poitier won as Best Actor for *Lilies of the Field* (1963). More than fifty years passed before another black woman won the prize in McDaniel's category: Whoopi Goldberg for *Ghost* (1990). Only ten black women have been nominated as Best Supporting Actress, and only two have won.

Eleven black men have been nominated as Best Supporting Actor, and three of those have been given the prize: Louis Gossett, Jr., in *An Officer and a Gentleman* (1982); Denzel Washington in *Glory* (1989); and Cuba Gooding, Jr., in *Jerry Maguire* (1996). In the lead acting categories, seven women have been nominated, and one has been given the prize, Halle Berry for *Monster's Ball* (2001); men have been nominated a dozen times, winning twice: Poitier in 1963, and Denzel Washington for *Training Day* (2001). The acting awards, however, do not tell the full story. In the seventy-six-year **history** of the awards, African Americans have garnered only eighty-four nominations regardless of category and have won just seventeen times, winning in eight acting and nine nonacting categories. The chronology of both nominations and victories shows a story of systemic racism and agonizingly slow progress. The first three decades of the Academy's ritual saw only five nominations (and one win) for supporting performances by blacks.

Not until the 1960s did an African American receive a nomination in a nonacting category, and not surprisingly, that nomination was for music— Duke Ellington for *Paris Blues* (1961); not for yet another decade (over forty years after the beginnings of the awards) did a black person win a nonacting category. That distinction went to Isaac Hayes for his theme from *Shaft* (1971). The hierarchy of racist **stereotypes** placed entertainment right after servitude as a major purpose and pleasure of the black person in mainstream cinema. Thus, it is almost logical that, within an illogical system, performance and music would be the first avenues of success for the black film artist. The less visible but equally telling technical categories were closed to African American nominees until 1969; the first nomination came in film editing. Although Quincy Jones is the most-nominated African American person, his nominations span three categories. Willie D. Burton has been nominated six times for Best Sound, winning for *Bird* (1988). The 1980s has been the most successful decade at the Oscars for African Americans so far: thirty-one nominations (twelve for acting) and nine wins (two in performance categories).

The larger story implied by the statistical analysis of nominations is a complicated one of sexism and racism. First, and clearest, an organization that has grown up within a racist culture and that is overwhelmingly dominated by nonblacks has found it difficult even to suggest excellence by nomination and nearly impossible to declare superiority through awarding a black person a designation as "Best" in any category. Only three black women and five black men have won the award for "Best" performances. When it comes to what might be considered the more intellectually demanding technical **work** in cinema, it is not surprising that such an organization might withhold both opportunity and applause on the combined basis of **race** and sex. Of the forty-four nonacting African American nominees since 1961, only six have been women. Overall, only four black women have won Academy Awards—three for acting and one for songwriting. Thus, Hattie McDaniel's triumph in 1939 was a monumentally misleading omen.

While there are black women, such as Dorothy Dandridge, Ruby Dee, and Butterfly McQueen, whose names are part of film history in spite of the system within which they worked, many other talented African American women—Fredi Washington, Nina Mae McKinney, and Diana Sands—also found themselves at the peak of their careers, far from the peak of their talents, with nowhere to go because there were no lead roles, either developed for them or offered to them, as complex, dynamic characters. As poorly as black women fared in front of the camera, the situation was predictably worse for women in film production. Nevertheless, African American women have been filmmakers for as long as African American men. **Zora Neale Hurston** both wrote and filmed ethnographies, and Eloyce Gist made and marketed her evangelical films, during the same period Oscar Micheaux worked, especially the 1920s to 1930s.

While the number of categories in which black people are nominated has indeed increased over the years, the very limited number of nominations and even more limited number of awards demonstrate an inherent inequality in the industry's system of self-evaluation and self-reward. The crux of the problem is this: Membership in the Academy is a prerequisite for the privilege of nominating and voting, and membership is predicated on invitation by the Board of Governors, extended to those whose film work reflects the Academy's standards, to those who themselves have been nominated for the award, or to those who have been deemed candidates for their significant contributions to cinema. This set of subjective and restrictive criteria makes clear how it is that African Americans remain an Academy membership and ballot minority. It is the cumulative result of a century of racist conventions in film. Two of the most significant contributors have been race types and the industry code.

In the earliest of American films, black characters frequently were portrayed by nonblack actors in blackface and occasionally by absurdly made-up black actors in blackface. In *Toms, Coons, Mulattoes, Mammies, & Bucks*, Donald Bogle traces the history of typed roles into which African American actors were cast, ironically forced into situations where their performances in mainstream media perpetuated those very stereotypes that marginalized them by race. Further, he describes the persistent existence of these basic types and their predictable qualities in contemporary black characters. With roles restricted to minor characters and those determined by stereotypes, opportunities in front of the camera for African Americans have been frustratingly limited. Part of the problem has been the fact that fundamentally racist attitudes were enshrined in the motion picture industry's self-censorship codes that were in place from 1920 until 1964.

Arising from the complex problems associated with censorship boards at the state level, some of which would allow a pregnant woman to appear on screen and some not, for example, and since producing multiple versions of every film in order to placate local quirks was logistically unfeasible, the movie studios collectively arrived at the more practical solution of a production code. The code was devised in order not to offend either overarching national attitudes or the local sensibilities of each state and thus to protect the studios' capital investment in the making of films and guarantee the widest possible audience pool with the result of the greatest possible profit. Among the many restrictions the industry imposed on itself, which touched on every aspect of society, two items are particularly noteworthy in a discussion of African Americans in film: white **slavery** and miscegenation. White slavery could not be depicted; black slavery was neither mentioned nor proscribed. Portrayals of miscegenation were "forbidden." This prescribed apartness and superiority, born of racist convictions, assured racial inequality on-screen and implicitly encouraged it off-screen by constructing a color bar on human interactions of all kinds, but particularly intimate relationships.

Independent black cinema, however, was not bound by the rules and practices of the Hollywood studios. Here, black actors played black lead characters, black secondary characters, black villains, and black heroes, living everyday life and engaging with black themes. Segregated theaters and screenings meant ready-made audiences for "race movies." Hundreds of screening spaces opened, and the independents thrived during the 1920s and 1930s. The advent of sound and its requisite expensive technologies disrupted an energetic underground cinema begun by people like William Foster, Noble Johnson, and Oscar Micheaux and which had produced hundreds of movies (many of them now lost) for black audiences. Another determining factor was that Hollywood began producing race movies of its own to satisfy a clearly identified market and appetite for black images on the screen.

Following on the heels of an ideological shift from pursuing nonviolent means to social equality during the **civil rights movement** to the militancy of **Black Nationalism**, the blaxploitation films of the early 1970s energetically undermined as many of the "Don'ts and Be Carefuls" of the obsolete Production Code as possible. These independent movies, starting with Melvin Van Peebles's *Sweet Sweetback's Baadasssss Song* (1971), portrayed urban corruption, their heroes often the very pimps and drug dealers the code had prohibited from positive portrayals, their villains often the very law enforcement groups the code had protected from negative portrayals. *Sweetback's* protagonist is a porn star turned radical in the face of police corruption. The early race movies had focused primarily on the interests of the black bourgeoisie; the blaxploitation films that made Fred Williamson, Pam Grier, Tamara Dobson, and others into cult stars unabashedly flaunted black **sexuality** and realistically represented the speech and movement and concerns of less privileged black people.

The history of African Americans in film is a mixed history, and a discouraging one if only major studio productions are weighed, but it is a far deeper and varied tradition than those productions suggest. Black people have always found ways to tell black stories, and as documentarians such as Yvonne Welbon retrieve filmed documents and situate them and their makers in their legitimate place in the historical record, overall perception of the black contribution to cinema history is changing inevitably, both inside and outside African American communities. Contemporary filmmakers are adding to that continuum as black cinema and blacks in cinema expand exponentially.

Works About

Bobo, Jacqueline, ed. *Black Women Film and Video Artists*. New York: Routledge, 1998.

Bogle, Donald. *Toms, Coons, Mulattoes, Mammies, & Bucks: An Interpretive History of Blacks in American Films*. 4th ed. New York: Continuum, 2001.

Bowser, Pearl, Jane Gaines, and Charles Musser. *Oscar Micheaux and His Circle: African American Filmmaking and Race Cinema of the Silent Era*. Bloomington: Indiana University Press, 2001.

Everett, Anna. *Returning the Gaze: A Genealogy of Black Film Criticism, 1909–1949*. Durham, NC: Duke University Press, 2001.

Jones, G. William. *Black Cinema Treasures: Lost and Found*. Foreword Ossie Davis. Denton: University of North Texas Press, 1997.

Mapp, Edward. *African Americans and the Oscar: Seven Decades of Struggle and Achievement*. Lanham, MD: Scarecrow Press, 2003.

Midnight Ramble: Oscar Micheaux and the Story of Race Movies. Dir. Bestor Cram and Pearl Bowser. Northern Light Productions, 1994.

Rhines, Jesse A. *Black Film/White Money*. Piscataway, NJ: Rutgers University Press, 1996.

Sisters in Cinema. Dir. Yvonne Welbon. Our Film Works, 2003.

Sylvester, Melvin. *African-Americans in Motion Pictures: The Past and the Present.* Brookville, NY: Long Island University, B. Davis Schwartz Memorial Library, 1999. www.liu.edu/cwis/cwp/library/african/movies.htm#place.

A. Mary Murphy

FINNEY, NIKKY (1957–)

Nikky Finney was born Lynn Carol Finney in Conway, South Carolina, on August 26, 1957, to Ernest A. Finney, a civil rights attorney, and Frances Davenport Finney, an elementary school teacher. Although a poet rooted in the folk traditions of the African American **South**, Finney's work relies upon the spiritual and aesthetic influence of West African tradition, the **womanist** wisdom of her maternal grandmother, Beulah Lenorah Davenport, and her **family**'s political commitment to equality and social justice.

After receiving her undergraduate degree from Talladega College, Finney began graduate work at Atlanta University and then worked as a writer/ photographer for the Black Women's Health Project. During her time in Atlanta, she befriended **fiction** writer/cultural worker/activist, **Toni Cade Bambara**. Bambara's talent for appreciating the voices of black people, particularly black women, was more than literary device. Bambara welcomed black writers, one of whom was Finney, into her home for workshops, food, and nurturing. The group would be known formally as the Southern Collective of African American Writers, and Bambara would fulfill the role of mentor for Finney until Bambara's **death** in 1995 of cancer.

Finney's first collection of **poetry**, *On Wings Made of Gauze* (1985), mixes renderings of black family and issues of equality and social justice. In this early collection, Finney explores the themes she would develop fully in later works. After living in Atlanta, Finney moved to Oakland, California, before taking a teaching position at the University of Kentucky. Like her mentor Toni Cade Bambara, Finney worked with young writers. In Kentucky, Finney founded the Affrilachian Poets with then emerging writers Frank X. Walker, Crystal Wilkerson, Kelly Norman Ellis, and Ricardo Nazrio-Colon. Finney's **work** with the group emerged from the need to represent African Americans and other people of color in Appalachia. The group exemplifies her desire to reclaim the contributions of African peoples in the **history** of the American South. While in Kentucky, she completed her second collection of poetry, *Rice* (1995). Again, Finney was able to foster and preserve the legacy of black southern culture. *Rice*, she reaffirms in narrative, free verse, is the African heritage of South Carolina. The collection's title harkens to South Carolina's slave past and the cultivation of the state's cash crop by West Africans. Her collection includes personal poems that celebrate grandmother **love** in "The Vertigo" as well as persona poems like "Cotton Tea," which depict methods slave women used to induce abortion once impregnated by the captors. Other poems examine **domestic violence**, the love of women (both sexual and nonsexual), and the universal oppression of women.

In 1999, she won the PEN American Open Book Award for *Rice* and completed a collection of short stories titled *Heartwood* (1997). In 2003 she published *The World Is Round*, a mixture of poetry and memoir. Much of Finney's aesthetic blends the feminist/womanist perspectives of **Alice Walker** and **Audre Lorde** with the fierce sense of self-determinism of **Black Arts Movement** poets **Nikki Giovanni**, **Sonia Sanchez**, Haki Madhubuti, and **Carolyn Rodgers**.

Works By

For Posterity's Sake: The Morgan and Marvin Smith Story. Script. Dir. Heather Lyons. Lexington, KY: Little City Productions, 1995.
Heartwood. Lexington: University Press of Kentucky, 1997.
On Wings Made of Gauze. New York: William Morrow, 1985.
"Pluck and Guts." *Kindness*, by Toshi Reagon. Washington, DC: Folkways Records, Smithsonian Institution, 1997.
Rice. Toronto: Sister Vison Press, 1995.
"Salt-water Geechee Mounds." *Bloodroot: Reflections on Place by Appalachian Women Writers*. Ed. Joyce Dyer. Lexington: University Press of Kentucky, 1998. 120–127.
"To Be Beheld." *Good and Bad Hair*. Photographs by Bill Gaskins. New Brunswick, NJ: Rutgers University Press, 1997.
The World Is Round. Atlanta, GA: Innerlight Press, 2003.

Work About

Dawes, Kwame. "Reading 'Rice': A Local Habitation and a Name." *African American Review* 31 (1997): 269–279.

Kelly Norman Ellis

FISHER KING, THE

In **Paule Marshall**'s most recent novel, *The Fisher King* (2000), Marshall investigates similar themes as in her other stories, especially those of integrating the past and the present into the lives of her characters. This story layers voices and generational tales like ***Daughters***, but *The Fisher King* adds a different twist. Telling the story through an eight-year-old boy, Marshall weaves the narratives of several generations of the boy's **family** and the tragic decisions that led to their estrangement. These elements all hinge on the backdrop of the African American **jazz** movement.

The Fisher King is primarily the account of the young boy's grandfather, Sonny-Rett Payne. When Sonny-Rett determines to defy his West Indian mother in both his choice of wife and career, he flees the country. His marriage to Cherisse McCullum angers both the bride's and groom's families, and Sonny-Rett's decision to become a jazz musician is even more unacceptable to them. As a result, the young couple joins the American expatriates in Paris, never to reconnect with their families in New York again. The novel begins with young Sonny, the jazz musician's grandson, confronting the extended families in America for the first time since Sonny-Rett's **death**.

In *The Fisher King*, Marshall again attacks the themes of integrating one's personal past with a larger cultural heritage in order to most fully discovery oneself. The characters are of West Indian heritage, like those in many of Marshall's other stories, and they must not only face racism in America but also must integrate the pressures of a close-knit immigrant **community** with their own dreams and aspirations. This novel also incorporates the racism associated with jazz in America, often considered evil by mainstream American culture throughout the early twentieth century. Young Sonny listens to the story of how these many pressures cause Sonny-Rett's and Cherisse's exile from their families, and the grandson discovers with the readers how familial stubbornness can damage relationships forever. Despite Sonny-Rett's death in poverty and exile, Marshall opens a space for hope in the reconnection between young Sonny and his still-living American great-grandmothers. In *The Fisher King*, as in all of Marshall's writing, narrative offers an opportunity for remembering, retelling, and thus **healing** for many generations of family.

Work About

Wallhead, Celia M. "Myth, Ritual and Racial Identity in Paule Marshall's *The Fisher King*." *Revista Canaria de Estudios Ingleses* 45 (2002): 205–214. (Spanish summary.)

Laura Baker Shearer

FOLKLORE

One cannot assay the richness of African Americans' contributions to national folklore without acknowledging the diverse voices, expertise, and creative ingenuity of black women over the long trek from the horror of **slavery** to the political and social prominence enjoyed by many today. African American folklore as a field of knowledge production has often been overlooked by readers, educators, and cultural historians who disparage it as being facile, dated, derivative, quaintly impressionistic, or unworthy of serious scholarly regard. By the same token, folklore dealing with black women's experience has suffered further marginalization due to the combined hierarchies of **race**, **class**, and gender. This slight is ironical given the prominence of *Mules and Men* (1935), **Zora Neale Hurston**'s seminal folklore collection.

This work combines **autobiography** and anthropological analysis to detail the folklore in her native state of Florida, as well as Louisiana, **home** of the legendary voodoo icon Marie Leveau.

As economic objects, most slave women were severely restricted to manual labor in either the fields or the plantation household. Because of this constraint, early women-centered folk knowledge had its source in the **domestic** arts (for instance, needlecraft, **quilting**, cooking, child care, textile and clothes production, and traditional **healing**). These tributaries of knowledge intermingled with less gender-specific expressions of black vernacular **identity**: songs and melodies, oral storytelling, games, jokes, religious rites, chants, sermons, traditional **community** customs (for example, jumping a broomstick to symbolize wedlock), superstition and the occult, and later, the visual arts and folk **literature**. The underlying difficulty in establishing a comprehensive vision of early (proto)feminist folklore exists in its dearth of public advocates, as well as a probable lack of artistic self-awareness. In other words, collectors were not actively archiving or publishing material during the time of slavery because of racist and sexist devaluation (that is, the impression that the inner workings of blacks' lives—especially black *women's* lives—were not worth cataloguing for posterity). The folk practitioners themselves were not consciously engaging in their art as such, primarily because of a scarcity of means (including education, **literacy**, and leisure time), and the oppressively unpredictable nature of life under the "peculiar institution."

Social gatherings, including religious worship, **family** bonding, and occasional celebrations, would have been prime opportunities for the dissemination and reproduction of folk knowledge. However, as would be expected, these gatherings depended on the whims and demands of masters, mistresses, overseers, and the local night-riders (patrollers) who used terror tactics to prevent regular fraternizing among slaves. Fear of insurrection and a reversal of servitude back onto whites (the rhetoric of "Negro domination" that permeated the postbellum era), especially after Nat Turner's 1831 rebellion, were among the principal reasons for curtailing free exchange and slave recreation. Similarly, the intergenerational relay of folklore, especially the learning between mothers and daughters, was stymied by the specter of the auction block and the usually irreparable separations that ensued once children and other family members were sold away. A system of surrogacy and mentorship resulted in some households, with older or more experienced black women serving as teachers and mother figures to their younger peers. Sometimes, white children, or even the mistress herself, were recipients of the slave woman's care and expertise. Such emotional and practical generosity, likely a function of necessity as much as choice, contributed in part to the "**Mammy**" **stereotype** that indirectly praises black women for their domestic savvy but simultaneously divests them of the agency to adopt a host of other, more intellectually challenging social roles.

The thousands of autobiographical interviews compiled for the depression-era Federal Writers' Project (FWP) of the Works Progress Administration showcase the complexity and underlying volatility of many such relationships.

An avid concern for these intimate aspects of slave life helped form the standard oral questionnaire for the Slave Narrative Collection. The majority of the fieldworkers who conducted interviews were white, but black women like Ida Belle Hunter and Bertha P. Tipton were contributors to this legacy. Derived from the recollections of an aging black population, these accounts prove searing in their descriptive accuracy. As first-person testimonials, they offer a veritable goldmine of historical, anthropological, and sociological information that valorizes the resourcefulness and emotional resilience of the tellers. Female interviewees often describe such chores as cooking, carding, weaving, dye- and mattress-making, and the allocation of various household duties. They also recall local housing, types of furniture, agricultural methods, **conjuring** and superstitions, ghost stories, popular songs, and clandestine attempts to attain some form of religious or educational instruction despite the dangers of exposure and punishment. The salaried **work** provided by this important government initiative also contributed indirectly to the insertion of African American folklore into other genres of black literature. Such would-be novelists as **Ralph Ellison**, **Richard Wright**, and Hurston herself were among those writers on the FWP payroll who found themselves better equipped to pursue their creative interests at a time when opportunities and financial security were scarce. Elements of folklore—the Brer Rabbit allusion in Ellison's *Invisible Man* (1952), the Badman stereotype reconfigured in Wright's *Native Son* (1940), and the verbally dexterous Eatonville community portrayed in Hurston's ***Their Eyes Were Watching God*** (1937) suggest how two very different imaginative helixes—one that can be traced back to ancestral West African, Euro-American, and Native American beginnings, another that has its roots in the gritty social realism of the years spanning mass migration, lynch law, Jim Crow segregation, pervasive social alienation, and political disenfranchisement—can intertwine to form the genetic material of mid-twentieth-century African American **fiction**.

Talking a step backward in literary **history**, folk practices in the formative genre of the **slave narrative** played a somewhat peripheral role to the overarching preoccupation with character, abolitionist moral suasion, carefully honed rhetorical effects, and political efficacy. Popular slave narratives like that of Henry Bibb (1849) describe the typical diversions of nonreligious slaves on Sabbath day: banjo-playing, gambling, singing, brawling, gaming, dancing, and drinking. A seminal passage in **Frederick Douglass**'s *Narrative of the Life of Frederick Douglass* (1845) contemplates the singing of slaves at the Great House Farm. These codified utterances reveal the paradoxical marriage of a joyous form with miserable but effectively veiled content. It is this nascent formula combining laughter and tears that would eventually find popular reiteration in African American musical forms like the **spirituals**, **blues**, and **jazz**. More sensitive to the female slave's particular struggles, and ostensibly a "writing back" to Douglass's robust masculine persona, **Harriet Jacobs**'s ***Incidents in the Life of a Slave Girl*** (1861) juxtaposes the brief but permissible merrymaking of Christmas with the tragic sale of slaves on New Year's Day. Many of the most popular narratives tend to focus more on the evolution of the male speaker's consciousness and his quest for intellectual and physical **freedom** than the plight of the female slave under similar, if not more abusive, circumstances. An appreciation of mutual hardship often exists, but a pervasive and unanimous sense of equality is difficult to discern in most of the texts and contexts presented by popular male narrators.

The slave narratives are a specialized genre, but they function symbolically as folk literature by imparting a representative voice for a larger community, one of the underlying objectives of folklore as a *communal* tool for cultural survival. Many of the recurrent motifs in the genre, including a victory for the underdog and the deception of the powerful, emerge in classic African American folktales, especially trickster tales (animal and human) and etiological fables (the "why" stories). Highly recognizable, the Brer Rabbit cycle offers a primarily male cast of characters: Brer Fox, Brer Deer, Brer 'Gator, Brer Dawg, and Brer Rabbit himself. Sis Cat is one of a few female characters who appears consistently (if at all), along with miscellaneous **love** interests who are often of indeterminate species. Brer Rabbit and the story of Tar Baby, originally brought to public prominence by Joel Chandler Harris's Uncle Remus collection of 1881, was reapplied in **Toni Morrison**'s 1981 novel *Tar Baby*. As a racist epithet, "tar baby" refers disparagingly to any African American, especially an individual of a darker complexion. As feminist symbol, it evokes a full range of significant connotations. On the negative side, the feminized tar baby suggests black women's voicelessness, emotional denigration by males, external constructions of black femininity, racist suggestions of pollution and contamination, and victimization through implied and actual physical **violence**. On the more positive side, the tar-covered figure comes across as a female refusing to acknowledge the dominating male presence, an embodiment of enigmatic or aggressive female power, and the attractive cohesiveness of black sisterhood (a society to which Brer Rabbit, playing the role of the representative male figure, is denied both easy entry and clean exit).

The abuse and denigration of black women is not a theme foreign to either early or more recent manifestations of African American folk culture. Such critics as Roger D. Abrahams, Lawrence W. Levine, and Geneva Smitherman have discussed the fascinating array of socially conscious, artistically innovative techniques used in verbal sparring (that is, signifying) between African Americans. Particular attention has been directed toward black males in historically rural but now largely urban locales. The assumption that females have little part in this discourse is a problematic one. For instance, in "the dozens" (the art of clever insult, whether categorized as "dirty" or "clean"), the role of the mother is a given. Although the subject of mockery and subsequent defense, her symbolic centrality as a life source, caregiver, sexual and social being, and powerful presence remains stark and irrefutable. At the same time, the verbal abuse of the mother also signals her contradictory position as the subject *and* the object of imaginative play. Such play can be constructive and critical, but it can also prove misogynistic and demeaning to black women and to women in general. Recent feminist theories have placed the exploitation and exchange of women at the core of many masculinist cultural rituals. As a result, the verbal affirmation of male power in folk-based oral culture often occurs at the expense of grandmothers, mothers, sisters, wives, daughters, and other female kin. Women are increasingly asserting their own individualities through intervention into, and participation in, such contests and witty exchanges. Janie Crawford's ability to hold her own in *Their Eyes Were Watching God* exemplifies the talent and verve that black women can offer, given the opportunity to participate fully on the discursive playing field.

Concerns about representations of black women also arise in early folk literature. The tale "Why the Sister in Black Works Hardest" details a chain of command originating with a white woman ("Ole Missus") who demands that her husband ("Ole Massa") retrieve a large, antiquated box from the middle of a road. The reversal of the standard patriarchal model (the white man at the top of the hierarchy of social power) is at best a reflection of the Reconstruction-era apotheosis of white womanhood, especially in the southern states, as a response to rampant fears about race purity, chastity, and caste disruption. Unwilling to follow through with his wife's demand that he retrieve the box, Ole Massa directs his black servant (typically a clever slave named John in other tales) to perform the assigned task. The black male, equally reluctant, commands his wife to do so, exploiting her—just as he was exploited—for her free labor, ignorance, and inability to refuse. Once open, the box presents the black woman with a large reserve of hard work, making her a modern-day Pandora and the center of much-needed political and social struggle.

A slight reversal of this abject status occurs in the folktale "Why Women Always Take Advantage of Men," where the black female adopts the role of trickster and so-called badwoman, bargaining with God and the Devil (but particularly with the latter) to make her more powerful than her husband. While the home may appear to be a place of incarceration for some black women, especially those relegated to housework because of a lack of education and better employment opportunities, it is a site of ultimate female mastery in this instance. The wife wields power over the three domains that her husband frequents or values most: the kitchen, the bedroom, and the nursery. In this tale, the articulateness of the black characters emerges, as well as the humorous juxtaposition of God and the Devil, no longer untouchable or vastly antithetical entities. Such contentious topics as the idea of original sexual equality, man's justification of power through recourse to **religion**, and the shortsightedness of his domination based on physical superiority are all placed in stark yet humorous relief.

An area in which black women have wielded considerable, albeit largely unacknowledged, power is the field of folk medicine. Among other slave narrators, Bibb describes the practice of medicating sick slaves by means of an indigenous pharmacopoeia, the content of which ranged from pungent salts, castor oil, and red pepper tea to more creative and dubious concoctions like boiled chimney soot (which the master would compel the slave to drink). More conventional ingredients with therapeutic properties included assorted leaves, camphor, oil of cloves, sulfur flowers, asafetida (often tied around the neck to ward off infection), various roots like High John the Conqueror, and an array of patented formulas that appeared well after the demise of slavery. To save the time and expense of calling a physician, rootworkers, "witch doctors," and herbalists were often depended on by slave owners to administer to the sick among the black plantation communities. These healers tended to be mature and trustworthy females. Some were even free agents and businesswomen like Aun' Peggy of **Charles Waddell Chesnutt**'s *The Conjure Woman and Other Conjure Tales* (1899). Such females stood as redoubtable figures and early feminist role models. While they inspired fear in those who believed them to be witches, they earned the respect of others for their ability to offer tangible assistance when few such avenues were available—save recourse to prayer.

Douglass's text includes an incident with a "magical" root given to him as protection by a fellow (male) slave, Sandy Jenkins. He adds that **deaths** were often ascribed to trickery, imbalance, or ill will rather than to natural causes. Such a belief finds a more contemporary echo in **Alice Walker**'s *The Color Purple* (1982) when Celie suffers insomnia after having wronged Sophia, a fellow black woman who hardly deserves to be beaten for the sake of her husband's lack of self-esteem. As Chesnutt's collection attests, male and female rootworkers, counselors, and conjurers ("two-headed doctors") were not anomalies but acknowledged spirit-mediators and guides who could reassert the tenuous balance between the human and nonhuman world. Their ability to infuse the mundane with the magical, and distill faith and **myth** into the physiological process of healing, resonates with contemporary naturopathic and related alternative therapies.

As Hurston reflected in her treatise "Characteristics of Negro Expression" (1934), black folklore is neither a dead language nor a finite and static collection of anecdotes, expressions, and behavioral orientations. Rather, in a constant state of flux, it offers a site for creative and cultural invigoration. Its diversity, adaptability, and capacity to reconfigure conventional power relations offer a metaphor for America's continuing need to accommodate the voices of African Americans, especially those of black women.

See also Ancestor, Use of; Memory; South, Influence of the; Spirituality

Works About

Abrahams, Roger D., ed. *African American Folktales: Stories from Black Traditions in the New World.* New York: Pantheon, 1999.

Billingslea-Brown, Alma Jean. *Crossing Borders Through Folklore: African American Women's Fiction and Art.* Columbia: University of Missouri Press, 1999.

Dance, Daryl Cumber. *From My People: 400 Years of African American Folklore.* New York: Norton, 2002.

Hamilton, Virginia. *Her Stories: African American Folktales, Fairy Tales, and True Tales.* New York: Blue Sky Press, 1995.

Hurston, Zora Neale. "Characteristics of Negro Expression." *The Norton Anthology of African American Literature*. Ed. Henry Louis Gates, Jr., and Nellie Y. McKay. 1st ed. New York: Norton, 1997. 1019–1032.

Levine, Lawrence W. *Black Culture and Black Consciousness: Afro-American Folk Thought from Slavery to Freedom*. New York: Oxford University Press, 1977.

Smitherman, Geneva. *Black Talk: Words and Phrases from the Hood to the Amen Corner*. Rev. ed. Boston: Houghton Mifflin, 2000.

Sundquist, Eric J. *The Hammers of Creation: Folk Culture in Modern African-American Fiction*. Athens: University of Georgia Press, 1992.

Nancy Kang

FOOTE, JULIA A. J. (1823–1900)

Born in Schenectady, New York, in 1823, Julia A. J. Foote was one of the most notable women preachers of the nineteenth century. In her struggles against the limitations that the church imposed on women preachers, Foote developed a strong feminist perspective on her life as a wife and churchwoman. Like **Zilpha Elaw**, Foote was affiliated with the African Methodist Episcopal (AME) Church from childhood. At age fifteen, Foote was converted and joined the AME Church. She studied the Bible diligently and attended church services faithfully. When she was eighteen years of age, she married George Foote, a sailor. She accompanied her husband to Boston shortly after their marriage and there joined the African Methodist Episcopal Zion Church, where she urged church members to seek sanctification, as Elaw had done. It was during this period that Foote felt her call to preach.

In her spiritual **autobiography** *A Brand Plucked from the Fire*, published in 1879, Foote describes the circumstances of her call to preach. For a few months prior to her call, she felt inspired to exhort and pray for people in a house-to-house ministry. Since spiritual exhortation was not classified as preaching, the male leadership of the AME Zion church voiced no objections to her ministry. Fully aware of the obstacles that women preachers faced from **family** and church leaders, Foote was reluctant to acknowledge or accept her call to preach. An angel appeared to her three times in a vision before she accepted the call. Each time the angel brought a message from God commanding her to preach. The final message assured her that her soul would be lost unless she obeyed "God's righteous commands." Ironically, Foote's call to preach was problematic because she had spoken out against women preachers. However, the angel's third message left her no choice; she must yield to God's authority.

Almost immediately, she encountered opposition. Her husband, embarrassed by her preaching, threatened to send her back to her parents or to the "crazy house" if she did not obey his command to stop preaching. Moreover, her pastor, Reverend Jehiel Beman, ordered her to stop preaching. When she refused to obey, he charged her with violating church discipline and excommunicated her. Foote appealed her excommunication, but the male church leaders upheld Reverend Beman's decision. Reflecting on her pastor's attempts to silence her, Foote makes a bold feminist response in her autobiography: "There was no justice meted out to women in those days." Because her calling came from God, Foote would not allow her husband, her pastor, or any other man to override God's authority.

Consequently, Foote's autobiography is a feminist text that speaks specifically about the spiritual and cultural liberation of women. Her own life is an object lesson in independent thinking and resistance to male dominance. Indeed, Foote invites women to declare their independence from male authority when she writes: "You will not let what man may say or do, keep you from doing the will of the Lord or using the gifts you have for the good of others." Although "man" includes women, Foote's experience with dominant men suggests an emphasis on men who want to control women.

Work By

A Brand Plucked from the Fire: An Autobiographical Sketch. Cleveland, OH: W. F. Schneider, 1879.

Work About

Andrews, William L. Introduction to *Sisters of the Spirit: Three Black Women's Autobiographies of the Nineteenth Century.* Bloomington: Indiana University Press, 1986. 1–22.

Elvin Holt

FOR COLORED GIRLS WHO HAVE CONSIDERED SUICIDE/ WHEN THE RAINBOW IS ENUF

This 1975 innovative, dramatic piece by **Ntozake Shange** (*en*-toe-zah-kay–*shang-ay*) marked the beginning of her career. An experimental blend of dance, **poetry**, music, and **drama**, *for colored girls* created a new space for women of color to declare themselves. Through the seven women's voices/ dances that grace the various "choreopoems," as Shange defines them, the reader enters a network of **womanism** covering a wide range of political, sexual, and spiritual concerns of black people. Begun in San Francisco as improvisational poetry/dance/music pieces performed in various clubs in the early 1970s, *for colored girls* took shape in New York City in 1974 with the collaboration of Paula Moss (choreography) and Oz Scott (directing). It was staged under African American producer Woodie King, Jr., at the New Federal Theatre, having a successful run there from November 1975 until June 1976. Joseph Papp subsequently produced *for colored girls* at the New York Shakespeare Festival's Anspacher Theatre and later at the Booth. It was published in 1976 and became one of the most famous works of the new African American womanist sensibility of the 1970s. Like no contemporary **literature** before her, Shange's *for colored girls* brings the life of the African American woman out in the open.

Shange's first work launched an important new era in black theater, for she redefined it to include the choreopoem as a legitimate dramatic form. It also draws on African dramatic/theatrical forms: a blending of chant, poetry, music, dance, and rituals. Many women identified with the black women in her pieces, which argue eloquently for females to **love** and believe in themselves enough to become visible, independent agents in creating, first and foremost, themselves. Shange's work gave not only shape but also color to later-twentieth-century feminism. Thematically, the twenty poems in the piece concern black women's abilities to overcome loneliness, abuse, self-effacement in relationships with men, **rape**, and invisibility. In the choreopoem "Sorry," women who have been mistreated through the patriarchal "I'm-sorry-I-cheated-on-you-baby" response are through with excuses. They simply will not absorb them anymore. A rainbow can be enough, Shange's work seems to suggest, because it offers new possibilities after the storm. And so her work marks a new beginning in the forms of African American art, for the choreopoem allows for several emotional tones to be struck at once.

There are seven black women whose names are lady in brown, yellow, orange, red, purple, blue, and green. Their voices intermingle within many of the poems, and together they attempt to rewrite language to allow for black women's reality. Using a complicated mixture of realism and magic, Shange creates a world where women are together, helping one another and acknowledging their place in the larger scheme of society. The introduction explains that such a language is necessary because, otherwise, the black girl is made invisible by English discourse conventions. This new choric form, furthermore, was necessary for the attempt to reintegrate the **body** with the mind. Literature and the arts had so long been dominated by individual rather than collective voices and shaped by museumlike decorums instead of by the raucus cultural expressions of the 1960s—youth culture, black influences in rock and **jazz** music, the **civil rights movement**, and the black liberation movement. With the appearance of *for colored girls*, there was now a new form of artistic expression that black women could identify as their own. Boldly, Shange's play made a definitive announcement: An African American woman will not identify with cultural forms that were developed primarily by whites. She will make her own new forms and create her own realities and through them break old silences and taboos.

Shange has stated that she writes for "colored girls" who need to read wonderful things about themselves in order to develop some self-esteem and a defense system against internalized racism and sexism. The women in her vignettes create that self-loving. The language manages movement, like dancing in the text, for the cadences and rhythms have a central significance in the sequence as a whole. As the lady in yellow explains, all she has going for her is the music and the dance. By exploring the expressive potential of the body through dance, the seven women in the choreopoem search for, and find, various ways of making meaning of their experiences. Through them, Shange portrays black women fighting for their integrity and self-respect. Knowing how one's own body moves, and moving it, connects the mind and emotions to one's physical embodiment, thus **healing**, if only momentarily, the mind/body split. The women strengthen their newly created visibilities to one another by telling their many stories, sometimes painful, sometimes beautiful, but always real. They tell their stories to other struggling women and are bolstered by that. They sway with each other and themselves as the words move them to laughter and tears. But there is a language that they can understand and experiences that they can share that make the hurt and pain easier to endure. "Latent Rapist" is a good example of this, as the women echo the observation that a rapist is more likely to be a man whom you know than the "stranger" you/we/I usually assume a rapist to be. Dancing in this section is more like crouching in pain, but even so the dance movements of *for colored girls* are generally self-affirming, erotic, spiritual, communal, defiant, and playful.

Dance liberates bodily pleasure from **sexuality**. It conveys thinking through the body, and it plays a central role in *for colored girls*, where the exploration of being a black girl/woman can be undertaken without inhibition or fear. The women of the play possess creative energy based in the erotic, as **Audre Lorde** wrote about in her essay on the "Uses of the Erotic" in black women's lives, especially in artistic and political realms. Movement through dance also emphasizes a fluid temporality, and each choreopoem segues effortlessly into the next. The piece "one," performed by the lady in red, is about a woman who enhances her erotic power beyond sexuality, waking up the men after sex and making them leave her place so that she can write, which is her art. She claims the power that many women wish they had more of: power to attract and, then, to turn away men. The lady in red treats herself to body art—butterflies, sequins, and passion flowers—which she lets fall off of her later in the night as she bathes in scented oils. In "no more love poems #4," the lady in yellow says that being alive, a woman, and black is a "metaphysical dilemma": Staying alive emotionally is a challenge, and a chorus of dance movements and voices must enter into the moment in order to keep it from collapsing.

One of the most evocative and memorable metaphors to come out of *for colored girls* is the piece "somebody almost walked off wid alla my stuff," meaning somebody has taken all of my best parts, somebody has stolen my **identity** from me, somebody does not know me. Shange's *for colored girls who have considered suicide/when the rainbow is enuf* enacts the means whereby that "stuff" comes back; women of color speak, dance, and sing it back into their realities. In this work, Shange lays the foundation for what follows in her subsequent artistic efforts. She takes hold of the language that has hobbled African American women's subjective realities through the operations of **stereotypes** and categories, then she bends it. Shange creates written/oral/kinetic forms of resistance within English, accomplishing what Ezra Pound wished the modernists would do: "make it new." Shange's influence on black theater in the late twentieth century is enormous. Through the inimitable argument of the choreopoem, she addresses the subjugation of black women, not to elicit pity or sorrow but to encourage, to bolster, the women who are "searching for the ends of their own rainbows."

See also Beauty; *Betsey Brown*; Black Feminism; Community; Folklore; *Liliane: Resurrection of the Daughter*; *Sassafrass, Cypress & Indigo*

Works About

Brown-Guillory, Elizabeth, ed. *Their Place on the Stage: Black Women Playwrights in America*. Westport, CT: Praeger, 1990.

Gofrit, Leslie. "Women Dancing Back: Disruption and the Politics of Pleasure." *Postmodernism, Feminism and Cultural Politics*. Ed. Henry A. Giroux. Albany: State University of New York, 1991. 174–195.

Tate, Claudia. "Ntozake Shange." *Black Women Writers at Work*. Ed. Claudia Tate. New York: Continuum, 1983. 149–174.

Waxman, Barbara Frey. "Dancing Out of Form, Dancing into Self: Genre and Metaphor in Marshall, Shange, and Walker." *MELUS* 19.3 (1994): 91–106.

Sharon Jessee and Fayme Perry

FORMAN, RUTH (1968–)

Ruth Forman was born in Cape Cod, Massachusetts, and grew up in Rochester, New York. She is a poet whose work celebrates woman, particularly African American womanhood. Reviews of Forman's **poetry** frequently situate her within the tradition of female poets like **Sonia Sanchez**, **June Jordan**, **Nikki Giovanni**, **Audre Lorde**, and **Alice Walker**. These groundbreaking writers have enabled young female poets, like Forman, to spread their wings to the winds and speak the truth sitting before them. Forman's work illustrates a talent that seizes the legacy and carries it forward for others to build upon as she celebrates female power, connection, and sensuality.

Forman's poetry addresses the innumerable phases of womanhood and the roads traveled to obtain each plateau and speaks to the hope and potential that lives in the midst of near hopelessness. Her work conveys power, truth, and attitude, at times subdued but frequently in your face. Forman's poetic strength finds voice in its presentation of the power attained by woman in the reality of her situation, be that circumstance joyous or painful. Forman writes, although not exclusively, in black urban vernacular, and her poetry often focuses on situations confronting African Americans, especially women.

The richness of Forman's poems mirrors and captures the complexity and multifaceted nature of African American culture and experience as it streams through the voices of her poetic protagonists. In her verses are the unheard voices of previous generations as her poetry celebrates what it is to be black and female, in all its expressions. While "You So Woman" and "Five" celebrate black female sensuality and influence, works such as "Young Cornrows Callin Out the Moon" and "If You Lose Your Pen" contain the **love**, joy, sadness, and hope found in African American experience.

Forman's poems like "Up Sister" and "Stoplight Politics" evoke an inseparable connection found in female experiences regardless of the placement of woman along a socioeconomic or political spectrum and a shared consciousness that resists splintering. Poems such as "In the Mirror Too Long," "In a Darkroom," and "Today You Dial Me" address female ownership of self as woman and as African American, in the wake of past occurrences that threaten to alter its course.

Forman was the recipient of the Barnard New Women Poets award for her first book of poetry, *We Are the Young Magicians* (1993), and the 1999 Pen Oakland Josephine Miles Award for Poetry for her second book, *Renaissance* (1997). Forman has also performed her work at the United Nations, the National Black Arts Festival, the Frederick Douglass Creative Arts Center's Black Roots Festival, the Poetry for the People Series, on National Public Radio, and PBS's The United Nations of Poetry. In 2001 Forman received the Durfee Artist Fellowship to complete her first novel titled *Mama John.*

Works By

Renaissance. Boston: Beacon Press, 1997.
We Are the Young Magicians. Boston: Beacon Press, 1993.

Works About

Oden, Gloria. Review of *We Are the Young Magicians*, by Ruth Forman. *MELUS* 18 (1993): 111–113.
Review of *Renaissance*, by Ruth Forman. *Publisher's Weekly,* January 26, 1998, 88.
Selman, Robyn. "The New Shape-Changers" Review of *We Are the Young Magicians*, by Ruth Forman. *Kenyon Review* 16.2 (1994): 174–184.

Wanda G. Addison

FRANKLIN, J. E. (1937–   )

Jennie Elizabeth Franklin—playwright, short-story writer, educator, and theater director—was born in Houston, Texas, to Robert Franklin, a cook, and Mathie Randle Franklin, a maid. One of thirteen children living in tight quarters, Franklin was banned from making noise, a restriction that heightened her attentiveness to sound. After learning to write, Franklin hoarded found pens and paper to "re-play" these sounds, which still echo in the distinct voices of her characters.

Franklin graduated from the University of Texas in 1964 and continued her studies at Union Theological Seminary. In 1964 she married Lawrence Seigel (now deceased) with whom she had one daughter, Malike N'Zinga. After receiving her B.A., she taught with the Freedom School in Carthage, Mississippi, and with the Congress of Racial Equality (CORE) Student Nonviolent Coordinating Committee program to interest students in reading. Her **work** with CORE led to her first full-length play production, *A First Step to Freedom* (1964), performed at the Sharon Waite Community Center in Harmony, Mississippi. Her belief that theater should educate is currently reflected in her "Open Script" project that invites students to collaborate in writing texts that reflect their own lives and values. Franklin was also youth director of Neighborhood House in Buffalo, an analyst in the U.S. Office of Economic Opportunity in New York City, lecturer in education at the City University of New York, visiting professor at the University of Iowa, resident director of Skidmore College, and playwright-in-residence at Brown University. In 1997 she was the Resident Scholar at the Schomburg Center for Research in Black Culture, where she wrote *Grey Panthers*, a series of ten-minute plays on the lives of black elders. She is currently a faculty member of the Harlem School of the Arts and producing artistic director of Blackgirl Ensemble Theatre, which she founded.

In 1971 Franklin earned acclaim for her play *Black Girl*, which opened at the Theater de Lys in New York and was later released as a **film**, a process she recounts in her book *Black Girl: From Genesis to Revelations* (1977). *Black Girl* centers around the choices of Billie Jean, a seventeen-year-old high school dropout who struggles to escape her **family**'s expectations of marriage and **motherhood** in order to go to college to pursue a career as a dancer. Similar themes of becoming and survival pervade Franklin's work, along with reflections on the **violence** that results when the black **community** internalizes oppressions imposed on them by white society. Franklin was also recognized for *Christchild* (1981)—the first in an octet of plays that charts the lives of four black children born to an intergenerational marriage—which explores the question of whether moral virtue can emerge from histories of suffering and sacrifice.

Her work has earned her numerous awards and grants, including a National Endowment for the Arts Creative Writing Fellowship, a Rockefeller Fellowship, and two National Endowment for the Arts Fellowships. She was awarded the New York Drama Desk Award for Most Promising Playwright in 1972 for *Black Girl* and won the 1992–1993 John F. Kennedy Center New American Play Award for *Christchild*.

See also Drama

Works By

Black Girl. New York: Dramatists Play Service, 1971.

Black Girl: From Genesis to Revelations. Washington, DC: Howard University Press, 1977.

Christchild. 1981. *Women Playwrights: The Best Plays of 1993*. Ed. Marisa Smith. Newbury, VT: Smith and Kraus, 1994. 41–94.

"The Enemy." *Black Short Story Anthology*. Ed. Woodie King. New York: Columbia University Press, 1972. 349–359.
Miss Honey's Young'uns. 1989. *Black Drama in America: An Anthology*. Ed. Darwin T. Turner. Washington, DC: Howard University Press, 1994. 615–665.
The Prodigal Sister. New York: Samuel French, 1974.
Two Mens'es Daughter. *The Best American Short Plays 1994–1995*. Ed. Howard Stein and Glenn Young. New York: Applause Theatre, 1995. 43–53.

Works About

Beauford, Fred. "A Conversation with *Black Girl*'s J. E. Franklin." *Black Creation* 3 (Fall 1971): 38–40.
Curb, Rosemary K. " 'Goin' through Changes': Mother-Daughter Confrontations in Three Recent Plays by Young Black Women." *Kentucky Folklore Record: A Regional Journal of Folklore and Folklife* 25 (1979): 96–102.
Lester, Elenore. "Growing Up Black and Female." Review of *Black Girl*. Dir. Shauneille Perry. *New York Times*, July 11, 1971, 5.
Parks, Carole A. "J. E. Franklin, Playwright." *Black World* 21 (April 1972): 49–50.

Stacy Grooters

FREEDOM

What is freedom? What does it mean to be free? In Western culture and **literature**, the ideal of freedom tends to turn upon certain ideological mainstays. Autonomy, independence, and, perhaps most important, individualism frame Western claims of freedom, certainly within an American context. Freedom is not simply an ideological concept, however; it is experiential. As experience, freedom is shaped by, indeed determined by, one's **identity** and subjectivity. Freedom, then, turns on difference. The language of personal liberty, articulated in such critical texts as the Declaration of Independence and the Constitution, creates a rhetoric of freedom that in its claims of inclusivity and universality perhaps intends to transcend difference but tends simply to deny the realities of those experiences shaped and determined by difference, especially those of **race**.

African Americans have been critically engaged in the project of crafting a concept of freedom in terms relevant to their lived experience. For a people whose original experience in America was one of chattel **slavery**, African Americans have of necessity been fiercely invested in both the material reality and ideological rhetoric of freedom. Just as the **history** of African-descended people in America has been a complex one, so, too, have the definitions and parameters of the ideal of freedom been complicated and evolving. Understandably, African Americans, in life and literature, have frequently framed freedom as the absence of subjugation or oppression. But like the Western rhetoric of liberty and individualism that neglects the experience of race, freedom as the simple absence of subjugation becomes an ahistorical frame that fails to take into account both critical historical shifts and experiences of difference within the African American experience, specifically those related to gender.

An inquiry into freedom within African American history, culture, and literature reveals a changing dynamic rather than a static ideal, discourse, or experience. At different points in history, African Americans have framed freedom in different ways, by turns as a material reality, a social experience, a psychic state, and a metaphysical condition. The particular vision of freedom in African American life, as reflected in African American literature, correlates with the particular manner in which freedom was threatened or denied. That is to say, within the bonds of chattel slavery freedom was envisioned as a physical reality; when one's physical self is considered the property of another, freedom would certainly be framed as the legal possession of one's **body**. Once emancipation occurred, physical bondage ended and the struggles for freedom moved from the material realm to the social; the challenge was to negotiate a place, both literally and figuratively, for these newly freed selves. Later, as civil rights battles were being fought on the social front, the quest for freedom turned inward: The psychic landscape became the site of the quest for a different kind of freedom, the liberation of consciousness.

Arguably, freedom, as rhetoric, discourse, and experience, serves as the critical point of departure in African American **literature**. The historical trajectory tracing freedom from material reality to metaphysical condition unfolds in the literature.

Nineteenth-century **slave narratives**, the autobiographical accounts of fugitive or former slaves, serve as testimonials to the brutal subjugation of an entire race and the indomitable will of an enslaved people to be free. These firsthand accounts of slavery and the quest for freedom reveal the extraordinary incongruities between the nation's rhetoric of freedom and the experience of hundreds of thousands of men, women, and children, close to 2 million human beings during the course of the Atlantic slave trade.

These narratives also reveal the gendered nature of slavery and, consequently, of freedom. To begin to understand the divergent lived and literary experiences of African American men and women with regard to freedom, it is crucial to consider the historical intersection of race and gender. For while men and women of African descent have a shared history based on their racial identity, their experiences have been fundamentally shaped, too, by their gender.

Any exploration of African Americans' struggles for freedom must begin with the experience of slavery. Slavery, while pernicious physically and psychically for all enslaved people, was a gendered experience. Both enslaved men and women were subjected to the dehumanization and subjugation of being considered the physical property of white slaveholders, but black women's physical selves, their gendered bodies, created a dimension to their experience of slavery that would later influence their vision of freedom. For the black female body itself has been the site of a singular kind of subjugation from the earliest presence of African-descended women on American shores. Enslaved women's gender, their female bodies, determined the contours of their captivity and their experience of enslavement. As the legal, physical property of their masters, black women's bodies were subjected not only to grueling labor but also to sexual exploitation at the hands of white slaveholders. Moreover, as children followed the condition of the mother, enslaved women gave birth to enslaved children; their bodies were used, then, to perpetuate the very system that enslaved them.

Just as it is critical to illuminate the particular and gendered experience of slavery endured by enslaved women, enslaved men's experiences within slavery must also be examined in order to fully understand the manner in which particular experiences of captivity determine specific, arguably gendered visions of freedom. No text speaks more directly to the gendered nature of captivity than the slave narrative. Studies of the literary depictions of African Americans' ideological and experiential engagement with the issue of freedom begin, expressly or implicitly, with these firsthand accounts of slavery and African Americans' original quests for freedom.

For years, **Frederick Douglass**'s *Narrative of the Life of Frederick Douglass, an American Slave* (1845) was the most widely read and studied work in this genre. In his narrative, Douglass describes his life as a slave and his quest for **literacy** and liberty. The story of his physical and psychic journey was for years *the* slave narrative, the voice of the authentic slave experience. What Douglass actually offers, however, is a very specific account of one enslaved person's experience, one enslaved *man's* experience. For Douglass's gender defines the nature of his enslavement and determines the course of his quest for freedom.

The stories of enslaved women began to emerge as part of black feminist scholars' recovery project in the late 1960s and 1970s. Only in the decades since has the impact of gender on the experiences of slavery begun to unfold in earnest, with Deborah Gray White's *Ar'n't I a Woman* (1985) serving as one of the earliest scholarly explorations of the ways in which gender shaped the slave experience for black women. The 1980s also brought a newly recovered and authenticated black woman–centered and –authored slave narrative to light, giving life and voice to the enslaved black woman's experience. This narrative, now considered a crucial one in the genre, is **Harriet Jacobs**'s *Incidents in the Life of a Slave Girl* (1861). Her text serves as a critically important companion work to Douglass's *Narrative*. Read together, these two works serve as the most compelling depictions of the gendered nature of slavery and, consequently, of freedom.

Douglass's account of slavery centers on his inability to be an autonomous, independent being with the right to reap the rewards of his labor and intellect. He writes to his sense of what slavery and freedom mean to him in the often-quoted line: "You have seen how a man was made a slave; you shall see how a slave was made a man." Within this declaration, Douglass expresses a vision of freedom not only as the antithesis of slavery but as the realization of manhood. Douglass's definition of freedom and manhood, crafted in relation to white constructions of manhood, a publicly recognized, agentic autonomy and individualism, would serve as points of departure for later black male writers. Arguably, then, African American male writers, from Douglass forward, have framed their literary visions of freedom within the Western cultural framework of individualism.

Jacobs's narrative is anchored in more corporeal and relational realities within the private sphere. Her narrative attests to the particularly gendered nature of slavery when she speaks to the particular experiences of women within the peculiar institution upon the birth of her second child, a girl. "When they told me my newborn babe was a girl, my heart was heavier than it had ever been before. Slavery is terrible for men; but it is far more terrible for women."

For Jacobs, slavery meant the perpetual threat of sexual violation, the denial of her desire to be chaste and, later, to marry her choice of mate and to mother her children. It becomes clear at many points in the narrative that Jacobs' role as a mother, this primary relational role, defines Jacobs's sense of herself as a woman. It is her inability to fulfill that relational role that defines her experience of slavery and drives her quest for freedom.

Douglass gained literacy and the liberty to go out into the world to write and lecture about his experiences; he became a self-authoring, autonomous individual. In contrast, Jacobs's freedom was defined by the negation of the threat of **rape** and the opening up of a space for her to mother her children; hers was a relational freedom. In simple terms, Douglass establishes a trajectory for black male writers in which freedom is posited as the realization of individualism, while Jacobs's literary legacy to black women writers is a decidedly relational vision of freedom.

Writers along both trajectories are steeped in a cultural ethos that informs their visions of freedom, however, frequently requiring a negotiation with the very dynamics of individualism and the relational. It is an ethos that emerges from a commitment to **community**. For despite the social forces that impacted them from the outside, perhaps even because of them, the black community has served throughout African American history as the space within which to lay claim to their humanity, to be free. The African American emphasis on community gives rise, then, to a particular vision of freedom, centered not on the individual but on the communal.

It is little wonder that the communal is a touchstone in African American culture and ideals of freedom, given the historic denial of black people's connections, both through kinship and within community. During slavery, displacement and separation were natural consequences of a system that treated black people not as members of humanity but as commodities; market value preceded, indeed generally negated, familial or emotional bonds. Children could be sold away from parents, spouses could be sold away from one another; relational bonds could simply be dissolved at the discretion or whim of the slaveholder. After centuries of enslavement and impermanence, **family**, relationship, and community would become central not only to African American culture and life but to African American identity itself.

By contrast, the self as individual is very much central to Western ideology and to a distinctly Western cultural ethos, the ethos of individualism. Not an ahistorical reality, radical individualism supplanted the classical understanding of human society in which the collective was the fundamental unit of human society. The modern concept of the self posits the individual as the critical unit of human society, preeminent to the collective, even engaged in a struggle to thwart the claims of the collective. Radical individualism, not simply a Western cultural ideal but a white, Western, patriarchal model of selfhood, serves as the wellsprings for the Western ideal of freedom.

By contrast, African American culture, defined by a particular and "peculiar" social experience, has historically centered on the communal as ethos and as the framework for identity. Arguably, African Americans, despite centuries of geographic and cultural separation, have drawn upon and retained African social and cultural patterns in which the self is a communal entity, a part of a larger, vitally important whole. Traditional African society organizes itself along kinship lines, and communal life is essentially the way of life. By virtue of the cultural retention of African models, the American slave experience that denied and dissolved kinship and relationship ties, and another century of collective struggle against the social, economic, and psychological forces of racism, African Americans have been deeply invested in the communal. The African American communal ethos serves, then, as a critical departure from the Western ethos of individualism and informs African Americans' visions of freedom in life and literature.

African American literature from the early twentieth century reveals black writers engaged in the negotiation for social freedom, both for the individual and the collective. The turn of the century and the early decades of the century saw the erection, fortification, and entrenchment of rigid, legally and socially sanctioned segregation and disenfranchisement that served as America's bulwark against the perceived threat of this newly freed caste to the white, patriarchal social order. African American writers such as W.E.B. Du Bois with his articulation of "double consciousness" gave voice to this experience of being "legally" free but still socially subjugated. Du Bois and Alain Locke became the leaders or deans of the New Negro movement, a movement of the black artists and intelligentsia that took as its charge to keep the renegotiation of African Americans' place in the American consciousness and social order, to forge a space for African-descended people to be truly free.

This period served as the context for the burgeoning of arts and literature traditionally referred to as the **Harlem Renaissance**. The writers of this period were, too, given the charge of using their literary works to forward the cause of this political and social project, by addressing the ills of racism and/or creating in the realm of **fiction** depictions of a sector of African American society who, by virtue of their educational, cultural, and professional achievements and their economic status, bore a resemblance to a certain segment of white America. By illuminating the harrowing effects of racism, while emphasizing the similarities across racial lines between these two classes, black writers' works might serve to make white Americans reenvision the African American race as a whole, and the sanctioned racism of social segregation and political and economic disenfranchisement might be mitigated. Works like **Nella Larsen**'s *Quicksand* (1928) and *Passing* (1929) and Jessie Redmon Fauset's *There Is Confusion* (1924) contributed to this project by focusing on characters from the black upper classes often engaged in a struggle against the strictures of racial discrimination. In many ways, these works made explicit the need for an end of strife between the races and, implicitly, proffered a case for racial equality, the opening up of a greater social freedom for black people.

A second generation of Harlem Renaissance writers, however, had no qualms about focusing on the folk, both in the rural **South** and the urban North, while simultaneously laying claim to an equal share of the national ideal of freedom. Writers like **Zora Neale Hurston** and **Langston Hughes**, in their works *Their Eyes Were Watching God* (1937) and *The Ways of White Folks* (1934), did not engage the issue of interracial strife by focusing on African American characters and life or offering critiques of European Americans. These writers focused on a cultural specificity without wavering from an implicit claim to racial equality and, with the attendant social, economic, and political enfranchisement, freedom.

Writers in the second half of the twentieth century, heirs to the legacies of the **civil rights movement**, moved the search for freedom onto psychic and metaphysical terrains. As legally sanctioned segregation and disenfranchisement gave way to a newly negotiated social space for African Americans, African American literature moved beyond the modernist focus on order and identity to a postmodern concern with dis-order and the expansive or liberatory possibilities of rewriting narratives of history and identity. For while African American writers were turning in the direction of the postmodern, a number of them also turned back to the past and the experience of slavery. **Neo-slave narratives** and other fictional works like **Octavia Butler**'s *Kindred* (1979), **Charles Johnson**'s *Oxherding Tale* (1982), **Sherley Anne Williams**'s *Dessa Rose* (1986), and **Toni Morrison**'s *Beloved* (1987) return to the past, illuminating within the narrative space the historical experience of African-descended people, retrieving them from historical narratives that had rendered them slaves to reveal them as enslaved people crafting lives out of the most life-denying of circumstances, physically, psychically, and spiritually resisting a would-be dehumanizing subjugation to engage in the quest for freedom.

The literary trajectory from nineteenth-century slave narratives to twentieth-century postmodern fictions of slavery traces the transformations in the historical discourses of freedom within African American history. Clearly, as African Americans moved through various phases of oppression and subjugation, physically, socially, psychically, and spiritually, they have also found ways in which to move beyond or rise above the forces that denied them claim to their own visions of freedom.

Works About

Andrews, William L. *To Tell a Free Story: The First Century of Afro-American Autobiography.* Urbana: University of Illinois Press, 1988.

Carby, Hazel. *Reconstructing Womanhood: The Emergence of the Afro-American Woman Novelist.* New York: Oxford University Press, 1995.

Giddings, Paula J. *When and Where I Enter: The Impact of Black Women on Race and Sex in America.* New York: Amistad, 1996.

Patterson, Orlando. *Slavery and Social Death: A Comparative Study.* Cambridge: Harvard University Press, 1985.

Stepto, Robert. *From Behind the Veil: A Study of Afro-American Narrative.* Urbana: University of Illinois Press, 1991.

Sundquist, Eric. *To Wake the Nations: Race in the Making of American Literature.* Cambridge, MA: Belknap Press, 1994.

Yolanda M. Manora

 **G**

GAINES, ERNEST (1933–)

Ernest J. Gaines was born on the River Lake plantation in Oscar, Louisiana. Although he moved to the San Francisco, California, area in his teens, his **plantation** youth shaped his novels and short stories. All of his works are set in fictional St. Raphael Parish, with its towns of Bayonne and Morgan, on the west side of the Mississippi River. The capital city of Louisiana, Baton Rouge, east of the Mississippi River, acts as a geographical marker. Gaines's works are set in the years from the mid-1940s to the early 1970s, an era that marked a transition in the **South** from the Jim Crow era to the **civil rights movement** era. All of Gaines's novels and short stories focus on African American characters but include the presence of whites, generally Cajuns and Creoles. He also focuses on the shift from black-centered plantation farming and ties to the land for the descendants of slaves to a land that is taken over by white farmers.

Gaines's first novel, *Catherine Carmier* (1964), centers on Jackson Bradley, a twenty-two-year-old young man who returns to his Aunt Charlotte's **home** on the plantation after completing college in California. Charlotte is convinced that Jackson has returned home to teach the children of the area, but he already knows he will not stay. When he returns, Jackson realizes his **love** for his childhood friend/sweetheart Catherine, who is devoted to her **family** and committed to staying on the plantation to care for her parents, especially her father, Raoul, as they age. Catherine is Creole, separated from Jackson by skin color and by her father's vehement opposition to mixing with "common" black people. Even as children, Jackson and Catherine had to keep their friendship secret from her father. Raoul is the last remaining farmer who has not been run out by the whites who want to plow under the black quarters, graveyards, and churches for crops. He holds on to Catherine like he holds on to his land.

In the battle between Jackson and Raoul for Catherine we have the embodiment of common themes in Gaines's work: old versus new, young versus old, tradition versus change, city versus country. All of the young people have left the plantation for **work** in cities or to go to school, like Jackson. There is the common battle of fair economic access to resources and income. There is also the battle for justice under a legal system that does not recognize the black man as equal, deserving equal protection. In addition to these feminist themes that transcend gender boundaries—economics, justice, opportunity—we see a feminist battle uniquely Catherine's own in the novel. She is torn between two men who identify themselves through her. Unlike her sister Lillian, who leaves the area and feels no attachment to the people or the place, Catherine remains bound by what she sees as her duty to her father. She refuses to see that she deserves a life of her own, that they have had their youths and lives, that she is entitled to being with the man of her choice.

Even Jackson, however, defines Catherine through himself. That she deserves an education, a chance to see a bigger world than that of the plantation, that she is someone more than her daddy's precious girl or the lover/fiancée Jackson wants her to be, is never discussed. The culminating battle between Raoul and Jackson is discussed in terms of how it affects each of them, not what it means for Catherine. Only Lillian attempts to help Catherine realize that she is a woman of worth, a lesson Catherine rejects, for she ultimately chooses to remain on the plantation with Raoul. The novel ends abruptly at the end of the fight between the two men, with no last commentary on or from Catherine, who remains as voiceless as she has been throughout the novel.

Gaines's second novel, *Of Love and Dust* (1967), continues his exploration of the relationships between men and women, men and the land, black men against white law. In this novel Gaines includes more of the "aunt" characters who figure prominently in much of his work. Miss Julie Rand is the old woman who enlists the narrator, thirty-three-year-old Jim Kelly, a respected, steady plantation hand, to watch out for her godson, Marcus, who has stabbed a man but has been bailed out by the white owner of the plantation, Marshall Hebert. Marcus is young, arrogant, and determined not to serve time anywhere, either in jail or on the plantation. Miss Julie wants Jim to help Marcus learn to rein himself in, to learn to take responsibility for himself and his actions. While learning the backbreaking work of pulling corn, Marcus is driven by Jim, by other farmhands, and by the white overseer of the plantation, Sidney Bonbon.

Marcus is determined to take up with Bonbon's black mistress, Pauline, with whom he has two children. Bonbon is in love with Pauline, more than with his white wife, Louise. The whole plantation is alarmed when Marcus makes known his interest in Pauline, and no one can stop him from making advances toward her. Pauline rejects Marcus, and for this he seeks revenge on Bonbon. Marcus then turns his attentions to Louise, thinking that cuckolding Bonbon is the solution to asserting his **freedom** and his manhood. The other black people on the plantation know that if Marcus and Louise are caught, Marcus will be killed. Aunt Margaret, Louise's housekeeper, is especially appalled because she is, in essence, a coconspirator with Marcus and Louise, since she did not tell Bonbon immediately when the couple first started their relationship. Marcus and Louise decide to leave together to go North, where interracial couples are more accepted. Their plans are discovered, and Bonbon kills Marcus at the time he and Louise have set to run away.

From a feminist perspective, this novel makes clear how women are pawns in men's games. At first, Pauline has no choice about Bonbon taking her for his mistress. While he loves her and she does grow to love him, both understand that they can never have an "open" relationship anywhere but on the plantation. Louise, too, has no say about her husband's infidelities. Nor does she have a say with other men in her life. Her father and brothers have thrown her to Bonbon, Bonbon throws her aside, and Marcus, at first, uses her to attack Bonbon, but then realizes he has feelings for her. However, she still is the excuse for him to run away, which he threatens to do throughout the novel, even before he is involved with her. She remains an appendage to his wants and desires. Other women are also bound by white men's, then black men's rules. Aunt Margaret must be quiet to protect herself; Miss Julie must enlist Jim's help, for she has no "pull" with Marcus; Marcus rejects his mother's influence as well.

Bloodline and Other Stories (1968) sees somewhat of a transition away from the rather single-dimensional female characters of the first two books. "A Long Day in November" tells the story of a couple's daylong separation through the eyes of six-year-old Sonny. His mother, Amy, is fed up with her husband's, Eddie's, reckless attention to his car. Eddie is gone too long too often, so she packs up and moves down the quarters to her mother's home. The separation affects Sonny in each part of his life. He has trouble with school, he is torn between the parents, he is bewildered by his grandmother's anger at his father, he must examine his allegiances.

The women in this story are more fully realized than female characters in the earlier works. Even though her move to her mother's finally acts to wake up Eddie and commands his attention, Amy is weak and vacillates in her feelings for Eddie. She even has him beat her (despite his opposition to it) at the end of the story to justify his manhood and solidify their separate roles. But her mother is the strong, no-nonsense woman of much of Gaines's work. She readily takes a shotgun to Eddie, twice. She is independent and wants that same strength for her daughter. Madame Toussaint, the fortuneteller and adviser, also acts as a strong presence, perhaps the female character who most reflects Eddie's weaknesses. Eddie whines to her, first about what she charges (thus his rejection of her need to make a living and her need to exact payment for services rendered), then about the advice she gives (he does not want to burn his car; he wants to sell it). Madame Toussaint is adamant about burning the car, and eventually Eddie does it. Doing so is the show of good faith Amy needs to return to him.

Another story in *Bloodline*, "Just Like a Tree," recognizes more women in the strong-aunt tradition Gaines develops so extensively in his work. Aunt Fe is the **community** mother who is to leave to go live with family in the city. The story is told through the eyes of those around her, with the common threads being her goodness, her generosity, her indomitable spirit.

"The Sky Is Gray" is the portrait of perhaps one of Gaines's strongest women characters, Olivia. Her son, James, narrates. The story focuses on having to take a day away from the fields to have James's tooth pulled. As they journey through town, we see Olivia in a number of ways. James tells us repeatedly about Olivia's strength and how she does not like to show weakness or for anyone around her to do so, but in their travels it is clear that, despite her seeming hardness (Olivia makes eight-year-old James kill for food birds he wanted to play with), Olivia is altruistically maternal. She is silent during an argument about God in the dentist's office; James is allowed to reach his own conclusions. She feigns buying an ax handle so James can get warm. She is aware of her own honor: She pulls a knife and threatens a man who comes on to her. She is independent: She rejects the charity of a white storekeeper. Throughout all of these events, she teaches James to be a man, exemplifying those traits she deems worthy—care, honor, dignity, self-reliance, self-respect, work—in her own carriage.

It is in Gaines's earliest well-known book that we have his strongest woman: *The Autobiography of Miss Jane Pittman* (1971). The reader meets Jane when she is 110. She is a former slave who has lived to see the civil rights era. Jane is, from the beginning, well aware of herself and the need to speak up and act how she knows she needs to, no matter the consequences. As a freed child, Jane is determined to go north, to Ohio. But she is unaware of how far Ohio is from Louisiana, and thus we see her as she lives from day to day, in her quest to realize her freedom. In the first part of her journey, she cares for the orphaned Ned, a boy she takes as her own. She must work very hard for them to live, doing plantation work, cooking. As Ned grows up and away, she "marries" Joe Pittman, a man she loves and who, in turn, loves her. When he is killed after they have 10 years together, she must once again face the world around her through hard work and the boundaries white society puts on her. Jane must exist in what white people determine are her opportunities: fieldwork, housework, child care. Her interests outside of work are her own: boxing and baseball. Through all of her life, including Ned's devastating **death** because of his civil rights work, Jane remains stable, strong, and dignified. Whether she fends off black and white oppressors in the Reconstruction era or seeks to end segregation, Jane is at the end of her life what she is when we first meet her: willing to take risks for what she believes in.

In My Father's House (1978) is a predominantly male-centered book. By the absence of women, however, the plight of females during the middle part of the twentieth century is made abundantly clear. The Reverend Phillip Martin sowed a wild youth before he found God. As a young man he had three children with a woman with whom he had a long relationship; she moved to California, and he did not see or hear of them for more than twenty years. The older son from that relationship returns when he is twenty-eight, but Phillip does not recognize him right away. The young man, Etienne, first calls himself "Robert X." He is jailed for vagrancy; he is dirty, mysterious, and cryptic to the community. When Phillip recognizes who Etienne is at a civil rights meeting, he collapses, explaining why to no one. Etienne is then arrested, and Phillip goes to bail him out. He is only allowed to do so by the white sheriff because he promises to stop his involvement in a picketing action against a white storekeeper. Phillip is seen as a traitor, and no one knows why.

As Phillip learns about Etienne's past, we see the condition of women. Etienne has come to kill Phillip because of the hardships he, his single mother, and his siblings faced without Phillip. Etienne's sister was raped, and the other brother killed the rapist. The mother, Johanna, wasted away, and Etienne blames Phillip. We also see Phillip's wife Alma pushed aside, alienated, and ignored by Phillip as he runs his church and civil rights activities, then also later as he seeks to discover what happened to Johanna and to deal with Etienne. Phillip is slow to learn about the effect he has on the women in his life.

A Gathering of Old Men (1983), like *In My Father's House*, is focused on men, with women, more specifically black women, generally background characters. Eighteen men gather to say each has killed the white bully Beau Boutan. They are determined to confound the sheriff's investigation, even though he is sure he knows which did it. Only one could have done it. Each man takes the killing as his opportunity to assert, finally, near the end of his life, the manhood that white plantation owners and law have stripped from him.

When it is discovered at the end that Beau was killed by Charley, a very large, very black man whom Beau has tormented, and who has run away, letting the other men stand for him, we see the men changed and with a bit more pride in their steps. Charley dies after killing a second white man in a gun battle, saying repeatedly that he finally is a man, no longer a "boy." So he is the one who most remains in the state of manhood he claims that day, even though the others stand in a way they did not figure they had left in themselves.

What remains a problem of feminist inquiry in this story is that each black man who asserts that he killed Beau is prompted to do so by a white woman, Candy, the heiress of the plantation upon which the killing takes place; this underscores the powerlessness of the men to do and act for themselves. With Candy orchestrating the stand against the sheriff, the question remains as to how independent each man truly is. Charley, however, does indeed declare his manhood without Candy at the helm of his actions and is proven to be the man he claims to be.

It is finally in *A Lesson before Dying* (1993) that we see much of the web of stories, themes, and characters come together in what is perhaps Gaines's finest work to date. When Jefferson, a young field hand, is convicted of a murder he did not commit, he is sentenced to death by electric chair. In the closing arguments of his trial, his own attorney refers to Jefferson as a hog. His godmother, Miss Emma, enlists the help of the schoolteacher, a man named Grant Wiggins, who is restless, angry at life in the quarters, and angry at the system that falsely convicted Jefferson, to help Jefferson learn to be a man before he is electrocuted. Grant's battles with himself, his Aunt Lou, Miss Emma, and his girlfriend and the plight of the children in the quarters all reveal the racism, segregation, and hopelessness that produced Jefferson. Grant feels his efforts are futile, that the damage done Jefferson reaches far beyond being called a hog.

Because the women of the novel—Miss Emma and Aunt Lou—are exemplary "strong-aunt" community women as Gaines has repeatedly appear in his works, they are the driving forces of the novel: They are, to borrow phrasing, irresistible forces and immoveable objects. They will not be told "no," neither about Jefferson's resistance to see himself as a man nor in Grant's reluctance to teach Jefferson. In the end, they get exactly what they want: Jefferson recognizes his manhood.

Works By

The Autobiography of Miss Jane Pittman. New York: Dial, 1971.
Bloodline and Other Stories. New York: Dial, 1968.
Catherine Carmier. New York: Atheneum, 1964.
A Gathering of Old Men. New York: Knopf, 1983.
In My Father's House. New York: Knopf, 1978.
A Lesson before Dying. New York: Knopf, 1993.
Of Love and Dust. New York: Dial, 1967.

Works About

Babb, Valerie Melissa. *Ernest Gaines*. Boston: Twayne, 1991.
Byerman, Keith. "Negotiations: The Quest for a Middle Way in the Fiction of James Alan McPherson and Ernest Gaines." *Fingering the Jagged Grain: Tradition and Form in Recent Black Fiction*. Athens: University of Georgia Press, 1985. 41–103.
Estes, David, ed. *Critical Reflections on the Fiction of Ernest J. Gaines*. Athens: University of Georgia Press, 1994.
Gaudet, Marcia, and Carl Wooton. *Porch Talk with Ernest Gaines*. Baton Rouge: Louisiana State University Press, 1990.
Lowe, John. *Conversations with Ernest Gaines*. Jackson: University Press of Mississippi, 1995.

Catherine E. Lewis

GETTING MOTHER'S BODY

Suzan-Lori Parks's 2003 debut novel is set in west Texas, where she herself spent time as a youth while her father was in Vietnam. The characters emerged from her fondness for and **memories** of the landscape, the big sky, and arid landscape. The novel resembles William Faulkner's *As I Lay Dying* (1930) in that both stories focus on the burials of dead women and are told by **family** members and the women themselves. Each story has a journey and a pregnant woman; however, where the Bundren family journeys to bury the mother the way she has instructed them, Billy Beede and her accomplices in *Getting Mother's Body* are sojourning to exhume the body of Willa Mae, her own mother.

It is 1963, and Billy Beede, a sixteen year-old black girl in rural Lincoln, Texas, finds herself pregnant and unmarried. After Billy travels to Texhoma to marry Snipes, the unborn child's father, and realizes that he is already married, she is determined to rid herself of everything that is associated with him. This includes the wedding dress, which she begins to burn but then opts not to because the return of it may help her to pay for a safe abortion. She is catapulted into a larger self-motivated quest once she sees that piecing together the little money she has will not be enough to pay for the abortion. In her desperation, she realizes she is very similar to her mother who surfaces in the novel as a **blues** singer performing songs about her ability to see a person's "hole," or weak spot, that helps her to get their money. Billy Beede, too, learns to see "holes" or make them in order to free herself from Snipes.

Parks tells the story of a young girl willing to take up the dead in order not to end up like her mother, who bled to death from a self-botched abortion. Billy Beede steals her mother's ex-lover's truck and travels to LaJunta, Arizona, to dig up her mother's **body** for the jewels that Dill said are buried with her. There is urgency for Billy; not only must she abort the baby before it is unsafe to do so, but she has to get to LaJunta before the new shopping center is built on the land where her mother has been buried. She is accompanied by her Aunt June and Uncle Teddy, who raised her and who also hope that they will be able to relish in Willa Mae's treasure. Aunt June, who has been one-legged since her childhood, wants to buy a new limb if there is one in her color for sale, and Uncle Teddy wants a new house and church for his family. And Dill Smiles, who was betrayed by Willa Mae when she exposed to the town that she was **passing** for a man, is in fast pursuit because she never buried the treasure. A scorned Dill Smiles used the money to finance her own pig farm that reaps her the rewards of financial independence, something few black Lincoln residents, let alone women, are able to attain.

Parks is successful at infusing comedy, desperation, and the meaning of family into the novel. In addition, *Getting Mother's Body* is also important as it creates a **community** of people who in the segregated **South** have not lost hope; many people in the novel join Billy in the journey to change their lives. Equally significant is Parks's creation of nontraditional female characters who win and lose on their journey to autonomy.

Works About

"*Getting Mother's Body*: An Exclusive Excerpt from the Pulitzer Prize–Winning Playwright's Sexy Debut Novel." *Essence* (May 2003).

McHenry, Susan L. Review of *Getting Mother's Body*, by Suzan Lori-Parks. *Black Issues Book Review* (July–August 2003): 54.

Review of *Getting Mother's Body*. *Publisher's Weekly.com*, May 19, 2003. publishers weekly.com.

Brandon L. A. Hutchinson

GIBSON, PATRICIA JOANN (1951–)

Patricia Joann Gibson, also known as P. J. Gibson, was born in 1951 in Pittsburgh, Pennsylvania. She was raised by her grandparents until the age of five, when she moved to Trenton, New Jersy. After high school, Gibson went on to attend Keuka College, an all-women's college in upstate New York, where in 1973 she received a B.A. in drama, religion, and English. After receiving a prestigious Schubert Fellowship to study at Brandeis University, Gibson pursued an M.F.A. in theater arts. Upon graduation, she taught creative writing at Boston College from 1975 to 1976 and then went on to teach at the Frederick Douglass Creative Arts Center, a nonprofit arts center in New York City.

Gibson is first and foremost a playwright, having written thirty-two plays to date, three of which have been published and seventeen of which have been produced for stage. Her work is noted for often including educated and professional African American characters in stark contrast to many depictions of African Americans in popular culture. She has also written **poetry** and short stories, including two short stories and a poem in the anthology *Erotique Noire/Black Erotica*. The source of her creative inspiration is black women, and she is often quoted as saying, "If I live to be 150, I still won't have enough time to write about all the black women inside of me."

Gibson's plays have been performed throughout the world, including across the United States, Europe, and Africa. Over the years she has also accumulated numerous awards and honors including a grant from the National Endowment for the Arts, two Audelco Awards, which are given to black theatrical artists and producers, as well as six playwriting commissions. She has laid her hands on the Sidewalk of Fame of the Bushfire Theatre of Performing Arts in Philadelphia, served as artist-in-residence at the University of Michigan, guest lectured at Yale University, and holds a key to the city of Indianapolis.

Her most recognized work is the play *Long Time since Yesterday*, written in 1985 and published by Samuel French in 1986. The story focuses on five sorority sisters who reunite twenty years after college at the **home** of a classmate who has recently committed suicide. Alisa, Panzi, Thelma, Babbs, and Laveer have all reached individual levels of success when they reunite in

New Jersey to mourn the **death** of Janeen, their classmate who committed suicide at the age of thirty-eight. Through a series of flashbacks, the women examine both the past and the present. They come together to mourn, to understand, and to examine their own lives. *Long Time since Yesterday* is a story about women negotiating the complex web of relationships, secrets, **sexuality**, politics, gender, life, and death. Over the years, *Long Time since Yesterday* has been performed throughout the country, including at Johns Hopkins University and the New Horizon Theater. Gibson is currently an associate professor of English at John Jay College of Criminal Justice in New York City.

Works By

Destiny's Daughters: 9 Voices of P. J. Gibson. New York: 1st Books, 2002.
Erotique Noir/Black Erotica. Ed. Miriam DeCosta-Willis, Reginald Martin, and Roseann Bell. New York: Anchor Books, 1992.
Long Time since Yesterday: A Drama in Two Acts. New York: Samuel French, 1986.

Works About

Jordan, Shirley. *Broken Silences: Interviews with Black and White Women Writers.* New Brunswick, NJ: Rutgers University Press, 1993.
Perkins, Kathy, and Roberta Uno, eds. *Contemporary Plays by Women of Color.* Boston: Routledge Press, 1995.
Wilkerson, Margaret. *Nine Plays by Black Women.* New York: New American Library, 1986.

Roxane Gay

GIOVANNI, NIKKI (1943–)

One of the most popular black American poets of the second half of the twentieth century, Nikki Giovanni was born Yolande Cornelia Giovanni, Jr., in Knoxville, Tennessee. She was the second of two daughters born to Gus Jones and Yolande Cornelia Giovanni. Though born in Knoxville, Giovanni was raised in Cincinnati, Ohio, but she returned to the city of her birth to live with her maternal grandparents while she completed two years of high school there. Her grandmother, Louvenia Terrell Watson, had a profound influence on Giovanni's life, encouraging her to stand up for social justice and to always speak her mind. This outspokenness has become a lifelong trait and a hallmark of her **poetry**.

But as a young woman, this characteristic was often seen as threatening to others, and in 1961 she was expelled from Fisk University after her first semester for not following rules that seemed to her archaic and out of touch. Three years later, with a new dean in place, Giovanni was encouraged to reenter Fisk, which she did—with great success. While there, she reestablished the Student Nonviolent Coordinating Committee on campus, served as editor of the campus literary magazine, and participated in the Fisk Writers Conference, which allowed her the opportunity to meet several prominent black writers such as Robert Hayden, **Margaret Walker**, and **Amiri Baraka** (then LeRoi Jones). In January 1967, she graduated with honors and a degree in **history**.

Just two months later, her beloved grandmother died. Working through the grief of such a loss, Giovanni focused her attention on her writing, creating the poems that would go into her first book of poetry, *Black Feeling Black Talk* (1968). Meanwhile she also organized the first Black Arts Festival in Cincinnati and attended the Detroit Conference of Unity and Art, meeting many protest leaders while there and becoming more and more involved in the fight against social injustice for black Americans. She received a grant from the Ford Foundation that allowed her to move to Wilmington, Delaware, and enroll in the University of Pennsylvania's School of Social Work. With borrowed money, Giovanni published *Black Feeling Black Talk* herself. In its first year of publication, the book sold more than 10,000 copies, garnering Giovanni a lot of popular and critical attention. She dropped out of the School of Social Work, and in 1968, she received a grant from the National Endowment for the Arts. She moved to New York to begin taking classes in the M.F.A. program at Columbia University's School of Fine Arts.

At the end of 1968, Giovanni received a grant from the Harlem Arts Council and, along with the money made from sales of her first book, published her second book of poems titled *Black Judgment*. This volume also did extremely well, selling 6,000 copies within its first three months of publication. These first two books of poetry, which she later combined into one volume, offer many poems that protest the condition of black Americans within a racist white system. She, like many other writers of the **Black Arts Movement**, wrote in experimental forms using lowercase letters, fused words, and slang words, including epithets previously excluded from literary works. The experimental forms echoed the mood and themes of the poems themselves, poems that were fueled on rage and hope, poems that called for change now, and a change that was taken, not passively accepted.

Giovanni's poetry was widely popular but not always critically accepted, even by other writers within the Black Arts Movement. But she chose to forge her own path in life. For instance, in 1968 she gave birth to her only child, a son she named Thomas Watson, as a single woman, never revealing the father's name. At the time, this decision was as revolutionary as her poems. Her poetry was not all militant protest, though. Poems such as "The True Import of Present Dialog Black vs. Negro," which takes an urgent, militant tone, are also juxtaposed with poems such as "Nikki-Rosa," one of the most anthologized and beloved of all her work. The latter poem's title is taken from Giovanni's childhood nickname, and it examines the poet's childhood remembrances. But the poem explores what it means for a black poet to do the very act of remembering. She points out that too often the childhoods of black people are seen in negative ways; poverty and abuse are emphasized, especially by white biographers who, by their very nature, cannot comprehend that there was far more in these childhoods that was positive. While the negative was there, Giovanni shows that the **love** and nurturing of black **families** overwhelm and overcome it to produce happy **memories** and healthy families.

While her poems were finding great success, Giovanni began teaching college classes. She edited and published a book of poems by black women; perhaps one of the first such anthologies ever, *Night Comes Softly* (1970) included poems by well-known poets as well as by the new and unknown. That same year, 1970, Giovanni also saw her first two volumes of poems published together as a single volume by William Morrow Publisher, and she published her third book *Re: Creation* through Broadside Press. By this time she had become so well known that she was named "Woman of the Year" by *Ebony* magazine.

A year later, Giovanni published *Gemini: An Extended Autobiographical Statement on My First Twenty-five Years of Being a Black Poet*, a piece that was part **autobiography**, part polemic, and part personal statement of belief. It reveals a poet struggling to make sense of her personal history within the larger story of black women and black history. *Gemini* was nominated for the National Book Award in 1973, and her successes continued to grow. Boston University offered to house her papers within its Mugar Memorial Library, an agreement that continues to this day. She also received a number of honors and awards, including being named "Best Poet" by *Contact* magazine in 1971 as well as being named "Woman of the Year" by *Mademoiselle* in 1971 and by *Ladies' Home Journal* in 1972.

Unafraid of change and a prolific writer, Giovanni began working in other genres, and through the 1970s her poetry continued to explore other thematic material. In particular, she began writing poems for children: *Spin a Soft Black Song* in 1971, *Ego-Tripping* in 1973, and *Vacation Time* in 1980. She also began appearing on the television show *Soul*, an entertainment and talk show produced by Ellis Haizlip, one of the first black producers at PBS. The show hosted a number of black luminaries, and Giovanni made several appearances. In 1971, she taped special segments of the show with **James Baldwin**, transcripts of which she would later edit to create the book *A Dialogue: James Baldwin and Nikki Giovanni* (published in 1973). She would go on to establish another famous dialogue, this one with Margaret Walker. Giovanni published *A Poetic Equation: Conversations between Nikki Giovanni and Margaret Walker* in 1974. These dialogues reveal a theme that can be found consistently through Giovanni's work—how individuals come to their own **identity** via the larger backdrop of black history, especially through their experience within black families.

This theme can be found in her book of poems *My House*, which she published in 1972 and which was named one of the best books of the year by the American Library Association. That same year she joined the National Council of Negro Women and became the youngest person ever to receive an honorary doctorate from Wilberforce University, the nation's oldest black college. She became the frequent subject in dozens of magazines and even made an appearance on *The Tonight Show*. Far from slowing her down,

Giovanni's success seemed to spur her onward. She began publishing in yet another format when she began releasing spoken-word albums, one of which, *Truth Is on Its Way*, won the National Association of Television and Radio Announcers award for Best Spoken Word Album in 1972. She published other spoken-word albums to great success: *Like a Ripple on a Pond* (1973), *The Way I Feel* (1975), *Legacies* (1976), and *The Reason I Like Chocolate* (1976).

In 1978, her father had a stroke and was subsequently diagnosed with cancer. Giovanni and her son moved back to Cincinnati to help out her family. Her father died that same year, one day after her thirty-ninth birthday. She remained in Cincinnati with her mother for several years. During the decade of the 1980s, Giovanni continued to adhere to an impressive **work** ethic. While she kept a busy schedule of speaking engagements and readings, she also held teaching posts: first, at Ohio State University as a visiting professor, and then at Mount Saint Joseph's College as a professor of creative writing. In 1983, the same year that she published *Those Who Ride the Night Winds*, she also was named Woman of the Year by the Cincinnati YMCA. In fact, the honors seemed to grow during this time period. In 1985, Giovanni was named to the Ohio Women's Hall of Fame as well as named an Outstanding Woman of Tennessee, and in 1986 she served as the Duncan Artist in Residence for the Taft Museum in Cincinnati. A year later, she was the subject of a PBS documentary, *Spirit to Spirit*.

All the while, she continued writing, producing a collection of essays called *Sacred Cows...and Other Edibles* in 1988. Her volume of children's poems, *Vacation Time* (1980), was awarded the Children's Reading Roundtable of Chicago Award. She moved to Blacksburg, Virginia, after accepting a permanent position as a full professor of English at Virginia Tech, but her teaching efforts went beyond the traditional classroom when she began a creative writing group at a retirement home. She later edited a collection of writings from this writing group. She published another collection of essays on surviving academic life in her book *Racism 101* (1994), as well as the twentieth-anniversary edition of her book *Ego-Tripping and Other Poems for Young Readers*.

While she continued to win numerous awards, honors, and even keys to cities, Giovanni also earned the title of cancer survivor after she was diagnosed with lung cancer in early 1995. Though she lost one of her lungs and three ribs to the cancer, she survived to continue writing and teaching. Though her recovery might have been expected to slow down her considerable schedule, her poetic output seemed to keep apace with the wide variety of awards and honors she continued to win. For instance, Giovanni was named the Gloria D. Smith Professor of Black Studies at Virginia Tech, and she published a number of books in the latter half of the 1990s. In 1996 alone, she published *The Selected Poems of Nikki Giovanni*, *The Genie in the Jar*, and *The Sun Is So Quiet* (the last two are children's books). And in 1997 she published another book of poems, this one called *Love Poems*.

While she has received numerous honorary doctorates from universities, Virginia Tech named Giovanni to its highest honor when it awarded her the

University Distinguished Professor in 1999. That same year she published another collection of poetry, *Blues: For All the Changes*, for which she received an NAACP (National Association for the Advancement of Colored People) Image Award. She won another Image Award for her 2002 book *Quilting the Black-Eyed Pea: Poems and Not Quite Poems*, and her spoken-word CD, *The Nikki Giovanni Poetry Collection*, was a finalist for the 2003 Grammy Award in the spoken-word category. Finally, and most fittingly, Giovanni won the first Rosa Parks Woman of Courage Award, and it is an award well deserved for a writer who so warmly embraces change, who welcomes growth, and who writes fearlessly. Currently, Giovanni works at Virginia Tech, and she continues to inspire students, readers, and audiences everywhere.

Works By

Black Feeling Black Talk. 1968. Detroit: Broadside Press, 1970.
Black Feeling Black Talk/Black Judgment. New York: Morrow, 1970.
Black Judgment. Detroit: Broadside Press, 1968.
Blues: For All the Changes: New Poems. New York: Morrow, 1999.
Cotton Candy on a Rainy Day. New York: Morrow, 1978.
A Dialogue: James Baldwin and Nikki Giovanni. Philadelphia: Lippincott, 1973.
Ego-Tripping and Other Poems for Young People. Chicago: Lawrence Hill, 1973.
Gemini: An Extended Autobiographical Statement on My First Twenty-five Years of Being a Black Poet. Indianapolis: Bobbs-Merrill, 1971.
The Genie in the Jar. New York: Holt, 1996.
Love Poems. New York: Morrow, 1997.
My House. New York: Morrow, 1972.
Night Comes Softly: An Anthology of Black Female Voices. Ed. Nikki Giovanni. Newark, NJ: Medic Press, 1970.
Poem of Angela Yvonne Davis. New City: Afro Arts, 1970.
A Poetic Equation: Conversations between Nikki Giovanni and Margaret Walker. Washington, DC: Howard University Press, 1974.
Racism 101. New York: Morrow, 1994.
Re: Creation. Detroit: Broadside Press, 1970.
Sacred Cows . . . and Other Edibles. New York: Morrow, 1988.
The Selected Poems of Nikki Giovanni (1968–1995). New York: Morrow, 1996.
Spin a Soft Black Song: Poems for Children. 1971. New York: Farrar, Straus, 1987.
The Sun Is So Quiet. New York: Holt, 1996.
Those Who Ride the Night Winds. New York: Morrow, 1983.
Vacation Time: Poems for Children. New York: Morrow, 1980.
The Women and the Men. New York: Morrow, 1975.

Works About

Becerra, Cynthia S. "The Poetry of Nikki Giovanni." *Masterpieces of African-American Literature*. Ed. Frank N. Magill. New York: Salem Press, 1992. 399–401.

Evans, Mari, ed. *Black Women Writers (1950–1980): A Critical Evaluation.* Garden City, NY: Anchor Press/Doubleday, 1984.

Fowler, Virginia, ed. *Conversations with Nikki Giovanni.* Jackson: University Press of Mississippi, 1992.

——. *Nikki Giovanni.* Boston: Twayne, 1992.

Norris, Emma Coburn. *"Gemini: An Extended Autobiographical Statement on My First Twenty-five Years of Being a Black Poet." Masterpieces of African-American Literature.* Ed. Frank N. Magill. New York: Salem Press, 1992. 182–185.

Tate, Claudia, ed. *Black Women Writers at Work.* New York: Continuum, 1983. 60–78.

Walters, Jennifer. "Nikki Giovanni and Rita Dove: Poets Redefining." *Journal of Negro History* (Summer 2000): 210+.

Amy Sparks Kolker

GOLDEN, MARITA (1950–   )

Literary activist, novelist, memoirist, and editor, Marita Golden is committed to producing and recognizing a broad range of writing. Born in Washington, D.C., in 1950, Golden was encouraged to pursue her **love** of writing by her parents, Sherman, a taxi driver, and Beatrice, a landlord. In her teens, she voraciously read novels by William Thackeray, Jane Austen, Gustave Flaubert, and Leo Tolstoy, whose writing, in her words, "spoke across the ages" to her own life. As a college student at American University in the 1960s—a time when **civil rights movement** leaders were reevaluating black **literature** and literary traditions—she was inspired by the scope and ambition she found in works by authors of African descent. According to Golden, writing for her Web site, "All the writers I love have taught me a lot about the role of courage in the writer's life. The writer is supposed to be brave and daring and to ask the questions others fear asking."

Golden's desire to question led her to Columbia University, where she earned a master's in journalism in 1973. It was there that she met Femi Kayode, an African man whom she followed to Nigeria and later married. However, as she describes in the autobiographical *Migrations of the Heart* (1983), her transition from a black activist and New York City television executive to a traditional African wife and mother was difficult and, ultimately, untenable. She returned to the United States with her son, Michael, in 1979 and assumed various professorships in the fields of English and journalism as her writing career developed.

Since **Alice Walker** praised Golden's *Migrations of the Heart*, Golden has published four novels, three anthologies, and two nonfiction works inspired by her experiences as a single mother. Her novels center on the unique concerns of African American women ensconced in networks of **family**, **race**, politics, and **history**. Focusing on a range of characters—including students at a New England university (*A Woman's Place*, 1986), a farmer's daughter in the streets of Washington, D.C. (*Long Distance Life*, 1989), female civil rights workers (*And Do Remember Me*, 1992), and a mother released from prison (*The Edge of Heaven*, 1997)—Golden's **fiction** refuses to furnish easy solutions to the complex problems of black women. Also notable is her anthology *Wild Women Don't Wear No Blues* (1993), in which African American women writers offer frank reflections on love and sex. In her recent book *Don't Play in the Sun* (2004), Golden returns to **autobiography**, candidly revealing her struggles as a woman with dark skin.

Today, Golden encourages other writers to dare through her groundbreaking work with the **Zora Neale Hurston/Richard Wright** Foundation, which she founded in 1990. Established to recognize and foster **community** among writers of African descent, the foundation has distributed over $100,000 in annual literary awards and scholarships to Hurston/Wright Writers' Week, a summer workshop. A self-described "literary cultural worker," Golden interweaves art, activism, courage, and candor, inviting both readers and writers to join her.

Works By

And Do Remember Me. New York: Doubleday, 1992. (Novel.)
Don't Play in the Sun: One Woman's Journey through the Color Complex. New York: Doubleday, 2004.
The Edge of Heaven. New York: Doubleday, 1997.
Gumbo: An Anthology of African American Writing. Ed. Marita Golden and E. Lynn Harris. New York: Harlem Moon Books, 2002.
Long Distance Life. New York: Doubleday, 1989.
Migrations of the Heart. New York: Doubleday, 1983.
A Miracle Every Day: Triumph and Transformation in the Lives of Single Mothers. New York: Doubleday, 1999.
Saving Our Sons: Raising Black Children in a Turbulent World. New York: Doubleday, 1995.
Skin Deep: Black Women & White Women Write about Race. Ed. Marita Golden and Susan Richards Shreve. New York: Nan A. Talese/Doubleday, 1995.
Wild Women Don't Wear No Blues: Black Women Writers on Men, Love, and Sex. Ed. Marita Golden. New York: Doubleday, 1993.
A Woman's Place. New York: Doubleday, 1986. (Novel.)

Works About

Ambrose, D'Lena. "Novelist Sponsors Annual Contest to Nurture Black Writers." *Chronicle of Higher Education*, June 14, 1996, n.p.
Hill, Lynda. Review of *Wild Women Don't Wear No Blues*. *African American Review* 29.4 (Winter 1995): 691–693.
Marita Golden. www.maritagolden.com.

Warren, Nagueyalti. Review of *Long Distance Life*. *Black American Literature Forum* 24.4 (1990): 803–808.

Rebecca Meacham

GOMEZ, JEWELLE (1948–)

Jewelle Gomez is a significant contemporary poet, novelist, journalist, essayist, activist, teacher, and public speaker who explores the multicultural, lesbian experience in her works. Gomez was born in Boston on September 11, 1948, and reared in Boston and Washington, D.C., by a supportive, extended **family** of African American and Native American ancestry. Despite experiencing material poverty in her childhood, Gomez earned a B.A. from Northeastern University in 1971 and an M.S. in 1973 from Columbia University's School of Journalism, where she was a Ford Foundation Fellow. Her early life was influenced by the major political movements of the 1960s and 1970s—the civil rights movement, the antiwar movement, and the **Black Arts Movement**.

Gomez's early **work** was in journalism and television. She worked in television production for WGBH-TV's *Say Brother* in Boston and for WNET-TV's Children's Television Workshop in 1970s. She later worked in off-Broadway theater in New York. In the 1980s and the early 1990s, Gomez worked for the New York State Council on the Arts. She has also worked as a high school teacher and a professor of creative writing. Additionally, Gomez has devoted considerable energy to activist causes such as being a founding board member of the Gay and Lesbian Alliance against Defamation (GLAAD) and a member of the Feminist Anti-Censorship Task Force (FACT).

Gomez is a prolific writer and speaker. She has contributed essays to many feminist and lesbian publications and has written countless book and **film** reviews. Gomez is a vigorous proponent of feminism, **lesbianism**, and multiculturalism with a commitment to social justice. Much of her work has the critical engagement of aspects of her **identity** as its centerpiece. She writes from multiple, simultaneous perspectives in a way that preserves and celebrates the complexities of the human experience.

Gomez's work is influenced by literary writers such as **Ntozake Shange** and **Toni Morrison** and lesbian and feminist critics such as **Audre Lorde**, Barbara Smith, and **Cheryl Clarke**. Her earliest creative works are self-published **poetry** (*The Lipstick Papers* [1980] and *Flamingoes and Bears* [1986]). In her poetry, Gomez describes the lesbian experience in sensual and intimate terms.

Her first novel, *The Gilda Stories*, was published in 1991 and won Lambda literary awards for **fiction** and science fiction. *Gilda*, a fine example of speculative fiction, blends elements of the traditional, gothic vampire story with elements of the romantic novel, historical novel, and mystery novel, as well as elements of fantasy and science fiction genres. Gomez skillfully uses time and geographic space to convey the personal experience of the self-titled protagonist who is an African American lesbian vampire. *Gilda* is written within the framework of shifting scales ranging from the lived experience of the individual to the larger dynamics of **community** and family. In the stories about Gilda, Gomez interrogates the links between the exercise of social power and social responsibility. In the late 1990s the Gilda stories were adapted to the stage as *Bones and Ash* by the Urban Bush Women; the script of this adaptation was subsequently published.

Works By

Bones and Ash: A Gilda Story. New York: Quality Paperback Books, 2001.
Don't Explain. Ithaca, NY: Firebrand, 1998.
Flamingoes and Bears. Jersey City, NJ: Grace, 1986.
Forty-three Septembers. Ithaca, NY: Firebrand, 1993.
The Gilda Stories: A Novel. Ithaca, NY: Firebrand, 1991.
The Lipstick Papers. Jersey City, NJ: Grace, 1980. (Poetry.)
Oral Tradition: Selected Poems Old & New. Ithaca, NY: Firebrand, 1995. (Poetry.)

Works About

Bronski, Michael. "Jewelle Gomez." *Gay and Lesbian Biography.* Detroit: St. James Press, 1997. 163–164.
Nelson, Linda L. "Jewelle L. Gomez." *Contemporary Lesbian Writers of the United States.* Ed. Sandra Pollack and Denise D. Knight. Westport, CT: Greenwood Press, 1993. 213–219.
Sanchez, Brenna. "Jewelle Gomez." *Contemporary Black Biography.* Vol. 30. Detroit: Gale, 2002. 68–70.

Kimberly Black-Parker

GOSSETT, HATTIE (1942–)

Poet, writer, performance artist, and teacher, Hattie Gossett describes her early life in her introduction to *Presenting . . . Sister NoBlues* (1988). Her parents came north to New Jersey during World War II with an energetic belief that they could achieve the American dream but, disappointed, ended up focusing on their daughter's success. She reacted against their genteel expectations in a way reminiscent of **Lorraine Hansberry**'s account of her own character formation. Despite pressure to be, in Gossett's words, "a lady and a good negro," like Hansberry she learned resistance from the ghetto/project kids who beat her up and, in the process, discovered a new intensity directing her unconventional life. When Gossett discovered the pleasures of reading and music, especially **jazz**, they gave her a sense of belonging to "a whole lineage of people . . . who aint gonna go along with the program."

Forced to be a debutante, in the early 1960s she dropped out of college, fled to the Lower East Side, got married and divorced twice in quick succession, wore Afros and dashikis, and took a militant stance. For a while she specialized in temporary jobs that allowed her to get by in order to create. She has been an editor at magazines as different as *True Story* and *Black Theater*. She has published in works of feminist criticism, like *Heresies*, and been part of black women's collectives like **Kitchen Table: Women of Color Press** but also written a sex column for *Essence*. *Presenting... Sister NoBlues*, however, is a landmark, combining the **Black Arts Movement**'s commitment to orality and antielitism with a great sense of comic timing and feminist critique.

At the end of her introduction, she writes that she is beginning another book, but that work has not yet been published; instead, her writing has increasingly emerged as performance, especially in music and/or dance collaborations with other multiform artists, including Vinie Burrows, Jawole Willa Jo Zolar of Urban Bush Women, Casselberry-Dupree, Evelyn Blakey, Robbie Maccauley, Edwina Lee Tyler, Andrea E. Woods of SouloWorks, and composer Fred Carl. A series of recent high-profile awards, including the New School University David Randolph Distinguished Artist-in-Residence Award in 2002, may finally help Gossett realize her old dream of escaping the edges of necessity with enough drive left to keep producing a passionate art.

The theme of rebellion/anger that runs through Gossett's work can disconcert critics, but themes define her life more accurately than chronological lists of degrees and awards. She carefully totes up the costs of economic vulnerability and, in *Sister NoBlues*, transforms the nickel-and-dime encounters of working women into angry and hilarious letters from a tenant, a **domestic**, a cleaning woman, a woman trying to collect a debt. Another set of poems ("a night at the fantasy factory," "setting up," and the deft "butter" sequence) describes the humiliations of being a waitress. She intersperses them with monologues—variously irritating, grandiose, seductive, and pathetic—spoken by the waitress's black male customers.

In Gossett's work, poverty and rebellion do not preclude betrayal by one's comrades: the "progressive" clinic that cannot imagine the plight of its cleaner, the left-wing scholars whose self-righteous sexism she neatly refutes in "on the question of fans." She recognizes the limits and contradictions of various alliances, even those black women forge, excoriating "mammys" as "daddy's enforcer," but (usually) keeps her eyes on the prize. Her affinity for performance tends to blur her own life as a "diva" with that of "Sister NoBlues," a collective black woman whose formidable contributions to individuals, communities, and world culture have often been erased and/or exploited; however, many people recognize Sister's genius when she is "on"—an apt description of Gossett's own legendary performances.

Sections 3 and 4 of *Sister NoBlues*, in particular, are often reprinted because they speak to a global audience in the distinctive voice of a cosmopolitan black woman revolutionary, who—in Cuba, Dakar, Barbados, or New York— takes great pleasure in her alliances and victories and, from a distance, laughs at her defeats. Many of these poem/performance pieces are chants and ceremonies of an alternative artistry determined to activate those working for change. "Is it true what they say about colored pussy?" improbably turns that query to uplift; "woman mansion" rewrites the heaven a churchwoman can expect; "21rst century black woman warrior wimmins chant" recognizes the vulnerabilities of tough, loving, "bad" women, even as it celebrates their courage.

Living in Harlem, "at the crossroads," Gossett retains her trickster wit and sassy voice, reminding her aging generation that there is still a lot to do. She makes laughter, music, the inventive rhythms of speech, and pleasure serve the struggle for justice, but she turns a critical ear to American lies and individuals' compromises and strategies inside and outside of movements. She belongs in books like this but resists the form.

Works By

"at the crossroads #1." Hattie Gossett. Poetry: Writer's Portfolio. 2002. www .writersregister.com/artists/NY6.

"billie lives! billie lives." *This Bridge Called My Back: Writings by Radical Women of Color*. Ed. Cherríe Moraga and Gloria Anzaldúa. Foreword by Toni Cade Bambara. Watertown, MA: Persephone Press, 1981. 109–112.

"BRAS AND RUBBERS IN THE GUTTERS: its enough to have my mother turning over in her grave!" *High Risk: An Anthology of Forbidden Writings*. Ed. Amy Scholder and Ira Silverberg. New York: Dutton, 1991. 105–112.

"intro & 10 takes; a satire." *Heresies #12: Sex Issue* 3.4 (1981): 15–18.

"jazzwomen: they're mostly singers and piano players. only a horn player or two. hardly any drummers." With Carolyn Johnson. *Jazz Spotlight News*, August 1979. Reprinted in *Rock She Wrote*. Ed. Evelyn McDonnell and Ann Powers. New York: Delta, 1995. 57–65.

"mins movement??? a page drama." *Women Respond to the Men's Movement: A Feminist Collection*. Ed. Kay Leigh Hagan. Foreword by Gloria Steinem. San Francisco: Pandora, 1992. 19–25.

Presenting . . . Sister NoBlues. Ithaca, NY: Firebrand Books, 1988.

Texts for "Shelter" from *Heat*. With Laurie Carlos. Dance Concert, Urban Bush Women, 1988. Alvin Ailey American Dance Theater, 1992.

"who told you anyone wants to hear from you? you ain't nothing but a black woman!" *This Bridge Called My Back: Writings by Radical Women of Color*. Ed. Cherríe Moraga and Gloria Anzaldúa. Foreword by Toni Cade Bambara. Watertown, MA: Persephone Press, 1981. 175–176.

Works About

Albrecht, Lisa Diane. *The Woman Writer Empowered: A Study of the Meanings of Experience of Ten Published Feminist Women Writers*. Ph.D. diss., SUNY Buffalo, 1984.

Giddings, Paula. "Word Star." Review of *Presenting . . . Sister NoBlues. Essence* (April 1989): 40.

Ross, Gregory. "African Voices and Jazz Festival: A Special Combination." *New York Amsterdam News*, April 30, 1998, 26.

Susan Nash

GRAHAM, SHIRLEY (1896–1977)

Gerald Horne's *Race Woman: The Lives of Shirley Graham Du Bois* says the Rev. David A. and Elizabeth Etta (Bell) Graham named a daughter born on November 11, 1896, Lola Shirley Graham. Papers archived at the Radcliffe Institute for Advanced Study at Harvard University corroborate the details that began the future author and human rights advocate's uncommon quest.

From the time Graham was born, her father, an itinerant African Methodist Episcopal minister with a **love** for cultural politics, answered calls in cities such as Chicago, Detroit, Colorado Springs, Spokane, and Seattle and churches throughout Indiana, Michigan, Minnesota, and Louisiana. The nomadic life played havoc with Graham's education; nonetheless, she graduated in 1915 from Lewis and Clark High School in Spokane. She married Shadrach McCants three years later.

After they divorced in 1927 in Portland, Oregon, her mother largely raised their sons Robert, four, and David, two. Shirley McCants, as she was known, built a career. During the next three years Graham was a music librarian at Howard University and taught at Morgan College in Baltimore while she studied music at Howard, New York's Institute of Musical Arts, and in Paris at the Sorbonne. In 1931, Graham signed on at Oberlin College in Ohio. She earned a bachelor's degree in 1934 and a graduate music degree the following year. She spent the next year as a fine arts instructor at the Tennessee Agricultural and Industrial Normal School for Negroes, now called Tennessee State University, in Nashville.

At the end of the 1936 school year, she became director of the Chicago Federal Theatre, an appointment that might have a connection to the good reviews her musical *Tom-Tom* received in 1932 at Cleveland's "Theatre of Nations" summer festival. Regardless of the reason, the job launched Graham on a three-decade journey as an international activist and writer.

During the 1940s she wrote biographies of famous blacks such as George Washington Carver, Paul Robeson, Jean Baptiste du Sable, and **Phillis Wheatley**. In 1961 she founded and edited *Freedomways* magazine. In the 1970s she wrote biographies and memoirs of her late, second husband William Edward Burghardt Du Bois and former presidents Gamal Abdel Nasser of Egypt and Tanzania's Julius K. Nyerere. Graham founded the Graham Artists Bureau to broker talented performers. In 1941, she joined the United Service Organizations (USO) as entertainment director for black troops at Fort Huachuca, Arizona.

In 1943, spurred by a more than platonic involvement with still-married civil rights advocate W.E.B. Du Bois, Graham became a field secretary for the National Association for the Advancement of Colored People (NAACP). After they married in 1951, the pair spent the rest of their lives as human rights advocates with associates that included communists. The House Un-American Activities Committee indicted her husband, but he was acquitted for lack of evidence. Still, federal authorities dogged them. The couple grew frustrated with the timid 1950s progress in civil rights. At the invitation of President Kwame Nkrumah, they moved to Ghana in 1961 and became citizens. The U.S. government never let her live in this country again. After her husband died in 1963, Graham remained to help build Ghana's national television and telecommunications network. When Nkrumah was unseated in the 1966 coup, she and son David moved to Cairo, Egypt. Her human rights work continued until she died of breast cancer on March 27, 1977, in Beijing, China, seeking treatment.

Graham's papers may be found as follows: The Shirley Graham Du Bois papers [MC 476], Radcliffe Institute for Advanced Study, Harvard University, Cambridge, Massachusetts; The Schomburg Center for Research in Black Culture, Harlem, New York; W.E.B. Du Bois Manuscript Collection, Library of Congress, Washington, D.C.; The Julius Rozenwald Archives, Fisk University, Nashville; The Black Oral History Collection, Fisk University.

Works By

Booker T. Washington and the Negroes' Place in American Life. With Samuel R. J. Spencer. 1955. Toronto: Pearson Education, 1998.
Gamal Abdel Nasser, Son of the Nile: A Biography. New York: Third Press, 1972.
His Day Is Marching On. Philadelphia: Lippincott, 1971.
Julius K. Nyerere, Teacher of Africa. New York: Julian Messner, 1975.
Zulu Heart. New York: Third Press, 1974.

Works About

Coles, Robert. *Black Writers Abroad: A Study of Black American Writers in Europe and Africa.* New York: Garland Press, 1997.
Du Bois, W.E.B. *Autobiography of W.E.B. Du Bois: A Soliloquy on Viewing My Life from the Last Decade of Its First Century.* New York: International Publishers, 1968.
Hamalian, Leo, and James V. Hatch, eds. *The Roots of African American Drama.* Detroit: Wayne State University Press, 1992.
Horne, Gerald. *Race Woman: The Lives of Shirley Graham Du Bois.* New York: New York University Press, 2000.
Lewis, David Levering. *W.E.B. Du Bois: The Fight for Equality and the American Century, 1919–1963.* New York: Henry Holt and Company, 2000.

Perkins, Katherine, ed. *Black Female Playwrights: An Anthology of Plays before 1950 (Blacks in the Diaspora)*. Bloomington: Indiana University Press, 1991.

Vincent F. A. Golphin

GREENFIELD, ELOISE (1929–)

Eloise Greenfield, a major and prolific author for children, was born in North Carolina but moved with her **family** to Washington, D.C., then a segregated city, when she was a baby. She grew up in a housing project in which the **community** cared about each other and together tried to face the problems caused by racism. She attended Miner Teacher's College (now University of the District of Columbia) but dropped out after two years. After a career as a federal employee, she started writing songs and short stories, none of which were published. Her first picture book, *Bubbles* (1972), is about a small boy who is excited about learning to read. After trying to share his joy with busy adults, he finds the perfect audience: his baby sister. Her next few books were among the first biographies of African Americans for young children: *Rosa Parks* (1973), *Paul Robeson* (1975), and *Mary McLeod Bethune* (1977). Many of her picture books sensitively portray strong multigenerational black families facing everyday and crisis situations, such as *William and the Good Old Days* (1993), in which a young boy remembers how vibrant his grandmother was and deals with her deteriorating health, and *Grandmama's Joy* (1980), in which the young heroine tries to comfort her grandmother when they are about to be evicted. Some of her major themes are developing a positive **identity**, a sense of African and African American **history**, and the courage and resilience to follow dreams, as in *Africa Dream* (1977), a Coretta Scott King Award book, in which a child's dreams are filled with African images.

Greenfield turned to **poetry** with *Honey, I Love* (1978), in which a young girl expresses her joy in everyday life. *Nathaniel Talking* (1988) is a series of poems told by nine-year-old Nathaniel B. Free, in which he talks about events and people important in his life, including the **death** of his mother and his father's strength. Each member of his family has a poem echoing the musical tradition of that generation, including a rap poem for Nathaniel. Three years later, *Night on Neighborhood Street* (1991), another collection celebrating an African American neighborhood, was published. Both were King Honor Award books. *For the Love of the Game: Michael Jordan and Me* (1997) examines the experiences of two children who find inspiration and purpose in the life of their hero. Her lyrical, rhythmical poetry, true to children's experiences, is perhaps her strongest literary contribution.

One of her major achievements is *Childtimes: A Three-Generation Memoir* (1979), written with her mother, Lessie Jones Little, with contributions by her grandmother. The three women recount the challenges they have faced as black women in this country and the ways in which family **love** can help overcome obstacles. These are the **memories** of a particular family, but the author believes they also represent the feelings and experiences of other black families. She has written many other works, including board books for the youngest child and several novels for young readers.

Works By

Africa Dream. New York: John Day, 1977.

Bubbles. Washington, DC: Drum and Spear Press, 1972. (Republished as *Good News* by Coward, McGann, and Geoghegan, 1977.)

Childtimes: A Three-Generation Memoir. New York: Harper and Row, 1979.

For the Love of the Game: Michael Jordan and Me. New York: HarperCollins, 1997.

Grandmama's Joy. New York: Putnam, 1980.

Grandpa's Face. New York: Philomel, 1988.

Honey, I Love and Other Love Poems. New York: Crowell, 1978.

How They Got Over: African-Americans and the Call of the Sea. New York: HarperCollins, 2003.

Nathaniel Talking. New York: Black Butterfly, 1988.

Night on Neighborhood Street. New York: Dial, 1991.

Paul Robeson. New York: Crowell, 1975.

Rosa Parks. New York: Crowell, 1973.

William and the Good Old Days. New York: HarperCollins, 1993.

Works About

Children's Literature Review. Vol. 38. Detroit: Gale Research, 1996. 76–96.

Murphy, Barbara Thrash. *Black Authors and Illustrators of Books for Children and Young Adults: A Biographical Dictionary.* 3rd ed. New York: Garland, 1997. 153–155.

Pendergast, Sara, and Tom Pendergast, eds. *St. James Guide to Children's Writers.* Detroit: St. James Press, 1999. 455–457.

Silvey, Anita, ed. *Children's Books and Their Creators.* Boston: Houghton Mifflin, 1995.

Something about the Author. Vol. 105. Detroit: Gale Research, 1999. 205–209.

Susan L. Golden

GRIMKÉ, ANGELINA WELD (1880–1958)

Born in Boston in 1880, Angelina Weld Grimké knew both the relative privilege and the attendant tensions of her mixed-race heritage, a dynamic that her writing reflects. Her father, a diplomat and National Association for the Advancement of Colored People (NAACP) officer, was the nephew of Sarah Grimké and Angelina Grimké Weld, white abolitionists whose plantation-owning brother had fathered him and his brothers with Nancy Weston, a slave. The Grimké sisters offered their nephews the recognition that their brother did not, and in response, Angelina's parents, Archibald and Sarah Stanley Grimké, named her after the younger of the two women. Angelina's mother left Archibald Grimké in 1883, taking the child with her, only to return the girl to her father after four years. Significantly, then, while Angelina Grimké's own writing confronts issues like racial **identity**, it also recounts personal loss.

Grimké attended schools in Massachusetts and Minnesota. Her earliest poem dates to around her eleventh birthday, and at thirteen she published a poem to her uncle Theodore Weld. Even her earliest literary efforts addressed social issues, including short stories that decried lynching, a subject that she later revisited. Through her uncle and aunt, Francis and **Charlotte Forten Grimké**, she became familiar with the African American social circles in Washington, D.C., when she lived with them while her father was U.S. consul to Santo Domingo. In a series of 1896 letters, Grimké and Mary "Mamie" Burrill recorded their erotic longing for one another, hinting at the personal motifs that would later inform Grimké's literary work.

By 1900, Grimké was publishing **poetry** in journals like the *Boston Transcript*. In 1902, she moved again to Washington and began teaching, eventually working at what would become Dunbar High School, where she knew **Anna Julia Cooper** and **Jessie Redmon Fauset**. Injured in a railway accident in 1911, she would not recover robust health. Nevertheless, Grimké imagined compiling a collection of poems called "Dusk Dreams," encompassing both private passions and public critiques. On one hand, Grimké's poetry commemorates historically significant figures, including **family** members and others. Yet her 1909 poem "El Beso," published in the *Transcript*, bespeaks the quiet personal intensity and vibrant imagery that would characterize many of her later lyrics.

In 1916, Grimké's antilynching play *Rachel* was performed in Washington and later in New York and Boston. Publishing the **drama** extended its influence, and by 1921 this work about prejudice against a black family was earning mostly supportive reviews. Grimké's next play, the incomplete *Mara*, in ways shared subject matter, as did many of the short stories that she wrote during this time. In the 1920s, her poems appeared widely in anthologies by **Harlem Renaissance** writers, and she contributed more poems than any other woman to **Countee Cullen**'s *Caroling Dusk* (1927). Some critics see her father's 1930 **death** as a turning point for Grimké, and she produced no known poems after 1932, a fact that other critics attribute to the uncertain reception that Grimké's imagistic treatments of homoerotic desire would have faced during this era. After a long illness, she died in 1958.

Works By

Rachel. Boston: Cornhill Co., 1920.
Selected Works of Angelina Weld Grimké. Ed. Carolivia Herron. New York: Oxford University Press, 1991.

Works About

Hull, Gloria T. *Color, Sex, and Poetry: Three Women Writers of the Harlem Renaissance.* Bloomington: Indiana University Press, 1987.

Shockley, Ann Allen. *Afro-American Women Writers, 1746–1933: An Anthology and Critical Guide*. Boston: G. K. Hall, 1988.

Katharine Rodier

GRIMKÉ, CHARLOTTE FORTEN (1837–1914)

Charlotte Forten Grimké, poet, essayist, teacher, and civil rights advocate, is also now renowned for her personal writing. Her lifelong dedication to education and emancipation was in part a legacy from her **family**, especially her grandfather, James Forten: patriot, entrepreneur, and abolitionist. Although her mother died when she was only three years old, Forten was not without female exemplars as well as male during her youth in Philadelphia, as many members of the extended Forten family, including her aunts, publicly advanced reform causes and opportunity for their **race**.

In 1853, Forten went to study in Salem, Massachusetts, living there with the Remond family, themselves noted black abolitionists. In Salem, she joined the local Female Anti-Slavery Society and met many outspoken activists of her age, including William Lloyd Garrison. In 1856, she began teaching, a vocation to which she devoted much of her life, despite the illnesses that persistently afflicted her. An avid reader, she did not produce a volume of poems in her lifetime but despite her own professed reticence did publish close to a dozen individual poems, including several between 1858 and 1860.

Moving between teaching appointments despite periods of ill health between 1857 and 1862, Forten relocated frequently between Pennsylvania and Massachusetts. Then, inspired by an 1862 visit to John Greenleaf Whittier, she joined the Port Royal Experiment teaching former slaves in the Union-occupied islands off South Carolina. Forten's vivid journal entries at the time supplied the basis for letters in the *Liberator* and would again inform her publication in the *Atlantic Monthly*, "Life in the Sea Islands" (May/June 1864).

In May 1864, Charlotte Forten resigned her Port Royal commission and returned once again to Philadelphia, moving back to Boston in 1865 to work for the New England Branch of the Freedmen's Union Commission. In 1869, she translated *Madame Thérèse*, a novel about the French Revolution. Publishing personal sketches, short descriptions, and critiques of racism and segregation in the 1870s, Forten taught briefly in South Carolina and later in Washington, D.C. Employed subsequently at the U.S. Treasury, she met and married Francis J. Grimké, pastor of the Fifteenth Street Presbyterian Church. Their daughter, Theodora Cornelia, born in 1880, lived only six months.

In 1885, the Grimkés moved to Florida, returning to Washington in 1889, whereupon they became central figures in the city's flourishing black cultural life. Forten published several more poems and some lighter **fiction** and also produced essays on the race issue, art criticism, and a vignette of **Frederick**

Douglass. Having helped found the National Association of Colored Women, she focused as well on **work** at church and **home**. From 1894 to 1898, the Grimkés were legal guardians to their niece, **Angelina Weld Grimké**, who with her father would again reside with the couple in 1905. Increasingly frail and eventually bedridden by 1913, Charlotte Forten Grimké died in 1914, having maintained a measured public voice through **poetry**, through editorial and descriptive prose, and in her public service as teacher and **community** leader.

See also Cooper, Anna Julia

Works By

The Journal of Charlotte Forten: A Free Negro in the Slave Era. Ed. Ray Allen Billington. New York: Dryden Press, 1953.
The Journals of Charlotte Forten Grimké. Ed. Brenda Stevenson. New York: Oxford University Press, 1988.
The Life and Writings of Charlotte Forten Grimké. Vol. 2 of *Life and Writings of the Grimké Family.* Ed. Anna J. Cooper. N. p., 1951.
Two Black Teachers during the Civil War: Mary S. Peake; the Colored Teacher at Fortress Monroe. Life on the Sea Islands [by] Charlotte Forten. Ed. Lewis C. Lockwood. New York: Arno Press, 1969.

Works About

Braxton, Joanne M. *Black Women Writing Autobiography: A Tradition within a Tradition.* Philadelphia: Temple University Press, 1989.
Peterson, Carla L. *"Doers of the Word": African-American Women Speakers and Writers in the North (1830–1880).* New York: Oxford University Press, 1995.
Shockley, Ann Allen. *Afro-American Women Writers, 1746–1933: An Anthology and Critical Guide.* Boston: G. K. Hall, 1988.
Sterling, Dorothy. *We Are Your Sisters: Black Women in the Nineteenth Century.* New York: Norton, 1984.

Katharine Rodier

GUY, ROSA (1925–   )

Born in Trinidad, Rosa Guy moved with parents Henry and Audrey Cuthbert and younger sister Ameze to Harlem, New York, in 1932 at the age of seven. Two years later, the girls' mother died, and their uninvolved father paid a neighbor to watch them. Later, the girls would live in a succession of institutions and foster homes. At the age of fourteen, she quit school and took a job in a factory to help support Ameze. Two years later, one week before World War II, she married Warner Guy. He served in the military, and she gave birth to their son, Warner Guy, Jr. It was at this time that Rosa Guy first became involved with the American Negro Theatre.

At the end of the war, Guy worked in a clothes factory and attended night school. Because of the dearth of satisfying dramatic opportunities for a black woman at this time, she turned to writing. She enrolled in New York University, studying writing and theater. By the late 1940s, she was involved in the Committee for the Negro in the Arts. She also, with John Killens, formed the Harlem Writers Guild, a forum for her to air the plays and short stories she wrote.

Activism was also an important part of Guy's life. In 1961, after the assassination of Patrice Lumumba, the first prime minister of the independent Republic of Congo, Guy, **Maya Angelou**, and **Paule Marshall** held a sit-in at the chambers of the Security Council of the United Nations. It was in large measure due to this incident that the United Nations enacted stricter controls on access to the Security Council.

Five years later, Guy's first book was published. Set in black Harlem, *Bird at My Window* (1966) is the story of a **family** that fled the **South** after the father is accused of **rape** by a white woman whom he had rebuffed. The father is subsequently killed at a gambling table, and the family struggles to survive in spite of racism and burdensome responsibilities.

In the 1960s, Rosa turned her attention to youth. Curious about what they were feeling and thinking in response to the riots and assassinations of the **civil rights movement**, Guy took to the road. She traveled across the United States to talk to youth ages thirteen to twenty-three, rural and urban, high school and college, in a wide variety of settings. *Children of Longing* (1971), her second book, is an edited collection of their words. The universal themes the youth she talked to voiced—their hopes and fears, their difficulties dealing with parents and school—would appear in her later writing.

Rosa Guy's first book for youth, *The Friends*, was published two years later. The start of a trilogy about the Cathy and Jackson families, the book focuses on daughters Phylissia and Edith. The motherless girls are united by their longing for their mothers and their struggles with their families. The book also addresses the hostility and misunderstanding that can characterize relationships between black Americans and black West Indians. It was for this book that Rosa first received an American Library Association Notable Book Award.

Perhaps in part because of her own family experiences, responsibility is a theme that Guy visits often in her writing. Other common themes are the problems of discrimination and poverty faced by black youths in Harlem. Guy's writing is sometimes controversial. The second book in the Cathy-Jackson trilogy, *Ruby* (1976), involves a homosexual theme, and the third book, *Edith Jackson* (1978), involves abortion and police brutality. Her books for adolescents often seem to be a warning cry about a society that fails to meet the needs of youth.

Guy's work is often influenced by her international travel. Her first picture book, *My Love, My Love: or, the Peasant Girl* (1985) is a retelling of the beloved Hans Christian Andersen classic with Caribbean speech, rhythm, and flair. Her most recent novel, *The Sun, the Sea, a Touch of the Wind* (1995), involves Haitian characters and setting.

Works By

And I Heard a Bird Sing. New York: Delacorte, 1989.
Billy the Great. New York: Delacorte, 1992.
Birago Diop, Mother Crocodile: An Uncle Amadou Tale from Senegal. New York: Delacorte, 1981.
Bird at My Window. Philadelphia: Lippincott, 1966.
Children of Longing. New York: Holt, Rinehart and Winston, 1971.
The Disappearance. New York: Delacorte, 1979.
Edith Jackson. New York: Viking, 1978.
The Friends. New York: Holt, Rinehart and Winston, 1973.
A Measure of Time. New York: Holt, Rinehart and Winston, 1983.
Mirror of Her Own. New York: Delacorte, 1981.
The Music of Summer. New York: Delacorte, 1992.
My Love, My Love: or, the Peasant Girl. New York: Holt, Rinehart and Winston, 1985.
New Guys around the Block. New York: Delacorte, 1983.
Paris, Pee Wee and Big Dog. New York: Delacorte, 1985.
Ruby. New York: Viking, 1976.
The Sun, the Sea, a Touch of the Wind. New York: Dutton, 1995.
The Ups and Downs of Carl Davis III. New York: Delacorte, 1989.

Works About

Norris, Jerrie. *Presenting Rosa Guy.* Boston: Twayne, 1988.
Wilson, Judith. "Rosa Guy: Writing with a Bold Vision." *Essence* (October 1979).

Heidi Hauser Green

 **H**

HALEY, ALEX (1921–1992)

Alex Haley was born in Ithaca, New York, on August 11, 1921. His father was a college professor, and his mother was a grade school teacher. He was the oldest of three sons. After graduating high school at the age of fifteen, he attended college for two years and then joined the U.S. Coast Guard in 1939.

While at sea, Haley started writing short stories. In 1952, he was designated as the chief journalist by the Coast Guard, and he handled public relations assignments. After retiring from the Coast Guard in 1959, he started his new career as a freelance writer. He became an assignment writer for *Reader's Digest* magazine. Later he worked for *Playboy* magazine. He started a new interview feature at *Playboy*. His interview with **Malcolm X** while at *Playboy* led to his first book, *The Autobiography of Malcolm X: As Told to Alex Haley* (1965). This book was translated into eight languages and established him as a serious writer.

Next, he embarked upon the twelve long years of research into his maternal **family**'s **history**, inspired by the family stories he heard from his maternal grandmother in his youth in the 1920s and 1930s. To find clues about the roots of his ancestry, he used "the pronunciations of the African words repeated . . . by family members" and help from the linguists at several universities. These linguistic specialists verified the language, as well as the village where the words originated. He conducted research in the Library of Congress and in Great Britain Maritime records to trace the history of slave ships. His search led him to a sixteen-year-old boy named Kunta Kinte who was kidnapped and then sold into **slavery** from the small village of Juffure in Gambia, West Africa.

During this period, Haley wrote several magazine articles and was awarded honorary doctorates for his work. This work culminated in his most widely celebrated autobiographical work of **fiction**, *Roots: The Saga of an American Family* (1976). The book won the 1976 National Book Award and was translated into thirty-seven languages worldwide. The American Broadcasting Company/ABC-TV turned the book into a twelve-hour miniseries in 1977. That year Haley won the Pulitzer Prize and the Spingarn Medal from the National Association for the Advancement of Colored People. In 1979, ABC-TV produced his next book, *Roots: The Next Generation*. In 1988, he published *A Different Kind of Christmas*, a story about slave escapes in the 1850s. The U.S. Coast Guard Academy awarded him an honorary doctorate in 1989.

Haley suffered a heart attack and died on February 10, 1992. Before his **death** he was researching his paternal grandmother Queen, who was born to a black slave mother and her white master. The book was later finished by David Stevens and published as *Queen: The Story of an American Family* (1993).

Works By

Alex Haley's Queen: The Story of an American Family. With David Stevens. New York: W. Morrow, 1993.
The Autobiography of Malcolm X: As Told to Alex Haley. New York: Grove, 1965.
A Different Kind of Christmas. New York: Doubleday, 1988.
Mama Flora's Family: A Novel. New York: Scribner, 1998.
Roots: The Saga of an American Family. New York: Doubleday, 1976.

Work About

Shirley, David. *Alex Haley: Author*. New York: Chelsea House Publications, 2005.

Pratibha Kelapure

HAMILTON, VIRGINIA (1936–2002)

Virginia Hamilton was born in the farming **community** of Yellow Springs, Ohio, a setting that is prominent in her **fiction**. Hamilton is the author of more than thirty books, including adolescent fiction, **folklore**, and critical studies. Her books have received numerous awards, including the Newbery Medal, the National Book Award, the Coretta Scott King Award, the MacArthur Foundation prize, and the Hans Christian Andersen Medal.

Hamilton's fictional subjects and characters, both female and male adolescents, often face feminist challenges. They may feel at odds with their communities, families, bodies, and selves and see themselves as voiceless, powerless, and misunderstood. They see themselves as different and apart from those around them. Often they retreat into their imaginations in order to reckon with the world around them.

In *Zeely* (1967), Elizabeth, a.k.a. Geeder, is imaginative and restless. She is enamored of tall, beautiful Zeely, whom Geeder imagines is a Watutsi queen. Geeder longs for the attention of Zeely, seeing her as an ideal woman.

The Planet of Junior Brown (1971), while centered on male characters, reflects the feminist concerns of isolation, **body** image, madness, and the need for a nurturing community. Junior's weakening grasp on reality helps reveal the strengthening humanity of Junior's friend Buddy, a janitor.

One of Hamilton's most celebrated novels, *M. C. Higgins, the Great* (1974), also focuses on a teenage boy, but he, too, must contend with adult concerns as his **family** fights for their land and the environment. Another character, the female outlaw Lurhetta, is alienated and a stranger, but she helps M. C. learn the value of the world around him and his family's ties to the land.

Arilla Sun Down (1976) continues many of the themes of the novels that came before it. Arilla Sun Down Adams is biracial (African American and Native American). She is overshadowed by her brother, Jack Sun Run Adams, who is preoccupied with his Native American heritage and is wildly charismatic. Arilla knows her friends hang out with her in order to be near her brother. Dreamy thoughts and memories of childhood reveal Arilla to us as she tries to reconcile her feelings of unworthiness as she compares herself with her brother, cope with school and friends, and express her **love** and admiration for her beautiful mother and somewhat capricious father. Arilla searches for self-awareness and eventually discovers her strong sense of endurance.

Several years after *Arilla*, the novel *Sweet Whispers, Brother Rush* (1982) continues the themes of coming of age in the character Tree. The novel also continues to explore the folk beliefs and elements of the supernatural that occur frequently in Hamilton's work. The ghost who appears to Tree, Brother Rush, helps her understand a family illness, her retarded older brother Dab, and her sometimes chaotic relationship with her mother and the mother's boyfriend.

In her folklore collections *The People Could Fly* (1985) and *Her Stories* (1995) Hamilton collects tales of characters who overcome oppression by ingenuity, strength, and perseverance. *Her Stories* focuses on varying tales of larger-than-life women who defy traditional female conventions. "Annie Christmas" tells of a woman keelboat captain on the Mississippi River in the Reconstruction **South**. While Hamilton notes in the collection that the tales come from sources that are fantastic or from sources about which to hypothesize, the collection ends with three stories of women who did exist. All of the stories reinforce the strengths of women in the most adverse conditions.

Works By

Anthony Burns. New York: Knopf, 1988.
Arilla Sun Down. New York: Greenwillow, 1976.

The Bells of Christmas. San Diego: Harcourt, Brace, Jovanovich, 1989.
Bluish. New York: Blue Sky Press, 1999.
Bruh Rabbit and the Tar Baby Girl. New York: Blue Sky Press, 2003.
Charlie Parker Played Be-Bop. New York: Econo-clad Books, 1997.
Cousins. New York: Philomel, 1990.
The Dark Way. San Diego: Harcourt, Brace, Jovanovich, 1990.
Drylongso. San Diego: Harcourt, Brace, Jovanovich, 1992.
Dustland. New York: Greenwillow, 1980.
The Gathering. New York: Greenwillow, 1981.
The Girl Who Spun Gold. New York: Blue Sky Press, 2000.
Her Stories: African American Folktales, Fairy Tales, and True Tales. New York: Blue Sky Press, 1995.
The House of Dies Drear. New York: Macmillan, 1968.
In the Beginning: Creation Stories from Around the World. San Diego: Harcourt, Brace, Jovanovich, 1988.
Jaguarundi. New York: Blue Sky Press, 1995.
Jahdu. New York: Greenwillow, 1981.
Junius Over Far. New York: Harper, 1992.
Justice and Her Brothers. New York: Greenwillow, 1978.
A Little Love. New York: Philomel, 1984.
The Magical Adventures of Pretty Pearl. New York: Harper and Row, 1983.
Many Thousand Gone. New York: Knopf, 1993.
M. C. Higgins, the Great. New York: Macmillan, 1974.
The Mystery of Dies Drear. New York: Greenwillow, 1987.
Paul Robeson: The Life and Times of a Free Black Man. New York: Harper and Row, 1974.
The People Could Fly. New York: Knopf, 1985.
Plain City. New York: Blue Sky Press, 1993.
The Planet of Junior Brown. New York: Macmillan, 1971.
A Ring of Tricksters. New York: Blue Sky Press, 1997.
Second Cousins. New York: Scholastic, 2000.
Sweet Whispers, Brother Rush. New York: Philomel, 1982.
Time-Ago Lost: More Tales of Jahdu. New York: Macmillan, 1973.
The Time-Ago Tales of Jahdu. New York: Macmillan, 1969.
W.E.B. Du Bois. New York: T. Y. Crowell, 1972.
When Birds Could Talk and Bats Could Sing. New York: Blue Sky Press, 1996.
A White Romance. New York: Philomel, 1987.
Willie Bea and the Time the Martians Landed. New York: Greenwillow, 1983.
Zeely. New York: Macmillan, 1967.

Work About

Mikkelson, Nina. *Virginia Hamilton.* Boston: Twayne, 1994.

Catherine E. Lewis

HAND I FAN WITH, THE

The Hand I Fan With (1996), **Tina McElroy Ansa**'s third novel, brings us back to Lena McPherson from *Baby of the Family* (1996) and to Ansa's Mulberry, Georgia. By the time of this novel, all of Lena's **family** has died: her parents in an accident in their small airplane and her brothers in their own untimely **deaths**. Lena has become a very successful businesswoman and is intimately involved with the issues and crises of the lives of the people of Mulberry. She has become the hand that all of Mulberry fans with. Caught up in all of her business and good works, Lena is profoundly lonely, except for the friendship of Sister, her best friend since college. *The Hand I Fan With* is a novel about letting go of the world in order to tend to one's personal emotional and spiritual needs.

Before leaving for a year's sabbatical in Africa, Sister has performed a man-calling ceremony for Lena. The man, however, is a ghost, Herman, who has died 100 years earlier. Herman teaches Lena to take care of her own needs and to reconnect with nature. Together they work her garden and tend her horses. When Herman leaves, exactly one year after he has appeared, Lena is a different woman. She has turned her parents' former **home** into a shelter for homeless teens and has begun to have closer, more parental relationships with some of those teens.

The Hand I Fan With is frankly erotic and sensual. Ansa's usual descriptive skills reveal Lena's overtly sexual relationship with Herman and the joy both Herman and Lena take in food, in gardening, and in maintaining close contact with the landscape of Lena's hundred-acre estate, situated on a bend in the Ocawatchee River. Running through the novel and the river is "Cleer Flo'," a phenomenon of the Ocawatchee River in which the river's normally muddy waters turn clear green. Herman explains that Lena has caused this natural phenomenon by cursing the river and spitting into it. After Herman returns to the spirit world, we see that Lena's anger and unhappiness cause a literal storm in her world, flooding the river and taking out the bridge from her property to the highway. This sets the scene for the novel's climax when Lena has to deliver a foal by herself. Herman's spirit returns to guide her, and she succeeds in delivering the baby colt and in accepting the loss of Herman's physical presence for the guidance of his spiritual reality.

The Hand I Fan With unites Ansa's themes of the reality of the spirit world and the value of familial relationships as an essential source of emotional satisfaction. For Lena, family comes from her friendship with Sister and her growing maternal relationships with the children at her shelter. Guidance from Herman, the ghosts of her family, and other female spirits, including Rachel from *Baby of the Family*, helps Lena find her way toward a fully satisfying life, both emotionally and spiritually.

See also Love; Sexuality; Spirituality

Works About

Farrell, Beth. Review of *The Hand I Fan With*, by Tina McElroy Ansa. *Library Journal* 122.6 (April 1, 1997): 144–145.

Farrington, Carol Cain. Review of *The Hand I Fan With*, by Tina McElroy Ansa. *New York Times Book Review* 101 (November 24, 1996): 18.

Johnson, Rhonda. Review of *The Hand I Fan With*, by Tina McElroy Ansa. *Entertainment Weekly* 350 (October 25, 1996): 108–109.

Lewis, Lillian. Review of *The Hand I Fan With*, by Tina McElroy Ansa. *Booklist* 92.22 (August 1996): 1852–1853.

Warren, Nagueyalti. "Echoing Zora: Ansa's Other Hand in *The Hand I Fan With*." *CLA Journal* 46.3 (2003): 362–382.

Woods, Paula L. Review of *The Hand I Fan With*, by Tina McElroy Ansa. *Emerge* 8.1 (October 1996): 75–76.

Harriette C. Buchanan

HANSBERRY, LORRAINE (1930–1965)

Lorraine Hansberry was born and raised in Chicago in a **family** with social and intellectual advantages. Her mother, Nannie Perry Hansberry, a teacher and ward committeewoman, and her father, Carl A. Hansberry, a U.S. deputy marshall and successful realtor, had an active commitment to social justice. Through her uncle, William Leo Hansberry, a respected scholar and teacher of African **history** at Howard University, Hansberry first associated the efforts of Africa for independence with the struggle of black America for **freedom**, a connection that would later figure significantly in her creative work. During Hansberry's childhood and youth, visitors to the Hansberry **home** included such major figures of black American culture and politics as W.E.B. Du Bois, Duke Ellington, **Langston Hughes**, and Paul Robeson.

Her family's economic prosperity never blinded Hansberry to the social oppression under which most black Americans lived before the civil rights legislation of the 1960s. Activism was a part of the Hansberry family life. When Hansberry was eight, her father, with the support of the NAACP, the National Association for the Advancement of Colored People, challenged Chicago's discriminatory real estate covenants by moving his family to Hyde Park, an affluent, all-white Chicago neighborhood. Hansberry's experience of racism in this privileged enclave was immediate, brutal, and violent. The white "howling mobs" hurled a brick into the Hansberry home that barely missed her head. While the Illinois courts evicted the family, the U.S. Supreme Court eventually ruled residential restrictions unconstitutional, but Carl Hansberry's victory was hollow, for the ruling had little effect in establishing precedent. His legal challenge exacted a personal toll in his disillusionment with America as a place of equality. He was planning to move his family permanently to Mexico when he died in 1946 of a cerebral hemorrhage.

The **death** of her father when she was only fifteen may have influenced Hansberry's **memories** of him as an exceptional presence always doing "something brilliant," and throughout her life, Hansberry had male mentors, but as *To Be Young, Gifted and Black* (*TBYGB*) (1969) suggests, the recollections of her mother and other maternal figures in her family provide her most vivid images. While Nannie Hansberry's indulgence in luxuries at times troubled her youngest daughter, Hansberry remembered a long car ride to Tennessee to visit her maternal grandmother, a former slave; her mother, pointing to the Kentucky hills, informed her children that her own father as a boy had hidden from his "master" there and had survived by his mother's secret midnight forays to bring him food. In a letter to the *New York Times* when she was twenty-four, Hansberry recalled the image of her mother during the Hyde Park siege "desperate and courageous . . . patrolling our house all night with a loaded German lugur doggedly guarding her four children, while my father fought the respectable part of the battle in the Washington court" (April 24, 1964). Hansberry dedicated her best-known play, *A Raisin in the Sun* (1959), "to Mama: in gratitude for the dream." The heroic potential of **motherhood** finds its way into her plays through the strong presence of characters like Lena and Ruth Younger in *Raisin*, and the slave mother Rissa in the posthumously published *The Drinking Gourd* (commissioned by NBC but never produced). Hansberry's art shows a deep sensitivity to the intricacies of women's lives under challenging, possibly devastating, social conditions.

As the youngest of the Hansberry children by seven years, Lorraine's way for making her own decisions had been paved by three older siblings. Instead of attending a black college as her siblings had done, she spent two years at the University of Wisconsin, Madison, a large, mostly white institution where she became president of the Young Progressive Association, a national left-wing student organization. Without completing her degree, she moved to New York City in the fall of 1950, started attending classes at the New School for Social Research, and began a more active involvement with the protest movement.

Hansberry was supporting herself through freelance writing and odd jobs when the progressive magazine *Freedom*, published by Paul Robeson, and edited by Louis Burnham, hired her as full-time staff and quickly promoted her to associate editor. At the same time, her activism intensified. When Robeson's passport was revoked under suspicion of his communist activities, Hansberry delivered his speech at an international peace conference in Montevideo, Uruguay. She began speaking more frequently at public rallies and protests critical of American society. On a picket line at New York University protesting the exclusion of blacks from the basketball team, Hansberry met a graduate student of **literature** from a Russian-Jewish background who shared her interests in social causes and art. On June 20, 1953, she and Robert Nemiroff were married at the Hansberry home in Chicago. They spent June 19, the day before the wedding, marching in front of the Chicago Federal Building to protest the imminent execution of Ethel and Julius Rosenberg. The day after the wedding, they returned to their Greenwich Village apartment.

Hansberry's increased activism in New York seems the natural outcome of her early Chicago years. She saw her **identity** as inextricably linked to place (Chicago's Southside) and to **race** and gender: "I was born black and a female." Living and attending public schools among Southside's working-class blacks, she witnessed the enduring determination to embrace life despite the hardships of relentless poverty and fatigue. "Each piece of our living," she wrote, "is a protest." From her position of economic privilege, she admired the working **class** and underprivileged black children for their readiness to fight—"the girls as well as the boys" (*TBYGB* 41, 45, 65). In her view, their fighting spirit helped to equalize the sexes. Her New York articles reflect and extend these central formulations of her early years. According to Anne Cheney, Hansberry wrote over twenty articles for *Freedom* during her five-year association with the magazine, addressing events in Africa, articulating social issues such as the educational problems faced by black ghetto children, and covering women's protests against discrimination and war. In letters and articles in other publications, she denounced the social expectations of womanhood that could result in the destructive life and senseless death of a Marilyn Monroe; in letters, albeit anonymous, to the lesbian journal *Ladder*, she connected homophobic, racist, and sexist attitudes, recognizing the dominant culture's routine denial of the rights of gays, people of color, and women; and in her *Ebony* article, "This Complex of Womanhood," she called on black women to resist notions of woman's proper place.

After her marriage, Hansberry quit her job at *Freedom* to devote more time to writing and thinking. She began studying African history with W.E.B. Du Bois at the Jefferson School of Social Science, where she taught black literature. For the next three years she and Nemiroff supported themselves through a variety of jobs. In 1956, a song, cowritten by Nemiroff, "Cindy, Oh, Cindy," became a financial success, providing Hansberry with the opportunity to write full-time.

Since seeing a production of Howard Richardson and William Berney's *Dark of the Moon* in high school, Hansberry had been enchanted by the theater. She was impressed by performances of Shakespeare's *Othello* and *The Tempest* starring family friend Robeson. At Wisconsin, she became familiar with the social **drama** of playwrights like Ibsen, but it was a production of Sean O'Casey's *Juno and the Paycock* that affected her most profoundly. His powerful drama lingered in her consciousness, affirming the power of theater to convey human experience more fully than any other kind of writing. Earlier in 1956, Hansberry had begun working on a play about a struggling black family in Chicago's Southside. When, on March 11, 1959, *A Raisin in the Sun* opened on Broadway, Hansberry's own Mama Lena Younger moved audiences as deeply as she had been moved by Juno Boyle. Hansberry was the first black female playwright to have her work produced on Broadway. At twenty-nine, she became the youngest and first black playwright to win the New York Drama Critics Circle Award for Best Play. Her competition in the 1959 season included plays by Tennessee Williams and Eugene O'Neill.

A Raisin in the Sun tells the story of the five-member, three-generation Younger family, who live together in cramped quarters but have separate and large dreams. Their struggles in a social system that disadvantages blacks translate into familial tensions when Mama, the family matriarch, becomes the recipient of the $10,000 life insurance policy on her deceased husband. Mainstream white critics and audiences embraced the play, ensuring its commercial success. Hansberry's more personal triumph was the confirmation that through drama she could effectively serve her commitment to social justice. Despite the criticism of more militant black playwrights, like Ed Bullins and **Amiri Baraka** (who later changed his mind), that the play was melodramatic, *A Raisin in the Sun* brought universal recognition to specifically black social problems and an enhanced understanding of the social oppression of black Americans.

The next few years did not diminish Hansberry's activism and artistic productivity. She was among the prominent group of black artists and intellectuals, which included **James Baldwin**, who met with Attorney General Robert Kennedy in May 1963 to discuss America's racial crisis; according to Baldwin, Hansberry assumed leadership, refusing to endorse Kennedy's assertion that America was a land of equal opportunity for all races. Hansberry continued to pursue several artistic projects, but her only other play to be produced during her lifetime was *The Sign in Sidney Brustein's Window* (1965), whose protagonist, a white, Jewish, liberal intellectual living in New York's Greenwich Village, struggles with constant disillusionment in his commitment to moral action. Through the play's female characters, and Sidney's male homosexual neighbor, Hansberry questioned social attitudes toward women and homosexuals. An ambitious play in terms of both ideas and plotting, it lacked the dramatic clarity of *Raisin*, resulting in mixed reviews, but at the time of its opening in October 1964, Hansberry was already dying of pancreatic cancer. *Sidney* was not a commercial success, but the efforts of Nemiroff and their many friends financed its Broadway run until the day of her death.

In the spring of 1964, Hansberry and Nemiroff divorced, partly because of Hansberry's growing realization of her **lesbianism**, but they remained close friends and artistic collaborators. As her literary executor, Nemiroff published several finished and unfinished works posthumously, including her African play *Les Blancs* and *What Use Are Flowers?* which deals with nuclear holocaust. *To Be Young, Gifted and Black*, his compilation of Hansberry's writings into an **autobiography**, and a play, indicates the range of talents and interests that her early death left unfulfilled.

Hansberry's plans and unpublished manuscripts further suggest her engagement with feminist thinking. Her 1960 list of Projected Works (*TBYGB* 137) included a play about Mary Wollstonecraft, whose *A Vindication of the Rights of Woman* (1792) is a pioneer work of feminist analysis. In her unpublished essay on Simone de Beauvoir, she proposed *The Second Sex* (1949; English translation 1953) as one of the century's most significant books. Adrienne Rich has questioned a pattern in Hansberry's plays whereby characters, originally conceived as female, emerge as male in the final version. Sidney Brustein, for instance, starts out as Jenny Reed. In *Les Blancs*, a daughter and dead mother turn into the male protagonist and his dead father. The changes, however, do not marginalize the female presence in these plays. Even in *Les Blancs* where the female warrior goddess remains silent, her movements exude power. In her feminism, as in so much else, Hansberry was ahead of her time. Margaret B. Wilkerson has called her "the complete feminist," for she sought to address both race and gender within a social context. As black and female, Hansberry remained well aware that privileging gender over race offered no solutions. As Wilkerson also points out in her article "Lorraine Hansberry: The Complete Feminist," Hansberry did not see her sympathy for the situation of black men as contradicting her advocacy for women's rights. Both her commitment to human rights and her feminism remained inclusive.

See also Black Feminism; Civil Rights Movement

Works By

Lorraine Hansberry: The Collected Last Plays (Les Blancs, The Drinking Gourd, What Use Are Flowers?). Ed. Robert Nemiroff. New York: New American Library, 1983.

The Movement: Documentary of a Struggle for Equality. New York: Simon and Schuster, 1964.

"On Arthur Miller, Marilyn Monroe, and 'Guilt.'" *Women in Theatre: Compassion and Hope*. Ed. Karen Malpede. New York: Drama Book Publishers, 1983. 173–176.

A Raisin in the Sun. New York: Random House (Vintage), 1959.

A Raisin in the Sun. Unfilmed Original Screenplay. Ed. Robert Nemiroff. New York: Penguin (Plume), 1992.

The Sign in Sidney Brustein's Window. New York: Random House, 1965.

"Simone de Beauvoir and *The Second Sex*: An American Commentary." Unpublished, 1957.

"This Complex of Womanhood." *Ebony* 15 (August 1960): 40.

To Be Young, Gifted and Black: A Portrait of Lorraine Hansberry in Her Own Words. Adapted by Robert Nemiroff. New York: New American Library, 1969.

To Be Young, Gifted and Black: A Portrait of Lorraine Hansberry in Her Own Words (Acting Edition). Adapted by Robert Nemiroff. New York: Samuel French, 1971.

"*Touissant*: Excerpt from Act I of a Work in Progress (1961)." *9 Plays by Black Women*. Ed. Margaret B. Wilkerson. New York: New American Library, 1986.

Works About

Abramson, Doris E. *Negro Playwrights in the American Theatre 1925–1959*. New York: Columbia University Press, 1969.

Adler, Thomas P. *American Drama, 1940–1960: A Critical History*. New York: Twayne Publishers, 1994.

Ashley, Leonard R. N. "Lorraine Hansberry and the Great Black Way." *Modern American Drama: The Female Canon*. Ed. June Schlueter. Rutherford, NJ: Fairleigh Dickinson University Press, 1990. 151–160.

Bigsby, C.W.E. *Confrontation and Commitment: A Study of Contemporary American Drama 1959–66*. London: MacGibbon and Kee, 1967.

——. *Modern American Drama, 1945–2000*. Cambridge: Cambridge University Press, 2000.

Brown-Guillory, Elizabeth, ed. *Their Place on the Stage: Black Women Playwrights in America*. Westport, CT: Praeger, 1990.

Carter, Steven R. *Hansberry's Drama: Commitment amid Complexity*. Urbana and Chicago: University of Illinois Press, 1991.

Cheney, Anne. *Lorraine Hansberry*. Boston: Twayne Publishers, 1984.

Friedman, Sharon. "Feminism as Theme in Twentieth-Century American Women's Drama." *American Studies* 25.1 (1984): 69–89.

Leeson, Richard M. *Lorraine Hansberry: A Research and Production Sourcebook*. Westport, CT: Greenwood Press, 1997.

Rich, Adrienne. "The Problem With Lorraine Hansberry." *Freedomways* (Special issue on Lorraine Hansberry, ed. Jean Carey Bond) 19.4 (1979): 247–255.

Shinn, Thelma J. "Living the Answer: The Emergence of African American Feminist Drama." *Studies in the Humanities* 17.2 (1990): 149–159.

Wilkerson, Margaret B. "Excavating Our History: The Importance of Biographies of Women of Color." *Black American Literature Forum* 24.1 (Spring 1990): 73–84.

——. "Lorraine Hansberry: The Complete Feminist." *Freedomways* (Special issue on Lorraine Hansberry, ed. Jean Carey Bond) 19.4 (1979): 235–246.

——. "Political Radicalism and Artistic Innovation in the Works of Lorraine Hansberry." *African American Performance and Theater History: A Critical Reader*. Ed. Harry J. Elam, Jr., and David Krasner. Oxford: Oxford University Press, 2001. 40–55.

——. "The Sighted Eyes and Feeling Heart of Lorraine Hansberry." *Essays on Contemporary American Drama*. Ed. Hedwig Bock and Albert Werheim. München: Max Hueber Verlag, 1981. 91–104.

Rita Bode

HANSEN, JOYCE (1942–)

Joyce Viola Hansen grew up in the Bronx, New York City. From her parents she learned to appreciate books and the magic of storytelling. She received her B.A. in English from Pace University in 1972 and her M.A. in English education from New York University in 1978. Hansen began teaching English and reading in the New York City schools and, through her students, became aware of the need for books with settings, characters, and themes reflecting the lives of the black children in her classes.

Hansen began to write for these children, publishing her first novel, *The Gift-Giver*, in 1980. She quickly followed with her next novel, *Home Boy*, in 1982 and then *Yellow Bird and Me* in 1986. Hansen explores the problems young males experience within the inner city with sensitivity and understanding, yet she endows her female characters with strength to enable their own and the male characters' self-affirmation through dignity, **love**, and compassion.

After the success of her first three novels, Hansen branched into **historical fiction**. While all her narratives stem from the African American experience, Hansen chronicles that experience from varied perspectives. Both *Out from This Place* (1988) and *I Thought My Soul Would Rise and Fly: The Diary of Patsy, a Freed Girl* (1997) feature young girls who find courage during the unstable times following Emancipation. *Which Way Freedom?* (1986) is about an escaped slave who joins a black Union regiment and fights heroically at Fort Pillow in Tennessee. *The Captive* (1994) details the journey of a young boy who is captured in Africa and sold as a slave but eventually finds hope and **freedom**.

Hansen relates that before embarking on historical fiction, she researched the time periods extensively, combing histories and interviews with former slaves to gain an understanding of the environments into which she places her characters. She reports that the experience has left her with a newfound appreciation for the complexity of historical interpretation.

Hansen made her mark in children's nonfiction with *Between Two Fires: Black Soldiers in the Civil War* in 1993. She retired from the school system in 1995 but continued to write. In 1997, she collaborated with Gary McGowan on *Breaking Ground, Breaking Silence: The Story of New York's African Burial Ground*, which was published in 1998. The subject is a once-forgotten African burial site discovered during a 1991 excavation for a new building in Manhattan. Her latest **history** is *Freedom Roads: Searching for the Underground Railroad* (2003). Again teaming with Gary McGowan, Hansen drew information from archaeological sites, Negro **spirituals**, **quilting** patterns, **slave narratives**, oral histories, diaries, letters, and church and government records. In concluding that the **Underground Railroad** constituted a network of routes and way stations, Hansen acknowledges the difficulties inherent in reaching a completely accurate impression of the past through historical interpretation.

Nevertheless, her well-researched books shed much-needed light on the beginnings of African American history for new generations of schoolchildren. Three of her books have received the prestigious Coretta Scott King Author Honors: *The Captive*, *Breaking New Ground*, and *I Thought My Soul Would Rise and Fly*.

See also Children's and Young Adult Literature

Works By

Between Two Fires: Black Soldiers in the Civil War. New York: F. Watts, 1993.
Breaking Ground, Breaking Silence: The Story of New York's African Burial Ground.
   With Gary McGowan. New York: Henry Holt, 1998.

"Bury Me Not in a Land of Slaves": African Americans in the Time of Reconstruction. New York: Watts, 2000.

The Captive. New York: Scholastic, 1994.

Freedom Roads: Searching for the Underground Railroad. With Gary McGowan. New York: Cricket Books, 2003.

The Gift-Giver. New York: Houghton/Clarion, 1980.

The Heart Calls Home. New York: Walker, 1999.

Home Boy. New York: Clarion, 1982.

I Thought My Soul Would Rise and Fly: The Diary of Patsy, a Freed Girl. New York: Scholastic, 1997.

Out from This Place. New York: Walker, 1988.

Which Way Freedom? New York: Walker, 1986.

Women of Hope: African Americans Who Made a Difference. New York: Scholastic, 1998.

Yellow Bird and Me. New York: Clarion, 1986.

Works About

Diouf, Sylviane A. Review of *African Princess: The Amazing Lives of Africa's Royal Women. H-Net Review* (October 2004). www.h-net.msu.edu/reviews/showrev.

Horak, Lisa. Review of *Women of Hope.* "Children's Book Page." www.book page.com.

McGlinn, Jeanne M. Review of *The Captive. Alan Review* (Winter 1995): 23.

Moore, Opal, and D. MacCann. "On Canon Expansion and the Artistry of Joyce Hansen." *Children's Literature Association Quarterly* (Winter 1995–1996): 183–185.

Reardon, Elizabeth M. Review of *Breaking Ground, Breaking Silence. School Library Journal* (May 1998): 57.

Tolson, Nancy D. "Regional Outreach and an Evolving Black Aesthetic." *Children's Literature Association Quarterly* 20.4: 183–185.

Anne Mangum

HARLEM RENAISSANCE

The Harlem Renaissance is known as a period of unprecedented artistic production by African Americans. As the aesthetic counterpart to the social and political movement known as the Negro movement during the early twentieth century, the Harlem Renaissance represents a revolution in the ways African American artists would perceive themselves and their art and thus in the ways they would express themselves verbally, artistically, and musically.

Though both the geographical and historical boundaries of the Harlem Renaissance continue to be questioned, there is no doubt that Harlem had become the center of African American culture by the time of the Great Depression. Just as New York had become one of the cultural capitals of the United States by the

1920s, Harlem had become the geographical center for American blacks who had migrated North to seek better opportunities than those they encountered in the **South**. In Harlem, African Americans were able to live freely, **work** profitably, and attain an education in schools that were far superior to those in the South. As a sort of haven for African Americans to assert their African **identity** and heritage, Harlem was nicknamed "Black Manhattan" by **James Weldon Johnson** and the "Negro Metropolis" by **Claude McKay**.

Harlem's proximity to the publishing metropolis that was New York in the 1920s helped black artists who migrated there as well. New organizations and publications were established to promote African American art. Harlem Renaissance artists were largely inspired and enabled by figures such as **Charles Johnson**, editor of *Opportunity*, Carl Van Vechten, and Alain Locke, who actively sought out black artists and rewarded them for their creativity. The National Association for the Advancement of Colored People (NAACP) funded the magazine the *Crisis: A Record of the Darker Races* and offered grants to black writers, artists, and performers. Two of the most influential political leaders during this time, civil rights advocate A. Philip Randolph, editor of the *Messenger*, and political activist Marcus Garvey, who encouraged African Americans to celebrate their heritage, would inspire a new generation of free black artists to take pride in their cultural identity, and their public visibility helped to legitimate the artistic achievements of black America.

Regarding the dates of the renaissance, some draw a narrow boundary between 1925, when the anthology of writings about African American culture and creativity *The New Negro* was published, to the Great Depression of the 1930s. Others contend that it began in 1910 during what is known as the Great Migration, when the population of black people in Harlem almost tripled, and ended around 1937 when **Zora Neale Hurston** published *Their Eyes Were Watching God*, the last prominent novel to share characteristics with Harlem Renaissance **literature**. But still others note that the creative material produced during the Harlem Renaissance develops themes and reflects thoughts that were advanced much earlier, by notable figures such as **Frederick Douglass** and W.E.B. Du Bois, whose *The Souls of Black Folk* (1903) inspired a number of Harlem Renaissance writers. In fact, some have argued that the opposite philosophies of Du Bois, who encouraged African Americans to develop a strong sense of their African cultural identity, and Booker T. Washington in *Up from Slavery* (1901), who encouraged them to blend into American culture by striving to achieve economic prosperity and assimilating, are reflected in the tension between economic success and exploitation of African culture for the artists of the Harlem Renaissance.

The writers of the Harlem Renaissance address the continued persecution of African Americans by complicating simplified **stereotypes** assigned to them by white culture in various ways. The poet **Countee Cullen**, whose work appeared in such mainstream publications as *Vanity Fair*, *Bookman*, and *Harper's*, helped shape the aesthetic goals of the Harlem Renaissance by analyzing art in his regular column "The Dark Tower." His **poetry** stylistically resembles that of British Romantics from Shelley to Keats, but its message sharply critiques **race** and **class** prejudice. Quite unlike Cullen, **Langston Hughes** avoided traditional forms and brilliantly combined black dialect and musical rhythms to protest various forms of racial injustice. Hughes, who published several volumes of poetry and short stories, two novels, two autobiographies, and nine books for children, was a living example of the great potential African Americans possessed as writers. **Jean Toomer**, whose pastiche of poetry, prose, and **drama** titled *Cane* (1923) was recognized by some as a masterpiece hallmark of the Harlem Reniassance, recalled the music and content of Negro **spirituals** even as it reflected modernist principles of writing. Claude McKay, whose *Home to Harlem* (1928) celebrated the cabaret life of Harlem in the 1920s and aroused controversy for its uninhibited representation of male African American desire, overtly protested racial inequality and even at times generated criticism from the African American **community** for his views. Other writers of the Harlem Renaissance, from the novelist and short-story writer Rudolph Fisher, journalist and essayist Eric Walrond, playwright Willis Richardson to writer, editor, and librarian Arna Bontemps, are also seen as important in displacing, challenging, and rebuking assumptions about the inferiority of black writers.

The visual art of the Harlem Renaissance not only reflected the political, social, and cultural awakening of what came to be known as the New Negro but also introduced new images of African culture into American culture. Painter and muralist Aaron Douglas, who was called "the father of African American art," created illustrations for what is recognized as one of the defining texts, the *New Negro* (1925), as well as for the writing of James Weldon Johnson and Langston Hughes. Painter Palmer Cole Hayden, who transformed his career from janitor to an internationally recognized award-winning painter, was known for his controversial caricatures of black subjects. Other painters such as William Henry Johnson, Jacob Armstead Lawrence, Romare Beardon, and Archibald John Motley, Jr., attempted to represent realistically the experience of African Americans during the early twentieth century. Sculptor Sargeant Claude Johnson brought together images from African and Mexican culture, while painter and sculptor Richmond Barthé brought life to African American historical figures through busts and bas-reliefs.

The Harlem Renaissance also encompasses the achievements and prominence of musicians and performing artists that generated what is known as the Jazz Age. The success of black musicals such as *Shuffle Along* (1921), the first Broadway production that was written, produced, and performed by African Americans, and *Runnin' Wild* (1923), which inspired the phenomenon of the dance known as the Charleston, announced a new era of American music. Along with Louis Armstrong, who is known as one of the founding fathers of **jazz**, musicians such as pianist and composer Duke Ellington, pianist and bandleader Count Basie, and singer and bandleader Cab Calloway showcased their talent in musical venues such as the Apollo Theatre, the Savoy Ballroom, the Plantation Club, the Ciro Club, Connie's Inn, Small's Paradise, Barron's Exclusive Club, and the Cotton Club, most of which denied access to African American patrons.

Though the male writers, artists, and performers of the Harlem Renaissance have dominated many studies of the period, feminists have recently generated great interest in the female artists who were often seen as marginally representative of the movement. Scholars such as Barbara Christian, Gloria Hull, Deborah McDowell, Nellie McKay, Hortense Spillers, Claudia Tate, Cheryl Wall, and Mary Helen Washington significantly revised old conceptions of the Harlem Renaissance by bringing out its misogyny and focusing on women's contributions. Gloria Hull writes in her landmark study *Color, Sex, and Poetry: Three Women Writers of the Harlem Renaissance* (1987) that one of the most influential figures in the Harlem Renaissance, Alain Locke, editor of the *New Negro*, aided novelist Zora Neale Hurston even as he perpetuated the misogyny that characterized the era by expressing dislike for women and promoting male authors. As Cheryl Wall pointed out recently in *Meridians*, organizers and speakers at the Civic Club dinner on March 21, 1924, known by some as a formal induction of the Harlem Renaissance, seriously marginalized the woman writer it was supposed to celebrate, **Jessie Redmon Fauset**.

As the literary editor of the *Crisis*, Fauset not only encouraged collaboration of ideas among African American writers and artists by hosting intellectual evenings that brought them together but also was a prolific writer herself and one of the major figures of the Renaissance. In addition to Fauset, many other women—both white and black—enabled black artists during the Renaissance, such as heiress A'Leila Walker, who opened the doors of her town house she named the "Dark Tower" to black artists and writers. Both Ethel Ray Nance, secretary to Charles Johnson at *Opportunity*, and Regina Andrews, librarian at Harlem public library, encouraged women's artistic production by hosting notable figures such as Countee Cullen and Langston Hughes in their shared apartment. **Georgia Douglas Johnson** not only entertained many of the famous figures of the Harlem Renaissance at her "S Street Salon" but also organized writing workshops where many of their ideas developed.

Writers such as Fauset and Johnson were part of a large group of women poets, novelists, and playwrights to explore the complicated experience of African American female identity during the Harlem Renaissance, a group that also included **Marita Bonner**, **Alice Moore Dunbar-Nelson**, **Angelina Weld Grimké**, **Nella Larsen**, **Pauline Hopkins**, Zora Neale Hurston, **Helene Johnson**, **Ann Petry**, and **Dorothy West**. Other less known women writers such as Anita Scott Coleman, who published several short stories and poems on women's issues in *Crisis* and *Opportunity*, Clarissa M. Scott Delaney, who was both a respected poet and a social worker, the African poet Gladys Mae Casely Hayford (Aquah Laluah), who was an important figure in the Pan-African movement, poet and playwright **May Miller**, children's writer and poet Mary Effie Lee Newsome, the prolific poet Anne Bethel Bannister Spencer Scales, and others have been recovered impressively in *Harlem Renaissance and Beyond* (1990), though they have yet to be analyzed extensively.

Many African American women artists shared experiences of discrimination that reflected a complex mixture of racism and misogyny during the Harlem Renaissance and rebelled by establishing their own organizations or by successfully expressing their sense of alienation creatively. Though sculptor Augusta Fells Savage was turned away from an art school because of her **race**, for example, she would eventually not only establish her own school, the Savage Studio of Arts and Crafts, but also begin the Harlem Community Art Center and aid in the organization of the Harlem Arts Guild. Also a sculptor, Meta Vaux Warrick Fuller turned her experience of solitude as a black woman who experienced severe racial discrimination during her lifetime into widely celebrated art that brought together the images of African **folktales** and the painful experience of being an African American woman in the early twentieth century. Several other African American female sculptors flourished during this period, from Selma Burke, Elizabeth Alice Catlett, and May Howard Jackson, who produced busts of such notable figures as **Paul Lawrence Dunbar** and Du Bois, to Nancy Elizabeth Prophet, who earned international recognition as a sculptor. Painters Louis Mailou Jones, who brought the cultures of Haiti and Africa together in her impressionist paintings, and Laura Wheeler Waring, who not only illustrated for the *Crisis* but also composed portraits of many of the African American leaders of the period, also made important contributions to the world of African American art.

Some of the most notable musical and theatrical performers during the Harlem Renaissance were women as well. The most famous of these were **blues** singers such as Ma Rainey, commonly recognized as one of the earliest blues singers, and Bessie Smith, who called herself the "Empress of the Blues" and became a national phenomenon as one of the most successful singers of the early twentieth century. The unrelated Clara Smith was considered second only to Bessie. Jazz vocalist and songwriter **Billie Holiday** (Eleanora Fagan) continues to be celebrated as one of the most accomplished performers of jazz and blues and is also revered for her recording of "Strange Fruit" (1939), the first song by an African American that chastises the practice of lynching. Other singers such as Ida Cox, who successfully headlined her own shows, Marian Anderson, who was the first African American opera singer to perform at the Metropolitan Opera House, and Adelaide Hall, a singer whose impressive career had her performing from the time of the Renaissance until she was ninety years old, lived as examples that African American women could achieve great and lasting success as musicians. Performers such as Gladys Bentley (Bobbie Minton), an openly gay singer who cross-dressed, embraced and reflected the sexually liberal nature of the Harlem Renaissance and the Jazz Age in general. Singer, dancer, and actor Florence Mills, whose career ended tragically early when she was only thirty-two, had become one of the most famous and popular black performers of her time in Europe and the United States. Singer and dancer **Josephine Baker** not only rose to international fame from complete poverty but also pushed the boundaries of the Harlem Renaissance world set by Du Bois and Locke in her risqué performance in *La Revue Negre* (1925). Actors Rose McLendon, who starred in plays such as Langston Hughes's *Mulatto*, which had become the longest-running play on Broadway at the time, and Ethel Waters, who lived through the horrific experiences of extreme poverty and child abuse to become one of the most prominent singers and actresses of the Harlem Renaissance, also visibly contributed to the achievements of African American culture.

The creative art produced by both women and men of the Harlem Renaissance would inspire numerous African American artists, writers, and musicians of the future such as **Amiri Baraka** (LeRoi Jones), **Ishmael Reed**, **Audre Lorde**, **Paule Marshall**,**Toni Morrison**, and **Alice Walker**. But the legacy of women's contributions to the Harlem Renaissance is just beginning to be perceived as feminists work to uncover and explore the unique achievements of African American women artists.

Works About

Hull, Gloria T. *Color, Sex, and Poetry: Three Women Writers of the Harlem Renaissance.* Bloomington: Illinois University Press, 1987.

Kramer, Victor A., and Robert A. Russ. *The Harlem Renaissance Re-examined: A Revised and Expanded Edition.* Troy, NY: Whitston Publishing, 1997.

Musser, Judith. "African American Women's Short Stories in the Harlem Renaissance: Bridging a Tradition." *MELUS* 23.2 (1998): 24–47.

Roses, Lorraine Elena, and Ruth Elizabeth Randolph, eds. *Harlem Renaissance and Beyond: Literary Biographies of 100 Black Women Writers 1900–1945.* Boston: G. K. Hall, 1990.

——, eds. *Harlem's Glory: Black Women Writing, 1900–1950.* Cambridge, MA: Harvard University Press, 1996.

Wall, Cheryl A. "Histories and Heresies: Engendering the Harlem Renaissance." *Meridians* 2.1 (2001): 59–76.

——. *Women of the Harlem Renaissance.* Bloomington: Illinois University Press, 1995.

Kathleen M. Helal

HARPER, FRANCES E. W. (1825–1911)

Born on September 24, 1825, in Baltimore, Maryland, Frances Ellen Watkins Harper was a novelist, orator, essayist, poet, journalist, and activist. All of Harper's written and oratorical works were part of her efforts toward bringing about that "brighter coming day" she believed was on the horizon for women, African Americans, and indeed, all Americans.

Harper was born free in the slave state of Maryland and was orphaned at an early age. She was raised by her uncle William Watkins, who headed the William Watkins Academy for Negro Youth in Baltimore, a school recognized for its rigorous training in languages, biblical study, and elocution. As Frances Smith Foster notes, by age fourteen, Harper had acquired an education that was superior to most nineteenth-century Americans of any color or **class** at that time. Despite her education, it appears that Harper was only able to find **work** as a seamstress, nurse, and housekeeper when she left the academy. Harper worked for the Armstrong **family** who owned a bookstore; they appear to have granted her access to their books in her spare time.

At age twenty, Harper published her first book, *Forest Leaves*, of which no extant copy appears to exist. In the early 1850s, Maryland laws prohibited free blacks from entering the state; if caught, they would be reenslaved. Baltimore was an increasingly dangerous place for free African Americans, and William Watkins closed his school and moved to Canada. For unknown reasons, Harper, aged twenty-five, did not travel with the family but moved to Columbus, Ohio, where she became the first woman professor at the newly formed Union Seminary (later Wilberforce University). Harper taught for a time at Little York, Pennsylvania, and eventually realized she was not well suited for teaching.

In response to an incident involving a free black man being sold back into **slavery**, Harper gave up teaching and devoted the rest of her life to abolition and other social reform agendas. In 1853, she moved to Philadelphia, where she published in abolitionist publications and lived with the family of noted abolitionist and **Underground Railroad** activist William Still, whose home was the main "depot" in Philadelphia. At this time, Harper contributed widely to numerous abolitionist publications, and in 1854 she combined her **poetry** and essays into *Poems on Miscellaneous Subjects*. As its title suggests, Harper addressed a wide range of topics including slavery, abolition, **religion**, women's rights, temperance, and African American **history**. This volume sold 10,000 copies in its first three years and was enlarged and reissued in 1857. In 1871, it entered its twentieth edition. Harper is also listed as an editor and contributor to what is now considered to be the first African American literary journal, the *Anglo-African Magazine*. In 1859, she published what is generally considered to be the first short story by an African American woman, "The Two Offers."

In 1854, after her first lecture in Boston, Harper accepted a position as a lecturer with the Maine Anti-Slavery Society and thus became one of the first professional orators in the United States. Harper was reported to be a highly articulate, persuasive, and fiery speaker who did not violate the rigid codes of female decorum. In 1866, Harper spoke at the Eleventh National Woman's Rights Convention at which Susan B. Anthony, Elizabeth Cady Stanton, Lucretia Mott, and Frances D. Gage also spoke. Harper's speech "We Are All Bound Up Together" established her presence with the national feminist organizations.

When she was thirty-six, she married Fenton Harper, a widower with four children. Together they had one child, Mary, who lived with Harper throughout her life. Little is known about Fenton or why Harper married at such a late age. When Fenton Harper died in 1864, everything that was jointly owned was taken from her to pay off debts she knew nothing about. This experience reinforced Harper's understandings of the powerlessness of women and reinvigorated her commitment to equal rights for all. Within months of his **death**, she and Mary moved to New England, and she returned to the lecture circuit.

Less is known about Harper's life after this point, and most of what is known about her comes from newspapers and other public documents. During the Civil War, she published writings and gave lectures. Between 1864 and 1870, she traveled to every southern state (except Texas and Arkansas), where she lectured to whites, blacks, and integrated audiences, teaching former slaves **literacy** and homemaking skills. She wrote letters to northern newspapers urging support for Reconstruction efforts. After the failure of Reconstruction, Harper argued for reformed voting rights and attempted to build strong African American communities from within.

In 1872, Harper published what is likely her most innovative work, *Sketches of Southern Life*. This work introduced the character of Aunt Chloe who, according to Frances Smith Foster, helped shape emerging interests in literary realism and local color through her use of dialect, folk characters, and culture. In 1892, Harper published her best-known novel, ***Iola Leroy***, in response to the inaccurate and increasingly popular Plantation School novelists and in answer to the need for more books that would inspire and instruct African American readers.

Throughout her life, Harper was a committed social activist in printed word and deed for causes ranging from abolition to suffrage to temperance. She was one of the first African American women to hold office in the almost exclusively white Woman's Christian Temperance Union, was active in founding of the National Association of Colored Women, and from 1893 until her death, was involved in the Universal Peace Union. Harper's health began failing in 1901, and despite numerous offers of assistance, Harper declined them all, citing her desire for independence and liberty. Harper died on February 22, 1911, in Philadelphia, Pennsylvania.

Twentieth-century critics such as Barbara Christian, Frances Smith Foster, Mary Helen Washington, and many others have helped to recover and contextualize Harper's contribution to the American literary tradition and to show that Harper's belief in the "brighter coming day" remains as important today as it was in her own time.

Works By

A Brighter Coming Day: A Frances E. W. Harper Reader. Ed. Frances Smith Foster. New York: Feminist Press, 1990.

Iola Leroy: Or, Shadows Uplifted. Ed. Frances Smith Foster. New York: Oxford University Press, 1988.

Minnie's Sacrifice, Sowing and Reaping, Trial and Triumph: Three Rediscovered Novels by Frances E. W. Harper. Ed. Frances Smith Foster. Boston: Beacon Press, 1994.

Poems on Miscellaneous Subjects. Boston: Yerriton and Sons, 1854.

Sketches of Southern Life. Philadelphia: Merrihew and Son, 1872.

Works About

Carby, Hazel. *Reconstructing Womanhood: The Emergence of the Afro-American Woman Novelist*. New York: Oxford University Press, 1987.

Foster, Frances Smith. "Frances Ellen Watkins Harper." *Black Women in America: An Historical Encyclopedia*. Ed. Darlene Clark Hine, Elsa Barkley Brown, and Rosalyn Terbourg-Penn. Bloomington: Indiana University Press, 1993. 532–537.

Logan, Shirley Wilson. *"We Are Coming": The Persuasive Discourse of Nineteenth-Century Black Women*. Carbondale: Southern Illinois University Press, 1999.

Peterson, Carla L. *Doers of the Word: African American Women Speakers and Writers in the North (1830–1880)*. New York: Oxford University Press, 1995.

Sale, Maggie Montesinos. "Frances Ellen Watkins Harper." *American Women Prose Writers, 1870–1920*. Ed. Sharon M. Harris, Heidi L. M. Jacobs, and Jennifer Putzi. Detroit: Gale Research, 2000. 182–192.

Heidi L. M. Jacobs

HARRIS, E. LYNN (1955–   )

E. Lynn Harris was born in Flint, Michigan, and raised in Little Rock, Arkansas. He attended the University of Arkansas at Fayetteville, where he completed a B.A. in journalism. Following graduation, Harris enjoyed a successful thirteen-year career as computer salesperson before quitting that **work** to write his first novel, *Invisible Life*. Given the difficulties facing black gay authors in getting publishers to take on their work, Harris, notably, self-published *Invisible Life* in 1991 and sold it through black-owned bookstores, beauty salons, and even from the trunk of his car. When the first edition quickly sold out of its 10,000 copies, Harris won a reissue with Anchor Books, which simultaneously published his follow-up novel *Just as I Am* in 1994. This began a highly successful run of novels, stories, and a published memoir. Harris's works to date have all become bestsellers, while several have won a variety of awards, including the James Baldwin Award for Literary Excellence for *If This World Were Mine* (1997).

For literary critics and academic commentators, Harris's works, especially his breakthrough novel *Invisible Life*, are particularly significant in foregrounding bisexuality and exploring the complicated intersections of sexual **identity**, sexual behavior, and racial identity, particularly for black males. That these writings have gone on to achieve widespread mainstream popularity is significant in the **history** of publishing in the United States. The publication of Harris's *Invisible Life* in 1991 marked one of the first instances in which a U.S. novel addressed black male bisexuality as its central theme. While other black authors, including Wallace Thurman with *Infants of the Spring* (1932), **Claude McKay** with *Home to Harlem* (1928), and **James Baldwin** with *Another Country* (1962), had discussed black male bisexuality, it was not presented as a primary theme. Although critics do not consider Harris's work to be among the same rank of **literature** as that of McKay or Baldwin, his work is important in bringing into the open a direct discussion of the experiences of bisexual black men.

In the United States, **race** and **class** converge to influence the development of discourses around sexual identities. Homophobia and racist **stereotypes** of black **sexuality** have contributed to a silencing of voices concerning black male bisexuality, forcing many black male bisexuals into positions of adopting invisible or dual lives. This invisibility sexuality has been matched by an invisibility in terms of political organizing and social movements. While bisexual political and social organizing in the United States is at a later and less developed stage than gay organizing, what organizations, publications, and networks do exist are predominantly white and middle class. This has created a certain disaffection and alienation among Black male bisexuals as their needs, interests, and experiences have been largely unarticulated, at least nationally.

This silencing has been reflected and reproduced in the publishing industry in the United States. Despite the emergence and proliferation of lesbian and gay presses as part of the growth of lesbian and gay movements, much of the work that is published is written by white men and women. The experiences of gay and bisexual black men have not found expression in much of the published work, certainly not in terms of **fiction**. Despite important breakthroughs for black women novelists, similar advances have not been made by black male novelists, especially among sexual minorities.

In light of these facts, the broad success of Harris's novels is particularly remarkable. Harris's popular writings have broken through the silence that has enveloped black male bisexuality.

In his treatments of black male sexuality, Harris's works suggest that supposedly stable or fixed identities such as gay or bisexual are inadequate for understanding black male sexuality or sexual practices. His works resist the essentializing, within dominant cultures and discourses, of black and gay identities. Instead, he offers glimpses into the often contradictory or conflictual experiences of black male sexuality. Harris's writings both problematize and reenvision conventional, racialized notions of **black masculinity** through the author's complex explorations of bisexuality. For Harris, bisexuality evades attempts to capture an inherent, essential sexual identity.

For Harris, repression relates as much or more to racialized experiences and the formation of racial identities as to sexual identities. Thus the processes of coming out and addressing one's emotional conflictuality are complexly bound up with the formation or reformation of racialized identities in his stories. In dealing with these contradictory experiences and understandings, Harris emphasizes his characters' attempts to forge some solidarity in the context of sexual diversity.

The extent to which Harris's discussions of bisexuality upset conventional approaches to sexual or identity politics have led some commentators to claim Harris as a postmodern writer. Still others have identified rather conventional identity symbolism in Harris's works. Traci Carroll, for example, points to Harris's tendency to associate dark skin with traditional heterosexual masculinity and stable sexual identity. Other conventional aspects of Harris's works include his use of straightforward narrative structures focused on plot, the narrator's middle-class voice, and the privileging of personal upward mobility.

Elsewhere, Lisa Frieden criticizes the rather stereotypical portrayal of Basil, the sole character in Harris's work who maintains a bisexual identity throughout, as predatory and deceitful. While Harris's earlier works began a tentative process of dealing openly and thoughtfully with the complexities of bisexuality, his later works have settled into a more mainstream treatment that some critics suggest falls back on a discrediting of bisexuality as a transitional stage between heterosexuality and homosexuality. Even worse, Harris identifies bisexual men as deceivers primarily responsible for bringing HIV (human immunodeficiency virus) into the heterosexual **community**. This plays into conventional stereotypes that similarly attribute the spread of HIV into heterosexual and lesbian communities to the supposed promiscuity of bisexuals. These stereotypes, which downplay alternative explanations such as intravenous drug use or unsafe sex practices, reinforce notions that bisexuals are somehow more dishonest and irresponsible than monosexuals. While Harris does highlight social pressures, most notably homophobia, that force people to closet their sexuality, his failure to deconstruct these stereotypes, even as they contribute to the very processes Harris challenges, remains problematic.

Indeed, critics have also argued that Harris's works have retreated into a conservative defense of monogamy in which the bisexual character (Basil) poses the constant looming predatory threat to gay and straight couples alike. While Harris comes to pose bisexuality as a threat to heterosexual black women and African American families, he proposes a version of "**family** values" narratives as a means to repair divisions in African American communities in the context of more openly diverse sexual identities.

Part of this may be expressive of the tensions between Harris's understandings of his sexuality and his faith. In his second novel, *Just as I Am*, which takes its title from a **spiritual**, these tensions are expressed outwardly in the emphasis on **healing** and therapy, and confession within therapy, in that work. They are also reflected starkly in the decision by the series' protagonist Raymond to return to the **South**, where he moves back in with his parents and undertakes a period of chastity.

While Harris's discussion of homophobia, presentations of nonessentialist sexual and racial identities, and notions of healing and collective well-being touch upon values expressed in some **black feminist** theory, his work overall is conflicted and contradictory, torn between liberatory and conservative sentiments. In this regard, it may well be truly postmodern work.

Works By

Abide With Me. New York: Doubleday, 1999.
And This Too Shall Pass. New York: Doubleday, 1996.

Any Way the Wind Blows. New York: Anchor, 2001.
If This World Were Mine. New York: Doubleday, 1997.
Invisible Life. New York: Anchor Books, 1994.
Just as I Am. New York: Doubleday, 1994.
A Love of My Own. New York: Doubleday, 2002.
Not a Day Goes By. New York: Anchor, 2000.
What Becomes of the Brokenhearted. New York: Anchor, 2003.

Works About

Carroll, Traci. "Invisible Sissy: The Politics of Masculinity in African American Bisexual Narrative." *Representing Bisexualities: Subjects and Cultures of Fluid Desire.* New York: New York University Press, 1996. 180–204.
Foxxe, Austin. "A Visible Life." *Advocate,* July 8, 2003. http://www.dynomind .com/p/articles/mi_m1589/is_2003_ July_8/ai_105367800.
Frieden, Lisa. "Invisible Lives: Addressing Black Male Bisexuality in the Novels of E. Lynn Harris." *Bisexual Men in Culture and Society.* Ed. Brett Beemyn and Erich Steinman. New York: Harrington Park, 2002. 73–90.

J. Shantz

HEALING

African American feminist **literature** is richly textured with images of the healing of **body**, mind, and soul that echo the struggles of African American women to overcome white abstract beliefs about their femininity and humanity. Images of healing in the **poetry**, songs, and stories of African American women are a testament to their struggle for self-validation. The female healer character, often in the form of grandmother or spiritual **ancestor**, functions as part of a gynocentric discourse that strengthens the matriarchal bond through which **family history** and culture traditionally are passed down. For African American women writers, their literary images of healing are inextricably linked to a shared history of **slavery**, **motherhood**, and patriarchal domination that work to affirm the forces of **love** and hope.

Many images of healing in African American feminist literature concern dissipated and fractured motherhood through the loss of a child[ren]. One of the most horrific images in literature, and history, is the tearing away by slaveholders of a child from its mother. In ***Incidents in the Life of a Slave Girl*** (1861), **Harriet Jacobs**'s relationship with her grandmother demonstrates the bond between mothers, as both women lose children through slavery. The grandmother is a strong female character whose healing strength provides a solid foundation throughout *Incidents*. She affirms the bond of motherhood, as her healing love and wisdom are cornerstones of silent and subtle strength within the narrative. In **Toni Morrison**'s ***Beloved*** (1987), the women of the **community** gather around the house at 124 and loudly sing and pray for Sethe when the ghost of the murdered infant Beloved sucks the life from her. Sethe's crime went against the very notion of motherhood, yet she becomes the recipient of the healing love and strength of her sisters.

Gloria Naylor's works often utilize the natural and supernatural world, which then become the source of strength and healing. In *Linden Hills* (1985), Willa Nedeed is healed through the writings left by the previous Mrs. Nedeeds, creating a compelling bond between women that transcends time and gives Willa the strength to move past the loss of her infant and to embrace her own autonomy. In *Mama Day* (1988), it is the healing power of a family in crisis that becomes a testament to the infectiousness of human perseverance and the efficacy of believing. In **Toni Cade Bambara**'s *The Salt Eaters* (1980), healing power is woven through a splendid array of characters ebbing in and around the life of Velma Henry. Minnie Ransom's bond to Old Wife is repeated in Ransom's bond to Velma as their unity demonstrates the radiant power of healing.

Framed around the desire to cure the soul from the repressiveness of slavery and the white belief in black inhumanity, frequent images of healing in African American literature unite physical **freedom** of the body with spiritual self-determination. For African American women the yearning for freedom of the body from patriarchal restraints becomes intertwined with the need for autonomy and selfhood. The spiritual narrative worked to validate African American women's humanity through the power of personal revelation, enabling the healing of both mind and soul. The act of owning one's story—of being free to *speak*, to tell, to relive experiences—became both a liberating and healing power. Such examples include **Jarena Lee**'s *The Life and Religious Experience of Jarena Lee, a Coloured Lady, Giving an Account of Her Call to Preach the Gospel* (1836), in which Lee attempts suicide but is saved by a divine awakening from within and the discovery of Scripture. Her journey is one of self-discovery, and her narrative is a lyrical account of her determination to preach the Gospel despite the confines of patriarchal authority. Such spiritual healing and affirmation of female selfhood can also be found in the narrative of **Sojourner Truth**, **Maria Stewart**'s *Religion and the Pure Principles of Morality* (1831), and **Harriet Wilson**'s *Our Nig* (1859).

Voice is a source of empowerment in the act of healing and African American women's unabating will to speak without fear, to tell a story, and to relay experiences externalized an autonomy that challenged social attitudes toward African American women's intelligence and humanity. Healing images of freedom in song and verse are keenly captured in **Frances E. W. Harper**'s "Eliza Harris" and "Songs for the People" where "music pure and strong" heals the heart and soul of all who hear. The lyrical grace and redemptive power of verse fosters a unique power to heal and celebrate womanhood. **Maya Angelou**'s poetry presents deliciously positive visions of African American **beauty** and **sexuality**, contrary to restrictive white standards of beauty. Angelou's **autobiography** *I Know Why the Caged Bird*

Sings (1969) is a testament to her unflinching strength and resilience and exhibits a sense of the spiritual healing that comes from her ever-present awareness of the voice of her ancestors.

Zora Neale Hurston's "How It Feels to Be Colored Me" expresses how it feels to be African American in a white community, how being colored should be but a small part of her wholeness. The act of *having* to explain her humanity outside of her color becomes a healing act of self-validation. The healing properties of self-revelation also run throughout Hurston's ***Their Eyes Were Watching God*** (1937) as Janie sets herself in a comfortable position and proceeds to relate her story to Pheoby because " 'tain't no use in me telling you somethin' unless Ah give you de understandin' to go 'long wid it." It is the act of sharing stories, of passing down wisdom between women, that creates a lush network of healing, of sisters whose resplendent array of experiences and knowledge heals each other, their families, and their community. The healing power within community is a theme in **Alice Walker**'s ***The Color Purple*** (1982), where Shug Avery's vivacious self-determination and captivating presence slowly heal the horrors of **rape** and **domestic** abuse Celie has suffered.

Images of healing in African American women's stories carry added significance as bearers of the black female experience both past and present. African American feminist writings reach beyond the color line and out to the whole community of women, sharing their healing power within the common bonds of motherhood, child rearing, and patriarchal bondage.

Works About

Birch, Eva Lennox. *Black American Women's Writing: A Quilt of Many Colors*. New York: Harvester Wheatsheaf, 1994.

Blair, Barbara, and Susan E. Cayleff, eds. *Wings of Gauze: Women of Color and the Experience of Health and Illness*. Detroit: Wayne State University Press, 1993.

Puhr, Kathleen M. "Healers in Gloria Naylor's Fiction." *Twentieth Century Literature* 40.4 (1994): 518+.

Debbie Clare Olson

HERRON, CAROLIVIA (1947–   )

Although Carolivia Herron's first novel *Thereafter Johnnie* (1991) won wide critical acclaim, she is best known for her controversial children's book *Nappy Hair* (1997), an **identity**-affirming celebration of African American female **beauty**.

Herron's *Nappy Hair* is a delightful autobiographical sketch about Brenda and her unruly hair. Herron's story utilizes the African American call-and-response tradition that works rhythmically to incorporate much more than a commentary on Brenda's nappy hair. Herron's story is really an affirmation of black beauty in the face of an increasingly narrow white standard of what constitutes attractiveness. Herron's tale celebrates Brenda's nappy hair by weaving a lyrical **history** around Brenda's hair and keenly connecting a sense of pride to the heritage her nappy hair represents. Herron's tale is an important contribution to black children's **literature** as it works to affirm black standards of beauty in a society that continuously bombards black children with a predominantly white paradigm.

Herron's first and only novel to date, *Thereafter Johnnie*, is a richly textured epic set in Washington, D.C., with numerous allusions to **myth** and biblical prophecies. Herron's novel discombobulates father-daughter incest, patriarchal **family** structure, and the intricacies of seduction. *Thereafter Johnnie* contains a complex structure that draws heavily on ancient Greek myths and African American folk legends. Herron's Johnnie, the child of Patricia and her father, John Christopher, is mute as a child but finds her voice at age fourteen. Johnnie's muteness parallels Herron's own childhood lack of awareness about sexual abuse she suffered. Herron's Johnnie does not slip into a melancholy victimhood but rather is a strong character who embarks on a search for her identity. The story is told from multiple female points of view, thereby negating the traditional patriarchal exclusivity of history and myth, as it explores the multifaceted history of modern racial conflict within the milieu of a global **race** war. The novel traces the destruction of the family and its ultimate **healing** through a second coming—Johnnie as messiah—that births a new society.

Herron was born on July 22, 1947, in Washington, D.C., to Oscar and Georgia Herron. In 1969 she earned her B.A. in English from Eastern Baptist College and, in 1973, an M.A. in English from Villanova University. She completed a second M.A. in comparative literature and creative writing and her Ph.D. in comparative literature and literary theory from the University of Pennsylvania in 1985. Herron taught at Harvard University as an assistant professor of Afro-American studies and comparative literature from 1986 to 1990. In 1985 Herron was awarded a Fulbright Research Scholarship and in 1989 was awarded the Folger Shakespeare Library Post-Doctoral Research Fellowship. Herron was a Bunting fellow at Radcliffe College from 1988 to 1989. She was a visiting professor at Carleton College in 1989, and from 1990 to 1992 Herron was the director of the Epicenter for the Study of Epic Literature and associate professor of English at Mount Holyoke College. Herron is a founding member of Jews of African Descent and continues her research in the interconnectedness of Judaic and African cultures.

See also Children's and Young Adult Literature

Works By

Nappy Hair. New York: Knopf, 1997.
Selected Works of Angelina Weld Grimkè. Ed. Carolivia Herron. New York: Oxford University Press, 1991.
Thereafter Johnnie. New York: Random House, 1991.

Works About

Breau, Elizabeth. "Incest and Intertextuality in Carolivia Herron's *Thereafter Johnnie.*" *African American Review* 31.1 (Spring 1997): 91–103.

Daly, Brenda O. "Whose Daughter Is Johnnie? Revisionary Myth-making in Carolivia Herron's *Thereafter Johnnie.*" *Callaloo* 18.2 (Spring 1995): 472–491.

Lester, Neal A. "Nappy Edges and Goldy Lockes: African-American Daughters and the Politics of Hair." *Lion and the Unicorn* 24.2 (April 2000): 201–224.

Debbie Clare Olson

HISTORICAL FICTION

Historical fiction is a narrative form that combines research with imaginary elements in order to recreate a historical event, period, or figure. African American **literature** reworks the nineteenth-century European tradition of the historical novel in order to challenge versions of **history** established by white hegemonies. African American historical fiction, therefore, privileges the lives of the socially marginalized who remained outside the pages of history. **Slave narratives**, in their double role of contributing to the abolitionist cause and to the making of history, establish one of the most prevailing concerns of the black historical narrative—the production of the historical record.

Frederick Douglass's novella *The Heroic Slave* (1853) is one of the first texts to combine slave and fictional narratives in order to recover African American history. In this text there is a conscious effort to challenge the gaps and distortions of the American annals. In the recreation of the story of the slave rebel Madison Washington, Douglass established those unrecorded elements through **fiction**. The narrative is constructed around the oral exchanges between characters. From Madison's soliloquy to the final recounting of the mutiny on board the *Creole* by its surviving first mate, Douglass promotes the spoken word as a means of recovering history, thus establishing another significant paradigm in African American historical fiction. In this work, Douglass also illustrates that in the African American text history is simply not the story of the past but a means of explaining and understanding the present.

This dual process of entering into a dialogue with contemporary readers, calling their attention to the plight of a disenfranchised people while recording and reimagining history, also informs the fictional work of **Frances E. W. Harper**. As a women's rights activist, Harper is particularly keen to register the role of black women during **slavery**, the Civil War, and its aftermath. In *Minnie's Sacrifice* (1867–1868), slave women risk their lives to cross rebel lines in order to aid suffering soldiers. In ***Iola Leroy*** (1892), a female slave ingeniously spies for the Union army by hanging her sheets in different ways, which corresponded to different movements of the rebel forces, while Iola works as a nurse, relieving the suffering of the wounded. After the war the women continue to have an active role, working side by side with men in a continuous effort to reunite families and establish communities. The past, in Harper's work, functions less as a nostalgic era of courageous endurance and deliverance and more as a period from which directions for the future can be drawn. An interesting aspect of Harper's work is her call for the establishment of a literary tradition that would assist the "uplifting" of the **race**, proving intellectual parity with whites, overturning the stereotypical images of blacks, and operating as a didactic medium for both. In this way, Harper summons the creation of a literary body that would reflect the history of African Americans reimagined and written by themselves.

Nineteenth-century African American literature, however, presents limitations in its treatment of history. Writers such as Harper and **Pauline Hopkins** in *Contending Forces* (1900) approach the past from a didactic and moral point of view. Confined by the corset of the conventions of the time and too preoccupied with the creation of a black middle-class role model for, and leader of, the masses, they write about exceptional characters, generally educated and very often light enough to pass for white. In doing so, they set aside a black protagonist who could be considered representative.

The silences and the gaps left by both the slave narratives and nineteenth-century historical fiction constitute the open spaces from which the stories of contemporary writers begin to take shape. As Houston A. Baker observes, only in the last four decades have African American writers traveled "as an extensive and articulate group . . . all the way back to the origins and recorded their insights in distinctive forms designed for a black audience" (53). In fact, Arna Bontemps's *Black Thunder*, a fictional account of Gabriel Prosser's insurrection published in 1936, is the only significant work to deal with slavery before the publication of **Margaret Walker**'s benchmark novel *Jubilee* (1966).

Led by the desire to record her great-grandmother's story, Walker extensively researched the historical texts available in the 1940s and 1950s, concluding that not only was African American history practically unwritten but that black women's history was still in a state of tabula rasa. Studying a myriad of documents, Walker created a historical context in which to give shape to her grandmother's oral narrative. The novelist creates a patchwork made up of fact and fiction in order to bring to life history and story. To validate the uniqueness of her grandmother's narrative and the distinctiveness of African American history and experience, Walker uses **folklore** as the framework of her novel. Music is an important element in this context. Walker shows her understanding of the central role that music occupies in black American culture by opening each chapter of her novel with a passage from a song. These passages function as epigraphs that establish the theme or set the tone of each chapter. In a European tradition, these excerpts are, generally speaking, taken from influential works, which inspired authors and helped to shape texts and traditions. Choosing oral texts as epigraphs, Walker clarifies the tradition within which her work is set. She also uses folk speech patterns, storytelling, and sayings; superstitions, beliefs, **religion**, and rituals; food, herbal medicine, and household customs; quilt making, clothing, and games in order to represent and express African American history in folk terms. In others words, Walker weaves her prose with those African

American traditions and skills that were communicated via word of mouth, revealing a rich and whole culture that survived and developed devoid of the printed word. Walker's thorough research, concern with historical accuracy, and meticulous representation of the quotidian freed other writers from the constrictions of verisimilitude, allowing them to enter the more complex psychological landscapes of the enslaved subject.

In the 1970s, with the emergence of black studies departments and the publication of studies on the history of slavery such as John Blassingame's *The Slave Community* and George Rawick's *From Sundown to Sunup*, both published in 1972, the novelist could be less preoccupied with her or his role as social historian. The historical fiction of this period is dominated by two main trends, representations of the early twentieth century and of the antebellum **South**. Novels such as **Louise Meriwether**'s *Daddy Was a Number Runner* (1970), **Toni Morrison**'s *The Bluest Eye* (1970), *Sula* (1973), and *Song of Solomon* (1977) and **Alice Walker**'s *The Third Life of Grange Copeland* (1970) explore the era of their parents' generation and their own childhood and early adulthood, portraying the endurance of both rural and urban communities in a segregated society from the 1920s to the 1960s. These novels reexamine and reinvent the African American experience as a part of a literary process that points toward a revision and redefinition of black **identity** from an imaginative perspective.

The exploration of slavery continues to dominate the historical novels of this decade such as **Ernest Gaines**'s *The Autobiography of Miss Jane Pittman* (1971), **Gayl Jones**'s *Corregidora* (1975), **Ishmael Reed**'s *Flight to Canada* (1976), **Alex Haley**'s *Roots* (1976), **Barbara Chase-Riboud**'s *Sally Hemings* (1979), and **Octavia Butler**'s *Kindred* (1979). With the exception of *Flight to Canada*, which tells the story of Raven Quickskill, an escaped bondman who returns to the plantation to free other slaves, and *Roots*, a genealogical narrative that traces the origins of a black American **family** to Africa, these novels privilege the female slave.

The most innovative works of this period are those that attempt to find different modes of exploring slavery, developing and reworking the African American historical novel. In *The Autobiography of Miss Jane Pittman*, Gaines validates oral tradition by recreating the past through the voice of a storyteller, a representative figure whose chronicle is simultaneously the narrative of her personal story and the collective history of African Americans. *Flight to Canada* presents a parody of Harriet Beecher Stowe's *Uncle Tom's Cabin* (1852) in a text that revises the conventions of the slave narrative. Reed's use of anachronistic elements such as a slave's escape by jumbo jet and the television broadcast of Lincoln's assassination blurs the boundaries and draws parallels between slavery and the Civil War and the present of the bicentennial anniversary of the country. In *Kindred*, Butler uses time travel to transport her protagonist from California in 1976 to an 1813 plantation, where her grandmother was born, testing her survival skills with the knowledge of the present. In Butler's novel, black history is marked by its discontinuity. On her last trip to the past, Dana, the main character, loses an arm—a metaphor for a history that cannot be retrieved.

In *Corregidora*, the chronological narrative is abandoned in favor of a narrating mode that is fragmented and at times seemingly disjointed in order to mirror the mental processes by which one remembers, selects, and recreates different aspects of personal history. Jones's first-person narrative constitutes an innovative approach to the use of folk speech. In order to solve the tension between the third-person narrator's standard English and the characters' dialogue or monologue in vernacular, Jones breaks out of this narrative frame. By doing so she not only removes the hierarchical relationship between standard English and black vernacular, but she also authenticates African American oral tradition by creating a narrator who is essentially a storyteller. Jones also initiates a new trend in the African American historical novel by exploring those events that, owing to their horrific nature, compromise the notion of historical continuity not because the past remains irremediably cut off from the present but because it remains a ghostly presence in the present day. This novel is also influential in its use of **blues** patterns of call and response to recreate a notion of history that is circular rather than linear. The blues function as a creative synthesis in which the tensions and contradictions of African American history can be contained.

In the 1980s and the subsequent decades, slavery remained a central theme in African American historical fiction. The emphasis of the works from this period is the representation of the heterogeneity of the experience of the enslaved self along with the exploration of facets of that experience that, in both slave narratives and nineteenth-century literature, remained in the realm of the unspeakable. In *Dessa Rose* (1986) and *Beloved* (1987), **Sherley Anne Williams** and **Toni Morrison**, respectively, also create fiction from fact in order to transform the fragmented past into what Margaret Walker calls the "muscle and flesh for the real and living bones of history" (*How I Wrote Jubilee* 58). In the "Author's Note" to *Dessa Rose*, Williams explains that her story is based on two unrelated historical episodes: a 1829 uprising on a coffle in Kentucky led by a pregnant slave and the story of a white woman who, living in a remote area of North Carolina in 1830, offers refuge to runaway slaves. Morrison bases her novel on the story of Margaret Garner, a slave who in Cincinnati in 1856 attempted to kill her four children, trying to save them from a life of bondage. Both these novels move away from linear modes of narration, reflecting blues patterns of repetition and variation. From the silences to the half-told tales, the fabric of the narrative leaves many loose threads to be picked up at a later stage. The act of reading becomes one of following the retelling of certain episodes until a more complete picture emerges. In these novels, **memory** is a critical issue not only because the way one remembers shapes the structure of the narrative but also because it is crucial to the reconstruction of an unwritten past. In *Dessa Rose*, historical continuity is assured by the ex-slave's passing on of her memories to next generation. In *Beloved*, Morrison reworks Jones's notion that a past of slavery can hold a grip on the present. However, Morrison's concept of "re-memory," a recollection that untold or unclaimed remains a ghostly presence in the present, is more ambiguous. Although the prefix "re" suggests repetition, the never-ending resurfacing of the same memory, the final chapter of the novel reiterates that Beloved's story was not one to pass on. In this way, Morrison illustrates the paradox inherent in recreating the past, recalling and reimagining what the ancestors chose to forget.

In *Oxherding Tale* (1982), **Charles Johnson** dramatizes the sexual exploitation of enslaved men. Edward P. Jones explores the contradictory world of black slaveholders in *The Known World* (2003). In *Free* (1992), Marsha Hunt writes about the legacies of slavery in a small northern town in the early twentieth century, exploring the rigid divisions of **class**, race, and sex of the age in the context of a homosexual relationship and thus uncovering another silenced aspect of American history.

This period also witnessed the publication of critically acclaimed fictional biographies. **Virginia Hamilton**'s *Anthony Burns* (1988) dramatizes the life of the eponymous runaway slave, his trial and return to slavery under the Fugitive Slave Act of 1850. In *The President's Daughter* (1994), Barbara Chase-Riboud presents a sequel to *Sally Hemings*, which chronicles the life of Harriet, Sally's daughter with Thomas Jefferson. Louise Meriwether's *Fragments of the Ark* (1994) is based on the life of Robert Smalls and explores the African American participation in, and perspectives on, the Civil War. Jewell Parker Rhodes chronicles the intimate relationships of Frederick Douglass in *Douglass' Women: A Novel* (2003). Jacqueline Sheehan presents a fictional account of the life of **Sojourner Truth** in *Truth: A Novel* (2003).

Contemporary writers have experimented with ways of representing in their work the harrowing experience of the **Middle Passage**, the Atlantic crossing of kidnapped slaves from Africa to the New World. Examples of accounts of the Middle Passage occur in **Paule Marshall**'s ***Praisesong for the Widow*** (1983). The protagonist's symbolic experience of the ancestors' sea voyage, rather than signifying the moving away from homeland, family, language, and history, signals the character's redefinition of her racial identity by returning to the origins of the black people in the Americas. In *Beloved*, the spirit of the dead baby remembers the lives of several incarnations, recalling the memories of the slave ship in order to connect with the experience of the "Sixty Million and more" to whom the book is dedicated. However, it is not until the publication of Chase-Riboud's *Echo of Lions* (1989) and Charles Johnson's *Middle Passage* (1990) that the Atlantic crossing receives a full-scale treatment.

Chase-Riboud's novel recreates the story of Joseph Cinque, an African captive who led a mutiny on board the slaver *Amistad* in 1839. The mutineers attempt to find their way back to West Africa but are captured and imprisoned in New Haven. The novel dramatizes a trial case that finally ends in the Supreme Court, where the accused are defended by ex-president John Quincy Adams and, in a landmark decision, acquitted. Chase-Riboud explores the contradictions inherent to the American political and judicial system, while showing the impact of American slavery on the African continent. In the context of a land devastated by the illegal slave trade, Cinque's triumph is a partial one.

Middle Passage follows the adventures of a recently emancipated slave from Illinois, who ends up traveling first to New Orleans and then to Africa aboard an illegal slave ship. In the characterization of his protagonist, Johnson re-works the type of the trickster, who is made to review his identity in his encounter with the Allmuseri tribe. The novel is clearly influenced by texts of the Western tradition such as Herman Melville's *Moby Dick* (1851) and "Benito Cereno" (1856) and Edgar Allan Poe's *The Narrative of Arthur Gordon Pym* (1838), while rewriting the slave narrative by drawing on different gen-res, including **autobiography**, diary, logbook, and travel narrative.

In their short stories "Damballah" (1981) and "The Education of Mingo" (1977), **John Edgar Wideman** and Charles Johnson, respectively, represent the lives of the abducted Africans and their adjustment to the New World. Johnson's tale focuses on the slave/master relationship and how the dynamics of slavery affect both blacks and whites. In Wideman's text, the figure of the African functions as a more obvious link between America and Africa. The memory of Africa passed on to a younger slave reshapes both the young man's identity and the historical map of the Americas, partially recovering the cultural loss of the Middle Passage.

Other novels published in the last two decades have turned to exploring the quest for integration during the civil rights era in works that favor the child's perspective of the world. **Ntozake Shange**'s *Betsey Brown* (1985) and **Maxine Clair**'s *Rattle Bone* (1994) are two coming-of-age narratives set against the background of school desegregation. **Tina McElroy Ansa**'s *Baby of the Family* (1989) follows the first years of Lena McPherson in an evocation of black middle-class life in 1950s Georgia. Set in the turbulent years of the early 1960s, A. J. Verdelle's *The Good Negress* (1995) describes a young girl's struggle to come to terms with her identity, divided between the rural world of her grandmother and the more sophisticated and somewhat unsettling realm of her mother's house in Detroit. In *Only Twice I've Wished for Heaven* (1997), Dawn Turner Trice explores the emergence of a black middle class in the 1970s that separated themselves from the rest of the **community** by living in different areas and attending distinct schools and churches. Narrated from the perspective of eleven-year-old Temmy, the novel examines the cultural losses intrinsic in the establishment of social boundaries, which contribute to a homogenization of the experience. In these narratives, the child's point of view allows the writers to register the disquietude and uncertainty of an evolving society.

Recent portrayals of the slavery era emphasize the genealogical narra-tive. **Linda Beatrice Brown**'s *Crossing Over Jordan* (1995), Sandra Jackson-Opoku's *The River Where Blood Is Born* (1997), Connie Briscoe's *A Long Way from Home* (1999), and Lalita Tademy's *Cane River* (2001) explore the lives of several generations of African American women of the same family, dealing with issues of racism, sexual exploitation, miscegenation, and **passing**, which not only blur racial boundaries but also expose the complexities of African American history. **J. California Cooper**'s *Family* (1991), *In Search of Satisfaction* (1994), and *The Wake of the Wind* (1998) are also tales told across generational lines in order to reconstruct African American history by drawing on family chronicles.

See also Neo-Slave Narrative

Works About

Baker, Houston A., Jr. *The Journey Back: Issues in Black Literature and Criticism.* Chicago: University of Chicago Press, 1980.

Beaulieu, Elizabeth Ann. *Black Women Writers and the American Neo-Slave Narrative: Femininity Unfettered.* Westport, CT: Greenwood Press, 1999.

Bell, Bernard W. *The Afro-American Novel and Its Tradition.* Amherst: University of Massachusetts Press, 1987.

Carby, Hazel V. *Reconstructing Womanhood: The Emergence of the Afro-American Woman Novelist.* New York: Oxford University Press, 1987.

Christian, Barbara. *Black Women Novelists: The Development of a Tradition, 1892–1976.* Westport, CT: Greenwood Press, 1980.

——. "'Somebody Forgot to Tell Somebody Something': African-American Women's Historical Novels." *Wild Women in the Whirlwind: Afra-American Culture and the Contemporary Literary Renaissance.* Ed. Joanne M. Braxton and Andrée Nicola McLaughlin. New Brunswick, NJ: Rutgers University Press, 1990. 326–341.

Rushdy, Ashraf H. A. *Remembering Generations: Race and Family in Contemporary African American Fiction.* Chapel Hill: University of North Carolina Press, 2001.

Walker, Margaret. *How I Wrote Jubilee and Other Essays on Life and Literature.* Ed. Maryemma Graham. New York: Feminist Press at CUNY, 1990.

Ana Nunes

HISTORY

The exploration of history as narrative and the ways in which such narratives shape the understanding of **identity** and the world have been at the heart of African American **literature** from the earliest **slave narrative** through the modernist novels of **Ralph Ellison** and **Toni Morrison**. Feminist African American literature adds a new and important lens to the examination of historical narrative, not only to illuminate the construction of **race** and **class** but to reveal and interrogate the heteropatriarchal standards that inform judgments and values about gender and **sexuality**. Just as **Harriet Jacobs**'s *Incidents in the Life of a Slave Girl* (1861) exposed the particular effects of **slavery** on women and the rampant sexual abuse perpetrated against them, so feminist African American literature exposes sexist assumptions that inform works of art.

Thus the interests of African American women writers in the re-presentation of history is twofold: to uncover the racist and sexist assumptions that have shaped historical narratives and priorities, on the one hand, and to articulate a positive historical narrative of cultural complexity and survival in African American cultural history and, specifically, history as viewed through women's experience, on the other. Even as black women artists were re-presenting history, they were making history of their own. As black women's writing has flourished in America between 1970s and the present, it has done so in tandem with **black**

feminist criticism, which offers a hermeneutic for reading the writing of black women, and **black feminism**, which has created an activist agenda for change in the lives of black women and the systems that oppress them.

Because **fiction** relies on narrative, the African American novel has been a rich resource for alternative versions of history and challenges to official interpretations of the past. Ralph Ellison's *Invisible Man* (1952), now considered one of the classic novels of the twentieth century, is an intricate narrative that explores the persistence of the past in the present through such double-edged legacies as African American music and American **stereotypes** of blackness. Ellison's exploration of history as internalized racism and the resulting double consciousness in his central male character is a landmark in African American fiction, but his treatment of female characters in this novel remains problematic because Ellison uses them in order to reflect the psychological dilemmas of his central male character, rather than as subjects in their own right. Thus he resorts to "types"—either the "forbidden fruit" of the erotically charged white, blond woman or the sturdy, reliable "**Mammy**" archetype, as in his landlady Mary Rambo. Such representations are answered by the work of the many fine African American women novelists writing today.

African American women novelists present women as subjects as they reveal internalized racism *and* sexism, often showing how internalized racism creates sexist hierarchies in black American culture. Before Ellison, **Nella Larsen, Zora Neale Hurston**, and **Ann Petry**, among others, sought to explore the consciousness and experience of women caught in sexist scenarios. Hurston, in particular, reveals the ways in which hierarchies are inscribed in history and serve to oppress both women and cultural minorities such as African Americans and Bahamians. Since the publication of Ellison's *Invisible Man*, such novelists as **Toni Cade Bambara, Barbara Chase-Riboud, Gayl Jones**, Toni Morrison, **Gloria Naylor, Alice Walker**, and **Sherley Anne Williams** have made women's lives, characters, and situations central to their historical novels.

Two African American women novelists in particular have contributed to African American women's history not only in their fiction but through their criticism. Alice Walker's articulation of a matrilineal history for black women artists in her groundbreaking essay "In Search of Our Mothers' Gardens" (1984) and a literary history for black women writers through her essays on Zora Neale Hurston have provided inspiration for many black artists and critics engaged in the acts of recovery and identity formation. Her Pulitzer Prize–winning *The Color Purple* (1985) ignited a controversy in the black **community** among a number of male critics who felt that she was casting black men in a bad light by exposing **domestic** and sexual abuse within the black community. Their fury was, in retrospect, a measure of her success in challenging internalized sexism as well as racism. Toni Morrison, whose novels also expose sexism, writes fiction with textured details drawn from specific moments in American history—post–World War I Ohio in *Sula* (1974), reconstruction Ohio in *Beloved* (1987), westward migration in *Paradise* (1998), and the culture of African American seaside resorts in *Love*

(2003). Her influential essays on the reading of American literature, *Playing in the Dark: Whiteness and the Literary Imagination* (1992), have profoundly affected the ways in which race is discussed and American literature, in particular, is interpreted.

Poets and dramatists have also contributed to the representation of history, especially as it concerns the lives of black women, in their work. In **poetry**, **Sonia Sanchez** and **Carolyn Rodgers** have articulated the perspectives of women so often missing from the **Black Arts Movement. Lucille Clifton** personifies history as female and gives voice to mythic female characters such as Eve. **Elizabeth Alexander** creates a voice for the Venus Hottentot in the title poem of her first collection, *The Venus Hottentot: Poems* (2004), and explores the personas of Betty Shabazz and Toni Morrison in her later work. **Anna Deveare Smith** creates a tableaux of living history in her docudramas based on live interviews such as *Fire in the Mirror* (1993).

While black women writers were exploring history in their work, they were also making history. Although the label "feminist" was not widely used to refer to black women until the 1970s, women's strategies for survival during the preceding years have increasingly become the subject of black feminist art and scholarship. In 1970 Toni Cade Bambara edited a collection titled *The Black Woman*, celebrating the contributions of black women to history and culture. In the same year, Toni Morrison, then an editor at Random House, published her first novel, **The Bluest Eye**, and also edited *The Black Book*, a collection of pictures, newspaper articles, advertisements, and other documents revealing an African American cultural legacy. Morrison continued to **work** to bring the writings of other black women writers into print, notably those of Gayl Jones and Toni Cade Bambara, as she developed her own career as a novelist. In 1973 the National Black Feminist Organization (NBFO) was formed at the offices of the National Organization for Women (NOW). This organization was formed partly in response to the continued media coverage of the feminist movement as white and middle class and sought to bring visibility to a black female leadership to address women's issues in African American contexts. As black feminists sought to articulate an agenda, a number of prominent black women writers objected to the label "feminist," including Toni Morrison, who argued in a *New York Times* interview that black women were the original working women and that their agenda differed significantly from that of white middle-class feminists. Alice Walker, in response to the controversy, coined the term "**womanist**" to refer to those who loved women and who collaborated with them in order to foster health and creativity. Patricia Hill Collins, a sociologist, has been one of the leading thinkers shaping theories of black feminist thought.

Writers such as **Audre Lorde**, Margaret Sloan, and Barbara Christian focused on black lesbian issues to address the interlocking oppressions of patriarchy and heterosexism in the lives of black women, owning black feminism and adding strength to its social analyses. Audre Lorde's embrace of the label "black lesbian feminist," and her argument that this term embraced all black women who supported each other through female community, redefined the lesbian dimensions of black feminist criticism in ways that made it central to the movement. As these women artists and writers developed a feminist critique, they were also engaged both in the re-vision and in the making of history.

One of the first acts of black feminist criticism was that of historical recovery. Mari Evan's *Black Women Writers* (1984) and Mary Helen Washington's anthologies *Black-Eyed Susans* (1975) and *Invented Lives* (1987) made a chronological array of black women's writing available to a wide reading public. The rise of black feminist criticism was a response to the need for new historical paradigms that inform critical values and evaluation. In tandem with the development of this criticism, the recovery of black women's texts from obscurity began. Jean Fagin Yellin's scholarship on Harriet Jacobs has canonized that text as one of the most important slave narratives and the leading female slave narrative. Her analysis of Jacobs's narrative revealed the ways in which the paradigm of female writing differed, not only in terms of experience but structurally from male narratives such as the self-made-man pattern of **Frederick Douglass**'s *The Narrative of the Life of Frederick Douglass* (1845). In contrast to Douglass's narrative, Jacobs's reveals the networks of connection and interpersonal relationships that made her escape possible. Nonetheless, Douglass himself was a strong supporter of women's rights and was present at the first Seneca Falls Convention in 1848.

A number of male African American scholars have done work or collaborated to further the study of history in black feminist literature and criticism. Henry Louis Gates's work of anthologizing black feminist criticism and editing the **Schomburg** series, which reproduces nineteenth-century literature by black women, has contributed significantly to the prominence of both historical scholarship on black women writers and theory written by contemporary black women critics, as has his recent discovery and edition of **Hannah Crafts**'s *The Bondwoman's Narrative* (2002). Michael Awkward's *Inspiriting Influences: Tradition, Revision, and Afro-American Women's Novels* (1989) wove together historical analysis with contemporary theory as it provided a new standard of theoretical sophistication for the discipline.

Certain historical moments have become of particular interest to black feminist writers and critics. Among them are slavery and emancipation, migration, the **blues**, domestic work, the representation of the **body**. In addition to moments of physical struggle, such as escape from slavery and abusive situations, and moments of historical achievement, such as emancipation and the **civil rights movement**, women writers pay special attention to domestic life and female friendships. Both black male and female writers have explored in depth the legacy of the **South** and African American music. Black women writers in particular have paid attention to the ways in which migration and the blues have created mobility, space, and a variety of new roles for women to play in culture. They have explored the ways in which the "**beauty myth**" has distorted the self-images of black women. And they continue to explore the intersection of domestic spaces and technology, communication, and mass media. The most recent criticism coming from African American women writers invested in historical interpretation is influenced by cultural criticism, as exemplified in the work of Jacqueline Bobo. Telling histories continues to be a vital part of African American women's writing and criticism, even as the theories and perspectives continually shift to find a more accurate lens through which to expose racism, sexism, and the brilliant survival strategies of black women, as well as their creative triumphs today.

See also Historical Fiction; Neo-Slave Narrative

Works About

Awkward, Michael. *Inspiriting Influences: Tradition, Revision, and Afro-American Women's Novels*. New York: Columbia University Press, 1989.

Collins, Patricia Hill. *Black Feminist Thought: Knowledge, Consciousness, and the Politics of Empowerment*. New York: Routledge, 1990.

Evans, Mari. *Black Women Writers (1950–1980): A Critical Evaluation*. Garden City, NY: Anchor Press/Doubleday, 1984.

Griffin, Farah Jasmine. *Who Set You Flowin': The African-American Migration Narrative*. New York: Oxford University Press, 1996.

Morrison, Toni. *Playing in the Dark: Whiteness and the Literary Imagination*. Cambridge, MA: Harvard University Press, 1992.

Rody, Caroline. *The Daughter's Return: African American and Caribbean Women's Fictions of History*. New York: Oxford University Press, 2001.

Russell, Sandi. *Render Me My Song: African-American Women Writers from Slavery to the Present*. New York: St. Martin's Press, 1990.

Ann Hostetler

HOLIDAY, BILLIE (1915–1959)

The white gardenia in her hair was as much her trademark as the soulfulness of her voice. Billie Holiday, who has been described as kind, maternal, volatile, happy, sad, irresponsible, and gentle, is certainly one of the most well known **jazz** singers in America.

Born Eleanora Fagan in early-twentieth-century Baltimore, Holiday experienced the hardships of segregation and poverty. For the first ten years of her life she lived intermittently with her mother, her extended **family**, and a Catholic school for wayward black girls while her mother sought employment and relationships in New York and Philadelphia. Once finally reunited with her mother in New York, she contributed to the household by running errands, babysitting, and scrubbing house steps.

Holiday ran errands for one particular woman, the owner of a brothel, who allowed her to listen to the music of Louis Armstrong and Bessie Smith on the phonograph. That music changed her life.

Although women were not encouraged to sing or play jazz, Holiday began singing in Harlem night clubs. These performances led to her first recordings in 1933, "Your Mother's Son-in-Law" and "Riffin' the Scotch." Between the years of 1935 and 1938, she recorded over eighty songs. While there were some who did not appreciate her style of singing or the music she sang, most who heard her were captivated by the soul in her voice and the artistry with which she used it.

Her subject matter is perhaps less desirable for many modern feminists. For instance, in "My Man," the speaker is content to stay in a relationship with a man who is unfaithful and abusive. In "Billie's Blues," although the speaker seems to have a strong sense of self at times, she also remains in a relationship with a man whom she laments treats her as a slave. While there is no justification for such relationships, one must recognize the impact these songs had on Holiday's audiences: Many women felt that she was singing their story. One should also consider that these songs of bad relationships and loss could quite possibly be drawn from her own life. Holiday suffered through many bad experiences with men, beginning with a distant relationship with her father and including her **rape** by a neighbor, unwanted sexual advances by a cousin, a brief stint as a prostitute, and involvement with abusive men.

Holiday's experiences also led her to record "Strange Fruit" in 1939. This song about the surreal horror of southern lynching expressed the anger Holiday felt about the racism she and other blacks suffered. She was initially reluctant to record the song for fear that people would hate it, but the song was a turning point in her career and one of her most well known.

In her 1956 **autobiography** *Lady Sings the Blues* (written with William Duffy), Holiday recounts not only the triumphs of her life and music but the dark times as well. While many agree that this story is lyrical and captivating, there is some doubt as to the truth of many of the details. Finding it a story worth knowing, however, Paramount Studios released a **film** loosely based on the book in October 1972. Starring Diana Ross and Billy Dee Williams, the movie received favorable reviews and five Academy Award nominations, including Best Actress.

In 1959, Holiday succumbed to chronic alcohol and drug abuse. While such behavior is an unforgettable part of her life, Holiday is best remembered as a woman who sang the heartache and struggle of the black people but who also showed them the **beauty** that life can bring.

Work By

Lady Sings the Blues. With William Duffy. 1956. New York: Penguin Books, 1984.

Works About

Gourse, Leslie, ed. *The Billie Holiday Companion: Seven Decades of Commentary.* New York: Schirmer Books, 1997.
Griffin, Farah Jasmine. *If You Can't Be Free, Be a Mystery: In Search of Billie Holiday.* New York: Free Press, 2001.

Nicholson, Stuart. *Billie Holiday*. Boston: Northeastern University Press, 1995.

Oliphant, Dave. *The Early Swing Era, 1930 to 1941*. Westport, CT: Greenwood Press, 2002.

White, John. *Billie Holiday: Her Life and Times*. New York: Universe Books, 1987.

RaShell R. Smith-Spears

HOME

For the African American **community**, home has often been perceived as a site of conflict. Forcibly removed from Africa, African Americans lost physical contact with their indigenous home. The "slave culture debate," which has gone on for decades, argues whether or not African Americans brought certain values, traditions, and customs with them when they were forced to migrate to the Americas. The evidence of the continued influence of African aesthetics on the African American culture is highly noticeable. Contemporary African American music owes its development to the slave songs and **work** songs that were created during **slavery**. In these work songs and in other aspects of communication, Africans in the Americas used the drum, a distinctly African music form, to express themselves. More important, Africans in the Americas carried with them the **memory** of Africa and an oral tradition that allowed them to pass on their personal and group **history**.

It is through the oral tradition that the most viable connection to Africa as the lost home has been maintained. In most slave communities, slaves who escaped from the plantations formed Maroon communities in the hills. These communities maintained a strong connection to Africa through the oral telling of stories. The oral tradition has been an instrumental part of the black experience in the Americas. It is often incorporated in African American **literature** as a means of culture communication and cultural transcendence. From the oral tradition, African Americans developed "call and response," a form of communication that has been incorporated into African American culture. Perhaps the most noticeable use of call and response in African American literature comes in **Toni Morrison**'s novel **Beloved** (1987), which uses the tradition as an affirmation of the spirit of the African in the African American.

The idea of Africa as the "true" home of African Americans is not simply an impression that comes from the psychological maintenance of African values. Early African American writers were identified as *transatlantic writers*, a term that reflected their multiple local affiliations. Olaudah Equiano is perhaps the most well known of these writers. Equiano, unlike many slaves, carried with him a strong memory of his African home and the traditions by which he was raised. Although Equiano is forced to mask his relationship to his indigenous home behind a developed interest in **Christianity**, he continually lets his readers know that he has not forgotten his past. When Equiano is first introduced to the Christian **religion**, his acceptance comes with an assertion that he can follow this religion because he identifies in these written words the customs and traditions of his African home. Equiano spends most of his life after capture sailing the Atlantic; his identification as a transatlantic writer captures the true nature of his physical alliances, as an individual tied not only to the Atlantic but also to the African, American, and European continent that borders it.

For slaves who, unlike Equiano, were not able to traverse the Atlantic, the connection to Africa as home is not as evident. Although many slaves acknowledge that their true home existed elsewhere, the desire for survival became a longing to find place where they could live as free men in the Americas. Thus, we find in the narrative of **Frederick Douglass** one of the first claims of America as home. Douglass can, in effect, be seen as the beginning of **Black Nationalism** in America. Douglass speaks not on behalf of himself as an individual but for the African American community as a whole when he calls for **freedom** and an acceptance of his humanity. With these words comes an acknowledgment that African Americans belonged here. Henry Garnett and David Walker further establish this idea by articulating in their writings that it is the labor of blacks in America that has made it what it is, establishing that African Americans belong here not simply because this is the space that they occupy but, most important, because this is the space that they have built with their sweat and labor. Ironically, despite his emphasis on seeing the black population as a community, Douglass deemphasizes the role that gender played in the slave system that developed in the United States.

With the Emancipation Proclamation and the end of the Civil War, life changed for African Americans. Some scholars have argued that with the abolishment of slavery and the onset of Jim Crow laws and lynching, life got much worse for the black population in America. Although African Americans gained their freedom, they did not gain access to the resources they would need to establish themselves as viable "citizens" in America. African Americans found themselves after the Civil War without "40 acres and a mule"—without property or work. A sharecropping system was established, but instead of providing African Americans with access to wealth, it was another system by which mainstream Americans used black labor without proper forms of compensation. Thus African Americans found it hard to identify America as home. It is within this environment that Booker T. Washington developed his "Atlanta Compromise." Born a slave, Washington spent much of his life as a laborer. He saw the future of blacks in America as being tied to the question of economics. African Americans needed to prove themselves productive members of American society in order to gain access equality. With his "Cast Down Your Buckets" speech, given in Atlanta, Georgia, on September 18, 1895, Washington became one of the most controversial figures in African American history. Washington suggests that blacks needed to begin at the bottom of American society as laborers and work their way into the American economic system. He likewise calls to white Americans, who were at the time looking to recent immigrants for labor, to rely on the population of newly freed slaves. Washington was highly critiqued by his contemporaries including W.E.B. Du Bois, who saw his uplift ideology as assimilationist. Du Bois critiqued Washington for asking African Americans to give up the basic rights that would allow them to legally and psychologically make a claim of America as home. Du Bois asserted that Washington's ideology asked blacks to give up the right to vote as well as their civil rights. Du Bois was very critical of having all African Americans establish themselves as laborers.

For Du Bois the question of racial uplift was a question of representation. His solution was to have the "Talented Tenth" of the black community gain economic and social stability and then be responsible for uplifting the rest of the **race**. He believed African Americans could gain access to mainstream America through its talented artists and scholars. Du Bois's ideology was not without its limitations; it is questionable whether or not Du Bois saw women as possible candidates for the Talented Tenth.

Du Bois's ideas about racial uplift and representation proved to be instrumental in the development of the **Harlem Renaissance** (a.k.a. the New Negro movement). His assertion that all art produced in the African American community be a form of propaganda helped to structure the movement. Du Bois was particularly interested in the ways that the white mainstream viewed African Americans; he was concerned with the image of the black community that was presented in literature and art. Du Bois therefore asked artists to produce positive images of African Americans in all forms of art, images of middle-class, upwardly mobile, educated African Americans. Du Bois can be seen as attempting to write the African American into American citizens, to create a sense of home, or nation, through literature. Du Bois's endeavor was not an impossible or a new one. Early settlers of America had in effect used literature as a means for creating the nation. Benjamin Franklin's notion of the self-made man became a template for American citizenship and American individualism.

Du Bois's call for art as a form of propaganda, however, created much controversy among artists during the Renaissance. Du Bois's notions centered on middle-class sensibilities, and younger artists, like **Claude McKay** and **Langston Hughes**, felt that they did not want to be restricted to presenting images that would appeal to white America. These Harlem School writers, as they became known, wrote literature that represented all aspects of life, particularly focusing on the working-class people of Harlem. By writing against Du Bois and Alain Locke's base for the Harlem Renaissance, the Harlem School writers opened themselves to criticism that frequently left them in the position of interloper. As harmful as Du Bois's ideas were for the Harlem School, they were perhaps even more complicated for the women writing during this time period.

Women played an important role in the Harlem Renaissance. It was in the home of women that artists met to share, develop, and discuss their work. Women were the foundation of the Renaissance, and they helped to establish many of the scholars who are associated with the Renaissance today. Despite the instrumental role that women played, they were often unrecognized by their peers and by the publishing world. It is only recently that works by women during the Harlem Renaissance have been "recovered." One such text, **Jessie Redmon Fauset**'s **Plum Bun** (1929), directly questions the Talented Tenth and the focus on middle-class ideals. Fauset uses her novel, ironically subtitled *A Novel without a Moral*, to demonstrate the limitations of the middle **class**, which she portrays as politically unaware and powerless to see the reality of life in America.

During the Harlem Renaissance, Du Bois's belief in the ability of African Americans to function within the American mainstream is critical to his insistence that artists write themselves into American society. He founded the National Association for the Advancement of Colored People (NAACP) in an attempt to actuate this belief. Du Bois's greatest critic at this time was Marcus Garvey. Garvey, unlike Du Bois, did not see any potential for the African American in America. Garvey believed that America could never be a true home for African Americans. Garvey therefore developed the "Back to Africa" movement in order to facilitate the return of African Americans to their true home, Africa. Garvey felt that there was no possibility for equality or racial uplift for blacks in the Americas. Unfortunately, Garvey himself had never been to Africa, and he did not have a "real" image of what Africa was like. Garvey saw Africa as the "mother" country that needed her displaced citizens to return and free her from the continued impact of colonialism. It was Garvey's hope that Africans in the Americas would return to Africa and develop her into a world power. Despite the divergence in their ideas, it is ironic that at the end of this life W.E.B. Du Bois would deny his American citizenship and return to Africa, making a clear and distinct statement about his determination of where his home truly was.

Garvey and Du Bois were not the only figures during this time who were attempting to define the relationship that African Americans had with America. George Schuyler, a contemporary of both scholars, saw African Americans solely as a product of American society. At a time when African American artists were attempting to distinguish their work as a by-product of the hybrid influence of African and American values and traditions, Schuyler suggested that there was no difference between African Americans and other cultural and ethnic groups that made up American society. In a roundabout way, Schuyler was in effect suggesting that African Americans were already Americans. He presented an image of African Americans that located them solely within the boundaries of the United States. Home was therefore not a site of conflict; the African American was just another product of American society. Schuyler's definition of the African American dismissed the real and imagined connection to Africa that had thus far been critical to the survival of African Americans in the United States.

Defining and determining what home was during the 1900s was complicated by the experience that African Americans encountered in the United States at that time. During this period there were over 3,000 documented lynchings, a figure that does not take into account the undocumented lynchings that occurred. For many African Americans this act, although not legalized, was a government-sanctioned policy of control that relegated African Americans to a position of noncitizen.

Du Bois's influence during this time was not limited to his desires for artists during the Renaissance. In his seminal text *The Souls of Black Folk*, Du Bois suggests that to truly understand black culture, one must comprehend southern black culture. Du Bois presents the **South** as the site of authentic blackness; the home of "real" and "true" African American culture was the South. This notion would have great literary impact as it has been incorporated into much of the literary work that has been written during and since the Harlem Renaissance. Literary characters, on a search to define who they are, often make a physical or metaphoric journey to the South. Texts where we see a literal movement South include **James Weldon Johnson**'s *Autobiography of an Ex-Colored Man* (1912) and **Jean Toomer**'s *Cane* (1923). In **Ralph Ellison**'s *Invisible Man* (1952) when the unnamed protagonist has lost control of his surroundings, he finds himself in the home of a southern woman who takes on a maternal, nurturing role, in effect facilitating a metaphoric return to the South. The South as the home of black culture is also presented in **Nella Larsen**'s ***Quicksand*** (1928). However, for Larsen this idea is one that limits the agency of African American women. At the end of *Quicksand*, the main character, Helga Crane, who has spent most of the novel attempting to define who she is, returns to the South, where she marries a preacher. Helga's return to the South restricts her, rather than enhancing her as an individual. Returning to the South, Helga is trapped by her gender; as the novel ends, she is laboring in childbed, yet again, with no sense of place other than the maternal role she is limited to.

It is during the **Black Arts Movement**—with its "I'm Black and I'm Proud" motto—that we see a shift from the emphasis on the U.S. South back to Africa as home. The Black Arts Movement is the literary arm of the Black Power movement, and it is a moment in time when African Americans demonstrated pride in their "Africanness." It is a period celebrating all things black, and at the center of this celebration is an acknowledgment of, and a sense of pride in, Africa. This recognition of Africa as a central part of African American culture and tradition has continued to play a significant role in how contemporary African Americans see and define themselves. The African American community is itself a hybrid community that reflects the influence of both African and American value systems.

Since the 1970s, the number of Caribbean writers who have migrated to the United States has complicated the question of defining home within the African American community. For these writers, such as **Paule Marshall**, **Michelle Cliff**, and **Jamaica Kincaid**, defining home must incorporate a reevaluation of the colonial influence on the Caribbean. These writers have a triple alliance to negotiate—Africa, the Caribbean, and the United States. Although many of these writers have been incorporated into the African American literary tradition, their literature primarily focuses on the Caribbean. Noticeable in the works of Jamaica Kincaid, the postcolonial question takes a gender-specific approach. Kincaid's critique of home is centralized on a critique of her mother, whom she imagines as manifestation of the colonial presence in Antigua.

Works About

Chancy, Myriam. *Searching for Safe Places*. Philadelphia, PA: Temple University Press, 1997.

Du Bois, W.E.B. *The Souls of Black Folk*. New York: New American Library, 1969.

Favor, J. Martin. *Authentic Blackness*. Durham, NC: Duke University Press, 1999.

Josie Brown-Rose

HOMEMADE LOVE

Homemade Love, **J. California Cooper**'s second short-story collection, was published in 1986 and received an American Book Award. The collection of contemporary **folktales** is composed of thirteen stories and focuses on the lives of everyday people and their ability to survive life's obstacles. All of the stories contain a life lesson.

Cooper's use of vernacular has caused her narrative style to be compared to **Zora Neale Hurston** and **Alice Walker**, and this is very apparent in this collection. Like Janie in Hurston's *Their Eyes Were Watching God* (1937) and Celie in Walker's *The Color Purple* (1985), the characters in *Homemade Love* speak in black dialect. The narrators are both male and female, but there is a feminist pattern in the work: There is a strong emphasis on the ability of women to empower one another; as well, an important theme in many of the stories is that a woman must learn to be independent and, especially, that she can survive without the aid of a man.

The characters in this collection live basic country lives. A few, however, are drawn to city life and its perceived glamour. The man in "Living," for example, leaves his wife and their country life, where everything seems old and worn, for the big city, but he quickly learns that the city is not all that he imagines and returns **home** within three days with a greater appreciation for the simplicity of his country life. Similarly, the narrator in "Funny Valentines" recognizes the authenticity of life in the country as opposed to the superficial life that she observes in the city.

Most of the characters are seeking satisfaction, and often they find fulfillment late in life. Many have a deep-seated **love** for home and **family**. They also recognize that education and a strong **work** ethic are key elements to living a better life. Characters such as those in "Without Love" find that they can live the American dream of owning a home that is full of the love of children and grandchildren, but Cooper's message is that work is necessary to achieve this success.

Throughout the collection, Cooper's characters acknowledge their hatred for white exploiters who "runs this world," but many also realize that not all white people are bad. In "Happiness Does Not Come in Colors," the narrator learns that love, like happiness, "does not come in colors."

Not all of Cooper's narrators are admirable. Some are nosy neighbors such as "The Watcher," who is too concerned about her neighbors' lives to notice the decline within her own life. Others are outright sinners who easily justify their bad behavior. In "Swingers and Squares," for example, the narrator selfishly lives her life and disregards her responsibility to her children. The narrator's ironic comment that some people are fools and do not learn from their mistakes is Cooper's moral message in this tale.

See also Family; In Search of Satisfaction

Works About

Naroisse, Judy A. "Book Sense: *Homemade Love*." *Sentinel*, June 21, 1990, A8.

Schumacher, Michael. Review of *Homemade Love*, by J. California Cooper. *Writer's Digest* 67 (1987): 21.

Steinberg, Sybil. Review of *Homemade Love*, by J. California Cooper. *Publishers Weekly* 230.2 (1986): 53.

Diane Todd Bucci

HOPKINS, PAULINE (1859–1930)

Through the pages of her prose, the columns of her journalistic essays, and the **drama** of her theater—written and performed—Pauline Elizabeth Hopkins showed herself to be a dynamic and subversive figure in the early African American literary tradition.

A descendant of a long line of impressive racial activists that includes James Whitfield and Nathaniel and Thomas Paul, Hopkins was born in 1859 in Portland, Maine, to Northrop Hopkins and Sara Hopkins (née Allen). Raised and educated in Boston, Hopkins demonstrated literary promise when she was merely fifteen, winning first place in an essay contest sponsored by **William Wells Brown**. Six years later, in 1880, Hopkins's first play *Peculiar Sam; or, The Underground Railroad* premiered at Boston's Oakland Garden. The cast was her own troupe, the Hopkins Colored Troubadors, and Hopkins herself sang the lead role. Until she eventually left the stage in the 1890s to pursue stenography training, Hopkins not only gave recitals and concerts throughout the Boston area but also lectured on black **history**.

Ever committed to creative endeavors, Hopkins temporarily abandoned stenography in 1900 to join the board of directors of *Colored American* magazine, the United States's first black journal. The journal's publisher, the Colored

Co-operative Publishing Company, also released Hopkins's first novel, **Contending Forces**: *A Romance Illustrative of Negro Live North and South* (1900), and she was named editor of the magazine's Women's Department from 1901 to 1903 as well as literary editor in 1903. Under both her own name and her mother's maiden name, the magazine published Hopkins's essays, short stories, and her novels *Hagar's Daughter: A Story of Southern Caste Prejudice* (1901–1902), *Winona: A Tale of Negro Life in the South and Southwest* (1902), and *Of One Blood; or the Hidden Self* (1902–1903). Hopkins also lectured nationwide to raise funds for publication.

Hopkins's tenure ended in 1904, however, when *Colored American* was purchased by Fred R. Moore, a man who was closely allied with Booker T. Washington and who did not approve of Hopkins's outspokenness on racial issues or her protest-oriented politics. Though Washington and his supporters denied ill will, citing failing health as motivation for her separation from the magazine, critics—including W.E.B. Du Bois—vehemently declared the move a coup. After this dismissal, Hopkins began publishing her work in *Voice of the Negro*, the first African American magazine in the **South**, and in 1916, she became the editor of *New Era Magazine*, which failed after only two issues.

In the wake of this disappointment, Hopkins left the public gaze. She never married, and little is known about her life until 1930 when, while employed as a stenographer at the Massachusetts Institute of Technology, Hopkins was killed at **home** in an accidental fire.

Hopkins survived over half a century of critical obscurity to be rediscovered in the 1980s through both critical revival and the reprinting of *Contending Forces* and her magazine novels as part of Oxford University Press's **Schomburg Library of Nineteenth-Century Black Women Writers** series. This revival reaffirms Hopkins's artistic versatility as well as her continuing relevance to African American literary and cultural study.

Works By

Contending Forces: A Romance Illustrative of Negro Life North and South. Boston: Colored Co-operative Publishing Company, 1900. Reprint, New York: Oxford University Press, 1988.

Hagar's Daughter: A Story of Southern Caste Prejudice. 1901–1902. London: XPress, 2003.

The Magazine Novels of Pauline Hopkins. 1901–1903. New York: Oxford University Press, 1988.

Of One Blood; or the Hidden Self. 1902–1903. New York: Washington Square Press, 2004.

Peculiar Sam; or, The Underground Railroad. 1879. *The Roots of African American Drama.* Ed. Leo Hamalian and James V. Hatch. Detroit: Wayne State University Press, 1991. 100–123.

A Primer of Facts Pertaining to the Early Greatness of the African Race and the Possibility of Restoration by Its Descendants—with Epilogue. Cambridge, MA: P. E. Hopkins, 1905.

Works About

Carby, Hazel. *Reconstructing Womanhood: The Emergence of the Afro-American Woman Novelist*. New York: Oxford University Press, 1987.

Gruesser, John Culler, ed. *The Unruly Voice: Rediscovering Pauline Elizabeth Hopkins*. Urbana: University of Illinois Press, 1996.

Pryse, Marjorie, and Hortense J. Spillers, eds. *Conjuring: Black Women, Fiction, and Literary Tradition*. Bloomington: Indiana University Press, 1985.

Wall, Cheryl, ed. *Changing Our Own Words: Essays on Criticism, Theory, and Writing by Black Women*. New Brunswick, NJ: Rutgers University Press, 1989.

Jennifer Larson

HOTTENTOT VENUS: A NOVEL

Barbara Chase-Riboud's works attract controversy because the author tends to take on stories about the oppression of African people in the Americas and abroad. Moreover, readers are forced to regard the incidents, but the main characters do not always think and act the way many might expect. She gives black women voices that grate against contemporary expectations. For example, in the early 1980s most Americans did not imagine a man like Thomas Jefferson involved in a romantic relationship with an African slave. Those familiar with the **history** of **slavery** in this country would harbor the **stereotype** of the black woman raped by the white master. In **Sally Hemings** (1979), Chase-Riboud portrays Hemings as an African slave who chooses to have children and an unrewarded lifelong affair with Jefferson. The story elevates their intimacies from sexual oppression and abuse to romance. *Hottentot Venus* (2003) is written in a similar spirit.

Sarah Baartman, protagonist of *Hottentot Venus*, shows a mind-set many contemporary readers will find difficult to understand. The 2003 novel's title character accepts debasement and captivity as a means to escape colonialism and genocide. Those imbued with today's empowerment notions will find that hard to understand.

In 1810, twenty-year-old Ssehura, an orphaned girl from the Khoikhoi tribe, in Britain's then–Cape Colony, near the tip of South Africa's Cape of Good Hope, abandoned her homeland for a shot at fame in England. Historians say William Dunlop, a ship's doctor, promised the former shepherdess money, marriage, and adulation if she went **home** with him. She was tricked and betrayed. The four-foot-seven-inch woman, whose Anglicized name, Sarah Baartman, comes from an Afrikaner translation of Ssehura, ended up in a sideshow for six years. After her **death** scientists turned her into a freak in a museum exhibition. Her **body** was dissected. The skeleton was encased in a plaster likeness that accented the drooping breasts and the legendary bulbous buttocks that once drew the curious crowds to see and scoff at the "Hottentot Venus." The brain and genitalia were put in glass jars, along with a portrait and wax model that highlighted the labia. Those objects, displayed until 2002 in the Museum of Natural History in Paris, were preserved as "scientific proof" of blacks as subhuman.

Based loosely on the true story, Chase-Riboud's Sarah refuses the aid of British abolitionists such as Robert Wedderburn, who sues to free her. The woman clearly understands her dire predicament yet accepts being poked, prodded, pawed, and paraded as an animal because she is paralyzed by personal demons and a great fear of returning to South Africa, where her tribe members face genocide.

Chase-Riboud's description and dialogue make readers squirm but help unveil an oppressed mind and soul. French scientists created the Hottentot Venus as the antithesis of the Roman goddess of **beauty** and **love**. Baartman's dark skin, large buttocks, and drooping genitals are used to establish a standard for ugliness and otherness. The novel leads the reader to wonder who is most primitive.

Works About

Duke, Lynn. "Listening to the Lady in the Glass Case; With *Hottentot Venus* Barbara Chase-Riboud Writes a Historical Wrong." *Washington Post*, November 16, 2003, D1.

Graham, Renee. "Harrowing Novel Gives Strong Voice to Victim of Cruelty." Review of *Hottentot Venus*, by Barbara Chase-Riboud. *Boston Globe*, January 5, 2004, B9.

James, L. Raven. Review of *The Hottentot Venus*, by Barbara Chase-Riboud. The R.A.W. Sistaz Reviewers, January 19, 2004. www.rawsistaz.com.

Johnson, Vanessa F. Review of *The Hottentot Venus*, by Barbara Chase-Riboud. *Copperfield Review* (Summer 2005). www.copperfieldreview.com.

"Revisiting Rosetta Stone of Scientific Racism." Review of *The Hottentot Venus*, by Barbara Chase-Riboud. *Atlanta Journal-Constituion*, December 7, 2003, 10L.

Vincent F. A. Golphin

HOW STELLA GOT HER GROOVE BACK

Written in less than a month, **Terry McMillan**'s 1996 novel *How Stella Got Her Groove Back* is described by the author as the closest to **autobiography** that she has written so far. Following the **death** of both her mother and her best friend, McMillan journeyed to Negril, Jamaica, for a much-needed respite. Enter Jonathan Plummer: a twenty-year-old hotel worker who stole McMillan's heart.

Following her vacation to Jamaica, McMillan began **work** on this fourth novel that chronicles the romance between forty-something Stella Payne and twenty-something Winston Shakespeare. In this romantic tale, Stella Payne, a successful securities analyst and a single mother of a preadolescent son, is in need of a spur-of-the-moment Jamaican vacation after assessing her life only to realize that she has lost her "groove." In other words, Stella recognizes her need for romantic companionship. Although not traveling to Jamaica in order to find romance, by chance, Stella meets young Winston, and soon their friendship turns romantic.

Often criticized for its structure, *Stella* is written in stream-of-consciousness form; there are moments when the lack of punctuation reflects the characters' emotions. *Stella* can be described as an allegorical form of *Romeo and Juliet* where two star-crossed lovers must endure the difficulties that come with forbidden **love**. In the case of Stella and Winston, the forbidden elements of their relationship have much to do with their age difference. In *Stella*, McMillan departs from the typical pattern of the romance narrative in that both characters make slow and deliberate decisions regarding their future. Thus, McMillan helps readers to unravel the complexities of a love relationship where there are not only social taboos to worry about but also societal ills (racism and sexism) that will influence the outcome of the relationship. Although their romance is speckled with a mixture of objections and doubts, Stella and Winston decide to persevere in their relationship despite the age gap. Such a move challenges conventional notions of **sexuality** as they relate to gender and age. Both Winston and Stella are aware of the double standard that exists between men and women.

In *Stella*, McMillan reminds her readers that personal **freedom** happens when one looks inside oneself for affirmation rather than looking externally. Moreover, the novel challenges patriarchal notions of masculinity where the romantic tale ends with the female character having to give up erotic and spiritual parts of herself. And although the novel features a younger man with an older woman, McMillan does not create a **Mammy** figure out of Stella. Instead, readers witness a balanced relationship where Stella and Winston reawaken and discover their passions.

How Stella Got Her Groove Back was made into a film in 1998.

Works About

Putnam, Amanda A. "Hot Combs, Curling Irons, and Contradictions: Portrayals of African American Women in Mid-1990s Pop Fiction." *Alizés* 22 (2002): 35.

Review of *How Stella Got Her Groove Back*. *Publishers Weekly* 244.20 (1997): 74.

Catherine Ross-Stroud

HUGHES, LANGSTON (1902–1967)

Born in Joplin, Missouri, in 1902 and raised by his maternal grandmother until the age of twelve, Hughes led a largely peripatetic lifestyle. This was partly due to his mother's difficulty in securing menial employment. Included in his early travels were Kansas, Illinois, and perhaps most important for Hughes's later playwriting, Ohio. Under the direction of Russell and Rowena Jelliffe, the Gilpin Players of the Karamu House Theater in Cleveland would eventually stage some of his most important dramatic works (although *Mule Bone*, his aborted collaboration with **Zora Neale Hurston**, never made it past the planning stage). Marital instabilities and the eventual divorce of his parents led to a lifelong struggle to nurture what **love** and affection, had it been forthcoming from both parents, could have provided: emotional stability, a sense of belonging, and a respite from childhood loneliness.

Feminist readings of Hughes's early life may focus on the effects that Carrie Hughes's poverty had on her son's artistic development. *The Big Sea* (1940), Hughes's jovial but emotionally guarded **autobiography**, juxtaposes the harried life of his working mother to the authoritative and unabashedly capitalistic drives of his father, an expatriate American living in Mexico. This text would be followed by the more politically inflected *I Wonder as I Wander* in 1956. James Hughes's reasons for repudiating America (but not its ideals of self-sufficiency and personal gain) enact the utopian desire for a place where a black American could be enterprising and independent and thereby escape the soul-corroding harassment of the color line. His vision is reminiscent of Dr. Brian Redfield's in the novel *Passing* (1929) by **Nella Larsen**, which details the struggle of Irene Redfield to keep her **family** together despite her husband's obsession with emigration to Brazil.

Although Hughes credits his mother (herself a poet) for helping him to develop an appreciation for the arts through plays and books, their relationship appears marked by ambivalence. A typical example is the chapter in *The Big Sea* titled "Mother of the Gracchi," where Carrie Hughes attempts to present an oral recitation for the Inter-State Literary Society but is thwarted by her elder son's distracting onstage antics. A similar incident has Langston deliberately forget his **poetry** for a church presentation, an event to which his mother traveled just to hear him speak. While his behavior may be an expression of juvenile rebellion, it also communicates a deep longing for maternal attention and approbation. One brief source of such attention was Hughes's grandmother, a proud woman who used stories to instill in her grandson a sense of ancestral heroism. Honored as the last surviving widow of John Brown's raid (1859), Mary Langston carried a stalwart sense of her own genealogical investment in the abolitionist and revolutionary **history** of the area. Her obstinate thrift, while not as severe as that of **Richard Wright**'s fundamentalist grandmother, still constrained her charge both physically and emotionally. This discipline did not rival that of his father, whom Hughes eventually declared he hated. While admirable for her commitment to her own economic and social welfare, she also remained distanced from Langston, her personality quite unlike the sympathetic, rustic grandmother Hager in *Not Without Laughter* (1930), Hughes's award-winning first novel. Upon her **death**, Hughes was transferred to the **home** of acquaintances, Auntie and Uncle Reed, whose relatively simple life offered the writer a measure of happiness without the constant financial fretting of his mother or the harassment from his father about the young writer's inability to conform to his filial ideals.

Despite his mother's protests, Hughes spent some time teaching and living on his father's ranch in Mexico. In 1921, during the train ride to the border, he composed "The Negro Speaks of Rivers," a lyrical meditation on worldwide sites of black civilization. These were all connected by the powerful trope of flowing rivers that enacted the transit of blood in human veins. This piece would be published in the *Crisis*, the official journal of the National Association for the Advancement of Colored People (NAACP), and put him in contact with such emerging **Harlem Renaissance** luminaries as Alain Locke and the journal's immensely gifted editor, **Jessie Redmon Fauset**. During his time at Columbia University, Hughes's mother joined him in New York, and he felt bound to support her with the funds provided by his father. Only when she left for Cleveland did he find the burden lifted somewhat, although he continued to live in poverty.

Unmoored by the lackluster experience of college, and driven by the eventual withdrawal of his father's already conditional financial aid, Hughes failed to earn a degree and spent his adolescence in poorly paid manual labor jobs, made more difficult by pervasive color prejudice. Many of the jobs he acquired put him in only occasional contact with women. During the formative experience of working on a freighter (the SS *Malone*) bound for the African coast, Hughes's main encounter with women involved witnessing two young African girls prostituting themselves to the foreign sailors. The writer's description in *The Big Sea* errs on the side of objective reportage rather than involved commentary, revealing his passive position as an observer, not participant. Such is again the case in a scene involving a bar brawl in Paris over the ethics of male violence against women. The author had taken up a kitchen job in Le Grand Duc, a nightclub that featured Florence Embry, a black performer from Harlem, as the star attraction. Little would Hughes know, this glittering atmosphere, a momentary reprieve from the constant threat of financial destitution, would serve as a modest precursor to the many social functions that awaited him when he returned to America. Hughes also details the experience of rooming with a poverty-stricken white dancer, as well as a short-lived romance with an Anglo-African girl. Both of these are passing portraits, although the latter incident has interpretive potential for critics who seek to explore (or posit) the dimensions of Hughes's submerged homosexuality.

The most prominent female influence in Hughes's artistic life would prove to be Mrs. Charlotte Osgood Mason, a wealthy white patron who began to support the writer while he was attending Lincoln University in Pennsylvania. A year earlier, in 1926, Hughes published his first poetry collection *The Weary Blues*, an innovative fusion of **blues** and **jazz** rhythms into richly stylized portraits of lower-class black life. Another poetry collection, *Fine Clothes to the Jew* (1927) would follow, although its critical reception and sales were less than stellar in comparison. Many of the poems from these and subsequent efforts meditated upon the **beauty** of black women ("When Sue Wears Red," "Red Silk Stockings," "Juke Box Love Song"), their social and economic struggles ("Mother to Son"), and the psychological toll of racism and unfulfilling relationships ("Song for a Dark Girl," "Gal's Cry for a Dying Lover"). Hughes does not shy away from adopting the persona of a black woman ("Lament over Love," "Hard Daddy"), or the lover that alternatively exalts or abuses her ("Bad Man") in order to depict the complexity of black women's experience in Harlem.

Hughes's "Godmother" provided generously for her charge and was highly devoted to nurturing black artists (including Hurston and Locke) during the period of literary efflorescence known as the Harlem, or "New Negro," Renaissance. "The Blues I'm Playing," a short story included in *The Ways of White Folks* (1934), may be construed as a veiled commentary on the exigencies of Mrs. Mason's artistic direction. With its prose treatment of lynching, **passing**, ingrained racism, and the aftershocks of **slavery** and miscegenation, the text presents a more pessimistic reflection of black/white relations in America than the soulful mélange of laughter and tears that characterized Hughes's blues poetry. It was published after the patron and artist had a bitter falling out, an incident that could be described as a slow and lethal buildup of tension between contrasting artistic visions. Mrs. Mason's increasingly specific and resolute demands pressured Hughes, who was unwilling to conform to her ideals of black "primitivism." The situation was exacerbated to a large extent by his quarrel with Hurston over *Mule Bone: A Comedy of Negro Life* (1930; not published in full until 1991). Intent on creating an authentic **drama** based on black vernacular forms, the pair collaborated on a humorous reinvention of a (hetero)normative romantic cliché: two men's attempts to win the hand of a desirable, sexually available female. The folkloric flair, rollicking but nuanced humor, and romantic tension inherent in this love triangle belie the gravity of the dispute. Although speaking with relative restraint in his autobiography, Hughes characterizes Hurston as erratic and emotionally unstable, throwing tantrums in front of their friend Carl Van Vechten, accusing the typist Louise Thompson of interference and undue personal investment, and plotting with Locke and Mason to discredit him, her sometime friend and collaborator.

After this personal nadir, Hughes pursued leftist politics through his writing, choosing to publish in a communist-run journal, *New Masses*. He became more vocal about inequalities endemic to American society, traveling extensively in the **South** and later the Soviet Union both to disseminate his work and hone his ideological orientation. Politics and critical awareness of black life never strayed far from Hughes's artistic aims. Despite later attempts during the McCarthy era to discredit him for socialist sympathies, the integrity of Hughes's choices remained more or less intact. Even noted black educator Mary McLeod Bethune (1875–1955) encouraged his efforts to bring poetry to a greater cross section of the African American populace. It was this kind of accessibility and willingness to immerse himself in the concerns of his black brothers and sisters that eventually made Hughes the male "Poet Laureate of the Negro Race," if not officially, at least in the minds of those who enjoyed his work.

In the twilight of Harlem's high days, Hughes's attention turned to drama and a vast spectrum of literary forms: librettos, children's writing, edited collections, histories, and even spoken-word poetry. He would eventually found his own company, the Harlem Suitcase Theater. Many of his plays were staged at the Karamu House, although often to mixed reviews. Among others, *Mulatto* (1935) paved the way for ***A Raisin in the Sun*** (1959), **Lorraine Hansberry**'s bittersweet drama of the Younger family in Chicago and their attempts to recuperate their deferred dreams of self-respect and financial stability. Not only does the play's title allude to a line from one of Hughes's signature poems, "Harlem," it also replaced his drama of miscegenation and longing as the most popular black production on Broadway.

During the war years, the antics of Hughes's phenomenally popular character Jesse B. Semple ("Simple") appeared in the black-owned *Chicago Defender*, starting in 1943. Over two decades, the newspaper column yielded five volumes of Simple stories. Central to Simple's life was the juggling of his relationships with women: his would-be (and later) wife Joyce, his girlfriend Zarita, his ex-wife Isabel, and his landlady. Two cousins, Minnie and Lynn Clarisse, map the intellectual complexity of black urban women, although not all characters appear in each collection. Simple is noted for his verbal jousting, his lack of pretension, and his searing inferences about the city, the nation, and the state of **race** relations. These stories pivot upon the colloquial repartee between Simple and the unnamed narrator, later identified as a Mr. Boyd, over an evening beer. Although women's voices do appear in context, they are usually filtered through the masculine narrative perspective. Insofar as Simple was conceived as a composite of numerous male Harlemites, the women in his life also showcase a blend of hardworking, high-living, and assertively self-aware individuals. This obtains despite their being largely distanced from the site of actual narrative exchange. Misogynistic commentary exists but is mitigated by Simple's obvious dependence on his female companions for health, happiness, and basic self-understanding.

Toward the end of his career, Hughes remained active. The scope of his interests included emerging black writers, one of whom was **Alice Walker**. Although the Civil Rights struggle and the **Black Arts Movement** demanded more radical shifts toward Afrocentric and avant-garde art forms, Hughes's lifelong contributions to African American **literature** have remained indelible.

Works By

The Big Sea: An Autobiography. New York: Knopf, 1940.

The Book of Negro Folklore. Ed. Langston Hughes and Arna Bontemps. 1958. New York: Dodd, Mead, 1983.

The Collected Poems of Langston Hughes. Ed. Arnold Rampersad and David Roessel. New York: Vintage-Random, 1995.

I Wonder as I Wander: An Autobiographical Journey. 2nd ed. New York: Hill and Wang, 1993.

Mule Bone: A Comedy of Negro Life. By Langston Hughes and Zora Neale Hurston. Ed. Henry Louis Gates, Jr., and George Houston Bass. New York: HarperPerennial, 1991.

Not Without Laughter. 1930. New York: Simon and Schuster, 1994.

Simple Speaks His Mind. New York: Simon and Schuster, 1950.

The Ways of White Folks. 1934. New York: Vintage, 1990.

The Weary Blues. New York: Knopf, 1926.

Works About

Bernard, Emily, ed. *Remember Me to Harlem: The Letters of Langston Hughes and Carl Van Vechten, 1925–1964.* New York: Knopf, 2001.

Bloom, Harold, ed. *Langston Hughes.* New York: Chelsea House, 1989.

Gates, Henry Louis, Jr., and Kwame Anthony Appiah, eds. *Langston Hughes: Critical Perspectives, Past and Present.* New York: Amistad-Penguin, 1993.

Miller, R. Baxter. *The Art and Imagination of Langston Hughes.* Lexington: University Press of Kentucky, 1989.

Ostrom, Hans. *A Langston Hughes Encyclopedia.* Westport, CT: Greenwood Press, 2002.

Rampersad, Arnold. *The Life of Langston Hughes.* 2nd ed. 2 vols. New York: Oxford University Press, 2002.

Tracy, Steven C., ed. *A Historical Guide to Langston Hughes.* New York: Oxford University Press, 2003.

Nancy Kang

HUGHES, VIRGINIA. See Rahman, Aishah

HUNTER, KRISTIN. See Lattany, Kristin Hunter

HURSTON, ZORA NEALE (1891–1960)

Zora Neale Hurston was an African American female novelist, ethnographer, and essayist who is known for her celebration of the richness of language and culture that emerged from a unique, expressive black **community**. Most of her works are situated in the **South**, specifically in Florida, and capture the black southern vernacular and traditions of that region.

Although Hurston was born in Notasulga, Alabama, on January 15, 1891, she always claimed to have been born in Eatonville, Florida, the first incorporated all-black city in the United States. She also routinely shaved ten or more years from her actual birthdate, usually asserting that she was born in 1901. It appears that the Hurston **family** moved to Eatonville when Zora Neale was just a toddler, and it was that location that shaped her and her **literature**. During these early years, until she was anywhere from eleven to fourteen years old, Hurston states that she never experienced racism in Eatonville, her only experience with white people being her observation of them as they passed through the town on their way to somewhere else. All of that changed with the **death** of her mother; she was sent to school in Jacksonville, Florida, and became just another "little colored girl" in this large urban center.

Hurston did not complete her education at that time; instead, she was bounced around from relative to relative, eventually taking on a number of odd jobs and living a life of independence, separate from her brothers and sisters most of the time. After several years, the desire for an education took hold of her and would not let go. She completed high school in Washington, D.C., and immediately entered Howard University, still doing odd jobs to support herself. Upon graduation from Howard, Hurston, like so many other black artists, headed for Harlem and the phenomenon known as the **Harlem Renaissance**. By this time she had already published her first short story, "John Redding Goes to Sea" (*Stylus*, May 1921), and her first nationally published story, "Drenched in Light" (*Opportunity*, June 1925). "Drenched in Light" is particularly telling because of its portrayal of Watts, a poor black girl so full of light she does not feel the weight of oppression. Obviously patterned after Hurston herself, "Drenched in Light" serves as the model around which Hurston chose to live her life. She was so confident in herself as a person that, as she writes in "How It Feels to Be Colored Me," she cannot imagine anyone depriving themselves of the pleasure of her company.

Hurston took Harlem by storm. Also, with the sponsorship of Annie Nathan Meyer, she received a scholarship to Barnard College and became its only black student. There, her study of anthropology under the tutelage of Franz Boas opened her eyes not only to the power of ethnography but, more important, to the culturally rich resources of her own little section of the country, Eatonville, Florida. This discovery offered an outlet for the release of her literary genius. So much material had been right under her feet, but it took the distance between Florida and New York to make her realize it. Once these floodgates opened, however, there was no turning back. Her career moved in two directions simultaneously; as a writer, she developed a passion for recording and reproducing black folkloric traditions; as a performer, she became the toast of Harlem parties as a storyteller and performing artist. She was thus doubly committed to the African American oral tradition. Like many other black artists during this time, Hurston had a wealthy white patron who was fascinated by and invested in what was called the "primitive" black arts. For Hurston, this patron was Mrs. Charlotte Osgood Mason. Also like other black artists learned, one of the negative results of this type of financial relationship was that the patrons exerted a certain amount of control, and often approval or censorship, over what and in what form the artists could publish. While other artists severed their relationships with their patrons, Hurston, being resourceful, found ways to mask the chastising messages within her literature while retaining the financial support of Mrs. Osgood Mason.

Hurston, fiercely independent when it came to her subject matter and its presentation, was not particularly popular with the black male intellectual and literary leaders of the Harlem community because she refused to align her work with anybody's political ideologies. Rather than using her art as a weapon to overtly challenge the oppressive conditions under which blacks in America lived, she chose to present a folkloric picture celebrating the rich traditions of the African American community. Her challenges to racism, sexism, and classism were, for the most part, more covert, blended into her beautiful lyrical narratives. One of her main critics, **Richard Wright**, was particularly outspoken regarding Hurston's most celebrated novel, *Their Eyes Were Watching God* (1937), asserting that it brought to the black community no theme, no thought, and no message but instead exploited the "quaint" aspects of Negro life to satisfy the tastes of a white audience. Such criticism demonstrates that the story of a black woman searching for her voice had no place in the male-dominated Negro literature of that time. In addition to the dozens of short stories, essays, plays, musicals, and newspaper articles that Hurston produced, she also published an **autobiography** and a total of six novels and ethnographies during her lifetime: *Jonah's Gourd Vine* (1934), *Mules and Men* (1935), *Their Eyes Were Watching God* (1937), *Tell My Horse* (1938), *Moses, Man of the Mountain* (1939), *Dust Tracks on a Road* (1942), and *Seraph on the Suwanee* (1948).

The last few years of Hurston's life were marked by poverty. This black female writer who defied the models laid out by patrons and the black male "literati," who was the winner of a number of awards including the Guggenheim, who published more books than any other black woman during her time (and more than many afterward), was discovered working as a maid in Miami in 1950 in order to support herself. Deteriorating health eventually led her to a position working as a columnist for a weekly black newspaper, the *Chronicle*, in Fort Pierce, Florida, in 1957 and as a substitute teacher with Fort Pierce's black high school, Lincoln Park Academy. When she could no longer **work**, she lived on county assistance and with the help of friends until she died in relative obscurity on January 28, 1960. Black feminist scholar **Alice Walker** is credited for her diligence in finally locating Hurston's unmarked grave site in the 1970s and lifting her out of obscurity, coordinating a proper tribute to the woman now regarded by many to be Florida's first daughter of literature; the inscription on her gravestone reads "A Genius of the South." Since then, documents that she left behind have been preserved in a special collections section of the University of Florida library, an official Zora Neale Hurston postage stamp has been released, the house in which she lived in Fort Pierce has been made a historic landmark, and the city of Fort Pierce has established a Zora Neale Hurston Dust Tracks Heritage Trail patterned after a similar trail established several years ago in the city that Hurston claimed as her home—Eatonville, Florida.

Hurston was a woman who spoke her mind—about American democracy, black literature, integration, and a score of other topics—without seeking anyone's approval or affirmation. Some critics called her arrogant; however, she was a black woman who was very comfortable with herself, someone who did not write to "uplift her race" because, in her opinion, it was already uplifted.

Works By

The Complete Stories: Zora Neale Hurston. New York: HarperCollins, 1996.

Dust Tracks on a Road. 1942. New York: HarperCollins, 1996.

Every Tongue Got to Confess: Negro Folk-Tales from the Gulf States. Ed. and Intro. Carla Kaplan. New York: HarperCollins, 2001.

I Love Myself When I Am Laughing . . . & Then Again When I Am Looking Mean and Impressive: A Zora Neale Hurston Reader. Ed. Alice Walker. Old Westbury, NY: Feminist Press, 1979.

Jonah's Gourd Vine. 1934. New York: HarperCollins, 1990.

Moses, Man of the Mountain. 1939. New York: HarperCollins, 1991.

Mule Bone: A Comedy of Negro Life. With Langston Hughes. 1931. New York: HarperCollins, 1991.

Mules and Men. 1935. New York: HarperCollins, 1990.

The Sanctified Church. Ed. Toni Cade Bambara. Berkeley: Turtle Island, 1981.

Seraph on the Suwanee. 1948. New York: HarperCollins, 1991.

Tell My Horse. 1938. New York: HarperCollins, 1990.

Their Eyes Were Watching God. 1937. New York: HarperCollins, 1990.

Zora Neale Hurston: A Life in Letters. Ed. Carla Kaplan. New York: Doubleday, 2002.

Works About

Bethel, Lorraine. " 'This Infinity of Conscious Pain': Zora Neale Hurston and the Black Female Literary Tradition." *All the Women Are White, All the Blacks Are Men, But Some of Us Are Brave.* Ed. Gloria T. Hull, Patricia Bell Scott, and Barbara Smith. Old Westbury, NY: Feminist Press, 1982. 176–188.

Boyd, Valerie. *Wrapped in Rainbows: The Life of Zora Neale Hurston.* New York: Scribner, 2003.

Hemenway, Robert E. *Zora Neale Hurston: A Literary Biography.* Urbana: University of Illinois Press, 1980.

Lowe, John. *Jump at the Sun: Zora Neale Hurston's Cosmic Comedy.* Urbana: University of Illinois Press, 1994.

Meisenhelder, Susan Edwards. *Hitting a Straight Lick with a Crooked Slick: Race and Gender in the Work of Zora Neale Hurston.* Tuscaloosa: University of Alabama Press, 1999.

Peters, Pearlie Mae Fisher. *The Assertive Woman in Zora Neale Hurston's Fiction, Folklore and Drama.* New York: Garland, 1998.

Johnnie M. Stover

 **I**

IDENTITY

Negro, colored, black, Afro-American, African American. This partial list of names for racial identity suggests the rapid mobility of thought about racial identity in African American culture and in American culture generally. One of the major themes of African American **literature**, therefore, has been the question of identity. African American literature and literary studies have, consequently, greatly contributed to the critical theorization of identity, a major critical concern of the late twentieth century.

Racial identity was originally imposed on "Negroes" from without—that is, not as an internally developed identification but as a classification system developed by Europeans. The concept of "**race**" is understood by contemporary critical theory to have developed in conjunction with practices of colonization and **slavery**. In the era of imperialism and empiricism (beginning in the European Renaissance and expanding into the eighteenth century Age of Enlightenment and on), the concept of race displaced region and **religion** as the primary marker of human "types." "Race" (a nonnatural, man-made concept and system of classification) came to be posited and even lived, by colonizers and colonized, as a natural, biological, and scientific fact. In the Americas, this system of racial classification both enabled and abetted slavery by demarcating a fundamental distinction between "Caucasians" and "Negroes."

However, in the context of eighteenth- and nineteenth-century America, a high incidence of miscegenation between "whites" and "Negro" slaves challenged the system of racial classifications. An elaborate terminology for fractionalized racial identity—for example, "**mulatto/a**" (half black, half white), "quadroon" (one-fourth black), "octoroon" (one-eighth black)—came into play. Legally, though, the "one-drop rule" became institutionalized in the United States. This "one-drop rule" stated that anyone with any black African ancestry at all (even "one drop of black blood") is "Negro." This "one-drop rule," which served to increase the slave pool, was, over the years, accepted by both whites and blacks as a natural and true determinant of racial identity.

But the one-drop rule meant that a person could look white but "really" be black. Such a possibility created—and reflected—instabilities in the concept of racial identity. These instabilities are dealt with almost obsessively through two major motifs of nineteenth- and early-twentieth-century American literature: "**passing**" and the figure of the "tragic mulatta." (*Mulatta* came to mean any woman of mixed race, whatever the fraction of mixing.) Novels by both whites and blacks, from Harriet Beecher Stowe's *Uncle Tom's Cabin* (1852) to **Nella Larsen**'s *Passing* (1929), and popular plays and **films** from the musical *Show Boat* (1951) to **Adrienne Kennedy**'s *Funnyhouse of a Negro* (1964), display an American cultural fascination with these motifs. Most typically, these motifs appear in the form of a light-skinned woman who tries to live in the white world but fails and comes to a tragic (usually fatal) end. While this typical narrative can be read as ultimately punishing the mulatta for crossing racial barriers, she is also generally treated with great sympathy by the narrative. Hence the ambiguities and ambivalences of American racial identities were both revealed and contained in the figure of the passing mulatta, who embodies anxieties not only about (literal and figurative) miscegenation but also about the inherent impurities of racial identity classifications.

With the **civil rights movement**, a more humanist approach to racial identity gained political prominence. In Martin Luther King, Jr.'s, famous "I Have a Dream" speech (1963), individuals, ideally, "will not be judged by the color of their skin but by the content of their character." In this formulation, the content of an individual's character is separable from (if not irrelevant to) the color of that individual's skin. Individual identity is distinct from, and more important than, racial or cultural identity. While the civil rights movement was very conscious of racial inequities in American culture, its goal was for American culture to achieve "color blindness," as opposed to color consciousness, at least in hiring and funding practices and ultimately in economic distribution and political representation. Racial identity was seen as a *product* of racial inequality, which was to be overcome. While the civil rights movement did not necessarily promote assimilation, it saw racial identity as less important than cross-racial cooperation and racial equality. A work such as **Lorraine Hansberry**'s play *A Raisin in the Sun* (1959) exhibits this humanist, equality-oriented approach to racial identity.

Concomitant with the civil rights movement was the emergence of a more separatist movement (or set of interrelated submovements). Loosely associated with terms and phrases like "Black Power," "Black Pride," "Black Is

Beautiful," and "Afrocentrism," and with groups like the Black Panthers and Nation of Islam (among many others), this mode displaced terms like *colored* and *Negro* with *black*. This movement tended to pose racial identity as fundamental, not incidental, and to see black identity as preexisting and transcending socioeconomic racial inequality. Indeed, it built its politics upon the foundation of racial identity; in some circles, its politics consequently came to be referred to as "identity politics." This approach saw racial identity not, finally, as manmade but as essential. Indeed the metaphor of "blackness," reflected in the terminological shift from "Negro" or "colored" to "black," emphasizes the physicality of this identity and its stark difference from (if not polar opposition to) **whiteness**. Ironically, this mode accepted and affirmed the "one-drop rule" of racial identity, but this time it revalued blackness over whiteness.

In the 1980s and 1990s, as poststructuralism took hold in academia, "identity politics" was criticized for its essentialism. **Body**-based identities were conceived of not as biological facts but as constituted through "performative acts." A performative model of identity (developed by Judith Butler first in regard to gender identity) suggests that identity is not something we *have*; it is something we *do*. The illusion of an essence underlying identity categories is a product, not a precursor, of our endlessly reiterated performances of those identity categories.

In the case of racial identity, the sense of an "authentic black identity" is, in the poststructuralist model, performatively produced. Like other concepts constructed within and reified through language, "blackness" (or racial identity, generally) is more a discursive entity than a prediscursive fact. Hence a terminological and conceptual shift from "black" (connoting a seemingly factual, biologically and body-based racial identity) to "African American" (connoting a more culturally produced identity, one based not in biological fact but in the occupying of national and ethnic positions and self-identifications). In this model of identity, it is not just the terminology of racial identity that is culturally constructed and historically specific but the very identity category divisions themselves and even the very concept of racial identity. To say that racial identity is a construct, though, is not to say that it is not real but to say that its reality is produced within its sociocultural moment—and hence not inevitable. As Henry Louis Gates, Jr., put it in *The Signifying Monkey*, his groundbreaking book on African American literary identity, "Blackness exists, but 'only' as a function of its signifiers" (151). Or as Frantz Fanon put it earlier in his prescient *Black Skin, White Masks*, "The Negro is not. Any more than is the white man" (151). In other words, neither racial identity category ("Negro" or "white") has any absolute, extradiscursive or extracultural grounding.

The language of "man" in the above Fanon quotation embodies the implicitly male-gendered nature of much of the discussion of racial identity. But racial identity is gender inflected, just as gender identity is racially inflected. Many African American women and other women of color were finding a white bias in the feminist movement even as they were finding a male bias in African American, Native American, Latino, and other racial identity–based movements. This frustration is encapsulated in the title of the 1982 book *All the Women Are White, All the Blacks Are Men, But Some of Us Are Brave*. Another important anthology of critical writings in this mode is the 1981 book *This Bridge Called My Back: Writings by Radical Women of Color* (and the more recent update *This Bridge We Call Home: Radical Visions for Transformation*). A feminist approach to identity that refuses to single out any one coordinate—race, gender, sexual orientation, **class**, even health and disability status—as primary is sometimes referred to as a "womanist" approach and is associated with writers such as **Alice Walker**, **Audre Lorde**, and **Ntozake Shange**. **Womanism** observes how a culture of white privilege (if not white supremacy) such as the United States tends to reinforce the power of the dominant group by marginalizing and dividing subordinate groups. Womanist politics seeks to overcome such divisions and hence offers the terminological category "people of color" to emphasize political unity among racial subdivisions. This shift in terminology reflects yet another shift in the conceptual experience of racial identity, now as a political construction that can temporarily unite nonidentical groups. Such an approach sees identity as always already multiple, intersected fundamentally with other primary coordinates, and inherently political.

Some critics have noticed a decline in focus on identity in contemporary literary theory and even an emerging critique of the need to identify. The ability to move beyond or refuse racial identification, though, lies in the domain of the privileged race. For African Americans, the question of identity remains crucial to representation, both in the body politic and in the arts. Identity questions are certainly not disappearing from contemporary African American literature.

Representing, both politically and aesthetically, is bound up with identifying practices. Much critical work remains to be done in respectfully reevaluating the personal, political, and aesthetic functions of identity and of identification in African American literature.

Works About

Anzaldúa, Gloria E., and AnaLouise Keating, eds. *This Bridge We Call Home: Radical Visions for Transformation*. New York: Routledge, 2002.

Fanon, Frantz. *Black Skin, White Masks*. Trans. Charles Lam Markmann. New York: Grove Weidenfeld, 1967.

Gates, Henry Louis, Jr. *The Signifying Monkey: A Theory of African-American Literary Criticism*. New York: Oxford University Press, 1988.

Hull, Gloria, Patricia Bell Scott, and Barbara Smith, eds. *All the Women Are White, All the Blacks Are Men, But Some of Us Are Brave: Black Women's Studies*. Old Westbury, NY: Feminist Press, 1982.

Moraga, Cherríe, and Gloria Anzaldúa, eds. *This Bridge Called My Back: Writings by Radical Women of Color*. Watertown, MA: Persephone Press, 1981.

Deborah Thompson

I KNOW WHY THE CAGED BIRD SINGS

A lyrical blend of realism, emotional gravity, and candid reflections on segregation-era America, *I Know Why the Caged Bird Sings* (1970) is **Maya Angelou**'s feminist intervention into the primarily male tradition of African American **autobiography**. The first installment in Angelou's serial autobiography, it conveys the vicissitudes of growing up black and female in an atmosphere of pervasive uncertainty, racist and sexist devaluation, and precarious self-fashioning. The stability and nurturing provided by human relationships, especially those within the **family**, are forces that counteract the constant threat of dissolution, despair, and **death**. Its title derived from poet **Paul Laurence Dunbar**'s "Sympathy" (1899), the text combines the themes of knowledge (and the imperative for *self-knowledge*) with the artist's desire for voice amid the pervasive silencing of a hostile but not irredeemably corrupt society.

The work begins with the two Johnson children, Maya (a shortened form of Marguerite) and her brother Bailey, riding on a train to Stamps, Arkansas, from California. Moving from the West Coast to the **South**, through to the Midwest briefly, and ultimately back to the West again, the textual and geographic itinerary of the novel forms a symbolic circle, tacitly enunciating a yearning for wholeness as well as respectful and open-minded reciprocity between writer, reader, and the whole chiaroscuro of individuals making up the American republic. For these passed-around children, the **home** provided by the strong female presence of their paternal grandmother, Mrs. Annie Henderson, offers a catalyst for their educational and emotional development. Rural Stamps provides the earliest scenes of instruction both in and outside of the home, and San Francisco emerges as the site where the older Maya explores a more diverse spectrum of opportunities from which to forge a life path. Her accomplishments include becoming the city's first black streetcar conductor and, at the conclusion of the text, courageously accepting the responsibility of teenage **motherhood**.

Buoyed by lucid, unsentimental prose, an awareness of racialized corporeality—the black female **body**—figures prominently in the text. Maya often feels self-conscious about her appearance (her height, angularity, and perceived ugliness), but these pale in juxtaposition with her intellectual curiosity, her refreshing sensitivity, and her finely wrought, imaginative "I." The repudiation of white American standards of **beauty** (the "Black Is Beautiful" credo) is prefigured in Maya's dismemberment of a blonde, blue-eyed baby doll, a Christmas gift from her absent parents. This episode resonates with similar acts of **violence** in **Toni Morrison**'s *The Bluest Eye* (1970). In Angelou's text, the simultaneous vulnerability and resoluteness of the female body and mind are prefigured in the first chapter's image of a razor threatening a young girl's throat. Childhood **rape**, which the speaker experiences at the hands of her mother's boyfriend, is the materialization of this threat. Posttrauma, Maya slips into a state of aphasic shock, unable to speak in a combination of fear, guilt, and powerlessness. Her rebirth from paralyzing introversion is catalyzed by a **love** for **literature**, language, and the nonjudgmental guidance of Bertha

Flowers, a schoolteacher who emphasizes the importance and intrinsic beauty of the human voice. Later, after an awkward and worry-plagued journey to sexual awareness, Maya finds joy in dance, **drama**, and motherhood, occasions that celebrate the dexterity, communicative power, and creative potential of the female body.

In Stamps, the narrator expresses her frustration with the treatment of the blacks in the rural **community**: the drudgery and alienation resulting from toil in the cotton fields, the victimization by local racists, and the small but searing indignities faced by her loved ones, a daily reminder of color prejudice. One memorable episode bears witness to the indignities endured by Maya's grandmother at the hands of some neighborhood poor whites. A robust widow, "Momma" Henderson exudes respectability and feminine agency. Her personal qualities are a stalwart **work** ethic, religious devotion, and dutiful generosity. Her power echoes that of **Harriet Jacobs**'s grandmother in *Incidents in the Life of a Slave Girl* (1861). Like the latter, Momma is particularly admirable for her business acumen. The store she runs with her disabled bachelor son (Uncle Willie) is a concentrated site of community power. Provisions for the body *and* the mind (in the form of chatting, gossip, and opportunities for public assembly) are exchanged and explored with equal vigor.

Distanced from this rural scene is Vivian Baxter, Maya's mother, a woman whose aura of fun flirtatiousness almost diametrically opposes Momma's organic simplicity. Whether portrayed as a latter-day goddess, a black version of a Hollywood starlet, an earthy Madonna, or a kite borne aloft above the heads of her children, this performer and ego ideal diversify our often narrow image of what a mother is or should be: desirable, imaginative, and heavily invested in the pursuit of her own goals. She bears no trace of the pancake-flipping **Jemima** or baby-minding **Mammy**. Grandmother Baxter, Vivian's mother, is also striking, primarily for her ability to function within an almost amoral zone of civic influence. Almost white in skin color, she serves as a precinct police captain, holding political and legal sway over gamblers and other shady personalities. This station is rather atypical of a black woman in depression-era St. Louis. Between Momma, Vivian, Grandmother Baxter, and Maya herself, the text clearly reveals the diversity and vividness possible in the maternal narrative genre.

Apart from underscoring female friendship and kinship bonds, *I Know* suggests that the best platform for the negotiation of a confident self is lived experience. After a skirmish with her father's girlfriend, Maya find solace with a community of indigent youths inhabiting a southern California junkyard. The ultimate vision is not gender exclusive but rather collaborative, highlighting for today's readers **Alice Walker**'s theory of **womanist** empowerment. Maya's enduring love for Bailey, his rapid initiation into a racist society, and even his inadvertent complicity in black women's oppression complement his sister's understanding of personal tragedy and its racial and sexual implications. Beyond these, issues as diverse as **lesbianism**, the collective wisdom of "mother-wit," and the integrity of naming converge and merge in the engaging eloquence of Angelou's earliest recollections.

See also Black Feminist Criticism; Healing; Identity; Memory; Religion; Sexuality

Works About

Bloom, Harold, ed. *Maya Angelou's "I Know Why the Caged Bird Sings."* Philadelphia, PA: Chelsea House, 1998.

Braxton, Joanne M., ed. *I Know Why the Caged Bird Sings—A Casebook.* New York: Oxford University Press, 1999.

Kent, George E. "Maya Angelou's *I Know Why the Caged Bird Sings* and the Black Autobiographical Tradition." *African American Autobiography: A Collection of Critical Essays.* Ed. William L. Andrews. Englewood Cliffs, NJ: Prentice Hall, 1993. 162–170.

Megna-Wallace, Joanne. *Understanding "I Know Why the Caged Bird Sings": A Student Casebook to Issues, Sources, and Historical Documents.* Westport, CT: Greenwood Press, 1998.

Walker, Pierre A. "Racial Protest, Identity, Words, and Form in Maya Angelou's *I Know Why the Caged Bird Sings.*" *College Literature* 22.3 (October 1995): 91–108.

Nancy Kang

IMAGO. See Xenogenesis Trilogy

INCIDENTS IN THE LIFE OF A SLAVE GIRL

In 1861 when **Harriet Jacobs** first published *Incidents in the Life of a Slave Girl*, it was promoted as a tool with the power to end the vicious enslavement of blacks. In a voice shocking for its strength and vehemence, Jacobs chronicles her plight as a young woman caught in the bonds of **slavery** in Edenton, North Carolina. Throughout her narrative she explicitly appeals to northern white women, hoping to elicit their sympathy and rouse them to action in support of the abolitionist cause. In her narrative, Jacobs takes on the arguments of proslavery factions, as she categorically disproves the **myth** of the "happy slave." She tells stories of those around her that exhibit the brutality and inhumanity of slavery, and she uses her own life as an example of its degrading effects upon even the most virtuous of young women. Finally, she examines the conditions of her enslavement that forced her to hide for seven years in a crawl space in her grandmother's **home**. Throughout her story, Jacobs uses the pseudonym "Linda Brent," and she loosely masks the **identity** of her cast of characters, while, at the same time, claiming the veracity of her account. Perhaps her greatest accomplishment in her narrative is that she forces her readers to see her or "Linda" as someone not all that different from themselves.

Jacobs's narrative begins with her awakening to her condition as a slave. Upon her mother's **death** when she was six years old, Jacobs, or "Linda," learns that she is the property of her mother's mistress and that she will now take her mother's place at this mistress's side. She notes that her mother had been a slave in name only, and she finds her treatment in this new home to be pleasant and her life to be as carefree as that of a white child. When this kind mistress dies, however, Jacobs learns that she has been willed to the woman's five-year-old niece. This incident is the first in a series of moments in the text where Jacobs learns to distrust the intentions and actions of white people.

Jacobs goes to live in the home of Dr. and Mrs. Flint—her new mistress's parents—and it is here that Jacobs spends the bulk of her enslavement. In *Incidents*, Jacobs tells of growing up in the Flint household and of Dr. Flint's attempts to manipulate her into a sexual relationship. Judging a consensual relationship with a man that she did not loathe to be better than a forced encounter with one she did, Jacobs enters into a liaison with a prominent white citizen, referred to in the narrative as "Mr. Sands." She bears two children—a son and a daughter—by this man, which serves to infuriate the "jilted" Flint—so much so that he vows he will never sell her or her children. She also has to contend with Mrs. Flint's jealousy at her husband's perceived infidelity. Jacobs describes how, in a near pathological fit of distrust and resentment, Mrs. Flint would haunt her bedside at night. Mrs. Flint ultimately succeeds in having Jacobs expelled from the house, and after living with her grandmother for a time, she is sent to the plantation to serve the Flints' son and his new wife.

In her narrative, Jacobs describes awakening to the fact that, despite the best interests of Mr. Sands and his intentions to buy her and her children, neither she nor her children will ever see **freedom** unless she takes matters into her own hands. Prompted by the information that her children will be brought to the plantation to **work**, Jacobs devises a plan for escape. She flees the household one night, to be taken in by a sympathetic white woman, who is also, ironically, a slaveholder. When this arrangement proves too dangerous, Jacobs's uncle constructs a garret above her grandmother's storage shed where Jacobs will spend the next six years and eleven months confined to a space so small that she cannot stand upright within it. Although her narrow space is cramped and subject to the elements—cold in the winter, hot in the summer, wet and unhealthful during the rainy season—Jacobs is close to her children and at least marginally safe from her pursuers.

Despite Jacobs's long absence from Dr. Flint's household, he does not give up his obsessive search for her. Over time, Jacobs realizes the threat she poses to her grandmother's own safety (and peace of mind), and she emerges from her garret to make her final bid for freedom aboard a ship bound for the North. Her daughter, Louisa Matilda (Ellen in the book), had preceded her when Mr. Sands had, in fact, purchased his daughter (but not freed her!) and taken her north to live with (and serve) his new wife and child. When Jacobs reaches New York, she is reunited with her daughter and befriended by Nathaniel Parker Willis and his first wife, Mary Stace Willis (Mr. and Mrs. Bruce in the book), who become her employers and protectors.

Ever fearful of being caught and returned to enslavement in Edenton and even more so after the passage of the "Fugitive Slave Act," Jacobs flees the city on several occasions when she learns of the arrival in town of people from her hometown who could identify and possibly arrest her. Jacobs is finally liberated when Mr. Bruce's second wife is successful in purchasing her from her mistress—now married and in dire financial straits. Although Jacobs is bitter that her freedom must be purchased and is not considered a natural right, at the conclusion of her narrative she is grateful to be rid once and for all of the yoke of slavery.

Jacobs was encouraged by her friend Amy Post to write her story in order to help the cause of abolition, but the publication of her story was not without trial itself. Fearful of taking on the task herself, Jacobs initially desired to pass along her story for another writer to tell. Harriet Beecher Stowe was a natural choice, and, when Jacobs learned that Stowe would be touring England, she proposed to send her daughter, Louisa, to join the company with the hopes of persuading Stowe to write her mother's story. Stowe responded to this proposal by claiming that Louisa, as a young black woman, would be spoiled by the attention she would receive there and that the plan was not logistically feasible despite the fact that Jacobs was prepared to pay Louisa's way. Jacobs responded to this slight with predictable anger but also with renewed vigor for her project. She knew that if her story were to be told, she herself must tell it. Although Jacobs initially considered a British publisher, her biographer Jean Fagan Yellin notes that it is unclear why that plan fell apart. Two of the American publishers Jacobs contacted about publishing her narrative failed before the book reached print, but Thayer and Eldredge was instrumental in encouraging Jacobs to work with Lydia Maria Child, who would eventually become the book's editor and write a preface for the text. After Thayer and Eldredge went bankrupt, Jacobs, tired of waiting, bought the plates and had the book printed herself.

Although it was initially well received and even published in London as *The Deeper Wrong; or, Incidents in the Life of a Slave Girl. Written by Herself,* over the years, Jacobs's story passed into obscurity. When it was read, it was assumed to be the work of abolitionist Lydia Maria Child and not the factual account its author claimed it to be. In her preface to her critical edition of *Incidents,* Yellin describes her own initial doubts about the text and her gradual awareness of its accuracy over the course of her research into women abolitionists. Yellin identified the characters in the story long thought to be types rather than actual people, and she successfully connected places and events to Jacobs's recollections in order to reveal the veracity of Jacobs's claim to truth and to reconnect the text with its original author.

See also Slave Narrative

Works About

Garfield, Deborah M., and Rafia Zafar, eds. *Harriet Jacobs and "Incidents in the Life of a Slave Girl": New Critical Essays.* Cambridge: Cambridge University Press, 1996.

Jacobs, Harriet. *Incidents in the Life of a Slave Girl: Written by Herself.* Boston: For the Author, 1861. Cambridge: Harvard University Press, 1987–2000.

Yellin, Jean Fagan. *Harriet Jacobs: A Life.* New York: Basic Civitas Books, 2004.

Jennifer Dawes Adkison

IN LOVE & TROUBLE: STORIES OF BLACK WOMEN

In Love & Trouble: Stories of Black Women is the first published collection of short stories by **Alice Walker**. Some stories were previously published, but the collection as a whole appeared in 1973. It was preceded by four other works by Walker, including her first novel, *The Third Life of Grange Copeland* (1970).

Walker, who grew up in Georgia, wrote the stories between 1967 and 1973 on the heels of the **civil rights movement** and during the **Black Arts Movement**. Consisting of thirteen stories, *In Love & Trouble* addresses many concerns that recur in Walker's work. She takes a critical look at the oppression that black women face. Important to Walker's view is not only how black women are affected but also how oppressive forces such as racism and sexism pollute the black **community**.

Most of the stories take place in the **South**. Each one involves a black woman and her experience with **love**. As the title suggests, however, their experience is not always positive. For Walker's women, love can include misplaced loyalty to black men who are often characterized as abusive and dismissive (as in "Really, Doesn't Crime Pay?" and "Her Sweet Jerome"). Walker explores these women's lives and surroundings with an eye toward revealing how oppression affects their physical and mental states of being, namely, in trying to fulfill definitions of self and resisting conventional definitions imposed on them. Individual relationships and social institutions, such as marriage and **religion**, are both scrutinized.

The collection begins with "Roselily," setting the example for Walker's critical and insightful stories. The story takes place during the title character's wedding ceremony. Roselily is a southerner with three children and no husband. She hopes that marriage to a black Muslim from Chicago will bring her and her children some respectability and security. Knowing little about her future husband's religion, she expects her role as a wife will be subservient and confining. Her love for him exists only as the recognition of his ability to improve her condition as a single, working mother. Roselily acknowledges feeling trapped and unfulfilled, yet marriage and life in a northern city seem better than her current situation.

Throughout the collection, women often act against their notions of **freedom** and fulfillment because societal conventions limit what they can do. Yet these women are not simply victims. At the least, they define fulfillment for themselves even if they cannot act in support of that fulfillment. The development of a definition of self-fulfillment in the face of racism and sexism is itself a valuable process for Walker's women. It is a necessary struggle without which change would be impossible.

In Love & Trouble was met with mixed critical reception. Critics charged that the depiction of black men was stereotypical and that the women came across as damaged victims. Supporters contend that Walker's women are not victims but women with hope who are capable of growth in spite of the difficulties they may face. Some have described the stories as examples of **womanist** prose, a term Walker popularized that refers to black feminists or feminists of color.

See also In Search of Our Mothers' Gardens: Womanist Prose; Womanism; *You Can't Keep a Good Woman Down*

Works About

Bradley, David. "Novelist Alice Walker Telling the Black Woman's Story." *New York Times*, January 8, 1984, sec. 6, 24.

Brown, Julie, ed. *American Women Short Story Writers: A Collection of Critical Essays.* New York: Garland, 1995.

Christian, Barbara. "The Contrary Women of Alice Walker." *Black Scholar* 12.2 (1982): 21–30.

Evans, Mari, ed. *Black Women Writers (1950–1980): A Critical Evaluation.* Garden City, NY: Anchor Press/Doubleday, 1984.

Gates, Henry Louis, Jr., and K. A. Appiah. *Alice Walker: Critical Perspectives Past and Present.* New York: Amistad Press, 1993.

Petry, Alice Hall. "Alice Walker: The Achievement of the Short Fiction." *Modern Language Studies* 19.1 (1989): 12–27.

Winchell, Donna Haisty. *Alice Walker.* New York: Twayne Publishers, 1992.

Raquel Rodriguez

IN SEARCH OF OUR MOTHERS' GARDENS: WOMANIST PROSE

Written between 1966 and 1982, this 1984 text is a collection of essays, articles, reviews, and speeches by **Alice Walker** divided into four sections. In part one, Walker describes in "Saving a Life That Is Your Own: The Importance of Models in the Artist's Life" the frustration she felt for the lack of black women writers as models. However, in her pursuits of a factual account of voodoo, she stumbles across the footnoted name **Zora Neale Hurston**, which leads her to Hurston's works and the marking of her grave site in Florida. Though Walker found herself drawn to Flannery O'Connor, **Jean Toomer**, and **Langston Hughes**, she claims her pursuit of black women writers as a search for the texts she should have been able to read during her education. Another essay in part one relates her difficulties devising a curriculum to teach ninety black women how to pass on black heritage to their students. Other essays review authors Walker considers as models: Jean Toomer, Buchi Emecheta, and **Rebecca Cox Jackson**.

Part two characterizes the **civil rights movement** and how it affected black communities and herself. In these essays she discusses place, **community**, **home**, her role as a writer during the revolution, her anxiety at combining **motherhood** and writing, Langston Hughes, Cuba, and a **film** made by a black sorority.

Part three contains the namesake essay of the collection that describes the need to reevaluate how creativity, art, and **literature** are defined and asserts, as Virginia Woolf did, that women have always been creative but often were disallowed to produce because of oppression. That is, Walker looks low to find creativity in her own mother's garden as proof of a black women's **history** of creativity. Also in this section is an interview, a published letter to *Ms.*, and a rejected one to *Black Scholar*.

In part four she delineates on topics such as antinuclear activism, imperialism, civil rights, and motherhood. In "Writing *The Color Purple*," she reveals the impetus for the novel, her own struggles to write the novel in New York, her eventual move to San Francisco, and how quickly the story was written there. The estimable collection culminates with an essay from *Ms.*, "Beauty: When the Other Dancer Is the Self," which chronicles the experience that led her to accept her once disfigured and completely blinded eye. Scholars have written on numerous aspects of this text.

See also Womanism

Works About

Banks, Erma Davis, and Keith Byerman. *Alice Walker: An Annotated Bibliography 1968–1986*. New York: Garland, 1989. 127–138.
Lauret, Maria. *Alice Walker*. New York: St. Martin's Press, 2000. 1–29.
Winchell, Donna Haisty. *Alice Walker*. New York: Twayne Publishers, 1992. 14–28.

Laura Madeline Wiseman

IN SEARCH OF SATISFACTION

The novel *In Search of Satisfaction* was published in 1994 by **J. California Cooper**. It is an epic saga about the lives of three families. Cooper's use of vernacular has caused her narrative style to be compared to **Zora Neale Hurston** and **Alice Walker**, and this is very apparent in this novel. Like Janie in Hurston's *Their Eyes Were Watching God* (1937) and Celie in Walker's *The Color Purple* (1985), the characters in *In Search of Satisfaction* speak in black dialect. At the same time, the need to learn standard English as a means of becoming more successful is emphasized, as is the importance of education. Cooper conveys the idea that knowledge gives one power and that this is especially true for the doubly oppressed black woman.

The Bible and **religion** play prominent roles in much of Cooper's work, but this is perhaps most apparent in *In Search of Satisfaction*. The novel explores the role of good and evil as the characters attempt to become upwardly mobile after **slavery** has been abolished. God and, especially, Satan appear to guide the characters as they make important life decisions. As she does in much of her work, Cooper has many moral lessons to convey in *In Search of Satisfaction*, and a major theme in the novel is the idea that life may be difficult, but it is important to do the right thing and follow the Ten Commandments. As well, there is a warning to be wary, for there is much evil in the world; therefore, one must beware of those who do not respect the Commandments.

The hardships of poverty and the superficiality of wealth are visible in the novel. Many characters find that they cannot escape poverty because of their limited education and experience. For example, characters such as Joel and Ruth have the simple, respectable dream of owning a **home** and sending their son, Lincoln, to college. Other characters are seduced by the trappings of the rich and are willing to sacrifice their values in order to live in luxury. Yin, for example, is full of envy and craves the abundance of the material world. Even the wealthy, white, and powerful Befoes, who are worth millions, are so consumed by greed that they take advantage of the town's poorest inhabitants. Ultimately, some, but not all, recognize that this superficial lifestyle does not bring them complete fulfillment, and they realize that they will find greater satisfaction through **love** and **family**.

Cooper acknowledges that we are all "in search of satisfaction" but that we pay for the choices that we make; therefore, we must choose wisely.

See also Family; *Homemade Love*

Diane Todd Bucci

INTERRUPTION OF EVERYTHING, THE

Reflective in tone, **Terry McMillan**'s sixth novel explores the trials and tribulations of midlife. Forty-four-year-old Marilyn Grimes is ready to settle down to a comfortable life that includes a peaceful marriage. Unfortunately, Marilyn learns that life is not so simple; there are always interruptions.

First, there is her husband, Leon, who is going through a midlife crisis of his own. His distant moods and rebellious behavior wreak havoc on their marriage. Authorine, Leon's mother, lives with the Grimes **family**. Although elderly, she begins a relationship and eventually marries Prezelle, an elderly man who is still full of life.

Marilyn's children do not give her much peace either. Sabrina, Marilyn's oldest child, lives a bohemian lifestyle in Berkeley. Marilyn struggles to hold back her opinion as she witnesses her daughter deferring her dreams in order to fulfill family obligations—a path Marilyn once took. Simon and Spencer are

Marilyn's college-age twins. Each has a different view of success, and Marilyn keeps her fingers crossed that they will accomplish all of the goals they set for themselves.

While her **home** life is nothing less than chaotic, Marilyn also struggles with the declining health of her mother, Lovey; she later discovers that Lovey's unusual behavior is due to the onset of dementia. Marilyn's adopted sister, Joy, behaves irresponsibly and has two children. The rapid decline of her mother's health and the tragedy that later strikes Joy figure in Marilyn's decision to open her home to her extended family and begin the job of primary caretaker all over again.

Interruption is a vivid portrait of the foibles that come with aging. Marilyn learns that life is not a straight trajectory, but a recursive cycle of progress and defeats.

Works About

Review of *The Interruption of Everything. Publishers Weekly* 252.35 (2005): 58.
Smolowe, Jill. "A Shakeup for Stella: With Terry McMillan's Novel about Midlife Crises Hitting Stores This Month, Her Marriage to the Man Who Inspired *How Stella Got Her Groove Back* Hits the Skids." *People Weekly* 64.2 (2005): 97.

Catherine Ross-Stroud

IOLA LEROY

Poet, orator, journalist, and activist **Frances E. W. Harper** published her novel *Iola Leroy* in 1892 at the age of sixty-seven. Harper's novel was published both in Boston and Philadelphia, and within its first year of publication, it had gone through five printings. Frances Smith Foster suggests that *Iola Leroy* was probably the bestselling novel by a pre-twentieth-century African American writer.

Written in response to the political and social exigencies of the post-Reconstruction United States, *Iola Leroy* can be read in the context of Harper's lifelong activism and social reform **work**. Throughout her life, Harper advocated a universal **love** realized by a commitment to humanity. In her speeches, writings, and activism, Harper was committed to securing equal rights for all and was active in word and deed for causes such as abolition, temperance, and suffrage. After the failure of Reconstruction, Harper was particularly committed to **healing** the personal and communal wounds caused by the "cancer" of **slavery** and to building strong African American communities from within.

Iola Leroy looks at America's past, present, and future and the role black women could play in the future of the nation. The eponymous Iola is the daughter of Eugene Leroy, a white plantation owner, and Marie, the descendant of a black woman. Although Leroy manumits Marie and establishes their children as his rightful heirs, an avaricious cousin challenges the legality of Marie's manumission upon Eugene's **death** and declares Eugene's will invalid. The cousin claims Eugene's property and sells Marie and her children into slavery. Iola is lured from the North and sold as a slave; her **beauty** makes slavery particularly perilous for her. Harry is forewarned of his fate and joins the Union army, where he enlists with a black regiment. Iola is rescued by another slave who, charmed by her beauty, brings her to the Union army, where she works as a nurse. Significantly, Iola and her brother Harry are both able to pass for white, yet they choose to "link their fortunes" to the black **race** and to work toward its healing and elevation. Both Leroy children embody the characteristics of ideal citizens: Harry is a "manly and self-respecting" man, and Iola is a "useful and self-reliant" woman.

Much of the novel is concerned with **family** members searching for and finding each other, establishing happy homes, and helping to raise strong future leaders and citizens. In promoting these traditionally female endeavors, Harper underscores the centrality of African American women in the processes of healing and elevating not only the race but the nation as well.

When Iola asks what she can do for her race, she is told to write a book that will "inspire men and women with a deeper sense of justice." Harper's own *Iola Leroy* is such a book, and Iola's ideas frequently echo those found in Harper's other writings, particularly those of love, hope, and optimism. Iola and Harper both believe there is "a brighter coming day" on the horizon and that African American women are especially suited for ushering it in.

Works About

Carby, Hazel. *Reconstructing Womanhood: The Emergence of the Afro-American Woman Novelist.* New York: Oxford University Press, 1987.

Foster, Frances Smith. Introduction. *Iola Leroy: or, Shadows Uplifted.* New York: Oxford University Press, 1988. xxvii–xxxiv.

Peterson, Carla L. " 'Further Liftings of the Veil': Gender, Class, and Labor in Frances E. W. Harper's *Iola Leroy.*" *Listening to Silences: New Essays in Feminist Criticism.* Ed. Elaine Hedges and Shelley Fisher Fishkin. New York: Oxford University Press, 1994. 97–112.

Tate, Claudia. *Domestic Allegories of Political Desire: The Black Heroine's Text at the Turn of the Century.* New York: Oxford University Press, 1992.

Young, Elizabeth. "Warring Fictions: *Iola Leroy* and the Color of Gender." *American Literature* 64.2 (June 1992): 273–297.

Heidi L. M. Jacobs

 **J**

JACKSON, ANGELA (1951–   )

Angela Jackson is a recognized African American poet whose verse unifies her African heritage, small-town southern roots, and urban experiences. Jackson was born in Greenville, Mississippi, the fifth of nine children born to George and Angeline Jackson. Her family relocated to Chicago when she was a young child. It was in Chicago where she began to forge her distinctive poetic voice that plumbs heartfelt, accessible, and everyday subjects. Her poems, continually drawing from African motifs, resonate with an innocent southern childhood charm and an eclectic cosmopolitan culture. Jackson attended Northwestern University, where she quickly gained a reputation as a gifted poet for her unmistakably inventive style, penetrating voice, and accessible subject matter.

Jackson is primarily a poet who has published many collections of verse, including *Voo Doo/Love Magic* (1974), *The Greenville Club* (1977), *Solo in the Boxcar Third Floor E* (1985), *Dark Legs and Silk Kisses* (1993), and *And All These Roads Be Luminous: Poems Selected and New* (1998). Her **poetry**, enriched by her deeply rooted cultural voice and complex yet mundane metaphors, explores the abstract and prosaic. Her subjects are the familiar and everyday: **love**, **family**, cultural **memory**, politics, and African American heritage. In "Transformable Prophecy," the poet develops the metaphorically rich language, centered on the traditional African folktale of a spider that appears in many of her poems, to describe the recreation of the world: "When the world ends / a great spider will rise like a gray cloud / above it." Her authentic voice resonates with the here and now in "The Autumn Men," as Jackson describes the familiar scenes and smells of men raking leaves in the family yard, while young girls think about falling in love. Her images are sharply focused, distilled down to basic emotions. Although love in the prose piece "Witchdoctor" may be elusive, the language is poignant and vivid.

As an emerging playwright, Jackson's repertoire includes *Witness!* (1978), produced in Chicago and Milwaukee by the Ebony Talent Readers Theatre; *Shango Diaspora: An African-American Myth of Womanhood and Love* (1980), produced in Chicago, Cleveland, and New York; and *When the Wind Blows* (1984) produced in Chicago.

Jackson's artistic style and sensitivity have been shaped through her involvement with Chicago's Organization of Black American Culture (OBAC) during the 1970s. OBAC is a conclave of writers and other artists that promotes the articulation of the African American aesthetic. She joined the organization in 1970 and helped to fashion the group's manifesto that stresses high standards for literary expression and critical evaluation of creative works within the black context. Her first book *Voo Doo/Love Magic*, a collection of fifteen poems, strongly reflects the aesthetic and sociopolitical foundation of OBAC. The small volume carries a dedication to the members of OBAC and to Hoyt Fuller, the workshop's leader until 1976, when Jackson assumed the direction of OBAC.

Included among the many awards she has received are a fellowship from the National Endowment for the Arts and an American Book Award for *Solo*. She was elected chairperson of the board of directors for the Coordinating Council of Literary Magazines. She received international recognition when she represented the United States at the Second World Festival of Black and African Arts and Culture (1978). In 1983 Jackson received the Hoyt W. Fuller Award for Literary Excellence.

In her early poem "Voo Doo/Love Magic," Jackson declares that she is going to get into the reader's soul, where she will place a magical love spell. The poem's final line declares: "I'm gonna put a hex on you." Jackson's spirited and ebullient canon of writing does indeed place a hex on the reader.

Works By

And All These Roads Be Luminous: Poems Selected and New. Evanston, IL: Northwestern University Press, 1998.

Dark Legs and Silk Kisses: The Beatitudes of the Spinners. Evanston, IL: Northwestern University Press, 1993.

The Greenville Club. Kansas City, MO: Bk Mk Press, 1977.

Shango Diaspora: An African-American Myth of Womanhood and Love. Chicago, Parkway Community House Theatre, October 1980.

Solo in the Boxcar Third Floor E. Chicago: OBAhouse, 1985.

Voo Doo/Love Magic. Chicago: Third World Press, 1974.

Witness! Chicago, Showcase Theatre, March 1978.

Works About

Harris, Trudier, and Thadious M. Davis, eds. "Angela Jackson." *Dictionary of Literary Biography*. Vol. 41: *Afro-American Poets since 1955*. Detroit: The Gale Group, 1985. 176–183.

Herman, Edith. "Verse Things Could Happen When a Poet Visits the School." *Chicago Tribune*, May 30, 1977, II: 5, 7.

"Women to Watch." *Ebony* 37 (August 1982): 56.

Michael D. Sollars

JACKSON, ELAINE (1943–)

Elaine Jackson, actress, playwright, and teacher, was born in Detroit, Michigan, and later graduated from Wayne State University, where she studied speech and education. Upon graduation, Jackson pursued a career as an actress. She moved to the West Coast and as an off-Broadway actress performed in a number of plays including the Negro Ensemble Company's production of *Liberty Call* (1975). Jackson became a published playwright and a part of the black theater movement in 1971 when *Toe Jam* appeared in Woodie King and Ron Milner's *Black Drama Anthology*, a collection of plays by a number of notable African American dramatists, including **Amiri Baraka**, **Kathleen Collins**, and **Langston Hughes**. The New Federal Theatre, the Greenwich Mews Theater, and the American Folk Theatre produced many of Jackson's plays.

Black feminist perspectives are presented in most of her work. In three acts and seven scenes, *Toe Jam*, produced by the New Federal Theatre, features Xenith Graham as she struggles to carve out a creative space for herself, a space that will bring her into her own. She dreams of becoming a famous poet, actress, and playwright, though her mother demands that she stop pretending and find financial security and "honor" for herself by marrying Kenneth, the son of a doctor. *Cockfight* (1976) focuses on relationships between black men and women as the premise of the play surrounds the dissolution of a marriage. According to the Schomburg Center, *Cockfight* (1976) was originally titled *Kenya Cowboys* ("Cockfight" is handwritten on the title page of *Kenya Cowboys*). Apparently the Greenwich Mews Theater produced the play in 1976 under the title *Cockfight*.

Paper Dolls (1979) is a satire concerned with mainstream ideas of **beauty**. Margaret-Elizabeth, Miss Emancipation of 1930, and her colleague, Lizzie, who was first runner-up, have traveled to Canada to judge an international beauty pageant. Along the way, they reminisce about their days as beauty pageant contestants. Pinched noses, straightened hair, tightened lips, and bleached skin are among the many efforts these aging beauty queens have used to obtain "beauty." The play exposes the destructive nature of hair and skin politics on women's lives. Margaret-Elizabeth and Lizzie decide it is not too late for them to reinvent themselves in order to help future generations realize the beauty that rests in black women's natural appearances.

Other works by Jackson include *Birth Rites* (1978), a comedic **drama**, produced by the American Folk Theatre of New York. The action of the play takes place in a hospital in New York where several expectant mothers of diverse backgrounds contemplate **motherhood** as they look forward to the birth of their newborns.

Jackson has received several awards for her work. She was awarded the Rockefeller Award for Playwriting in 1978–1979, the Langston Hughes Playwriting Award in 1979, and a National Endowment for the Arts Award for playwriting in 1983. Jackson's work is reflective of her interest in black female **identity** development, empowerment, and self-actualization. Jackson is applauded for her work as a dramatist who recognized the need to make the voices of young black women audible in the theatrical world.

Works By

Paper Dolls. 9 Plays by Black Women. Ed. Margaret B. Wilkerson. New York: New American Library, 1986. 347–423.
Toe Jam. Black Drama Anthology. Ed. Woodie King and Ron Milner. New York: Meridian Book, Penguin Group, 1971. 641–671.

Works About

Curb, Rosemary K. " 'Goin' through Changes': Mother-Daughter Confrontations in Three Recent Plays by Young Black Women." *Kentucky Folklore Record: A Regional Journal of Folklore and Folklife* 25 (1979): 96–102.
MacDonald, Erik. *Theater at the Margins.* Ann Arbor: University of Michigan Press, 1993.

KaaVonia Hinton-Johnson

JACKSON, MAE (1946–)

Mae Jackson, poet, playwright, activist, and educator, was born on January 3, 1946, in Earl, Arkansas. She studied at the New School for Social Research in New York City from 1966 to 1967 and later during the 1970s. Her work has appeared in numerous periodicals, including *Black Creation, Essence, Journal of Black Poetry,* and *Negro Digest/Black World* and anthologies, such as *The Poetry of Black America* (1973), *BlackSpirits* (1972), *Night Comes Softly* (1970), and *Black Out Loud* (1970).

Jackson published *Can I Poet with You* (1969) during the height of the **Black Arts Movement**. In the introduction, **Nikki Giovanni**, one of Jackson's mentors, suggests that Jackson is a natural poet, a "people poet," committed to addressing the concerns of the **community**. The volume of **poetry** contains nearly thirty poems on a range of topics from black pride and Black Power to black **love** and black art. Above all, *Can I Poet with You* demands that the black female presence in the revolution (and the Black Arts Movement) is recognized and documented. In the poem "For Some Poets," from which the book's title comes, Jackson asks several leading poets—"roi" (LeRoi Jones/Amiri Baraka), "nikki" (Nikki Giovanni), Marvin X (Marvin Ellis Jackmon), and others— "Can I . . . poet with you please?" In 1970, Jackson received the Conrad Kent Rivers Memorial Award of *Negro Digest/Black World* for *Can I Poet with You*.

During the 1970s, Jackson turned to writing plays. She was a playwright with the Negro Ensemble Company Playwrights Workshop and a member of the Brewery Puppet Troupe. Three unpublished plays—*Sketches in Black and White* (1976), *When I Grow Up I Want to Be* (1976), and *Cafe Who* (n.d.)—written by Jackson are housed in the Schomburg Collection. She has also authored several children's plays: *The Harriet Tubman Story*, *The Jackson Five Meets Malcolm X*, and *When Kwanzaa Comes*. She has also worked as an instructor at Cell Block Theatre, Bronx Men's House of Detention, Queens Men's House of Detention, Metropolitan Correctional Facilities, Loft Film and Theatre Center, and South Jamaica Senior Citizens Center. Jackson also wrote a documentary titled *The Prison Movement* for Pacifia Radio. Jackson has been a Pacific News Service commentator and director of "Children without Walls," a program teaching art to the children of women in prison. In 1997, Jackson wrote a moving commentary titled "The Fire Next Time—Lessons of the Shabazz Tragedy" for *Jinn Magazine*. The article discusses the implications of fire around, first, the house of **Malcolm X**'s youth, then the apartment he lived in, in 1965, and finally the fire set by Malcolm's grandson that resulted in his wife Betty Shabazz's **death**. Further, she laments that fire continues to consume her own generation. Jackson was a member of the Student Nonviolent Coordinating Committee (SNCC) and the H. Rap Brown Anti-Dope Movement. Jackson's work reveals her commitment to activism and **community** uplift.

Works By

Can I Poet with You. New York: Black Dialogue; Detroit, MI: Broadside Press, 1969.
"The Fire Next Time." *Jinn Magazine*, 1997. www.pacificnews.org/jinn/.

Works About

Adoff, Arnold, ed. "Jackson, Mae." *The Poetry of Black America: Anthology of the 20th Century.* New York: Harper and Row, 1973. 526–527.
Bailey, Leonead Pack, ed. *Broadside Authors and Artists: An Illustrated Biographical Directory.* Detroit, MI: Broadside Press, 1974. 65.
King, Woodie, ed. "Jackson, Mae." *BlackSpirits: A Festival of New Black Poets in America.* New York: Random House, 1972. 245.

KaaVonia Hinton-Johnson

JACKSON, MATTIE (1843–?)

Forging hope under seemingly insurmountable circumstances, Mattie Jane Jackson's life is a testament to never giving up and always believing that a better day would come. Jackson's life story is also the celebration of the woman as heroine as she witnessed firsthand the heroics of her mother, Ellen, in standing up to her owners and in sacrificing her **freedom** so that her children could gain their freedom first.

Born in St. Louis in 1843 to slaves Ellen and Westley Jackson, Jackson endured separation from her **family** early in her life; her father and mother lived on separate plantations when she was born. Her father eventually escaped with the assistance of his wife and with the hope of reuniting with his family, but **slavery** would prevent such a reunion and would leave Jackson's mother to raise her and her sister alone.

Jackson's life unfolded under several different slave owners. One owner, William Lewis, was the result of the family being sold after attempting to escape some two years after the father's departure. A partnership between Lewis and his brother-in-law further separated the already broken family by sending Jackson to live with the brother-in-law and his wife. Jackson eventually returned to the Lewis residence and to her mother, who had remarried and had two more children. Ellen would again be left alone to care for her family because this husband, too, escaped to freedom.

Change was on the horizon, though, for Jackson and her family, for the Civil War had begun. Jackson's owner held out hope of victory until the Union army took New Orleans. Jackson and her mother were overjoyed that freedom was almost at hand because their owner, mostly in retaliation, treated them horribly. A beating by Lewis left Jackson with a permanent scar on her head, one that she said would be a constant reminder of her treatment as a slave.

Yet another owner would gain possession of Jackson and her family and separate them. She would fare far worse under this owner; she was not fed enough and was given constant and difficult **work**, but this did not stop her from plotting her escape. Daily for six months Jackson awoke in the early morning hours to find someone to help her escape using the **Underground Railroad**. She finally succeeded and arrived in Indianapolis a free woman for the first time.

Once there she was encouraged by the Unionists to read, write, and pursue her literary interests. The dreams that Jackson had held for as long as she could remember were finally coming true. The hopes that she had for her family would come true as well; Jackson's mother joined her in Indianapolis, finally successful after six escape attempts and more than forty-three years as a slave. Jackson and her mother returned to St. Louis, where Ellen remarried. Jackson moved on to Lawrence, Massachusetts, and in 1866 dictated the story of her life to her stepmother.

Work By

The Story of Mattie J. Jackson: Her Parentage, Experience of Eighteen Years in Slavery, Incidents During the War, Her Escape from Slavery: A True Story. Lawrence, MA: Sentinel Office, 1866.

Lamara Williams-Hackett

JACKSON, REBECCA COX (1795–1871)

An early African American feminist, Rebecca Cox Jackson was born free around 1795 near Philadelphia. A religious visionary, Jackson believed that she had been chosen to make known God's will to His people. For Jackson and many other women in the nineteenth century, a call to serve God as a preacher brought with it a sense of personal empowerment that frequently conflicted with patriarchal restrictions on women's participation in the public sphere. Not surprisingly, Jackson faced opposition from her brother Rev. Joseph Cox, her husband Samuel Jackson, and clergymen in the African Methodist Episcopal (AME) Church. But despite strong resistance from men who viewed her call to preach as nothing more than female impertinence/arrogance, Jackson persevered and gained considerable recognition as a preacher and founder of a black Shaker **community** in Philadelphia.

First published in 1981, Jackson's writings detailing her spiritual journey are compelling and easy to read. Readers will be fascinated by Jackson's brilliant descriptions of her extraordinary dreams and visions. Women readers may feel a special connection to the dreams involving **domestic** activities such as women taking care of children, sewing, cleaning house, and preparing meals. These traditionally feminine tasks assume symbolic meanings in Jackson's writings.

According to Jackson's spiritual **autobiography**, her religious awakening occurred during a thunderstorm in 1830. An inner voice told her she will die and go to hell. Jackson then prayed and asked for forgiveness. Subsequently, she was converted and felt a tremendous **love** for God and all humankind. Another turning point in Jackson's spiritual development was her decision to embrace a celibate lifestyle. Influenced by her inner voice, Jackson perceived sex as sin. Therefore, she refused to engage in sex with her husband, thereby liberating herself from male sexual dominance. Moreover, Jackson's inner voice led her to preach and pray in public without the approval of the male leadership of the AME Church. Following her conversion, Jackson received spiritual guidance and authority from God through visions and dreams. Consequently, she did not feel bound by limitations that men set for her in the church or elsewhere.

In 1831, Jackson received a vision of "God's true people," the Shakers. She was impressed by the Shakers' commitment to celibacy and their feminist theology, which included a Mother and Daughter as well as a Father and Son in the godhead. She was also enticed by the idea of Holy Mother Wisdom balancing the traditional Almighty Father. Because Jackson believed Shakers were God's chosen or "true people," she felt compelled to bring other blacks into the predominantly white Shaker community. While living in the Watervliet Community of Shakers in 1851, Jackson requested permission from Eldress Paulina Bates to evangelize among blacks in Philadelphia. Displeased with Jackson's strict obedience to her inner voice, Bates denied Jackson's request. Undeterred by Bates's refusal, Jackson left Watervliet and devoted six years to preaching among blacks in Philadelphia. In the "Dreams of Home," Jackson was welcomed back into the Watervliet community, where she acknowledged Eldress Bates's authority as leader and received her blessing. Jackson and her friend, Rebecca Perot, returned to Philadelphia and established a community of black Shakers that survived forty years after Jackson's **death**.

Work By

Gifts of Power: The Writings of Rebecca Jackson, Black Visionary, and Shaker Eldress. Ed. Jean McMahon Humez. Boston: University of Massachusetts Press, 1987.

Works About

Bassard, Katherine Clay. *Spiritual Interrogations: Culture, Gender, and Community in Early African American Women's Writing.* Princeton, NJ: Princeton University Press, 1999.

Evans, James H., Jr. *Spiritual Empowerment in Afro-American Literature.* Lewiston, NY: Edwin Mellen Press, 1987.

Humez, Jean McMahon. Introduction to *Gifts of Power.* Boston: University of Massachusetts Press, 1987. 1–64.

Elvin Holt

JACOBS, HARRIET (1813–1897)

In her long and tumultuous life, Harriet Jacobs fought not only for the **freedom** of enslaved blacks but also for their dignity. In her narrative ***Incidents in the Life of a Slave Girl*** (1861), which she wrote pseudonymously as "Linda Brent," **race** and gender intersect to underscore the particular trials of the female slave. Jacobs masterfully weaves a tale of **love** and hope, fear and degradation, as she appeals to her largely white audience in the North.

Jacobs was born in 1813 in Edenton, North Carolina, to Delilah, daughter of Molly Horniblow (both enslaved), and her husband, Elijah Knox, a carpenter by trade, who, although a slave himself, was allowed to **work** and live with his **family**. As a girl, Hatty (as she was called) had no knowledge of her own enslavement. Upon her mother's **death** in 1819, when Hatty was only six, she first learned of her position as a slave. Her family was of mixed race, with her grandmother, Molly, the daughter of a white man who had been Molly's mother's master, and race and concerns about race figure prominently in Jacobs's narrative. The family had been allowed to live together and must have maintained some semblance of normalcy for Jacobs to write at middle age that her awareness to her condition of enslavement occurred when she was sent to serve her mother's mistress after her mother's death.

Although Delilah's mistress, Margaret Horniblow, promised that she would protect Delilah's children, Miss Margaret died prematurely while still in her twenties. During Miss Margaret's lifetime, Hatty led a comfortable life in service to her young mistress. Doing the almost unthinkable, Margaret taught Hatty to read and write and supervised her religious education. Despite the strong bond that clearly developed between the mistress and her slave, in a deathbed codicil to her will Margaret bequeathed the girl to her three-year-old niece Mary Matilda Norcom. (Interestingly, the fact that the codicil was never signed by Margaret Horniblow has led Jacobs's biographer Jean Fagan Yellin to question whether it was Margaret's intention to will Jacobs to her niece or whether this was the result of the machinations of Margaret's lecherous brother-in-law, Dr. James Norcom.)

Nothing about her experiences up until age twelve when she came to live in the Norcom household could have prepared Jacobs for her life there. From that time and for the next quarter of a century, Jacobs would live in fear of Dr. Norcom's power over her very life. In her narrative, Jacobs describes Dr. Norcom's (he is named "Dr. Flint" in the text) attempts to manipulate her into a sexual relationship despite the fact that she was only fifteen years old, and he was over fifty. Retelling the stories of the indignities she suffered at Norcom's hands was clearly troubling to Jacobs as she wrote her narrative. Nonetheless, she explicitly claims in her narrative that she uses these episodes, even though her modest sensibility shrinks at their recounting, in order to stir the sympathy of northern white women for the plight of southern black women still enslaved. It becomes clear to Jacobs that for the young slave girl virtue is not an option, and she loses no opportunity to share this appalling situation with her readers.

Because of her status as a slave, Jacobs was denied the basic right of marriage to the man of her choice. When she fell in love with a local freeborn black man, Dr. Norcom scoffed at her choice and, like a jealous lover scorned, told her that if she ever spoke to the man again, he would have him whipped. Determining that a lover of her choosing is better than concubinage with the despised Norcom, Jacobs began a relationship with a local lawyer, Samuel Tredwell Sawyer, who was sympathetic to her plight. Her relationship with Sawyer produced two children, Joseph and Louisa Matilda, whom, along with herself, Jacobs hoped Sawyer would purchase and free. Through her relationship with the affluent and aristocratic Sawyer, Jacobs was able to sidestep Dr. Norcom's attentions. As Norcom's social superior, Sawyer could offer a modicum of protection to young Harriet.

In her narrative, Jacobs makes the claim that **slavery** is degrading to both black and white women, which is vividly illustrated in her contentious relationship with Mrs. Norcom. Well aware of her husband's attention to Harriet, Mrs. Norcom first keeps a nighttime vigil over the slave girl and then, as her jealous passions erupt, bans her from the house altogether. Despite the fact that Jacobs moved out of the Norcom home to once again live with her grandmother, Dr. Norcom kept up his sexual entreaties and threats, although it appears that he was too cautious to act upon them.

Jacobs lived with her grandmother Molly for six years, but upon once again rejecting Dr. Norcom's sexual advances, she was sent to live on the family plantation to serve Norcom's son and his new wife. During this time, Jacobs learns that Norcom plans to send her children to the plantation, too, so they can be "broken in" to the life of the slaves. This knowledge coupled with her growing awareness that Norcom will never sell her (or her children) to Sawyer compelled her to formulate a plan for escape. Although she could not have known it at the time, true freedom was over seventeen years away—seven of which would be spent hiding in a space so small she could not even stand erect.

Jacobs's conviction that she must either run away or die a slave began a new era in her life. On the night that would mark this change, Jacobs completed her chores, locked up the house, and retired to her room to wait. At midnight she crept down the stairs, opened the parlor window, jumped out, and never looked back. Although she would remain a slave on paper for another seventeen years, she never again lived as one. On that fateful night, she ran to her grandmother's house, asked a friend to hide her clothing (to make it look as if she had fled northward), and lit out for a hiding place at an unidentified friend's house. When a snake bit her in her hiding place, she was taken into the home of a sympathetic white woman (also a slaveholder) and concealed there until the fear of discovery became too great.

While Jacobs waited in the snake-infested swamplands nearby, her uncle constructed a tiny garret room (what Jacobs, referencing William Cowper's "The Task" (1785), called in her narrative "The Loophole of Retreat") above the storage shed at her grandmother's house where she spent the next six years and eleven months in near-constant confinement. Unable to stand up or move about freely in the space, Jacobs's only consolation was that her children were never far away, and she could occasionally catch a glimpse of them from a peephole she had fashioned in the wall. The little "room" to which she had retreated may have saved her life, but she suffered the physical effects of this dramatic confinement for years afterward, at times being unable to climb stairs or walk without pain.

In the meantime, Dr. Norcom, enraged at Jacobs's flight, jailed all of her relatives under his authority—both of her children, her brother, and her aunt Betty. Using a slave trader as an intermediary to mask his own involvement,

Sawyer stepped up his negotiations to buy the children, and Norcom eventually relented. The children became the property of their father (as did Jacobs's brother, John) but were still not emancipated, as Jacobs had years before hoped. Several years later, Sawyer took John north with him, where John proceeded to run away. Two years after that, when Sawyer moved north with his new wife and baby, he brought Louisa along, leaving her in New York with his cousins. Following their lead, two years after her daughter's departure, Jacobs finally fled to the North aboard a ship accompanied by another slave woman. Terrified and exhausted by the experience, Jacobs made friends among the abolitionists in Philadelphia, who offered her financial assistance for her train fare to New York (which she did not need, thanks to her grandmother's support) and, perhaps even more important to the young woman who had never been out of Edenton and its environs, a kind welcome in a strange new world.

Making her way to New York, Jacobs was reunited with her beloved daughter but was distressed to learn that the child's father had "given" her to his cousin as a maid and she had been ill-treated and neglected by her new "mistress." Jacobs found employment in the home of writer Nathaniel Parker Willis and his first wife, Mary Stace Willis, tending to their baby daughter, Imogen. Upon learning that her whereabouts had been betrayed to Dr. Norcom by one of Samuel Tredwell's relatives, Jacobs confessed her story to Mary Willis, who helped Jacobs and her daughter flee to Boston. She had previously fled to Boston on another occasion and had at that time called for Joseph to be sent to her. That time she had returned to the Willis employ in New York; this time she did not—at least not immediately.

The Jacobs family spent several years together in Boston, but upon the death of Mary Willis, Jacobs was once again called upon to help tend Imogen. Jacobs's sympathy for the motherless child, as well as the extra earnings she would make as her caregiver, prompted Jacobs to accompany Willis and his daughter to England in 1845 on a visit to Mrs. Willis's relatives. Jacobs found her travels in England to be a liberating experience, not only because according to British law she was not chattel but, even more significantly, the British people never treated her as such. In her experience abroad with the Willis family, she found the British to be curiously egalitarian. She was even allowed to ride in the same railway car as her white employer. Jacobs and the Willises returned to the United States after a ten-month absence.

Jacobs returned to Boston to find that Norcom, still in hot pursuit, had given the New York police a detailed description of her appearance and offered a $100 reward for her capture. She also received letters from Norcom's son John, from his son-in-law Daniel Messmore, and from Mary Matilda Norcom Messmore, Jacobs's "mistress," all entreating Jacobs to return to them. Several years later in 1852, after having been cut out of her father's will, Mary Matilda and her husband arrived in New York in pursuit of Jacobs. In a panic, Jacobs went into hiding, and her friend Cornelia Grinnell Willis, Willis's second wife for whom she had been employed, purchased her freedom from the Messmores for $300. Although Jacobs was relieved to be finally rid of the yoke of slavery, she was disturbed that she could be bought and sold like so much property in the free state of New York.

Once this period of her life ended, Jacobs was better able to put her experiences as a slave into perspective. Prompted by her friend abolitionist and reformer Amy Post, Jacobs wrote the story of her years of enslavement and her road to freedom. Jacobs's first thought was to give her story to someone else to write; however, she was rebuffed in her efforts by Harriet Beecher Stowe, who suggested incorporating Jacobs's story as an example in her *Key to Uncle Tom's Cabin* rather than publishing it on its own. Jacobs secured the support of Lydia Maria Child, who also edited her text and wrote an introduction to it; however, in the economically volatile publishing world of the mid to late nineteenth century, Jacobs was initially unable to find a publisher who did not go bankrupt before the book's publication. Eventually, Jacobs bought the plates to her book and had it published herself. Her story was well received, and it, along with her brother's activism, put her into contact with a number of leading abolitionists, among whom she became something of a celebrity.

In the years that followed, Jacobs devoted herself to the plight of her fellow African Americans—the enslaved, the fugitives, and during the Civil War, the refugees. She volunteered at a refugee camp in Alexandria, Virginia, and was shocked and overwhelmed by poor treatment of the refugees streaming in from the **South**. In 1864, she and Louisa opened a school in the refugee settlement in Alexandria to teach the formerly enslaved children. In 1865 they also established a school in Savannah, Georgia.

In 1867, Jacobs returned to Edenton, North Carolina, for the first time since she had fled so many years before. She hoped her visit would ascertain whether or not she could feasibly make Edenton her **home** once more. Over the course of her visit, she found that although the former slaves were free, they were still subject to some of the same brutal and unjust laws and attitudes that had been the foundation of their enslavement. The visit clearly illustrated for Jacobs that Edenton could never truly be home to her.

In 1878, Jacobs and Louisa moved to Washington, D.C., where Jacobs spent the remaining years of her life. As Jacobs aged and suffered from illness and poverty, her old friend Cornelia Grinnell Willis came to her aid, helping her settle into a small house. Forced to nurse her mother, Louisa was unable to earn money to support them. Friends and activists took up a small collection to help her out; however, following a fall from a wheelchair that injured her hip, Jacobs died on March 7, 1897. She was buried in Mount Auburn Cemetery in Cambridge. By the time of her death, she and her narrative had already faded into obscurity and would remain so until the republication of *Incidents* in 1987.

See also Slave Narrative

Work By

Incidents in the Life of a Slave Girl: Written by Herself. Boston: For the Author, 1861. Cambridge: Harvard University Press, 1987.

Works About

Garfield, Deborah M., and Rafia Zafar, eds. *Harriet Jacobs and Incidents in the Life of a Slave Girl: New Critical Essays.* Cambridge: Cambridge University Press, 1996.

Yellin, Jean Fagan. *Harriet Jacobs: A Life.* New York: Basic Civitas Books, 2004.

Jennifer Dawes Adkison

JAZZ

The roots of this rapidly evolving music can be traced back to the methods of communication used by slaves working on plantations and in private homes. Both field hollers and the nineteenth-century "ring shouts" performed in New Orleans's Congo Square were interpreted by white observers as mere entertainment, but for the participants themselves, they helped to preserve African heritage, convey plans for escape, and defy the oppressive social customs of America. A similarly complex agenda defined the work of the early-twentieth-century "classic **blues**" singers. Blues music evolved from the call-and-response strategies of early African American gospel music and the themes of loss and hope that characterize **slavery** songs. It is the central musical precursor to modern jazz. Classic blues vocalists such as Gertrude "Ma" Rainey, Bessic Smith, Clara Smith, and Ethel Waters enjoyed an economic **freedom**, social mobility, and expressive potential rare for black women of the time. Their lyrics' exploration of social inequality, **domestic** abuse, sexual autonomy, and other controversial topics has been cited by cultural critics like Hazel Carby and **Angela Davis** as important evidence of **black feminist** sensibilities.

Jazz styles, such as the ragtime piano of Jellyroll Morton and the Dixieland bands that featured soloists like trumpeter Louis Armstrong, emerged as a tradition independent of blues in the 1910s and 1920s. These evolutions, while affording new opportunities for black male musicians to profit by their art, offered little compensation for women musicians. Classic blues' popularity declined in the late 1930s as the Great Depression limited African American consumers' ability to purchase "**race** records" and a new crop of male "urban blues" singers usurped performance spaces. The development of a highly commercialized style, swing, also redefined jazz in the 1930s as a dance music. Swing music usually featured a big band with stringed, brass, and wind instruments playing rapid, upbeat tunes and a vocalist who served as both soloist and the visually attractive symbol of the band. This style encouraged women in jazz to pursue careers as singers. Such a venture was considered more ladylike than instrumental performance, and women singers often found that their medium was more acceptable to their male colleagues. Ella Fitzgerald, one of jazz's most celebrated singers, began performing at New York's Savoy Ballroom in 1935, at the age of seventeen. Just four years later, after making recordings of hits like "A-Tisket, a-Tasket" and "My Last Affair," she became the leader of Chick Webb's band, a position she held for two years. Singer **Billie Holiday**, later nicknamed "Lady Day," joined the Count Basie band in 1937, leaving after a year to join Artie Shaw's band. Her voice's gritty quality, her talent in improvisation, and her **beauty** helped to secure her a successful solo career and many recordings, including her signature denunciation of lynching, "Strange Fruit."

Bebop developed in the early 1940s as a reaction against swing's commercialism and uniformity of style. Its practitioners were interested in monophonic tunes, chromatically inflected improvisation, complex solo riffs, and the equal participation of all ensemble members. Many African American women jazz singers who began their careers with swing bands gained acclaim in later years for their scat singing and solo improvisations. Ella Fitzgerald scatted with ease and brilliance; her recordings from the period include "Lady Be Good," "How High the Moon," and several Tin Pan Alley show tunes. Billie Holiday was a featured soloist at clubs around the country, often earning more than $1,000 per week. Sarah Vaughn, who claimed saxophonist Charlie Parker and trumpeter Dizzy Gillespie as her major influences, made many recordings of jazz standards, pop tunes, and religious ballads. She is admired for her skill in scat improvisation and her strong, full voice. Betty Carter, nicknamed "Betty Bebop," is known for the speed of her improvisations and the richness of her voice's lower register. She toured with several blues and jazz artists, including Muddy Waters and Sonny Rollins, and eventually formed her own record company.

Black women instrumentalists also contributed to the technically difficult, improvisatory creations of bebop. Some of these players were associated with bandleaders or their already famous spouses at the beginnings of their careers. Many were pianists for reasons similar to those of the women vocalists. Lil Hardin Armstrong, who was married to Louis Armstrong from 1924 until 1932, began her career playing with bands like King Oliver's. She also led several of her own groups and composed tunes such as "My Heart" and "Lonesome Blues." Mary Lou Williams, one of jazz's most gifted pianists and wife to baritone saxophonist John Williams, started her career in Kansas City, where she performed with such jazz greats as Art Tatum. She became a sought-after arranger and composer, producing experimental pieces like *Zodiac Suite*. Alice McLeod Coltrane, a pianist who married saxophonist John Coltrane in 1965, collaborated with her husband on modal compositions. The International Sweethearts of Rhythm, a group formed at a high school in Piney Woods, Mississippi, in 1938, was the country's first integrated all-women jazz group. They performed extensively in the United States, toured Europe, and were featured in some short **films**.

Other black women instrumentalists have helped to define the unique position that women hold in jazz. Their involvement in many facets of the music reflects the proliferation of styles—cool, free, modal, fusion, neoclassical, and so on—that occurred post-bebop. Trumpeter Clora Bryant became famous during the 1960s for her skills in improvisation but has pursued composition, singing, and bandleading into the twenty-first century. Trombone player Melba Liston worked as a performer and arranger with Dizzy Gillespie for several years, led the jazz division of the Jamaica School of Music in the 1970s, and returned to bandleading in the 1980s. Most black women in jazz play in ensembles, make recordings, and teach music; many also play blues, rock, and classical music to support their main interest. Today the work of these and other African American women jazz musicians, including vocalists like Cassandra Wilson, belies traditional conceptions of women as participants on the sidelines of jazz.

Works About

Dahl, Linda. *Stormy Weather: The Music and Lives of a Century of Jazzwomen.* New York: Limelight Editions, 1984.

Gourse, Leslie. *Madame Jazz: Contemporary Women Instrumentalists.* New York: Oxford University Press, 1995.

Handy, Antoinette. *Black Women in American Bands and Orchestras.* Metuchen, NJ: Scarecrow Press, 1981.

Placksin, Sally. *American Women in Jazz, 1900 to the Present: Their Words, Lives, and Music.* New York: Wideview Books, 1982.

Jennifer Denise Ryan

JAZZ

Jazz (1992), **Toni Morrison**'s sixth novel, is set primarily in "the City" in the 1920s, the decade that witnessed the peak of the Jazz Age, the height of the **Harlem Renaissance**, and the effects of the Great Migration of rural African Americans to northern urban centers. Reflecting the cacophony of the city itself, the novel is composed of various narrative voices, including those of the primary characters and an unreliable, semiomniscient narrator that at times seems to be a person, the city, or the book itself and that initiates readers into the private, female discourse of **community**. The voices combine to tell the story of Joe and Violet Trace, a Virginia couple who danced into the city on a train in 1906 and end up knowing each other only after Joe shoots and kills his young lover Dorcas and Violet is thrown out of the church for trying to stab the dead girl at the funeral.

On a larger level, the novel centers on **motherhood** and tells the tale of broken families and broken people putting themselves back together. Dorcas's parents were killed in the 1917 East St. Louis riot. Her best friend Felice saw her parents only 600 days out of seventeen years because they worked for whites in another town. Violet's mother, Rose Dear, jumped into a well two weeks before her long-gone husband returned bearing gifts and laughter, too late to save his wife. By then True Belle, Violet's grandmother, had already come and put the world right-side up, but (as a slave) True Belle herself had years before left her two daughters to go to Baltimore with her white, unmarried mistress who was pregnant with a black man's child.

When True Belle returned to Virginia to help Rose Dear raise her five children, she told Violet stories of the golden-haired Golden Gray, the son of Vera Louise, who grew up thinking he was white and went to the **South** to find his father when he found out he was not. On his trip to the South, the narrator muses, Golden Gray first scares, then saves, a naked, pregnant black woman who embodies the untamed, unfettered, female independence that lurks within all the text's women. When Henry Lestory returns from a hunting trip, he finds a woman in labor and a white-skinned son that he never knew was in the world. Lestory names the woman Wild after she bites him in the cheek. Refusing to talk or to nurse her baby boy, she rejects her role as mother and returns to the woods and the redwings that always mark her presence.

Her baby, Joe, names himself Trace, because that is what his parents disappeared without. Joe tries to find Wild three times, only wanting to know if, as Lestory had hinted, she was indeed his mother. On the third trip he finds the cave she lives in, but she refuses to show herself or speak. Her silence drives him away from the country and himself and sends him dancing with Violet into the pulse of the City and the illusion that you can lose yourself without losing. When Joe hunts through the streets looking for Dorcas, not intending to use his gun, he is as much hunting for his mother Wild as he is for the girl who exchanged stories with him beneath the sheets and who filled the silence his wife surrounded herself in.

Violet Trace does hair, but not in the legally licensed parlor, and drinks milkshakes to try to fill in the behind she swears she once had or, at least, the Violet who lived in Virginia once had. Her husband's infidelity forces her to confront and reconcile the fragments of her self, to mend the cracks in the world that made her sit down in the street one day instead of taking the next step forward, the cracks that made her steal a baby and laugh out loud, the cracks that let *that* Violet through to find a missing knife and disrupt a funeral. When she realized she could not count on the words that came out of her mouth, she stopped talking rather than sound crazy and lose Joe. Her silence, however, does more than protect her. It conceals the rage, hunger, fear, and weariness that pulses within the text's women, each of whom find their own ways to conceal it, to resist, to sew the next stitch or take the next step. But when the silence no longer holds the pieces of her self together, when rage slips through a crack and drives a knife toward a dead girl's face, Violet must face the losses in her life: her mother's suicide, her father's absence, the specter of a golden boy, her three miscarried or aborted children, the parrot that she turned out in freezing weather because she could not hear him say "**Love** you" anymore. She develops a friendship with Alice Manfred, Dorcas's aunt, and with Alice can admit that another time she might have loved the girl young-enough-to-be-her-daughter. After nights staring at Dorcas's picture, days full of Joe's tears, and visits from a girl with gone-too-much parents, Violet finally finds the "me" that she had lost.

The novel closes with stories rather than silence. Felice visits the Traces, purportedly looking for a ring she had let Dorcas borrow but even more to tell Joe that he should stop crying. Dorcas, the girl who swallowed fire watching her house and her mother inside burn and whose voice owns less than five pages of the text, fed off danger, secrets, and the power of pushing people. Felice also confesses that Dorcas let herself die by insisting that no one call the police or an ambulance (which did not come even after Felice did call) and tells Joe privately that Dorcas's last words were of him. Her message: that there is only one apple in the garden. Joe tells Felice that he shot Dorcas because he did not know how to love. The three dance out of the novel a reconstructed **family**: Felice becomes a surrogate daughter for Joe and Violet; Joe stops crying and gets a job; Violet gives up the doll baby she had slept with since mother love had hit her hard. Finally, Joe and Violet begin to tell each other their stories. The fissures of dislocation, abandonment, and isolation begin to heal, as they become the necessary things for their nights.

See also Beauty; Identity; Jazz

Works About

Albrecht-Crane, Christa. "Becoming Minoritarian: Post-Identity in Toni Morrison's *Jazz*." *Journal of the Midwest Modern Language Association* 36.1 (2003): 56–73.

Brown, Caroline. "Golden Gray and the Talking Book: Identity as a Site of Artful Construction in Toni Morrison's *Jazz*." *African American Review* 36.4 (2002): 629–642.

Cannon, Elizabeth M. "Following the Traces of Female Desire in Toni Morrison's *Jazz*." *African American Review* 31.2 (Summer 1997): 235–247.

Cornell, Drucilla. "The Wild Woman and All That Jazz." *Feminism beside Itself.* Ed. Diane Elam and Robyn Wiegman. New York: Routledge, 1995. 313–321.

Jones, Carolyn M. "Traces and Cracks: Identity and Narrative in Toni Morrison's *Jazz*." *African American Review* 31.3 (Fall 1997): 481–495.

Knadler, Stephen. "Domestic Violence in the Harlem Renaissance: Remarking the Record from Nella Larsen's *Passing* to Toni Morrison's *Jazz*." *African American Review* 38.1 (2004): 99–118.

Mbalia, Dorothea Drummond. "Women Who Run with Wild: The Need for Sisterhoods in *Jazz*." *Modern Fiction Studies* 39.3–4 (Fall–Winter 1993): 623–646.

Mori, Aoi. "Embracing Jazz: Healing of Armed Women and Motherless Children in Toni Morrison's *Jazz*." *CLA Journal* 42.3 (March 1999): 320–330.

O'Reilly, Andrea. "In Search of My Mother's Garden, I Found My Own: Mother-Love, Healing, and Identity in Toni Morrison's *Jazz*." *African American Review* 30.3 (Fall 1996): 367–379.

Pearce, Richard. "Toni Morrison's *Jazz*: Negotiations of the African American Beauty Culture." *Narrative* 6.3 (October 1998): 307–324.

Treherne, Matthew. "Figuring In, Figuring Out: Narration and Negotiation in Toni Morrison's *Jazz*." *Narrative* 11.2 (2003): 199–212.

Julie Cary Nerad

JEZEBEL

Along with **Mammy** and **Sapphire**, Jezebel is one of the three most widely recognized **stereotypes** applied to African American women. The Jezebel stereotype takes its name from the biblical Queen Jezebel, wife of King Ahab. Jezebel's foreignness (as the Phoenician wife of the king of the Israelites), her active support for the worship of pagan deities, and her influence over her husband have earned this figure, one of the Bible's more notable women characters, a lasting reputation as the incarnation of female evil, gender transgression, idolatry, and sexual indiscretion. Applied to African American women, the Jezebel stereotype draws most heavily on the biblical queen's strong association with sexual indiscretion and what has been perceived as her undue influence over her male partner. When used as a negative stereotype, the term *Jezebel* refers to the black woman-as-seductress, the sexually indiscriminate African American female who uses her erotic appeal to attract and manipulate men.

The Jezebel stereotype perpetuates the damaging but widespread perception that African American women are always already aroused, available for, and open to sexual activity. As such, this stereotype has played an instrumental role not only in justifying but in sanctioning and normalizing the sexual exploitation of black women. During the antebellum period, the **myth** of the black Jezebel's insatiable sexual appetite was invoked to excuse white owners' abuse of their female slaves. During the century that followed, the Jezebel myth formed the underpinnings of a social hierarchy that tolerated and even encouraged the white, male sexual exploitation of black women servants (housekeepers and child-care workers). This exploitation was compounded by the inability of black women so victimized to seek legal recourse against their attacks. Viewed by the white-dominated legal establishment through the lens of the Jezebel stereotype, African American women's accusations of **rape** and molestation were viewed as categorically unfounded.

The Jezebel stereotype differs from the Mammy stereotype in that it seeks to underscore rather than repress or deny the **sexuality** of African American women. The Jezebel stereotype is similar to the Sapphire stereotype in its emphasis on black women's interactions with men. In addition, like Sapphire, the Jezebel stereotype is predicated on the myth of black women's capacity to exercise power and control over males. Whereas the Sapphire figure controls men through her emasculating insults and jibes, the seductress Jezebel undermines men's control (especially white men's control) over their own sense of sexual propriety through her primal and irrepressible erotic advances.

The influence of the Jezebel stereotype on African American **literature** is most evident in black women's writing of the antebellum period. **Harriet Jacobs**'s *Incidents in the Life of a Slave Girl* (1861), **Harriet E. Wilson**'s *Our Nig* (1859), and the antebellum **poetry** of **Ann Plato** and **Frances E. W. Harper** each are meticulous in their representation of African American women whose sexual propriety is unimpeachable. Similarly, black male writers of the period take special pains to underscore the plight of their African American women characters as innocent victims of a **race**-based economic system that facilitates their sexual exploitation. Most notable among this second group of texts is the autobiographical *Narrative of the Life of Frederick Douglass* (1845) and **William Wells Brown**'s pioneering novel *Clotel, or the President's Daughter* (1853).

The influence of the Jezebel figure on African American literature of the antebellum period, and in subsequent decades as well, highlights the function of this and other stereotypes as controlling images. The popular understanding of African American womanhood as an **identity** category defined by a narrow range of negative typologies that justifies the limitation of black women to certain occupations, social strata, and economic classes creates for African American women writers a circumstance in which black women's occupation of roles and settings that fall outside of those defined by the established stereotypes as the rightful place for African American womanhood is perceived as an aberration. As such, the representation of, for example, a sexually modest African American woman, as in Jacobs's *Incidents in the Life of a Slave Girl*, is received by the broader reading public as counterhegemonic (as in counter to the popular understanding of black women's sexual status), and thus the author, in order to tell the story of her young protagonist, must first explain away the perceived aberration of her sexual propriety.

As well-established paradigms against which African American women writers must first position themselves or their characters in order to depict ways of being black women that run counter to the visions that they offer up, Jezebel, Mammy, Sapphire, and other stereotypes have effectively controlled the terms on which African American women writers have been able to depict their black female subjects. As such, the stereotypes, constructed as tools to facilitate the continued subjugation of black people, have also come to shape the way that blackness becomes visible and thus the means by which African American writers can.

See also Aunt Jemima

Works About

Bennett, Crystal, and Marilyn Yarbrough. "Cassandra and the 'Sistahs': The Peculiar Treatment of African American Women in the Myth of Women as Liars." *Journal of Gender, Race and Justice* 4 (Spring 2000): 626–657.

Gilman, Sander. "Black Bodies, White Bodies: Toward an Iconography of Female Sexuality in Late Nineteenth Century Art, Medicine, and Literature." *Race, Writing, and Difference.* Ed. Henry Louis Gates, Jr. Chicago: University of Chicago Press, 1986. 223–261.

Ajuan Maria Mance

JOHNSON, AMELIA E. (1858–1922)

Amelia Etta Hall Johnson's early life is found mainly in government records. Yet what they tell us is revealing. According to her **death** certificate, Johnson was born in Toronto in 1858, a time when Ontario's black population had swelled due to the Fugitive Slave Law. The 1880 Baltimore census tells us that her mother Eleanora was from Maryland; her father Canadian. From Toronto, the **family** relocated to Montreal, a multilingual society that, to Amelia's benefit, did not enforce segregation in education. It is likely that she encountered less racism in Montreal than she would have in Maryland, especially given her fair skin. Nevertheless, following the pattern of many blacks who returned from Canada following the Civil War, in 1874 the family relocated to Maryland. There Amelia met, and in 1877 married, Rev. Harvey Johnson, pastor of Baltimore's Union Baptist Church.

The wife of a minister was expected to assume substantial responsibilities, and Johnson was no exception. Certainly her literary productions—Christian and educational—would have assisted in establishing the reputation of her husband's congregation. After the birth of her children, Harvey, Jr. (n.d.), Jessie Eleanor (1878), and Prentiss (1883), Johnson began publishing for youth. In 1887 she established the *Joy*, a literary periodical for youth, where she also hoped African American women might publish. A year later the *Ivy* appeared, directed at the same audience but with **history** as its subject. Johnson's writing was also included in *National Baptist*, *American Baptist*, and *Sower and Reaper*.

In 1890 the first of Johnson's religious novels, *Clarence and Corinne; or, God's Way*, appeared, followed by *The Hazeley Family* (1894) and *Martina Meriden; or What Is My Motive?* (1901). All were imprints of the American Baptist Society, one of the era's largest publishers, and marketed across **race**. While Johnson has been criticized for creating characters who are not identifiably black, in featuring characters without racial markers Johnson's characters were not so much "white" as they were ambiguous. Yet race is inevitable in the reception of her novels, as readers were aware of hers. Her texts' assertion of Christian morality, then, resonates within a history of linking it with racial justice.

For Johnson this yoking of **Christianity** and racial advancement would have been unremarkable. Notably, her husband's church was socially and politically active, and he was instrumental in bringing **Frederick Douglass** to Baltimore in 1898–making their meeting likely. Reverend Johnson was also active in agitating against laws that penalized unwed black mothers and in integrating Maryland's legal and teaching professions.

Johnson's involvement in the activities of her husband merits consideration. Reports state she "read, typed and edited the numerous articles written and published by her husband," and in 1903, when her husband published his only book, Johnson wrote the introduction–in addition to any other input. After her death her son recalled, "We always kept our mother busy in telling us stories, fairytales, etc. She was so interesting to us, for she was a writer, you know. . . . My mother was my father's best friend, and his chief comfort, his guide in all his business matters. Looking back over fifty years, I still consider this union a perfect one" (Kroger 22). In this light, it is worth reconsidering Johnson's designation as a potentially apolitical author, instead recognizing her as integral in the social activism of turn-of-the-century black Baltimore.

Works By

Clarence and Corinne; or, God's Way. Philadelphia: American Baptist Publication Society, 1890.
The Hazeley Family. Philadelphia: American Baptist Publication Society, 1894.
Martina Meriden; or What Is My Motive? Philadelphia: American Baptist Publication Society, 1901.

Works About

Christian, Barbara. Introduction to *The Hazeley Family*. New York: Oxford University Press, 1988. xxvii–xxxvii.
Koger, A. Briscoe Koger. *Dr. Harvey Johnson*. Baltimore, MD: N.p., 1957.
Majors, Monroe Alphus. *Noted Negro Women, Their Triumphs and Activities*. Chicago: Donahue and Henneberry, 1893.
Penn, I. Garland. *The Afro-American Press and Its Editors*. 1891. New York: Arno Press, 1969.
Shockley, Ann Allen. *Afro-American Women Writers, 1746–1933: An Anthology and Critical Guide*. Boston: G. K. Hall, 1988.
Spillers, Hortense J. Introduction to *Clarence and Corinne; or, God's Way*. New York: Oxford University Press, 1988. xxvii–xxxviii.
Tate, Claudia. *Domestic Allegories of Political Desire: The Black Heroine's Text at the Turn of the Century*. New York: Oxford University Press, 1992.

Jennifer Harris

JOHNSON, ANGELA (1961–)

Angela Johnson was born in Tuskegee, Alabama, and grew up in a small farm town in northeastern Ohio, where she was encouraged by her parents but reports she was a bitter teenager who wrote very dark **poetry** and read the Beat poets. She enrolled at Kent State University, thinking she wanted to be a social worker or teacher. Johnson did not write at all while in college but began again after she dropped out of school. Her first picture book, *Tell Me a Story, Mama* (1989), was well reviewed and won an Ezra Jack Keats New Writers Award. This story, and other picture books that followed, such as *Do Like Kyla* (1990), *When I Am Old with You* (1990), and *One of Three* (1991), emphasized warm, loving, African American intergenerational families who helped children facing typical developmental challenges and **family** situations. Even in her picture books, her writing tended to be spare and both realistic and poetic. *When I Am Old with You* won her the first Coretta Scott King Honor Award of her career.

Toning the Sweep (1993), a Coretta Scott King Award winner, was her first book for older readers. This touching story combines a present-day coming-of-age novel in which fourteen-year-old Emmie and her mother drive to the California desert to help Emmie's beloved, independent grandmother, Ola, settle her life as she is dying of cancer, with a back story about the brutal killing of Ola's husband by the Ku Klux Klan in 1964. Rich in symbolism, Ola's life is celebrated by her friends as she prepares to move back to the Midwest with her daughter. The story is told by all three generations, each a strong, resilient female. Other powerful novels followed including *Humming Whispers* (1995), in which a teenager fears she will develop schizophrenia at the same age as her older sister did. Two books of poetry from the viewpoint of adolescent girls, *The Other Side* (1998), about a teenager in a small Alabama town, and *Running Back to Ludie* (2001), in which a girl reunites briefly with her almost unremembered mother, explore the pains and triumphs of growing up female in particular times and places, again with universal resonance.

A giant step for Johnson was the novel *The First Part Last* (2003), her first novel with a male main character, a sixteen-year-old unwed father who is determined to raise his newborn daughter when the young mother tragically dies. His parents and friends are skeptical, but Bobby perseveres until he finds a solution. This book won the Michael Printz Award for young adult **literature** and another King Award. Johnson believes it is her most accessible novel. In 2003, Johnson, who lives in Kent, Ohio, was awarded a prestigious MacArthur Foundation fellowship, which she feels reflects the current respect given to young people's literature.

See also Children's and Young Adult Literature

Works By

Do Like Kyla. New York: Orchard Books, 1990.
The First Part Last. New York: Simon and Schuster, 2003.

Humming Whispers. New York: Orchard Books, 1995.
Running Back to Ludie. New York: Orchard Books, 2001.
Tell Me a Story, Mama. New York: Orchard Books, 1989.
Toning the Sweep: A Novel. New York: Orchard Books, 1993.
When I Am Old with You. New York: Orchard Books, 1990.

Works About

Engberg, Gillian. "The Booklist Interview: Angela Johnson." *Booklist* 100.12 (2004): 1074.
Holtze, Sally Holmes, ed. *Seventh Book of Junior Authors and Illustrators.* New York: H. W. Wilson, 1996.
Pendergast, Sara, and Tom Pendergast, eds. *St. James Guide to Children's Writers.* 5th ed. Detroit: St. James Press, 1999. 156–157.
Something about the Author. Vol. 102. Detroit: Gale Research, 1999. 125–128.

Susan L. Golden

JOHNSON, CHARLES (1948–   )

One of the most interesting and unusual contemporary African American novelists, Charles Johnson draws on an eclectic background in writing his **fiction**, including journalism, cartooning, advanced study in philosophy, and a long-standing interest in Eastern religions and martial arts. His novels are both densely intellectual and extremely comic, with highly visual imagery and sharp dialogue. He credits the influence of John Gardner, with whom he studied creative writing in college, for helping him to develop an original voice and to break free from what he found to be the restrictive conventions of naturalism. In Johnson's view, African American writers have only begun to plumb the complex depths of African American experience and have too often narrowly depicted the limited views of sociologists, resulting in stereotypical portrayals.

Born in Evanston, Illinois, in 1948, Johnson came of age during the 1960s and was politically active through his writing from the beginning of his college career at Southern Illinois University, where he wrote for the campus newspaper and published cartoons in a number of publications. As an undergraduate, he majored in journalism but switched to philosophy when he entered graduate school, first receiving a master's degree from Southern Illinois and then pursuing his doctorate at the State University of New York at Stony Brook. He published his first collection of cartoons, *Black Humor* (1970), while still an undergraduate, and his second, *Half-Past Nation Time* (1972), followed shortly thereafter. His first novel, *Faith and the Good Thing,* written after six unsuccessful novels were discarded, was published in 1974. Johnson's next two novels, *Oxherding Tale* (1982) and *Middle Passage*

(1990), which won the National Book Award, are both historical novels of **slavery** written in the first person, or **neo-slave narratives**, and both play philosophically with the **slave narrative** form. His collections of short stories, *The Sorcerer's Apprentice* (1986), and *Soulcatcher and Other Stories* (2001), like these two novels, deal largely with slavery, both historical and philosophical. Johnson's most recent novel, *Dreamer* (1998), also deals with **history**, this time with the 1960s and the assassination of Dr. Martin Luther King, Jr. Johnson currently holds the Pollock Professorship for Excellence in English at the University of Washington, where he teaches creative writing.

Another substantial area of production for Johnson has been screenwriting. With over twenty screenplays to his credit, Johnson has been active in shaping the presentation of African American history through **work** on such projects as "Booker" (1985), a children's television **drama** about the life of Booker T. Washington, which received the international Prix Jeunesse Award and a Writer's Guild Award, and the PBS series *Africans in America.*

While critics were initially slow to deal with Johnson's work, Johnson has been repeatedly honored for his contributions to **literature**. His short stories in particular have been well received, included in the collections *Best American Short Stories of the Eighties, Best American Short Stories* (1992), and the *O. Henry Prize Stories* (1993), as well as in many anthologies. *Oxherding Tale* was awarded the 1983 Washington State Governor's Award for Literature, and when *Faith and the Good Thing* was produced, in 1995, as a stage play by City Lit Theatre and the Chicago Theatre Company, it was awarded two Black Theatre Alliance awards. In addition, Johnson has won a National Endowment for the Arts fellowship, in 1979; a Guggenheim Fellowship in 1986; a MacArthur Foundation grant in 1998; and an Academy Award in Literature from the American Academy of Arts and Letters in 2002.

In addition to writing novels, Johnson has also published a book of criticism, *Being and Race: Black Writing since 1970* (1988), which analyzes African American fiction in philosophical terms, particularly in light of phenomenology. As the title suggests, Johnson first confronts the ontological problem of "being" as it is played out in racial terms, then considers how recent writers have confronted this issue in their writing. Historically, Johnson argues, African Americans have produced a tradition of tragedies in which African American characters primarily react to white oppression and live as socially alienated persons who seek but never find real homes. He praises writers such as **Ishmael Reed** and **Clarence Major**, whom he considers to have broken out of this tradition of tragedy and whose play with form and narrative allows them to write novels that reimagine and transform conceptions of **race** and **identity**. He considers male and female writers separately and, by and large, is more critical of the women. While he recognizes that the intersections of **race** and gender oppression have presented unique issues for African American women writers, and praises individual writers such as **Toni Morrison**, for creating Sula, a character he believes transcends race, he generally concludes that, as a whole, the women he discusses have not been as innovative formally or philosophically as the men.

Critics of Johnson's own fiction have often praised him for just this type of formal innovation. His two neo-slave narratives turn the tables on expected conventions, inviting readers to "decalcify" their perceptions of race and of history in the process. In fact, much of the humor in Johnson's fiction as a whole stems from these inversions of reader expectations and parodies of genre conventions. In *Oxherding Tale*, for instance, the main character, Andrew Hawkins, is mixed race, but rather than being the son of the white slave-master and a female slave, Andrew is conceived when the master decides to trade places for the night with his slave, George, and sends George to the white mistress's bed. Sexual **stereotypes** are again inverted when Andrew, emerging into adulthood and intent on earning his way out of slavery, becomes the sexual companion to Flo Hatfield, the owner of a neighboring plantation. *Middle Passage* begins with a freed slave who stows away on board an illegal slave trader in the 1830s and travels back to Africa, thus reversing as well as reimagining the seminal event in African American history. Both Rutherford Calhoun, *Middle Passage*'s trickster protagonist, and Andrew Hawkins are highly educated and shift easily between philosophical observations, street savvy, and jokes. Other characters, too, shift quickly and easily between discussions of slavery and anachronistic commentary on affirmative action, for example, and this pastiche of discourses offers new and often comically liberating perspectives on the way race has historically functioned.

Other critics, however, particularly early critics of *Oxherding Tale*, have considered Johnson's philosophical play with the concept of race to be ultimately troubling. The plot of *Oxherding Tale* might seem to invite this critique, as Andrew Hawkins, after his sexual enslavement to Flo Hatfield, ultimately escapes slavery by **passing** for white, marries a white woman, and becomes a schoolteacher. When, after his marriage, his former slave lover, Minty, whom he had intended to buy and then seemingly forgot, is sold at auction in the town in which Andrew has settled, Andrew feels guilt but is quickly relieved of this burden of the past when Minty, horribly ill with pellagra, forgives him, approves of his wife, and then conveniently dies. One possible reading of this turn of events is that the black female **body** remains the site of racial inscription and is defiled by it, while the male, apparently unencumbered by racialized embodiment, can simply choose to free himself from the past through an act of philosophical imagination. In other words, in the view of some critics, Johnson's depictions of race and identity as performative liberate only some characters and not others, and access to this liberation is marked by gender.

But nothing is that simple in Johnson's fiction, and other critics have focused on the ways in which female characters in these novels, like many of his other characters, are drawn as composites of cultural stereotypes, whom the protagonists must learn to understand and see differently. Rutherford Calhoun initially sees Isadora Bailey, in *Middle Passage*, as a staid, conventional schoolmarm, intent on trapping him in a life of boring respectability and unimaginative social conventions. He is thus unprepared when she acts completely outside of these stereotypes even while partially fulfilling them, enlisting the aid of the gangster, Papa Zeringue, to blackmail Calhoun, agreeing to pay off his debts, and thus save him from prison, if he will marry her and reform his trickster ways in return. After Calhoun's months on the slave trader, where he is exposed to the enslaved Allmuseri's philosophy of the unity of being, he is transformed into someone who sees Isadora not only as a desirable woman but also as an independent actor, able to break free herself from the very conventions he had assumed dictated her life.

Johnson's first novel, *Faith and the Good Thing*, offers his only female protagonist, the symbolically named Faith, who, at the age of eighteen, sets out on a quest for the "good thing" after the **death** of her mother. This novel is part folktale and part philosophical inquiry into the place of faith in the modern world. Prompted by the mystical Swamp Woman, a woman who is both conjurer and trickster, Faith leaves her rural Georgia home and travels to Chicago, following the historical migration of African Americans in the twentieth century. In the city, Faith, a naive idealist not unlike the young protagonist of **Ralph Ellison**'s *Invisible Man* (1952), is raped, becomes a prostitute, then a housewife, and finally dies in a fire after experiencing a grim life. After her death, however, her soul returns to Georgia, where she becomes the Swamp Woman and completes her quest. The novel, while drawing heavily from the African American folk tradition, also blends this with Eastern philosophy, as well as references to Western philosophers from Plato to the present. It juxtaposes the Baptist tradition of Faith's past with Buddhism, and many of the male characters in this novel function as symbols of separate Ways, in the Buddhist tradition: Faith's high school lover, Alpha Omega Holmes, is dedicated to the "Way" of romantic art; her husband, Isaac Maxwell, is dedicated to money; and others to philosophy or traditional **religion**. None of these, though, offer Faith the "good thing" she pursues. This novel has not received as much critical attention as Johnson's later work, and reading his later work in light of this novel would offer new territory for considerations of gender in his work.

In *Dreamer*, Johnson takes a different approach to considering the nature of the self and its relation to history. This novel offers a philosophical examination of Dr. Martin Luther King, Jr.'s vision of integration, ironically by considering a kind of disintegration of King through providing him with a doppelganger, Chaym Smith. Rather than functioning as a fully human and rounded character here, King becomes simply the locus of an idealized vision, and Smith, who shares his birthday, physical appearance, and intellectual heritage, functions as the locus of the human and flawed, the center of self-consciousness and unfulfilled desire, who may or may not have a hand in assassinating King at the end of the novel. Two young acolytes, Matthew and Amy, work to protect and promote King's vision and are left, after his death, to sort out its legacy.

Recently Johnson's work has received greater critical attention, with a number of books devoted to his fiction, but much work remains. Johnson's complex portrayal of history, his deep philosophical interrogations of race and identity, and his narrative innovations and experimentalism are substantial contributions to the tradition of African American literature and will continue to provide a fruitful field for critical investigation.

Works By

Being and Race: Black Writing since 1970. Bloomington: Indiana University Press, 1988.
Black Humor. Chicago: Johnson Publishing, 1970.
Dreamer. New York: Scribner, 1998.
Faith and the Good Thing. New York: Viking, 1974.
Half-Past Nation Time. Westlake Village, CA: Aware Press, 1972.
Middle Passage. New York: Plume-Penguin, 1990.
Oxherding Tale. New York: Plume-Penguin, 1982.
The Sorcerer's Apprentice. New York: Atheneum, 1986.
Soulcatcher and Other Stories. New York: Harvest Books, 2001.
Turning the Wheel: Essays on Buddhism and Writing. New York: Scribner, 2003.

Works About

Byrd, Rudolph P., ed.. *I Call Myself an Artist: Writings by and about Charles Johnson.* Bloomington: Indiana University Press, 1999.
Hardack, Richard. "Black Skin, White Tissues: Local Color and Universal Solvents in the Novels of Charles Johnson." *Callaloo* 22 (1999): 1028–1053.
Hayward, Jennifer. "Something to Serve: Constructs of the Feminine in Charles Johnson's *Oxherding Tale.*" *Black American Literature Forum* 25 (1991): 689–703.
Little, Jonathan. *Charles Johnson's Spiritual Imagination.* Columbia: University of Missouri Press, 1997.
Muther, Elizabeth. "Isadora at Sea: Misogyny as Comic Capital in Charles Johnson's *Middle Passage.*" *African American Review* 30 (1996): 649–658.
Nash, William R. *Charles Johnson's Fiction.* Chicago: University of Illinois Press, 2002.
Robbins, Sarah. "Gendering the History of the Antislavery Narrative: Juxtaposing *Uncle Tom's Cabin* and *Benito Cereno, Beloved* and *Middle Passage.*" *American Quarterly* 49 (1997): 531–573.
Rushdy, Ashraf. *Neo-Slave Narratives: Studies in the Social Logic of a Literary Form.* New York: Oxford University Press, 1999.
Whalen-Bridge, John. "Waking Cain: The Poetics of Integration in Charles Johnson's *Dreamer.*" *Callaloo* 26 (2003): 504–521.

Suzanne Lane

JOHNSON, GEORGIA DOUGLAS (1877–1966)

Georgia Douglas Johnson was one of the first black female poets to gain distinction as a poet. Born in Atlanta, Georgia, to Laura (Jackson) and George Camp, she was educated in public schools and completed the "normal course" at Atlantic University before pursuing music studies at Oberlin Conservatory of Music and Cleveland College of Music in Ohio. Returning to Georgia, she taught school in Marietta and became an assistant principal in Atlanta. On September 28, 1903, she married Henry Lincoln (Link) Johnson, an attorney and active member of the Republican Party. She and Henry had two sons, Henry Lincoln Johnson, Jr. (b. 1906) and Peter Douglas Johnson (b. 1907). In 1910 the **family** moved to Washington, D.C., where, in 1912, President Howard Taft named Henry Johnson recorder of deeds, a post he held until 1916.

Despite the discouragement of a husband who felt that her duties lay with being wife, mother, and homemaker, Johnson continued with her music and began to write stories and poems, sending them to newspapers and small magazines. Johnson was introduced to poet William Stanley Braithwaite, who became her mentor, and by 1928 she had published three volumes of **poetry**, *The Heart of a Woman and Other Poems* (1918), *Bronze* (1922), and *An Autumn Love Cycle* (1928).

One of the more prolific black women writers of the **Harlem Renaissance**, Johnson wrote numerous dramatic works during the 1920s and 1930s, but only a few of her scripts have survived. In 1926, her play *Blue Blood* won honorable mention in *Opportunity*'s playwriting contest and was later produced by the Krigwa Players. *Blue Blood* touches on the subject of white men's sexual exploitation of black women and deftly leads to a disturbing revelation as two black mothers discover their children, who are engaged to be married, have the same white father. *Plumes*, which concerns the struggle of a poor rural southern black mother who must deal with poverty and her daughter's **death**, won *Opportunity*'s first prize in 1927 and was produced by the Harlem Experimental Theatre. Johnson, who became active in the antilynching movement of the 1920s, used theater to speak out against social injustices by writing plays with powerful antilynching themes: *Safe* (c. 1920), *Blue-Eyed Black Boy* (c. 1920), *A Sunday Morning in the South* (1925), *A Bill to Be Passed* (c. 1920), and *And Still They Paused* (1920s).

After the death of her husband in 1925, Johnson became conciliatory for the Labor Department for eight years, during which time she continued to feverishly produce literary work, maintaining a column for a number of weekly newspapers, editing books, and writing songs. Johnson hosted literary gatherings at her home on S Street in Washington, D.C., which became known as "Saturday Night Soirees" where leading political and literary figures, black and white, would gather, including **Langston Hughes**, **May Miller**, **Marita Bonner**, Mary Burrill, **Alice Moore Dunbar-Nelson**, and **Zora Neale Hurston**. While Johnson ultimately found more success as a poet than as a dramatist, perhaps her more lasting legacy was that of nurturing **community** among the promising black literary talent of her day.

Works By

An Autumn Love Cycle. New York: H. Vinal, 1928.

A Bill to Be Passed. Unpublished, c. 1920.

Blue Blood. C. 1926. *Black Female Playwrights: An Anthology of Plays before 1950.* Ed. Kathy A. Perkins. Bloomington: Indiana University Press, 1990. 38–46.

Blue-Eyed Black Boy. C. 1920. *Black Female Playwrights: An Anthology of Plays before 1950.* Ed. Kathy A. Perkins. Bloomington: Indiana University Press, 1990. 47–51.

Bronze: A Book of Verse. Boston: B. J. Brimmer, 1922.

Frederick Douglass. Unpublished, 1935.

The Heart of a Woman and Other Poems. Boston: Cornhill Company, 1918; reprinted North Stratford, NY: Ayer, 2000.

Plumes. New York: Samuel French, 1927. *Plays by American Women, 1900–1930.* Ed. Judith Barlow. New York: Applause Books, 1985. 162–170; *Black Female Playwrights: An Anthology of Plays before 1950.* Ed. Kathy A. Perkins. Bloomington: Indiana University Press, 1990. 24–30.

Safe. C. 1929. *Strange Fruit: Plays on Lynching by American Women.* Ed. Kathy A. Perkins and Judith L. Stephens. Bloomington: Indiana University Press, 1998. 110–115.

Share My World, a Book of Poems. Washington, DC: Halfway House, 1962.

And Still They Paused. Unpublished, 1920s.

A Sunday Morning in the South. 1925. *Black Female Playwrights: An Anthology of Plays before 1950.* Ed. Kathy A. Perkins. Bloomington: Indiana University Press, 1990. 31–37.

William and Ellen Craft. Unpublished, 1935.

Works About

Dover, Cedric. "The Importance of Georgia Douglas Johnson." *Crisis* 59 (December 1952): 633.

Fletcher, Winona. "Georgia Douglas Johnson." *Notable Women in the American Theatre.* Ed. Alice M. Robinson et al. Westport, CT: Greenwood Press, 1989. 473–477.

Honey, Maureen. *Shadowed Dreams: Women's Poetry of the Harlem Renaissance.* New Brunswick, NJ: Rutgers University Press, 1989.

Hull, Gloria T. *Color, Sex, and Poetry: Three Women Writers of the Harlem Renaissance.* Bloomington: Indiana University Press, 1987.

Sherry Engle

JOHNSON, HELENE (1906–1995)

Helene Johnson was the youngest and among the most talented of the **Harlem Renaissance** poets. Her circle of friends included most of the major writers—**Zora Neale Hurston**, **Langston Hughes**, **Countee Cullen**, **Claude McKay**, **Gwendolyn B. Bennett**, and Wallace Thurman, among others. They praised and encouraged her work and clearly expected her to find literary success. Hurston, for example, promoted Johnson's work on book tours throughout the **South**, and Thurman observed in 1928 that Johnson "alone of all the younger group seems to have the 'makings' of a poet" (210).

Helen Virginia Johnson was born in Boston on July 7, 1906, to Ella Benson Johnson of Camden, South Carolina, and George William Johnson of Nashville, Tennessee. Her parents migrated north around the turn of the century, married, and apparently separated shortly after their daughter's birth. An only child, Johnson was reared in a large, female-centered household, which included her maternal first cousin, the novelist and short-story writer **Dorothy West** (1907–1999), and several of her mother's sisters. The **family** pooled their resources and purchased a small cottage on Martha's Vineyard, where they summered, and leased a large four-storied brick house in Boston's Brookline neighborhood. It was there, at 478 Brookline Avenue (the property is now a playing field with a baseball diamond) that cousins West and Johnson came of age.

According to West, Johnson was shy, something of a jokester, and the family genius: "Helen was the kind of person who'd buy herself four doughnuts and go sit down at the Battery and stare at the water all day" (Guinier 211). While admitting that she was painfully shy and that she did well in her coursework, Johnson insists that she was not particularly bright. Her **poetry**, however, along with her studies at the prestigious Boston Girls' Latin School and at Columbia University, suggests otherwise. Before beginning elementary school, West and Johnson took dance and piano lessons and were tutored at **home** by their mothers' friend, Maude Trotter, sister of Monroe Trotter, founding editor of the influential Boston *Guardian*. A few of Johnson's early poems were first published in the *Guardian*. Asked in a 1987 interview when she initially started writing poetry, eighty-year-old Johnson replied, "Ever since I can remember" (Wall n.p.).

Johnson's earliest verse, such poems as "Metamorphism," "Trees at Night," and "Fulfillment," focus on nature and draw their inspiration from the hills, trees, and beaches of her beloved Massachusetts. Her verse became more experimental and more concerned with issues of **class**, **race**, and gender after she and Dorothy West moved to New York City in 1926 and began living on their own. For example, the July 1926 poem "Fiat Lux," Latin for "let there be light," dramatizes the flogging of an imprisoned black woman, while "A Southern Road," published four months later, protests the lynching of a black man.

More often, however, Johnson focuses on romantic **love**. "Cui Bono," Latin for "of what good," satirizes a young woman who sits all day, dreaming of love. When a potential beau approaches, she refuses his offer, reasoning that it was made too hastily. And so she continues sitting, dreaming of love, and growing quite anemic. Because Johnson was raised as a proper Bostonian, perhaps unduly concerned with decorum, it is tempting to read this poem as a gently mocking self-portrait. The long dramatic monologue "Widow with a Moral Obligation," also concerned with love and decorum, is clearly not autobiographical since Johnson, who wed William Warner Hubbell (1914–2002) in December 1932, was never a widow. The poem canvasses a widow's complex emotional, physical, and psychological torment as she begins to date. By poem's end, the widow realizes her obligation is not to her late husband but to herself and her new friend: Thus she determines to have a night of love (her gown undone) and **death** (burying her late husband's intruding **memory**) in one.

Whether exploring the hurly-burly of young love or the passion and sensuality of more mature lovers, Johnson's love poems repeatedly call for women to parry the wide array of social constraints used to limit them, especially as sexual beings. The young speaker in the arresting poem "Futility" is characteristic. Weary of restrictive, bourgeois rituals of courtship (much like the heroine of **Gwendolyn Brooks**'s "a song in the front yard"), Johnson's young woman determines to search for love out back, in the alley, consequently defying the teachings of family, class, and church. Other prominent themes in Johnson's oeuvre include the importance of the African past; the sensuousness of nature; joy gained from music, color, and dance; and black cultural pride. Stylistically, Johnson was one of only a handful of poets who was as comfortable and adept with the sonnet as with free verse.

Johnson's last published poem, "Let Me Sing My Song," appeared in 1935, three years after her marriage. She gave birth to a daughter, Abigail, in 1940 and then, apparently busy working inside the home and outside (as a correspondent for Consumers Union), she largely disappeared from public view. Although she continued to write, it is nonetheless unfortunate that such a remarkable poet faded from the literary scene.

Work By

This Waiting for Love: Helene Johnson, Poet of the Harlem Renaissance. Amherst: University of Massachusetts Press, 2000.

Works About

Bryan, T. J. "The Published Poems of Helene Johnson." *Langston Hughes Review* 6.2 (Fall 1987): 11–21.

Ferguson, SallyAnn H. "Dorothy West and Helene Johnson in *Infants of the Spring.*" *Langston Hughes Review* 12.2 (Fall 1993): 22–24.

Guinier, Genii. "Interview with Dorothy West, May 6, 1978." *The Black Women Oral History Project.* Ed. Ruth Edmonds Hill. Vol. 10. Westport, CT: Meckler, 1991. 143–223.

Honey, Maureen. *Shadowed Dreams: Women's Poetry of the Harlem Renaissance.* New Brunswick, NJ: Rutgers University Press, 1989.

McGrath, Abigail. "Afterword: A Daughter Reminisces" to *This Waiting for Love: Helene Johnson, Poet of the Harlem Renaissance.* Amherst: University of Massachusetts Press, 2000. 123–130.

Miller, Nina. *Making Love Modern: The Intimate Public Worlds of New York's Literary Women.* New York: Oxford University Press, 1998.

Mitchell, Verner D., and Cynthia Davis, eds. *Where the Wild Grape Grows: Selected Writings by Dorothy West, 1930–1950.* Amherst: University of Massachusetts Press, 2005.

Stetson, Erlene. *Black Sister: Poetry by Black American Women, 1746–1980.* Bloomington: Indiana University Press, 1985.

Thurman, Wallace. "Negro Poets and Their Poetry." *The Bookman* 67 (July 1928): 555–561. Rpt. in *The Collected Writings of Wallace Thurman: A Harlem Renaissance Reader.* Eds. Amritjit Singh and Daniel M. Scott III. New Brunswick, NJ: Rutgers University Press, 2003. 205–216.

Wall, Cheryl A. Unpublished mail interview with Helene Johnson. June 1987.

——. *Women of the Harlem Renaissance.* Bloomington: Indiana University Press, 1995.

Verner D. Mitchell

JOHNSON, JAMES WELDON (1871–1938)

James Weldon Johnson is well known for composing "Lift Every Voice and Sing," which he wrote along with his brother John Rosamond Johnson (1873–1954) in 1900 for a special celebration of Abraham Lincoln's birthday. Twenty years after composing the song, the National Association for the Advancement of Colored People (NAACP), for which Johnson served as field secretary in 1916 and later became its secretary, adopted the song as the Negro National Anthem. However, Johnson was also an author and a poet, producing an important body of work during the **Harlem Renaissance**. Concerned about the negative image black Americans suffered, Johnson combined his artistic endeavors with civic and political involvement to undermine racist attitudes in America. He used writing positively to present the complexity of black life in America. Although he has a substantial body of work to cull from, some of his most memorable are *God's Trombones* (1927), *Along This Way* (1933), and *The Autobiography of an Ex-Colored Man* (1912).

God's Trombones, a slim book of **poetry**, illustrates the importance of ministers to the black **community**, and it demonstrates the oratorical prowess of those ministers. The book consists of seven poems or sermons often delivered to black congregations and a preface that Johnson uses to explain how to read the sermons for maximum enjoyment and understanding. Like other artists during the Harlem Renaissance, Johnson writes the book of poetry for reasons other than art for art's sake. He argues that the poems can be used to garner respect for black ministers and, by extension, blacks in general. By demonstrating his artistic ability and providing positive representations of his subject, white America would be challenged to reassess its prejudiced and racist attitudes. Johnson's belief that art is beneficial in breaking **stereotypes** and undermining racism is illustrated in the preface to his book *The Book of American Negro Poetry* (1922), where he writes, "No people that has produced great literature and art has ever been looked upon by the world as distinctly inferior." Still promoting this vein of thought, Johnson posits in "Race Prejudice and the Negro Artist" that racism was being fought on religious, education, political, industrial, ethical, economic, and sociological fronts but that individual artists were playing a very important role in helping to combat racism. To that end, Johnson's poems/sermons in *God's Trombones* illustrate from a historical biblical perspective through the present the importance of the minister to contemporary American culture in general and black Americans in particular.

Johnson's choice of poems/sermons portrays his intimate knowledge of what most ministers deemed essential messages for their congregations to know and to internalize. These messages are timeless in that they are still delivered today. For example, the first poem is "The Creation." In "The Creation," the biblical account is given, but Johnson's depiction of God creating is at once playful and human. God is portrayed not only as omnipotent but also as maternal. Johnson's version of the creation and the minister delivering the sermon serves to conjure up in the audience's mind a picture of a God who is tender, loving, and kind.

Other poems/sermons included in the book are titled "Go Down, Death," "Noah Built the Ark," "The Crucifixion," "Listen, Lord-A Prayer," "The Prodigal Son," and "The Judgment Day." As can be seen, the poems cover the gamut from alpha to omega and other crucial sermons in between.

Johnson illustrates his ability as a nonfiction writer in his **autobiography** *Along This Way*. In it he relates an incident in a Jacksonville bicycle shop that caused him to reflect on and to investigate his life. During a bit of verbal exchange among Johnson and other somewhat unfamiliar white men, Johnson is sarcastically asked by a nondescript white man what he would give to be a white man. Briefly taken aback, Johnson replies, "I am sure that I wouldn't give anything to be the kind of white man you are. No, I am sure I wouldn't; I'd lose too much by the change." As a result of this exchange, which occurred at the end of the nineteenth century when Johnson was a high school principal in Jacksonville, Florida, he began a method of self-examination that culminated in the writing of the autobiography. Most whites would assume that all black Americans wanted to become white, thereby giving up their birthrights, heritage, and culture. Indeed, many fair-skinned blacks decided to pass for white to escape the harshness of black life at that time. Subsequently, Johnson constantly critiqued his motives, words, actions, and reactions to people, events, and racism to be sure that his response to the white man was genuine. In *Along This Way*, Johnson raises questions about the social privilege accorded to whites in America at the expense of nonwhites. He invokes the Constitution and its precepts that all men are created equal and have the right to pursue happiness. In doing so, Johnson fantasizes about a genie offering and granting four gifts to Johnson. The gifts are any amount of wealth, a desired boon, a change of place with another person, and a change of **race**. Johnson readily requests a modest amount of money, and the democratic rights enumerated in the Constitution and Declaration of Independence, which would give him the opportunity to pursue happiness and be equally rewarded for his **work**. However, Johnson is perplexed about becoming another person and changing race. He realizes that to change either his person or race would constitute a loss of self. Consequently, Johnson ends the fantasy by refusing a change of person and race. He deduces that to participate in such an exchange would suggest that a person could totally remake himself or herself, obliterating his or her **identity**.

In an earlier novel, *The Autobiography of an Ex-Colored Man*, Johnson depicts his unidentified narrator's attempt to obliterate his identity as a black or biracial man by **passing** as Caucasian. At a time in American **history** when being black and proud was not popular, mixed-race people who looked white sometimes chose to pass for white and cut all ties with their racially marked families. Some African Americans in the arts like **Josephine Baker**, **James Baldwin**, and others left America for Europe to escape harsh American racist treatment and to receive better compensation and recognition of their talents. Similarly, the fictional narrator in the novel is a musician who, along with his white patron, goes to Europe to live and perform. The ex-colored man is by blood, by appearance, by education, and by tastes a white man. Although the ex-colored man resembles his white father more on the outside, in order to assume the identity as white only, he has to deny his black mother and his black birthright and culture. Choosing to be white causes him to publicly deny and change his person, thereby resulting in psychological self-doubt and feeling a sense of loss. Upon returning to America, the ex-colored man is faced with the dilemma of choosing to be white or black in a society that has changed geographically but not much socially, depending on the location.

Johnson was a multifaceted man who was involved in the arts, politics, and education during his lifetime. He was also a leader in pushing for advancement of black people through his work with the NAACP, becoming its secretary, the first black American to serve in that position at the time. Furthermore, he exemplified a productive life through his work as a lawyer, as a U.S. consul in Venezuela and Nicaragua, and a contributing editor for the *New York Age*. At the time of his **death** in 1938, Johnson was a professor of creative writing at Fisk University in Nashville, Tennessee. His contributions to the arts and to humanity stand the test of time.

Works By

Along This Way: The Autobiography of James Weldon Johnson. 1933. New York: Viking, 1968.

The Autobiography of an Ex-Colored Man. 1912. New York: Dover Publications, 1995.

Black Manhattan: The American Negro: His History and His Literature. 1930. New York: Arno Press and the New York Times, 1968.

The Book of American Negro Poetry. Ed. James Weldon Johnson. 1922. New York: Harcourt, Brace and World, 1931.

The Book of American Negro Spirituals. With J. Rosamond Johnson. 1925–1926. New York: Viking Press, 1940.

God's Trombones: Seven Negro Sermons in Verse. Drawings by Aaron Douglas. Lettering by C. B. Falls. New York: Viking-Penguin, 1927. New York: Vintage-Penguin, 1990.

Negro Americans: What Now? 1934. New York: Da Capo Press, 1973.

"Race Prejudice and the Negro Artist." *Harper's Magazine*, November 1928, 769–776.

Works About

Carroll, Anne. "Art, Literature, and the Harlem Renaissance: The Messages of *God's Trombones*." *College Literature* 29.3 (Summer 2002): 57–78.

——. "Introduction–James Weldon Johnson." *James Weldon Johnson and Arna Wendell Bontemps: A Reference Guide.* Boston: G. K. Hall, 1978.

——. *James Weldon Johnson.* Ed. David J. Nordloch. Boston: G. K. Hall, 1987.

Marren, Susan, and Robert Cochran. "Johnson's *The Autobiography of an Ex-Colored Man*." *Explicator* 60.3 (Spring 2002): 147–150.

Schulze, Jennifer L. "Restaging the Racial Contract: James Weldon Johnson's Signatory Strategies." *American Literature* 74.1 (March 2002): 31–59.

Juluette Bartlett Pack

JONAH'S GOURD VINE

Originally titled *Big Nigger*, *Jonah's Gourd Vine* (1934) was the first novel published by **Zora Neale Hurston**. Based on the lives and deaths of her parents, this account is thought by some critics to be a more accurate representation of John and Lucy Ann Hurston than that found in her **autobiography *Dust Tracks on a Road*** (1942).

The principal characters representing Hurston's parents are John Pearson and Lucy Potts. The novel centers around the power of verbal play. Lucy is skilled in these word games, and she eventually teaches the techniques to John, whose command of them is instrumental in his assumption of a place of leadership in the **community**. John, who already had a gift for speech but not for the nuances of performative or persuasive speaking, is initially attracted to Lucy because of her possession of these attributes. He had grown up on the other side of the creek with his mother and stepfather, Amy and Ned Crittendon, and it appears that he gets his natural gift of gab from Amy Crittendon. But Amy's gift is not appreciated by Ned, who resents her linguistic wit and regularly beats her, using his fists to assert his manhood because he is no match for her verbal skills. Soon John's male ego also begins to suffer, and he starts to resent Lucy's superior talent with words.

John comes to realize how powerful voice and the ability to sway others is, and this realization leads to problems in the Pearson marriage. He resents not only Lucy's natural verbal talent but also the role she has played in his own success. All of the men in Eatonville know that John is a "wife-made man," and they do not hesitate to throw it in his face, especially when he becomes a little too full of himself. His male pride wounded, John seeks ways to elevate himself while at the same time to silence Lucy.

In order to demonstrate the power of his masculine **identity**—to himself as well as to Lucy—he commits flagrant infidelities to prove that he is not "wife-made." When John fails silencing Lucy by outtalking her, he slaps her. He crosses a line here that he has never crossed before, and the damage is irreparable. When Lucy starts to deteriorate and eventually dies, John finds that her voice comes back stronger than ever.

A number of critics make an obvious comparison between Lucy and the character of Janie Crawford in Hurston's *Their Eyes Were Watching God* (1937). Lucy's only marriage leads to attempts by her husband to take away her voice as he forces her deeper and deeper into silence and into a subordinate position in their marriage. Janie's journey is one in which she successfully fights off the attempts of two husbands to silence her, eventually finding a voice and her own sense of self. Ironically, through her **death**, Lucy seems to find power again, as John cannot escape the guilt and shame he feels for striking her. Even though he seems to have found himself later in the novel through the earnest respect he shows his new wife, Sally, his tragic death soon after this revelation appears to suggest that he does not get off easily for his treatment of Lucy. In the end, it is Lucy's voice that comes through loud and clear.

Works About

Beilke, Debra. " 'Yowin' and Jawin': Humor and the Performance of Identity in Zora Neale Hurston's *Jonah's Gourd Vine*." *Southern Quarterly* 36.3 (Spring 1998): 21–33.

Hutchings, Kevin D. "Transforming 'Sorrow's Kitchen': Gender and Hybridity in Two Novels by Zora Neale Hurston." *English Studies in Canada* 23.2 (June 1997): 175–199.

Johnnie M. Stover

JONES, EVERETT LEROY. See Baraka, Amiri

JONES, GAYL (1949–   )

Gayl Jones was born in 1949 in Lexington, Kentucky, and grew up in the **South** listening to the stories that her grandmother and mother told. Her mother, Lucille, wrote stories for the children, and her grandmother, Amanda Wilson, had been a playwright. This maternal legacy of storytelling is thematized in Jones's novels, as her narratives are concerned both with the literary legacy of the oral tradition and with the sounds of storytelling—the cadences and dialects of African American speech. Jones attended Connecticut College, where she won the prize for original **poetry** two years in a row, in 1969 and 1970, and also won the Frances Steloff Award for **fiction** in 1970 for her short story "The Roundhouse," which was later included in her collection of stories *White Rat*, published in 1977. After graduating in 1971, she enrolled at Brown University for her doctorate, where she worked with Michael Harper, producing a play, *Chile Woman*, in 1974, and her first novel, ***Corregidora***, in 1975, the year she received her Ph.D. Her second novel, ***Eva's Man***, followed in 1976. Both of these novels were edited by **Toni Morrison** at Random House. Jones's work, particularly *Corregidora*, has been critically acclaimed from the beginning, and she received the Howard Foundation Award in 1975, a National Endowment for the Arts Fellowship in 1976, and one from the Michigan Society of Fellows from 1977 to 1979.

After her marriage to Robert Higgins, Jones left the United States in the early 1980s to live in Europe for a half dozen years, where she published *Die Vogelfangerin* (*The Birdwatcher*; 1986) in Germany. Jones is not only a playwright and novelist but also a poet, publishing the collections *Song for Anninho* (1981), *The Hermit Woman* (1983), and *Xarque and Other Poems* (1985). Her criticism, too, encompasses multiple genres; in her detailed scholarly examination *Liberating Voices: Oral Tradition in African American Literature* (1991), she considers the development of voice and the use of **folklore** in poetry, short stories, and novels by African American writers from **Paul Laurence Dunbar** to Morrison. More recently, Jones has returned to fiction, publishing two more novels, *The Healing* (1998), which was a finalist for the National Book Award, and *Mosquito* (1999).

Almost all of Jones's writing presents a first-person narrator who uses the cadences and dialect of southern African American speech, and both the poetry and the fiction read as either oral tale told to an intimate listener or lyric meditation. While most of her characters are of the lower **class** and not classically educated, often working with horses, as beauticians, or in tobacco factories, the narratives are embedded with allusions to classical **literature** and **myth**, and the names of her characters are frequently symbolic. Ursa Corregidora, for instance, is derived from the Latin word for "bear" and the Portuguese for "magistrate" or "judge," and Ursa's life is dictated by her need to bear judgment or witness against the original Corregidora, the slave master of her grandmothers. Eva Medina Canada's name links to both Eve, calling up echoes of how Genesis characterizes woman as made for man, and Medusa, who holds the power to kill men. In *Mosquito*, the main character is Sojourner Jane Nadine Johnson—an obvious reference to **Sojourner Truth**, who redefined what it meant to be an African American woman and who worked to abolish **slavery**—an apt name, then, for Johnson, a.k.a. "Mosquito," a truck driver who comes to **work** in a contemporary underground railroad, helping provide safe passage and sanctuary for illegal Mexican immigrants. Jones's vast reading in multiple languages and scholarly knowledge of African American **history**, combined with her ear for the sounds of everyday speech, make her novels multilayered, rich, and complex reading experiences.

Jones's thematic concerns as a writer have been consistent throughout her career: the influence of history, particularly the legacy of enslavement, **rape**, and sexual abuse, on the lives of African American women; female familial relationships; African American women's **sexuality**; the role of narrative in dealing with trauma and **healing**; and the relationship between African American fiction and the oral tradition—folklore, **sermons**, the **blues**, and **family** stories. She has been both praised for her vivid and unflinching depictions of troubled sexuality and gender relationships and criticized for what some readers have felt to be negative images of both African American men and women. Jones's early work in particular is filled with painful stories of **domestic** abuse, loss, and trauma, while her more recent fiction, as the title *The Healing* suggests, offers the possibility of redemption and reclamation of self in spite of this legacy. The relationship between self and other, between personal independence and commitment to family, lover, culture, and history, is worked out positively in *Mosquito* as well. Because Mosquito refuses to join the trucking union, and instead creates her own company, she remains economically and politically independent and can therefore fulfill her commitments to the illegal immigrants, whom she transports in her trucks.

In both her novels and her poetry, most notably the critically acclaimed *Corregidora* and *Song for Anninho*, Jones explores the history of slavery and its effects on African American **identity** and family relationships. *Corregidora* is a haunting and lyrical narrative that examines the legacy of racial and sexual oppression on the lives of four generations of African American women. The main character, Ursa Corregidora, is a blues singer whose mother, grandmother, and great-grandmother have produced her as a "witness" to replace the destroyed documentary evidence of their enslavement and rape by the Portuguese slave master Corregidora, who used Ursa's great-grandmother and grandmother as prostitutes and who fathered both her grandmother and mother. These women raise Ursa to "make generations"—to procreate in order to produce more witnesses, but within months of her marriage, Ursa's husband throws her down the stairs while she is pregnant with her first child, and she loses her womb. The novel intersperses the grandmothers' narratives of enslavement with Ursa's attempts to define herself and build a lasting relationship with a man, so that these oral tales, which Ursa has heard her entire life, seem more her own memories than those of her **ancestors** and shape her actions and identity a century after slavery has ended. *Song for Anninho*, set in Brazil in the seventeenth century, is narrated by a female slave, Almeyda, who has also listened to her grandmother's stories and gained an identity through this narrative connection. This prose poem narrates the **love** between Almeyda and Anninho, two slaves who have escaped to Palmares, a maroon colony that was destroyed in 1695. In both texts, the women lose a physical symbol of gender, sexuality, and **motherhood** to **violence**; like Ursa's lost womb, Almeyda's lost breasts (a Portuguese soldier cuts them off) denote the lasting loss and scars resulting from slavery that impede African American women's ability to love and nurture their families.

Eva's Man deals most explicitly with the **stereotypes** of African American female sexuality that are a direct legacy of slavery. Eva Medina Canada, the main character and narrator, has grown up hearing and experiencing mostly negative stories about male-female relationships, and snatches of these re-membered stories and encounters are interspersed with her meditations on why she committed her crime of murdering and orally castrating one of her lovers. Eva's choices as a sexual being seem culturally circumscribed; she hears repeatedly that women who are not whores ought not to be outside the house; that once a woman has sex she will not be able to control her desire for it; that women who do not immediately agree to men's desires are mean and evil. In her memories, every man she has ever met, whether a little boy or an old man, her own cousin, her mother's lover, or a random man on a bus, has assumed she wants to have sex with him and has tried, often violently, to force her into it. Eva thinks of herself as Medusa because she has the power to make men stiff, and she eventually thinks of herself as a Queen Bee because she stings men who want sex from her (before the murder, she had stabbed a man who solicited her in a bar). Her act of biting off her lover's penis echoes the violent acts that result in the loss of Ursa's womb and Almeyda's breasts, as well as the act of resistance Ursa's great-grandmother performed on the slave master Corregidora before escaping.

In *Corregidora*, this act of resistance, biting Corregidora's penis during fel-latio, is something that Ursa must imagine on her own, as her great-grand-mother would never say what she had done. This is just one example of the tension between what is told—the legacy of slavery—and what is not told—fruitful modes of resistance and healing—that dominates many of these nar-ratives as well. Familial stories can be either liberating or entrapping, as Ursa discovers in *Corregidora*, and for many of Jones's protagonists, the information they most need handed down from mother to daughter never arrives but instead remains shrouded in secrecy and silence. Both Ursa and Eva have mothers who do not tell them anything useful about desire, love, or marriage, and they are left to discover and fend for themselves, while the narratives they do receive (Ursa from her grandmothers, Eva from her mother's friend Miss Billie, and both from girls slightly older than they are) constrain their relationships with men and inhibit their desire. They see themselves as the women in the historical narratives, rather than as individual actors able to define their own lives and relationships.

All of the novels employ a quest for self-reclamation and healing, in which telling one's own story plays a large part, but these plots are often not obvious as such because they are not linear. Within the fragments of disordered memories, *Eva's Man* offers the possibility of empowerment and obliquely suggests that Eva has turned to **lesbianism** in jail as a way to fulfill her desire without fulfilling a stereotype. *The Healing* is narrated backward from the present, in which Harlan is about to perform a faith healing, to the past, through Harlan's careers as rock-star manager and beautician and her affairs with various men, including an African German horse breeder and a medical anthropologist. The novel suggests that all of these earlier identities continue to constitute Harlan's identity as healer, that Harlan, unlike the protagonists of Jones's first two novels, has been able to integrate her history in a useful and fulfilling manner, rather than be entrapped by it. *Mosquito*'s plot development is often displaced by narrative disquisitions on everything from the Central Intelligence Agency's illegal activities to movie stars' hair color, so that often this cultural commentary, rather than Mosquito's acts of providing sanctuary, seems to be the main point of the novel.

Because Jones skillfully controls African American idiom, parodies other texts, and signifies on American culture, reviewers have favorably compared her work to that of **Zora Neale Hurston**, **Ralph Ellison**, and **Ishmael Reed**. Both *Mosquito* and *The Healing* are replete with references to, and analysis of, other novels from *Invisible Man* to *Huckleberry Finn*. Much of Jones's brilliance lies in her ability to use the colloquial voice of working-class African American women to provide not only extensive social commentary but also intriguing metafictional discourse on the nature of narrative.

Works By

Corregidora. New York: Random House, 1975.
Eva's Man. New York: Random House, 1976.
The Healing. Boston: Beacon Press, 1998.
The Hermit Woman. Detroit: Lotus Press, 1983.
Liberating Voices: Oral Tradition in African American Literature. Cambridge, MA: Harvard University Press, 1991.
Mosquito. Boston: Beacon Press, 1999.
Songs for Anninho. Detroit: Lotus Press, 1981.
White Rat: Short Stories. New York: Random House, 1977.
Xarque and other Poems. Detroit: Lotus Press, 1985.

Works About

Dubey, Madhu. "Gayl Jones and the Matrilineal Metaphor of Tradition." *Signs* 20 (1995): 245–267.

Harris, Trudier. "A Spiritual Journey: Gayl Jones's *Song for Anninho*." *Callaloo* 5 (1982): 105–111.

Robinson, Sally. *Engendering the Subject: Gender and Self-Representation in Contemporary Women's Fiction*. Albany: SUNY Press, 1991.

Verge, Shane Trudell. "Revolutionary Vision: Black Women Writers, Black Nationalist Ideology, and Interracial Sexuality." *Meridians* 2 (2002): 101–125.

Ward, Jerry. "Escape from Trublem: The Fiction of Gayl Jones." *Callaloo* 5 (1982): 95–104.

Suzanne Lane

JONES-MEADOWS, KAREN (1953–   )

Like many artistic women, Karen Jones-Meadows possesses a wide range of talents. Her first career was as an elementary school teacher. For three years, she taught in both Boston and North Carolina public schools. When Jones-Meadows became disillusioned with the bureaucracy of the public education system and realized that writing, not teaching, was her true passion she began writing **poetry**. Those verses evolved into plays, and a career was born. In 1984, Jones-Meadows wrote *Henrietta*, a play set in New York City, that follows a bag lady and a black urban professional who become friends and whose lives grow as a result of learning from each other's differences. The play was produced by the critically acclaimed Negro Ensemble Company, and her reputation as a talented playwright was born.

Her career has since been marked by the success of the play *Harriet's Return* (2003), which she wrote and stars in. The **drama** chronicles both the public and private lives of Harriet Tubman, the revered conductor of the **Underground Railroad** who emerged during the twentieth century as an icon for African American people. The narrative begins with Tubman's childhood in Maryland, continues through her marriages, years on the Underground Railroad, her Civil War tour, and social rights activism. There are more than thirty characters in the play, all played by Jones-Meadows. The work has impressed audiences throughout the country and garnered numerous awards. Actors including Phylicia Rashad, Moses Gunn, and Oscar choreographer Debbie Allen have played the characters she has written. Jones-Meadows also wrote the plays *Tapman* (1987), *Major Changes*, and *Sala: An African Cinderella Tale* (1996).

In addition to traveling throughout the country performing *Harriet's Return* and *Henrietta* (1984), Jones-Meadows also gives workshops to promote **literacy**, writing, and the theatrical arts. She participates in her local **community**, serving as a member of the Screenwriting Conference in Santa Fe Board of Advisors. She has also set her sights toward Hollywood. In 1987, she had a small role as an emergency room nurse in the movie *Critical Condition*, starring Richard Pryor. She has written for television, including a teleplay titled *The*

Trials of Juanita, which was optioned but has not yet been picked up by a network. Other television writing endeavors include a series titled *Hip Hop in the Promised Land* for Comedy Central and a series of public service announcements for the Fox station in New York City. Most recently, Jones-Meadows has worked with entrepreneur Cleveland Hughes to bring Harriet Tubman's life to the silver screen in a **film** titled *The Life of Harriet Tubman*. Jones-Meadows moved to New Mexico in 1995, where she currently resides.

Work By

Henrietta. The National Black Drama Anthology. Ed. Woodie King. New York: Applause, 1995.

Work About

Andrews, Laura. "Harriet Tubman Shown as Romantic Figure." *New York Amsterdam News*, April 15, 1995, n.p.

Roxane Gay

JORDAN, JUNE (1936–2002)

As an author and as an activist, June Jordan was distinguished by her clarity, her conscience, and her unfailing commitment to the creation of a just society. Jordan's passion for language—for the feel, sound, and rhythm of words—is evident in all her works, and those works cover a wide range of genres: political essays, **poetry**, **fiction** for young readers, screenplays, even the libretto for an opera set in post–earthquake Los Angeles, "I Was Looking at the Ceiling and Then I Saw the Sky" (1995). Born in Harlem to Jamaican immigrants, Jordan began writing early, earning money by producing **love** poems and poetic put-downs for her schoolmates. After several years of public schooling, she received a scholarship to an elite New England preparatory school, then returned home to New York City to begin her studies at Barnard College. While in school, she met and married Michael Meyer; this interracial marriage (then illegal in forty-seven states) led to a son, Christopher, and then to a divorce, about ten years later. Shortly after her marriage, Jordan left school, finding little connection between her **community** in Bedford-Stuyvesant and the culture and curriculum of Barnard College. This experience is detailed in "Notes of a Barnard Dropout," a lecture given in 1975 while she and **Alice Walker** shared the Reid Lectureship at that school (1975; in *Civil Wars*).

During these years, Jordan cared for her son Christopher, primarily as a single mother, and continued studying independently. Her interest in architecture led to a friendship with Buckminster Fuller and to one of her first major published pieces, a 1964 essay in *Esquire* proposing a plan to redesign

Harlem for maximum community and livability. The essay helped her to garner the 1970 Prix de Rome Environmental Design Award; she also won an Architectural Design Award from the American Institute of Architecture, for a joint proposal for the African Burial Ground in New York, New York. It was by chance that, in the fall of 1967, Jordan began teaching English composition at the City College of New York, where **Toni Cade Bambara**, Barbara Christian, Adrienne Rich, and **Audre Lorde** were among her colleagues. Her teaching career took her to institutions including Connecticut College, the State University of New York at Stony Brook, and the University of California at Berkeley, her academic **home** at the time of her 2002 **death** from breast cancer. Throughout these years, she remained a dynamic writer and educator whose interactions with her students nourished her writing and theirs. In fact, her inspiration and assistance led to publications such as *The Voice of the Children* (1970), a volume of poetry she produced with children from writing workshops she taught as a participant in New York's Writers and Teachers Collaborative, and *June Jordan's Poetry for the People: A Revolutionary Blueprint* (1995), the result of her popular Poetry for the People classes at Berkeley.

Across all the decades of her writing and teaching careers, and across all the genres in which she published, Jordan circled repeatedly back to a number of issues that she examined and reconsidered in the context of a changing—and not so changed—American sociopolitical landscape. Although the body of Jordan's work and the singular, crisp beauty of her style cannot be reduced to any set of themes, those themes do identify some of her crucial areas of concern. Because Jordan truly believed in "liberty and justice for all"—and also in equality—regardless of **race**, gender, **class**, sexual orientation, or any other potential identifying characteristic—she tackled issues like racism, affirmative action, women's rights, education, **violence** of all kinds, and economic inequity, over and over again. She was not one to back down from a fight, and language was her chosen means of joining the fray.

In her memoir *Soldier: A Poet's Childhood* (2000), Jordan describes how, as an infant and toddler, she "could not help but fall in love with words," as her mother recited nursery rhymes, connecting each noun to a part of the girl's **body** and touching her at the moment she pronounced it. This love for language was reinforced by Jordan's attendance at church services where, even if she did not always understand what was happening, she was nonetheless transported by the unusual and incantatory, repetitive nature of the words used there—words clearly associated with a certain power. The power of words themselves, and the responsibility of their speakers and writers to ensure that those words express their own truths to bring about meaningful acts of communication, is affirmed by Jordan in essays and poems from throughout her career.

This concern surfaces in "The Voice of the Children," a 1967 essay from *Civil Wars* detailing her involvement with the Teachers and Writers Collaborative. In her essay about this experience, Jordan comments on what will become a central element in her work, an element linking her concern for language as the expression of an individual who participates in a particular culture with her insistence that educators see, understand, and respect their students as individuals. Although this concern initially grew from her demand for recognition of black English as a distinct, viable, and valuable form of expression, in "White English/Black English: The Politics of Translation" (1972; in *Civil Wars*), it eventually developed into a broader call for a "legitimately American language" in "Problems of Language in a Democratic State" (1982; in *On Call* [1985]). Her most impassioned statement on this subject is perhaps her 1985 essay, "Nobody Mean More to Me Than You and the Future Life of Willie Jordan" (*On Call*). Here, her defense of black English is sparked by her black students' initial rejection of Alice Walker's **The Color Purple** (1982), a shock that leads her to undertake teaching a course on black English. When the brother of a student in that new course is killed by the New York City police, her students wrestle with the problem of how to express their outrage: in standard English, which may get published, or in black English, which allows them to be true to themselves? Jordan clearly sees the connection between devaluing a people and devaluing their language.

Because she saw this connection, much of Jordan's time and energy as an educator and as an author was devoted to helping students recognize the quality of their own authentic languages and voices and the power of speaking about their own experiences. With this goal in mind, she also produced several books exploring black life from the inside for children and young adult readers. *His Own Where* (1971), an inner-city story of young love written entirely in black English, was a finalist for the National Book Award the year it was published. *Who Look at Me* (1969), an innovative text combining her own poetic text about double consciousness with paintings and sketches depicting African Americans, was also designed for young readers. Others of these books include *Dry Victories* (1972), which uses a dialogue format to compare Reconstruction with the civil rights era; the biography *Fannie Lou Hamer* (1972); *New Life: New Room* (1975); and *Kimako's Story* (1981).

The pedagogical drive was an important aspect of Jordan's writing, and she was devotedly committed to the ideal of truly democratic education. From her 1969 essay "Black Studies: Bringing Back the Person" (*Civil Wars*), supporting open admissions at City College and demanding change in the New York City school system, to "Of Those So Close Beside Me, Which Are You?" (1986), "Finding the Haystack in the Needle, or, the Whole World of America and the Challenge of Higher Education," and "Toward a Manifest New Destiny" (1991; all in *Technical Difficulties* [1992]), Jordan continued to argue for multicultural education as vital to a pluralistic, democratic society existing in a heterogeneous world. Following the 1996 passage of California Proposition 209, gutting affirmative action in that state, Jordan once again turned her attention to policies for affirmative action, which she defined as "life on behalf of more life" in one of several essays on the subject in *Affirmative Acts* (1998).

Consistent with her views on education, Jordan's writing often considers the political from a personal point of view, or the impact of the political on the personal, and juxtaposes in surprising ways issues that are often seen as unconnected. Thus, her 1982 essay "Report from the Bahamas" (*On Call*) moves from her own experience as a black woman tourist in the Bahamas to the dangerous situation faced by one of her students, a black South African woman abused by her alcoholic husband. In the essay's startling conclusion, Jordan describes how this student is helped by another when solidarity develops across color lines, solidarity based on a similar **history** of suffering. She then calls for a new, universally human solidarity, based not on fear and danger but on positive connection—before it is "too late."

Jordan insisted on the interconnectedness of all struggles for **freedom**, justice, and equality and especially resented attempts by others to reduce these campaigns down to either/or oppositions in which only one type of pain, hope, or suffering was considered legitimate or worthy of concern. She tackles this topic playfully in "A Short Note to My Very Critical and Well-Beloved Friends and Comrades," from her 1980 collection of poetry titled *Passion*. Elsewhere, however, her treatments of this subject are more serious, as in the many essays documenting her refusal to be pressured into privileging or denying her **identity** as a woman, as a black person, as a bisexual. A survivor of **rape**—not once but twice—she recalls, in "Notes toward a Model of Resistance" (*Affirmative Acts*), that she could not resist her first attacker, a white man, until she thought of herself as a black woman being ordered about by a white man. Her second attacker, years later, was black; her racial consciousness did not help her to resist him, and her gender consciousness was not enough. She describes the experience in a short poem called "Case in Point" (*Passion*) and also in "Waking Up in the Middle of Some American Dreams" (*Technical Difficulties*). In a manifesto-style poem in *Passion*, Jordan unites all the aspects of her history and her identity, demanding justice for them all, simultaneously, *now*. Jordan understood that identity politics were grounded in the experiences of people's everyday lives, but she expressed her frustrations with their limits, too, as in "Waiting for a Taxi" (*Technical Difficulties*).

Jordan's acute awareness of her own gender identity stemmed in part from her father's disappointment at her birth and determination to raise her as a son, an experience detailed in *Soldier*. She fought back against her father's physical abuse and witnessed her mother's silent struggle, which ended in suicide. Later in life, Jordan's struggle with breast cancer was another reminder of the particular difficulties faced by women. These difficulties include a sometimes cavalier health system and a federal government that sees women's health issues as only a distant second priority, if that. "Besting a Worst Case Scenario" (1996; in *Affirmative Acts*) offers a detailed description of Jordan's own experience in dealing with breast cancer and the medical system; it also offers statistics on women's health in the United States and a call to action to change this lamentable situation. The problematic outcome of her mastectomy left her physically unable to write for months; "First Poem after

Serious Surgery" evokes her fear of this silence, in its temporary and menacingly more permanent forms (*Kissing God Good-Bye* [1997]).

Jordan maintained a steadfast devotion to her principles despite pressure when her positions did not fit into others' political orthodoxies. For instance, her regularly repeated demands for a new foreign policy approach toward Israel and the Palestinians were not always well received. But she would not compromise and held to an unwavering sense of what was right. Principles, however, preclude neither a sense of humor nor an appreciation of **beauty**. And Jordan's writing often testifies to both her comic sense and the lyrical aspect of her vision. "Letter to the Local Police" (*Passion*), a complaint about rioting roses, synthesizes the two, while many others represent her delight in the natural world.

Jordan's notion of success was not limited to the merely individual, as is evidenced by her many collaborative endeavors. In 1979, she joined forces with Sweet Honey in the Rock and **Ntozake Shange** to produce a night of music, song, and poetry, "In the Spirit of Sojourner Truth." Another collaboration with Bernice Reagon yielded the famous poems/ songs, performed by Sweet Honey, "Alla Tha's All Right, But" and "Oughta Be a Woman." Jordan's individual accomplishments were, nonetheless, acknowledged and rewarded with numerous prizes and awards, including the Lila Wallace *Readers Digest* Award (1995) and the National Black Writers' Conference Lifetime Achievement Award (1998), which she dedicated to her parents. Jordan's legacy lives on in her writing and in the writing of her many students.

Works By

Affirmative Acts: Political Essays. New York: Anchor Books, 1998.
Civil Wars. Boston: Beacon Press, 1981.
His Own Where. New York: Crowell, 1971.
"In the Spirit of Sojourner Truth." Produced at New York Public Theater, 1979.
"I Was Looking at the Ceiling and Then I Saw the Sky." Music by John Adams. Produced at Lincoln Center, New York, NY, 1985. Available on compact disc from Nonesuch.
June Jordan's Poetry for the People: A Revolutionary Blueprint. Ed. Lauren Muller. Intro. by June Jordan. New York: Routledge, 1995.
Kissing God Good-Bye: New Poems, 1991–1997. New York: Doubleday, 1997.
Living Room: New Poems, 1980–1984. New York: Thunder's Mouth Press, 1985.
"The Music of Poetry and the Poetry of Music." Music by Adrienne B. Torf. Produced in New York, NY, and Washington, DC, 1984.
Naming Our Destiny: New and Selected Poems. New York: Thunder's Mouth Press, 1989.
On Call: Political Essays, 1981–1985. Boston: South End Press, 1985.
Passion: New Poems, 1977–1980. Boston: Beacon Press, 1980.

Soldier: A Poet's Childhood. New York: Basic Books, 2000.

Some of Us Did Not Die: New and Selected Essays. New York: Basic Books, 2002.

Technical Difficulties: African American Notes on the State of the Union. New York: Pantheon, 1992.

Things That I Do in the Dark: Selected Poetry. New York: Random House, 1977. Rev. ed., Boston: Beacon Press, 1981.

Who Look at Me. New York: Crowell, 1969.

Works About

Brogan, Jacqueline Vaught. "From Warrior to Womanist: The Development of June Jordan's Poetry." *Speaking the Other Self: American Women Writers.* Ed. Jeanne Campbell Reesman. Athens: University of Georgia Press, 1997. 198–209.

Comfort, Juanita Rodgers. "Becoming a Writerly Self: College Writers Engaging Black Feminist Essays." *College Composition and Communication* 51:4 (June 2000): 540–559.

Eagleton, Mary. "Working across Difference: Examples from Minnie Bruce Pratt and June Jordan." *Caught Between Cultures: Women, Writing & Subjectivities.* Ed. Russell, Elizabeth. Amsterdam: Rodopi, 2002. 129–150.

Flynn, Richard. " 'Affirmative Acts': Language, Childhood, and Power in June Jordan's Cross-Writing." *Children's Literature: Annual of The Modern Language Association Division on Children's Literature and The Children's Literature Association* 30 (2002): 159–185.

Gomez, Jewelle. "June Jordan: July 9, 1936–June 14, 2002." *Callaloo: A Journal of African-American and African Arts and Letters* 25:3 (Summer 2002): 715–718.

Harjo, Joy. "An Interview with June Jordan." *High Plains Literary Review* 3:2 (Fall 1988): 60–76.

Jocson, Korina M. " 'Taking It to the Mic': Pedagogy of June Jordan's Poetry for the People and Partnership with an Urban High School." *English Education* 37:2 (January 2005): 132–148.

Keating, AnaLouise. "The Intimate Distance of Desire: June Jordan's Bisexual Inflections." *Journal of Lesbian Studies* 4:2 (2000): 81–93.

MacPhail, Scott. "June Jordan and the New Black Intellectuals." *African American Review* 33:1 (Spring 1999): 57–71.

Norman, Brian. "June Jordan's Manifest New Destiny: Allegiance, Renunciation, and Partial Citizens' Claims on the State." *Michigan Feminist Studies* 18 (2004): 77–96.

Walsh, Rebecca. "Where Metaphor Meets Materiality: The Spatialized Subject and the Limits of Locational Feminism." *Exclusions in Feminist Thought: Challenging the Boundaries of Womanhood.* Ed. Mary Brewer. Brighton, England: Sussex Academic, 2002. 182–202.

Monika Giacoppe

JUBILEE

Margaret Walker Alexander exerted her most powerful literary effort in the crafting of her only work of **fiction**, *Jubilee* (1966). Drawing on the power of **history** and the significant importance to her of personal **family** history and the preservation of both, the author created a mock biography that explored the atypical life of her great-grandmother, Margaret Duggins Ware Brown.

The novel was inspired by stories that the writer heard told by her grandmother, Elvira Ware Dozier, and from family heirlooms and artifacts that had been stored for years in a trunk that came into her possession. She found enough information in the trunk to explore on behalf of her recreated **ancestor**, Vyry, vital questions of **freedom**, **race**, and **class** as well as the devastation of life in **slavery**.

The foundation of *Jubilee* was begun in 1942, nearly a decade after Walker had graduated from Northwestern University in 1935 with a Bachelor of Arts degree. She then went on to pursue and completed her Master's in Creative Writing at the University of Iowa in 1942, and there the **work** on *Jubilee* seemed for a time to come to an end.

Walker married hastily because she dearly wanted a family; in 1943 she wed Firnist Alexander. Together, they had two sons and two daughters. Over the years of rearing her family and to ensure their economic stability, she moved to Jackson, Mississippi, in 1946. At Jackson State University, a long academic teaching career ensued.

Well into a settled family life, Walker did not abandon *Jubilee*. Her youngest daughter Margaret with her, she returned to the University of Iowa to work on her Doctor of Philosophy degree. At the end of that endeavor, and after a hiatus from teaching at Jackson State, twenty-three years of incubating *Jubilee*, she returned to Mississippi with her degree in hand and the completed novel *Jubilee*.

Jubilee has stood the test of time. In the work, Walker gave dimension to Vyry that startled readers. Walker portrayed Vyry as the bedrock of strength, perseverance, and wisdom while she and company moved westward through Alabama to find a suitable place to settle. Vyry's husband, Innis, had learned that there was ample land to which no one held title that could be claimed by freed slaves.

Still, in search of a place to lay roots, the family was forced to go from place to place. Finally, Providence seemed to intervene. While passing through a white neighborhood, Vyry answered cries for help and gave assistance to a young woman in labor. The entire town was grateful to Vyry, and there she triumphed when her white neighbors promised her and her family protection. They then built a **home** for Vyry and her family.

Works About

Egejuru, Phanuel, and Robert Elliott Fox. "An Interview with Margaret Walker." *Callaloo* 2.2 (1979): 29–35.

Graham, Maryemma. "The Fusion of Ideas–An Interview with Margaret Walker Alexander." *African American Review* 27.2 (Summer 1993): 279–286.

Miller, R. Baxter. "The 'Etched Flame' of Margaret Walker: Biblical and Literary Re-creation in Southern History." *Tennessee Studies in Literature* 26 (1981): 157–172.

Pettis, Joyce. "Margaret Walker: Black Woman Writer of the South." *Southern Women Writers: The New Generation*. Ed. Tonetta Bond Inge. Tuscaloosa: University of Alabama Press, 1990. 9–19.

Tate, Claudia. "Margaret Walker." *Black Women Writers at Work*. Ed. Claudia Tate. New York: Continuum, 1983. 188–204.

Elisabeth S. James